THE JEWS IN THE CARIBBEAN

THE LITTMAN LIBRARY OF
JEWISH CIVILIZATION

Dedicated to the memory of
LOUIS THOMAS SIDNEY LITTMAN
who founded the Littman Library for the love of God
and as an act of charity in memory of his father
JOSEPH AARON LITTMAN
and to the memory of
ROBERT JOSEPH LITTMAN
who continued what his father Louis had begun

יהא זכרם ברוך

'Get wisdom, get understanding:
Forsake her not and she shall preserve thee'
PROV. 4:5

The Littman Library of Jewish Civilization is a registered UK charity
Registered charity no. 1000784

THE JEWS IN
THE CARIBBEAN

Edited by
JANE S. GERBER

London
The Littman Library of Jewish Civilization
in association with Liverpool University Press

The Littman Library of Jewish Civilization
Registered office: 4th floor, 7–10 Chandos Street, London W1G 9DQ

in association with Liverpool University Press
4 Cambridge Street, Liverpool L69 7ZU, UK
www.liverpooluniversitypress.co.uk/littman

Managing Editor: Connie Webber

Distributed in North America by
Oxford University Press Inc, 198 Madison Avenue,
New York, NY 10016, USA

First published in hardback 2014
First published in paperback 2018

Catalogue records for this book are available from
the British Library and the Library of Congress

ISBN 978–1–906764–99–9

Publishing co-ordinator: Janet Moth
Copy-editing: Mark Newby
Proof-reading: Philippa Claiden
Index: Caroline Diepeveen
Designed and typeset by Pete Russell, Faringdon, Oxon.

Printed and bound in Great Britain by
TJ International Ltd., Padstow, Cornwall

To Roger, Dina, Debbie, and Tamar

ACKNOWLEDGEMENTS

THIS VOLUME emerged from an international conference, 'The Jewish Diaspora of the Caribbean', convened in Kingston, Jamaica, from 12 to 14 January 2010. Participants included scholars and members of the general public from Europe, North America, and many parts of the Caribbean. Jamaican participants included high-school students from Hillel Academy of Jamaica, students and faculty from the Mona campus of the University of the West Indies, members of the local Jewish community, and representatives of the Jamaican government, who gathered together to learn of a shared history stretching back more than 300 years. Formal lectures alternated with field trips as historic sites became an alternative lecture hall: a visit to Kingston's Sha'ar Hashamayim Synagogue stimulated lively speculation on the origins and symbolic meaning of the sand-covered floor in its main sanctuary; the Portuguese inscriptions on the seventeenth- and eighteenth-century tombstones at the Hunt's Bay cemetery historic restoration evoked the Iberian and Dutch roots of Jewish life in Jamaica; while a tour of the Jamaican National Museum highlighted the art of Jamaican Sephardi artist Isaac Mendes Belisario. The subject matter of the formal sessions was wide-ranging—from Jamaican art, architecture, and literature; relations between Sephardi Jews and slave society; and the use of genealogy as a tool in understanding the Portuguese diaspora in the Caribbean to questions of gender and family and the construction of Jewish history in the Caribbean today. Veteran Jamaican families rubbed shoulders with North American guests as meals were shared in fellowship, followed by a rousing Bendigamos, the traditional Ladino grace after meals. The spirit of the conference was celebratory, with warm hospitality and fellowship abounding. Yet the aim was scientific. While the long-range impact of the conference on the communal identity and future of the Jewish community of Jamaica defies prediction, some of its fruits can be found in this volume of the proceedings. Most of the following chapters were presented as papers at the gathering in Kingston, with the addition of three invited chapters that bear upon the subject matter of the conference.

Two institutions served as co-sponsors of the Kingston conference, the Institute for Sephardic Studies at the Graduate Center of the City University of New York and the United Congregation of Israelites of Kingston. Their respective heads, myself and Mr Ainsley Cohen Henriques, jointly planned the academic and social content of the programme. In addition, two individuals deserve special mention, Stanley Mirvis of the Graduate Center of the City University of New York and the late Edward Kritzler of Jamaica. Ed Kritzler, a New Yorker by birth and a Jamaican for many decades, introduced me to Jamaica and its dynamic Jewish and Jamaican leader Ainsley Henriques in

2006. When Ainsley and I subsequently explored the possibility of convening an academic gathering in Jamaica, I realized that I had met not only an ideal conference co-chair, but an extraordinary citizen of Jamaica whose roots in the country reached back centuries to the Portuguese Jewish diaspora in colonial times. His pride in the harmonious coexistence of his Sephardi and Jamaican heritages is well known. He brought attention to detail, personal tact, and a lively sense of humour to the complex planning of an international conference, ensuring that the gathering would be both substantive and expertly executed. The flawless co-ordination and communication between New York and Kingston were the result of the outstanding role played by Stanley Mirvis. Stanley's organizational, technical, and editorial skills were also invaluable in the preparation of these proceedings. My thanks to all the scholars who contributed to this volume, as well as to those who do not appear in the volume but whose contributions at its sessions were significant.

The Institute for Sephardic Studies and the Center for Jewish Studies at the Graduate Center of the City University of New York generously offered staff and facilities for the planning of the conference, and several foundations and institutions provided grants for its support and implementation. It is a pleasure to acknowledge the donations of the family of the late Honourable Aaron J. Matalon, the Maduro and Curiel Bank, the French Embassy of Jamaica, the Tourism Enhancement Fund of Jamaica, the Goren Foundation, the George Washington Institute for Religious Freedom and Ambassador John L. Loeb, Jr., Stanton Estates Ltd, and Heritage Muse, Inc., of New York. Individuals who contributed to the conference included Mr Jonathan de Sola Mendes of New York, Dr John de Mercado of Kingston, and Laurence and Ronnie Levine of Oakland, New Jersey. The production of this volume and the inclusion of its maps and photographs were made possible through the generosity of the Cahnman Foundation.

The academic gathering in Jamaica brought together senior scholars who have been working for decades in the archives of Europe and the Caribbean and young scholars contributing the first fruits of their research. Their shared deliberations reflect several academic disciplines and touch upon many aspects of Jewish life in the Caribbean in general and Jamaica in particular. It is hoped that this endeavour will encourage more joint explorations in the fields of Jewish studies, Atlantic studies, and the history of the Jews in the early modern world.

JANE S. GERBER
Editor and Conference Co-Chair
Director, Institute for Sephardic Studies
Graduate Center of the
City University of New York

THERE ARE a few occasions in life in which one is privileged to participate. The Jewish Diaspora of the Caribbean International Conference was one such event. The conference was born out of a conversation at a luncheon, then it morphed into proposals, and evolved into a 'happening' that gave credibility to the rich history of a partly forgotten people—the Jews of the Caribbean. Now only a remnant of larger and more influential congregations, the Portuguese Jews of the Caribbean have been in the region for over 350 years. Before that they had been expelled from Spain, baptized in Portugal, subjected to the Inquisition, and only gradually permitted to settle throughout western Europe. They became proud inhabitants in the New World, establishing dynamic settlements when they were allowed to do so. These histories, now being researched more fully, need to be told in the place where they occurred. This was the purpose of the conference.

That we attracted a most significant and erudite panel of experts to present their papers over three days was in itself noteworthy. To have attracted a consistent audience of over 200 people daily over these three days was especially gratifying. To have the proceedings published is yet another reason to celebrate. To all those who contributed to the success of this conference, to the scholars who made it to Kingston, Jamaica and presented most willingly, I would like to express a heartfelt thank you. To the participants who attended, so interested in these presentations that they sat until the last words were spoken each day, many thanks are due.

The conference could not have taken place without the generosity of many people, especially those donors who chose to dedicate conference sessions in honour or to the memory of distinguished family members: Isaac Mendes Belisario (1794–1849), Charles Gomes Casseres (1921–2006), Ernest Henriques da Souza (1933–2000), Avram (Dolphy) Goldstein Goren (1905–2005), and Aaron Joseph Matalon (1918–2008). My special appreciation goes to the many unsung heroes and heroines who helped the presenters and participants energetically and anonymously.

Finally, to co-chair Professor Jane Gerber and conference co-ordinator Stanley Mirvis, I would like to express my gratitude not just for a job very well done, but as colleagues without whom it could not have happened and this book would still be a dream unfulfilled.

A vital segment of our history is preserved in these pages. Our children and their offspring will now have the opportunity to know more about their legacy in the Caribbean in general and Jamaica in particular.

AINSLEY COHEN HENRIQUES
Conference Co-Chair
Past President, Jamaica Historical Trust
President, United Congregation of Israelites

CONTENTS

List of Illustrations   XV

Note on Transliteration   xvii

Introduction   I
JANE S. GERBER

PART I
THE HISTORICAL BACKGROUND OF THE
CARIBBEAN SEPHARDI DIASPORA

1. The Formation of the Portuguese Jewish Diaspora   17
    MIRIAM BODIAN

2. Curaçao, Amsterdam, and the Rise of the Sephardi Trade System   29
    in the Caribbean, 1630–1700
    JONATHAN ISRAEL

3. To Live and to Trade: The Status of Sephardi Mercantile   45
    Communities in the Atlantic World during the Seventeenth and
    Eighteenth Centuries
    NOAH L. GELFAND

PART II
AUTHORITY AND COMMUNITY IN
THE DUTCH CARIBBEAN

4. Amsterdam and the Portuguese *Nação* of the Caribbean in   67
    the Eighteenth Century
    GÉRARD NAHON

5. 'A flock of wolves instead of sheep': The Dutch West India   85
    Company, Conflict Resolution, and the Jewish Community of
    Curaçao in the Eighteenth Century
    JESSICA ROITMAN

6. Religious Authority: A Perspective from the Americas   107
    HILIT SUROWITZ-ISRAEL

PART III

MATERIAL AND VISUAL CULTURE

7. Jonkonnu and Jew: The Art of Isaac Mendes Belisario (1794–1849)   121
JACKIE RANSTON

8. Testimonial Terrain: The Cemeteries of New World Sephardim   131
RACHEL FRANKEL

9. Counting the 'Sacred Lights of Israel': Synagogue Construction   143
and Architecture in the British Caribbean
BARRY L. STIEFEL

PART IV

JEWS AND SLAVE SOCIETY

10. The Cultural Heritage of Eurafrican Sephardi Jews in Suriname   169
AVIVA BEN-UR

11. Shifting Identities: Religion, Race, and Creolization among   195
the Sephardi Jews of Barbados, 1654–1900
KARL WATSON

12. Sexuality and Sentiment: Concubinage and the Sephardi Family   223
in Late Eighteenth-Century Jamaica
STANLEY MIRVIS

13. The 'Confession made by Cyrus' Reconsidered: Maroons and   241
Jews during Jamaica's First Maroon War (1728–1738/9)
JAMES ROBERTSON

14. Jewish Politicians in Post-Slavery Jamaica: Electoral Politics in   261
the Parish of St Dorothy, 1849–1860
SWITHIN WILMOT

PART V

REASSESSING THE GEOGRAPHICAL BOUNDARIES
OF CARIBBEAN JEWRY

15. The Borders of Early American Jewish History   281
ELI FABER

16. Port Jews and Plantation Jews: Carolina–Caribbean Connections   289
DALE ROSENGARTEN

PART VI
PERSONAL NARRATIVES

17. The Strange Adventures of Benjamin Franks, an Ashkenazi   311
Pioneer in the Americas
MATT GOLDISH

18. Daniel Israel López Laguna's *Espejo fiel de vidas* and the Ghosts of   319
Marrano Autobiography
RONNIE PERELIS

19. 'My heart is grieved': Grace Cardoze—A Life Revealed   329
through Letters
JOSETTE CAPRILES GOLDISH

PART VII
THE FORMATION OF CONTEMPORARY
CARIBBEAN JEWRY

20. Refugees from Nazism in the British Caribbean   343
JOANNA NEWMAN

21. Inscribing Ourselves with History: The Production of Heritage in   361
Today's Caribbean Jewish Diaspora
JUDAH M. COHEN

Notes on the Contributors   389

Index   395

ILLUSTRATIONS

COLOUR PLATES

between pages 126 and 127

7.1 *The Queen or 'Maam' of the Set Girls* (Isaac Mendes Belisario)

7.2 *Jaw-Bone, or House John-Canoe* (Isaac Mendes Belisario)

7.3 *Koo, Koo, or Actor Boy* (Isaac Mendes Belisario)

7.4 *Red Set Girls and Jack-in-the-Green* (Isaac Mendes Belisario)

7.5 *Bevis Marks Synagogue* (Isaac Mendes Belisario)

7.6 *Portrait of a Lady or The Lady in Black* (Ellen Tree) (Isaac Mendes Belisario)

7.7 Portrait of an unknown man (Isaac Mendes Belisario)

7.8 Portrait of Samuel Sharpe (Isaac Mendes Belisario)

7.9 Portrait of the Reverend Isaac Lopez (Isaac Mendes Belisario)

between pages 300 and 301

16.1 *An Exact Prospect of Charles Town* (Bishop Roberts)

16.2 Prayer book manuscript by Isaac Harby

16.3 'Calendar of Fasts, Festivals, and other days, Observed by the Israelites'

16.4 *Biblia Hebraica*

16.5 Miniature of Jacob de Leon (John Ramage)

16.6 Miniature of Abraham Moïse (Unknown artist)

16.7 Portrait of Rebecca Isaiah Moses, née Phillips (C. W. Uhl)

16.8 Portrait of Isaiah Moses (Theodore Sidney Moïse)

16.9 Portrait of Isabel Rebecca Lyons Mordecai (Theodore Sidney Moïse)

FIGURES

8.1 Tombstone of Mordecai, son of Solomon, son of Isaiah. Old Ashkenazi cemetery of Paramaribo, Suriname   132

8.2 Tombstone of Rebecca, wife of Benjamin Henriquez da Costa. Cassipora Creek cemetery, Suriname   136

9.1 Front elevation of Bevis Marks Synagogue, London   148

9.2 Detail of *Governor Robinson Going to Church* (Unknown artist)   150

9.3 Front elevation of Neve Shalom Synagogue, Spanish Town, Jamaica   154

9.4   Sha'ar Hashamayim Synagogue, Kingston, Jamaica   155
9.5   Thumbnail sketch of Shearith Israel Synagogue, New York   156
9.6   Front elevation of Jeshuat Israel's Touro Synagogue, Newport, RI   160
9.7   Front elevation of the Great Synagogue, Gibraltar   162
11.1   *Mikveh*, Nidhe Israel Synagogue, Bridgetown, Barbados   198
11.2   Front elevation of Nidhe Israel Synagogue, Bridgetown, Barbados   199
11.3   The Daniels family   202
11.4   Nancy Daniels   219
21.1   'Cordovan' menorah   365
21.2   St Eustatius Hanukah menorah   366
21.3   Cover of Isidor Paiewonsky, *Jewish Historical Development in the*   371
       Virgin Islands, 1665–1959
21.4   Cover of Judah M. Cohen, *Through the Sands of Time*   384

MAPS

13.1   Parish boundaries and eastern Jamaica, 1723–69   244
13.2   Parish of Portland, Jamaica, 1723–69   245
14.1   Jewish trading networks, St Dorothy, Jamaica, 1841–65   267
14.2   Settlements, St Dorothy, Jamaica, 1841–65   270

TABLES

9.1   Synagogues in English colonies of the first imperial period (1583–1783) 158
9.2   Sephardi synagogues built in the Dutch empire before the Patriot   159
       Revolt (1787–9)
11.1   Jewish wills registered in Barbados   200
11.2   Jewish residential patterns, Bridgetown, Barbados, 1749   208
11.3   Racial/religious profiles of house owners/occupants, Bridgetown,   209
       Barbados, 1804
14.1   Landholding of voters for Moses Lyon and Peter Harrison, St Dorothy,   269
       Jamaica, 1849
14.2   Regional distribution of voters, St Dorothy, Jamaica, 1850   271
14.3   Occupation of voters for Solomon Rodriques and David Smith, St Dorothy, 274
       Jamaica, 1854

NOTE ON TRANSLITERATION

THE transliteration of Hebrew in this book reflects consideration of the type of book it is, in terms of its content, purpose, and readership. The system adopted therefore reflects a broad approach to transcription, rather than the narrower approaches found in the *Encyclopaedia Judaica* or other systems developed for text-based or linguistic studies. The aim has been to reflect the pronunciation prescribed for modern Hebrew, rather than the spelling or Hebrew word structure, and to do so using conventions that are generally familiar to the English-speaking reader.

In accordance with this approach, no attempt is made to indicate the distinctions between *alef* and *ayin*, *tet* and *taf*, *kaf* and *kuf*, *sin* and *samekh*, since these are not relevant to pronunciation; likewise, the *dagesh* is not indicated except where it affects pronunciation. Following the principle of using conventions familiar to the majority of readers, however, transcriptions that are well established have been retained even when they are not fully consistent with the transliteration system adopted. On similar grounds, the *tsadi* is rendered by 'tz' in such familiar words as barmitzvah. Likewise, the distinction between *ḥet* and *khaf* has been retained, using *ḥ* for the former and *kh* for the latter; the associated forms are generally familiar to readers, even if the distinction is not actually borne out in pronunciation, and for the same reason the final *heh* is indicated too. As in Hebrew, no capital letters are used, except that an initial capital has been retained in transliterating titles of published works (for example, *Shulḥan arukh*).

Since no distinction is made between *alef* and *ayin*, they are indicated by an apostrophe only in intervocalic positions where a failure to do so could lead an English-speaking reader to pronounce the vowel-cluster as a diphthong—as, for example, in *ha'ir*—or otherwise mispronounce the word.

The *sheva na* is indicated by an *e*—*perikat ol, reshut*—except, again, when established convention dictates otherwise.

The *yod* is represented by *i* when it occurs as a vowel (*bereshit*), by *y* when it occurs as a consonant (*yesodot*), and by *yi* when it occurs as both (*yisra'el*).

Names have generally been left in their familiar forms, even when this is inconsistent with the overall system.

INTRODUCTION

JANE S. GERBER

IT IS MORE than a decade since the first academic gathering dedicated to the subject of the Jews and the expansion of Europe in the West convened at the John Carter Brown Library at Brown University in 1997.[1] In the interim new research has led to the expansion of Atlantic studies, Sephardi studies, and diaspora studies as discrete fields of enquiry, suggesting a redrawing of the temporal and geographical boundaries of the history of the Jews in the early modern period. A second conference, 'Atlantic Diasporas', was held at Johns Hopkins University in March 2005, its papers appearing in published form in 2009.[2] The presentations at the two gatherings emphasized the importance of transnational and interdisciplinary perspectives in studying the early modern period and its Jews. Since new research often tends to proceed along parallel lines, with little communication and few points of intersection across specialities, one of the goals of the conference on the Jewish diaspora in the Caribbean convened in Kingston, Jamaica, in January 2010 entitled 'The Jewish Diaspora of the Caribbean' was to bring together senior scholars from several disciplines and junior scholars in the early stages of their research to explore the Jewish diaspora in the Atlantic world. The second goal of the gathering was to shed light specifically on the history and culture of the Jews in Jamaica and to emphasize the importance of local developments in understanding broader regional and international currents.

Existing scholarship on the Jewish experience in the Americas has tended to focus on its New Christian antecedents in the Spanish- and Portuguese-speaking world. This emphasis reflects the dramatic Iberian origins of the earliest Jewish and crypto-Jewish enclaves in the Atlantic, as well as the richness of Spanish archival sources, a result of the zeal of the Spanish and Portuguese Inquisitions in ferreting out information from their victims. In contrast, research on the Jewish settlements in the Dutch and British colonial empires in the Caribbean has been frequently hampered by the paucity of sources, a consequence of the recurrent hurricanes and earthquakes in the region. The burgeoning field of Atlantic studies has raised new questions and provided alternative

---

[1] Paolo Bernardini and Norman Fiering (eds.), *The Jews and the Expansion of Europe to the West, 1450–1800* (New York, 2001).

[2] Richard L. Kagan and Philip D. Morgan (eds.), *Atlantic Diasporas: Jews, Conversos, and Crypto-Jews in the Age of Mercantilism, 1500–1800* (Baltimore, 2009).

perspectives on the study of Jewish history in which conventional views of 'centre' and 'periphery' in early modern history have been challenged. It is increasingly apparent that the parameters of early modern Jewish history require significant modification as the dramatic reconfigurations of Jewish identity played out globally in varying fashions. At the same time, newer notions of ethnicity, as distinct from religion, have challenged conventional definitions of sephardicity. To say that Caribbean Jewry became part of a heterogeneous New World with changing and multivalent ethnic and racial identities is to state the obvious. Yet traditional depictions of Sephardi cosmopolitanism have not usually included the rich local texture of the Caribbean diasporas. Similarly, Sephardi Jewish economic life acquires new dimensions when viewed from the colonial periphery rather than the European metropolitan centre. Considered through a Caribbean, as opposed to a continental European lens, Jewish life in the early modern period assumes new contours. England's colonial empire, for one, was centred in the Caribbean for centuries. When the Jewish community of Barbados was awarded residency rights provided that they 'behaved themselves civily and conformably to the Government of this Island' a milestone in the saga of Jewish emancipation was achieved. Similarly, when viewed from the Caribbean, the concession of a lawful niche for Jewish settlement in England had less to do with Menasseh ben Israel's petition to Oliver Cromwell than with the Sephardi role in the development of colonial trade. Nor can the affluence and mobility of Amsterdam's celebrated seventeenth-century Jewish community be fully understood without reference to its ongoing economic ties to Curaçao and Suriname. With the expansion of Europe in the west and the formation of multiple Jewish diasporas, alternative interpretations of Jewish identity and Jewish community appeared. Issues such as the emergence of modernity and the attainment of civic emancipation for the Jews acquired new meanings. In short, Caribbean Jewish life was neither simply an extension of the Jewish communities of London and Amsterdam nor an appendage of North America.

Jewish life in the western hemisphere begins with the crisis precipitated by the Expulsion of the Jews from Spain and Portugal at the close of the fifteenth century. As a result, a transnational Sephardi diaspora began to take shape, stretching eastwards from Iberia to the Balkans, the Levant, and Asia Minor and westwards to Brazil, several other points in South America, and the Caribbean islands. In the immediate aftermath of 1492 the majority of Spanish Jews moved directly over the border into Portugal, only to find themselves trapped there five years later and forcibly converted.[3] When King Manuel I ascended the throne of Portugal in 1496, he faced two contradictory pres-

---

[3] For a full discussion of the Expulsion, see Haim Beinart, *The Expulsion of the Jews from Spain* (Oxford, 2002). The connection between Portugal's expansionist policies and the king's preference for Jewish conversion rather than expulsion can be found in François Soyer, *The Persecution of the Jews and Muslims of Portugal: King Manuel I and the End of Religious Tolerance* (Leiden, 2007). Soyer's thesis contradicts the older and more widely accepted view that Manuel acceded to the Expulsion in order to gain the hand of Princess

sures. On the one hand, he aspired to expand the Portuguese empire into North Africa and around the Horn of Africa eastwards. His Portuguese Jewish population could play a positive economic role in such colonial ventures. On the other hand, however, he sought the hand of Princess Isabella of Spain and the eventual union of Spain and Portugal that such a betrothal promised. Reluctant to lose his talented Jewish population as demanded by the Spanish royal house, yet eager to embark upon his royal marriage, Manuel opted for the forced conversion of the Jews. By prohibiting any further practice of Judaism on Portuguese soil while simultaneously closing Portugal's borders to emigration, the Portuguese government imposed a de facto forced conversion to Christianity on all Jews remaining on Portuguese soil. A unique sociological phenomenon emerged as a result of this cynical and cruel measure. Portuguese society suddenly contained a large and distinctive social group—perhaps as much as 10 per cent of the total population of the country—that was neither fully Catholic nor any longer (in the eyes of the Church) Jewish. In Portugal's few urban areas Jews may have comprised as much as 25 per cent of the population. Aside from their concentration in cities and their distinctive socio-economic roles, the new converts included some of the most stalwart émigrés from the 1492 Spanish Expulsion, the people least likely to passively accept the new Christian faith imposed upon them. The formerly Jewish population (known variously as *la naçao* or *Cristãos novos* in the Portuguese domain and as *la nación*, Conversos, or Marranos in the Spanish realm), formed a definable entity whose integration, even under the best of circumstances, was problematic. In this instance, social integration of such a large and distinctive ethnic group was rejected by the Christian majority.

The New Christians who remained in Portugal after the deadline for departure were assured by the government that no ecclesiastical body would be established to question their religious practices and beliefs. The absence of an Inquisition in Portugal for at least one generation facilitated the establishment of crypto-Jewish practices among individuals and groups of former Jews. Perhaps the majority of the formerly Jewish population proceeded initially to go 'underground', practising those aspects of Judaism that could be expressed in the absence of synagogues, schools, books, and a formal community or religious leadership. Since crypto-Judaism, by its nature, leaves few traces, it is difficult to follow the evolution of Jewish practice after its official demise in Iberia. The preservation and transmission of Judaism were dangerous and circumscribed, especially after the establishment of the Portuguese Inquisition in 1536. In this context, fraught with suspicion and peril, the newly discovered lands in the west offered the possibility of refuge. Removed from Iberia, New Christians could conceal their Jewish ancestry and evade the economic restrictions imposed on them as a result of

Isabella. For another perspective, see Benjamin R. Gampel, 'Ferdinand and Isabella and the Decline of Portuguese and Navaresse Jewries', in Yom Tov Assis and Yosef Kaplan (eds.), *Jews and Conversos at the Time of the Expulsion* (Jerusalem, 1999), 65–92.

their Jewish roots. They could also cultivate clandestine forms of Jewish practice and identity far from informers and the surveillance of the Iberian inquisitions. Many New Christians who emigrated probably also hoped to eventually participate in a Jewish life that they had never known or only dimly recalled.

But western European ports also beckoned. Before long, New Christian enclaves emerged in European commercial centres such as Antwerp, Bordeaux, London, Hamburg, and, especially, Amsterdam, as well as in the New World colonies across the Atlantic. New Christians who emigrated often remained in touch with relatives in the Iberian ports of Lisbon, Porto, Seville, and Madeira and retained commercial and familial ties that transcended imperial boundaries. These Iberian émigrés were widely valued for their entrepreneurial skills as well as for their long-distance trading contacts.

One favourite destination of Portuguese New Christians during the sixteenth century was Brazil, where sugar production was emerging as an increasingly important factor in international commerce. Between 1550 and 1650 modest investors could participate in sugar cargoes and even acquire fortunes in the sugar trade. When the Dutch conquered Portuguese Brazil in 1630, the New Christians who had gravitated to Brazil under the Portuguese were now finally able to espouse Judaism openly. The newly found religious freedom of Brazil also enticed hundreds of Portuguese New Christians and Jews from various parts of western Europe to cross the Atlantic to participate in the new economy as well as to join the faith of their forebears. With their right to profess Judaism in Brazil under the newly proclaimed Dutch administration (1630–54) temporarily assured, Sephardim began to assist actively in the shaping of Dutch transatlantic commerce. Indeed, so significant were the Jews of Brazil to the colony's prosperity that the Dutch West India Company granted them rights and privileges still denied their co-religionists in Holland, including commercial protection and the right to engage in retail trade.[4] But their well-being in Brazil was short-lived. With the Portuguese reconquest in 1654, the Jews were forced to flee. The dispersal of some 1,500 Jews from Dutch Brazil came at a propitious moment, greatly enhancing the colonizing capacity of Dutch Jewry. Its resources increased dramatically and new opportunities were opening up in the Caribbean. Many Brazilian Jews returned to Amsterdam, others spread throughout the Caribbean, a relatively large number migrating to the Guianas, Barbados, Martinique, and in Jamaica, as well as New Amsterdam. These Brazilian émigrés, now openly practising Jews, successfully negotiated the establishment of new Jewish

[4] New Christians and Sephardi Jews were responsible for developing at least 20 per cent of Brazil's sugar production capacity (see James C. Boyajian, 'New Christians and Jews in the Sugar Trade, 1550–1750: Two Centuries of Development of the Atlantic Economy', in Bernardini and Fiering (eds.), *The Jews and the Expansion of Europe to the West*, 476; for an overview, see Anita Novinsky, 'Sephardim in Brazil: The New Christians', in Richard D. Barnett and Walter M. Schwab (eds.), *The Sephardi Heritage: Essays on the History and Cultural Contribution of the Jews of Spain and Portugal*, vol. ii: *The Western Sephardim* (Grendon, Northants, 1989), 431–44).

communities and played a significant role in the development of the non-Spanish Caribbean. Among those who returned to Holland, many subsequently joined other Jews from Amsterdam and London in the emerging commercial opportunities in the Dutch and British Caribbean. It was during the 1650s, as a result of the demographic shifts following the Dutch defeat in Brazil, that Amsterdam Sephardi Jews established a Jewish settlement in Dutch Curaçao.[5]

Sephardi Jews were deemed to be valuable settlers by European Protestant colonial powers. Their family networks spanned the globe, while their surviving web of business ties in Iberia could be especially beneficial to commerce. Moreover, they were conversant with trading conditions in Europe and the Ottoman empire and spoke the languages of both regions. They shared with the English and the Dutch a common hostility to Spain and Portugal based, in the case of the Sephardim, on their tormented past and the continuing plight of crypto-Jews and New Christians on Iberian soil. The presence among them of merchants, planters, artisans, and experts in tobacco, sugar, dye-woods, and other commercially significant products of South America enhanced their attractiveness as a source of manpower and utility to the colonial powers. In the opinion of historians David Sorkin and Lois Dubin the Sephardi Jews constitute a distinct social type that they identify as 'Port Jews', noteworthy for their mobility and their roles as cultural brokers and purveyors of products.[6] The enterprising Dutch recognized the commercial assets the Sephardim could bring to the Low Countries and the Dutch colonies and acknowledged their presence by granting them the right to practise Judaism in Amsterdam, albeit inconspicuously, in the early seventeenth century. Amsterdam's Jews also actively pursued agricultural as well as commercial endeavours after the Dutch seizure of Curaçao from the Spanish in 1634 and Suriname from the British in 1667.

The history of the Jews of Jamaica forms an integral chapter in the life of the New Christians of Iberia. Secret Jews and descendants of former converts probably numbered among the first Spanish settlers to the island. According to some reports, they even served as guides to the conquering British fleet when it took the Spanish port of

[5] Isaac S. Emmanuel and Suzanne A. Emmanuel, *A History of the Jews in the Netherlands Antilles*, 2 vols. (Cincinnati, 1970), i. 40–1, 46–7. Amsterdam's chocolate-manufacturing industry, a typical Jewish industry in the seventeenth century, began on a significant scale soon after the rise of the Curaçao trade in the 1650s (see Jonathan I. Israel, 'The Economic Contribution of Dutch Sephardi Jewry to Holland's Golden Age, 1595–1713', *Tijdschrift voor Geschiedenis*, 96 (1983), 505–35).

[6] Lois C. Dubin, 'Researching Port Jews and Port Jewries: Trieste and Beyond', in David Cesarani (ed.), *Port Jews: Jewish Communities in Cosmopolitan Maritime Trading Centres, 1550–1950* (London, 2002), 47–58; ead., '"Wings on their feet . . . and the wings on their heads": Reflections on the Study of Port Jews', *Jewish Culture and History*, 7 (2004), 16–30; ead., 'Introduction: Port Jews in the Atlantic World "Jewish History"', *Jewish History*, 20/2 (2006), 117–27; ead., *The Port Jews of Hapsburg Trieste: Absolutist Politics and Enlightenment Culture* (Stanford, Calif., 1999); David Sorkin, 'The Port Jew: Notes Toward a Social Type', *Journal of Jewish Studies*, 50/1 (1999), 86–97; id., 'Port Jews and the Three Regions of Emancipation', in Cesarani (ed.), *Port Jews*, 31–46.

St Iago de la Vega (Spanish Town) in 1655. Almost immediately after the British occupation of Jamaica in 1655, the so-called 'Portugals' established an openly Jewish presence in the commercial centre of Port Royal. In contrast to Dutch Curaçao, Danish St Thomas, or English Barbados, where the Jews were concentrated in a few urban centres, or to Dutch Suriname, with its distinctive plantation economy and unique ethnic intermixing, Jamaican Jewry was widely dispersed in several towns and villages, as well as in the main population centres on the island, and soon possessed numerous synagogues and cemeteries. As the island flourished, the Jewish population grew apace. At the time of the American War of Independence, when only 120 Jews resided in Newport, Rhode Island's famous Jewish community, and 600 Jews resided in Charleston, South Carolina, Jamaica housed a Jewish population of 900 and Suriname, in 1787, contained 1,292 Jews, forming, in both instances, a significant proportion of the resident European population. At its peak in 1881, the Jewish population of Jamaica numbered approximately 2,500 (out of a total white population of 14,432), constituting the most important Jewish community in the Caribbean.[7] By the eighteenth century distinctive Ashkenazi communities existed alongside the Sephardim in the region.

The contributions to this volume are dedicated primarily to the Jewish settlements of the Dutch and English colonies in the Caribbean, with a focus on the Jews of British Jamaica in the seventeenth and eighteenth centuries. It would be incorrect, however, to over-emphasize any specific national loyalties or identities of the Jews in the proto-nationalist societies of the seventeenth and eighteenth centuries. Jews enjoyed varying political conditions under the several European powers, despite the economic and political competition among the European nations throughout the region. Jewish inter-communal trading, social, and familial networks straddled the various empires. Distinctions based upon different sovereign powers were muted among the Jews. The Dutch language, for example, scarcely figured in either naming patterns or cemetery inscriptions for generations. The Portuguese Jews of the seventeenth and eighteenth centuries circulated among the various imperial systems, fairly insulated from the raging theological divisions and political rivalries characterizing the European powers of their day.[8] As we shall see in several of the chapters in this volume, the favourable status of the Jews in the Caribbean frequently anticipated their legal emancipation in

---

[7] Mordechai Arbell, *The Portuguese Jews of Jamaica* (Kingston, Jamaica, 2000), 36; see also Jacob A. P. M. Andrade, *A Record of the Jews in Jamaica from the English Conquest to the Present Time* (Kingston, Jamaica, 1941); Richard D. Barnett and Phillip Wright, *The Jews of Jamaica, Tombstone Inscriptions* (Jerusalem, 1997); Benjamin Schlesinger, 'The Jews of Jamaica: A Historical Review', *Caribbean Quarterly*, 13 (1967), 46–53. On comparative population statistics, see Seymour Drescher, 'Jews and New Christians in the Atlantic Slave Trade', in Bernardini and Fiering (eds.), *Jews and the Expansion of Europe to the West*, 460, table 21.3. See also Chapters 15 and 16 below on reassessing early American Jewry.

[8] Evelyne Oliel-Grausz, 'Networks and Communication in the Sephardi Diaspora: An Added Dimension to the Concept of Port Jews and Port Jewries', in David Cesarani and Gemma Romain (eds.), *Jews and Port Cities, 1590–1990: Commerce, Community, and Cosmopolitanism* (London, 2006), 61–76.

Europe. Culturally, Caribbean Jews bore some resemblances to their co-religionists in Europe. Portuguese persisted among the Portuguese Jewish diaspora, largely as a language of symbolic importance, particularly in religious life. At the same time unique cultural expressions and manifestations of ethnicity emerged in the ethnically diverse slave societies of the Caribbean. In constant contact with one another, they frequently moved from one island to the next, often criss-crossing the Atlantic to the ports of western Europe. Early on the Jews were ousted from the French Caribbean. Banished by the Code Noir (1685), they moved to more favourable conditions in Curaçao. Regardless of the European power in control, Amsterdam and its Jewish authorities loomed large in all the Caribbean Jewish settlements in the seventeenth and eighteenth centuries, with London gradually gaining in importance in the eighteenth and nineteenth centuries.

Part I of this volume focuses on the historical background of Jewish communities in the Dutch and British Caribbean and explores some of their defining features. Miriam Bodian, a prominent historian of Portuguese Jewry, traces the roots and migratory patterns of the 'western Sephardi diaspora'. Describing a highly mobile international trading community that dealt in colonial commodities such as indigo, cacao, and sugar, Bodian also notes that the Portuguese Jewish diaspora tended to experience a looser form of adherence or affiliation to Judaism after discarding its crypto-Jewish masks and formally adopting Judaism. The widespread and generally accepted Jewish ideal of the merchant and communal leader who was also a learned Talmud scholar never took root in this diaspora. In weighing the comparative roles of kinship networks and economic factors in dictating the direction of Sephardi migration, Bodian notes that the Portuguese New Christians of the sixteenth and seventeenth centuries anticipated the changing patterns of world trade and migration.

Jonathan Israel, an eminent historian of the Dutch Republic in the seventeenth century, explores the rise of the Sephardi trading system between 1630 and 1700, offering new insights into when and why Jewish participation in Caribbean commerce became a prominent feature of Dutch trade. Israel posits that the key factor in the ascendancy of Curaçao and its Jews was not the policies of the West India Company and its shareholders but new patterns of navigation and maritime technical innovations. The small craft that replaced the large long-distance Dutch ships could enter the many lagoons, inlets, and peninsulas between Rio de la Hacha and Coro. This mode of trading provided the basis for the long-term stability of the Sephardi community of Curaçao, a community comprising merchants, ship-owners, suppliers, and brokers, many of whom were familiar with the Spanish language. The increasing trade in cash crops, such as cacao, tobacco, and sugar, between Curaçao and western Europe, coupled with Jewish adaptability to new commercial conditions, lay at the heart of Jewish prosperity in Curaçao. Israel's study pinpoints precisely when these changes occurred, revising other scholarly theories on the emergence of Curaçao as a centre of Jewish commerce.

The seventeenth century was the century of Dutch global economic hegemony. As Amsterdam emerged as the entrepôt of European commerce, her Sephardi Jews assumed significant roles in the economic development of Suriname, Dutch Brazil, and Curaçao. Their colonial contributions, in turn, were recognized by the Dutch (and British) with the concession of unprecedented charters and privileges to the Jews. Noah Gelfand presents a broad overview of the negotiated rights and privileges of the early Jewish settlements in the Atlantic world and rejects the notion of any consistent 'Jewish policy' on the part of the British and Dutch empires. Rather, Jewish rights and privileges were achieved on an ad hoc basis depending upon a variety of situational factors in the metropolitan centres or the peripheries of the empires.

The three essays in Part II on authority and community in the Dutch Caribbean illustrate how Amsterdam's Jewish community and the West India Company wielded considerable influence in shaping local Jewish life in the Caribbean. In his analysis of the centrality of Amsterdam in the lives of the Jews of the Caribbean, Gérard Nahon, senior historian of the western Sephardi diaspora, stresses the centrality of Amsterdam's Jewish community as a source of religious leadership and religious artefacts for Jewish communities in the Dutch Caribbean. His chapter includes the texts of several letters preserved in the *Copiador de Cartas* detailing the various religious connections of Amsterdam Jewry and its Mahamad with the Jews of the West Indies and tracing the waning of Amsterdam's pre-eminence in the eighteenth century.

The ties between the Jewries of Amsterdam and Curaçao were complex and multi-layered. The West India Company and the Mahamad of Amsterdam were only two of several official bodies empowered to exercise control over the religious affairs of the Jews in Curaçao. Although the local Mahamad theoretically possessed absolute authority to protect and discipline the Jews of Curaçao, members of the community would sometimes appeal directly to the Dutch government, the West India Company, or the Amsterdam Mahamad, if they found the decisions of the local authorities unacceptable. Plagued by internal factionalism during the seventeenth and eighteenth centuries, Curaçao's Jews had recourse to Amsterdam repeatedly and also turned to overlapping authorities locally. Tensions between dependence and autonomy in the Dutch Caribbean are the subject of complementary studies by Hilit Surowitz-Israel and Jessica Roitman. Both scholars explore specific instances of Jewish communal conflict in which thorny questions regarding the locus of authority surfaced. Surowitz-Israel uses the *ascamot* of 1688 and a responsum from 1767 to highlight the contest for decision-making powers among the Jews. Jessica Roitman presents a lively chronicling of the complex unfolding of events during an acrimonious communal conflict in Curaçao in 1746, adding nuance to standard histories of the West India Company and its powers vis-à-vis the Jews. Both studies demonstrate that the western Sephardi Jews proved unable to resolve their communal conflicts in the early modern period as many areas of life began to elude the all-embracing hold of the religious community and its oligarchic rule. Yosef Kaplan has shown elsewhere how misuse and overuse of the *ḥerem* in Amsterdam in the eighteenth century was one important index of this growing phenomenon.

Although the Caribbean never ranked among the main cultural centres of Sephardi Jewry, its history is not devoid of artistic interest or achievements. Part III examines the material and visual culture of Jamaican Jewry in chapters by art historian and biographer Jackie Ranston, architect Rachel Frankel, and architectural historian Barry Stiefel. Ranston is the biographer of Isaac Mendes Belisario (1794–1849), the first island-born Jamaican artist and an iconic figure in Jamaican cultural history considered by many to be the national painter of Jamaica. His greatest work is a series of warm and very human lithographs depicting the local Jamaican Christmas masquerade known as Jonkonnu, an annual festival that 'included multiple African cultures and European masquerade alongside British mumming plays and even Shakespearean monologues'. In his representation of the Jonkonnu celebration, Belisario sympathetically depicts this authentic survival of African culture among Jamaica's slaves and provides unique visual depictions of its elaborate costumes and costly masks. Ranston suggests speculatively that the disguises donned during the Jonkonnu carnival might have struck a sympathetic chord in Belisario, a descendant of former Marranos. She also comments on the specific economic and human contacts that developed among Jewish shopkeepers and the slave population of Jamaica at the time of the annual Jonkonnu.

Architect Rachel Frankel's cemetery restoration project at Hunt's Bay in Jamaica provides hints of the religious beliefs of Jamaica's Jews in the seventeenth and eighteenth centuries. Frankel compares her findings at the Jamaican restoration project with those she uncovered at the Cassipora Creek cemetery excavation in the plantation colony of Suriname, contrasting the Jewish settlement in the British empire with the one in the Dutch empire. Jews in both empires have left traces of shared messianic traditions in some of their interment practices.[9] Frankel includes the texts of several tombstones in her study and notes the conspicuous absence of the Dutch language among Surinamese inscriptions. In his survey of synagogue construction in the English-speaking world, Barry Stiefel stresses the global reach of Sephardi settlement in the late seventeenth century, noting the relative numerical unimportance of the Jewish population in the British Isles compared with that of the Caribbean. He quantifies the population shifts of New World Jewry reflected in the dates of synagogue construc-

---

[9] Rachel Frankel, 'Antecedents and Remnants of Jodensavanne: The Synagogues and Cemeteries of the First Permanent Plantation Settlement of New World Jews', in Bernardini and Fiering (eds.), *Jews and the Expansion of Europe to the West*, 394–439; on the messianic traditions of colonial Jewry and Dutch Jewry in general, see Aviva Ben-Ur and Rachel Frankel, *Remnant Stones*, vol. i: *The Jewish Cemeteries of Suriname: Epitaphs* (Cincinnati, 2009).

tion and also seeks signs of mutual influences among the many synagogue construction projects in the Dutch, British, and Danish territories.

In Part IV the relationships between slaves and Jews are explored by Aviva Ben-Ur, Karl Watson, Stanley Mirvis, James Robertson, and Swithin Wilmot. The five contributions in this section approach the subject of the relations of Jews and blacks in Caribbean slave society from the perspectives of gender and family, political history, and popular culture, adding to the growing body of literature in this field. Historian Aviva Ben-Ur examines the cultural heritage of Eurafrican Sephardi Jews of Suriname in her fascinating study of the Jewish identity of enslaved and manumitted mulattoes who were the offspring of Sephardi Jews and their former slaves. Focusing on a few dozen Eurafricans in eighteenth-century Suriname, Ben-Ur invokes naming patterns from tombstone inscriptions, wills, and communal registers; oral testimonies combined with genealogical research; and archives in The Hague to recreate Eurafrican cultural identity. Conversion to Judaism, according to Ben-Ur, was only one index of identity and not necessarily the most important one. She emphasizes the heterogeneity of the Surinamese Jewish community and the complexities of discussing Surinamese issues of race and Jewish identity.

Stanley Mirvis uncovers new evidence of bonds of affection between Sephardi men and their black or mulatto slaves or concubines and offspring through a close reading of wills and probate records in Jamaica. Mirvis's study provides new evidence of an evolving Sephardi identity in the Caribbean during the eighteenth century and relates Sephardi family developments to the social history and evolving family patterns in the broader society. Karl Watson's detailed description of the stipulations in the wills and records of Sephardi Jews in Barbados provides a vivid illustration of the creolization of the Barbadian population and the familial interconnections among its Portuguese Jewish population.

Jews were far more prominent in Jamaica during the eighteenth century than in either Great Britain proper or any of her other colonies. Nevertheless, their political loyalties were subject to question and suspicion in Jamaica, particularly during the eighteenth-century slave revolts. Jamaican historian James Robertson examines an incident of Jewish 'treason' that allegedly occurred during the First Maroon War (1728–1738/9), a war that was waged between Jamaica's self-emancipated former slaves and their descendants (Maroons) and the colonial government. It was rumoured at the time that runaway slaves and Maroon insurgents were purchasing gunpowder from a Jewish merchant. One possible source of this allegation was the confession extracted from a captured Maroon agent, described in colonial records as 'Cyrus the slave'. Robertson examines the precise wording of the 'confession of Cyrus', a testimony replete with seemingly authentic details that the captive had concocted. Robertson's *explication de texte* unveils the inconsistencies in the text and the historical context in which the accusation of Jewish treason was upheld. The text of Cyrus's 'confession' is included as an appendix to the chapter.

The Jews of Jamaica gained full civil rights in 1831, six months after the free blacks and three years before the general abolition of slavery. (Significantly, it took another twenty-seven years before the Jews in England were emancipated.) Nevertheless, colour remained a divisive political issue long after the legal emancipation of the slaves. Prominent Jamaican historian Swithin Wilmot explores the social cleavages in Jamaica's society in the nineteenth century, tracing black–Jewish relations between 1849 and 1860 as reflected in the electoral politics of St Dorothy, a parish west of Spanish Town. Wilmot analyses the ways in which the white Protestants, perceiving Jews as 'off-white' although socially inferior, sought to make common cause with the Jewish merchant class and the wealthy free coloureds. Wilmot's examination of the voting records in St Dorothy Parish reveals an emergent alliance between the newly freed black people and the Jews, despite these white Protestant overtures. Between 1838 and 1866 Jewish representation in the Jamaican Assembly rose from 4 per cent to 28 per cent. Wilmot suggests that amicable ties among blacks, coloureds, and Jews were forged in the commercial relations and social connections that developed in the Sunday markets in Kingston and other towns during the period of slavery. He demonstrates how Jewish retailers and black small settlers and coloured artisans were able to build upon their earlier amicable relations to create a solid electoral partnership, noting that Jewish electoral candidates also addressed issues, such as education and more equitable property qualifications for suffrage, that were of central concern to the new class of black small settlers.

The field of Atlantic studies has drawn a new map of European settlement in the west, one that takes into account a broad arc stretching from Brazil to Newfoundland. The far-flung Sephardi diaspora fits comfortably into this revised geographical sweep. Two scholarly considerations of the parameters of Jewish settlement are presented in Part V. American colonial Jewish historian Eli Faber redraws the boundaries of early American Jewry, placing it within an arc in which the Jews of London, Amsterdam, and the Caribbean are all linked to the North American mainland, and suggests alternative ways in which American Jewry can be integrated into a new global history. Both Faber and curator Dale Rosengarten invoke the family histories of long-familiar colonial American Jews to illuminate their more expansive definition of American Jewry. Faber turns to the Jews of Jamaica to inform colonial Jewish history in New York, while Rosengarten invokes the history of Jews in Barbados to illuminate colonial Charleston, South Carolina. Both scholars call for a reframing of the parameters of American Jewish history and suggest a reassessment of the connections between the Caribbean and colonial North America.

Traditional histories of Caribbean Jews have tended to concentrate on depicting the lives of the wealthy, the prominent, and the successful among the Sephardi merchants, as has Sephardi history in general. In contrast, the portraits presented in Part VI are of unknown or little-known Jews of the Caribbean whose experiences add texture and depth to our knowledge of the emergence of the Ashkenazi diaspora in the region, of early cultural life among Jews in the Caribbean, and of the lives of Sephardi women.

The early Caribbean Jewish experience is generally and correctly depicted as an extension of the Sephardi diaspora. In his chapter, Matt Goldish paints a colourful portrait of an otherwise unknown peripatetic Ashkenazi Jew of the seventeenth century, Benjamin Franks, forebear of the famous Franks family of colonial New York. Benjamin Franks, a victim of the great earthquake of 1692 in Port Royal, Jamaica, would have remained anonymous were it not for his ill-fated decision to seek to regain his fortune in India by signing on as a member of Captain Kidd's crew. The distinction between privateer and pirate, the one legal and the other not, was often blurred in the seventeenth and eighteenth centuries. Matt Goldish reconstructs Franks's misadventures from his humble beginnings in Jamaica to his eventual role as star witness against Captain Kidd in Bombay and London. As Franks criss-crossed the globe his wanderings mirror the migration patterns of many seventeenth- and eighteenth-century Ashkenazi Jews seeking a livelihood on the heels of the successful western Sephardim. Using the biography of Franks as paradigmatic, Goldish also demonstrates the ease with which a Jewish trader, whether Ashkenazi or Sephardi, could set up shop on any continent in that age.

The first Jewish poet to gain prominence in Jamaica was the Portuguese-born Daniel Israel López Laguna (1635–1730). Ronnie Perelis, a scholar of literary biographies, seeks hints of Laguna's tormented Marrano past in his Spanish paraphrase of the book of Psalms, *Espejo fiel de vidas*, an exceptional literary work composed in Jamaica. Perelis's task is particularly challenging since Laguna's interior life and any hints of his dramatic New Christian autobiography are well hidden. After examining the literary genre of self-disclosure among sixteenth- and seventeenth-century former Conversos in general, Perelis turns to Laguna's poetic paraphrase of the Psalms, noting the creative power of the poet's long sojourn in Jamaica.

The status of Sephardi women, as indeed of most women in the nineteenth century, was frequently lamentable. Josette Goldish presents a poignant account of an obscure nineteenth-century Jewish woman, Grace Cardoze, from Danish St Thomas, whose biography has come to light through the recent discovery of a cache of her letters in Denmark. Josette Goldish recreates her tragic and stoic life through a study of the decades-long correspondence between the Cardoze–Delvalle family and Rabbi Simonsen of Denmark. In introducing the reader to the personal trials of a woman who was the victim of hardships precipitated by her husband's infidelity and Victorian attitudes towards poverty, social convention, and mental illness, Goldish uncovers a human portrait that shatters many stereotypes about 'the Sephardi family'.

Few Jews reside in the Caribbean today and fewer still can trace their origins to the Sephardi settlers of the early modern period. Historic synagogues have been destroyed and cemeteries lie abandoned and eroded by the elements. The voluminous literature on Jewish migration in the twentieth century includes little research on the Jews of the Caribbean. The closing section of the book (Part VII) turns to two areas of current demographic and historical interest, the rescue and resettlement of the Jews of Europe during the Second World War and the construction of memory and the production of history among demographically declining or vanishing Jewish communities around the globe.

Apart from the saga of the admission of a small group of German Jewish refugees to Sosúa in the Dominican Republic as a result of the Evian Conference, the Caribbean is usually not associated with efforts to rescue and resettle the beleaguered Jews of Europe during the inter-war period.[10] Joanna Newman's research into Gibraltar Camp in Jamaica and the little-known story of the resettlement of Jews in Trinidad raises anew some of the thorny issues of the 'politics of rescue' of European Jews in the 1930s and 1940s. Newman contrasts Jewish resettlement projects in the islands of Jamaica and Trinidad and notes the tensions between British and West Indian immigration policies, on the one hand, and the Jewish resettlement agencies, on the other. While the British sought to limit Jewish access to the West Indies, advocates of Jewish resettlement searched vainly for asylum for the Jews of Europe in any likely or unlikely corner of the globe. Trinidad briefly offered the possibility of Jewish rescue, since it did not require entry visas during the 1930s. But fears of inundation by penniless Jewish refugees, reflected in the lyrics of a calypso that Newman includes in her discussion, led to the closing of Trinidad's borders in January 1939. In contrast to the accessibility of Trinidad during the 1930s, Jamaica was closed to Jewish immigration prior to 1941. At that time, the British decided to build an internment camp outside Kingston to relieve the growing number of refugees in Gibraltar. The camp, which came to be known as Gibraltar Camp, was prepared for an anticipated 9,000 European refugees, although the number of admissions was eventually reduced to 1,700. The Jewish inmates faced severe restrictions on mobility and the pursuit of a livelihood and dispersed soon after the end of the war. Today, the story of Gibraltar Camp is virtually unknown, and the site is part of the campus of the University of the West Indies in Kingston.

The past decade has witnessed many attempts to restore historic synagogues and Jewish cemeteries around the globe. Most of these projects, including those in the Caribbean, have occurred where Jewish communities no longer exist. In some places, remnants of former communities seek to reconnect with a more dynamic past through the excavation and rededication of historic sites. Many of the restorations in Europe have been commercialized and form part of Jewish 'heritage trails' that are promoted

[10] See Marian A. Kaplan, *Dominican Haven: The Jewish Refugee Settlement in Sosúa, 1940–1945* (New York, 2008).

for the explicit purpose of tourism. In the final chapter of the book, ethnomusicologist Judah Cohen explores the ways in which memory informs contemporary identity formation in one instance in the Caribbean, through an analysis of the events surrounding the bicentennial celebration of a historic synagogue in St Thomas. The celebration in question was planned and executed by the Hebrew Congregation of St Thomas, a congregation formally affiliated with the Union for Reform Judaism (1967) whose membership is heavily American Ashkenazi in origin and relatively recent by the standards of the Caribbean.

In 1996–7 the Hebrew Congregation of St Thomas organized a bicentennial celebration and sought to attach itself communally and symbolically to the historic congregation Beracha Veshalom Vegemiluth Hasadim, the original Sephardi congregation founded in 1797 under Danish rule. In a lively and perceptive analysis, Cohen suggests how 'heritage production' may simultaneously both inform and preserve the present St Thomas community. St Thomas Jewry shares some of the challenges, such as an unstable climate and uncertain financial and political conditions, confronting other Jewish settlements in the Caribbean. Like other dwindling Jewish communities around the globe, the community of St Thomas has tried to take advantage of the Jewish tourist trade through the preservation of a site of Jewish history. It seeks, according to Cohen, to present itself as 'a congregation of rooted islanders yet also as sophisticated travellers'. In the process, it has turned to a romanticized Sephardi past, appropriating it as its own. Cohen, who served as a participant-observer in the St Thomas celebratory events, notes the role that the 'Sephardi mystique' plays in the ongoing shaping of that community's identity.

The process of reconnecting with a more dynamic Jewish past that energized the St Thomas community also animates other recent Caribbean Jewish projects such as the Jewish cemetery restorations in Suriname and Jamaica and the restoration of the historic Sephardi synagogue of Bridgetown in Barbados. These efforts form part of global attempts to retrieve local Jewish history. As in St Thomas, such projects have often been accompanied by tenuous claims to an inherited Sephardi identity by the surviving remnant community, providing an ambiguous source of new identities and reconstructed histories. Such projects of memory construction and commemoration have also had salutary results as a by-product. They have led to the convening of conferences, the initiation of efforts towards archival preservation, the construction of local museums, and the recognition of the Jewish past as an integral part of local history. Such projects also serve to greatly expand the boundaries of Sephardi Jewish history, placing it squarely within the new fields of Atlantic and diaspora studies.

PART I

THE HISTORICAL BACKGROUND
OF THE
CARIBBEAN SEPHARDI DIASPORA

CHAPTER ONE

THE FORMATION OF THE PORTUGUESE JEWISH DIASPORA

MIRIAM BODIAN

CARIBBEAN JEWRY was a sub-diaspora with roots in an older and wider one that scholars refer to as the 'western Sephardi diaspora' or the 'Portuguese Jewish diaspora'. This chapter will explore the formation—geographical, cultural, and economic —of the older diaspora, from whose DNA, so to speak, Caribbean Jewry developed.

Although the origins of the western Sephardi diaspora, properly speaking, lie in Portugal, a coherent narrative must begin with events in late fourteenth-century Spain. Spanish Jewry at that time possessed a rich culture and sophisticated forms of communal organization that had developed over centuries. It constituted the largest Jewry in the world. The activity of the mendicant orders in town plazas and court circles had given new impetus to popular anti-Jewish feeling, but there was no obvious reason to anticipate the riots that broke out in Seville during the summer of 1391 and spread throughout the towns of Castile and Aragon. The scale of the riots was unprecedented. We have no statistics, but it is evident from the documents that many Jews were killed. Of those who survived, many did so because they lived in communities that were not struck. Many others survived only because they submitted to baptism. Indeed, by the time the riots ceased, a significant new population of Conversos had been created. And the newly baptized could not reclaim their status as Jews. Although technically the Church prohibited forced baptisms, such conversions had long been viewed as valid after the fact.[1] A baptized Jew who reverted to Judaism was a heretic and, if apprehended, was subject to severe punishment. This rarely happened before the establishment of the Inquisition, but public scrutiny and the threat of popular violence were effective in policing the public behaviour of Conversos.[2]

---

[1] See the note by Kenneth Stow in Solomon Grayzel, *The Church and the Jews in the XIIIth Century*, ed. Kenneth Stow, 2 vols. (New York, 1966; repr. Detroit, 1989), ii. 103 n. 3; Benjamin Ravid, 'The Forced Baptism of Jewish Minors in Early-Modern Venice', *Italia*, 13–15 (2001), 259–60.

[2] The most detailed and thorough account of the riots of 1391 and their aftermath is still Yitzhak Baer, *A History of the Jews in Christian Spain*, 2 vols. (Philadelphia, 1978), ii. 95–169; for a more recent, succinct account, see Jane Gerber, *The Jews of Spain: A History of the Sephardic Experience* (New York, 1992), 113–18.

The consequence was an unprecedented sociological situation. The existence side by side of practising Jews and backsliding Conversos, at a time of feverish anti-Jewish preaching by mendicant friars, was a recipe for trouble. Hostility to unbaptized Jews persisted, and hostility to Jewish converts and their descendants (whose sincerity was suspect) grew. Tensions led to the establishment of the Spanish Inquisition in the early 1480s in order to eliminate Converso 'judaizing'. These tensions also precipitated the expulsion of the unbaptized Jews in 1492 in order to eliminate Converso contact with the source of religious 'pollution'.

Genealogically, Caribbean Jewry had its roots in the Spanish Jews expelled in 1492, who were *not* descendants of the Jews baptized in 1391 or thereafter. These Jews, whose families had resisted Catholic missionizing pressures in the century leading up to the Expulsion, had come to view the Church with a high degree of revulsion. During their last decade in Spain—that is, after the establishment of the Inquisition—they had witnessed the Inquisition's terrorization of their erstwhile co-religionists, which surely rendered the option of choosing baptism over exile after the Edict of Expulsion an unpalatable one. Consider the cautionary remark of a Converso in 1491 to a young Jew who was contemplating conversion: 'You see how they burn them, and you want to become a Christian?'[3]

The exiles of 1492 took with them whatever they could salvage of their property as well as the texts and intellectual traditions of Spanish Jewish culture. The destination of choice for many was the Ottoman empire, where crucifixes and friars were rare. Some went to North Africa and some to Italy. But for many, the easiest and safest route out of Spain was across the Spanish border into Portugal. The exiles would have been aware of popular Portuguese hostility to Jews (especially towards Spanish Conversos who had escaped there and reverted to Judaism), but they would also have known of the consistent protection of Jews offered by the Portuguese Crown.[4]

The Portuguese monarch permitted streams of desperate exiles to enter Portugal. In exchange for a payment of 8 cruzados, they could reside there for eight months. For payment of a much larger fee, the members of 600 households were allowed to settle permanently, alongside the native Portuguese Jews. It would be nice to have exact numbers, but we don't. Chroniclers of the period estimated that up to 120,000 Spanish exiles entered Portugal in 1492, but this is certainly exaggerated. A more reasonable estimate by a contemporary scholar holds that the Jewish population of Portugal on the eve of the Expulsion was about 30,000, a figure that doubled—or more than

---

[3] Yitzhak Baer, *Die Juden im christlichen Spanien*, 2 vols. (Berlin, 1929; repr. 1936), ii. 405.

[4] See Humberto Baquero Moreno, 'Movimentos sociais anti-judaicos em Portugal no século XV', in Yosef Kaplan (ed.), *Jews and Conversos: Studies in Society and the Inquisition* (Jerusalem, 1985), 62–73; on the immigration of Spanish Conversos to Portugal, see Maria José Pimenta Ferro Tavares, *Los judíos en Portugal* (Madrid, 1992), 131–9.

doubled—with the arrival of the exiles.[5] An influx of Jews at this level would have had a palpable impact on the towns of a kingdom with only about a million inhabitants. Unfortunately, we know very little about relations between the native Portuguese Jews and the Spanish exiles. It seems significant, though, that the documents we possess reveal no use of terms to distinguish between the 'natives' and the newcomers, suggesting that the exiles quickly blended in with the native Jews. Both groups, after all, were heirs to the same late fifteenth-century Sephardi rabbinic culture, and Spanish Conversos who had earlier fled to Portugal were already part of Portuguese Jewry. (Such accommodating behaviour would not be characteristic in later generations, when the cultural profile of the Portuguese Jews had become strongly differentiated from that of any other Jewish group.)

The exiles were valued by the Portuguese Crown for their entrepreneurial skills, of which Portugal, now poised to take advantage of its imperial reach, was in need. But popular hostility in the face of the wave of émigrés, intensified by episodes of plague, threatened the relative equilibrium between Christians and Jews. Moreover, a potentially advantageous dynastic marriage produced a dilemma for the Crown. The Portuguese king was eager to wed a daughter of Ferdinand and Isabella and thus create the possibility that a son from this marriage would inherit the entire Iberian peninsula. However, as a condition for this, the Spanish monarchs demanded that the groom-to-be expel the Jews. The Portuguese king did issue an expulsion decree in late 1496, but it remained largely a dead letter. A series of draconian royal measures aimed to induce the Portuguese Jews to convert culminated in the voluntary or forcible conversion of most of them by the spring of 1497.[6] To ease the transition to life as Catholics, the new converts were offered immunity for two decades from enquiry into their religious practices. In fact, this provided many of them with a hiatus during which they could adapt to crypto-Judaism. It did not, however, protect them from the outbreak of dreadful anti-Converso riots in Lisbon in 1506.[7]

Escape from Portugal was certainly on the minds of many of the newly baptized. To avert this, the Crown closed the Portuguese borders to them in 1499. Efforts to prevent such emigration were never very successful, however, and in any case this first ban on emigration was soon lifted after the riots of 1506. In the first half of the sixteenth century, those who managed to leave Portugal mainly followed the path of the Spanish exiles of 1492, settling in Jewish communities in Italy, the Ottoman empire, and North Africa. Those who settled as Jews in Ottoman lands—Smyrna, Salonica, Aleppo, and elsewhere—maintained strong ties with Portuguese Jews in western Europe for some

---

[5] This is Tavares's conclusion (*Los judíos en Portugal*, 38–41, 129–31). Tavares is cautious, however, about offering even approximate figures.

[6] On the series of events culminating in mass baptism, see ibid. 159–69.

[7] See Yosef Hayim Yerushalmi, *The Lisbon Massacre of 1506 and the Royal Image in the 'Shebet Yehudah'* (Cincinnati, 1976).

time. But in the eighteenth century those ties weakened, as the western Sephardim increasingly came to view 'oriental' Jews as backward.[8]

The most attractive place of settlement in Italy was initially Ferrara, whose duke first offered the ex-Converso émigrés a charter to settle there as Jews in 1538.[9] In the 1550s the Portuguese Jews of Ferrara created a thriving centre of literary and printing activity aimed specifically at an ex-Converso audience.[10] Even at this early point, settling in a city that also harboured an older Jewish population, the 'Portuguese' recognized themselves as a group apart. This is evident in *Consolação as tribulações de Israel* by Samuel Usque, published in Ferrara in 1553, which became a classic in the Portuguese Jewish diaspora.[11] Usque wrote that he composed the work specifically for the benefit of *nossa nação portuguesa* ('our Portuguese nation'), a group that he also referred to collectively as the *desterro de Portugal* ('Portuguese dispersion').[12] This terminology, employed within two generations of the forced baptisms (and the first reference to the Portuguese ex-Conversos as a distinct group that I am aware of), reflects a clear awareness of the group's unique experience and fate. However, in Italy, with its Mediterranean orientation, its ghettos, and its overall rabbinic complexion, the pressures on Portuguese Converso émigrés to modify their exclusivist inclinations were strong. In Venice—a great centre of western Sephardi life until the plague of 1630–31—the Portuguese or 'Ponentine' Jews were recognized as a distinct group by the authorities in 1589, yet the broad cultural mix of Jewish types in the Venetian ghetto led to a moderation of 'Portuguese' difference there.[13] The mechanisms at play in Livorno, which succeeded Venice in the second half of the seventeenth century as the major centre of Portuguese Jewish life in Italy, were somewhat different. Yet there, too, friction between Jews of different backgrounds was moderated by the Mediterranean Jewish environment.[14]

The existence of the New Christians in Portugal became newly precarious once the

---

[8] See Francesca Trivellato, *The Familiarity of Strangers: The Sephardic Diaspora, Livorno, and Cross-Cultural Trade in the Early Modern Period* (New Haven, 2009), 64.

[9] Ferrara was the most important Portuguese Jewish centre in Italy until the 1570s, although from 1547 to 1556 Portuguese ex-Conversos also resided in Ancona in significant numbers. Venice succeeded Ferrara as the centre of Portuguese Jewish printing, culture, and communications until it was overshadowed by Amsterdam in the seventeenth century.

[10] See Cecil Roth, 'The Marrano Press at Ferrara, 1552–1555', *Modern Language Review*, 38 (1943), 307–17.

[11] As early as 1556 it was reported to be circulating among the crypto-Jews of London. On the dissemination of the book, see Yosef Hayim Yerushalmi, 'Introduction', in Samuel Usque, *Consolação as tribulações de Israel: Edição de Ferrara, 1553*, ed. Yosef Hayim Yerushalmi and José de Pina Martins, 2 vols. (Lisbon, 1989), i. 101–7.   [12] Usque, *Consolação as tribulações de Israel*, ii. 2ʳ, 3ʳ.

[13] On the formal distinctions between German–Italian, 'Levantine', and 'Ponentine' Jews, see David Malkiel, *A Separate Republic: The Mechanics and Dynamics of Venetian Self-Government, 1607–1624* (Jerusalem, 1991), 13–16, 93–113; on the pressures towards integration between groups in the Venetian ghetto, see Miriam Bodian, 'The "Portuguese" Dowry Societies in Venice and Amsterdam: A Case Study of Communal Differentiation within the Marrano Diaspora', *Italia*, 6 (1987), 30–61.

[14] See Trivellato, *The Familiarity of Strangers*, 92–6.

Crown launched a serious effort in the 1530s to gain papal approval for a Portuguese Inquisition. A protracted struggle ensued between the Crown and Portuguese New Christian lobbyists in Rome.[15] Papal approval was eventually granted: in 1536 a Portuguese Holy Office was established, and in 1540 it held its first auto-da-fé. The primary (though not sole) aim of this institution was to identify 'judaizing' heretics and punish them. Technically, it spared New Christians who were 'honest' Christians. But with its anonymous denunciations and secret trials, no New Christian could feel secure. Its psychological impact was enormous, compounding the stigma from which New Christians already suffered. In the literature of the western Sephardim, the Inquisition was represented as *the* villain—an essential actor in the quasi-historical collective memory of the Portuguese.

Some New Christians chose flight. But for others, who had by this time become conditioned to conform to Catholicism, it was not an opportune moment. Well before the Inquisition was established, a number of Portuguese New Christians had gravitated towards a lucrative new occupation—trade in colonial commodities.[16] Their network linked Lisbon with Antwerp and Venice, where they had 'Portuguese' contacts and agents. Among the wealthiest of these merchants was Francisco Mendes, whose brother was strategically located in Antwerp. By the time of his death in 1536, Francisco had built-up a powerful commercial house. (Today he is chiefly known for having been the husband of the young Dona Gracia Nasi.[17]) In the following decades, Portuguese New Christian merchants began supplying European markets with sugar produced in São Tomé (a Portuguese island off West Africa). From the 1560s, when it began to be cultivated in Brazil, New Christians moved quickly into transatlantic traffic in sugar. Many of them strengthened their commercial network by relocating to Brazil. The experience these merchants accumulated during this period would later facilitate the extension of their network far beyond the Portuguese sphere.[18]

The relationship between the Portuguese Conversos' long-distance trade network, their endogamous marriage patterns, and their beliefs is not easy to assess. It is clear that they, far more than Spanish Conversos, were likely to hold on to crypto-Jewish

[15] On this intrigue-filled story, see Alexandre Herculano, *History of the Establishment of the Inquisition in Portugal*, trans. John Branner (New York, 1968).

[16] On the early activity of Portuguese Jews in Atlantic trade—gold and slaves from Africa, sugar from Madeira—see Tavares, *Los judios en Portugal*, 67–9; on the entry of Spanish exiles into long-distance maritime trade in the Levant—an important step facilitating Sephardi entry into Atlantic trade—see Jonathan I. Israel, 'Jews and Crypto-Jews in the Atlantic World Systems, 1500–1800', in Richard L. Kagan and Phillip D. Morgan (eds.), *Atlantic Diasporas: Jews, Conversos, and Crypto-Jews in the Age of Mercantilism, 1500–1800* (Baltimore, 2009), 5–6.

[17] The standard work on Dona Gracia and her family is Cecil Roth, *Doña Gracia of the House of Nasi* (Philadelphia, 1948).

[18] See Jonathan I. Israel, 'The Sephardi Contribution to Economic Life and Colonization in Europe and the New World (16th–18th Centuries)', in Haim Beinart (ed.), *The Sephardi Legacy*, 2 vols. (Jerusalem, 1992), ii. 371–3.

beliefs over many generations. The simple explanation is that they were descended from Jews whose families had for a century or more resisted pressures to convert in Spain, and who had themselves chosen exile rather than convert in 1492. They were descended, that is, from Jews who were highly motivated to maintain their ancestral beliefs and who raised their baptized children accordingly.[19] Yet motivated though they might be, over time the crypto-Jews of Portugal lost touch with traditional Jewish life and culture. Unlike the exiles in Italy and the Ottoman empire, they were isolated from both medieval rabbinic sources and the remarkable flowering of Jewish culture in the post-Expulsion era. The long separation from rabbinic Judaism, and their extended immersion in Christian European ways, meant that the forms of crypto-Judaism many of them cultivated bore little resemblance to either medieval or early modern rabbinic Judaism. Not only did they know nothing of the *Shulḥan arukh* or Lurianic kabbalah, they had lost any significant knowledge of Hebrew, and they had 'forgotten' the very existence of the Talmud.[20] In any case, not all of them were 'judaizers'. Many were essentially indifferent religiously or had assimilated to Portuguese Catholic life.

As a long-distance trade network developed among these Conversos, the advantages of having agents or family members in the growing centres of the Atlantic trade beyond the Iberian peninsula increased. It is hard to know to what degree economic motivations lay behind decisions to emigrate. But what determined the new *direction* of flight was unquestionably the economic vitality of the Atlantic world (though some emigration continued to the older Mediterranean centres). In the late sixteenth century, a stream of Portuguese Conversos from both Portugal and Spain (where some Portuguese Conversos had gravitated after the annexation of Portugal to Spain in 1580) made their way northwards to Antwerp or south-west France, where they lived as Catholics and had little sustained contact with rabbinic Judaism. But by the early seventeenth century ex-Conversos were settling in Hamburg and Amsterdam as more or less openly practising Jews.[21]

Portuguese Converso émigrés began arriving in Amsterdam in significant numbers when the Twelve Years Truce between the Netherlands and Spain was signed in 1609, resulting in favourable conditions for merchants trading with the Iberian peninsula. The degree of freedom the émigrés enjoyed as Jews made the city doubly attractive. This freedom, together with the absence of any other Jewish presence in the region,

---

[19] See Yosef Hayim Yerushalmi, *From Spanish Court to Italian Ghetto: Isaac Cardoso: A Study in Seventeenth-Century Marranism and Jewish Apologetics* (Seattle, 1981), 3–8; Miriam Bodian, *Hebrews of the Portuguese Nation: Conversos and Community in Early Modern Amsterdam* (Bloomington, 1997), 12.

[20] See Miriam Bodian, *Dying in the Law of Moses: Crypto-Jewish Martyrdom in the Iberian World* (Bloomington, 2007), 37–9.

[21] For a concise English account of the trajectory of the Hamburg Portuguese Jewish community, see Klaus Weber, 'Were Merchants More Tolerant? "Godless Patrons of the Jews" and the Decline of the Sephardi Community in Late Seventeenth-Century Hamburg', in David Cesarani and Gemma Romain (eds.), *Jews and Port Cities, 1590–1990: Commerce, Community and Cosmopolitanism* (London, 2006), 77–92.

allowed them unique latitude in establishing the character of their community. By 1615 the leadership had grasped the potential of their community to do something new: to adopt a leadership role in the expanding diaspora of Portuguese Conversos and Jews. This imaginative leap was first expressed in the establishment of a dowry society 'to marry orphans and poor maidens of this Portuguese Nation . . . from St Jean de Luz to Danzig, including France and the Netherlands, England and Germany'.[22] Secret members—crypto-Jews—were admitted from Antwerp, reflecting the impact of the community on the previously isolated population there as well. In general, the dowry society symbolized the leadership role that Amsterdam's 'Portuguese' assumed in the western Sephardi diaspora in such activities as proselytizing among Conversos in Catholic lands (covertly), providing rabbinic guidance, and raising funds for charitable ends.[23] The contours of this diaspora were continually changing, as trade networks shifted and people moved, but the Amsterdam community remained a rather fixed point in the western Sephardi diaspora.

Portuguese New Christian entry into Atlantic states north of the Pyrenees, where Jews had not resided for centuries, was eased by their thorough conditioning to 'being Catholic'. In France, they were able to maintain a facade of Catholic conformity for several generations. Even where ex-Conversos could live openly as Jews, their acculturation was facilitated by the fact that, through their forced Catholicization in the Iberian peninsula, they had been successfully Europeanized. They spoke European languages (and members of their intellectual elite read Latin), dressed in European fashion, and were in close touch with the currents of European intellectual and political life. For many ex-Conversos, Jewish loyalties, however powerful, were anchored not in rabbinic tradition but in ethnicity, ancestry, and hostility to the Church. Building entirely new communities in Amsterdam, Bordeaux, or London gave them the freedom to shape community life according to their own tastes and outlook. That is, the new diaspora that emerged in the Atlantic states did not reproduce the characteristics of traditional Jewish societies, regardless of its leaders' rhetoric of 'return' and 'restoration'. Despite the connections it maintained with the 'old' Sephardim in the Ottoman empire and Italy, its adaptation to rabbinic life was distinctive, with, for example, greater emphasis on the Bible than was prevalent in other Jewish cultures and a high reliance on prayer books and Bibles in Spanish.[24] Moreover, in the literature and

---

[22] Bodian, 'The "Portuguese" Dowry Societies in Venice and Amsterdam', 41–2.

[23] See, inter alia, Gérard Nahon, 'Les Rapports des communautés judéo-portugaises de France avec celle d'Amsterdam au 17e et au 18e siècles', in *Métropoles et périphéries séfarades d'Occident: Kairouan, Amsterdam, Bayonne, Bordeaux, Jérusalem* (Paris, 1993), 99–183; Evelyne Oliel-Grausz, 'Relations, coopération et conflits intercommunautaires dans la diaspora séfarade: L'Affaire Nieto, Londres, Amsterdam, Hambourg (1704–1705)', in Henry Méchoulan and Gérard Nahon (eds.), *Mémorial I.-S. Révah: Études sur le marranisme, l'hétérodoxie juive et Spinoza* (Paris, 2001), 335–64.

[24] On the complex relationship of the Portuguese Jews to the 'old' Sephardim, see Bodian, *Hebrews of the Portuguese Nation*, 147–51.

behaviour of its non-rabbinic writers, Jewish pride was closely associated with Iberian notions of masculinity and nobility. More generally, the post-biblical traditionalism of the 'old' Sephardi world never became foundational for the everyday outlook and theology of most 'Portuguese'. It is true that Portuguese Jewish messianic enthusiasm during the brief Sabbatian episode may have tightened 'Portuguese' bonds to the wider Jewish world, but in the wake of this mass foray into the fantastic—which stressed the mythic, rather than the halakhic, content of rabbinic Judaism—the Portuguese Jewish communities soon re-established their aloofness from 'other' Jews. In retrospect, it seems evident that the aim of 'restoring' rabbinic patterns of belief and behaviour after a hiatus of many generations in new centres where the Europeanized ex-Conversos were the only significant Jewish population was a powerful but ultimately utopian dream.

This is not to say that rabbinic authority was not established in Amsterdam, Hamburg, London, Bayonne, Bordeaux, and elsewhere (though its power to discipline its members proved limited).[25] Indeed, the western Sephardi diaspora produced a number of its own rabbinic scholars trained in Sephardi traditions. But the widespread Jewish ideal of the merchant and communal leader who was also a learned Talmud scholar—indeed, the ideal of talmudic study as a life-long activity for male members of the community—never took root in this diaspora. It was no accident that the first open attacks on rabbinic Judaism among early modern Jews were launched by Portuguese Jews. It is true that the Amsterdam and Hamburg communities severely punished early vocal opponents of the 'oral law', but this should not lead to the conclusion that the community was rigidly Orthodox. The measures communal leaders took to silence heterodoxy can better be viewed as part of an ongoing struggle to achieve a collective public image of adherence to rabbinic norms.[26] In later generations neither the rabbinate nor communal leaders had the power (or perhaps the will) to enforce these norms. It should be emphasized, though, that traditional Jewish life played an enduring role and remained a key identity marker. When the Jerusalem-born Sephardi rabbi and emissary Hayim Yosef David Azulai visited Bordeaux in the 1770s, he noted in his diary that the influential Portuguese Jewish merchant Abraham Gradis was 'one of the greatest heretics, who do not believe in the Oral Torah and eat forbidden foods in public'. Nevertheless he noted that Gradis 'showed us very great honor'.[27]

[25] In France, the transition from clandestine to public practice of Judaism among the 'Portuguese' was gradual. Although Hebrew inscriptions began to appear on Bayonne gravestones in the late seventeenth century, it was only in 1723 that the Crown explicitly referred to the erstwhile 'Portuguese merchants' as Jews (see Gérard Nahon, 'From New Christians to the Portuguese Jewish Nation in France', in Beinart (ed.), *The Sephardi Legacy*, ii. 336–64); on mixed signals from the French authorities in the 1680s, see Gérard Nahon, *Juifs et Judaïsme à Bordeaux* (Bordeaux, 2003), 48–9.

[26] See Miriam Bodian, 'Les Juifs portugais d'Amsterdam et la question identitaire', in *La Diaspora des 'Nouveaux-Chrétiens*, Archives du Centre Culturel Calouste Gulbenkian, 48 (Lisbon, 2004), 112–16.

[27] This observation was made in Matthias Lehmann, '"Levantinos" and Other Jews: Reading H. Y. D. Azulai's Travel Diary', *Jewish Social Studies*, NS 13/3 (2007), 26.

But, to return to the changing shape of the diaspora, the population of northbound Converso émigrés in the seventeenth century included not only wealthy merchant families, but poor families as well—some of them chronically poor, some of them despoiled by the Inquisition, some of them ruined in business. Especially in the first half of the century, the poorer families tended to cluster in small towns in south-western France—in St Jean de Luz, Peyrehorade, Biarritz, La Bastide-Clairence, Bidache, and Dax—as well as in Bordeaux and Bayonne. Many of them eventually made their way to Amsterdam—an expensive city but one in which they could expect to receive support from the Portuguese Jewish community. Poor Sephardim began arriving from Italy as well, in the hope of finding work or at least communal charity. The burden on the community was such that its leaders established a board in 1622 to deal with the problem. The lack of adequate resources and employment for poor members of 'the Nation' (nação)—a term both Portuguese Conversos and Portuguese Jews used to refer to themselves—led the board to take active measures to discourage the influx of poor émigrés from France and to redirect those who did arrive to destinations in Italy or the Ottoman empire.[28] In the 1640s the deterioration of conditions for Portuguese New Christians in Spain and Portugal led to a new wave of emigration northwards, putting more strain on the already overtaxed welfare board in Amsterdam.

The expansion of the Dutch to the Americas had already opened up new opportunities for Portuguese Jewish settlement. Perhaps more than a thousand Dutch Jews made the crossing to north-eastern Brazil in the decade after 1635, following its conquest by the Dutch.[29] Among the early émigrés to Pernambuco were quite a few impoverished Jews, some of whom successfully petitioned the Dutch West Indies Company to pay their passage.[30] Some of the émigrés prospered—especially long-distance merchants who traded in sugar and slaves, among other commodities. Others went into debt (or deeper into debt).[31] By 1636 a congregation was established in Recife with its own communal institutions, using Amsterdam as its model. Among its members were local New Christians who, with the departure of the Portuguese, joined the openly practising Jewish community or participated at the margins.[32] Communal leaders soon brought a rabbi and other synagogue functionaries from Amsterdam. The institutional life of the community was a Jewish expression of the Dutch colonial effort to replicate familiar forms of life in an alien environment. Zacharias Wagener's

---

[28] On the problem of the émigré poor, see Bodian, *Hebrews of the Portuguese Nation*, 141–2; Tirtsah Levie Bernfeld, *Poverty and Welfare among the Portuguese Jews in Early Modern Amsterdam* (Oxford, 2012); Daniel Swetschinski, *Reluctant Cosmopolitans: The Portuguese Jews of Seventeenth-Century Amsterdam* (London, 2000), 182–7.

[29] On the problem of establishing figures for the Jewish population in Dutch Brazil, see José Antônio Gonsalves de Mello, *Gente da Nação: Cristãos-novos e judeus em Pernambuco, 1542–1654*, 2nd edn. (Recife, Brazil, 1996), 280–2.   [30] Ibid. 218–22.   [31] For some vivid examples, see ibid. 267–70.

[32] Bruno Feitler, 'Jews and New Christians in Dutch Brazil, 1630–1654', in Kagan and Morgan (eds.), *Atlantic Diasporas*, 123–51.

painting of the slave market in the Rua dos Judeus (Jews' Street), where the synagogue was located, serves as a reminder of how far these Jews actually were from the urban landscapes of Europe.

The imperial rivalries that had made possible the establishment of a Jewish community in Brazil also brought about its early demise. The decline began with an insurrection in 1645 by Portuguese Catholic plantation owners. This was followed by a successful military campaign by the Portuguese to reconquer north-eastern Brazil. The terms of capitulation, signed in early 1654, provided protection for the Jews, but only for a space of three months, during which time they were expected to liquidate their property. Most of the Jews still in Brazil at the time returned to Amsterdam, many of them desperately poor.[33]

The apparent contraction of the western Sephardi diaspora was, however, only temporary. In the 1640s and 1650s intense efforts were being made by Portuguese Jews to secure permission for Jews to settle in the Caribbean and the Guianas.[34] It was in this context, in 1655, that Menasseh ben Israel made his famous effort to persuade Oliver Cromwell to formally allow openly professing Jews to settle in England. (At the time there were a number of New Christian merchants in London, but they avoided involvement.) Menasseh's mission has often been described as unsuccessful because the opposition it aroused at the Whitehall Conference meant that no official permission was forthcoming. Yet in the wake of his petition, behind-the-scenes negotiations were undertaken, and quietly the necessary institutions for Jewish communal life were put in place. Within a couple of years, a religious functionary was brought from Hamburg, a building was rented for use as a synagogue, and land was purchased for a cemetery.[35] Portuguese Jews began arriving—after 1688, in considerable numbers. The London community never competed with that of Amsterdam in size or influence, and its members were often less than enthusiastic about traditional Jewish life,[36] but with Britain's emergence as a major imperial power, it naturally remained an important hub in the western Sephardi commercial network.

This was the point to which the western Sephardi diaspora had evolved when patterns of transnational trade, together with the exodus from Dutch Brazil, began drawing the attention of Portuguese Jews to the Caribbean. By this time, the centre of gravity of the western Sephardi diaspora had shifted decisively to the Atlantic, with sig-

[33] Wim W. Klooster, 'Networks of Colonial Entrepreneurs: The Founders of the Jewish Settlements in Dutch America, 1650s and 1660s', in Kagan and Morgan (eds.), *Atlantic Diasporas*, 36.

[34] Jonathan I. Israel, 'Menasseh ben Israel and the Dutch Sephardic Colonization Movement of the Mid-Seventeenth Century (1645–1657)', in Yosef Kaplan, Henry Méchoulan, and Richard Popkin (eds.), *Menasseh ben Israel and His World* (Leiden, 1989), 139–63.

[35] For a succinct account of events around Menasseh's mission, see Todd M. Endelman, *The Jews of Britain, 1656 to 2000* (Berkeley, Calif., 2002), 19–27.

[36] See Yosef Kaplan, 'The Jewish Profile of the Spanish-Portuguese Community of London during the Seventeenth Century', *Judaism*, 41 (1992), 229–40; Endelman, *The Jews of Britain*, 31–4.

nificant communities established in the Netherlands, France, and Britain—all nations with imperial designs on the Caribbean. Other chapters in this volume will deal with the complexities of Jewish settlement, trade, and culture in the sub-diaspora that emerged in the Caribbean (at a time when small Portuguese Jewish communities were also being established in North America). Over time this sub-diaspora developed its own characteristics and cultural style, but its formation and some of its enduring characteristics should be understood in the context of a wider linguistic, religious, cultural, and economic experience with roots in Portugal.

CHAPTER TWO

CURAÇAO, AMSTERDAM, AND THE RISE OF THE SEPHARDI TRADE SYSTEM IN THE CARIBBEAN, 1630–1700

JONATHAN ISRAEL

THE QUESTION of why and how a network of Sephardi Jewish merchants linking Curaçao, St Eustatius, St Thomas, Barbados, Jamaica, and Martinique came to play a uniquely prominent role in the mechanism of Caribbean commerce during the seventeenth and eighteenth centuries remains one of the most curious and interesting that can be posed about the maritime and commercial history of the Caribbean in early modern times. Of the various communities making up this network, that of Curaçao was consistently the largest and most important from the middle of the seventeenth century to the middle of the nineteenth and even beyond. What follows is an attempt to explain this phenomenon.

While the Sephardi merchants of the Caribbean eventually secured a significant trading role in the Caribbean colonies of all the European powers involved in the area —the English, French, Danes, Dutch, and Spaniards—the most important European entrepôt for the Sephardim of the Caribbean down to the end of the eighteenth century was consistently Amsterdam, and it was the Dutch trading system that provided the Sephardim with their best opportunities. However, as has been pointed out— most notably in an important thesis on Dutch commerce in the Caribbean, published in 1995—the system of Dutch trade in the Caribbean underwent a major change in the later seventeenth century, and the 'once so familiar sight of larger Dutch ships that had begun sailing directly from the United Provinces', after 1648, to Spanish America, especially along the northern coasts of South America, had all but disappeared before the end of the seventeenth century. By that time, 'another type of less direct trade with Hispanic America had gained the upper hand, revolving around Curaçao'.[1] This active small-craft navigation, we shall see, provided an enduring basis for the rise, prosperity, and long religious and cultural stability of the Sephardi community of Curaçao.

---

[1] Wim W. Klooster, *Illicit Riches: The Dutch Trade in the Caribbean, 1648–1795* (Leiden, 1995), 61.

Under this subsequent, more complex, system of commerce, large seagoing vessels crossed the Atlantic and landed their cargoes at Willemstad, the port of Curaçao, from where the goods were transported by sloops, and later schooners, plying back and forth between Curaçao and the coast of the Spanish Main. These same sloops and schooners also sailed to other parts of the Caribbean, in particular Cuba and Puerto Rico, widening the catchment area of Curaçao's active trade. To these islands, and also St Thomas and Barbados (but less commonly to Jamaica), they sailed to fetch cash crops of various kinds—sugar, indigo, tobacco, and so forth—that were then stored at Willemstad until seagoing shipping plying what the Dutch in the Caribbean called the *grote vaart*— as opposed to the *kleine vaart* handling the local coastal and island-hopping trade —became available to transport these goods, together with the cargoes of cacao transferred from Venezuela, back to Holland.

This transition from an earlier model of big-ship long-distance trade to the new model of two-stage commerce pivoting on Curaçao was clearly of decisive importance in the cultural and social as well as in the economic history of the Caribbean. In the first place, this shift to Curaçao-based trade offered concrete advantages in terms of fixing, stabilizing, and regularizing the traffic connecting the Dutch entrepôt with Spain's American empire. The concentration of negotiations and transactions at a single point enabled merchants to gain a far better perspective on supply and demand and create a regular market based on a steady flow of commercial information and consequently to stabilize prices and outlays and minimize uncertainty and risk as well as insurance premiums. In the second place, this transition transformed the function in Caribbean commerce not just of Curaçao but also of Sephardi Jewry. For besides the fine harbour that Willemstad offered, the change in trading method and the character of the new system provided a secure, well-supplied pivotal focal point that the earlier long-distance, single-stage commerce lacked, making it possible to concentrate at the main entrepôt all kinds of localized expertise and skills that could not be settled in one place under the earlier pattern of commerce.

The new system required storage, exchange, and insurance facilities in one protected and privileged locality, with a large and well-defended harbour, such as Curaçao provided, and also a local stock of shipping, support facilities for ships and seamen, reserves of naval stores—sail-canvas, ropes, pitch for the hulls, and the like—besides a fixed garrison that also needed regular supplies and stores, and a community of merchants, brokers, and ship-owners based there disposing of specialized knowledge of trading conditions in three or four different Caribbean empires. For the merchants could not operate without developing close ties with trusted correspondents in Amsterdam, in the non-Spanish Caribbean Antilles, *and* along the Spanish Main. Hence, these merchants required a Dutch background combined with local contacts and familiarity with the Spanish language and local conditions, and also knowledge of trading conditions in the non-Spanish Antilles requiring a network of correspondents and agents in such key commercial centres as Barbados, St Thomas, Jamaica, and Martinique. Since Curaçao is a relatively barren island unsuited to intensive food production and its indigenous (and Spanish) pre-1634 population had been extremely sparse, it also needed regular contacts with ports such as Newport (Rhode Island), Boston, and New York in the British North American colonies, the closest source of supply for salt fish and barrelled meat, grain, timber, ropes, and other essential supplies. At its height in the 1680s and 1690s the Curaçao-based fleet consisted of around eighty barques, manned by fifteen to eighty men each, many of these owned and fitted out by Jewish merchants.[2]

It was perhaps above all the requirement for knowledge of Spanish and expertise in collating cost, price, and general demand-and-supply information from around the region that provided the opportunity for a relatively large Jewish community to crystallize, stabilize demographically, and establish a firm and enduring framework of educational and charitable institutions. The complexity of the new trading context favoured a relatively large number of small traders rather than a few big ones and dispersal rather than concentration of risk. It also needed specialized brokers and experts in particular commodities, especially in the different qualities of tobacco, cacao, indigo, pearls, sugar, and so forth. Hence, while the privileges and rights granted to the Sephardi Jews in Curaçao, and the Dutch Caribbean generally, by the West India Company (WIC) were originally very restricted, far more grudging than those the company had granted the Jews in Dutch Brazil in the 1630s, and (as has been rightly stressed) were limited to strictly defined economic rationales,[3] the social and religious consequences of these charters were far more wide-ranging.

Yet we should not regard the emergence of this Curaçaoan Sephardi community with its flourishing trade with the Spanish Main as automatic. During the original phase of Dutch maritime expansion in the Caribbean, from the 1590s down to the resumption of the war with Spain in 1621, Curaçao played no significant role. Subsequently too, there were many obstacles to its emergence. The various obstacles and hindrances ensured that the dramatic rise of this commerce could only take place in a certain way, using particular specialized methods and at a certain time.

The barren island of Curaçao was originally seized by the Dutch from the Spaniards, in July 1634, by a small force sent from Dutch Brazil. Lacking any developed agriculture or other resources, it was easily taken from the few dozen Spaniards and an estimated 400 Indians living there, and a series of resolutions of the States of Holland,

---

[2] Algemeen Rijksarchief, The Hague, WIC 203, fo. 291ᵛ, Beck to Amsterdam directors, Willemstad, 4 Jan. 1710; Jonathan Israel, *The Dutch Republic: Its Rise, Greatness and Fall, 1477–1806* (Oxford, 1995), 944; id., 'The Jews of Dutch America', in Paulo Bernardini and Norman Fiering (eds.), *The Jews and the Expansion of Europe to the West, 1450–1800* (New York, 2001), 338, 348.

[3] Jonathan Carp, *The Politics of Jewish Commerce: Economic Thought and the Emancipation in Europe, 1638–1848* (Cambridge, 2008), 16.

of February and March 1635, secured the financial aid from the States that enabled the West India Company to establish a permanent garrison on the island and construct Fort Amsterdam at what became Willemstad, and a second, lesser, fort, as well as other defences. Originally, the company hoped that Curaçao would prove 'a suitable place where we can procure salt, hard-wood and other items and from where we can infest the enemy in the West Indies'.[4]

We should not underestimate the early Dutch involvement with Curaçao or the strategic shock that its capture administered to the Spanish colonial bureaucracy in the Caribbean area. If Curaçao had the best harbour anywhere in the southern Caribbean and a number of strategic advantages for a sea-power such as the Dutch, the nearby Venezuelan coast lacked good harbours capable of receiving larger vessels. According to a Spanish report of 1636, on hearing of the loss of Curaçao, the governor of Venezuela dispatched warnings all around the Caribbean. A reconnoitring party of Indians and Spaniards that was landed, from Venezuela, in May 1636, returned with two Dutch prisoners and word that the Dutch had already constructed two substantial forts manned by 400 soldiers.[5] However, while the war with Spain continued, down to 1647 (not, in practice, 1648 as is usually stated), the island turned out to be economically virtually useless, and there is no evidence of any significant commercial role before the later 1650s.

The emergence of a permanent Dutch trading system in the Caribbean area, we know, took place between 1647 and the 1690s. But there remains still a certain amount of vagueness as to why, how, and when this process occurred. In this chapter I shall try to establish with a little more precision than in the past the character and timing of the transition to indirect trade between Amsterdam and the Spanish Main and, as a result, clarify somewhat a number of social and cultural consequences. First, there is the question of timing. According to scholars such as Cornelis Goslinga and the thesis of Wim Klooster, the transition to the new mode of commerce 'took place between 1670 and the 1690s, when a staple market was created in Curaçao'. 'By the end of the 1660s', affirms Klooster, 'a regular trade with the Venezuelan coast had been established, and Spaniards were coming to Curaçao', while Curaçaoans likewise sailed to the nearby port of Coro. The West India Company recognized the island's importance and granted it the status of a free port.'[6] In support of this contention, Klooster cites three reports from the Spanish ambassador at The Hague, the first two dated 4 February and 26 May 1665 and the third dated 15 January 1669, and noticeably makes no particular mention of the Anglo-Spanish War of 1655–60. I myself, suggesting slightly different

---

[4] See the printed resolutions of the States of Holland for 19, 23, 27 Feb. and 9 Mar. 1635, and Jonathan Israel, *The Dutch Republic and the Hispanic World 1606–1661* (Oxford, 1982), 274, 294.

[5] British Library Add. MS 13,974, 'Breve relacion de Curaçao' (1636), fo. 65ᵛ.

[6] Klooster, *Illicit Riches*, 61; Cornelis Christiaan Goslinga, *The Dutch in the Caribbean and in the Guianas 1680–1791* (Assen, 1985), 156–9.

timing in my 1982 monograph, nevertheless also missed the significance of the late
1650s for the rise of Curaçao as a general Caribbean entrepôt, maintaining that Curaçao's failure to 'develop any regular contraband business with either the Spanish
American mainland or the Caribbean islands' continued 'from 1648, through the years
to 1661'.[7]

In the discussion that follows, I shall try to correct both myself and to an extent
Klooster by bringing out the crucial significance for the transition of the late 1650s and
early 1660s and by showing how this small correction to our timing of the process
affects the explanatory model that we use. What strikes me as chiefly problematic
about the explanation offered by Klooster, who sees the main shift as starting in the
1670s, is that it is entirely detached from any political and strategic pressures that might
explain the timing and suggests that what occurred was a more or less straightforward
exchange between Curaçao and the main centres of Spanish population in central
Venezuela, in particular Caracas. It relies on a purely economic model, the superiority
and advantages of the entrepôt system, as against depending on long-distance trade in
large vessels, sailing from Holland or, as was often the case in the 1650s and 1660s, via the
Canaries, to account for the change. Consequently, irrespective of whether the shift
began in the 1670s or earlier, his model suggests no real reason why it occurred at one
time rather than another.

Finally, I shall argue that historians need to distinguish between the semi-official
trade organized by the West India Company itself, dealing with appointees of the Spanish Crown in such major Spanish centres as Caracas, La Guaira, Cumaná, and Cartagena, and the furtive, smaller-scale, and more specialized, as well as difficult, smuggling
traffic directed to places easily accessible by boat from Curaçao, such as Coro, Tucacas
at the northern tip of the peninsula of Paraguaná, the closest point of the Spanish
American mainland to Curaçao, and the Lake Maracaibo depots that were, however,
unsuitable for larger vessels and exceedingly remote and inaccessible overland by mule
track—or by boat offshore—from either east or west, that is from either Caracas or
Cartagena de Indias.

The 1670s, moreover, seem rather problematic as a decisive point at which the
Curaçao-based trading system should commence and the Curaçaoan Sephardi community emerge as the largest and most stable in the Caribbean, because the Third
Anglo-Dutch War (1672–4) developed into a highly disruptive and discouraging hin-
drance to Dutch seaborne commerce generally. For around three years Dutch transatlantic navigation, like Dutch trade to the Mediterranean and the East Indies, was all
but paralysed. It would hardly have been a good time to establish stores of goods and a
shipping fleet at Curaçao. Postulating the 1670s is also problematic because such a
schema makes it difficult to see what kind of transition there can have been from the

---

[7] Israel, *The Dutch Republic and the Hispanic World*, 412.

religious and cultural framework developed by the Dutch Sephardi community at Recife and Olinda, in Brazil, under Dutch West India Company rule, ending in 1654 with the surrender of Dutch Brazil to the Portuguese. Yet historians, and here I think rightly, have hitherto always assumed close links between the rise of the Caribbean Sephardi Jewish community in the seventeenth century and the experiences and skills developed earlier by the Sephardim in Brazil.

If one postulates a long gap between 1654 and the rise of the Curaçaoan entrepôt, one has to explain the special role of Sephardi Jews on Curaçao purely in terms of their Iberian background and prior familiarity with handling of such Caribbean cash crops as sugar and indigo, in Amsterdam and other European emporia. But this would imply that Sephardi Jewish predominance in trade, credit operations, negotiation, and cultural exchange in Brazil was merely an earlier, parallel phenomenon, detached and more or less an accident as far as the emergence of Curaçao, Barbados, and Jamaica was concerned and not one reflecting a continuously unfolding, developing structural role in the forming of the Caribbean world in the seventeenth and eighteenth centuries. Klooster agrees that 'the Jewish communities that arose in the Caribbean and Guiana in the 1650s and 1660s were all established in the shadow of Dutch Brazil'.[8] But the close and pivotal connection between this development and the shift from the earlier to the later Dutch trading system in the Caribbean is left noticeably vague and unclear if we fix our attention on the 1670s as the key moment of transition, as there was no real basis for Sephardi communities to emerge vigorously in the Caribbean as long as Dutch navigation there remained an essentially long-distance traffic based on Holland or, alternatively, the Canaries.

However, the earliest reports of shops and stores of goods being established on Curaçao in order to service a local commerce with the Spanish Main using small vessels reach back considerably earlier than 1670 and, it should be noted, are specifically connected with a particular political and strategic context, the Anglo-Spanish War of 1655–60, a conflict provoked by Cromwell and extremely disruptive for Spain's regular transatlantic commerce via Cadiz and the main Spanish American emporia. In March 1661 the Spanish ambassador at The Hague remitted to Madrid reports obtained from Amsterdam. According to these, the Dutch on Curaçao now had 'large stores with all kinds of goods, and these they introduce on that coast by night using long boats, drawing their returns in silver bars and other products of those parts' (grandes almacenes de todos generos de haciendas, y que las introducen de noche con barcos luengos en aquella costa, sacando sus retornos en barras y otros generos de aquellas

---

[8]   Wim W. Klooster, 'Networks of Colonial Entrepreneurs: The Founders of the Jewish Settlements in Dutch America, 1650s and 1660s', in Richard L. Kagan and Philip D. Morgan (eds.), *Atlantic Diasporas: Jews, Conversos, and Crypto-Jews in the Age of Mercantilism, 1500–1800* (Baltimore, 2009), 34, 49.

[9]   Archivo General de Simancas (AGS), Libros de la Haya, vol. xlii, fo. 94; Jonathan Israel, *Diasporas within a Diaspora: Jews, Crypto-Jews and the World Maritime Empires (1540–1740)* (Leiden, 2002), 513–14.

partes).[9] Similarly, an anonymous Jewish informant in Amsterdam reported to the Spanish embassy in The Hague in September 1663 that 'with the war which His Majesty had with England, as the galleons and fleets were not able to cross regularly, the Dutch managed to introduce many cargoes of goods in the [Spanish] Indies by making [Curaçao] a shop for the entire coast of Tierra Firme' (con la Guerra que tubo su Magestad con Inglaterra no pudiendo yr continuadamente Galeones y Flotas, procuraron olandeses introducir en Indias muchas haziendas haziendo della almacen para toda la costa de Tierra Firme).[10]

In the archives we find some interesting details concerning specific voyages that seem to confirm these more general reports. In April 1661 the Spanish envoy at The Hague reported to Madrid the return voyage from Curaçao to Amsterdam of a ship called *The Prince* carrying 1,500 quintals of Campeche wood, an enormous consignment representing nearly half the Netherlands' annual consumption of this important product, brought to the island (Curaçao itself providing very little logwood) on a Spanish vessel that also carried a rich store of silver and pearls, having come to the island to purchase slaves and European goods.[11]

It is worth pausing for a moment to consider the question of Campeche wood. By interrupting the transatlantic traffic, the Anglo-Spanish war of 1655–60 caused a severe shortage of European merchandise, especially textiles, as well as slaves in the Spanish American colonies. But, strikingly, the war also caused chronic shortages of a different kind, presenting a serious challenge to the Dutch textile industry based at Leiden. For Caribbean Campeche or logwood had become the main base for a range of blue, black, red, and green textile dyes used in the Dutch and much continental European textile manufacture. The Spanish agent in Amsterdam, Don Manuel Belmonte, pointed out in a report to Madrid of December 1666 that some 100,000 quintals of Spanish American Campeche wood and other dyewood was sold in Europe every year, mainly in Holland, France, and Italy (since its use was officially banned in England), but that the Netherlands was the largest consumer.

In this important document Belmonte proposes that the Spanish Crown should reorganize the trade in 'palo de Campeche' and increase its profits from it, by monopolizing it and regulating its transportation from Seville to Amsterdam, imposing and collecting higher duties. This he thought perfectly feasible, 'for it was found in the year 1655 when we had the war with Cromwell that it was worth 120 florins [guilders] per quintal in Holland and this because it is very necessary for the manufacture of textile products . . . and in Holland it is in greater demand than in France, for in that province [Holland] they consume more than 30,000 quintals per year' (pues se experimento el

---

[10] AGS, Libros de la Haya, vol. xlvii, fo. 109, anonymous 'aviso' on Curaçao, dated Amsterdam, 4 Sept. 1663; Israel, *Diasporas within a Diaspora*, 513.

[11] Israel, *Diasporas within a Diaspora*, 514; AGS, Libros de la Haya, vol. xliii, fo. 163, Gamarra to Philip IV, The Hague, 5 Apr. 1661.

año de 1655 quando tubimos la guerra con Cromwell valió en Holanda a 120 florines el quintal, y esto por ser mui necesario para la fabrica de manufacturas . . . y en Holanda se necessita del in mayor cantidad que en Francia, pues se consumen el año en la provincia mas de 30,000 quintales).[12] With such an urgent and consistent demand for Spanish American logwood in Holland, it appears that it was not just shortage of slaves and textiles in Spanish America that helped forge the new entrepôt off the Venezuelan coast but also the urgent need for Spanish American dyewoods at the great textile centre of Leiden.

Equally, though, it would seem that this emergence of a wartime entrepôt trade on Curaçao, the development that laid the foundation for the Sephardi Jewish community of Curaçao as pivotal to the Caribbean *kleine vaart*, happened in spite of rather than because of the West India Company's strategy in the Caribbean. For we should not necessarily assume that the WIC saw it as being in its, and its shareholders', interests to favour or facilitate the rise of a Sephardi commerce based on Curaçao. Indeed, it is striking that the early settlement contracts between the company and the earliest Jewish settlers on the island stipulated that they were to engage in agriculture and conceded no right to participate in maritime trade. The first contract with João de Yllan, signed in 1651, provided for the settlement of fifty families for the purpose of cultivating the land and establishing plantations. There can be little doubt that the directors were not especially enthusiastic about this arrangement. Rather, they were distinctly suspicious of Yllan's intentions, and this whole enterprise reflects rather the social crisis and exigencies facing the Dutch Sephardi community in the years around 1650 than any long-term plans or ambitions of the WIC.

Other documents too confirm that in the early 1650s the WIC directors suspected that the real objective of the Jews was to trade in the Caribbean from Curaçao with other islands and the Spanish Main while they, the directors, remained opposed to any such development. They sought to discourage the Sephardim from developing a niche in this traffic because their objective was to promote a thriving commerce in the WIC's own hands, not encourage the emergence of a largely separate Sephardi sector such as had emerged earlier in Brazil. Clearly, at this stage, despite the post-1648 initial Dutch efforts to forge a new commerce with the Venezuelan coast, there was no such thing as a regular traffic of any kind, direct or indirect, between Holland and Venezuela. On 4 October 1651 a freight contract was jointly entered into in Amsterdam, before the notary Jan Volckertz Oli, by a Spanish citizen of Seville by the name of Captain Pedro Rodríguez Henríquez and the Amsterdam Sephardi merchant Manoel de Toralto (whose synagogue name was Isaac Henriques Faro), a trader with many connections with Spain, for a voyage via the Canaries to Caracas and Cumaná as well as Santo

---

[12] Biblioteca Nacional, Madrid MS 899, fo. 79ᵛ, Manuel de Belmonte, 'Propuesta de monopolio para el palo de Campeche'.

Domingo and Puerto Rico, the purpose of which was clearly exploratory and the initiative for which may well have come from the Spanish side.[13]

By late 1652, the directors had received definite information that João de Yllan and the other Jewish settlers on Curaçao were acting in violation of their undertakings, making no effort to 'plant tobacco, indigo, cotton and other staples', as they had been authorized to do, and were actually cutting logwood and using it to trade with other islands and also exporting the islands' horses.[14] João de Yllan, it should be noted, had lived in Brazil in the years 1639–40, when he engaged in provisioning the garrison and the white population of Recife. During the 1640s he traded as a Jewish merchant in Amsterdam. Before 1639 he probably lived in Lisbon. He remained the leader of the Curaçao Sephardi community only from 1651 to 1655, when he returned to Amsterdam, leaving his business on Curaçao in the hands of his brother-in-law and former business partner in Brazil, Joseph Frances.[15] In June 1653 there were again complaints that the Jews on Curaçao were not in fact cultivating the land but cutting dyewood and 'exporting horses from Aruba and Buenairo', the two subsidiary islands of Curaçao, to other parts of the Caribbean.

Bringing together the evidence provided by the WIC directors about the Jewish settlement on Curaçao in 1652–3 with the Spanish evidence of the years 1661–3, we can with some confidence draw several significant conclusions about Curaçao's rise to the status of a general Caribbean maritime entrepôt. First, the Sephardi settlers had already set out to evade company restrictions and establish their community as a Caribbean trading depot in the early 1650s and succeeded in doing so in a minor way. Secondly, it was clearly the Anglo-Spanish War of 1655–60, or rather its final phases, that acted as a trigger leading to the establishment of major stores of goods on Curaçao and the rise of the Curaçao fleet of sloops that serviced the regular commerce with the Spanish Main from the late 1650s onwards. Thirdly, the Jews were pivotal to this process from the outset. Fourthly, the often mentioned agreement of late 1662 between the Genoese slave *asentistas* in Madrid and the WIC, which converted Curaçao into a slaving depot for the Spanish Indies, was seemingly a less crucial milestone in the development of Curacao's Caribbean commerce than Simon van Brakel and other Dutch historians once claimed. Rather, the 1662 slaving contract, though it was doubtless important in consolidating the traffic, was a form of recognition that Curaçao had already secured an unparalleled and pre-eminent position in Caribbean trade some years before.

Several surviving documents from the late 1650s confirm that the main aim of the Dutch authorities was not to establish a local trade on Curaçao in the hands of a new merchant community based on sloops but, rather, to render the slave trade the chief

---

[13] Gemeentearchief, Amsterdam NA 1557a, p. 1007; Israel, *Diasporas within a Diaspora*, 239, 280–1.
[14] Israel, *Diasporas within a Diaspora*, 519–20; Klooster, 'Networks of Colonial Entrepreneurs', 42.
[15] Klooster, 'Networks of Colonial Entrepreneurs', 42.

focus of Curaçao's role and consolidate the company's grip over the flow of slaves, via Curaçao, to the Spanish colonies. A letter of June 1657 from the vice director of Curaçao, Matthias Beck, to the company directors in Amsterdam indicates that at that point, half-way through the Anglo-Spanish War, there was no regular small-vessel traffic between Curaçao and the Caracas–La Guaira central coastal zone of Venezuela. When Beck sent a sloop to La Guaira to make enquiries that year, he proposed that Spaniards interested in making purchases on the island should come there, if they had the opportunity, 'to purchase Negroes and merchandize, they would be welcome there and accommodated to their satisfaction either for specie, hides, tobacco or other commodities saleable in Europe'.[16] A few weeks later Beck reported to Amsterdam his having sold some items to visitors from Caracas 'all at a fair and reasonable price, in order to encourage and stimulate them to come to these ports to trade which I think is greatly for the Company's interest'.[17] Other documents of 1659–60 similarly show that Curaçao's role as a regular slave depot was then only just beginning, that several slave consignments had recently arrived, and that Beck considered the shipping in of black slaves by the company from Africa, as 'the only bait to allure hither the Spanish nation', as he put it in February 1660, 'as well from the Main as from other parts, to carry on trade of any importance'.[18]

Curaçao thus made the leap to being a substantial and regular slaving entrepôt in the years 1658–9 specifically, most of the slaves being sold to Spaniards from Venezuela but a few going elsewhere, including New Netherland. Between the 1670s and 1715, surviving statistics show that larger numbers of slaves were brought to Curaçao each year than to Suriname or any other New World destination.[19] The traffic reached its peak between 1678 and 1690.[20] Thus, in 1659, five slaves were delivered to New Amsterdam (i.e. New York), from Curaçao, with a larger group of thirty-nine being delivered from there in 1660. The latter arrived on two *fluit* ships—one having sailed from Holland via Guinea—which also brought horses. Another forty slaves arrived in New Amsterdam from Curaçao in 1661.[21] From the outset only a very small proportion of the slaves shipped by the Dutch from Elmina and elsewhere in Africa to Curaçao remained on the island, the bulk being promptly re-exported, principally to the Vene-

---

[16] Beck to Amsterdam directors, Curaçao, 11 June 1657, in *Voyages of the Slavers St John and Arms of Amsterdam, 1659, 1663; together with Additional Papers illustrative of the Slave Trade under the Dutch*, ed. Edmund Bailey O'Callaghan (Albany, NY, 1867), 113–16, 122.

[17] Ibid. 124–5: Beck to Amsterdam directors, Curaçao, 1657.

[18] Ibid. 151: Beck to Amsterdam directors, Curaçao, 4 Feb. 1660.

[19] Henk de Heijer, *Goud, ivoor en slaven: Scheepvaart en handel van de Tweede Westindische Compagnie op Afrika, 1674–1740* (Zutphen, 1997), 152.

[20] Ibid.; Goslinga, *The Dutch in the Caribbean*, 161–8; Jonathan Israel, *Conflicts of Empires: Spain, the Low Countries and the Struggle for World Supremacy, 1585–1713* (London, 1997), 330.

[21] O'Callaghan, *Voyages*, 178–9; J. M. Postma, *The Dutch in the Atlantic Slave Trade 1600–1815* (Cambridge, 1990), 25, 168.

zuelan coast but from the outset also to other Caribbean and New World colonies. Slaves were undoubtedly pivotal to Curaçao's emerging role as a specifically Dutch entrepôt. But were they also the major engine, the key economic factor, driving the so-called *kleine vaart* outside the company's hands? This seems a pertinent question despite the undoubted fact that a high proportion, perhaps approaching half, of all the slaves shipped across the Atlantic by the Dutch in the second half of the seventeenth century were brought first to Curaçao. For while Curaçao was indubitably a major transit port for slaves from the late 1650s until around 1720, there is no real evidence that involvement of the Jews in this traffic was the main factor behind their success in establishing themselves as the largest, most dynamic and diversified trading element in the Dutch Caribbean.

If some Jews were involved in buying and selling slaves, it was clearly WIC officials who administered the slave compounds on the island and sold or auctioned off the slaves on Curaçao, and these were invariably Protestants. Most, but not all, the slaves also arrived on Curaçao on WIC ships sailing from the Guinean coast. The point of raising this question is not to suggest that slaves were not a key commodity in which the Sephardi community dealt, for clearly they were, but rather to ascertain whether the slave traffic was really the main reason for the emergence of an active Sephardi community on Curaçao, and, equally, why it was that the collapse of the island's slave trade after 1715, when obstacles to the Dutch slave trade mounted and the British emerged as overwhelmingly dominant in the Caribbean slave trade, did not mean the immediate ruin, or even, as far as we can tell, any serious setback for the Sephardi community.[22] On the contrary, the early and mid-eighteenth century appears to be the most flourishing period in the history of Curaçaoan Jewry, with rising quantities of cacao, tobacco, indigo, silver, and goods from the British Caribbean colonies being remitted to Holland by Sephardi Jewish merchants trading between Curaçao and Amsterdam, regularly sending their cargoes on WIC ships.

The evidence for the late 1650s shows that Beck's aim was to establish a regular slave trade with Venezuela for the company's benefit. Given a degree of access to the Caracas area, where he tentatively established a Dutch presence in and around 1657-8, one might suppose there was no reason why a largely direct, semi-legal traffic between La Guaira and the company's officials in Curaçao should not have directly become the mainstay of Curaçao's commerce. But we must also consider the policies of the Spanish Crown and the post-war situation and not be too dismissive of the administrative apparatus of Spain. The interim governor of Caracas, Don Andres de Vera, was denounced to the Consejo de Indias, in Madrid in 1658, for allowing several Dutch ships

---

[22] Wim W. Klooster, 'The Jews in Suriname and Curaçao', in Bernardini and Fiering (eds.), *The Jews and the Expansion of Europe to the West*, 356; further on the collapse of the Dutch Curaçao slave trade after 1715, see de Heijer, *Goud, ivoor en slaven*, 152, 359–61.

to sell merchandise and load with cacao not only in the Caracas areas but also in and around Maracaibo and profiting personally, supposedly making 50,000 pesos from the arrangement.[23] Still more willing to deal with the Dutch was Don Felix de Zuñiga y Avellaneda, governor of Santo Domingo, simultaneously denounced for allowing the entry there of 'many Dutch ships' in 1657 with textiles, cargoes of slaves, and other goods and for being especially corrupt.

Some of these ships doubtless sailed from Curaçao even if most came direct from Holland or the Canaries.[24] But, evidently, the wartime situation was an exception and the end of the war with England enabled the Spanish Crown to exert political and administrative pressure and try to return to the status quo ante. Vera was reprimanded and replaced, and his replacement was much less accommodating towards the Dutch. In the first six months of 1661 the new governor counted no fewer than thirty Dutch vessels cruising along the coast off La Guaira hoping to trade, but steadfastly persisted in his policy of discontinuing the commerce instigated by his predecessor.[25] In one incident, he had a salvo of artillery fired into the air to warn Dutch intruders to depart. However, by his own admission, overland and coastal communications to the west of Caracas, with Coro and Maracaibo, the ports closest to Curaçao, were so tenuous that his firmness in central Venezuela could have little or no application there.[26] The unpredictable welcome the Dutch received in the main Venezuelan ports, then, was arguably the true reason that the main trade came to pivot on the Coro area, Maracaibo, Rio de la Hacha, and, later, the makeshift Dutch mainland port of Tucacas, and to evolve as a highly specialized smuggling activity conducted in small sloops. Its essence was its illicit character and its focus on the extreme west of Venezuela and east of New Granada —especially Coro, Maracaibo, Rio de la Hacha, and also the Indians of the Guajira peninsula.

Transportation of slaves from Africa to Curaçao, and their maintenance and then auctioning on Curaçao, was a WIC monopoly, and between 1662 and 1700 the company establishment on Curaçao did depend heavily on the import and re-export of slaves.[27] But this does not in itself prove that Curaçao's *kleine vaart* more generally also did. The fact that, after 1700, the *kleine vaart* to the Spanish Main and other parts of the Caribbean continued to flourish and the early and middle decades of the eighteenth century were the time of greatest prosperity for the Curaçao Sephardi community and its religious and cultural institutions not only raises doubts as to how vital the slave trade actually was in the Jewish trade in the early period but, more importantly, under-

[23] Archivo de Indias, Seville, Audiencia de Santo Domingo 2, *consulta* 28 Aug. 1658, fo. 3ᵛ.
[24] Ibid., *consultas* 28 Aug. (fo. 2), 15 Oct., 17 Sept. (fos. 2ᵛ–3), and 23 Nov. 1658.
[25] Ibid., Audiencia de Santo Domingo 195, Pedro de Porres to Philip IV, Caracas, 25 June 1661.
[26] Ibid., Pedro de Porres to Philip IV, Caracas, 8 Nov. 1661.
[27] Postma, *The Dutch in the Atlantic Slave Trade*, 44–5, 281, 301.

lines the need to distinguish between the WIC bulk slave trade based on Curaçao and the illicit small-craft coastal traffic to coastal destinations like Coro, Tucacas, and Maracaibo remote from Caracas and Cumaná.[28]

Postma was undoubtedly correct to state that 'after smuggling slaves into these colonies [Venezuela and New Granada] during the decades of the 1650s, the WIC obtained a major share in the legalized *asiento* trade in 1662' and that this new semi-legal traffic was based on Curaçao.[29] But the original intention of the scheme and the system implemented in practice was for the agents of the Madrid-based Genoese contractors Domingo Grillo and Ambrosio Lomelino, whose agents in Amsterdam signed the accord with the WIC, to come on vessels from Cartagena and Caracas to Curaçao to inspect and purchase slaves there, several hundred at a time. There was no essential logic in the *asiento* system or in the terms of the contracts servicing the ensuing expanded slave trade for why this development, so vital to Dutch interests and the WIC, should in itself have boosted Curaçao's illicit coastal and entrepôt trade with Coro, Tucacas, and Maracaibo, the mainstay of Sephardi commerce. The big slaving contracts of the 1660s clearly state that the contractors' agents were to pay for and receive the slaves on Curaçao and were responsible for shipping them in their own or hired vessels from Curaçao to their further destinations.[30]

With regard to slaves procured from the Guinean and Gold coasts, where the WIC exercised a general hegemony in the later seventeenth and early eighteenth century, there was neither any reason for third parties to be involved nor any desire for this on the company's part. The only segment of the transatlantic slave trade where the company had a clear reason to involve third parties, and Sephardi Jews specifically, was that part of the trade focusing on Portuguese Angola. No doubt for reasons of price, the company wished to procure some of its slaves there and in this case had to license the traffic to third parties with contacts with the Portuguese Crown. This seems to have been the specific reason why a number of major deliveries of slaves to Curaçao in the 1660s and later took place under the auspices of Portugal's Jewish agent in Amsterdam, Jeronimo Nunes da Costa (alias Moses Curiel) (1620–97), one of the wealthiest and most renowned Amsterdam Jewish merchants.[31] To give a notable example, it was reported to Madrid from Amsterdam, in September 1663, that the *Concordia*, a Dutch ship chartered in Amsterdam by a group of Jews, including Francisco Dias Jorge, Jeronimo's brother-in-law, and with the Jew David Abeniacar aboard as commissary,

---

[28] Ibid. 221, 237, 294.

[29] Ibid. 294; Simon van Brakel, 'Bescheiden over den slavenhandel der West-Indische Compagnie', *Economisch-Historisch Jaarboek*, 4 (1918), 49–50.

[30] 'Accoort om 2000 piece slaven ende meerder aan Curaçao te leveren' (van Brakel, 'Bescheiden over den slavenhandel', appendix 1 (pp. 61–6)); see also O'Callaghan, *Voyages*, 228–9: Beck to Stuyvesant, Curaçao, 16 Apr. 1665: 'I have sold here to the Genoese all the slaves which had come here on the Company's account in the last three ships.'   [31] On Jeronimo Nunes da Costa, see Israel, *Diasporas within a Diaspora*, 328–53.

sailed to Angola, where slaves were purchased and afterwards brought to Curaçao where they were sold to Grillo's agents.[32] Again, in December 1664 another vessel, the *Golden Tiger*, sailed from Amsterdam to Angola, where the commissary purchased 350 slaves; these were then shipped to Curaçao, where 200 were reportedly sold to Grillo's agents and the rest to local Spaniards who had crossed to Curaçao in boats loaded with cacao, tobacco, silver, and other Spanish American products.

After anchoring at Curaçao for many months, the vessel returned to Amsterdam in March 1666 carrying, according to Andrés de Belmonte in Amsterdam, no less than 45,000 pesos in silver as well as 120 canisters of Bariñas tobacco.[33] But there is no indication that this traffic between Angola and Curaçao had any particular connection with the small-boat traffic with the Venezuelan coast. In April 1666 Nunes da Costa was one of the organizers and main investors in another voyage from Amsterdam via Angola, for slaves, and on to Curaçao, though the ship was also carrying 15,000 pounds of cinnamon and other spices, valued at 30,000 pesos, and fine lace, to be traded in Venezuela under cover of the blacks.[34] What all this proves is the complex interconnectedness of the Dutch East and West India trades and their links with Dutch manufacturing, as well as the intricacy of the trade relations that came to focus on Curaçao at this time and also the impossibility of the WIC monopolizing a straightforward exchange of slaves for silver based on Caracas.

The war of 1655–60 was of course not the only war during the classic period of Curaçao Sephardi Jewry when Spain found herself locked in maritime and land conflict with Britain. During the War of the Spanish Succession (1701–14) and the Seven Years War (1756–63), as well as the War of American Independence during which Admiral Rodney perpetrated the notorious sack of St Eustatius, pillaging the Sephardi merchant and seafaring community in particular in February 1781, there was again heavy disruption. On all these occasions, the regular Spanish transatlantic navigation was severely interrupted, causing the illicit smuggling traffic between Curaçao and the Spanish Main to assume an expanded role, as also did the overland mule traffic from Maracaibo between the main spines of the Andes to Quito. A French report sent to Paris in 1707 asserts that around 150 Dutch craft a year were then unloading European goods in the Maracaibo–Rio de la Hacha area, sufficient to load 2,000 mules with cloth, linens, candles, and East India spices 'et inonder les provinces de Popayán, de Sancta Fé et de Quito'.[35]

Plainly, the main impetus behind this remarkable traffic, servicing a relatively wide span of Spanish America, was not the slave trade but the unique advantages of the lagoons, peninsulas, and inlets between Rio de la Hacha and Coro and the proximity of

---

[32] AGS, Libros de la Haya, vol. xlvii, fo. 196ᵛ; Israel, *Diasporas within a Diaspora*, 515.

[33] Ibid.   [34] AGS, Libros de la Haya, vol. liii, fo. 268; Israel, *Diasporas within a Diaspora*, 515.

[35] Georges Scelle, *La Traité négrière aux Indes de Castille, contrats et traités d'assiento*, 2 vols. (Paris, 1906), ii. 160, 309–10; Israel, *Conflicts of Empires*, 407–8; id., *Diasporas within a Diaspora*, 556.

this area to the splendid harbour of Willemstad. It is this, arguably, that really explains the unique concentration of Sephardi enterprise and commercial activity on Curaçao throughout the nearly two centuries down to the mid-nineteenth century. It is a story that shows how fitting it is that the history of South American Jewry as an organized community should have commenced in the seventeenth, eighteenth, and early nineteenth centuries at Tucacas and Coro.

CHAPTER THREE

TO LIVE AND TO TRADE

The Status of Sephardi Mercantile Communities in the Atlantic World during the Seventeenth and Eighteenth Centuries

NOAH L. GELFAND

Introduction

Jews occupied an unusual place in the social, political, and legal realm of the early modern Atlantic world. They were valued for the economic connections and cultural skills they possessed, but, ironically, they were often also despised for these same qualities. Their minority status in a Christian world made them easy targets of scorn and subject to regulatory policies. While some individual Jewish merchants, like Aaron Lopez of eighteenth-century Newport, Rhode Island, achieved wealth and respect, as a group Jews never gained full equality with Christians in the places they lived, remaining on the social and political margins.[1] Throughout the seventeenth and eighteenth centuries, Jews were a people within and without the Atlantic world—an economically important group, who nevertheless had to negotiate and then reaffirm specific privileges and rights to conduct business and practise their religion.[2]

---

[1] When Aaron Lopez died near Providence, RI, in May 1782, he was praised by the president of Yale College, Ezra Stiles, as 'a man unsurpassed in honor and extent of commerce', who was 'without a single enemy and the most universally beloved'. Yet despite these accolades and the high economic and social standing Lopez held in Newport, Jews were still second-class subjects, unable to acquire freeman status in colonial Rhode Island (see Franklin Bowditch Dexter (ed.), *The Literary Diary of Ezra Stiles*, 3 vols. (New York, 1901), iii. 24). In 1772 Aaron Lopez ranked first out of approximately 1,200 people as Newport's highest taxpayer, while Jacob Rodrigues Rivera was fifth and nearly all of the twenty-five Jewish heads of household ranked in the top 135 (see William Pencak, *Jews and Gentiles in Early America, 1654–1800* (Ann Arbor, Mich., 2005), 88). Aaron Lopez was denied freemanship, which would have granted him full political rights, in 1761. He was also denied naturalization privileges and had to seek them in Massachusetts (see Pencak, *Jews and Gentiles*, 101–2).

[2] The phrase 'a people within and without' is my own and is the title of my dissertation, 'A People Within and Without: International Jewish Commerce and Community in the Seventeenth and Eighteenth Centuries Dutch Atlantic World' (Ph.D. thesis, New York University, 2008). The phrase refers to the important role Jewish merchants played as cross-cultural brokers in the development of the early modern Atlantic world, operating within and between empires, while as a group Jewish mercantile communities nevertheless often occupied marginal spaces and were political outsiders.

One of the central reasons Jews occupied a space on the political margins of the early modern Atlantic world was their status as an alien population. Europeans and colonial Americans considered Jews to be members of a separate nation, while Sephardi Jews identified themselves as belonging to the Portuguese Jewish nation or Hebrew nation.[3] A diaspora people, Jews were without a homeland of their own and constituted a nation within a nation wherever they lived. Because of this and their inability to conform to the dominant religious culture of the societies in which they resided, they were subject to legal, social, and religious restrictions. Moreover, as aliens, they faced disabilities in commercial endeavours, including higher duties and taxes, and were occasionally prohibited from participating in some trades at all.[4]

While the restrictions and impediments Jews faced could be discouraging, most were not insurmountable. Sephardi Jews succeeded in forming communities in numerous locations in the Atlantic world during the early modern era. Indeed, historian Jonathan Israel has demonstrated that Sephardi Jews had the greatest geographical reach of any of the trading diasporas of the period.[5] The fact that as the seventeenth century progressed they were able to establish settlements in Dutch, English, and until 1685 French colonies was very important to their overall success.[6] Their dispersal throughout the Atlantic world meant that they did not owe allegiance to any single European power. Members of the Sephardi diaspora could play upon European rival-

---

[3]   The mercantile communities discussed in this essay consisted mostly of Sephardi Jews. While Ashkenazi Jews were present in the seventeenth century, most of the merchants conducting large-scale transatlantic commerce were Sephardim. In the eighteenth century Ashkenazi Jews were a much larger presence in Atlantic commerce, but Sephardi religious practices continued to predominate in the communities. The concept of the Portuguese Jewish nation is one that defies easy definition. The nation was made up of people who embraced a shared heritage, culture, language, and a remembrance of a common past in the Iberian peninsula. Ethnic and racial identification—the tribal aspects of Judaism, according to historian Jonathan Sarna—took precedence over religion in binding these people together and forging this collective identity (see Jonathan D. Sarna, *American Judaism: A History* (New Haven, 2004), 5).

[4]   For example, the Navigation Acts were sometimes employed to challenge and restrict Jewish commerce in the English Atlantic world (see Holly Snyder, 'English Markets, Jewish Merchants, and Atlantic Endeavors', in Richard L. Kagan and Philip D. Morgan (eds.), *Atlantic Diasporas: Jews, Conversos, and Crypto-Jews in the Age of Mercantilism, 1500–1800* (Baltimore, 2009), 53–6). Additionally, in England, Jews were excluded from retail trade in London, permitted only a fixed number of brokers at the Royal Exchange, and prohibited from joining the Levant Company (see Francesca Trivellato, 'Sephardic Merchants in the Early Modern Atlantic and Beyond: Toward a Comparative Historical Approach to Business Cooperation', in Kagan and Morgan (eds.), *Atlantic Diasporas*, 114).

[5]   Jonathan I. Israel, *Diasporas within a Diaspora: Jews, Crypto-Jews, and the World of Maritime Empires (1540–1740)* (Leiden, 2002).

[6]   Success here is defined as the ability of members of the Portuguese Jewish nation to conduct business and worship outwardly as Jews in the places they settled. Article 1 of the Code Noir issued in March 1685 by Louis XIV called on French officials to evict from their Caribbean islands 'all Jews who have established their residence there, who we order, as the declared enemies of the Christian religion, to leave within three months . . . or face confiscation of body and property' ('The Code Noir', in Laurent Dubois and John D. Garrigus (eds.), *Slave Revolution in the Caribbean, 1789–1804: A Brief History with Documents* (New York, 2006), 50).

ries, moving between empires to seek the greatest possible economic and religious concessions, thus helping at least partially to mitigate the disabilities they experienced.

For Sephardi Jews, the key to gaining economic and religious concessions in the Atlantic world lay in making themselves useful to the European powers. As Jonathan Israel has noted, their skills as cross-cultural brokers and the extent of their connections with New Christian kin, which enabled them to bridge the Protestant–Catholic divide and link the transatlantic seaborne empires of the Spanish, Portuguese, Dutch, English, and French, were extremely valuable and unparalleled among the trading diasporas of the era.[7] Ambitious Portuguese Jewish merchants recognized that this usefulness provided them with a degree of leverage with which to negotiate concessions from government agents and company officers, while pragmatic officials understood that allowing Jews certain liberties was in the best interests of their imperial projects. Nevertheless, securing charters and privileges to establish Jewish mercantile communities and then maintaining these privileges while enduring opposition and prejudice proved challenging.

This chapter seeks to explore the privileges and rights that the Sephardim were able to acquire in order to establish and maintain mercantile communities in the Caribbean and southern Atlantic world during the seventeenth and early eighteenth centuries. It focuses on people who were identified or who identified themselves as Jews and who had the dual purpose of engaging in transatlantic trade and worshipping openly as Jews. New Christian and crypto-Jewish populations in the Portuguese and Spanish Atlantic worlds—people who were critical to Sephardi trade networks but who did not or could not live as Jews—are therefore not central to my discussion. Since Jews were excluded from the French Caribbean after 1685, the French Atlantic is largely peripheral to this study as well. Instead, it focuses on the Dutch and English Caribbean and southern Atlantic worlds, where Jewish mercantile communities secured the greatest array of charters, privileges, and rights or were otherwise permitted to practise their religion and engage in commerce during the early modern era. Significantly, within these empires members of the Sephardi diaspora were best able to assert their identity as Jews.

In examining Jewish mercantile communities in both the Dutch and English Atlantic worlds, it quickly becomes apparent that there was no coherent policy regarding the Jews in either empire. Rather, privileges and rights were extended on a situational basis depending upon the needs of the Dutch and English in their metropolitan centres or their colonial peripheries. Factors such as imperial rivalries, population shortages in the colonies, and perceived commercial advantages from permitting Jewish trade networks to function within their territories all played a role in the privileges Sephardi merchants were able to negotiate for themselves. While the ad hoc

[7] Jonathan I. Israel, 'Jews and Crypto-Jews in the Atlantic World Systems, 1500–1800', in Kagan and Morgan (eds.), *Atlantic Diasporas*, 4.

nature of these privileges provided opportunities to press for greater concessions in certain circumstances, it also meant that community leaders sometimes had to assert and defend their position when circumstances changed.

The Sephardim and the Atlantic World

While the story of the Sephardi settlement in the Netherlands is by now a familiar one, certain aspects of this history deserve restating as the circumstances have significance for Jewish settlement in the Caribbean. Members of the Sephardi diaspora first began arriving in the Netherlands in the 1590s as New Christian merchants. Settling in Amsterdam, they would have been aware that no Inquisition existed in the Dutch Republic, but beyond that fact, there is no reason to suspect they initially believed they would be able to establish an openly Jewish community there. It is possible that some of these Portuguese New Christians would have known about article 13 of the Union of Utrecht, which established general freedom of conscience in the seven United Provinces.[8] Yet article 13 was specifically designed to prevent the persecution of Catholics and Protestants in the Netherlands, not to allow the practice of Judaism. As no Jews lived in the Netherlands at that time, they were not even mentioned in the document. Nevertheless, Portuguese New Christian émigrés to Amsterdam would have noticed that the city was a haven for persecuted Protestants from other European nations and may have sensed that article 13 'tended to inhibit action on the part of the authorities on any subject relating to religion'.[9] Thus the overall atmosphere of Amsterdam may have convinced the crypto-Jews among the Portuguese New Christians that they could practise Judaism in more obvious ways without negative consequences.

The formal practice of Judaism in Amsterdam is believed to have begun around 1602, when a rabbi arrived in the city to lead services.[10] By 1612 a second congregation had formed and its members arranged for Dutch carpenter Hans Gerritsz to construct a synagogue on Houtburgwal behind Breestraat.[11] Amsterdam's Reformed Church complained about the project to the city council. On 8 May 1612 the city council ruled that the Portuguese were prohibited from practising their religion in the building on penalty of having it demolished. Nevertheless, the building was finished and used as a

---

[8]   Article 13 of the 1579 Union of Utrecht, the Dutch Republic's constitutional document, states: 'each person shall remain free in his religion and that no one shall be investigated or persecuted because of his religion'. The full text is in Herbert H. Rowen (ed.), *The Low Countries in Early Modern Times* (New York, 1972), 69–74.

[9]   Daniel M. Swetschinski, *Reluctant Cosmopolitans: The Portuguese Jews of Seventeenth-Century Amsterdam* (London, 2000), 10.

[10]   Miriam Bodian, *Hebrews of the Portuguese Nation: Conversos and Community in Early Modern Amsterdam* (Bloomington, 1997), 42.

[11]   See 'Amsterdam Notarial Deeds Pertaining to the Portuguese Jews in Amsterdam up to 1639', trans. and ed. E. M. Koen, in *Studia Rosenthaliana: Journal for Jewish Literature and History in the Netherlands*, 5 (1971), 240–2.

synagogue, but ownership was actually transferred to Nicolaes van Campen, a member of the city council. In this way, the Sephardim and the Amsterdam authorities could claim that Judaism was being practised in a private home rather than publicly.[12]

In fact the legal right to public worship was not formally granted to Jews in Amsterdam prior to the emancipation of Dutch Jewry in 1795. Moreover, there was never any all-encompassing Jewry statute or law in the United Provinces.[13] Instead, each municipality dealt with the issue of Jewish privileges on a case-by-case basis. In Amsterdam, a policy of inaction was pursued, whereby magistrates, who were mostly elite merchants and keenly aware of the economic importance of the Sephardim, generally ignored complaints or requests for restrictions against the Jews.[14] The result of this ambiguity was that over the course of the seventeenth century Jews were able to worship very publicly in Amsterdam. In 1675, when the Portuguese Jewish population in Amsterdam was at its highest (about 2,500 people[15]), the community dedicated a very large new synagogue, which still stands today.

As the leaders of the Sephardi Jewish community began to thrive and feel secure in Amsterdam, fifteen merchants and brokers established a charitable organization that reflected their commitment to Judaism and their sense of identity as members of an Iberian diaspora. Called the Santa Companhia de Dotar Orphans e Donzeles Pobres (Holy Confraternity for the Provision of Dowries to Orphans and Poor Maidens) and commonly referred to as the Dotar, it aimed to give dowries to poor New Christian women of Iberian heritage who promised to marry in conformity to the 'Sacred Law' and live openly as Jews.[16] Based in Amsterdam, the Dotar had correspondents in St Jean de Luz, Bordeaux, Paris, Nantes, Rouen, Antwerp, and Hamburg, who were charged with finding suitable candidates.[17] Later, correspondents from Recife, Curaçao, and other areas of the Atlantic diaspora joined the organization as well. The activities of the Dotar highlight the sense of mission many of the members of the Sephardim had to bring New Christians back to Judaism. Its headquarters in Amsterdam reflected the city's status as the leading Sephardi community of western Europe.[18]

Whereas obfuscation was sufficient to protect the Sephardim in Amsterdam and foster its growth into a centre of Judaism, the Dutch offered—and Jews sought out—

---

[12] Swetschinski, *Reluctant Cosmopolitans*, 12.   [13] Ibid. 12–13.

[14] The importance of Portuguese Jewish merchants in the sugar trade to Amsterdam, for instance, has been well documented (see e.g. Christopher Ebert, 'Dutch Trade with Brazil before the Dutch West India Company, 1587–1621', in Johannes M. Postma and Victor Enthoven (eds.), *Riches from Atlantic Commerce: Dutch Transatlantic Trade and Shipping, 1585–1817* (Leiden, 2003), 49–76; James C. Boyajian, 'New Christians and Jews in the Sugar Trade, 1550–1750: Two Centuries of Development of the Atlantic Economy', in Paolo Bernardini and Norman Fiering (eds.), *The Jews and the Expansion of Europe to the West, 1450–1800* (New York, 2001), 472–3.

[15] Bodian, *Hebrews of the Portuguese Nation*, 2.

[16] Ibid. 135; Swetschinski, *Reluctant Cosmopolitans*, 179.   [17] Swetschinski, *Reluctant Cosmopolitans*, 179.

[18] Another indicator of Amsterdam's rising importance to the Portuguese Jewish nation and the sense that this could be a permanent home for the diaspora community was the founding in 1616 of the Academia e Yesiba Ets Haim to educate children in the Sephardi tradition.

more concrete freedoms and privileges in the Dutch colonies of the Atlantic world. The example of Dutch Brazil is instructive for the role the West India Company envisioned for Jews in the colony, the perceived identity of New Christians living there, and the freedoms articulated in the charters for the colony.

In 1621 the States General chartered the West India Company to deal with Dutch activities in the Atlantic world. While the WIC's primary goal was to generate profits for its investors, its charter also indicated that it was founded as a 'maritime war machine to fight both Habsburg Spain and Portugal'.[19] With these dual ends of profit and war, the WIC turned its attention to Portuguese Brazil. Jan Andries Moerbeeck, a leading advocate for the conquest of Brazil, presented the WIC's case to the prince of Orange and the States General in 1623. Among the arguments for taking Brazil in his *Redenen Wearomme de West Indische Compagnie dient te trachten het Landt van Brasilia den Coninck van Spangien te ontmachtigen* (Reasons why the West India Company must Seek to Take the Lands of Brazil from the King of Spain), two stand out as particularly informative about Dutch economic motivations and perceptions of the Portuguese New Christians in the colony. According to Moerbeeck, not only could the Dutch expect to make a huge profit from capturing and controlling the means of sugar production, but they could also make sugar refineries in the Netherlands more profitable in the process by lowering transportation costs.[20] Additionally, Moerbeeck offered a telling opinion about the Portuguese New Christians living in Brazil. Claiming almost all of them were actually Jews in disguise, he promised that if the WIC offered them religious freedom they would welcome the Dutch as liberators and assist in the conquest.[21]

While Moerbeeck's assessment of the true religious identification of the Brazilian New Christians was obviously an exaggeration, his overall argument for taking possession of Brazil was persuasive. In January 1624 a WIC expedition consisting of twenty-six ships under the command of Admiral Jacob Willekens and Vice Admiral Piet Heyn sailed for Bahia, the capital of Brazil.[22] After a few brief skirmishes, the Dutch captured Bahia in May 1624. Significantly, though actual evidence is scant, a perception existed in Spain and Portugal that crypto-Jews in Brazil did in fact help the Dutch.[23] A year later, in May 1625, when the Portuguese returned in force and recaptured the region, a number of New Christians were prosecuted for accepting passports and swearing allegiance to the Dutch. For the WIC and those Portuguese colonists who sided with them, this first Dutch attempt in Brazil proved a disaster.[24]

[19] Wim W. Klooster, *The Dutch in the Americas, 1600–1800: A Narrative History with the Catalogue of an Exhibition of Rare Prints, Maps, and Illustrated Books from the John Carter Brown Library* (Providence, RI, 1997), p. xvi.

[20] Jan Andries Moerbeeck, *Redenen Wearomme de west Indische Compagnie dient te trachten het Landt van Brasilia den Coninck van Spangien te ontmachtigen* (Amsterdam, 1624), 6.

[21] Ibid. 4.   [22] Arnold Wiznitzer, *Jews in Colonial Brazil* (New York, 1960), 51.

[23] Wiznitzer cites the discussion of this matter in the State Council in Madrid (ibid. 53).   [24] Ibid. 56–7.

When the Dutch planned another attempt to capture the world's greatest source of sugar in 1629, the WIC aimed for Recife, the capital port of Pernambuco. In planning this conquest, the WIC, in conjunction with the States General, devised a policy for the subsequent administration of a Dutch colony there. According to the charter, which was given to the commander of the expedition, the Dutch were to respect the religious practices of all the inhabitants of the conquered area. While the Reformed Church was to be the official religion of the colony—a regulation that was articulated in the 1621 founding charter of the WIC and hence a standard requirement for all Dutch Atlantic colonies—and missionary organizations such as the Jesuits were prohibited, the right of private worship was granted to Spanish, Portuguese, and indigenous peoples alike.[25] According to the charter, Jews were permitted to worship in the colony as well.[26] Thus, the charter effectively pledged the WIC to actively protect religious minorities in Dutch Brazil. Significantly, in including Judaism among the different religions to be respected, the Dutch became the first Atlantic power to explicitly grant Jews the freedom to practise their religion in their homes and the first to commit to defending them from enquiries and harassments because of their beliefs.[27]

The response of the Sephardim to the WIC's Brazilian charter was electric. Jews accompanied the Dutch to Brazil as part of the military expedition, and once the WIC was victorious in Pernambuco a flood of Portuguese Jewish merchants migrated from Amsterdam to the colony. They were joined by a number of Portuguese New Christians already living there who, under the protection of the WIC, no longer feared the threat of the Portuguese Inquisition and took the opportunity to return to Judaism. Moerbeeck had been correct, not in thinking that every New Christian was a Jew in disguise, but rather in arguing that offering religious privileges to Jews would benefit the WIC and the Dutch Republic as a whole. Indeed, Portuguese Jewish colonists in Dutch Brazil were extremely valuable as translators between company officials and Catholic Portuguese planters. Moreover, as historian Arnold Wiznitzer noted, Jews played a dominant role 'as financiers of the sugar industry, as brokers and exporters of sugar, and as suppliers of Negro slaves on credit, accepting payment of capital and interest in sugar'.[28]

Between 1630 and 1654, when the West India Company lost its hold on Pernambuco, the Sephardim created the first openly practising Jewish community in the New World. At its height in 1645 (before the onset of the Catholic Portuguese rebellion against WIC rule) the Jewish population of Dutch Brazil may have been as many as

---

[25] *Groot Placaet-Boek*, 2 vols. (The Hague, 1658–64), ii. 1236–7.

[26] Ibid. ii. 1236–7, art. 10: 'De Spaignaerts, Portugeisen ende Naturelen van den Lande, 'tzy Roomsch ofte Joots—gefinde, sullen gelaten werden by hare vryheyt, sonder moeyenisse ofte ondersoeck in hare conscientien, ofte particuliere Huysen' (The Spanish, Portuguese and Indians of this land, Catholics or Jews, should be left alone free without harassment or investigation into their religious practices within their private homes).   [27] Ibid. ii. 1236–7.   [28] Wiznitzer, *Jews in Colonial Brazil*, 70.

1,000, between a third and a half of the white civilian settler total.[29] A new charter arrived with Governor General Johan Maurits van Nassau-Siegen in August 1636. Responding to requests from Reformed clergy to curtail public worship by Jews and remonstrance from Christian merchants, who felt threatened by Jewish economic power in the colony, article 32 of the new charter reiterated the company's pledge to protect Jewish worship and confirmed the ability of Jews to engage in the retail trade, a privilege unavailable to them in Amsterdam.[30]

Because of these favourable privileges, at least two Sephardi communities formed in the colony: Tsur Israel congregation in Recife and Magen Abraham congregation just across the harbour in Mauricia. A number of rabbis, including Isaac Aboab, migrated to Dutch Brazil and the elite merchants among the Sephardi inhabitants were able to establish a Mahamad to govern the communities.[31] The Mahamad held administrative authority over all aspects of Jewish life in the colony—from granting admission to the religious school for children to regulating burial in the Jewish cemetery. While it exercised a considerable amount of coercive power, it was also instrumental in fostering a sense of common identity among the diverse Jewish inhabitants of the colony.

The long rebellion against WIC rule and the eventual fall of Dutch Brazil sent the Sephardim scattering across the Atlantic world. Having grown accustomed to worshipping freely, conducting transatlantic commerce, engaging in the retail trade, owning property, and enjoying the protection of a powerful company in Brazil, many Jews sought to replicate this experience elsewhere in the Atlantic. But, circumstances were different in other Atlantic locations, and members of the Sephardi diaspora had to adjust their expectations and in general take a more active role in securing privileges and freedoms for themselves.

Following the Dutch loss of Pernambuco, the influential Amsterdam rabbi Menasseh ben Israel undertook a journey to London to discuss readmitting Jews to England with Oliver Cromwell. Cromwell was interested in promoting overseas commerce and believed the widespread trade connections of the Sephardim would be beneficial to England. Portuguese New Christian merchants had been active in London since the mid-sixteenth century.[32] Now, however, the 1651 Navigation Act threatened their ability to conduct business, while openly practising Sephardi Jewish merchants were anxious to establish a legal presence in London whence they could engage with the developing English empire.[33] Ben Israel's meeting with Cromwell resulted in the Whitehall Conference of December 1655, where merchants and ministers voiced their opposition to the readmission of Jews on economic and religious grounds. Instead of a formal

---

[29] Wiznitzer, *Jews in Colonial Brazil*, 130.   [30] *Groot Placaet-Boek*, ii. 1252–3.

[31] In 1648 the two congregations were united for administrative purposes, but each held services in their own synagogue.   [32] Snyder, 'English Markets, Jewish Merchants, and Atlantic Endeavors', 52.

[33] Todd M. Endelman, *The Jews of Britain, 1656 to 2000* (Berkeley, Calif., 2002), 23.

ruling in favour of Jewish settlement in England, Cromwell was forced to adopt an unofficial readmission policy. Merchants of the Sephardi diaspora would be able to apply directly to him (and after the Restoration to the Crown) for endenization and thus live in England and trade legally within the English Atlantic. At least ninety Jews took this step between 1655 and 1680.[34] By 1702 a Portuguese synagogue was dedicated for public worship, and in 1720 there were over 1,000 Sephardi Jews living in London.[35]

The establishment of the Portuguese Jewish community in England may have gained momentum from concurrent developments in the Caribbean. Members of the Sephardi diaspora fleeing Dutch Brazil settled in Barbados, ostensibly to continue trading in a commodity with which they had great expertise: sugar. In 1652 several Jewish families set out from Barbados with an English expedition to take possession of Suriname, another location with the potential for sugar production.[36] Subsequently, individual Portuguese Jewish merchants began to acquire privileges to conduct business there. On 8 April 1661, for example, Benjamin de Caseres, Henrique de Caseres, and Jacob Fraso petitioned King Charles II to 'live and trade in Barbados and Surinam'.[37]

As other Sephardim arrived in the colony they settled near Cassipora Creek, a minor tributary of the Suriname River. Here they seem to have established a separate Jewish cemetery, which, more than just a practical consideration, was an essential physical manifestation of the Jews' effort to maintain, or for New Christians to reclaim, a sense of Jewish identity in the New World.[38] Perhaps as many as 100 Jews migrated to Suriname in 1664, after the French captured the Dutch colony in Cayenne. Added to this number were refugees from Jewish settlements in the Dutch Wild Coast colonies of Pomeroon and Essequibo, so that by 1667 the population of Jews in Suriname may have exceeded 200.[39] In this decade Jewish inhabitants continued to settle further along the Suriname River, clearing land and building houses in the area that would subsequently be known as Jodensavanne.

The migration of Jewish settlers from the Dutch Wild Coast colonies to Suriname is illustrative of the interconnected colonization endeavours of Jewish groups in the Caribbean and southern Atlantic world after the fall of Dutch Brazil. David Cohen

[34] Snyder, 'English Markets, Jewish Merchants, and Atlantic Endeavors', 54.

[35] Endelman, The Jews of Britain, 41.

[36] Historical Essay on the Colony of Surinam, 1788, trans. Simon Cohen, ed. Jacob Rader Marcus and Stanley F. Chyet (Cincinnati, 1974), 28–9. Essai historique sur la colonie de Surinam (Paramaribo, 1788), widely attributed to David de Isaac Cohen Nassy, is the main source of information on the early history of Jews in Suriname.

[37] See Herbert Friedenwald, 'Material for the History of the Jews in the British West Indies', Publications of the American Jewish Historical Society, 5 (1897), 46–7.

[38] The oldest surviving tombstone in the Cassipora Creek cemetery dates to 1669, while the latest of the two hundred or so graves is from 1840 (see Rachel Frankel, 'Antecedents and Remnants of Jodensavanne: The Synagogues and Cemeteries of the First Permanent Plantation Settlement of New World Jews', in Bernardini and Fiering (eds.), The Jews and the Expansion of Europe to the West, 409).

[39] L. L. E. Rens, 'Analysis of Annals Relating to Early Jewish Settlement in Surinam', in Robert Cohen (ed.), The Jewish Nation in Surinam: Historical Essays (Amsterdam, 1982), 29–36.

Nassy of Amsterdam (also known as Joseph Nunes de Fonseca), who had formerly lived
in Recife, was one such entrepreneur who attempted to settle Jews in several New
World locations. In February 1652, for example, he obtained a patent from the WIC to
bring fifty Jewish colonists to Curaçao.[40] He was also involved in supplying the Jewish
settlements at Essequibo and Pomeroon later in the decade.[41] On 12 September 1659
David Nassy and Company received a charter from the directors of the WIC to
establish a colony at Cayenne.[42] The privileges it received would have a great influence
on the Jewish experience in Suriname.

These economic privileges were designed to foster the colony's structural and pro-
ductive development and encourage settlement, which, it was hoped, would provide
the WIC with a critical mass of colonists, thus strengthening the Dutch hold on the
territory.[43] In exchange for clearing and cultivating land, David Nassy and Company
and all the Jewish settlers were exempted from paying tithes and imposts to the WIC for
twenty years and from taxes on crops, dyestuffs, and other wares produced in the
colony for five years and allowed free navigation and trade along the rivers and in the
bays of the colony.[44] The Jewish settlers were also entitled to engage in the slave trade,
albeit in a slightly proscribed manner. The WIC was to provide the bulk of the slaves for
the colony, but Jewish colonists were allowed to capture slaves at sea, bring them to
Cayenne, and then trade them anywhere in the Atlantic, on condition that every fourth
slave remain in the colony. Jews, like other colonists, were required to pay a 10-guilder
tax per slave to the WIC.[45] In religious matters, the charter granted to David Nassy and
Company provided Jewish settlers in Cayenne with freedom of conscience and the
privilege of public worship in a synagogue.[46] Moreover, Jews were to enjoy these privileges throughout the entire colony, not simply in Nassy's settlement.

The special privileges the Jewish refugees from Cayenne had enjoyed and those
secured by contemporaries in Curaçao and Barbados must have played a role in the
decision of the English authorities to offer the Sephardim similar freedoms in Suri-

---

[40] 'Grant of Land on Curaçao to Joseph Nunes de Fonseca by the West India Company' (22 Feb. 1652)
(*Curacao Papers, 1640–1665*, ed. Charles T. Gehring and Jacob Adriaan Schiltkamp (Interlaken, NY, 1987), 49).

[41] Receipts on account of the sale of slaves through the director of the Wild Coast, called Nova Zeelandia
(1659), Gemeente Stadsarchief Amsterdam (Amsterdam Municipal Archives, GSA), Notarieel Archief (NA)
334, 1350 (Wild Coast Documents).

[42] Documents concerning privileges issued to persons who establish themselves on the Wild Coast (12
Sept. 1659), GSA, NA 334, 1351 (Wild Coast Documents).

[43] The Jewish colonists were to develop their own area of land away from the already established Dutch
settlements. According to Mordechai Arbell, they 'settled on the western side of the island of Cayenne in a
place called Remire' (Mordechai Arbell, 'Jewish Settlements in the French Colonies in the Caribbean
(Martinique, Guadeloupe, Haiti, Cayenne) and the "Black Code"', in Bernardini and Fiering (eds.), *The Jews
and the Expansion of Europe to the West*, 396).

[44] Charter of David Nassy and Company, arts. 2, 8, 11 (*Historical Essay on the Colony of Surinam*, 183–6).

[45] Ibid., art. 17 (*Historical Essay on the Colony of Surinam*, 187).

[46] Ibid., art. 7 (*Historical Essay on the Colony of Surinam*, 184–5).

name. A formal grant of privileges was passed by the assembly and issued by Lieu-tenant Governor William Byam and the council on 17 August 1665.[47] Aimed at keeping recent immigrants and recruiting additional Jewish settlers to the colony, the 'General Privileges' had a similar logic to the WIC's charter in Brazil and granted freedoms comparable to David Cohen Nassy's patent in Cayenne. Byam and the council stated that it was in the best interests of the new colony to 'invite persons of whatever country and religion to come and reside here and traffic with us'.[48] Furthermore the 'General Privileges' stated that the Jews already settled with 'persons and property' had 'proved themselves useful and beneficial to this colony' and thus should be encouraged to continue 'their residence and trade here'.[49] The key, of course, to the acceptance of Portuguese Jews in Suriname and elsewhere was their usefulness. Jews such as Ben-jamin de Caseres, Henrique de Caseres, and Jacob Fraso had valuable trade connections with Barbados and England, while the refugees from Cayenne, including Samuel Nassy, were commercially connected to the Netherlands.[50] The inhabitants of Suriname were already well aware of the advantages that would accrue from trade with Jewish merchants based in the Netherlands.[51]

With developing the colony's economy clearly underlying the encouragement of Jewish settlement in Suriname, the 'General Privileges' granted the Portuguese Jews freedoms which actually went beyond those the Dutch had offered elsewhere in the Atlantic world and those the Jews in England itself enjoyed at the time. Every member of the Portuguese Jewish nation in the colony or who arrived to live and trade after the promulgation of the 'General Privileges' would 'possess and enjoy every privilege and liberty possessed by and granted to the citizens and inhabitants of this colony, and shall be considered as English-born'.[52] Significantly, while Jews in England and in the recently acquired North American colony of New York had to petition for endenization in order to participate in commercial activities, Jews in Suriname were granted outright 'every privilege and liberty which we [the English] ourselves enjoy, whether derived from laws, acts, or customs, either regarding our lands, our persons, or other pro-perty'.[53] Furthermore, the 'General Privileges' stated, in case the previous language

---

[47] 'General Privileges' (*Historical Essay on the Colony of Surinam*, 188–9).

[48] Ibid. (*Historical Essay on the Colony of Surinam*, 188).

[49] Ibid. (*Historical Essay on the Colony of Surinam*, 188).

[50] Samuel Nassy was the son of David Cohen Nassy.

[51] In May 1663 David Cohen Nassy, merchant in Amsterdam, contracted with shipper Joris Govertse of Rotterdam to deliver meat to Suriname in exchange for sugar (notarial document (10 May 1663), GSA, NA 1542, 65, 67). Food, in general, needed to be imported to Suriname as the soil was not good, and most of the agricultural effort on plantations went into producing sugar. Ships from New York and New England supplied the colony with butter, flour, stockfish, mackerel, and other products in exchange for molasses, Suriname brandy, and timber (see Roelof Bijlsma, 'Surinam's Trade from 1683 to 1712', in M. A. P. Meilink-Roelofsz (ed.), *Dutch Authors on West Indian History: A Historiographical Selection* (The Hague, 1982), 40–1).

[52] 'General Privileges' (*Historical Essay on the Colony of Surinam*, 188).

[53] Ibid. (*Historical Essay on the Colony of Surinam*, 188).

was not sufficiently clear, that on condition that 'they be true subjects of the King of England', Jews were to have 'full liberty to plant, trade, and do whatsoever they may consider conducive to their advantage and profit'.[54] Clearly, Suriname's marginal location and limited commercial development induced the English to grant privileges that would have been seen as unnecessary or even controversial elsewhere in the Atlantic.

In religious matters, the 'General Privileges' permitted the Jews 'to practice and perform all ceremonies and customs of their religion'.[55] Ten acres of land were also granted to the Jewish community for the express purpose of building a synagogue and a school, thus making the practice of Judaism in Suriname under the English a matter of public policy, rather than simply a tolerated private one. Additionally, Jewish marriages were deemed valid, inheritance practices upheld, and a promise made not to summon them before a court or magistrate on their sabbath.[56]

The far-reaching privileges granted by the English in Suriname ensured Jews protection in both the commercial and the religious spheres and probably persuaded the recently arrived refugees from Cayenne of the advantages of remaining in the colony.[57] However, this religious and economic security was called into question less than a year and a half later when the Second Anglo-Dutch War (1665–67) threw the colony into chaos. The Dutch were awarded the colony in the Peace of Breda, which officially ended the war on 31 July 1667.[58] Abraham Crijnssen, the Dutch privateer now in command of the colony, declared that the Jews should continue to enjoy the privileges granted by the English. Furthermore, Crijnssen added that all of the present inhabitants, whatever their nationality, 'shall have and enjoy the same privileges as the Dutch, among whom they shall dwell'.[59] Crijnssen's grants were endorsed by the States of Zeeland the following year.

The Portuguese Jewish inhabitants of Jodensavanne were eventually able to build a synagogue in 1685, on land donated by Samuel Nassy.[60] Named Beraha Vesalom, the

---

[54] 'General Privileges' (*Historical Essay on the Colony of Surinam*, 188–9).

[55] Ibid. (*Historical Essay on the Colony of Surinam*, 189).

[56] Ibid. (*Historical Essay on the Colony of Surinam*, 189).

[57] It is important to remember that Jews had other options during this period. For example, Curaçao was quickly developing into a major destination for Jewish migrants from Europe as well as for refugees from other colonial Atlantic locations.

[58] 'General Privileges' (*Historical Essay on the Colony of Surinam*, 407). That the English were willing to part with Suriname in the peace treaty suggests that the colony had a marginal place within England's overall empire. The Peace of Breda confirmed their conquest of New York, giving the English possession of an unbroken stretch of the North American coast from present-day Maine to the Carolinas. Moreover, the English possessed other valuable and more developed sugar-producing colonies in Jamaica and Barbados. For the Dutch, and more specifically the Province of Zeeland, taking Suriname represented another opportunity to get involved directly in the sugar trade after their loss of Pernambuco thirteen years earlier.

[59] Extract from the articles granted to the inhabitants of Suriname (6 May 1667) (*Historical Essay on the Colony of Surinam*, 191).

[60] Cornelis Christiaan Goslinga, *The Dutch in the Caribbean and in the Guianas, 1680–1791* (Assen, 1985), 273.

synagogue was constructed on high ground in a courtyard in the town centre. Made of brick and standing 33 feet high, it was the tallest structure in Jodensavanne.[61] Jewish rituals were observed according to Sephardi practices, though at least twelve Ashkenazi families were present in Jodensavanne during this period.[62] The community's first rabbi, Amsterdam-trained Isaac Nieto, had arrived in Suriname in 1680.[63] Five years later the synagogue was dedicated by Rabbi David Pardo, who had also moved to the colony from Amsterdam. Pardo came from one of the most respected rabbinic families in Amsterdam, perhaps suggesting the significance with which the parent community viewed this South American outpost.[64] Another rabbi, named Arias, is identified on a map of Suriname drawn during the 1680s.[65]

During the 1670s and 1680s the colony's economy began to accelerate, due in no small part to the Jewish inhabitants' previous plantation experiences and commercial connections.[66] Notarial records reveal the efforts of Jewish planters and merchants to develop the colony's infrastructure and commercial potential, including contracts for the delivery of goods to Suriname from Amsterdam in exchange for sugar produced by or consigned to Jews.[67] Sugar exports from Suriname to the Netherlands rose steadily throughout the 1680s from 3.5 million pounds weight in 1684 to 7 million pounds four years later.[68] As Jews made up almost a quarter of Suriname's population and owned forty plantations in 1694, their importance to the colony's overall economic production during the seventeenth century was quite significant.[69]

While Jews made important commercial, military, social, and political contributions (they were allowed to vote for members of the colony's assembly, but not serve in it) to seventeenth-century Suriname, they sought to retain as much communal autonomy as possible and remain on the margins. Indeed, much of the appeal

[61] Frankel, 'Antecedent and Remnants of Jodensavanne', 413, 416. Today, the synagogue is a ruin. According to Rachel Frankel, the remains of the synagogue measure 94 feet along the east–west axis and 43 feet along the north–south one.

[62] Goslinga, *The Dutch in the Caribbean and in the Guianas*, 360. Suriname's Ashkenazi Jews split from the Sephardi Jews and formed their own congregation in 1735.

[63] Of course, it is quite possible a rabbi was present earlier in Jodensavanne, but the documentary evidence has not survived (see Kenneth R. Scholberg, 'Miguel De Barrios and the Amsterdam Sephardic Community', *Jewish Quarterly Review*, 53 (1962), 133).

[64] David Pardo's great-grandfather was Joseph Pardo, Amsterdam's first Sephardi rabbi. Joseph was born in Salonica, had moved to Venice by 1589, and had settled in Amsterdam by 1608. David Pardo's grandfather was Amsterdam rabbi David Pardo, who was instrumental in uniting the city's three Sephardi congregations in 1639 (see Bodian, *Hebrews of the Portuguese Nation*, 50–1, 165–6).

[65] Laurentius Knappert, 'The Labadists in Surinam', in Meilink-Roelofsz (ed.), *Dutch Authors on West Indian History*, 266–7.

[66] A number of the first Jewish inhabitants of Suriname had been involved previously in the sugar trade in Dutch Brazil.

[67] See e.g. notarial documents (16 May 1679), GSA, NA 3791, 231; (18 Nov. 1682), GSA, NA 4104, 391; (19 June 1684), GSA, NA 4110, 293; (1 Feb. 1685), GSA, NA 4113, 287.

[68] Goslinga, *The Dutch in the Caribbean and in the Guianas*, 277.   [69] Ibid. 360.

of Jodensavanne must have been its relative isolation. There Jews could practise their religion and live their lives comparatively free from the watchful eyes of Reformed predikants or colonial officials. Nevertheless, they had to guard against encroachments upon or curtailments to their privileges and immunities. The situation in Suriname required particular diligence as the administration of the colony changed hands frequently. In 1682 the WIC assumed control of Suriname from the States of the Province of Zeeland. Later that same year the WIC sold two-thirds of its proprietary rights to two partners: the city of Amsterdam and the Aerssen van Sommelsdijck family. The WIC, the city of Amsterdam, and the Aerssen van Sommelsdijcks became equal partners in a new entity called the Chartered Society of Suriname.[70] From its headquarters in Amsterdam, the society gave the WIC the monopoly in the slave trade, banned Catholics from settling in the colony, and appointed Cornelis van Aerrsen van Sommelsdijck the new governor.[71]

Governor Van Sommelsdijck arrived in the capital Paramaribo in November 1683. Soon after, he wrote: 'I must give expression to the immense satisfaction I derive and continue to derive daily from the industry, zeal, affection, and honesty of those of the Jewish Nation . . . and I wish that I could say even one fourth the same of our Christians.'[72] Nevertheless, he began to make laws which contravened the privileges Jews had enjoyed since 1665. Specifically, he prohibited Jews from working their slaves and conducting business amongst themselves on Sundays. He also called into question the legality of Jewish marriage contracts, because they failed to include a civil certificate issued by the local government.[73] Van Sommelsdijck's sabbath policies, which meant that Jewish-owned businesses and plantations would cease production on both Saturdays and Sundays, threatened the economic position of Jews by putting them at a competitive disadvantage to their Christian neighbours. Moreover, his questioning of Jewish marriage contracts was seen as an attack on Jewish autonomy, which, if left unchecked, could lead to the curtailment of other Jewish practices in the colony. The Jewish community protested to the directors of the Chartered Society of Suriname on 20 May 1685.[74] The directors' response, dated 10 December 1685, was a victory for the Jewish community.[75]

[70] Goslinga, *The Dutch in the Caribbean and in the Guianas*, 271.   [71] Ibid.
[72] Cornelis van Aerrsen van Sommelsdijck to Board of Directors of the Society of Surinam, quoted ibid. 360.   [73] *Historical Essay on the Colony of Surinam*, 39.   [74] Ibid. 194.
[75] Accordingly, they wrote to Van Sommelsdijck that 'touching a request in regard to the continuation of such privileges and rights such as they, both under the English rule and otherwise, have acquired successively from time to time, we in consideration of the fact the same privileges in no sense would bring about a disadvantage or contempt to the colony, or any prejudice which anyone might expect to come, we have found it good to write this to your excellency, that you are to maintain the aforesaid privileges acquired by the Jewish community in Surinam, in the same manner as was formerly the case in the county' (Extract from a letter of the Lord Directors of the Chartered Society of the Province of Surinam, to his excellency, the Lord of Sommelsdyk (10 Dec. 1685) (*Historical Essay on the Colony of Surinam*, 194)).

On 10 July 1694, however, Governor Johan van Scharphuysen, who had replaced Van Sommelsdijck, reinstated the ban on Sunday work.[76] Once again, the Jewish community wrote to Amsterdam, this time to Baron de Belmonte and Samuel Nassy, who had recently moved there from Suriname. De Belmonte and Nassy succeeded in getting the directors of the society to intervene and once more they ruled in favour of the Jewish community. However, in the second decade of the eighteenth century, when a large number of Jews moved to Paramaribo, ministers from the Dutch and French Reformed churches petitioned to have Jewish shops in the city closed on Sundays. Considering the relative power of the Calvinists in Paramaribo, the directors decided to placate them, and this time the Jews lost their privilege to do business on Sundays.[77] Whereas the Jews of seventeenth-century Jodensavanne had been extremely useful contributors to the development and stability of Suriname, and thus capable of extracting privileges from colonial authorities, those of eighteenth-century Paramaribo were not so distinctly valuable or worthy of special exemptions.

While some members of the Sephardi diaspora were settling Suriname and other areas of the Wild Coast of South America, others migrated to Curaçao, which was then controlled by the WIC. As in Cayenne and Essequibo, Portuguese Jewish merchants were granted charters to settle whole communities in Curaçao. In 1652, for example, the directors of the WIC granted David Cohen Nassy permission to settle a colony of Jews on the island of Curaçao.[78] According to the terms of the contract, Nassy and his colonists were to farm and raise livestock along a two-mile coastal strip provided to them by the company. They were also given a ten-year exemption from paying taxes on any of the produce they succeeded in growing. They were not, however, permitted to cut down dyewood trees or establish saltpans—two valuable economic activities that the company reserved for itself. Additionally, they were encouraged to engage in privateering against Portuguese shipping. In return for the improvements the Jewish settlers were to make on Curaçao, the company promised to 'neither obstruct nor hinder the aforesaid patroon and colonists in any way, but rather give them as much help and assistance as possible'.[79] Finally, to prevent 'scandalous activities', Jews were prohibited from employing Christian servants on Sundays.[80]

In contrast to the explicit promise to protect Jewish worship granted to Jews in Dutch Brazil, Nassy's charter made no mention of any specific religious privileges. Whether this oversight was intentional is not known. Perhaps he felt that the recent

[76] Ibid. 46.

[77] Robert Cohen, *Jews in Another Environment: Surinam in the Second Half of the Eighteenth Century* (Leiden, 1991), 126.

[78] In the Curaçao charter, he is referred to by his other name, Joseph Nunes de Fonseca ('Grant of Land on Curaçao to Joseph Nunes de Fonseca by the West India Company' (22 Feb. 1652) (*Curacao Papers*, 49).

[79] 'Freedoms and Exemptions granted and Awarded by the directors of the West India Company at the Chamber in Amsterdam' (22 Feb. 1652) (ibid. 49–51).   [80] Ibid. 51.

experience in Dutch Brazil and the continued tolerance of Jewish practice in Amsterdam was sufficient proof that the WIC would not proscribe Jewish worship in Curaçao. Indeed, another Jewish community led by João de Yllan had already been practising Judaism in Curaçao for several months without any explicit protections and without any reported incidents. For David Nassy and his intended settlers, however, this issue ultimately proved to be irrelevant. No evidence exists to suggest that Nassy ever migrated to Curaçao or that his efforts resulted in any Jews going to the island to take possession of the land granted by the WIC.[81]

The issue of religious freedom would, however, be of paramount importance to the next group of Jewish settlers who contracted to go to Curaçao in 1659. Directed by Isaac da Costa, formerly a leading member of the Portuguese Jewish community in Recife and a nephew of controversial Amsterdam dissident Uriel da Costa, the settlers consisted of a number of experienced colonists and achieved a critical mass of over seventy men, women, and children.[82] Though Isaac da Costa's charter (31 March 1659) is now lost, a summary of the privileges was written in 1825 when it was still extant in Curaçao. Chief among them was 'the free exercise of their religion here', a guarantee of protection by the company, and the ability to build houses for themselves on the island.[83] Given the harassment and ill will that Peter Stuyvesant had demonstrated towards the Brazilian Jewish refugees in New Netherland earlier in the decade, it is not

[81] The *Curacao Papers* has no mention of Joseph Nunes de Fonseca or his colonists in residence on the island. Only João de Yllan and his settlers are mentioned. Furthermore, David Nassy, as he was referred to in the Jewish community, was a witness at his daughter Sara's wedding to Isaac Drago in Amsterdam in 1656 (see David Verdooner and Harmen Snel, *Trouwen in Mokum: Jewish Marriage in Amsterdam, 1598–1811*, 2 vols. (The Hague, 1991), i. 38).

[82] Many of these colonists had also previously lived in Brazil. Isaac da Costa was among the notable members of the Jewish community at Recife who signed a letter to Governor General Johan Maurits van Nassau Siegen in 1642 (Remonstrance of the Hebrew People, Samuel Oppenheim Collection, Box 30, American Jewish Historical Society (AJHS)). In addition, Isaac da Costa sold the WIC 600 cans of bee's brandy at Recife in November 1645 (Notulan van Brasilie (1 Nov. 1645), Samuel Oppenheim Collection, Box 27, AJHS). Da Costa's uncle, Uriel da Costa was a Jewish rationalist who was born Gabriel da Costa in Oporto, Portugal in 1585. He moved with his family to Amsterdam to practise openly, but in 1624 was excommunicated for criticizing the elaborate rules of rabbinical Judaism. In 1633 he recanted, only to offend again and be excommunicated until 1640. In that year, he once more recanted and was subjected to public humiliation, including being whipped, by the Amsterdam Mahamad. Soon thereafter, he committed suicide. Uriel da Costa's faith was based on natural law and reason. He is considered to have influenced the thinking of Spinoza.

[83] A letter from the Mahamad of Mikvé Israel to the governor of Curaçao of 2 December 1825 lists the privileges of 1659 (cited in Yosef Hayim Yerushalmi, 'Between Amsterdam and New Amsterdam: The Place of Curaçao and the Caribbean in Early Modern Jewish History', *American Jewish History*, 72/2 (1982), 189). Incidentally, in 1657 Dutch Jews were officially declared subjects of the Netherlands, entitled to the same protection abroad as all native Dutch subjects. According to Herbert Bloom this declaration was designed to facilitate trade between Dutch Jews and Spain by protecting Jews and their goods from illegal seizure by Spanish officials (Herbert I. Bloom, *The Economic Activities of the Jews of Amsterdam in the Seventeenth And Eighteenth Centuries* (Port Washington, NY, 1937), 22).

surprising that the Curaçaoan colonists received a written guarantee and positive affirmation from the WIC of their freedom to practise Judaism on the island.[84] They were also given permission to buy slaves, a privilege that would be important in their trans-Caribbean trade and would result in significant slave ownership by members of the community.[85]

Isaac da Costa and the other Jewish colonists probably left Amsterdam for Curaçao sometime after 11 May 1659. This date is known because a notarial document records that Isaac da Costa purchased from the Mahamad of Talmud Torah congregation in Amsterdam a Torah scroll with an orange cloth cover to take with him to Curaçao.[86] This also suggests the Mahamad approved of the project.[87] Taking such a precious object to the colony illustrates that Da Costa and the other participants had faith in the WIC's promise to uphold their religious liberties and that they also intended to make a permanent settlement in Curaçao.

Indeed, the Jews who arrived in 1659 and throughout the 1660s made an effort to create a sense of permanence and forge a community on the island. While they had much economic interaction with the Protestant inhabitants of the island, they occupied a negotiated social space within and without the larger Dutch population. Because of their traditional position on the margins and the fact that their lives were lived almost exclusively within Mikvé Israel congregation, the Sephardi Jews of Curaçao, like those of Amsterdam, tended to build houses close to one another and near the synagogue. Typically, Jewish merchants lived with their families in the Punda section of Willemstad, where a street called Joodestraat was located and which over time became a predominantly Jewish neighbourhood.[88]

By 1702 there were 126 mostly Sephardi families comprising over 600 Jews in Curaçao.[89] The following year, a fifth synagogue was built to accommodate the

---

[84] While Peter Stuyvesant lived in New Netherland, he was also responsible for the administration of Aruba, Bonaire, and Curaçao. Vice Director Matthias Beck was stationed in Curaçao and reported to Stuyvesant as well as the directors of the WIC in the Netherlands. Stuyvesant wrote to the WIC about the Jews in New Netherland: 'we have . . . deemed it useful to require them in a friendly way to depart; praying also most seriously in this connection, for ourselves as also for the general community of your worships, that the deceitful race . . . be not allowed further to infect and trouble this new colony' (Peter Stuyvesant to the Amsterdam Chamber of the WIC (22 Sept. 1654), in Morris U. Schappes (ed.), *Documentary History of Jews in the United States* (New York, 1971), 1–2). Stuyvesant and his council also initially tried to prevent Jews from owning houses in New Netherland.

[85] Curaçaoan Jews who had spent time in Brazil would certainly have been familiar with the commercial advantages of acquiring slaves.   [86] Notarial document (11 May 1659), GSA, NA 334, 457.

[87] Additionally, the Amsterdam *parnasim* later provided financial assistance to impoverished Jews wishing to go to Curaçao.

[88] Wim W. Klooster, 'The Jews in Suriname and Curaçao', in Bernardini and Fiering (eds.), *The Jews and the Expansion of Europe to the West*, 354.

[89] Jonathan I. Israel, 'The Jews of Dutch America', in Bernardini and Fiering (eds.), *The Jews and the Expansion of Europe to the West*, 336–7.

growing community.[90] Curaçao's Jewish population rose through continued immigration from locations throughout the Atlantic world and through natural increase.[91] That Curaçao could sustain a growing Jewish population had much to do with the economic opportunities available to the Jewish residents of the island. They were able to conduct legal and extra-legal trade throughout the Atlantic world, own ships and small plantations, and established themselves as brokers in Curaçao.

No fewer than twenty-five plantations were owned by Jews in Curaçao at the beginning of the eighteenth century. The climate of Curaçao prevented large-scale agricultural production, but plantation owners did grow indigo, lemons, oranges, eggplant, okra, and potatoes.[92] Plantation owners also engaged in livestock breeding and trading, sometimes providing the WIC with goats and sheep to feed the company's slaves.[93]

Jews made themselves valuable to the WIC through their commercial connections from their earliest moments in the colony. For example, in January 1656 Mordachay and Joshua Henriquez imported a wide array of goods to Curaçao, including earrings, pearls, knives, scissors, thimbles, and needles. All their goods were valued according to their weight in sugar. For example, the 100 thimbles in their shipment cost a 150-pound sack of sugar or one and a half pounds of sugar per thimble.[94]

While Mordachay and Joshua Henriquez provided important tools to help develop the fledgling colony and establish a stock of goods to trade with other islands and the nearby Spanish mainland, what Curaçao needed most in the mid-1650s was foodstuffs. In February 1656 a Jewish merchant named Isaac da Fonseca arrived aboard the *Constant Anna* from Barbados. Armed with a letter of introduction from the governor of Barbados and a request to be allowed to trade with the WIC or the island's inhabitants, Da Fonseca promised that in return the company would have the same trade privileges in Barbados.[95] Significantly, Da Fonseca also had 4,000 pounds of flour, a large barrel of hard bread, a pipe of brandy, six barrels of beer, oil, and parcels of goods.[96] After a long debate between Da Fonseca and Vice Director Matthias Beck he exchanged his cargo for fourteen horses and an unspecified amount of dyewood. The arrival of a greater number of Sephardi Jews with Isaac da Costa's colony in 1659 led to large-scale trading operations on the island.

Jewish settlers further developed trade relationships with Barbados and began a

---

[90] Isaac S. Emmanuel and Suzanne A. Emmanuel, *History of the Jews of the Netherlands Antilles*, 2 vols. (Cincinnati, 1970), i. 93.

[91] For example, about 100 Jews migrated from Martinique after they were expelled in 1685.

[92] Emmanuel and Emmanuel, *History of the Jews of the Netherlands Antilles*, i. 63.

[93] Ibid. 64. Matthias Beck purchased goats for the company from Joshua and Mordachay Henriquez as early as March 1656 (*Curacao Papers*, 120).

[94] 'Account by Messrs Josua and Mordakay Emriques' (1 Jan. 1656) (*Curacao Papers*, 116).

[95] 'Extraordinary session held in the residence of the honorable vice-director M. Beck' (21 Feb. 1656) (*Curacao Papers*, 87).   [96] Ibid. (*Curacao Papers*, 91).

commercial and communal exchange with co-religionists in Dutch New Netherland and, to a much greater extent, English New York. In 1676, for example, Jacob de Lucena sent food from New York City to Curaçao in exchange for slaves.[97] During the first half of the eighteenth century, the ties between Jews in New York and Curaçao were especially close. Daniel Gomez of New York married Esther Levy of Curaçao to cement the commercial relationship between these families. Subsequently, he sent over 100 vessels to the island, consigning the cargoes to thirty-five different correspondents, all of whom were Sephardi Jews.[98] Moreover, in religious matters, when New York's Shearith Israel congregation began a campaign to raise money to construct a new synagogue on Mill Street in 1729, the second-largest contribution to the building fund came from the Jews of Mikvé Israel in Curaçao.[99]

Family representatives in Europe, and Amsterdam in particular, helped make the commercial activities of Jewish colonists in Curaçao possible. According to historian Wim Klooster, commercial families constructed networks to sustain the activities of Jewish merchants across the Atlantic.[100] They supplied the goods that were so important in the exchange between Curaçao and the colonies of the Spanish Main and rest of the Caribbean, which was the mainstay of both Jewish and Christian merchants on the island. Many of the recent Sephardi immigrants had a language advantage, as they or their ancestors were originally from Spain, and they were thus able to communicate with their trade partners in the Spanish colonies. Textiles—linens, cotton cloths, and silk fabrics—were acquired from the major production areas of Europe by Amsterdam merchants and sent to Curaçao for trade with Spanish America, where these items were in high demand.[101] Venezuelan cacao, tobacco, indigo, coffee, vanilla, cochineal, lemon juice, dyewood, logwood, sugar, and ginger were the main commodities exported to Amsterdam from Curaçao.[102]

As the Sephardi population of Curaçao continued to increase during the first third of the eighteenth century, the Jews outgrew the 1703 synagogue. Between 1730 and 1732 another building was constructed. Modelled on the Sephardi synagogue in Amsterdam, the new Mikvé Israel Synagogue was 77 feet long, 57 feet wide, 50 feet high, and had a mahogany interior.[103] The floor was covered in sand imported from Jerusalem as a tribute to Portuguese crypto-Jews who were supposed to have covered the floors of their secret synagogues in the Iberian peninsula to muffle the sounds of their footsteps. The new synagogue was dedicated on the first day of Passover, 1732.[104] It remains in use today and is the oldest synagogue building in the Americas.

[97] Emmanuel and Emmanuel, *History of the Jews of the Netherlands Antilles*, i. 69.
[98] Klooster, 'The Jews in Suriname and Curaçao', 345.
[99] Emmanuel and Emmanuel, *History of the Jews of the Netherlands Antilles*, i. 131.
[100] Wim W. Klooster, 'Curaçao and the Caribbean Transit Trade', in Postma and Enthoven (eds.), *Riches from Atlantic Commerce*, 205. [101] Ibid. 205.
[102] Ibid. 213–4; Emmanuel and Emmanuel, *History of the Jews of the Netherlands Antilles*, i. 70.
[103] Emmanuel and Emmanuel, *History of the Jews of the Netherlands Antilles*, i. 123. [104] Ibid. 123.

Overall, the early Portuguese Jewish inhabitants of Curaçao negotiated charters (the 1659 grant to Isaac da Costa in particular) for their settlement, which protected their freedom to worship. Having secured this important privilege, Sephardim flowed to the colony from Amsterdam and other places in the Caribbean to take advantage of the island's location. As merchant traders with access to a wide variety of European products, the Jews not only made themselves valuable to local Dutch authorities and the WIC as a whole, but to the economies of the Spanish, English, and French Atlantic colonies as well. Because of these two factors—religious freedom and economic opportunity—Curaçao flourished as a haven for Sephardi Jews and developed into the capital of New World Jewry during the eighteenth century.

Conclusion

The Sephardim never achieved full parity with their Christian neighbours in the early modern era. Even after their emancipation in western Europe at the end of the eighteenth century, they still faced customary restrictions and prejudices. Nevertheless, as this chapter has demonstrated, Sephardi Jewish merchants were able to negotiate a space for themselves to live, work, and worship in the Caribbean and southern Atlantic. The privileges and freedoms they acquired often depended on the particular circumstances of the ports or colonies they settled and were subject to change over time. In actively engaging with imperial or company officials to secure charters and concessions, members of the Sephardi diaspora took advantage of the available opportunities, proved their usefulness, and helped develop the Atlantic world while making this world work for them. In the process, Sephardim exhibited a common purpose and fostered a sense of shared identity that transcended the bounds of empire.

PART II

AUTHORITY AND COMMUNITY
IN THE
DUTCH CARIBBEAN

AMSTERDAM AND THE PORTUGUESE *NAÇÃO* OF THE CARIBBEAN IN THE EIGHTEENTH CENTURY

GÉRARD NAHON

TRANSLATED BY DANIEL SCHERR

TO
RICHARD D. BARNETT
in memoriam

Introduction

On 16 December 1742 the New York merchant Mordechai Gomes pulled a book from his library shelf, the *Biblia en lengua española*, the Ferrara Bible, a Spanish translation of the Bible printed in Amsterdam (1660–1). On one of the pages he wrote in Spanish: 'On Thursday, the first day of Rosh Hodesh Kislev, the Hanukah moon, corresponding to 16 December 1742, God saw fit to take into His midst my son Moshe Gomes, in Jamaica. May God Almighty allow his soul to enjoy glory. Amen.'[1] Twenty years later, on 9 December 1764, on this same page, he would enter yet another inscription: 'On the 14th of Heshvan 5525, 9 November 1764, God saw it fitting to take into His midst, in Curaçao, Ishac, son of Mr Mordechai Gomes. May God protect him.' In this same Bible he also marked the passing of their mother, Esther Marques, whom he had married in Jamaica. Symbolically, in his Spanish Ferrara Bible, the seminal book of the western Sephardi diaspora, Mordechai Gomes introduced the two great Jewish communities of

---

[1] The volume is preserved in the library of the Séminaire Israélite de France in Paris, H 8° 2567 (see Gérard Nahon, 'Le Mémorial espagnol de Mordecay Gomes sur une *Bible de Ferrare*, New York 1716–1764', in Winfried Busse and Marie-Christine Varol-Bornes (eds.), *Sephardica: Hommage à Haïm Vidal Sephiha* (Berne, 1996), 465–81. On the Ferrara Bible, see *The Ladino Biblia de Ferrara (1553)*, ed. Moshe Lazar and Robert Dilligan (Culver City, Calif., 2004); Iacob M. Hassán and Ángel Berenguer Amador (eds.), *Introducción a la Biblia de Ferrara: Actas del Simposio Internacional sobre la Biblia de Ferrara, Sevilla, 25–28 de noviembre de 1991* (Seville, 1994). The funerary inscription for Moshe Gomes is transcribed in Richard D. Barnett and Philip Wright, *The Jews of Jamaica: Tombstone Inscriptions 1663–1880* (Jerusalem, 1997), 80 no. 285. Rosh Hodesh Kislev 5503 corresponds to 29 November 1742. I have no explanation for this mistake.

the Caribbean: Jamaica and Curaçao. In the seventeenth century the Portuguese Jewish community of Amsterdam, descended from Portuguese Marranos, had become the political, economic, religious, and cultural mother community of the entire western Sephardi diaspora.[2] Through its emigrants, its capital, its political backing, and, above all, through its model, Amsterdam contributed to the birth of the first Jewish communities—all of them Portuguese—in the New World, starting with Recife in Brazil and including Aruba, Barbados, Curaçao, Guadeloupe, Jamaica, Martinique, Nevis, St Christopher, St Eustatius, St Martin, St Thomas: islands under the colonial rule of the Netherlands, France, England, and Denmark. Amsterdam is omnipresent, because of the epistolary, commercial, religious, and family relations it maintained with each of these communities.[3]

Being new, these Portuguese communities, which had given themselves the Portuguese appellation *nação*, needed the continued support of Amsterdam. They built their institutions and their communal organization on the model of the mother community, and they did so using material and spiritual tools imported from Amsterdam. The ties between Amsterdam and the Caribbean communities are known to us through letters contained in Amsterdam's *Copiador de Cartas* (Letter Copybook). The historian Zvi Loker has accounted for 300 letters sent to the Caribbean: 229 to Curaçao, 9 to St Eustatius, 8 to Jamaica, 7 to Barbados, and 1 to St Croix. Even though Jamaica was a dependency of the British Crown, and the Spanish and Portuguese community of London helped the elders of the Jamaican community with political problems with the British government, the elders deferred to the authority of Amsterdam. Many of the letters from the Amsterdam *parnasim* responded not to communities, but to individuals, suggesting that these individuals considered Amsterdam their community.[4]

[2] Yosef Kaplan is the leading scholar in this field. See esp. Yosef Kaplan, *From Christianity to Judaism: The Story of Isaac Orobio de Castro*, trans. R. Loewe (Oxford, 1989); id., *An Alternative Path to Modernity: The Sephardi Diaspora in Western Europe* (Leiden, 2000); see also Renata G. Fuks-Mansfeld, *De Sefardim in Amsterdam tot 1795: Aspecten van een Joodse minderheid in een Hollandse stad* (Hilversum, 1989); Daniel M. Swetschinski, *Reluctant Cosmopolitans: The Portuguese Jews of Seventeenth-Century Amsterdam* (London, 2000); Miriam Bodian, *Hebrews of the Portuguese Nation: Conversos and Community in Early Modern Amsterdam* (Bloomington, 1997); Jonathan I. Israel, 'The Republic of the United Netherlands until about 1750: Demography and Economic Activity', in J. C. Blom, Renata G. Fuks-Mansfeld, and I. Schöffer (eds.), *The History of the Jews in the Netherlands* (Oxford, 2002), 84–115; Gérard Nahon, 'Amsterdam, métropole occidentale des Séfarades au XVIIe siècle', *Cahiers Spinoza*, 3 (1979–80), 15–50; repr. in Gérard Nahon, *Métropoles et périphéries séfarades d'Occident: Kairouan, Amsterdam, Bayonne, Bordeaux, Jérusalem* (Paris, 1993), 71–94.

[3] See Yosef Hayim Yerushalmi, 'Between Amsterdam and New Amsterdam: The Place of Curaçao and the Caribbean in Early Modern Jewish History', *American Jewish History*, 72/2 (1982), 172–92.

[4] Regarding the correspondence from the Portuguese Jewish community of Amsterdam, see Gérard Nahon, 'Une source pour l'histoire de la diaspora séfarade au XVIIIe siècle: le *Copiador de Cartas* de la communauté portugaise d'Amsterdam', in Issachar Ben-Ami (ed.), *The Sepharadi and Oriental Jewish Heritage: Studies* (Jerusalem, 1981), 109–22; for an overview of the Amsterdam network, see Jonathan I. Israel, *European Jewry in the Age of Mercantilism 1550–1750* (London, 1998); Evelyne Oliel-Grausz, 'Relations et réseaux inter-

This chapter explores the unequal networks linking the nations, people, and material objects of the Caribbean with Amsterdam. These networks were unequal because Amsterdam served as the virtual and actual mother community for the entire region. Despite its geographical distance from the Caribbean, Amsterdam was a religious resource that could not be overlooked. I will attempt to show how and to what extent the Portuguese Jews of the Caribbean copied the Amsterdam model, tried to free themselves from it, and even tried to replace it with a Caribbean model: so that in the eighteenth century Curaçao went on to become the model for North American Jewish communities.

Unequal Networks

Jewish emigrants to the Caribbean largely departed from Amsterdam. Amsterdam thus played the role of expediter for Portuguese Jews in other European countries. On 20 July 1660, 152 Jews from Livorno set sail on the *Monte de Cisne* bound for Cayenne. Among them was the poet Daniel Leví de Barrios and his wife Deborah Vaes, who would die in Tobago where the group landed. Others, such as Abraham Semah Cortissoz, who was born in St Eustatius in 1764, would travel in the opposite direction and come to Amsterdam. Semah Cortissoz went to Amsterdam in 1791 and then left again for Suriname and Jamaica. Children born of slave women were sent to Amsterdam to obtain a Jewish education. Seven Jews who wished to settle in Martinique appealed to relatives in Amsterdam to intervene with the governor on their behalf. Still in Amsterdam on 11 December 1670, Jacob Pereira da Silva, David da Costa d'Andrade, and David Lopez Henriques, before the notary Pierre Padthuÿsen, designated an agent in Paris to petition King Louis XIV to allow them to stay and trade in Martinique. The enforcement of the Code Noir in March 1685, expelling the Jews from the French islands in the Americas, drove not only the Jews of Martinique but also immigrants from Amsterdam to Curaçao. João de Yllan, who was born in Portugal and returned to Judaism in Amsterdam, contracted with the Dutch West India Company on 21 March 1651 to settle Jews in Curaçao to farm the land.

In addition to the movement of people, there were exchanges of merchandise.[5]

communautaires dans la diaspora séfarade d'Occident au XVIIIe siècle' (Ph.D. thesis, Universite Pantheon-Sorbonne, 2000); ead., 'La Diaspora séfarade au XVIIIe siècle: communication, espaces, réseaux', *Arquivos do Centro Cultural Calouste Gulbenkian*, 48 (2004), 55–72; Zvi Loker, *Jews in the Caribbean: Evidence on the History of the Jews in the Caribbean Zone in Colonial Times* (Jerusalem, 1991), 325. On the strong ties between the London and Jamaica communities, see Richard. D. Barnett, 'The Correspondence of the *Mahamad* of the Spanish and Portuguese Congregation of London during the Seventeenth and Eighteenth Centuries', *The Jewish Historical Society of England Transactions*, 20 (1959–61), 10–13.

[5] Miguel de Barrios, *La poesía religiosa*, ed. Kenneth R. Scholberg (Columbus, Ohio, 1962), 10; Wilhelmina C. Pieterse, *Daniel Levi de Barrios als geschiedschrijver van de Portugees-Israelitische Gemeente te Amsterdam in zijn 'Triunfo del govierno popular'* (Amsterdam, 1968), 16; Mordechai Arbell, *The Jewish Nation of the Caribbean: The Spanish-Portuguese Jewish Settlements in the Caribbean and the Guianas* (Jerusalem, 2002), 63; notarial documents,

For example, in the seventeenth century, Benjamin d'Acosta de Andrade had sugar plantations in Martinique. He introduced chocolate manufacturing to the colony and initiated trade with Amsterdam. The Jewish traders of the Caribbean had agents to whom they were related, not only in Amsterdam but also in Bordeaux, Livorno, London, and New Amsterdam, all communities that were themselves affiliated with Amsterdam.[6]

The frequency of travel and economic exchange led the Portuguese Jewish community in Amsterdam to become a banking house for the western and American diaspora. As a result, the Amsterdam Mahamad served as the economic intermediary for Portuguese Jews throughout the Atlantic. Individuals from the Caribbean would deposit their capital in Amsterdam savings associations, and the *parnasim* would use the funds to support trading ventures by other Portuguese Jews and attempt to get a good return on them. On 27 August 1750 the *parnasim* responded to a letter from Ishac Haim Rodrigues da Costa, residing in Curaçao, who notified them of the death of his father-in-law Mordechay Alvares Correa. The deceased 'had provided 300,000 guilders in trust to be administered by our college for the benefit of his cousin'.[7] The Portuguese Jewish community of Amsterdam would proceed, in accordance with the wishes of the deceased, to execute wills in favour of heirs residing in the islands. The *parnasim* acted as executors for Jeudit Henriques, who died in Amsterdam in May 1730, for the benefit of Abraham Ribeira de Paiva, Daniel Ribeira de Paiva, and Rachel Ribeira de Paiva, who were living in Jamaica. The *parnasim* sent them an affidavit sworn by a lady in London, Ribca Henriques, in order for them to be paid their inheritance.[8] The monies

Gemeente Stadsarchief Amsterdam (Amsterdam Municipal Archives, GSA), Notarieel Archief (NA) 2902, in Isaac S. Emmanuel, 'Les Juifs de La Martinique et leurs coreligionnaires d'Amsterdam au XVIIe siècle', *Revue des Études Juives*, 123 (1964), 511–16; Code Noir, art. 1: 'Voulons que l'édit du feu Roi de Glorieuse Mémoire, notre très honoré seigneur et père, du 23 avril 1615, soit exécuté dans nos îles; ce faisant, enjoignons à tous nos officiers de chasser de nos dites îles tous les juifs qui y ont établi leur résidence, auxquels, comme aux ennemis déclarés du nom chrétien, nous commandons d'en sortir dans trois mois à compter du jour de la publication des présentes, à peine de confiscation de corps et de biens' (That the edict be implemented in our islands, ordering all our officers to expel from our islands all the Jews who are residing there, and to leave in three months' time from the publication of the present under penalty of confiscation of all property for non compliance) (*Code noir ou recueil d'édits, déclarations et arrêts concernant les esclaves négres de l'Amérique* (Paris, 1743)); Abraham Cahen, 'Les Juifs de La Martinique au XVIIe siècle', *Revue des Études Juives*, 31 (1895), 110; for the notification provided by the Dutch WIC to Governor Stuyvesant of a contract entered into with João de Yllan, see G. H. Cone, 'The Jews in Curaçao According to Documents from the Archives of the State of New York', *Publications of the American Jewish Historical Society*, 10 (1902), 147.

[6] Regarding Benjamin d'Acosta, see A. Cahen, 'Les Juifs de La Martinique', 93–4; on trade, see Mordechai Arbell, *The Jewish Nation of the Caribbean*, 41, 76, 132; see also the many notarial documents published in Zvi Loker, *Jews in the Caribbean*.

[7] Isaac da Veiga Henriques and Jacob de David de Pinto to Ishac Haim Rodrigues da Costa in Curaçao (Amsterdam, 27 Aug. 1750), GSA, Private Archief (PA) 334 91, 354.

[8] Amsterdam *parnasim* to Abraham Ribeiro de Paiva, Daniel Ribeiro de Paiva, Rachel Ribero de Paiva in Jamaica (10 Sept. 1733), GSA, PA 334 91, 90–1 (see App. 3 below).

deposited could be lent to rich merchants to help them improve their trade. One Ishack Henriquez Cotinho, who arrived in Amsterdam from Curaçao for eye treatment, found that he lacked the necessary funds to set off to sea again. On 19 July 1765 he requested a loan of 100 guilders from the *parnasim*, a loan to be repaid two or three months after his return to Curaçao. As collateral he offered his three slaves, with an option to sell them in the event that he did not pay back the loan.[9]

Efficient communication across the Atlantic was critical in maintaining Amsterdam's hegemony. A letter sent by the historian Christian Wilhelm von Dohm to the *parnasim* of Suriname, dated 29 January 1787 from Cologne, reached Paramaribo five months later, on 29 June, thanks to the diligent efforts of one Captain Dalmeyer.[10] Letters might take longer if they had to wait for a ship heading for their destination. Since a letter might be held up for a long time or even lost, people took the precaution of sending copies by other routes. On 8 July 1750 the Amsterdam *parnasim* sent Jacob Jeudah Leão in Curaçao 'a copy of the one we wrote to Your Grace on May 25 by means of the ship *De Hoop*, Captain Jurian Hoop [sic], may God have steered it to safe passage'.[11]

The Amsterdam *parnasim*'s political protection was first applied not only to the islands under the aegis of the Dutch West India Company, but to English Jamaica as well. In 1699 the Baron de Belmonte, don Manuel, also known as Isaac Nuñes, Agent-General, later Resident, of Spain in The Hague, who was very closely linked to the Portuguese Jewish community of Amsterdam, wrote a letter in French to William Beeston, governor of Jamaica, on behalf of the Jews of the island.[12] He requested the elimination of a special tax and an exemption of the island's Jews from military service on the sabbath and Jewish holidays to 'enjoy their religion, without forcing them to take up arms on the sabbath and their feast days, unless the enemy is in view'.[13]

In the seventeenth century Amsterdam received immigrants from Brazil, Portugal, Spain, Antwerp, and Venice. Poor people also flooded into the Portuguese Jewish

---

[9] Ishack Henriquez Cotinho to the Amsterdam *parnasim* and *gabay*, GSA, PA 334 535, 566; English trans. in Zvi Loker, *Jews in the Caribbean*, 134–5 no. 28.

[10] *Essai historique sur la colonie de Surinam, sa fondation, ses révolutions, ses progrès, depuis son origine jusqu'à nos jours, ainsi que les causes qui depuis quelques années ont arreté le cours de sa prospérité; avec la description & l'état actuel de la Colonie, de même que ses revenus annuels, les charges & impôts qu'on y paye, comme aussi plusieurs autres objets civils & politiques; ainsi qu'un tableau des moeurs de ses habitans en général avec l'Histoire de la Nation Juive Portugaise & Allemande y Etablie, leurs Privilèges, immunités & franchises: leur Etat politique & moral, tant ancien que moderne: la part qu'ils ont eu dans la défense & dans les progrès de la Colonie. Le tout rédigé sur des pieces authentiques y jointes, & mis en ordre par les Régens & représentans de la dite Nation Juive Portugaise* (Paramaribo, 1788), pp. x–xi (see *Historical Essay on the Colony of Surinam 1788*, trans. Simon Cohen, ed. Jacob Rader Marcus and Stanley F. Chyet (Cincinnati, 1974)).

[11] Amsterdam *parnasim* to Jacob Jeudah Leão in Curaçao (8 July 1750), GSA, PA 334 92, 344.

[12] On Baron de Belmonte, see *Encyclopaedia Judaica* (Jerusalem, 1971–2), iv. 442–3; Loker, *Jews in the Caribbean*, 177–182; Mordechai Arbell, *The Portuguese Jews of Jamaica* (Kingston, Jamaica, 2000), 44–5.

[13] Z. Loker, *Jews in the Caribbean*, 177 no. 41; see App. 1 below.

community in the eighteenth century, some of whom the Amsterdam *parnasim* sent to the colonies, giving them a sum of money on a long-term loan.[14] In his *Political Reflections regarding the Establishment of the Jewish Nation* (1748), the economist Isaac de Pinto recommended a policy of systematically and forcibly sending excess indigents to the Caribbean and Suriname writing: 'It is necessary to begin evacuating this multitude through shipments capable of procuring for them some settlement, whether on islands or in colonies' to be accomplished by 'providing an incentive to the poor to accept shipment and offering them an alternative: either go to the colonies with the considerable advantages proposed to them, or no longer be recipients of public assistance'. He justifies these shipments by the very history of the colonies: 'Attention should be paid to the Colony of Suriname, which already makes up a nation, fairly numerous and opulent, and the other Colonies in the Americas, such as Curaçao, Jamaica, Barbados and related islands: all were formed by vagabonds, by destitute, poor, desperate people, whom hunger exiled from Europe.'[15] The Caribbean and Suriname thus extended, to use Jonathan Israel's expression, Amsterdam's 'living space', a living space that was in short supply along the banks of the Amstel.[16] The policy was instituted by the Mahamad, who had forms printed for each *despacho*, or shipment, on which were recorded the name of the person being shipped overseas, the destination, and the amount of the loan that he received on his departure. On 14 August 1750 the *parnasim* of Amsterdam suggested to their London counterparts that they provide a travel advance on their behalf to a certain Abraham Morales: 'It is appropriate for Your Graces to pay to this Ab[raha]m Morales the amount of 100 guilders, on our account, for his being dispatched to Jamaica.'[17]

These new communities included former New Christians freshly arrived from Iberia who were unfamiliar with rabbinic traditions and who continued to speak and read Portuguese or Spanish in islands where Dutch or English was dominant.[18] Lacking printing presses, they imported their prayer books, religious objects, and religious

---

[14] See Israel, 'The Republic of the United Netherlands until about 1750', 91.

[15] He necessario começar evacuando esta multidaõ por via de despachos capases a procurar-lhes alguns estabelecimentos, seja em Ilhas, seja em Colonias. . . . Impellando os pobres, a aceitar o despacho; offerecendolhes a alternativa, ou de hir as Colonias com as ventagens consideraveis que se lhes propoem, ou naõ ser mas assistidos do public. . . . Que se faça attençaõ que a Colonia de Surinam, que compoem ja huma naçaõ, bastantemente numerosa, & opulenta, & as demais Colonias que ha na America, como saõ Curacau, Jamaica, Barbadas &s: todas se formaraõ de pessoas vagabundas, desvalidas, pobres & desperadas, que a necessidade exilou de Europa' (Isaac de Pinto, *Reflexoens politicas tocante a constituição da Nação Judaica. Exposição do estado de suas finanças, causas dos atrasos e desordens que se experimentão e meyos de os prevenir* (Amsterdam, 1748), 13, 14, 17). On poverty, welfare, and the semi-forced departure of poor people to other lands, see Tirtsah Levie Bernfeld, *Poverty and Welfare Among the Portuguese Jews in Early Modern Amsterdam* (Oxford, 2012), 41–58.   [16] See Israel, 'The Republic of the United Netherlands until about 1750', 95.

[17] Amsterdam *parnasim* to Binjamin Mendes da Costa in London (14 Aug. 1750), GSA, PA 334 92, 353.

[18] On the linguistic aspect of the history of Caribbean Jews, see Isaac S. Emmanuel, 'El Portuguêz en la sinagoga "Mikve Israel" de Curaçao', *Tesoro de los judíos sefardíes*, I (1959), pp. xxv–xxxi.

directives almost exclusively from Amsterdam, the major centre for Hebrew printing in western Europe between 1650 and 1750.[19] In 1744 Josias Hizquiyahu de Cordova, a rabbi first in Curaçao and later in Jamaica, had a sermon printed in Amsterdam. In 1773, under the supervision of Gerard Johan Janson, Israel Mondovy printed the *Seder tefilot lishe'elat matar*, a special liturgy praying for rain, composed by the rabbi of Curaçao, Semuel Mendes Sola, who had since died. In 1780 Jahacob Lopez de Fonseca, the Curaçaoan rabbi, had Jahacob Proops's widow print his sermon delivered in Curaçao in Portuguese under the title: *Moral Sermon and Panegyric that was Preached on the Notable Holiday of the Bridegrooms of the Law.* The only known exception was Daniel Israel López Laguna, whose parents had lived in France. Laguna composed his *Espejo fiel de vidas que contiene los Psalmos de David en verso* (A Faithful Mirror of Lives Contained in the Psalms of David in Verse), a poetical paraphrase of the book of Psalms in Spanish, in Jamaica and had it printed in London in 1720.[20]

The leaders of the Caribbean communities often appealed to the authority of the *parnasim* of Amsterdam. For instance, the Amsterdam *parnasim* acknowledged receipt of letters from St Eustatius dated 20 August and 5 October 1756: 'with the news that in that colony there is a number [of Jewish inhabitants] sufficient to form a congregation, for which purpose [they desired] to build a house of prayer devoted to the worship of the divine'.[21] Indeed the elders of St Eustatius begged for permission and financial help in order to implement their vow. The *parnasim* of Amsterdam, who contributed strongly to the establishment of Jewish communities in the colonies, such as St Martin in 1783, were the natural recourse for disagreements in religious affairs, all the more so because they had contacts in the Dutch government in The Hague.[22] In one internal conflict, which went on for several years in Curaçao, a certain Moses Penso wanted to open another synagogue on the island. The Amsterdam *parnasim* notified the governor in 1749 that 'we will not consent to a second congregation on that island'.[23] After they turned to the Dutch government, the *stadhouder*, Prince William IV of Orange-Nassau, put an end to the conflict in 1750. The *Publicação e provizional Reglamento de Sua Alteza o senhor Principe de Orange e Nassau, consernente a Nação Judaica Portuguesa em Curaçao*

---

[19] See Yosef Kaplan, 'The Jews in the Republic until about 1750: Religious, Cultural and Social Life', in Blom, Fuks-Mansfeld, and Schöffer (eds.), *The History of the Jews in the Netherlands*, 138; Leo Fuks and Renata G. Fuks-Mansfeld, *Hebrew Typography in the Northern Netherlands 1585–1815: Historical Evaluation and Descriptive Bibliography* (Leiden, 1984–1987); Harm Den Boer, 'Amsterdam as "Locus" of Iberian Printing in the Seventeenth and Eighteenth Centuries', in Yosef Kaplan (ed.), *The Dutch Intersection: The Jews and the Netherlands in Modern History* (Leiden, 2008), 87–112.

[20] See C. Cabezas Alguacil, 'Un acercamiento a la obra de Daniel López Laguna: *Espejo fiel de vidas*', *Miscelánea de estudios árabes y hebraicos*, 37–8 (1988–1989), 151–62; see also Chapter 18 below.

[21] Amsterdam *parnasim* to St Eustacius *jehidim* (17 Jan. 1757), GSA, PA 334 91, 250–1; see App. 4 below.

[22] Isaac S. Emmanuel and Suzanne A. Emmanuel, *A History of the Jews of the Netherlands Antilles*, 2 vols. (Cincinnati, 1970), i. 528; see also Chapter 5 below.

[23] Amsterdam *parnasim* to Curaçaoan *parnasim* and *gabay* (14 Aug. 1749), GSA, PA 334 92, 301.

(Publication and Provisional Regulations of His Highness the Prince of Orange and Nassau concerning the Portuguese Jewish Nation in Curaçao) was published in the same year in The Hague at Jacob Scheltus's printing facility and included a Dutch translation on the facing page. Even though Barbados was under British rule, the Portuguese Jewish community there was nonetheless under the aegis of the Portuguese Jewish community of Amsterdam.[24]

Rabbinic authority emanated exclusively from the *parnasim* of Amsterdam which organized aid to the Holy Land. Emissaries from the Land of Israel, such as Semuel Acohen, emissary for Hebron from 1772 to 1774, would travel to the Caribbean, equipped with letters of accreditation issued and printed in Amsterdam.[25] These emissaries would collect funds, deliver sermons and religious teaching, and give small bags of soil from the Holy Land along with books they had written and had printed when passing through Amsterdam. On 17 July 1747 the Amsterdam *parnasim* acknowledged receipt of a 'nedava para a Terra santa' (donation for the Holy Land) from Curaçao, conveyed in a warship.[26] Rafael Haim Ishac Carrigal, another emissary from Hebron, where he was born, had been hired as the rabbi of Nidhe Israel congregation in Barbados, where he died at the age of 48. In 1955 his tombstone was discovered in Barbados, broken into five pieces.[27]

As early as the seventeenth century, Torah scrolls were sent from Amsterdam to Barbados, Pomeroon, Curaçao, Cayenne, and Martinique. In 1670 Benjamin d'Acosta de Andrade in Martinique acknowledged receipt of a scroll sent from Amsterdam. The *parnasim* of Amsterdam distributed dowries to young women from Pomeroon, Curaçao, Jamaica, and Barbados, who had been orphaned or were otherwise felt to be deserving, through the confraternity called the Santa Companhia de Dotar Orphas e Donzellas Pobres (Holy Confraternity for the Provision of Dowries to Orphans and Poor Maidens). In doing so, Amsterdam performed a social function for women of Portuguese Jewish ancestry even in the Caribbean.

In addition to occasional contacts with learned rabbis from the Land of Israel, Caribbean communities had rabbis from Amsterdam. The Amsterdam-trained *ḥakham* Josiau Pardo, son-in-law of Saul Levi Morteira, was hired as a rabbi in Curaçao in 1674. He founded the Ets Haim yeshiva in Curaçao and later held the post of rabbi in Jamaica. Amsterdam served to link the Jewish communities of the Caribbean to the Land of Israel and Turkey through the provision of rabbis. The Amsterdam community also sent rabbis and cantors from Istanbul to the Caribbean—to the point that *ketubot* in Curaçao were drawn up in accordance with the rules of Istanbul. These distant

[24] Jacob Rader Marcus, *The Colonial American Jew, 1492–1776*, 3 vols. (Detroit, 1970), i. 123.

[25] Emmanuel and Emmanuel, *A History of the Jews of the Netherlands Antilles*, i. 161.

[26] Amsterdam *parnasim* and *gabay* to Curaçaoan *parnasim* (17 July 1747), GSA, PA 334 92, 190.

[27] Eustace M. Shilstone, *Monumental Inscriptions in the Burial Ground of the Jewish Synagogue at Bridgetown, Barbados* (London, 1956), 100–1 n. 256.

Caribbean nations were thus incorporated into halakhic Judaism thanks to Amsterdam. In 1678 Hakham Eliahu Lopez signed a contract with Louis Dias in Amsterdam to occupy the rabbinical chair in Bridgetown, Barbados. In 1691 he occupied the prestigious rabbinical position in Curaçao.

Amsterdam also provided Torah scrolls to Curaçao, St Eustatius, Barbados, and St Croix. Thus materially as well as spiritually, the law emanated from Amsterdam. Certain individuals donated other ritual objects and ornaments: in 1662 the Cohen Henriques family donated lamps and Torah scrolls to the Barbados synagogue.

Throughout the eighteenth century the power of Amsterdam declined along with its economy. As Caribbean Jewish nations obtained their freedom, new relations between Amsterdam, the Caribbean, and North America emerged. Jacob de Rivera moved from Curaçao to Newport; Mordechai Gomes moved from Jamaica to New York. In 1764 Curaçao was offering Newport and New York the financial and religious services that Amsterdam had previously provided. The rabbinical tribunal of Curaçao resisted the power of the Beit Din of Amsterdam on 23 April 1747: 'The conclusion of our Beit Din is absolutely opposed to the conclusion reached by Your Graces' tribunal.' The Amsterdam *parnasim* thereupon reminded the *parnasim* of Curaçao that 'our Jewish nation is maintained only by the miracles of divine providence'.[28] Jamaica linked itself politically with England and the Portuguese Jewish community of London, as Richard Barnett's study of the correspondence of the Mahamad of London has shown. The authority of the Jamaican Mahamad was nevertheless recognized by the communal leaders of Amsterdam. A hitherto unpublished letter from the Amsterdam *parnasim* to their Jamaican counterparts on October 1708 urges them to use their authority, so that Ribca Blandon, the widow of Salvador de Palacios, whose son Jacob de Palacios had died in Jamaica, could gain possession of her son's assets, held by a certain Blanca Soeiro.[29]

Replicas and Replicas of Replicas

Venice, the first Portuguese community to emerge from Marranism in the sixteenth century, provided the model for the communal organization of Amsterdam's Portuguese Jews. The Portuguese Jewish communities of the Caribbean, in turn, drew upon the regulations of Amsterdam. In both instances the Mahamad had at its disposal binding power over its members, including the power of excommunication. The Mahamad would hire a rabbi, a *ḥakham*, to teach the law and act as a judge. It would pay a salary to a cantor to sing the public prayers in accordance with the Amsterdam rite. The Mahamad imposed strict discipline, both in the observance of religious precepts and in the monitoring of mores: for instance, it prohibited gambling. Basing itself on the

---

[28] Amsterdam *parnasim* and *gabay* to Curaçaoan *parnasim* and *gabay* (23 Apr. 1747), GSA, PA 334 92, 171.

[29] Amsterdam Mahamad to Jamaican Mahamad (23 Oct. 1708), GSA, PA 334 90, 52; see App. 2 below.

Amsterdam model, the Caribbean mahamads imposed two taxes: the *imposta* and the *finta*. As in Amsterdam, a confraternity gave dowries to orphaned or indigent young women.[30]

In the islands as well as in Suriname, synagogue construction drew its inspiration from the Esnoga Synagogue constructed in Amsterdam in 1675, although the Caribbean houses of worship were smaller. In each synagogue a section was reserved for the women, except in St Thomas. However, the Caribbean communities added an element unknown in Amsterdam, a fine layer of sand covering the floor. Several interpretations of this have been put forward: that it was sand from the Land of Israel, that it was intended to muffle people's footsteps, that it symbolized the trek through the Sinai desert.[31]

Like the first three communities in Amsterdam, each Caribbean Portuguese congregation adopted a Hebrew name taken from a meaningful verse of the Bible: Mikvé Israel (Hope of Israel: Jer. 17: 13) in Curaçao; Nidhe Israel (Scattered of Israel: Ps. 147: 2; Isa. 11: 12, 56) in Barbados; Sha'ar Hashamayim (Gate of Heaven: Gen. 28: 17) in Jamaica; Honen Dalim (He Who Shows Pity to the Poor: Prov. 19: 17) in St Eustatius. The choice of Mikvé Israel may have been inspired by Menasseh ben Israel's book of the same name (*Esperança de Israel*, written in Spanish and published in Amsterdam in 1650).[32]

Rabbis and cantors also attempted to produce literary works, although with limited success: Cantor Moshe Lopes composed prayers for circumcisions in Barbados. Literary salons, such as the Docendo Docemur (We are Taught by Teaching) school, founded in 1785 in Suriname, were inspired by the salons in vogue in Amsterdam in the seventeenth century and organized public readings of French books. The adoption of French—Jewish settlers in Suriname were often natives of the French islands Cayenne and Guyana—also imitated Amsterdam, where French was used in enlightened Jewish circles. The manuscript catalogues from the Ets Haim and Rosenthaliana libraries published by Leo Fuks and Renata G. Fuks-Mansfeld contain a number of unpublished works written in French by Jewish authors from Amsterdam: for example, Isaac de Pinto's *Paradoxe soutenu par plusieurs exemples pour prouver que la vérité nous conduit souvent à l'erreur et l'erreur à la vérité* (The Paradox, Supported by Several Examples, to Prove that Truth Often Leads Us to Error and Error to Truth, 1745) and David Franco Mendes's *Dictionnaire de Marine contenant l'Art de la Navigation et l'architecture navale* (Maritime Dictionary Containing the Art of Navigation and Naval Architecture, 1780).

[30] On the issue of the model, see Evelyne Oliel-Grausz, 'Patrocinio and Authority: Assessing the Metropolitan Role of the Portuguese Nation of Amsterdam in the Eighteenth Century', in Kaplan (ed.), *The Dutch Intersection*, 149–72.

[31] On the sand and more generally on the imitation of Amsterdam and innovation in the Caribbean, see Aviva Ben-Ur, '"Distingués des autres juifs": Les Sépharades des Caraïbes', in Shmuel Trigano (ed.), *Le Monde Sépharade: Histoire et civilisation* (Paris, 2006), 279–328.

[32] Menasseh ben Israel, *Espérance d'Israël*, trans. and ed. Henri Méchoulan and Gérard Nahon (Paris, 1979), 96.

The editors of the *Essai historique sur la colonie de Surinam*, published in Paramaribo in 1788, stated that French was not their native tongue. The *Essai historique*, the first history of a Jewish nation written by the nation itself, no doubt drew inspiration from the taste Amsterdam had for its own history.[33]

Amsterdam was also imitated in baroque funeral practices. Curiously, just as funeral processions would sail through the Venice lagoon to the Lido cemetery or up the Amstel river to the Amsterdam cemetery in Ouderkerk, in Jamaica the deceased were transported by water from Port Royal to the cemetery in Hunt's Bay.[34] On the horizontal tombstones characteristic of Sephardi graves, epitaphs would be engraved in Hebrew, Portuguese, or Spanish, with extremely polished calligraphy, using the same abbreviations used in Amsterdam. French appeared on an epitaph very late in Santa Domingo: 'Ci gît—le bien heureux: Abraham Moline / décédé le décembre 1789' (Here lies the blessed Abraham Moline, who died in December 1789) followed by the Portuguese acronym *SAGDEG: Sua [bendita] alma goze da Eterna Gloria* (May his [blessed] soul enjoy Eternal Glory)).[35]

The use of figurative representations on tombs, such as biblical scenes related to the deceased's first name or ships sailing the ocean for maritime merchants or ship's captains, characteristic of seventeenth-century Amsterdam, may be found in Curaçao and Jamaica well into the eighteenth century, although this ornamentation had already gone out of style in Amsterdam.[36] In what was the height of affluence, well-to-do Jews in Curaçao stipulated in their wills that marble tombstones be imported from Amsterdam. David Israel Bernal declared in 1716 that he intended to have a 'modest stone transported from Amsterdam'. Esther Henriquez Moron was more demanding: her tombstone was also to be sent from Amsterdam, but hers was to be blue.[37]

Conclusion

Despite the political differences of English, French, Spanish, or Danish rule, the Amsterdam community participated in the birth and rapid growth of the Portuguese

[33] David Franco Mendes, *Memorias do estabelecimiento e progresso dos Judeos Portuguezes e Espanhoes nesta famosa citade de Amsterdam*, ed. Leo Fuks, Renata G. Fuks-Mansfeld, and B. N. Teensma, Publications of the Bibliotheca Rosenthaliana, 5 (Assen, 1975), pp. xii, 233.

[34] Regarding the cemetery, see Marilyn Delevante, *The Knell of Parting Days: A History of the Jews of Port Royal and the Hunt's Bay Cemetery* (Kingston, Jamaica, 2008).

[35] The seminal publication in this area is Isaac S. Emmanuel, *Precious Stones of the Jews of Curaçao: Curaçaon Jewry, 1656–1957* (New York, 1957); see also Aviva Ben-Ur and Rachel Frankel, *Remnant Stones*, vol. i: *The Jewish Cemeteries of Suriname: Epitaphs* (Cincinnati, 2009); Aviva Ben-Ur with Rachel Frankel, *Remnant Stones*, vol. ii: *The Jewish Cemeteries and Synagogues of Suriname: Essays* (Cincinnati, 2012); for the French colonies with less exuberant tombstones, see Loker, *Jews in the Caribbean*, 310–12 no. 80.

[36] Michael Studemund-Halevy, 'The Persistence of Images: Reproductive Success in the History of Sepharadi Sepulchral Art', in Kaplan (ed.), *The Dutch Intersection*, 123–48.

[37] Emmanuel, *Precious Stones of the Jews of Curaçao*, 118.

Jewish communities of the Caribbean becoming the gateway to the Americas. Many North American families had close relatives on the islands, while others had families in Amsterdam. Amsterdam found itself at the head of a virtual federation united by the use of Portuguese for day-to-day living, sermons, and epitaphs; Spanish for reading the Ferrara Bible; and French for general culture and belles-lettres.

This federation included active relationships for the exchange of people, rabbis, and merchandise. It was associated with the activities in Amsterdam on behalf of the Land of Israel, such as the fundraising campaigns of emissaries. The proceeds were sent to Jerusalem, Hebron, Safed, and Tiberias via Istanbul. Sacks of earth from the Land of Israel bearing the label *KKTS* (*Kehilot Kedoshot Terra Santa*[38]) reached the Caribbean through Amsterdam. Their contents were possibly mixed with the sand of the synagogue and used to cover the eyes of the deceased during the ritual cleansing that preceded burial. When in 1788 the *parnasim* of Suriname evoked 'l'Auguste république d'Hollande, notre mère patrie',[39] it was certainly Amsterdam they had on their minds.

APPENDICES

1 Memorial from the Baron de Belmonte (Francisco *alias* Isaac Ximenes) to the King of England (15 Jan. 1699)[40]

Le Baron de Belmonte représente très respectueusement à V[otre] M[ajesté] qu'ayant eu l'honneur informer VM des justes plaints que les juifs Portugais habitans dans l'isle de la Jamaïque ont contre l'assemblée de la ditte isle puisque, sans avoir esgard aux Lettres de Denization et de Naturalisation que VM et les rois ses prédécesseurs leurs ont fait la grâce de leurs accorder pour ce qui concerne leurs privilèges, desquels ils ont jouï l'espace de plus de trente ans, nonobstant les fréquentes sollicitations des Anglois de la ditte Isle qui prétendoient que l'asssemblée les taxa particulièrement, ils ont enfin succombéz et ont esté obligez de payer par trois fois les taxes particulières de trois mille livres, outre les taxes générales faits par les paroissiennes, et ils ont meme esté sur le point dans le dernier assemblée d'estre taxés particulièrement en cinq mille deux cent cinquante livres et, comme VM a bien voulu accorder à la très humble prière du Baron

---

[38] Arbell transcribes it as *kahal kadosh* (*The Jewish Nation of the Caribbean*, 164). I suggested the plural for the first half of the acronym. The term appears in Hebrew letters in the Hebron *Publicação* in the Americas, a leaf printed in 1772 for the emissary Semuel Acohen (John Carter Brown Library, Providence, RI, FA 772 P976 I–SIZE).   [39] *Essai historique sur la colonie de Surinam*, p. xx.

[40] National Archives, Kew, Colonial Office 137.6 (Jamaica). The text is according to Charles Gross, 'Documents from the Public Record Office (London)', *Publications of the American Jewish Historical Society*, 2 (1894) 165–7; repr. in Jacob A. P. M. Andrade, *A Record of the Jews in Jamaica from the English Conquest to the Present Time* (Kingston, Jamaica, 1941), 10.

de Belmonte qu'elle donneroit ses ordres souverains pour faire maintenir à la nation Juifve Portugaise les privilèges dont ils ont toujours jouï dans l'isle de la Jamaïque, les Lettres pattentes des rois antécesseurs de VM; le même Baron de Belmonte supplie VM très humblement et très respectueusement de faire écrire au Gouverneur de la Jamaïque que il aye à maintenir et observer religieusement et sans délai les privilèges que VM et les Rois prédécesseurs ont fait la grâce d'accorder à la nation juif Portugaise par ses Lettres pattentes sans les singulariser par aucune taxe particulière et qu'on leurs laisse jouir du culte et due libre exercice de leur religion, sans les obliger à prendre les armes le jour du Sabat ou de leur feste sollemnelles, à moins que l'enemy ne soit à le veue, qu'en tel cas ils les prendront avec ardeur et tacheront de se montrer dignes sujets et vassaux de VM et le Baron de Belmonte espère de la royale bonté de VM.

(Sgd.) Le Baron de Belmonte

With all due respect, the Baron de Belmonte represents to Your Majesty that having had the honour of informing Your Majesty of the well-founded complaints that the Portuguese Jews living on the island of Jamaica have against the assembly of the aforementioned island because, without taking into account the Letters of Denization and Naturalization that Your Majesty and the kings who preceded you had the kindness to bestow upon them with regard to their privileges, privileges they have enjoyed for more than thirty years, despite the frequent requests from the Englishmen of the aforementioned island who maintained that the Jews should be subject to special taxes, they have finally succumbed and have been forced to pay three times the specific taxes of £3,000, in addition to the general taxes paid by the local folk, and during the last meeting of the assembly, they were even at the point of having a specific tax levied on them to the amount of £5,250 and, since Your Majesty was willing to accede to the very humble prayer of the Baron de Belmonte and agreed to issue sovereign orders to have the privileges of the Portuguese Jewish nation maintained, privileges they have always enjoyed on the island of Jamaica, the letters patent from the kings who preceded Your Majesty; the Baron de Belmonte himself very humbly and respectfully beseeches Your Majesty to have correspondence sent to the governor of Jamaica so that he will maintain and religiously observe, forthwith, the privileges that Your Majesty and the kings that preceded you have had the kindness to bestow upon the Portuguese Jewish nation through your letters patent, without singling them out by any specific tax, and so that they may be allowed to enjoy the worship and the free exercise of their religion, without forcing them to take up arms on the sabbath day or on their solemn feast days, unless the enemy is in view, in which case they will take up arms with ardour and will endeavour to show themselves as worthy subjects and vassals of Your Majesty and the Baron of Belmonte places his hopes in Your Majesty's royal goodness.

(Signed) The Baron de Belmonte

2   The *Parnasim* of the Amsterdam Portuguese Jewish Community to the Gentlemen of the Mahamad of Jamaica (23 Oct. 1708)[41]

Muy magnificos S[enho]res,

O motivo destas regras he reprezenta a V[uestras] M[ercede]s em como a a sra Ribca Blandon, viuva de Salvador de Palacios, hu remostrado aos sres do *Mahamad* desta cidade que, avendo falesido nessa seu filho Jacob de Palacios e levado consigo hua cargação bastante luzida por seu estado, lhe fao noticiado por cartas que tene dessa, que tudo o que deixou o dito seu filho pasa em poder de sra Blanca Soeiro, e nos suplico quizessemos interposnos com VMs suplicandolhes que, com sua autoridade, obriguem aa ditta s[enho]ra ou a outra qualquer pessoa que tenha algo effeito do ditto difunto, para que debaxo de juramento declarem o que tem e facão de sorte que lhe venha a mão a esta pobre viuva cargada com muitas obligaçoens e que se empenou em mais que do que podra para depachar o dito seu filho por ley divina e humana lle tocas, e como esto he hua obra de caridade nos não pudemos escusar, esperando de sua begninidade de VMs apiadarão este cazo tão justificado tudo lhes for possivel.

Most Magnificent Sirs,

The reason for this correspondence is to represent to Your Graces that, as Mrs Ribca Blandon, the widow of Salvador de Palacios, has demonstrated to the gentlemen who make up the Mahamad of this city that, her son Jacob de Palacios having passed away there, and having left behind a rather substantial estate, she was notified by letters she has from there that everything that was left by her son will revert to the possession of Mrs Blanca Soeiro,[42] and she entreated us to take it upon ourselves to intervene before Your Graces, pleading with you so that, using your authority, you can obligate the aforesaid lady or any other person holding any of the possessions of the deceased, so that under oath they can testify as to what they have, and can act in such a way that it comes within reach of this poor widow laden down with many obligations and who went into debt more than she will be able to deal with in order to dispatch her aforementioned son as is appropriate in accordance with divine and human law, and since this is an act of charity we could excuse ourselves. We hope in the clemency of Your Graces, and hope that you will show the utmost degree of compassion in a case that is so justified.

---

[41]   GSA, PA 334 90, 52.

[42]   A Branca Sueyro died on 2 Sept. 1729 at the age of 54 (see Barnett and Wright, *The Jews of Jamaica*, 24 n. 129).

3   The *Parnasim* of the Amsterdam Portuguese Jewish Community to the
     Gentlemen of the Mahamad of Jamaica (10 Feb. 1733)[43]

S[enho]res Abraham Ribeira de Paiva, Daniel Ribeira de Paiva
a sra Rachel Ribeiro de Paiva

Amsterdam 10 fev[re]ro 1733

Jamaica

Havendo falesido no mes de mayo 1730 a sra tia d[o]na Jeudit Henriques e nomeado
a os sres do *Mahamad* por executores de seu testam[en]to feito nesta em 12 mayo 1730
diante do notario Phelip de Maroles y deixado nelle a VM J. Ab[aham] Ribeiro f 400 de
caixa por hua vez, e a VM Dan[ie]l Ribeiro f 400 como asima por hua vez, y a VM sra
Rachel Ribeira f 450 como asima, a VMs o seus descendentes, e avendo nesta tempo
pedido a sra Ribca Henriques de Londres lhe defesse a VMs esta noticia, por como te
aqui não apareseo sua preuva para pagar dittos legados, supomos não lles chegaria
d[it]a noticia que lhe damos oje 1a e 2a via para que VM posão valerse do seu quanto
antes e nos descargar e segir a vondade da defunta, y dezejando VMs a verba de dicho
testamento autentica esta mandaremos o que agora deixamos por escuzarles gastos,
advertindo que a preuva de cada hum deve ser poder para cobrar de nos, como
executores o legado de cada qual deixado pela sra tia, em virtude do seu testamento,
com a data delle e notario que pasou como notamos ariba para que não terão retensão
no pagam[en]to ao qual estamos prontos, e D[eu] lhes conseda a VMs muita vida tera
em gloria a difunta e o guarde largos anos como lhes dezejamos.

Is[aac] de Pinto
Mandado 1a navia por Lond[res] e por via de Moseh D[avi]d Mend[e]s.

Messrs Abraham Ribeira de Paiva, Daniel Ribeira de Paiva and
Mrs Rachel Ribeira de Paiva

Amsterdam, 10 February 1733

Jamaica

Since Mrs Jeudith Henriques passed away in May of 1730, and since the members of
the Mahamad were named as executors of her will, drawn up in this city on 12 May 1730,
in the presence of the notary Philip de Maroles, and since, in said will, 400 guilders cash,
payable once, were left to Your Grace J. Abraham Ribeira, 400 guilders were also left to
Your Grace Daniel Ribeira, payable once, and the sum of 450 guilders was left to Mrs
Rachel Ribeira, payable to Your Graces or your descendants, and since during this

---

[43]   GSA, PA 334 91, 90–91.

period of time we requested Mrs Ribca Henriques of London to convey this news to you, and since no valid document has appeared here from you authorizing the payment of the aforementioned bequests, we suppose that this news that we are giving you today did not reach you. We are giving you a first and a second opportunity so that Your Graces can avail yourselves of what is yours as soon as possible and discharge us and enable us to follow the wishes of the deceased. Should Your Graces desire the authentic clause of said testament, we will send it to you, although we now set it aside to save you expense. We advise you that the valid document authorizing payment from each one of you should be in the form of a power of attorney for you to be able to receive payment from us as executors of the amount bequeathed to each of you by your aunt, by virtue of her testament, along with its date and the notary, who came, as we noted above, so there will be no withholding of payment, which we are ready to effectuate. May God grant Your Graces long life, may He hold the deceased in glory, and may He preserve you for many years. Such is our desire for you.

Isaac de Pinto
Sent by ship from London through Moseh David Mendes.

4   The *Parnasim* of the Amsterdam Portuguese Jewish Community to the St Eustatius Jewish Nation (17 Jan. 1757)[44]

St Eustasius
S[enho]res Jehidim del K[ahal] K[ados] en la Isla de St Eustaçius

Amsterdam 17 Henero 1757

En su tiempo reçevimos la que V[uestra]s M[erceds]s nos escriven, su data 20 agosto y de nuebo la de 5 otubre del año passado. Com notisia de hallarence en essa colonia en numero sufisiente para formar una congrega, para cuio efecto dezeavan fabricar uma caza de oraçion dedicado al culto divino, cuio intente como tan loable no podemos dexar de aplaudir y apadrinar como ya lo tenemos hecho a la suplica de VMs a estos ssres Bewinthebbert de la compaña del West. Pero dichos señores nos dilatan en la respuesta asta el mes de marco que se deven juntar todas las camaras. No dudamos alcansaremos favorable despacho que luego remitiremos a Vs Ms como tambien sobe la neuba quexa que, por su ultima, nos dan de quererles obligar el governador a hazer guarda en sabat y dias festivos. Y visto la favorable rezolusion que les Sres Bewinthebbert tomaron en el año 1730 hazemos quenta que pondran orden en que Vs Ms puedan exercitar el libre exercisio de nuestras festividades sin la menor interupsion. En el inter remitimos a Vs Ms copia de dicha rezolusion para su govierno. quando le

---

44   GSA, PA 334 91, 250.

enbiaremos a Vmds como esperamos la lisençia destes ssres para la fabrica de la sinagoga lo haremos del *Sepher Thora* que nos piden siendo, quanto por aora se nos ofrese, rogamos a D[io]s les guarde y prospere por muchos años como les dezeamos.

Mui afectos de a Vs Ms

Los Parnassim y gabay K[ahal] K[ados] de T[almud] T[ora]

Mosseh Israel Susso

Moses Alvares Bueno

St Eustatius

Messrs *Jehidim* of the holy community on the island of St Eustatius

Amsterdam, 17 Jan. 1757

Some time ago we received correspondence from Your Graces, dated 20 August, and again, on 5 October of last year, with the news that in that colony there is a number sufficient to form a congregation, for which purpose it was your desire to build a house of prayer devoted to the worship of the divine. We can only applaud and promote such a laudable effort as we already did at the request of Your Graces to those Messrs Bewinthebbert[45] from the West [India] Company. However, these persons have delayed their response to us through the month of March in which all the chambers should meet. We do not doubt that we shall reach a favourable resolution, which we shall later send Your Graces, as well as with regards to the new complaint, which has been conveyed to us in their latest correspondence, by which the governor wants to obligate you to do guard duty on the sabbath and feast days. And given the favourable decision handed down by Messrs Bewinthebbert in 1730, we assume they will see to it that Your Graces can engage in the free observance of our festivities without the least interruption. In the meantime, we are sending Your Graces a copy of the aforementioned decision for your use. When, as we expect, we send Your Graces the licences for the construction of the synagogue we will also ship the Torah scroll you are requesting. That is all we have on our agenda for the moment. We implore God to watch over you and cause you to prosper for many years. Such is our desire for you.

Our warm wishes go out to Your Graces

The *parnasim* and the *gabbai*, Holy Community of Talmud Torah

Mosseh Israel Susso

Moses Alvares Buenos

---

[45] The directors of the WIC.

CHAPTER FIVE

'A FLOCK OF WOLVES INSTEAD OF SHEEP'

The Dutch West India Company, Conflict Resolution, and the
Jewish Community of Curaçao in the Eighteenth Century

JESSICA ROITMAN

'D O WHAT A FREE, TOLERANT RELIGION DEMANDS' enjoined Isaac Faesch,
governor of the island of Curaçao, to his Jewish colonists in 1748.[1] His pleas came
in the midst of a situation of protracted strife amongst the Sephardi community of
Curaçao.[2] The Sephardim had split into two factions and were fighting in the streets,
obstructing burials, and refusing to circumcise newborn baby boys whose fathers
belonged to the other faction. The *parnasim* were also issuing proclamations of excommunication with abandon, causing a flood of appeals from those excommunicated to
come pouring into Governor Faesch's office. The only comfort for Faesch in this sorry
situation was that his was not the only Dutch West India Company colony beset by
such troubles. In Suriname, the *parnasim* had excommunicated Isaac Carilho after he
joined the opposition to the governor of the colony. Carilho appealed to the States
General of Holland and won his case, embarrassing Governor Mauricius and the
parnasim, as well as causing some confusion about how much authority the *parnasim*
had in WIC-controlled colonies.[3]

These cases illustrate an important and previously overlooked issue: how the WIC
administration adjudicated the all too frequent conflicts that arose within the Jewish
communities it administered in the Dutch West Indies. In this chapter I will focus on
the highly contentious and chaotic situation in the Sephardi community on the island
of Curaçao in the mid-eighteenth century. I will argue that the WIC-appointed governor, as the first point of contact with a (supposedly) impartial civil authority, was

---

[1] Isaac S. Emmanuel and Suzanne A. Emmanuel, *History of the Jews of the Netherlands Antilles*, 2 vols.
(Cincinnati, 1970), i. 194.

[2] Almost all Jews in Curaçao in the eighteenth century were Sephardim. In fact, until the 1920s there were
never enough Ashkenazim to form a *minyan* (see ibid. i. 496).

[3] *Historical Essay on the Colony of Surinam, 1788*, trans. Simon Cohen, ed. Jacob Rader Marcus and Stanley F.
Chyet (Cincinnati, 1974), 75, 206. The case is also discussed in Robert Cohen, *Jews in Another Environment:
Surinam in the Second Half of the Eighteenth Century* (Leiden, 1991), 129–31. The States General acted as a sort of
parliament and governing body for the United Provinces in the eighteenth century.

thrust into an adjudicatory role which he had neither the experience nor the authority to fulfil effectively. The governor of Curaçao was hampered in his ability to control the island's Jewish community by a lack of clear directives from the WIC itself, including on how much power the *parnasim* had on the island, as well as by the political power held by various factions amongst the Jewish congregants in the Dutch Republic.

The case I explore in this chapter demonstrates how several judicial systems and processes for the adjudication of conflicts ran parallel to one another. The Sephardim had their own systems of internal control; however, the situation in mid-eighteenth-century Curaçao was complicated by the fact that the congregation on the island was ultimately under the jurisdiction of the Amsterdam Sephardi community. Likewise, the Jews in Curaçao also answered to the island's civil judicial system, which was responsible to both the WIC's ruling council—the Heren X—and, ultimately, to the States General.

The long-recognized right within the Dutch Republic, and by extension in the WIC, of religious groups to self-government, especially in religious matters, which was the premise upon which Governor Faesch was working in Curaçao, might have been effective in the Dutch Republic. However, the multi-layered, overlapping judicial systems in the colony, combined with very real issues of wealth and class within the Sephardi community—issues which fanned the flames of fractiousness—were a recipe for disaster by the mid-eighteenth century. Thus the general expediency of having groups adjudicate their own conflicts led in many cases to a huge amount of confusion and inefficiency in their resolution—confusion and inefficiency that was ultimately detrimental to the peace and prosperity of the island.

Background of Jewish Settlement in Curaçao

The founder of the WIC, William Usselinx, was a fervent Christian who saw it as the company's duty to bring Calvinism to America. He was also known as an antisemite.[4] Though many of the company's directors may have shared Usselinx's ideas regarding Jews, they were pragmatically inclined to allow Jewish settlement in their territories. Thus, even though the Dutch Reformed Church was the only denomination officially recognized in the colonies, in a typically Dutch fashion, the Jews and Jewish worship were 'tolerated', and the Jews were given the right to exercise their religion. This is not to say that the WIC as an entity was in any way particularly positively inclined towards Jews. A letter written by the Amsterdam chamber of the WIC in 1652 stated that the Jews are 'sly and traitorous and we should not place too much trust in them'.[5]

---

    [4] Mordechai Arbell, *The Jewish Nation of the Caribbean: The Spanish-Portuguese Jewish Settlements in the Caribbean and the Guianas* (Jerusalem, 2002), 143.
    [5] Quoted in G. Herbert Cone, 'The Jews in Curaçao According to Documents from the Archives of the State of New York', *Publications of the American Jewish Historical Society*, 10 (1902), 147.

Despite this lack of trust, there were plans for (Sephardi) Jewish settlement on Curaçao from a quite early stage of its existence as a WIC possession. This was, in part, because Curaçao was somewhat different from other Caribbean colonies. The semi-arid climate meant that Curaçao developed an economy with far fewer plantations than other Caribbean islands, and those there were not profitable. In fact, plantations on Curaçao were generally maintained to provide status rather than income.[6] The economy was based on trade and trans-shipment. For instance, most slaves brought to Curaçao were intended to be sold on other islands in the Caribbean or on the South American mainland. Thus, there was a niche for Jewish merchants, most of whom traded with the nearby English and French colonies, but particularly with the Venezuelan and Colombian coasts.[7]

That said, the original plan of the WIC was to have Jews as planters on Curaçao. In 1651 João de Yllan, at that time living in the Dutch Republic, was given a permit to settle with other Jews on the island. In 1652 Joseph Nunes de Fonseca was also given a permit for settlement.[8] In the charters granted to both men, they were promised the 'same freedoms as were given to the [Jewish] settlers in New Netherland', meaning the freedom to practise their religion.[9] Not much came of these early charters for settlement, though, and the first group of any consequence, composed of twelve families, arrived on Curaçao in 1659. The 1659 charter, arranged by Isaac da Costa, has been lost.[10] On the basis of other evidence, however, we can deduce that it contained the official recognition and support of the Jewish Curaçaoan community as an entity, permission to purchase slaves and build houses, and religious freedom. The WIC had entered into a contract with these Jews to provide land which they could settle and cultivate. However, agriculture never became a major enterprise for the Jews. The few who had been engaged in agriculture turned to trade by the early eighteenth century, in part because from 1711 to 1722 the island went through a disastrous drought.

By 1746, the time the conflict I discuss below occurred, the organized Sephardi population on Curaçao had probably reached its demographic peak, numbering around 2,000 people.[11] Of these, only a very few could be said to belong to the middle class.[12] The Jewish population was divided between the wealthy, mostly large-scale

[6] A. F. Paula, *From Objective to Subjective Social Barriers: A Historico-Philosophical Analysis of Certain Negative Attitudes Among the Negroid Population of Curacao* (Curaçao, 1972).

[7] Wim W. Klooster, 'The Jews in Suriname and Curaçao', in Paolo Bernardini and Norman Fiering (eds.), *The Jews and the Expansion of Europe to the West, 1450–1800* (New York, 2001), 354–9.

[8] Also known as David Cohen Nassy.

[9] Jacob Adriaan Schiltkamp, *Bestuur en rechtspraak in de Nederlandse Antillen ten tijde van de West-Indische Compagnie* (Willemstad, Curaçao, 1973), 36. There were some restrictions. For instance, they were not allowed to work on Sundays in deference to the Christian sabbath.

[10] Yosef Hayim Yerushalmi, 'Between Amsterdam and New Amsterdam: The Place of Curaçao and the Caribbean in Early Modern Jewish History', *American Jewish History*, 72/2 (1982), 172–92.

[11] Frances Karner, *The Sephardics of Curacao: A Study of Socio-Cultural Patterns in Flux* (Assen, 1969), 29.

[12] In 1659 the Amsterdam Sephardi community began assisting the migration of poorer Sephardim to

merchants and international traders, as well as brokers of all sorts, on one side; and the poor, largely small tradesmen, on the other.[13] On Curaçao, class differences were clearly and externally visible, to the point of separate neighbourhoods and syn-agogues.[14] Rents in the main city of Willemstad had become too high for the growing number of impoverished Jews, who moved to an area known as Otrabanda. Rents in Otrabanda were cheaper, so it became a haven for the few middle-income and the many poorer Jews. However, traditional Jewish limits on the distance one can walk on the sabbath, plus the fact that a rowing boat was needed to get to the main synagogue, another clear violation of traditional Jewish practice on the sabbath, meant that a synagogue had to be set up there.

The Beginnings of Conflict and Jewish Governance on Curaçao

The original by-laws (*ascamot*) of the Sephardi congregation known as Mikvé Israel (Hope of Israel), drawn up in 1688, did not seem to allow for another synagogue on the island. In 1732, though, the *parnasim* relented and permitted the establishment of a synagogue called Neve Shalom (House of Peace: ironic, in the light of later events) in Otrabanda, for the mostly low-income residents, under the jurisdiction of the main congregation of Mikvé Israel. However, it seems that this synagogue may have been in a private home, and they were refused a Torah scroll, since possession of a Torah scroll would imply the establishment of a second synagogue, which would conflict with the *ascamot*. By 1746 the Jewish families in Otrabanda had increased their membership to about thirty-five and were forming an increasingly visible presence in the Jewish community.

Because of a rather confusing conflict between members of this synagogue, which included a fight, an arrest, and an excommunication, Neve Shalom was closed, though it is not clear if an actual synagogue building was shut down, or if worshippers were told not to gather together in a private house anymore. Whatever the case, seventeen families asked the *parnasim* of Mikvé Israel for permission to pray in a (different) private house. Moreover, because of the growth of the community in Otrabanda, a larger synagogue was required anyway. This caused a great deal of discord, which Governor

Curaçao, which added to the lower-income population on the island (see Robert Cohen, 'Passage to the New World: The Sephardi Poor of Eighteenth-Century Amsterdam', in Lea Dasberg and Jonathan N. Cohen (eds.), *Neve Ya'akov: Jubilee Volume Presented to Dr. Jaap Meyer* (Assen, 1982), 31–42; Yosef Kaplan, *An Alternative Path to Modernity: The Sephardi Diaspora in Western Europe* (Leiden, 2000), 85–6, 287; Evelyne Oliel-Grausz, 'A Study in Intercommunal Relations in the Sephardi Diaspora: London and Amsterdam in the Eighteenth Century', in Chay Brasz and Yosef Kaplan (eds.), *Dutch Jews as Perceived by Themselves and by Others: Proceedings of the Eighth International Symposium on the History of the Jews in the Netherlands* (Leiden, 2001), 51).

[13] Yosef Kaplan, 'The Curaçao and Amsterdam Jewish Communities in the 17th and 18th Centuries', *American Jewish History*, 72/2 (1982), 193–211, 206.

[14] Kaplan, 'The Curaçao and Amsterdam Jewish Communities in the 17th and 18th Centuries', 199.

Faesch was ill equipped to deal with. Though the conflict sounds relatively minor from the point of view of the WIC, the debate was bitter enough for Faesch to mention it in his report to the Heren X in 1746.[15] In this same letter, he asked for a copy of the rights and privileges given to the Jews in Curaçao because he was unsure of his authority in the matter.

As far as Faesch and the leaders of Mikvé Israel congregation were concerned, the *parnasim* were the sole authoritative body for the Jewish community in Curaçao. They were responsible for collecting the community tax levied by the civil authorities, and empowered to supervise the proper operation of congregation and ritual functions, and to resolve disputes between members, including public quarrelling. The *parnasim* ruled, for example, on gambling, dues, ritual duties, dietary compliance, and decorum in the synagogue. Violators were subject to fines and temporary or permanent excommunication.[16]

In this respect, Curaçao's Sephardi congregation was no different from those throughout Europe and the Near East. As historian Eli Faber notes, they all regulated dress, morals, reading matter, attendance at plays and operas, and sexual conduct. Sanctions took the form of fines, refusal of admission to the synagogue during services, exclusion of the children of offenders from the community school, denial of interment in the community cemetery, and confession before the entire congregation, which used public shame and humiliation to discipline offenders and to deter others.[17] The ultimate sanction, however, was the complete excommunication of the miscreant, requiring that all members of the community avoid contact of any kind whatsoever with the transgressor.

As historian Miriam Bodian has pointed out, the basic principle behind the Sephardi community's organization, both in Amsterdam and in places like Curaçao, was the concentration of authority in the hands of a few.[18] Bodian goes on to observe how the Mahamad dominated every aspect of community life—so much so that the very first article of the 1639 *ascamot* states that 'the Mahamad shall have authority over everything'.[19] The Mahamad was a communal body in which 'insiders' shared power among themselves, and each outgoing member helped to choose the new member coming in.[20] The regulations of the congregations in Venice, Amsterdam, and Curaçao bestowed supreme power on them in all matters.[21] In Curaçao, though, the Mahamad's power exceeded even that of other Sephardi congregations because they could petition

[15] National Archives of the Netherlands (NL-HaNA), Tweede Westindische Compagnie (Second Dutch West India Company, TWC) 1.05.01.316.

[16] To rejoin the congregation after excommunication, one had to confess publicly in the synagogue, without shoes, from a low bench, in a contrite voice, and often also to resolve the original issue in a satisfactory fashion, which might include a fine.

[17] Eli Faber, *A Time for Planting: The First Migration, 1654–1820* (Baltimore, 1992), 67.

[18] Miriam Bodian, *Hebrews of the Portuguese Nation: Conversos and Community in Early Modern Amsterdam* (Bloomington, 1997), 111.   [19] Ibid.   [20] Ibid.   [21] Faber, *A Time for Planting*, 57.

the governor to banish those who lived immorally.[22] In fact, the *parnasim* had used this prerogative and requested that the civil government banish a few people they deemed incorrigible. For example, in 1674 a Jewish woman who was suspected of being a prostitute was banished, as was David Aboab in 1746, as I will discuss shortly.[23]

Mikvé Israel congregation, then, was essentially a partially self-governing enclave within Curaçao, and it maintained a semi-separate judicial system.[24] Yet it was the very power held by the leaders of Jewish congregations, meant to keep intra-communal conflicts in check, which, ironically, was the source of a large amount of internecine quarrelling in the WIC's overseas territories, particularly Curaçao—quarrelling from which even the mother community of Amsterdam was not exempt. Therefore, disputes about decisions of the *parnasim* might be, and often were, appealed 'up the ladder' through either religious or civil institutions. At times, appeals went through both Jewish and civil institutions at the same time until finally arriving in the chambers of either the WIC or the Dutch government—or both. Different judgements at differing levels on the two institutional 'ladders' could make resolving the conflict quite complex.

We can see this complexity in the case of David Aboab. In 1746 Aboab, who probably grew up in Venice, moved from Jamaica to Curaçao. The conflict that his short stay on the island provoked is well documented.[25] Essentially, he clashed with rabbis Raphael Jesurun, who served on the island from 1717 to 1748, and Samuel Mendes de Sola, formerly a rabbi in the Amsterdam synagogue, who arrived as Jesurun's assistant in 1744, and pronounced a religious ruling contrary to theirs. As a result, he was excommunicated. When he refused to express the public contrition necessary to bring the excommunication to an end, the *parnasim* of Mikvé Israel appealed to Faesch to

---

[22] Emmanuel and Emmanuel, *History of the Jews of the Netherlands Antilles*, ii. 544–5. Mikvé Israel congregation in Curaçao was particularly independent. It chose to ignore the ordinances of its mother community in Amsterdam and refused to ban members who went to the 'countries of idolatry', those where Judaism could not be practised openly, though the term usually referred to Iberia and her overseas territories. For information on Sephardi proscriptions on travel, see Yosef Kaplan, 'The Travels of Portuguese Jews from Amsterdam to the "Lands of Idolatry" (1644–1724)', in id. (ed.), *Jews and Conversos: Studies in Society and the Inquisition* (Jerusalem, 1985), 294–324; id., 'The Struggle against Travelers to Spain and Portugal in the Western Sephardi Diaspora', *Zion*, 64 (1999), 65–100.

[23] Emmanuel and Emmanuel, *History of the Jews of the Netherlands Antilles*, i. 188.

[24] Alan F. Benjamin, *Jews of the Dutch Caribbean: Exploring Ethnic Identity on Curaçao* (London, 2002), 112. For example, in the eighteenth century, the Dutch government passed a law that Dutch community property arrangements would be in effect for all marriages. The Sephardim, however, objected and in 1740 received an exception for Jewish marriages in Curaçao and Suriname (Emmanuel and Emmanuel, *History of the Jews of the Netherlands Antilles*, i. 149). The objections were based on the fact that the Jewish wedding ritual involves the signing of a *ketubah*, a marriage contract, prior to the wedding ceremony. In case of a divorce, the *ketubah* includes provisions for distributing the property brought into the marriage.

[25] See Benjamin, *Jews of the Dutch Caribbean*, 112; Emmanuel and Emmanuel, *History of the Jews of the Netherlands Antilles*, i. 187–9.

have him banished. Faesch, bowing to the authority of the *parnasim*, as he felt it was his duty to do, based on his understanding of Jewish self-government on the island, agreed, despite the fact that Aboab had violated no civil laws. Nevertheless, Faesch felt that Aboab's exile was a religious matter and that he had been stirring up partisanship in the Jewish community. In his letter to the WIC, Faesch stated that Aboab's exile was based solely on the request of the *parnasim*.[26]

This was not the only conflict to be roiling the Jewish community in Curaçao at the time. It had been rocked by a bitter conflict over an inheritance between the Pereira and Leão families, which had taken ten years to resolve.[27] The case set something of a precedent for conflict resolution within the Sephardi community in mid-eighteenth-century Curaçao. The *parnasim* of Mikvé Israel could not resolve it satisfactorily and had to appeal to the Amsterdam *parnasim*, who (as would become typical for them) urged that the two families settle their differences and not go to the civil courts. In the end, this conciliatory approach did not work, and the Pereira family took the case to the civil authorities. The civil authorities ruled in their favour in 1750. The Leão family appealed to the States General, as was to ultimately become the norm for the litigious members of Curaçao's Sephardi community.[28] Thus we begin to see what could be termed 'judicial shopping', with litigants appealing to multiple adjudicatory entities in search of their favoured outcome. Moreover, we begin to see the confusion engendered by the overlapping jurisdictions of the WIC on Curaçao, the Heren X in the Dutch Republic, the Amsterdam *parnasim*, and the *parnasim* in Curaçao.

Around this time, we also see the beginning of a precedent for a rather heavy-handed use of excommunication in Curaçao. A Sephardi merchant, Isaac Pardo, was excommunicated by Rabbi de Sola over a somewhat minor commercial matter. Pardo then complained to the WIC fiscal controller, Jan van Schagen, claiming his excommunication was invalid. Van Schagen intervened with the *parnasim* on his behalf by writing a sharply worded letter.[29] While Aboab had been excommunicated ostensibly

---

[26] NL-HaNA, TWC 1.05.01.02/316. Aboab left for Amsterdam with a manuscript about the events in Curaçao which he intended to publish. In Amsterdam Aboab blamed Rabbi de Sola for his problems. He was denounced by the Amsterdam community, at the request of the Curaçaoan *parnasim*, who were afraid that Aboab would appeal against his exile to the States General and try to return to Curaçao. The Amsterdam *parnasim* forced Aboab to sign a statement saying that his charges against de Sola were untrue and that he would not publish anything without the consent of the *parnasim*. Moreover, they petitioned the States General to deny any request for a permit to return to Curaçao that Aboab might make, and their request was granted. Aboab proclaimed 'What could a lamb do amidst wolves?' In 1746 the governor stepped in, despite being unsure of what his authority over the matter was, and ordered a general amnesty, including the absolution of all those who had been excommunicated during the Aboab conflict (see Emmanuel and Emmanuel, *History of the Jews of the Netherlands Antilles*, i. 188).

[27] See Emmanuel and Emmanuel, *History of the Jews of the Netherlands Antilles*, i. 181–3.

[28] NL-HaNA, Oude Archief Curacao (Old Archive of Curaçao, OAC) 1.05.12.01.825.

[29] Emmanuel and Emmanuel, *History of the Jews of the Netherlands Antilles*, i. 183.

for religious matters, Pardo was not. His excommunication seemed to have been an attempt by de Sola to keep an increasingly fractious congregation in line. De Sola declared angrily that his congregation was 'a flock of wolves instead of sheep'.[30]

Perhaps the congregation had become more bellicose because this was a time of general trouble in Curaçao. There had been a rash of murders along with a severe drought from 1746 to 1749.[31] In addition, in 1747 France had invaded Holland, which meant that many Curaçaoans suffered financial losses. In 1750 a slave uprising on the island complicated matters further. Moreover, there was a clear precedent for resorting to civil authorities and a definite tendency for both the civil and the communal authorities to be rather ineffectual. The civil authorities deferred to the Jewish community, especially the Amsterdam *parnasim*, while the Sephardi congregation had a pattern of delegating decision-making to the litigants themselves. These competing authorities allowed the Leão–Pereira inheritance case to drag on, entailing multiple appeals to various adjudicatory bodies. The Sephardi communal authorities were deeply concerned with keeping conflicts out of the civil courts, but were often unable to accomplish this. Meanwhile, the WIC officials, particularly Faesch, was stymied by the legacy of what historian C. R. Boxer has called 'a policy of masterly inactivity' in the mediation of competing ethnic and religious interests in WIC-controlled territories.[32] That policy seemed to have become the unsanctioned model for governors of WIC territories.

Structure of WIC Governance on Curaçao

The WIC, unlike the better-known Dutch East India Company, had as one of its major goals the promotion of privateering against the Spanish. In exchange for the rights to all seized goods, privateers were awarded permits to attack enemies of the Dutch Republic. However, after years of mismanagement, the WIC folded in 1674, and a new and reorganized WIC emerged that eschewed privateering and, instead, focused on the African slave trade and the exploitation of its remaining possessions, including Curaçao. The second WIC was dependent upon the States General and was a semi-public entity. Curaçao was a possession of the WIC under the authority of the Dutch Republic and was represented by the States General.[33] The company was organized, as the first WIC had been, in five 'chambers' representing the interests of the various cities and regions in the Dutch Republic, each of which received a certain share of the profits.[34] Each 'chamber' had a certain number of directors who, in turn, answered to

---

[30] Emmanuel and Emmanuel, *History of the Jews of the Netherlands Antilles*, i. 184.

[31] NL-HaNA, TWC 1.05.01.02.597/584.

[32] C. R. Boxer, *The Dutch in Brazil, 1624–1654* (Oxford, 1957), 122.   [33] Schiltkamp, *Bestuur en rechtspraak*, 8.

[34] These chambers were Amsterdam, Zeeland, Maze, Noorderkwarter, and Stad en Lande (see Henk den Heijer, *De geschiedenis van de WIC* (Zutphen, 2002), 111, 114).

the overall governing board, comprised of nine WIC directors and one member of the States General.[35]

Unfortunately, as historian Cornelis Goslinga observed, 'the Company had a nearly impossible combination of tasks to fulfil. As a commercial enterprise it had to make profits, and as a governing institution it had to master the techniques of good government. . . . As a result, it never succeeded in both fields: bad management eroded the profits, and it never mastered the techniques of good government.'[36] Bad management was clearly a problem in Curaçao by the mid-eighteenth century. The colonial government was run by the WIC, and the governor of Curaçao was selected and appointed by the Heren X.[37] Despite being appointed by the Heren X, the governor's authority ultimately stemmed from the States General, and he ruled in the name of both the WIC and the States General.[38] Thus, the settlers in Curaçao had no direct influence over who was appointed governor of their island.[39]

This arrangement was particularly galling to the colonists, because the office of governor was so important, and the governor was the most influential person in the colony.[40] The colonial government's executive, legislative, and judicial powers were vested in him. His power was almost absolute, though dependent on orders from the Heren X, who were, in turn, dependent for certain decisions on the States General.[41] The operative word, though, was 'almost', because the governor shared the legislative and judicial power, to some degree, with the ruling council of the island. The council, which also acted as a court of justice, served mainly in an advisory capacity, although the governor needed its co-operation to hire, fire, or suspend any employee in the company's higher ranks. The Heren X functioned as a court of appeal in these matters. The governor was chairman of the council, voted with the other members, and, in case of a tied vote, could cast a double vote. He chaired the sessions in which the council acted as a court of civil or criminal justice.[42]

During the governorship of Isaac Faesch, the number of council members was increased from nine to ten, in order to have another citizen on the council.[43] Until then,

---

[35] The directors were known in Dutch as *bewindhebbers*, and the governing board was called the Heren X, or the Ten Gentlemen. The first Dutch West India Company, active from 1621 until 1674 was governed by the Heren XIX. With the establishment of the second Dutch West India Company, the governing board was whittled down to ten.

[36] Cornelis Christiaan Goslinga, *The Dutch in the Caribbean and in the Guianas 1680–1791* (Assen, 1985), 79.

[37] Ibid.   [38] Schiltkamp, *Bestuur en rechtspraak*, 11.   [39] Ibid. 59 n. 5.

[40] The position of governor on the island of Curaçao was an attractive one due to the perks he would receive. For instance, he received 1,200 florins for each slave that was sold and 4 per cent of the value of the food that was sold on the island (see Henk den Heijer, *De geschiedenis van de WIC*, 149).

[41] Goslinga, *The Dutch in the Caribbean and in the Guianas*, 80.   [42] Ibid. 81.

[43] Schiltkamp, *Bestuur en rechtspraak*, 43. It was lowered to nine again in 1764. For the three non-WIC employees, being a council member was often a burden. As the only real organ of government on the island, the members were often overwhelmed by all the business they had to deal with. This meant that the non-WIC council members often had to put their own business affairs aside.

six of the nine council members were WIC employees. Unfortunately, the make-up of the council of Curaçao gave no guarantee that good governance would follow. The council had to make decisions about issues with which its members were unfamiliar; there were far too many WIC employees on the council, even with the addition of an extra citizen, and the WIC's interests were promoted, even if they were at odds with those of the settlers; and the members' lack of judicial knowledge caused problems, especially in the latter part of the eighteenth century.[44] The council could only decide on matters, including judicial issues, which the governor brought to it.[45] Essentially, the organization of the colonies was modelled on the Dutch Republic, with as much as possible of the judicial and other systems of governance being exported to the overseas territories.[46] Unlike in the Dutch Republic, however, where the States General had to take into consideration the various rights and privileges of cities and provinces, it was possible to have a uniform set of rules and regulations with much more centralized government.[47] Despite this, the WIC still relied on a system of unofficial checks and balances to deal with the various issues raised by the diverse ethnic and religious population of the colonies. For instance, the Sephardi Jewish community in Amsterdam exerted a not inconsiderable influence on the directors of the WIC thereby serving as a counterweight to the power of the colonial governors.[48]

The influence of the Sephardi community in Amsterdam on Jewish affairs in Curaçao is perhaps best demonstrated in their famous intervention with the directors of the WIC in Amsterdam in 1655 on behalf of their fellow Sephardim against the antisemitic measures taken in the colony of New Netherland by Governor Peter Stuyvesant. Less well known was their intervention in a case involving Balthazar Beck, the brother of Curaçao's governor Matthias Beck. In 1668 Balthazar Beck was a slave commissioner, captain of the civil guard, member of the ruling council, and a judge on Curaçao. He complained about the Jews constantly, imprisoned them with little justification, and allowed the sailors on one of his Spanish slave ships to string up an effigy of Judas that happened to strongly resemble Rabbi Pardo. Little happened to restrain him until one of the company's Jewish shareholders in Amsterdam, Jeronimo Nunes da Costa (Moses Curiel) complained forcefully to the company. Beck was dismissed.[49] In 1701 Governor

[44] Schiltkamp, *Bestuur en rechtspraak*, 46. There were specific days on which the council would decide on legal matters. Interestingly, Jews and Christians were segregated, with matters concerning Jews being decided on Thursdays from 9 to 11 a.m. Matters concerning both Jewish and Christian mortgages were decided together (Schiltkamp, *Bestuur en rechtspraak*, 60–1).   [45] Ibid. 24.

[46] In the seventeenth century, both orphans and inheritance chambers were set up on Curaçao to deal with children who lost one or both parents, as well as to deal with estates and inheritance issues. This was modelled on the same entities in the Dutch Republic. As an aside, Jewish orphans also fell under the authority of the general orphans chamber until 1810, when they set up their own (see ibid. 8).   [47] Ibid. 39.

[48] In return, the Mahamad forbade the Jewish merchants on Curaçao from participating in actions against the government or from criticizing it. In instances of complaints, the Mahamad turned either directly to the head office of the WIC or to the States General, or appealed through the Jewish community in Amsterdam (see Arbell, *Jewish Nation of the Caribbean*, 145).   [49] Ibid. 143.

Nicolaas van Beek ordered Jews to send their slaves to work on Saturdays. When the conflict escalated, the Jews on Curaçao appealed to the Heren X and the Amsterdam *parnasim*. Two of these *parnasim*, Baron de Belmonte and Alexander Nunes da Costa, were shareholders of the WIC. The Heren X, therefore, ordered van Beek to back off, 'as otherwise the trade and population of the aforementioned island would suffer considerable damage'.[50]

The WIC, despite its employees and directors' personal expressions of anti-semitism, wanted to stem the flow of Jews to the British colony of Barbados, where they could compete against the Dutch in the growing commerce with the Spanish colonies and in the sugar trade.[51] Therefore, the governors were always under pressure from the Heren X to treat the Jews well, as they were vital to Curaçao's economy.[52] Though the WIC administration would almost always act to protect its Sephardi settlers from any perceived 'outside' threat, including, as we have just seen, from its own employees, at least in Curaçao and Suriname, they were often stymied in dealing with internal conflicts. These conflicts were expected to be resolved internally, if at all possible.

The Conflict

By 1746 there were several unresolved conflicts simmering within the Sephardi community on Curaçao. There was the long-running Leão–Pereira inheritance case, David Aboab had just been exiled from the island, and Isaac Pardo was excommunicated, causing much consternation among the community. Moreover, the debate about how to deal with the Neve Shalom Synagogue was unresolved, and there were very real class divisions. At the same time the economic situation was worsening as a result of drought and war. In this context of factionalism and strife, a new conflict broke out, though it could, rather, be seen as an extension of the previous ones, involving the controversial and divisive Rabbi de Sola, he who had found himself among wolves instead of sheep, and Moses Penso, who had already locked horns with de Sola over the financing of a new synagogue. Penso had also been a supporter of David Aboab. By examining this dispute, we can see the ways in which the WIC and the Sephardi community struggled to deal with intra-communal conflict that escaped the bounds of the communal systems of justice set up precisely to keep such disputes in check.

For reasons that are not entirely clear, Rabbi de Sola and the *parnasim* grew increasingly at odds with Moses Penso and others who supported him. In the beginning Penso was cited for violating communal laws by removing a letter written by de Sola, probably concerning the exile of Aboab, from the synagogue's files. Penso was brought before the *parnasim*, but refused to submit to their judgement because he viewed them as biased. Therefore, he turned to the civil authorities and went to the government

[50] NL-HaNA, TWC 1.05.01.02/357, 15.   [51] Arbell, *The Jewish Nation of the Caribbean*, 243.
[52] Goslinga, *The Dutch in the Caribbean and in the Guianas*, 80.

secretary, requesting that de Sola confront him before the governor and the island council. The second in command to the governor on the island, the quartermaster councilman Jan Gerard Pax, brought the two men in front of Governor Faesch and brokered a peace between them: it lasted ten weeks.

The conflict soon erupted again. The 'opposition' to Rabbi de Sola and the Curaçaoan *parnasim* first appealed to the *parnasim* of the mother community in Amsterdam for redress of their grievances. But the Amsterdam *parnasim* counselled their brethren in Curaçao to settle their differences and stop the case from reaching the civil courts. However, such vague directives did nothing to resolve the issues. Very soon thereafter Penso and two other members of the community were excommunicated. Penso sought to prove that the *parnasim* had no right to excommunicate, based on a case from 1712 in Curaçao when the governor ordered that the excommunication of David Senor be rescinded. All three complained to the governor and the island's council against the misuse of the ban, but Faesch ultimately ordered them to obey the *parnasim*. In light of this precedent, Penso looked to the States General.[53] The *parnasim* wanted to avoid this intrusion of civil authority into community affairs, so they backed down and absolved all three men. Nevertheless, it seems that Penso felt morally obliged to continue with the appeal in order to annul all excommunications and to ensure that there were no further excommunications for secular matters.

Meanwhile, the controversy grew and a spate of excommunications followed. Many of those excommunicated by Rabbi de Sola and the *parnasim* appealed to Faesch, who was in a bind as he was caught between civil precedent and the autonomy of the Jewish community.[54] He soon became swamped with appeals against excommuni-

---

[53] NL-HaNA, OAC 1.05.12.01.863/139; 1.05.12.01.1528; 1.05.12.01.818/47.

[54] There was a clear precedent in Amsterdam for the incursion of civil authority into the Sephardi practice of excommunication. In the seventeenth century, the Amsterdam city authorities ratified the Sephardi community ordinances and acknowledged its right to exercise the instrument of excommunication against deviants and rebels. This right was explicitly acknowledged on various occasions. Nonetheless, the city magistrates took action if members of the Sephardi community complained that they had been unjustly excommunicated (see Stadsarchief Amsterdam (Amsterdam Municipal Archives, SSA), Portugees-Israëlietische Gemeente te Amsterdam (Portuguese Jewish Congregation of Amsterdam, PIGA) 334, 88; SSA, PIGA 334, 20/67; SSA, Notarieel Archief (NA) 964/443). See also the fascinating case of heiress Rebecca Naar in Lydia Hagoort, 'Persons of a Restless Disposition: Conflicts between the Jewish Merchants Lopo Ramires and Manuel Dias Henriques and the *Parnassim* of the Portuguese Nation about the Inheritance of Rebecca Naar', *Studia Rosenthaliana*, 32/2 (1998), 155–72. Until 1683 the Amsterdam magistrate took no steps that might limit the right of the Jewish community to use excommunication, but then, after a complicated situation involving the excommunication of a congregant who bought poultry from an Ashkenazi butcher, the city authorities stated that the leaders of the Sephardi community could not excommunicate its members without the prior agreement and authorization of the city authorities. This was, according to Yosef Kaplan, the result of hidden pressure exerted by the city authorities, who preferred the more moderate measure of nullifying a member's rights rather than outright excommunication—probably because that was more in line with their Calvinist understanding of religious discipline. This nullification did not have any religious or sacral significance, nor did it prevent anyone who had been expelled from maintaining social and economic contacts with members of his community (see Kaplan, *An Alternative Path to Modernity*, 137).

cations. In fact, excommunication was wielded so freely that he wrote to the Heren X in the Dutch Republic asking for more information about when the ban could be imposed, so that 'the Jews are not given more power than they already possess'.[55]

De Sola preached offensive sermons against Penso and a few of his supporters. So Penso and forty-five others petitioned the governor to either forbid de Sola from preaching against them or to allow them to open another synagogue. A supporter of Penso's, Mordechay Alvares Correa, was then threatened with excommunication.[56] At the same time, the *parnasim* lobbied Faesch not to grant the request for a new synagogue, submitting a petition with 235 signatures. The *parnasim*, covering their bases, also urged the *parnasim* in Amsterdam to submit the petition directly to the Heren X. Faesch also wrote a letter to the Heren X, in which he stated that he would not allow another synagogue until he heard otherwise from them.[57] Two principal stockholders in the WIC, Jacob de David de Pinto and Manuel Lopes Suasso, presented the petition and it was accepted. The WIC, bowing to the power of the Amsterdam community, ordered Faesch to deny any permit for a third synagogue and to endeavour to enforce Jewish obedience to the *parnasim*.[58]

The Amsterdam *parnasim* submitted a thirty-eight-page report on the conflict in January 1747, in which it was disclosed that some of the 'opposition' had been beaten up in the synagogue courtyard. The report gives unequivocal support for de Sola and the *parnasim* in Curaçao. Nevertheless, the Curaçaoan *parnasim* were advised to be sparing in the use of the ban.[59] Meanwhile, Penso's appeal to the States General had been effective, and they had ordered that his excommunication be overturned.[60]

The conflict nevertheless kept escalating. A fight broke out in the synagogue itself, and the *parnasim* now asked the government authorities in the Dutch Republic to empower them to have anyone they considered unacceptable jailed and/or banished from the island. This last request was too much even for the Amsterdam *parnasim*, who had so far been deeply invested in supporting their fellow oligarchs in Curaçao, and they wrote that they could not agree to 'such unlimited power'.[61] The governor

[55] NL-HaNA, OAC 1.05.12.01.863/423. This played on fears of Jewish self-government common among the increasingly centralized governments of early modern Europe, who viewed such power as an infringement of the sovereignty of the state. Objections to Jewish self-government were not unique to Curaçao. There were lengthy debates on the subject in early seventeenth-century Venice. In fact, the Venetians refused the Jewish community the right to excommunicate certain offenders, saying problems should be referred to the state's magistrates. In the early fifteenth century the issue came up in Sicily. In 1639 the Florentine government allowed the leaders of its Jewish community to deal with legal disputes between Jews, but required governmental approval of decisions ordering offenders to be exiled (see David Malkiel, 'The Tenuous Thread: A Venetian Lawyer's Apology for Jewish Self-Government in the Seventeenth Century', *AJS Review*, 12/2 (1987), 223–50. [56] NL-HaNA, OAC 1.05.12.01.867/79, 211.

[57] NL-HaNA, TWC 1.05.01.03/403. [58] Ibid. 1.05.01.04.475/45.

[59] SSA, PIGA 344, 1029. [60] NL-HaNA, Resolutions of the States General 1.01.03.

[61] Emmanuel and Emmanuel, *History of the Jews of the Netherlands Antilles*, i. 194.

then issued an ineffective proclamation outlawing all fighting. However, he made the mistake of threatening troublemakers with prosecution according to Jewish law.[62] Although Penso's excommunication had been overturned, many of his faction were still being punished by excommunication—which they felt to be deeply unfair—and Faesch's proclamation, therefore, had little influence on their behaviour. More excommunications of those who were against de Sola and the *parnasim* followed.

The plot thickened, however, because the fiscal controller, Jan van Schagen became involved in a dispute with a supporter of de Sola and the *parnasim*. Governor Faesch, meanwhile, suspected van Schagen of plotting against him to take over the governorship of the island. Faesch thought that van Schagen was going to go to the Dutch Republic, ostensibly to argue the case of Penso and his supporters, but also to undermine Faesch's standing with the Heren X. Thus, Faesch wrote that Penso and his group should be ordered to obey the *parnasim*.[63]

As Isaac Emmanuel and Suzanne Emmanuel point out, it is clear from the archival evidence that Faesch supported the *parnasim* and was far from an impartial point of contact with the civil authority.[64] Whether this support was due to his personal dislike of Moses Penso, his suspicion of van Schagen, who backed the opposition, or out of some personal belief in the assertion of traditional religious authority, is unknowable. The island council itself appears to have been divided, while the WIC directors seemed to be trying to balance the recommendations of the governor, which most often coincided with that of the wealthy Jewish shareholders representing the Amsterdam *parnasim*, and the demands of the opposition and van Schagen, some of whom were also wealthy and who also had recourse to the authority of the States General. Meanwhile, the States General was inclined to favour the opposition, if only to prevent a 'government within a government', and thereby to rein in the power of the *parnasim*.[65]

Yet, clearly, nothing was being resolved among the Jewish community in Curaçao. Fights began to break out at burials, because the *parnasim* had ordered that certain prayers for the dead not be said over the bodies of deceased opposition members or their families.[66] Fifty-seven people petitioned the governor and his council to keep de Sola from making inflammatory sermons and imposing excommunication, and for permission for them to conduct services in their own homes. This time, perhaps finally recognizing the futility of directing the petitioners to appeal to the *parnasim*, the governor forbade the opening of another synagogue and urged them to appeal to the civil courts.[67] However, the opposition had already appealed to the civil authority, including the States General, which had ruled in their favour, and this had still not reined de Sola in, so this directive was particularly ineffectual. In fairness to Faesch, though, he was ordered to pursue a do-nothing policy in deference to pressures

---

[62] NL-HaNA, OAC 1.05.12.01.180/132.
[63] NL-HaNA, TWC 1.05.01.02/596.
[64] Emmanuel and Emmanuel, *History of the Jews of the Netherlands Antilles*, i. 206–7.
[65] Ibid. i. 207.
[66] NL-HaNA, OAC 1.05.12.01.183/27.
[67] Ibid. 1.05.12.01.12.

brought to bear by the Amsterdam *parnasim*.[68] Because of this, the strife worsened. The authorities were even worried it would affect the well-being of the entire colony, because the Jews made up such a large percentage of the white population.

Over several days in May 1749 there were near riots in the streets between the two groups. The governor sent out a sergeant and twenty-four men to put a stop to the violence. He also issued yet another proclamation commanding the Jews to stop fighting with each other. Moreover, he acknowledged in a letter to the Heren X that the trouble came from the excommunications and sought their advice about resolving the problem.[69] The governor's letters make clear that he felt the rabbi and *parnasim* were misusing their authority, which had been restricted to issuing edicts of excommunication solely in religious matters. It seemed clear to him that these congregants had been excommunicated on the grounds of personal and economic issues, not religious ones. The confused Faesch entreated his superiors for clarification on the right of the *parnasim* to excommunicate. He wrote: 'I am not a Jew that I can understand their law.'[70] The Heren X could do little, however, as they had already ceded the authority to excommunicate to the *parnasim*, and to challenge that authority would not only violate the charters upon which Sephardi settlement on the island was founded, but also undermine the authority of other religious groups, including the state-sponsored Dutch Reformed (Calvinist) Church, to police their own members. Nevertheless, it is clear that the WIC officials felt a deep discomfort with the liberal use of excommunication—a discomfort that went far beyond a desire to check the power of a small group of settlers.

Within Sephardi communities, excommunication, also known as the *ḥerem*, or ban, was not necessarily a severe measure. In fact, it was sometimes used fairly regularly to enforce communal norms.[71] Thus, as Henri Méchoulan has argued, it is quite misleading to translate *ḥerem* as 'excommunication', because the implication of the word was one of complete expulsion, which was only rarely the case.[72] For instance, even relatively minor infractions, such as buying meat from an Ashkenazi butcher, could incur the *ḥerem*. Sometimes it meant only a day's ban. At other times the *ḥerem* was confined to barring a man from being called to the Torah during a limited period of time. From time to time Christian scholars and theologians criticized the use of the *ḥerem* by the *parnasim* in order to suppress critical opinions.[73] For Calvinist sensibilities

---

[68] Goslinga, *The Dutch in the Caribbean and in the Guianas*, 111.   [69] NL-HaNA, TWC 1.05.01.02.596.

[70] Ibid. 1.05.01.02.597/768; quoted in Emmanuel and Emmanuel, *History of the Jews of the Netherlands Antilles*, i. 201.   [71] Kaplan, *An Alternative Path to Modernity*, 108–39.

[72] Henri Méchoulan, 'Le Herem à Amsterdam et "l'excommunication" de Spinoza', *Cahiers Spinoza*, 3 (1979–80), 117–34.

[73] This was in contrast to church discipline—in France, the Netherlands, and Germany, at least—which had as its prime objective penitence, not punishment. The aim was to reconcile people to each other and to the community at large. Reformed churches all tended to follow a number of steps in their disciplinary routine. The final and most drastic step was permanent excommunication, which was very rare. Of nineteen

however, the concept of excommunication, as they understood it, was at odds with the role of religious discipline and unduly harsh.[74]

Despite his personal distaste for the use of the *herem* by the Jews, the governor had little ammunition in his arsenal. The WIC's organization was deeply rooted in Dutch urban culture, a culture in which groups arbitrated their own disputes, by and large, but turned to a series of adjudicating entities such as the orphan's and bankruptcy chambers, small claims courts, and as a near last resort to the municipal council for disputes. Faesch did not have the authority to deal with these problems. He could and did turn to the Heren X for help, but its authority over the congregation was also not entirely clear, particularly because the boundaries of what constituted a religious infraction in the early modern period, especially in a community which, as we have seen, exerted so much control over all aspects of congregants' lives, were not well defined. Moreover, they were checked by the economic and political power of the Amsterdam *parnasim*, which had steadfastly supported their fellow oligarchs in Curaçao. The governor's desperation increased.

Meanwhile, one bridegroom was refused permission to marry, because his future father-in-law was in the opposition camp. The gravediggers' society was ordered not to dig a grave for one Samuel Touro who had died suddenly. Indeed, the situation deteriorated so severely that there were fights in the cemetery, and the opposition started burying their own dead clandestinely, passing coffins over the cemetery walls.[75] The governor was forced to send soldiers to keep the peace at Jewish funerals on the island.[76] For instance, after the death of Mordechay Alvares Correa, one of the opposition leaders, the *parnasim* refused to make the cemetery keys available to the next of kin. Penso and Correa's son-in-law hired sailors to help them gain access to the cemetery. This shocked even those in the Jewish community who had been neutral, and the opposition grew. Once again, the opposition complained to the governor.[77] By this

---

cases of disciplinary action recorded in Utrecht in the 1620s no one was excommunicated. Likewise, over nearly 125 years (from 1578 to 1700), there were only thirty-three excommunications in Amsterdam, and the last, with one exception, occurred in 1642, probably because Calvinism had 'won out', and there was less competition among churches (see Judith Pollmann, 'Off the Record: Problems in the Quantification of Calvinist Church Discipline', *Sixteenth Century Journal*, 33/2 (2002), 423–38; Raymond A. Mentzer (ed.), *Sin and the Calvinists: Moral Control and the Consistory in the Reformed Tradition* (Kirksville, Miss., 1994)).

[74] There were some who viewed it positively. As early as 1615 there is an approving mention of the right of the Jewish community to excommunicate in Hugo Grotius's *Remonstrantie*: 'The masters of the Jews or those who are appointed to that end among them, will have the right to excommunicate and ostracize Jews whose way of life or opinions are evil.' But he also writes: 'Nonetheless, anyone who wishes to complain that he was excommunicated even though he was innocent should submit his complaint to the local authorities, who will investigate the matter and decide according to the laws of the Old Testament', which allows for the intrusion of civil authority into Sephardi communal discipline (see J. Meijer, *Hugo de Groot, Remonstrantie nopende de Ordre dije in de Landen van Hollandt ende Westvrieslandt dijent gestlt op de Joden* (Amsterdam, 1949), 42; quoted in Kaplan, *An Alternative Path to Modernity*, 133).   [75] NL-HaNA, TWC 1.05.01.02.596/1261.

[76] Ibid. 1.05.01.02.597/765a–68.   [77] NL-HaNA, OAC 1.05.12.01.821.

point, the Amsterdam *parnasim* were beginning to lose patience with their brethren in Curaçao and ordered that 'communal matters should not be allowed to end in litigation'.[78]

By 1750 the back and forth between Rabbi de Sola, the Curaçaoan Sephardim (both opposition and 'loyalists'), Faesch, and the *parnasim* in Amsterdam had become too much. As chief of police, Jan van Schagen felt he had to ensure that Curaçao remained peaceful. He had been planning to go to Amsterdam for some time to broker a peace agreement for the Jews on Curaçao. Governor Faesch, as we have seen, had opposed this trip because he suspected that van Schagen was trying to affect a coup and have him removed as governor. Be that as it may, after several delays, van Schagen finally went to Amsterdam. He was initially greeted with little enthusiasm by the Amsterdam *parnasim*, who had heard defamatory things about him from Faesch, as well as from the Curaçaoan *parnasim*. They therefore rejected his plan for peace on the island. He trumped their authority and went directly to the States General. The States General endorsed his plan and referred it back to the Amsterdam *parnasim*. Perhaps under some pressure, they agreed to sign it.

This plan limited the authority of the rabbi. He was no longer to be allowed to attend meetings of the *parnasim*, in the hope that the *parnasim* would act as an independent and neutral body. Moreover, the rabbi was only to be consulted in religious matters and was not to take on the role of judge. Most importantly, he was only allowed to use excommunication in 'exceptional' cases regarding exclusively religious issues. Even then, the excommunication had to be ordered by the *parnasim*.[79] Thus, there was an acknowledgement of the need to limit the power the rabbi could exercise over the congregation. There was also a clear recognition that the States General was the ultimate adjudicator, despite the rights and privileges given to the Jewish community and the long tradition in the Dutch Republic of religious self-government. Essentially, then, members of the *parnasim* as well as of the ruling council of the island of Curaçao had to break down the boundaries between ecclesiastical and civil court, moral admonishment and legal punishment, in ways that they had not been able to do before, due to the lack of clear guidance on the part of the WIC and an increasingly outdated notion of the religious and social unity of communal life.[80] This dissolution of religious and civil boundaries was symbolized by the fact that the peace plan was signed by the *stadhouder*, Prince William IV of Orange-Nassau, as representative of the entire Dutch Republic.

---

[78] Quoted in Emmanuel and Emmanuel, *History of the Jews of the Netherlands Antilles*, i. 198–9.

[79] Ibid. ii. 604.

[80] Mark Valeri, 'Religion, Discipline, and the Economy in Calvin's Geneva', *Sixteenth Century Journal*, 28/1 (1997), 129.

Conclusion

Rabbi Joshua de Cordoba preached a sermon on one of the three days of fast and prayer proclaimed by the Jews of Curaçao around the time of these events. The sermon paints a vivid picture of the social conditions prevailing among them. In his sermon he details a plague and a drought which devastated the island. In addition, he deplores the distinct lack of community solidarity. Commercial competition through price-cutting was the norm. Jewish ship-owners attacked ships owned by their co-religionists on the high seas and even near port. These same Jewish ship-owners refused to band together in the face of attacks by Spaniards on boats owned by other Jews.[81]

Nor were the Jews the only ones suffering: plague, drought, and the depredations of the Spaniards affected everyone on the island. There were also bitter conflicts within the Protestant and Catholic communities. These conflicts had begun in the early 1730s, when there was an ill-fated attempt to depose the Protestant minister Wigboldus Rasvelt.[82] Meanwhile, the Catholics were, like the Jews, fighting with their brethren in the streets of Otrabanda. Among the reasons for Catholic unrest was the rumour that Catholic priests were stirring up the 'coloured' and black people against the white (Protestant and Jewish) minorities, giving rise to continual quarrelling among the various factions among the Catholics on the island.[83] The fights were so violent and frequent that Faesch threatened to exile the troublemakers. Much like the assertion of traditional religious authority he had promoted in the cases of intra-communal conflict among the Jews, he ordered that the congregants obey their pastor until a new one arrived. Clearly, then, as Goslinga noted, 'the small island community displayed the characteristic of vicious backbiting'.[84]

Yet despite the problems in the religious communities on the island, the default policy of 'masterly inactivity' promoted by the WIC remained the model on Curaçao. This inactivity, coupled with the long-recognized right in the Dutch Republic and the WIC of self-government for religious groups was diffused throughout the Dutch territories overseas. For the WIC officials, religion was necessary for society to function well. The clergyman—whether rabbi, priest, or Protestant minister—represented his congregation and was officially invested with authority over that congregation. He helped society to stay well ordered by ensuring that his congregants behaved in appropriate ways. Because values were asserted through religion in Dutch culture, religious institutions both in the Dutch Republic itself and in the territories overseas provided the means for the transmission of values.

[81] Kaplan, 'The Curaçao and Amsterdam Jewish Communities in the 17th and 18th Centuries', 206.

[82] NL-HaNA, TWC 1.05.01.02.243/53–61; 70–83; 135–6; 180–2.

[83] Goslinga, The Dutch in the Caribbean and in the Guianas, 261. Most of the blacks (both enslaved and free), as well as the people of mixed descent, were members of the Catholic church. Most of the white elite were either members of the Dutch Reformed (Calvinist) church or Sephardi Jews.   [84] Ibid. 261.

The expectations of citizens and municipal authorities alike were that religious institutions would resolve conflicts between their members, and almost everyone was affiliated in some way with a religious institution. Groups like the Sephardim and Mennonites, among other religious groups in Amsterdam, even prescribed heavy penalties for, as it were, airing intra-communal dirty laundry in public by not submitting their conflicts to communal arbitration.[85] Yet the religious institutions on Curaçao, particularly the Jewish congregation, could not resolve their communal conflicts, because the near all-encompassing social and even economic role that religious communities possessed in the early modern period was fading.[86]

This situation was complicated by the fact that the rights and privileges given to Jews in the territories governed by the WIC were not uniform and were often the result of commercial expediency. For instance, in an effort to stimulate settlement and profit from existing Sephardi trade networks in the region, the WIC had guaranteed the Sephardi settlers in Curaçao and Suriname freedom of religion. But this also meant that there was no standardized set of laws or regulations for the WIC governors which might help determine how and when they had the authority to intervene in Sephardi communal governance. Moreover, the Heren X did not always have the final word in adjudicating decisions. It was not uncommon for colonists of all stripes to appeal the decisions made by the WIC's Heren X to the States General of the Dutch Republic— and those making such appeals sometimes won and the directives of the WIC were overturned. In fact, in the conflict I have analysed here, the States General almost always took the side of the 'opposition', while the Heren X, perhaps influenced by its wealthy Jewish shareholders, tended to side with the *parnasim*.

Because the Heren X were strongly influenced by the wealthy shareholders representing the interests of the Amsterdam (and Curaçaoan) *parnasim*, it is tempting to cast the conflict solely in terms of class. The conflict looks, on one level at least, very much like the result of an explosion of tensions between the wealthy Jewish traders who lived in the main city of Willemstad and the oligarchic *parnasim* who represented them, on the one side, and the poor Jews living in Otrabanda struggling for representation and recognition, on the other. In fact, as a consequence of this conflict, in 1752 the notables of the Amsterdam community tried to mitigate the class conflict and dissent on Curaçao, by giving a degree of influence to people from the middle and lower middle classes and curbing to some extent the extreme oligarchic tendencies which marked the Curaçaoan community.[87] So the class-based analysis is partially true. But Moses Penso,

---

[85] For an excellent analysis of how the Dutch Reformed Church dealt with intra-communal conflicts, see Herman Roodenburg, *Onder Censuur: De Kerkelijke Tucht in de Gereformeerde Gemeente van Amsterdam, 1578–1700* (Hilversum, 1990).

[86] The Sephardi community in eighteenth-century France was also notoriously fractious (see Zosa Szajkowski, 'Internal Conflicts within the Eighteenth Century Sephardic Communities of France', in id. (ed.), *Jews and the French Revolutions of 1789, 1830 and 1848* (New York, 1970), 167–75).

[87] Kaplan, 'The Curaçao and Amsterdam Jewish Communities in the 17th and 18th Centuries', 203; see also

the opposition leader, was a wealthy merchant, as were several other members of the opposition. Moreover, not all opposition members lived in Otrabanda. There were already long-simmering tensions within the community based on intra-familial feuds, such as that between the Pereira and Leão families, and issues of religious interpretation, like those that arose during the short and turbulent tenure of David Aboab on the island. Therefore, a class-based analysis will only take us so far.

I am more inclined to view the conflict as stemming from bad leadership, at least in part. De Sola was known to be hot-headed and impetuous.[88] He was clearly autocratic and unwilling or unable to compromise at any turn and primarily concerned with asserting his own authority and that of the *parnasim* against any perceived challengers. He seemed to have had little concern for reconciliation and the promotion of peaceful coexistence. Faesch was known as a generally fair and reasonable governor through most of his long term, but it seems that he allowed his personal dislike for Penso to cloud his judgement.[89] For instance, he refused to annul Penso's excommunication, but a few days later he overrode the *parnasim*'s excommunication of other congregants— congregants who had been excommunicated at the same time and for the same alleged infractions as Penso. Moreover, he often behaved in a contradictory manner, especially regarding excommunications. Sometimes he asserted his authority to overrule them, at others he acted as though he did not have the authority to do so, demanding answers about Jewish law from the Heren X.

Bad leadership is nothing new. However, in mid-eighteenth-century Curaçao, this bad leadership was set within the context of inefficient governmental and judicial structures. The Jewish community was supposed to regulate itself, as religious affiliation was all-encompassing. Yet it could not do so, as it became ever easier for members to live outside their religious community. Moreover, no one seemed sure of what to do when the policy of having the Jews adjudicate their own conflicts failed, as it did quite frequently. The *parnasim* were deeply invested in maintaining their own power and control yet were under the authority of the *parnasim* in Amsterdam. The *parnassim* in Amsterdam would almost always support their fellow oligarchs in the colonies, because not to do so would have undermined their own authority—until such time as the conflict became so big that the States General and the *stadhouder* became involved. The governor was supposed to be an impartial authority, yet he was far from being so, at least regarding Penso. The island council was meant to represent the islanders, yet it had little or no judicial expertise. Moreover, it could only rule on issues that the governor brought to its attention, and its members were mostly WIC employees, who

'Sermao Pregado por R. Jeosuah de Cordova em 11 Adar Risson 5513, dia instituido de Jejum e Rogativas na jlha de Curacao' (Sermon preached by R. Jeosuah de Cordova on 17 March 1753, a day set aside for fasting and prayer on the island of Curaçao), Library Ets Haim–Livraria Montezinos, Amsterdam, MS 48D46, 17–18.

[88]   Emmanuel and Emmanuel, *History of the Jews of the Netherlands Antilles*, i. 204.

[89]   Goslinga, *The Dutch in the Caribbean and in the Guianas*, 109, 111.

acted in the interests of the company, which, in this case, generally seems to have meant keeping the largely wealthy *parnasim* and their supporters happy. The Heren X was intended to be the main authority, but was influenced by lobbying from the *parnasim* in Amsterdam, which complicated the overlapping and sometimes contradictory systems for the adjudication of conflicts. Ironically, we can also see that the unofficial system of checks and balances instituted by the WIC 'worked', to some extent, because the States General, as the ultimate adjudicating authority, balanced out the power of the conflicting interests. Nevertheless, the system of resorting to the States General was a painfully time-consuming and inefficient way to rule a colony. Little wonder, then, that the days of the WIC were numbered. Within fifty years, the company was no more.

CHAPTER SIX

RELIGIOUS AUTHORITY

A Perspective from the Americas

HILIT SUROWITZ-ISRAEL

In december 1999 Nicholas Canny contributed 'Writing Atlantic History: or, Reconfiguring the History of Colonial British America', to a special issue of the *Journal of American History*.[1] His essay was intended to alert scholars of both British and American history to the idea that 'colonial history was a transatlantic subject'.[2] Canny warned that narrowly defined studies bound by geography ignore historical context. He argued that if one is to understand the history of the Americas—or England, for that matter—one has to understand what was taking place on both sides of the Atlantic. The benefit of this perspective is the ability to explore and contextualize the continuities and discontinuities of identity in the encounter and exchange between Europe and the Americas more accurately.

Canny's approach has been fruitfully adopted by a growing number of scholars, so much so that 'most early modernists working today on the North Atlantic, or the islands within it, would unhesitatingly endorse the importance of transnational and intercontinental flows'.[3] Paul Gilroy is one of the leaders in this field, advocating an approach that considers the dialectical exchange of the Atlantic and the unique negotiations of identity within the Atlantic world. In *Black Atlantic: Modernity and Double-Consciousness*, Gilroy argues that scholarship on Africans in the Atlantic world has essentialized the construction and analysis of blackness, causing blackness and blacks to remain marginal and in many ways isolated from the history of modernity. Gilroy explains that de-exoticizing the African in the Atlantic space incorporates Africans as part of the narrative of modernity, while effecting a reconstruction of the Atlantic space, and its experiences more broadly.[4]

This chapter builds on Gilroy's ideas, as it brings together the hemispheric perspectives of the Atlantic world and American studies with Sephardi studies, a natural

---

[1] Nicholas Canny, 'Writing Atlantic History: Or, Reconfiguring the History of Colonial British America', *Journal of American History*, 86/3 (1999), 1093–1114.   [2] Ibid. 1095.

[3] Richard L. Kagan and Philip D. Morgan, *Atlantic Diasporas: Jews, Conversos, and Crypto-Jews in the Age of Mercantilism, 1500–1800* (Baltimore, 2009), 18.

[4] Paul Gilroy, *The Black Atlantic: Modernity and Double Consciousness* (Cambridge, Mass., 1993).

fusion 'as no other diaspora ranged as widely, linked so many empires, or cut across so many confessional divides as did that of the Sephardim'.[5] The argument of this chapter is that by more fully integrating Portuguese Jews into the broader history of the Atlantic world and the Americas, the Jewish presence in the New World becomes less marginal, exotic, and exceptional. And the correlate holds true as well: reframing Jews in the Atlantic world sheds light on the formation of religious community, and religious authority in particular, in the early modern Atlantic as a whole. More specifically, close study of the Portuguese Jewish communities of the Caribbean effects a reconceptualization of the Dutch Atlantic in early modern exploration and settlement.

As Portuguese Jews settled the Americas they negotiated questions of power and authority between the Old and New Worlds and navigated the social realities of the formation of new religious communities and identities in the Americas. However, despite scholarship on Portuguese Jews as an ethno-religious community and, later, on religious authority in nineteenth-century Ashkenazi migration to the Americas, the question of religious authority among the Sephardi Jews of Curaçao and other American settlements has been largely overlooked in favour of economic histories and mercantile explanations. Generally, these communities are understood as economic units, wherein religious concerns and Old World institutions are fundamentally absent. In the few instances that religious authority is considered in the New World, island communities like Curaçao are generally seen as satellites of mother communities like Amsterdam with little local autonomy or agency.[6] Though there were many similarities in terms of communal structures and regulation, as we will see, there was also much negotiation between the colonial Mahamad and that in Europe. Such tensions can highlight the importance of the communities' roles in confronting the questions and answers of the New World.

One community that brings such questions to the fore is the early modern Portuguese Jewish community of Curaçao located in the Netherlands Antilles, approximately 35 miles off the coast of Venezuela. This island was an entrepôt in the seventeenth and eighteenth centuries, serving as a hub for both transatlantic and intra-island trade. During the early modern period, Curaçao was home to over 1,000 Jews, at times comprising one-third of the white population and more than 10 per cent of the total population.[7]

---

[5] Kagan and Morgan (eds.), *Atlantic Diasporas*, p. viii.

[6] For more on the role of economics in Sephardi Jewish life in the early modern Atlantic world, see Jonathan I. Israel, *Diasporas Within a Diaspora: Jews, Crypto-Jews, and the World of Maritime Empires, 1540–1740* (Boston, Mass., 2002); Paolo Bernardini and Norman Fiering (eds.), *The Jews and the Expansion of Europe to the West, 1450–1800* (New York, 2001).

[7] Alan Benjamin, *Jews of the Dutch Caribbean: Exploring Ethnic Identity on Curaçao* (London, 2002), 60, 103; Isaac S. Emmanuel and Suzanne A. Emmanuel, *History of the Jews of the Netherlands Antilles*, 2 vols. (Cincinnati, 1970), i. 277, 103; Cornelis Christiaan Goslinga, *A Short History of the Netherlands Antilles and Surinam* (The Hague, 1979); Francis Karner, *The Sephardics of Curaçao: A Study of Socio-Cultural Patterns in Flux* (Assen, 1969), 29.

European explorers first arrived in Curaçao in 1499. Though there has been speculation that Columbus's voyages brought Marranos to the island, the first openly professing Jew to reside on Curaçao was Samuel Coheno, the interpreter for Johan van Walbeck, the Dutch commander who captured the island from the Spanish in 1634. Though Coheno 'spoke Portuguese and did not eat pork' and was on the island for eight years, he never established a Jewish community. There is speculation, however, that he may have encouraged Jewish emigration from Holland to Curaçao.[8] One decade later the official establishment of a Jewish community on Curaçao began. This occurred under the patronage of Amsterdam's João de Yllan. Like Yllan, Coheno was a member of the Amsterdam Portuguese congregation, though there is no evidence that Coheno played a role in Yllan's decision to lead a group of Portuguese Jews to establish an agricultural colony on the island in 1651. Yllan received a charter from the West India Company to settle up to fifty Jewish families in Curaçao—in the end only ten families made the journey. Upon arrival, the families founded their congregation, Mikvé Israel (Hope of Israel), and a plantation named De Hoop (The Hope).[9]

It was only in 1659, with the arrival of seventy Portuguese Jews from Amsterdam, that a more established Jewish community developed. These individuals, under the leadership of Isaac da Costa, brought with them a Torah scroll given to them by the leaders of Ets Haim congregation in Amsterdam.[10] The group's charter provided them with 'extensive grants of land along the bay, freedom from taxation, a guarantee of protection by the authorities, exemption of doing guard duty on sabbath in times of war, and freedom to openly practice their religion'.[11] Yllan's group had established the first meetinghouse for prayer, and shortly after the arrival of da Costa's group the first Jewish cemetery on the island, Beth Haim, was consecrated in 1659.

The leadership structure of Curaçao's Mikvé Israel congregation was modelled on that of Amsterdam. The governing body consisted of fourteen *adjuntos*, councillors, who were the wealthy members of the community (a *jahid* (community member)

[8] Charles Gomes Casseres, *Istoria Kortiku di Hudiunan di Korsou* (Curaçao, 1990).

[9] Yosef Kaplan, 'The Curacao and Amsterdam Jewish Communities in the 17th and 18th Centuries', *American Jewish History*, 72/2 (1982), 200; Benjamin, *Jews of the Dutch Caribbean*, 91–5. In order to understand the significance of the naming of New World Portuguese Jewish communal institutions during the early modern period, messianic fervour and the collective memory of the community must be considered (see Menasseh ben Israel, *The Hope of Israel*, trans. Moses Wall, ed. Henry Méchoulan and Gérard Nahon (Oxford, 1987); Yosef Kaplan, *An Alternative Path to Modernity: The Sephardi Diaspora in Western Europe* (Leiden, 2000); id., 'The Curacao and Amsterdam Jewish Communities', 198).

[10] 'A Resolution made concerning a Scroll of the Law with some ornaments delivered to Isack da Costa on Iiar 18 to take with him to Curaçao', wherein da Costa acknowledges: 'I have received from the gentlemen of the Mahamad a Sepher Torah of fine parchment with its yellow taffeta lining; a band of flowered blue damask; a cap of red damask with its fringe; a flowered green satin cloth for the reading desk; a cloth of orange tafeta to cover the Holy Scroll and another cloak of white damask with gold braid; all of which is given for delivery to Curaçao' (Emmanuel and Emmanuel, *History of the Jews of the Netherlands Antilles*, ii. 748).

[11] Casseres, *Istoria Kortiku di Hudiunan di Korsou*, 4.

could only seek office once all of his and his family's debts and loans to the community were paid in full). These fourteen *adjuntos* selected from among themselves three leaders called the *parnasim*, who made up the body of the Mahamad: the *presidente* (president), the *parnas* (vice president), and the *gabay* (treasurer).[12] The Mahamad had authority over congregational matters and all other aspects of Jewish life on the island. Until 1825, when Jews were permitted to become citizens of Curaçao (three decades after this occurred in Amsterdam), the Mahamad was the legal governing body of Curaçao's semi-autonomous Jewish community. Until 1864 the Mahamad had even further reaching powers as Curaçao's civil government recognized only one Jewish congregation.

Like its Amsterdam counterpart, the Curaçaoan Mahamad had absolute authority over the island's Jewish community and had the power to protect and discipline its members. Members could be punished with fines and bans of varying severity. Community members at times tried to appeal to the West India Company, the Dutch government, and the Amsterdam Mahamad against major punishments, like the ban and exile. These petitions were perceived as a public affront to the authority of the Mahamad and generally resulted in further regulations affirming its power and authority. Indeed, even when other sources of authority were petitioned and those bodies responded, the Mahamad was not always willing to comply. Such actions highlight a fundamental tension in the Mahamad's status as both subject to island law and a governing body of a community understood as a nation. This relative autonomy is evident in the Curaçaoan Mahamad's decision to use banishment from the island as a form of punishment, with the local governor's support. At the same time, the Mahamad was subject to the rules of the Amsterdam Mahamad and the Dutch authorities.

Members of the Curaçaoan Mahamad, all wealthy businessmen, understood themselves to be the communal nobility. This 'economic elite had critical authority in religious activities, including activities that now might be understood as either personal or secular'.[13] Appointed by the previous Mahamad, the Curaçaoan Mahamad tended to consist of men from the same dozen powerful families who were among the island's first Jewish settlers—the Senior, Maduro, Marchena, Pereira, and Levy families, to name just a few. The Mahamad was as much a political, social, and economic organization as it was a religious institution as the 'social life and religious life of the [Curaçaoan] Jew . . . were inextricably linked'.[14]

The Mahamad also served as a liaison between the Jewish community and the civil authorities—either the WIC or the Dutch governor. This role, established in the first decades of Jewish settlement, helped ensure the commercial success of the local

---

[12] At some points there were five such positions, but because it was necessary to have been cleared of all debt to the community, such a large Mahamad was difficult to fill.

[13] Benjamin, *Jews of the Dutch Caribbean*, 96.

[14] Emmanuel and Emmanuel, *History of the Jews of the Netherlands Antilles*, i. 234.

Portuguese Jews. In the 1680s Balthazar Beck, slave commissioner to Curaçao and brother of the governor, Matthias Beck, tried to restrict Jewish trade. He saw the trade network of the 'demon Jews'[15] as a threat to his own business. The *parnasim* appealed to the WIC and particularly to two prominent Jews, Jacob Brandon and Jeronimo Nunes da Costa (also known as Moses Curiel). The company heard the appeal and made it clear to the governor 'that the Jewish Nation on the Island of Curaçao is free to exercise its religion and also engage in the trades as is allowed [the Jews] in Amsterdam'.[16] Beyond establishing the commercial rights of the community, this exchange demonstrates, first, the desire of the Spanish-Portuguese Jews in Curaçao to 'exercise [their] religion' and, second, that both Jews and non-Jews recognized the relationship between Curaçao and Amsterdam, and used the civil liberties in the mother country as a model for Jewish communal rights in Curaçao.[17]

The role of the Mahamad and questions of religious community and authority are addressed throughout our three main documentary sources for the history of Curaçao's Jews: the *ascamot* and the *Memorias Curiel* and *Memorias Senior* documents. The *ascamot* were probably first written in Curaçao in 1659. However, the earliest extant *ascamot* are from 1688 and are revisions of those from 1659 and 1671. The *Memorias Curiel* and *Memorias Senior* documents were recorded by Ephraim de Solomon Curiel and Jacob de David Senior (and later one of his sons) in Curaçao during the late seventeenth and eighteenth centuries. Both chronicle Jewish communal activity on the island.

Religious Authority

Questions of religious authority represent a perennial challenge to Jewish communities. There is a broad consensus among scholars that, in this case, all religious authority resided in the Amsterdam community and that Curaçao functioned as its satellite. Indeed, throughout the often-turbulent history of Curaçao's Jewish community, we find time and again that it appealed to Amsterdam for social, religious, and financial guidance. According to Yosef Kaplan:

From the very beginning, the Jews of Curaçao considered themselves as a branch of the Portuguese community of Amsterdam. The regulations of the 'Mikveh Israel' community were laid down in accordance with the 'style of the holy congregation of Talmud Torah of Amsterdam, which may God increase and which we ought to follow'. . . . They considered the Amsterdam community as a model to be emulated, and the supreme authority in every aspect of the organization and leadership of their own community.[18]

---

[15] Ibid. i. 85.   [16] Ibid. i. 86.

[17] I specify Jewish communal rights rather than individual rights, as the Jews of Curaçao had fewer civil rights as individuals than did their co-religionists in Amsterdam. For more on the rights of Jews in Curaçao, see Emmanuel and Emmanuel, *History of the Jews of the Netherlands Antilles*; Mordechai Arbell, *The Jewish Nation of the Caribbean: The Spanish-Portuguese Jewish Settlements in the Caribbean and the Guianas* (Jerusalem, 2002).   [18] Kaplan, 'The Curacao and Amsterdam Jewish Communities', 198.

This is true in many instances, but in fact there were times when Amsterdam's authority was challenged or rejected outright. These instances shed light on the limits of local autonomy and issues of centre and periphery in colonial Jewish matters.

In 1744 Hakham Samuel Mendes de Sola was sent from Amsterdam to Curaçao to help lead the community. De Sola was born in Lisbon, and re-judaized in Amsterdam. His European religious training reflected the Amsterdam Mahamad's push towards religious homogenization. Often, his practices were at odds with the Caribbean community, which was religiously heterogeneous and more lax, informed by an atmosphere of cultural and religious hybridity and the constant stream of Conversos and newly re-judaized Conversos who joined the community. This situation often led to tensions between the island community and the European-trained leadership.

Hakham de Sola arrived from Amsterdam to be the assistant to Hakham Jesurun, who had long been the community's religious leader.[19] This appointment was made by the Amsterdam Mahamad and the various fees associated with it were shared between the Curaçaoan and Amsterdam mahamads. De Sola was appointed to be the 'second Hakham at the side of the worthy Hakham M[orenu] V[e Rabenu] R[ibbi] Raphael Jessurun. . . . He was to follow the orders of the *parnassim* of Mikvé Israel in everything . . . for the peace . . . and to bind himself inseparably with the aforesaid gentlemen.'[20] De Sola arrived in Curaçao to a community plagued by infighting. One of the primary areas of contention was the dispute over an inheritance between the families of Samuel Jeudah Leão and Lea Pereira, a married couple both of whom came from respected families. Some time after their marriage Lea became pregnant, but the child was stillborn and Lea became fatally ill. In her final days Samuel had her sign a civil will, which essentially nullified the *ketubah* that they had signed and vowed to uphold as part of their wedding ceremony. The civil will granted Leão the entire marriage dowry and half of the estate that Pereira had inherited from her father.

According to *minhag toledo* (Toledo custom), used by the Sephardi Jews in Curaçao, if a woman died without producing a child in her marriage, then half of the dowry was returned to her family.[21] Pereira's family expected Leão to uphold the terms of the contract and provide them with that sum in addition to the family estate, which had not been mentioned in the *ketubah*. When he failed to do so, they approached the *ḥakham* and the *parnasim*, who rendered the civil will void and submitted their ruling to Amsterdam for certification. The ruling from Amsterdam stated that Leão should submit to his local Mahamad and return 50 per cent of the dowry and the share of the

---

[19] Emmanuel and Emmanuel, *History of the Jews of the Netherlands Antilles*, i. 178. Initially the preference was for Hakham Aron Ledesma of Suriname to become the *ḥakham*, but he declined the appointment.

[20] Ibid.

[21] As one *ketubah* that follows this custom states: 'If (God forbid) the bride shall die without issue during the lifetime of the groom, he shall return to the bride's heirs half of the dowry which she brought him' (Louis M. Epstein, *The Jewish Marriage Contract: A Study in the Status of the Woman in Jewish Law* (New York, 1927), 270).

estate to Pereira's family. The ruling also advised that such matters be settled internally, without the involvement of the local civil authorities.

Leão did not comply with the decision and involved the Dutch legal system of Curaçao. Since island law generally allowed the Mahamad to govern the Jewish community, the local authorities upheld the Mahamad's ruling. The legal recrimination reverberated for years within the Jewish community and only ended when Leão, having exhausted all legal recourse, submitted to the authority of the Mahamad.

Unfortunately, the rabbinical resolution and de Sola's subsequent implementation of the Amsterdam ruling in the Leão–Pereira case further divided the community. Part of this tension stemmed from de Sola's failure to include Moses Penso, a community *parnas* who opposed the resolution, in the religious council. Furthermore, in his report to Amsterdam's *parnasim*, de Sola called Penso 'a seditious, malevolent, turbulent man, disrupter of the public welfare' and branded Leão 'a pious fraud and real hypocrite'.[22] The fighting caused by both social and religious disagreements effectively split the community into two opposing factions—one led by Hakham de Sola and the *parnasim* and the other by Moses Penso. The friction escalated as Penso supported the construction of a second synagogue in Curaçao, a proposition that the leadership strongly opposed, as it threatened their power.

This episode demonstrates both the recognition of Amsterdam as the supreme authority, as de Sola was not only sent by the Dutch community to Curaçao, but he continued to turn to it for guidance; and the fragility of the Curaçao community and the tensions that surrounded the centralization of power. Such disagreements were especially frequent, as assertions of religious authority were entangled with all aspects of Jewish communal life.

Another episode that demonstrates the complexity of religious authority is the contentious issue of the construction of a second synagogue in Curaçao. The St Anna Bay divides Willemstad, the capital of Curaçao, into two parts, Otrabanda and Punda, where Mikvé Israel is located. With the growth of the Jewish population during the 1730s, the need for a new synagogue became more pressing. Otrabanda's residents, often poorer and less influential than their Punda co-religionists, felt that they were looked down upon. The Mahamad, reticent to cede any power, prohibited the formation of a new congregation and the building of a new synagogue in Otrabanda, as well as religious meetings and prayer groups of which the Mahamad was not a part, claiming that these would lead to disunity with the community.[23] The Mahamad's

---

[22] Emmanuel and Emmanuel, *History of the Jews of the Netherlands Antilles*, i. 182–3 n. 7.

[23] According to Ascama 11 (12 Tishrei 5449 [1688]) of Mikvé Israel, 'there shall at no time be erected or procured in this fortress [Willemstad] another house as a Synagogue outside of what we now have. In the event that an arrogant, bold, or headstrong person attempts to do so, whoever he may be, he shall incur the penalty of *Beraha* [a curse or small ban], he and his followers. He shall be given an opportunity to desist with that plan within eight days. But if he continues with his intention of disrupting the general union, a report

opposition was probably strengthened by the fact that Penso was active in the formation of the second synagogue, which would have provided a meeting place for Hakham
de Sola's adversaries.

After the initial resistance, Penso and his followers presented a halakhic argument
for the construction of the new synagogue. They argued that in order to reach Mikvé
Israel they needed to row their boats across the St Anna channel, a clear violation of
Jewish laws of the sabbath and festivals, or to walk a prohibited distance.[24] There is no
doubt that the use of a halakhic argument resonated with the Mahamad, which had
become increasingly strict under de Sola's leadership. Finally, in 1746, more than a
decade after the initial proposal, Mikvé Israel's Mahamad granted permission for the
Otrabanda synagogue to be built and provided them with the necessary ritual objects.[25]
This was done with the explicit understanding 'that [the congregation] called Neve
Shalom, at the Otrabanda, shall be Subordinate'[26] and under the control of Mikvé
Israel's Mahamad.

The construction of Neve Shalom Synagogue in 1746 did little to clarify the question of religious authority, as Otrabanda's Neve Shalom congregants felt increasingly
stifled by Punda's Mikvé Israel Mahamad. These resentments resulted in general violence between community members. In 1749–50, after Amsterdam's Ets Haim Mahamad
failed to quell the infighting, several Portuguese Jews who sided with Moses Penso
appealed to the regional and Dutch authorities to intervene to resolve the dispute and
end the violence. The Dutch *stadhouder*, Prince William IV of Orange-Nassau, issued a
proclamation in Portuguese and Dutch that declared peace in the Curaçao Jewish community. The proclamation further granted the Amsterdam Mahamad a few months to
submit new community by-laws to the Dutch authorities and ensure peace on the
island.

In 1750 the Amsterdam Mahamad sent a nine-article resolution to Mikvé Israel,
including provisions that all community members were to make peace among
themselves and that all of Curaçao's Jews were to submit to the *ascamot* prepared by the
Amsterdam *parnasim*.[27] The *ascamot* delivered from Amsterdam addressed general

shall be given to the gentlemen of the Mahamad immediately to remedy the situation. They, in the company
of the other signatories, shall seek to prevent that design through the intermediation of the Honorable
Governor should all other means fail. The penalty shall not be removed until the payment of forty-eight
florins to the Sedaca [charity chest]. However, if in time some [planters distant from the city] for their
convenience find it best and have enough people for a congregation, they shall be given a Sefre [Torah scroll]
and the necessary assistance so that everywhere we may serve God as we should, etc.' (Emmanuel and
Emmanuel, *History of the Jews of the Netherlands Antilles*, ii. 544).

[24] Joseph Corcos, *A Synopsis of the History of the Jews of Curaçao from the Day of Their Settlement to the Present Time* (Curaçao, 1897), 28–9; René D. L. Maduro (ed.), *Our 'Snoa' 5492–5742* (Willemstad, Curaçao, 1982), 58.

[25] Jacob de David Senior, *Memorias Senior 1713–1763*, Mongui Maduro Library Archives, Curaçao.

[26] Ascama I (1756, 1786) (Emmanuel and Emmanuel, *History of the Jews of the Netherlands Antilles*, ii. 586).

[27] The author saw an uncatalogued copy of this resolution at the John Carter Brown Library in July 2010.

community maintenance and regulations as well as events from the years of fighting, such as prohibitions against entering the synagogue with a weapon or writing satires against the Mahamad or rabbi. Unhappy with the Amsterdam regulations, the *parnasim* of Mikvé Israel petitioned Ets Haim to amend the *ascamot* in 1752. Not only was the petition denied, but the Amsterdam community made clear its displeasure that the community had approached the prince.[28]

Generally, Curaçao's *ascamot* were amended annually in Curaçao, signed by the local *parnasim*, and read to the congregation on the Jewish New Year. They were written in Portuguese, the primary language of the community. Those written as a result of the conflict differed from other Mikvé Israel *ascamot*, as they were written in Amsterdam at the behest of the Dutch government and in Portuguese and Dutch since they were submitted to the Dutch government (at the *stadhouder*'s request). The government's intervention demonstrates that the Dutch authorities recognized the island's community as an extension of Amsterdam's. Mikvé Israel also recognized this relationship and accepted its responsibility in receiving religious direction from Amsterdam.

Mikvé Israel ultimately recognized the authority of the Amsterdam Mahamad and its connections with the Dutch Crown. However, the process was not simple. Curaçao's Mahamad had initially petitioned for the by-laws to be amended and tried to assert some autonomy.

New World Realities: Authority and Accommodation

Thus far, the models presented have been unidirectional, describing movement from Europe to the Americas. But in fact in order for Amsterdam to exercise its authority it had to grapple with the new social questions and categories of the Americas. The

---

[28] This ongoing tension is clearly demonstrated in Mikvé Israel's *ascamot* from 12 Tishrei 5449 [1688]. Insecurity and insularity are shown in Ascama 5: 'On leaving the Synagogue every person shall continue walking and [anyone] wishing to converse shall do so without raising his voice, as otherwise it might be construed as quarrelling. If this occurs in the presence of a member of the Mahamad, he shall separate them and if they refuse to obey, they shall incur the penalty of *Beraha* which shall not be removed before payment of the twelve florins fine. In the absence of one of said gentlemen [of the Mahamad], one of the oldest [members present] shall do what he deems best to pacify them in order to avoid scandal, it being understood within a radius of three houses on either side of the synagogue.' Comfort within the broader legal and political systems is shown in Ascama 6: 'Should any question arise between the Congregants, [then] through the Semas [sexton] to whom five placas shall be given for citation, they shall be obliged to present the matter to the gentlemen of the Mahamad for adjustment. If the latter cannot settle it, they will grant permission to refer the matter to the Governor if they deem it a proper one and will prevent anyone acting otherwise by imposing a fine of twelve florins payable in cash and by denying him admittance to the Synagogue until such payment [has been made].' Such *ascamot* are repeated throughout the seventeenth and eighteenth centuries. This is part of a larger discussion regarding Jews involving civil authorities in Jewish communal affairs (Emmanuel and Emmanuel, *Jews of the Netherlands Antilles*, ii. 543).

American communities looked to Amsterdam for help in navigating these realities and challenged existing assumptions about race, environment, and other facets of colonial life. The following example looks at a religious question from the Caribbean submitted to Amsterdam, a responsum from *Peri ets haim* of 1767 involving Reuben and Simeon, two generic names used in responsa literature.[29] Reuben, a Caribbean resident, owned a 'non-Jewish maidservant' who was his 'purchased property' and 'worth a great deal'. He decided to go to Amsterdam for business, and his friend, Simeon, told him that 'in the city of Amsterdam they do not have permission to purchase or hold slaves', so Reuben should leave the slave with him, since, if she accompanies him to Amsterdam, she will likely be 'cajoled into fleeing'. Simeon offered to provide the slave-woman with food in exchange for her labour and upon Reuben's return he would return the slave.

Reuben agreed and two years later, upon his return, learned that his maidservant had borne a son to one of Simeon's slaves. Reuben claimed that since his maidservant was his property, the 'profit', that is the child, belonged to him. Simeon claimed that the child was his property since 'the slave woman came to his home alone, and so she will leave', and moreover his own slave had fathered the child. Reuben's response was that a child follows the mother. Moreover, how can one know that Simeon's slave is the father? He continued: 'that since she was impregnated from the market then the default assumption, regarding a maidservant, is that she whores. And, just as she had sexual relations out of wedlock with one, so she had with others.' The Amsterdam leadership were asked to rule on this question.

The rabbis began by addressing the issue of the custody of a child born out of wedlock, drawing an analogy between the unwed maidservant who has a child out of wedlock and a donkey that has a colt, in which case the child is the mother's. Interestingly, this analogy applies to any non-Jewish woman who bears a child without *kidushin*, betrothal. In this initial response, the maidservant is placed in a general category of a non-Jewish woman: her race and enslavement are not mentioned as part of the argument. Even the likening of the woman to a beast is not racialized at this point, referring rather to the lack of genealogy attributed to non-Jews and animals. These discussions, focusing on the slave as a woman who 'whores' and bears a child out of wedlock, led the rabbis initially to conclude that the child belonged to the mother and thus to rule in favour of Reuben.

Then, in an interesting twist that reflects the New World realities of slavery, the rabbis shifted the focus of their argument from genealogy to property rights. First, they introduced the analogy of owned cattle, as a parallel to the rights of an enslaved person; and, second, they discussed the age of the child and the child's mobility as it

---

[29] David ben Refael Meldolah in *Peri ets haim* (1767), John Carter Brown Library, Providence, RI, accession no. 10–80. *Peri ets haim* was a Jewish periodical of halakhic responses published from 1691 to 1807 in Amsterdam. The questions and responses in these volumes reflect the re-engagement of Portuguese Jews with Jewish law and the setting of the Dutch world and its colonies.

relates to its status as property: 'If the child is a young servant or slave who couldn't walk on account of his infancy, he counts as the owner's movable property.' Here, the rabbis argued that if the child is considered as property, then the child belongs to Simeon, as the child was born in his home and of his slave.

This responsum (which ultimately decided in favour of Reuben) demonstrates a particularly New World predicament, and the use of traditional Jewish institutions and structures to resolve it. Like other New World European communities, America's Jews during the early modern period were negotiating their new environment within an existing framework. The Amsterdam Mahamad, in order to maintain its authority, had to shift its existing categories to consider the realities of the Americas.

Towards Local Authority

Until this point, the discussion has followed the dominant model and, though allowing for more tension then is commonly assumed, presumes that Amsterdam maintained authority over its colonial Portuguese Jewish communities. There are, however, a number of cases where Amsterdam's authority was challenged outright, either through petition or through increased local autonomy. One such area, introduced above, involved the tensions between European-trained leaders and their New World congregants.

Against the backdrop of the debate in Curaçao concerning the construction of a second synagogue, Hakham de Sola further complicated matters by attempting to change the custom of the *lulav*, the ritual palm frond used on the Jewish holiday of Sukkot. Though the custom enjoined by Rabbi Joseph Caro's *Shulḥan arukh* was the established rite on the island, de Sola sought to implement the Salonica–Land of Israel custom, the rite then used in Amsterdam.[30] In so doing, de Sola implied that religious authority lay on the other side of the Atlantic, essentially functioning as an agent of Amsterdam's push towards religious homogeny throughout the Portuguese Jewish diaspora. Changing local custom, however, was not as simple as de Sola and the Amsterdam authorities had hoped, and the move was met with tremendous resistance from all sides of the Curaçaoan Jewish community. The congregants of Mikvé Israel sent letters to the Amsterdam *parnasim* protesting the change of custom. As a result of intense pressure from members of the Curaçaoan community, the Amsterdam *parnasim* ultimately relented, and Hakham de Sola had to sign an agreement promising not to change the custom of the *lulav*.[31] Shortly thereafter, de Sola submitted a letter of

---

[30] Curaçaoan Jews, who followed the rite set forth by Rabbi Joseph Caro, would shake the *lulav* in the following sequence: east, south, west, north, up, down. The Salonica–Holy Land custom introduced by Isaac Luria used the sequence: south, north, east, up, down, west (see Emmanuel and Emmanuel, *Jews of the Netherlands Antilles*, i. 183).   [31] Senior, *Memorias Senior 1713–1763*.

resignation, angrily claiming that he had 'to tend a flock of wolves instead of sheep'.[32] However, both the island and mother congregations rejected his resignation and de Sola was forced to remain leader of the community.

Our final example of the emergence of local religious authority among the Portuguese Jews in the Americas comes from Dutch Suriname. Suriname, which Jews settled from the 1650s onwards, was the site of one of the most successful and autonomous colonial projects by Portuguese Jews during this period. Its communal structure was similar to that of Curaçao with an authoritarian Mahamad, so that the Surinamese Sephardim were also subject to imported and imposed *ascamot* and religious regulations.[33] This striking case, discussed at length by Robert Cohen, concerns a 1754 *ascama*, according to which: 'during those days [between Passover and Shavuot] no *Jahid* may shave or have a shave or haircut, for whatever reason, under penalty of *Herem* and a fine of fl. 100'.[34] This ruling was unpopular as being clean-shaven was a local custom and more suitable to the tropical climate of the mainland. In 1789 there was 'a sudden outburst of sickness among the Sephardi Jews', who blamed the growth of beards for the illness. When the local Mahamad ruled that 'all petitioners may shave for medical reasons . . . at least twenty members of the community submitted medical affidavits, all signed by Jewish physicians or surgeons, testifying to heavy colds, inflammation of the throats or heavy tightness of the chest, caused by a slight inflammation due to not shaving the beard during these our holidays'.[35]

While New World Jewish communities were similar to the mother communities in Europe, over time they sought autonomy. The American communities faced new challenges, which were both negotiated transatlantically, as in the case of Reuben and Simeon, and locally, as in the case of facial hair in Suriname. As Gilroy argues regarding Africans in the Atlantic world, Portuguese Jews of the early modern Caribbean straddled the Old and New Worlds: rooted and institutionally tied to Europe, they were transformed by the encounter with the Americas and thereby became the proper subjects of American and Atlantic religious history.

[32]   David Aboab, 'Emeth ve yazib', in Emmanuel and Emmanuel, *History of the Jews of the Netherlands Antilles*, i. 184.

[33]   Robert Cohen, *Jews in Another Environment: Surinam in the Second Half of the Eighteenth Century* (Leiden, 1991); Goslinga, *A Short History of the Netherlands Antilles and Surinam*; Samuel Oppenheim, *An Early Jewish Colony in Western Guiana, 1658–1666: And Its Relation to the Jews in Surinam, Cayenne and Tobago* (Ithaca, NY, 2010).

[34]   Cohen, *Jews in Another Environment*, 154.   [35]   Ibid.

PART III

MATERIAL AND VISUAL CULTURE

CHAPTER SEVEN

JONKONNU AND JEW

The Art of Isaac Mendes Belisario (1794–1849)

JACKIE RANSTON

O N 12 MAY 1837 the *Jamaica Despatch* informed its readers that 'we have seen a very beautiful lithographic print, the specimen of one of the work which is about to be published by Mr I. M. Belisario—It should be in the hands of every Jamaica family'. It was a significant statement to make the year before 'full freedom' was enacted on the first day of August 1838.

The print illustrated the Queen, or Maam, of the Set Girls (Plate 7.1), one of the participants in the annual Jamaican Christmas masquerade known as Jonkonnu—a complex and diverse mix of many traditions that included multiple African cultures and European masquerade alongside British mumming plays and even Shakespearean monologues. Commonly anglicized to John Canoe, the masquerade had its origins in the early days of slavery when the Christmas holidays provided the only real recreational opportunities for the enslaved.[1]

The illustrator was a Sephardi Jew, Isaac Mendes Belisario, Jamaica's first island-born professional artist, and the *Queen or 'Maam' of the Set-Girls* one of a series of twelve hand-tinted lithographic prints that Belisario published for local purchase between 1837 and 1838.[2] Entitled *Sketches of Character, In Illustration of the Habits, Occupation and Costume of the Negro Population in the Island of Jamaica* and accompanied by an extensive descriptive text known as letterpress, they represent the only visual representation of the Jonkonnu masquerade in its fully evolved, creolized form by a first-hand observer.

The central figure and principal dancer in the celebration or masquerade was Jaw-Bone, or House John-Canoe, who bewitched onlookers with the agility of his pirouettes while balancing a beautifully crafted headdress in the form of a house (Plate 7.2). He took his name from the headdress or one of the accompanying musicians who played the jaw-bone—the preserved lower jaw-bone of a horse across which a piece of

---

[1] The first account of such performances comes from Sir Hans Sloane who spent fifteen months in Jamaica from 1687 as physician to the governor, the second duke of Albemarle, Christopher Monck (Sir Hans Sloane, *A Voyage to the Islands Madera, Barbadoes, Nieves, S. Christophers, and Jamaica*, 2 vols. (London, 1707, 1725)).

[2] Belisario's grandfather, Alexandre Lindo, had an English coachman whose mistress was Bessie Ford, a Queen of the Blue Set Girls.

wood was passed to produce a rattling noise. The house was usually constructed of pasteboard and coloured papers and ornamented with beads, tinsel, spangles, and pieces of looking glass. His popularity was challenged by the revered Actor Boys with their extravagant costumes, costly masks, and wigs of long horse hair who would compete for the title of best-dressed masquerader (Plate 7.3). Belisario depicted the winning performer of 1836 on King Street (where Belisario himself lived) standing outside the Fancy Warehouse—a store owned by Moses Quixano Henriques, a Jewish merchant and close friend of Belisario. It was here, at Henriques's store, that many masqueraders purchased the muslins, satins, silks, shoes, and ribbons for their magnificent costumes.[3] Jewish stores had been patronized by slaves for decades and for obvious reasons: they were open on Sunday—the slaves' day off—and the Jewish shopkeepers were 'particularly benefited' wrote a local observer in 1797 as 'the negroes taking the sole opportunity of being in town to supply themselves with cloth, and foreign provision'.[4]

Belisario informs us that an Actor Boy would pay upwards of '5 Doubloons, equal to about £15 Sterling' for his costume—about £750 (US$1,200) today. But he could be easily compensated by his skill as an orator, for Actor Boys would also compete by reciting passages from Shakespeare—Richard III was a favourite—and they collected money from their spectators: sums amounting to £10 or £12 per day (£500–£600, US$800–US$1,000).

The Set Girls entered the masquerade towards the end of the eighteenth century (Plate 7.4). Each set consisted of fifteen to thirty young women, identically and elaborately dressed and graded not only according to the colour of their costumes but also that of their skin: 'There were brown sets, and black sets and sets of all the intermediate gradations of colour' who 'sang as they swam along the streets . . . beautiful creatures . . . elegant carriages, splendid figures—full, plump and magnificent'.[5] They distinguished themselves by their names, and early groups included the Golden Set and the Velvet Set but in 1775 there were 'none so fine as the Garnet Ladies'.[6] By the late eighteenth century they were ousted by the Red and Blue sets 'decked out with much taste, sometimes at the expense of their white or brown mistresses who took pride in showing them off' singing, dancing, and trying generally to outdo each other.[7]

In Belisario's time, a group of Set Girls could collect from £8 to £10 a day—£400–£500 (US$650–US$800) today—from spectators who supported one or other of the sets. There was another set, 'The House-Keepers', who never danced; it did not befit their station—house-keeper was a euphemism for the mistress of a white man.

---

[3] *Morning Journal* (28 Oct. 1836), 2.

[4] Barry Higman (ed.), *Characteristic Traits of the Creolian & African Negroes in Jamaica, &c. &c. (1797)* (Kingston, Jamaica, 1976), 12. This edition includes roughly half of the material originally published in *The Columbian Magazine* in 1797.   [5] Michael Scott, *Tom Cringle's Log* (London, 1836), 265.

[6] Higman (ed.), *Characteristic Traits of the Creolian & African Negroes in Jamaica*, 19.

[7] John Stewart, *An Account of Jamaica and Its Inhabitants* (London, 1808), 264.

By the early nineteenth century, many of the costumes and even the parades themselves came to be funded by planters and European residents. One contemporary observer noted how the female participants were 'loaded with jewels furnished for the occasion by the white ladies',[8] while another described how the great houses were opened, the slaves 'drank with their masters' and spoke 'with greater familiarity . . . the distance between them appeared to be annihilated for a moment'.[9]

During the masquerades of December 1835, the *Kingston Chronicle* reported that 'several FEMALES who would wish to be termed Genteel' were found 'going under the Mask. Their names have been handed to us, and should we find them again tripping . . . contrary to the rules of decorum and modesty . . . we shall consider ourselves justifiable in alluding to them in a future number.'[10] On another occasion when two sets of boisterous masqueraders were told to unmask by the police in Spanish Town, they were found to be of 'ALL COMPLEXIONS', the *Morning Journal* disclosed in capital letters.[11] If anything, over time, Jonkonnu had become a leveller of slave society— everyone was involved either as spectator, sponsor, or performer.

The artist in Belisario would have been attracted to these deep social forces in a society on the cusp of change. One of his motives 'for having intruded on public attention', he wrote in the preface to his *Sketches of Character*, was 'a desire to hand down faithful delineations of a people, whose habits, manners, and costume, bear the stamp of originality'. Belisario recognized that for well over a century and a half, enslaved Africans had succeeded in keeping many of their traditions alive under the guise of Jonkonnu. It was here that 'the Other within' found freedom and expression— the source of a new creativity.[12] Jonkonnu was the point at which Belisario's Jewish and Caribbean identities intersected. Of Converso descent, Belisario was aware of how his own people had used masquerade to guard their identity as a condition of survival. Coerced into converting to Christianity, their strategy was a combination of conformity and concealment that enabled them to slip in and out of Jewish and Christian company while constantly being on their guard.

Despite in-depth research, Belisario remains something of an enigma. Raised by a family of wealthy Jewish merchants and slave traders, his *Sketches of Character* have acquired an iconic status, and he is remembered for having preserved the culture of the slaves through his art. Born in Kingston in 1794, he was descended from two distinguished Sephardi families. On the distaff side was the Lindo family, whose name appears frequently in the records of both Portuguese and Spanish inquisitions. We rarely hear of Negro slaves in the households of crypto-Jews, but in 1655 Belisario's

[8] George Blythe, *Remonstrance of the Presbytery in Jamaica* (Edinburgh, 1843), 242.
[9] Stewart, *An Account of Jamaica and Its Inhabitants*, 262.
[10] *Kingston Chronicle* (31 Dec. 1835), 3.   [11] *Morning Journal* (4 Jan. 1842), 3.
[12] See Yirmiyahu Yovel, *The Other Within. The Marranos: Split Identity and Emerging Modernity* (Princeton, 2009).

great-great-great-maternal grandfather, Lorenço (Isaac) Lindo and his wife were denounced by Maria and Catalina, their household slaves.[13] 'The family does not eat
pork', Maria told the inquisitor, 'if any is sent to them, they give it away'. There was
little to be done to hide the Friday ablutions except to beg the slaves not to talk. Catalina
deposed that Lindo was so afraid of the slaves' gossiping that they were not allowed out
except to fetch water and she had 'escaped' with Maria to 'unburden her conscience and
not through ill will'. After two years' incarceration, the Lindos were released and fled to
London. Succeeding generations lived in the Jewish communities of Venice, Amsterdam, and Bordeaux. It was from the French seaport of Bordeaux that Belisario's
grandfather, Alexandre Lindo, migrated to Kingston around 1765, where he seized the
opportunities offered by the New World to become Jamaica's wealthiest Jewish merchant, plantation owner, and slave factor.[14]

On a business trip to London in 1786, Lindo hired Abraham Mendes Belisario, the
18-year-old son of Hebrew scholar, Reverend Isaac Mendes Belisario, to work in Lindo's
counting house in Kingston.[15] Five years later, Abraham married Alexandre's daughter
Esther, and they had five daughters and one son, the artist, named after his paternal
grandfather.[16] The year Isaac was born, Lindo made his son-in-law a co-partner[17] in his
business, which folded after a disastrous deal with the French government, involving a
loan of £500,000 to provision some 20,000 French troops in neighbouring Santo
Domingo.[18] Payment was at first postponed and later the bills returned to Lindo
unpaid. Facing bankruptcy and threatened with arrest by the payeur général of the
colony,[19] Alexandre Lindo left Jamaica for London in 1803, leaving his sons to salvage
what they could from the sale of properties and plantations. He was joined in London
by the Mendes Belisario family. Isaac was 9 years old at the time. Six years later, he came
under the guardianship of his stockbroking uncle, Jacob Mendes Belisario, after his

[13] Lucien Wolf, *Jews in the Canary Islands: A Calendar of Jewish Cases Extracted from the Records of the
Canariote Inquisition* (London, 1926), 143–63.

[14] Fragments from Alexandre Lindo's journal recording the death of his brother, Joseph: 'Decembre a
1765—a Kinston [*sic.*] Jamaica, le 3 emme jour de chanuqua' (Private collection/Lindo Family).

[15] Abraham Mendes Belisario to Lord Liverpool (3 Nov. 1811), National Archives, Kew (TNA), Colonial
Office (CO) 152/98. The Mendes Belisarios had resided in London from at least 1686 when they openly
professed Judaism and became members of the Creechurch Lane Synagogue and teachers in the congregational school (J. Ranston, *Belisario—Sketches of Character: A Historical Biography of a Jamaican Artist* (Kingston,
Jamaica, 2008)).

[16] As noted in the appointment of trustees (7 July 1824) following the death of Esther Mendes Belisario
(Island Record Office, Twickenham Park, Jamaica (IRO), Liber Old Series 725, fo. 191).

[17] Agreement (8 Apr. 1794), IRO, Liber Old Series 469, fo. 156.

[18] General Nugent, Lieutenant Governor of Jamaica to British Secretary of State (15 Jan. 1803), TNA, CO
137/110.

[19] Mons. Lanchamp, payeur général de la colonie to General Rochambeau (27 June 1803), George A.
Smathers Libraries, University of Florida, Rochambeau Papers.

father returned to the West Indies to manage seven sugar estates on the island of Tortola.[20]

It was during this time that Isaac Mendes Belisario entered the world of art under the tutelage of Robert Hills, the British landscape artist and drawing master. Belisario's watercolour showing the interior of the Bevis Marks Synagogue, painted in 1812,[21] is his first publicly displayed work and the earliest known impression of Britain's oldest synagogue (Plate 7.5). Belisario followed the watercolour with an engraving of the same view aquatinted by D. Havell and 'most respectfully dedicated to the members of the Congregation'.

Between 1815 and 1818 Belisario exhibited landscapes at the Royal Academy and the Society of Painters in Oil and Water Colours but put aside his artistic endeavours in 1820 to work as a stockbroker until 1831, when he exhibited a watercolour *Portrait of a Lady* (or *The Lady in Black*) at the Royal Academy (Plate 7.6).[22] The sitter was the actress, Ellen Tree, who played Desdemona to the Othello of the Afro-American actor Ira Aldridge at Covent Garden. Peer pressure forced the manager to discontinue Aldridge's performances after *The Times* slammed Aldridge for his colour—although they had to admit that he was 'extremely well received'—and the *Athenaeum* protested 'in the name of common propriety and decency' at Ellen Tree 'being subjected to the indignity of being pawed by Mr Wallack's black servant'.[23] Belisario saved his comment on the wranglings for the title page to *Sketches of Character*: 'Nothing extenuate, nor aught set down in malice', quoting Othello's final speech: 'Speak of me as I am.'[24] It was the plea also of Aldridge and Belisario, as the latter assures viewers that his 'characters' are an honest rendition, 'nature in her ordinary form alone', he notes in the preface, 'having been the source from whence all the original drawings were derived'.[25]

Belisario published another portrait of Ellen Tree,[26] and then learned that he had come into some money from his deceased mother's estate in Jamaica. Access to these funds, which would allow him to live as an independent artist, possibly inspired his return to Jamaica in 1834. But the main reason was probably respiratory problems, which necessitated living in a healthier climate. Belisario arrived at Port Royal on 6 December 1834, after an absence of 31 years. He still had relatives in Jamaica, including

[20]   Abraham Mendes Belisario to Lord Liverpool (3 Nov. 1811), TNA, CO 152/98.

[21]   Although the date for this work is generally understood to be 1812 (and printed as such on a card published by the Spanish and Portuguese Jews' Congregation), 'it is not certain' according to the congregation's archivist, Miriam Rodrigues-Pereira.

[22]   A rule of the Stock Exchange was that no member admitted after 1812 was to be 'engaged in any other business', but Belisario produced at least one other landscape, untitled but signed and dated 1823.

[23]   James Wallack, a British actor, hired Aldridge as his personal attendant in New York.

[24]   *Sketches of Character* was published in three parts. In Part 1 the quotation reads as given here; in Parts 2 and 3 it reads 'nor set down aught in malice'.

[25]   Isaac Mendes Belisario, 'Preface', in id., *Sketches of Character* (Kingston, Jamaica, 1837–38), n.p.

[26]   A lithographic study on stage as Mrs Cregan in *Eily O'Connor*, a melodrama by Irish playwright Dion Boucicault.

a cousin of the same name,[27] who had been involved in the local sale of domestic slaves until the abolition of slavery that same year, after which he became a wharfinger.[28]

Where did Belisario stand on the abolition movement? His father, Abraham Mendes Belisario, addressed the same question and declared that the Abolition Act of 1807 had 'done little for the cause which gave it birth. Humanity still suffers.' As for his thoughts on emancipation itself, however, Abraham concluded: 'I shall not canvass these.'[29] And yet he spent fifteen years of his life working for the amelioration of the slaves throughout the British West Indies from the time he landed in Tortola in 1809. On his arrival, Abraham Mendes Belisario was horrified to see how cruelly the slaves were treated, in particular by one man, Arthur Hodge, a member of His Majesty's Council for the Virgin Islands. Abraham Mendes Belisario helped bring Hodge to trial for the murder of one of his slaves, for which Hodge was found guilty and hanged. The case was exceptional: rarely was a white man prosecuted for the murder of one of his slaves with a free black woman as the chief prosecution witness. 'It is a very difficult matter, viewing the existing laws re Negro testimony to convict a white man', said Abraham Belisario, who took copious notes of the trial and, at his own expense, published the report in London as grist to the mill of the abolitionists.[30]

Isaac Mendes Belisario took a similar stance on his return to Jamaica. He did not express his views on emancipation openly, but through his art. No other artist had attempted to capture the Jonkonnu on canvas or in print. They confined themselves to portraits and plantation and urban landscapes, often commissioned by the plantocracy themselves. Belisario also produced works in these genres but a closer examination of his works reveal that they are layered with subliminal messages.

In a portrait of an unknown man, for example (Plate 7.7), the viewer's attention is drawn to a copy of the *Report from the Selection Committee on Negro Apprenticeship in the Colonies*, prominently displayed against the table leg. It suggests that the sitter was involved or in sympathy with the 1836 report that investigated labour conditions in Jamaica following a legislative attempt to change the terms of apprenticeship against the advice of the Colonial Office. Although slavery was abolished on 1 August 1834, a period of transitional 'apprenticeship' was introduced whereby the former slaves were required to work 40½ hours each week without wages for their erstwhile masters. 'Full free' was still four years away. The contested issues included hours of work, use of workhouses as punishment, using chains on women prisoners, discriminatory marriage-law provisions, and inadequate education.[31]

[27] The son of his uncle, Moses Mendes Belisario and his wife Rebecca (née Henriques) (see Ranston, *Belisario—Sketches of Character*, 179).   [28] *Jamaica Courant and Public Advertiser* (22 May 1830), 4.

[29] Abraham Mendes Belisario's views on the Ameliorating Act of the Leeward Charibbee Islands passed in the year 1798 (2 July 1811), TNA, CO 152/100.   [30] Ibid.

[31] The fact that Belisario chose to sign the painting in a cartouche on the map of Jamaica showing the county of Surrey (misspelt), suggests that the sitter might be Edward McGeachy, a land surveyor who was

Plate 7.1 *The Queen or 'Maam' of the Set-Girls*. Lithograph with watercolour. Isaac Mendes Belisario, 1837

Courtesy of the Hon. Maurice and Mrs Facey

Plate 7.2 *Jaw-Bone, or House John-Canoe*. Lithograph with watercolour. Isaac Mendes Belisario, 1837

Courtesy of the Hon. Maurice and Mrs Facey

Plate 7.3 *Koo, Koo, or Actor Boy*—winner of the 1836 competition for the best dressed masquerader.
Lithograph with watercolour. Isaac Mendes Belisario, 1837

Courtesy of the Hon. Maurice and Mrs Facey

Plate 7.4 *Red Set Girls and Jack-in-the-Green*. Lithograph with watercolour. Isaac Mendes Belisario, 1837

Courtesy of the Hon. Maurice and Mrs Facey

Plate 7.5 *Bevis Marks Synagogue*. From left to right the figures are said to be the beadle; the philanthropist,
Sir Moses Montefiore; and the young Abraham Haim Pinto, grandfather of Geoffrey de Sola Pinto of Jamaica.
Watercolour. Isaac Mendes Belisario, *c.*1812

Courtesy of the Spanish and Portuguese Jews' Congregation of London

Plate 7.6 *Portrait of a Lady, or The Lady in Black* (Ellen Tree). Watercolour on ivory. Isaac Mendes Belisario, 1831

Dorotheum, Vienna

Plate 7.7 Portrait of an unknown man. Watercolour. Isaac Mendes Belisario, 1837

National Gallery, Jamaica

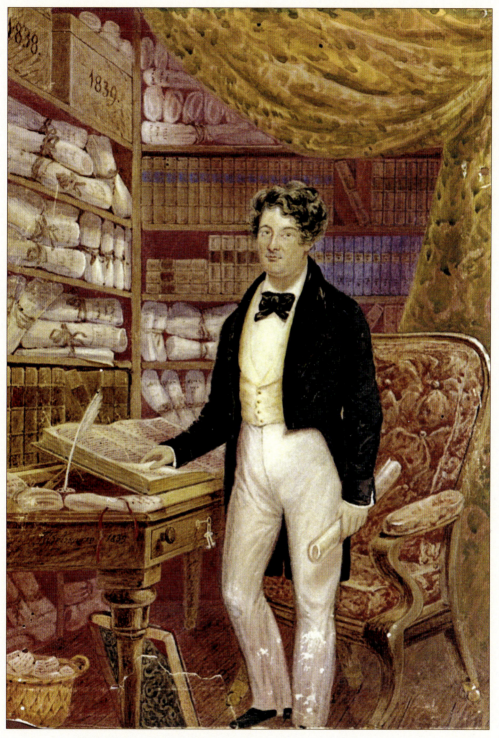

Plate 7.8 Portrait of Samuel Sharpe. Watercolour. Isaac Mendes Belisario, 1839

Photo: Kent Reid; private collection/Sharpe family

Plate 7.9 Portrait of the Reverend Isaac Lopez, cantor of the Spanish and Portuguese Jews' synagogue,
Kingston, Jamaica. Lithograph with watercolour. Isaac Mendes Belisario, 1846

Photo: Kent Reid; private collection

Another Belisario model was the chief justice of Jamaica, Sir Joshua Rowe, who, according to the Dublin-born doctor and special magistrate, Richard R. Madden, 'exhibited a bias in favour of blacks' during his time on the bench. 'Those same crimes with which Negroes stood charged in [the] colony', Madden continued, 'would be visited in England with far greater vigour'.[32] On completion of Rowe's portrait, Belisario was commissioned by the governor of Jamaica, the Marquess of Sligo, to produce a series of oil paintings of his Jamaican estates and surrounding areas.[33] Before his appointment as governor in 1834, Sligo had been an absent proprietor and confessed that he felt 'no repugnance to the continuance of slavery itself following the abolition of the trade in slaves'. After attending a meeting of West India proprietors in London in April 1832, however, Sligo became a convert to abolition based upon the very evidence adduced by the West Indian interest itself: 'I entered that room a colonial advocate', he admitted, 'I left it a decided abolitionist'.[34] Before Sligo left Jamaica in September 1836, he subscribed to Belisario's *Sketches of Character*.

These various abolitionist connections suggest Belisario held antislavery views, as does the story behind his portrait of Samuel Sharpe (Plate 7.8), a lawyer of Montego Bay and owner of Samuel Sharpe, a slave. The latter, popularly known as 'Sam', had adopted his owner's name, a servile custom, but one also exhibiting some measure of respect. 'As an individual', Sam said, 'he had no reason to find fault with the treatment he had received as a slave'. His master and the family were always very kind to him, but he 'felt acutely the degradation and the monstrous injustice of the system, and was bent upon its overthrow'.[35]

Sam Sharpe was the leader of the 1831 Christmas rebellion in Jamaica, intended as a strike by all the slaves in the western parishes in order to force plantation owners to pay them for their work. But his plan miscarried on the last night of the holidays, when militant elements, fuelled by the freedom of Jonkonnu, took over and set fire to a number of estates. Sam claimed responsibility, gave himself up, and was hanged—he was later declared a national hero of Jamaica. Samuel Sharpe tried to obtain Sam's body in order to give him a decent burial, but the authorities refused—such an act, he was told, would have 'an evil effect upon the minds of the slaves'.[36]

Another possible reason why Belisario did not express his political views openly was to protect himself and his community. In the same year as Sam Sharpe's rebellion,

made Crown Surveyor for Surrey in 1837, the same year he produced a plan of the Negro Grounds on Green Valley Plantation in the Port Royal Mountains.

[32] See William A. Green, *British Slave Emancipation: The Sugar Colonies and the Great Experiment, 1830–1865* (Oxford, 1991), 80; Richard Robert Madden, *A Twelvemonth Residence in the West Indies*, 2 vols. (Philadelphia, 1835), ii. 110.

[33] Marquess of Sligo's Account Book (20 May 1836), National Library of Ireland, Westport Papers MS 41,068/10.   [34] *Morning Chronicle* [London] (18 Mar. 1839).

[35] In an interview with Reverend Henry Bleby (Henry Bleby, *Death Struggles of Slavery* (London, 1853), 118).

[36] C. S. Reid, *Samuel Sharpe: From Slave to National Hero* (Kingston, Jamaica, 1988), 94.

Jamaican Jews obtained full political rights and began to take an active part in public life. Despite freedom to worship openly in Jamaica, Jews had nonetheless been subjected to discriminatory legislation. In 1711 it was made quite clear, under the Act of Regulating Fees, that 'no Jew, Mulatto, Indian or Negro shall be capable to officiate or write in for any offices upon any pretense whatsoever', and in the same year an act prohibiting non-Christians from voting was passed, to preserve Jamaica as a white Christian society. When political rights were extended to free blacks and the free people of colour in Jamaica in 1830, the Jews were the only class of free men who could not vote.[37]

Another untitled Belisario watercolour depicts a bespectacled Nonconformist minister about to preach in his chapel beside a table set for the Eucharist. It was originally owned by Joshua de Cordova—the Jewish co-proprietor of the *Gleaner*, founded in 1834 and still in print. Belisario's extensive letterpress was printed by de Cordova at the *Gleaner's* office. Why would de Cordova wish to own such a portrait? Was it a gift? Was it because it was painted by a Jew? (Approximately one-third of the 165 subscribers to Belisario's *Sketches of Character* were Jewish.) Did de Cordova donate land and/or funds for the chapel? It was not unknown for Jamaican Jews to assist members of other religions in this way. For instance, in 1827 Abraham Rietti, 'a Hebrew gentleman', donated land for the Ebenezer Wesleyan Chapel on the Spanish Town Road, near Kingston.[38]

Belisario had promised more pictures in his series of *Sketches of Character* but was forced to cease production through ill health. He was a victim of tuberculosis—that dreaded disease which either carried its victims off within months or lingered for years. For Isaac Mendes Belisario, it lingered, moving at a sluggish, tardy pace, and his torment is revealed in his inability to complete paintings and lithographs. Belisario returned to London in April 1839,[39] where he was nursed by his sisters and recovered enough to return to Jamaica, where he chronicled the great fire of Kingston in August 1843 with a set of vivid lithographs that showed close observation of domestic detail. But unlike earlier works, Belisario produced only the drawings, leaving the lithographer Adolphe Duperly to transfer them to the stone. Belisario returned to London where he died of tuberculosis on 4 June 1849.

Belisario's art ended as it began, with a Jewish theme: the first was the Bevis Marks Synagogue in London and the last his 1846 portrait of Reverend Isaac Lopez, cantor of the Spanish and Portuguese Jews' synagogue in Kingston where Belisario had been a vestryman from 1838 to 1839 (Plate 7.9).

As the late Professor the Honourable Rex Nettleford contended, the fact 'that

---

[37] See Samuel Hurwitz and Edith Hurwitz, 'The New World Sets an Example for the Old: The Jews of Jamaica and Political Rights 1661–1831', *American Jewish Historical Quarterly*, 55 (1965–66), 37–54.

[38] Peter Samuel, *The Wesleyan–Methodist Missions in Jamaica and Honduras, Delineated: Containing a Description of All the Principal Stations Together with A Consecutive Account of the Rise and Progress of Work at Each* (London, 1850), 55.   [39] *Jamaica Despatch and Kingston Chronicle* (5 Apr. 1839), 4.

Belisario was Jewish and not African or Christian European, merely speaks to the textured reality of the Jamaican persona which is multi-layered, multifaceted and multi-cultural but integrated in the subliminal unity manifested more than ever in the products of the collective and individual creative imagination'. This, Nettleford concluded, makes 'Isaac Mendes Belisario's story, the story of all Jamaica, indeed of all the Caribbean and the Americas'.[40]

[40]   Quoted in Ranston, 'Foreword', in *Belisario—Sketches of Character*, p. xvii.

CHAPTER EIGHT

TESTIMONIAL TERRAIN

The Cemeteries of New World Sephardim

RACHEL FRANKEL

THE JEWISH CEMETERIES of the New World, while not wholly preserved, accessible, or undisturbed, contain continuous centuries of gravestone imagery, epitaphic language, genealogy, burial patterns, and cemetery layout. They testify to the messianic beliefs of seventeenth-, eighteenth-, and, to some extent, nineteenth-century Jews living in an emerging and diverse environment characterized by political tolerance and abundant undeveloped terrain: quite different from the conditions on the eastern side of the Atlantic. They also convey a sense of cultural versatility, as evidenced by multi-lingual epitaphs, dual calendar systems, and fusion of artistic styles (see Figure 8.1). The cemeteries of Suriname and Jamaica, among others, help explain how these Sephardim, whether remnants of the Old World or pioneers in the New, established, practised, and expressed their religion in newly settled lands.

This essay focuses on three seventeenth-century cemeteries. Two are remotely located in the interior rainforest of Suriname, South America. The third is at Hunt's Bay, Jamaica. This Caribbean cemetery is now adjacent to a lawless squatter town on the industrial outskirts of Kingston. Burial in all three cemeteries ceased approximately 200 years ago. Subsequently, jungle flora obscured the sites, and only partial—but admirable and important—attempts were undertaken in the twentieth century to clear, restore, and inventorize them.

Until I and my architectural teams began our investigations in Suriname in 1998 and in Jamaica in 2007, no definitive map of the cemeteries or complete inventory of the extant gravestones existed. The result of the work in Suriname culminated in a book I co-authored with Aviva Ben-Ur, *Remnant Stones: The Cemeteries of Suriname: Epitaphs*. In this book, all the extant gravestones are transcribed, translated, and represented in a comprehensive architectural site plan. Many of the sepulchres represented are accompanied by a photograph. In our early research we discovered that burial registers for Suriname survive. However, the registers include entries that have no corresponding site in the cemeteries and there are names and dates of death incised on gravestones without a corresponding entry in the burial registers. I. S. Emmanuel, in his *Precious Stones of the Jews of Curaçao*, notes that this is typical. No burial registers for Jamaica's early cemeteries are known to have survived.

Figure 8.1 Tombstone of Mordecai, son of Solomon, son of Isaiah, with images of skull and crossbones, sugar cane, and coffee branch. Old Ashkenazi cemetery of Paramaribo, Suriname

Photo: Patrick Brunings, 2002

Owing to the remoteness, difficulty and danger of access, and obscurity of these cemeteries, scholarship has mostly neglected them. In Suriname, the communal archives include references to the cemeteries, but no survey, deed, extant fence, or gates remain. In Jamaica there is a deed of property acquisition with a sketch illustrating the parcels, but it describes only the metes and bounds; no fences, gates, or other landmarks are drawn.

I and my teams were the first to comprehensively map, inventory, photograph, transcribe, and translate the over 800 extant gravestones of the three cemeteries. Despite the stones having been exposed for centuries to elements that efface incised inscriptions, my teams—with fortitude, patience, and a light dusting of flour—deciphered most of the names, titles, birth and death dates, biblical passages, poems, biographical information, and illustrative imagery of the sepulchres. From this work, I have endeavoured to understand the site planning and burial patterns of the cemeteries —all different in layout but not without commonalities, including their proximity to water transport, recurrence of family names (Henriques, da Costa, Nassy, Pinto, etc.), and provenance in Europe, since neither the skilled craftsmen nor the marble and bluestone quarries which created the gravestones existed in the New World.

Jews began arriving in Suriname in the 1650s. They came from various parts of Europe, northern Africa, and other regions of the Americas. Under tolerant English and then Dutch colonial rule, they established an agrarian settlement on the Suriname River, south of what the English called Sands Point (later known as the town of Thorarica, not to be confused with the larger division of Thorarica).[1] By 1666 they had established a cemetery at Cassipora Creek.[2] The settlement quickly developed into the autonomous village of Jodensavanne, and by 1685 the community, by then in its second generation, had built Beraha Vesalom Synagogue, the first synagogue of architectural significance in the New World,[3] and established their second cemetery at Jodensavanne. By the early eighteenth century dozens of Jewish plantations lined the river. These Sephardi-owned plots of land, mostly devoted to the cultivation and processing of sugar and worked by enslaved Africans, formed the largest Jewish agricultural community in the world and the only Jewish settlement in the Americas granted virtual self-rule. By the eighteenth century Paramaribo, Suriname's capital city, included Ashkenazi and Sephardi communities. Each had its own cemetery, referred to today as the old Sephardi cemetery of Paramaribo and the old Ashkenazi cemetery of Paramaribo.

Jamaica became home to Jews at around the same time as Suriname. In 1661, in order to attract settlers to the colony, the English Crown offered grants of 30 acres to anyone who would settle in Jamaica within two years, together with all the rights and privileges of Englishmen to any children born there. But rather than establishing plantations and cultivating sugar, the first Jews who arrived took up residence in the colony's port, Port Royal, and involved themselves overwhelmingly in commerce.[4] Probably because the narrow peninsula had a high water table, they established their cemetery across the harbour at Hunt's Bay. The cemetery's earliest extant graves date from 1672.[5]

After the destruction of much of Port Royal by the earthquake of 1692, many Jews relocated across the harbour to the emerging commercial capital of the island, Kingston. Soon Jews also resided in Spanish Town, the seat of the colonial government, and in many of Jamaica's small seaport towns. While a few of Jamaica's Jews were planters,

---

[1] For a discussion of Thorarica the town, as opposed to Thorarica the division, see Rachel Frankel, 'Antecedents and Remnants of Jodensavanne: The Synagogues and Cemeteries of the First Permanent Plantation Settlement of New World Jews', in Paolo Bernardini and Norman Fiering (eds.), *The Jews and the Expansion of Europe to the West, 1450–1800* (New York, 2001), 434 n. 2.

[2] The earliest burial discovered by the 1998 Caribbean Volunteer Expeditions (CVE) fieldwork conducted under my leadership was that of Abraham Chyllon d Fonseca Meza, who, according to his epitaph, which was transcribed and translated by Aviva Ben-Ur, died on 22 Tishrei 5427 (1666) (Aviva Ben-Ur and Rachel Frankel, *Remnant Stones*, vol. i: *The Jewish Cemeteries of Suriname: Epitaphs* (Cincinnati, 2009), 98).

[3] See Frankel, 'Antecedents and Remnants of Jodensavanne'.

[4] Eli Faber, *Jews, Slaves, and the Slave Trade: Setting the Record Straight* (New York, 1998), 51–2.

[5] The oldest tombstone at the Hunt's Bay cemetery documented by CVE in 2008 under my leadership belonged to Abraham, son of Iahacob Gabay, who, according to his epitaph, died on 6 Nisan 5432 (1672).

most were merchants. By the beginning of the eighteenth century about eighty of Jamaica's families were Jewish. By 1730 their numbers had climbed to nearly a thousand,[6] and by the 1800s Jewish cemeteries ringed the island.[7]

While Jews in both eastern and western Europe were fleeing antisemitism, Jews in Suriname and Jamaica were incorporating refugees into their nascent communities. In seventeenth-century Suriname, Jews lived in an autonomous plantation milieu as landowners. In Jamaica, they lived mostly in heterogeneous port towns as a disenfranchised second class of free people. Their sociopolitical status more closely resembled that of most other New World Jews living in relatively tolerant British, Dutch, and Danish colonies. Nowhere else in the Americas, or for that matter in the world, in the seventeenth and eighteenth centuries did a community such as that of Suriname exist. It owned miles of contiguous plantations along a major conduit with a town of its own creation and its own administration at its centre. Jews in Barbados, Curaçao, St Eustatius, Nevis, Tucacas (Venezuela), St Thomas, and New York also established synagogues, cemeteries, schools, businesses, and institutions and succeeded, even if they did not thrive, in the socio-economic climate of their adoptive lands. But they did so within a Christian context where they were, at most, important players but never founding fathers in autonomous lands of their own settlement. The special privileges granted to the Jews of Suriname, coupled with their long-term commitment to plantation life, resulted in the unique creation of Jodensavanne. The effaced stones of Curaçao, the buried tombs of Spanish Town, and the lost sepulchres of Barbados contain vital clues to these communities. Until the epitaphs, imagery, and layout of these extensive (both chronologically and quantitatively) cemeteries are resurrected, we will not know how the distinctive social status of Jodensavanne's Jews was manifested in the construction of their cemeteries. Neither the cemetery of Jodensavanne in Suriname nor that of Hunt's Bay in Jamaica can be precisely placed in context: they can only be examined independently or in relation to each other. However, what can be surmised from the massive, expensive, and lasting stone sepulchres extant in Suriname, Jamaica, Barbados, and Curaçao, as well as in the smaller settlements of St Eustatius, Nevis, and New York, is that they testify to a common sense of permanence in the New World. Close examination of Cassipora Creek and Jodensavanne cemeteries testifies as well to a socio-religious autonomy unique to Jodensavanne's Jews.

A preliminary examination of tombstone inscriptions in Suriname reveals important data about the families in general and women in particular. Rebecca, wife of Benjamin Henriquez da Costa, died and was buried in Suriname's Cassipora Creek cemetery in 1771 (see Figure 8.2). By that time the cemetery had been in continuous use for over a century and contained hundreds of burials, many marked with elaborate

---

[6]   Faber, *Jews, Slaves and the Slave Trade*, 58.
[7]   Richard D. Barnett and Philip Wright, *The Jews of Jamaica: Tombstone Inscriptions 1663–1880* (Jerusalem, 1997), diag. 1, showing the main towns of Jamaica in which Jews settled.

gravestones of European origin and cut. It is likely that a European poet composed Rebecca's bilingual epitaph and that a stone carver in Amsterdam incised its imagery. The same European origins hold true for most pre-nineteenth-century New World Jewish gravestones.

The Hebrew portion of the epitaph, as transcribed and translated by Aviva Ben-Ur, is a poem written in the voice of the deceased:

> On the day of my abundant joy illness
> suddenly overcame me
> Birth pangs and rupture overwhelmed me
> I gave birth and died, like a blossom I turned away
> And the fruit of my womb was brought with
> me to the grave
> Alas, instead of joy, birth pangs, instead
> of song, tears are what I brought to
> my kin here and in lands beyond
> You who pass by, if you have a human heart,
> Shed your tears upon my bones.[8]

This dramatic poem is not surprising, for it is known that at this time Hebrew poetics was a subject in Sephardi schools in Amsterdam and employed rules developed in the Hispano-Arabic world and Renaissance Italy. However, the creative use of Hebrew poetry to express sentiments and conditions unique to the New World is novel and contributes to and reshapes the body of Sephardi literature. In Rebecca's Hebrew epitaph, for example, the experience of the transatlantic family is expressed in biblical language. Preceding the Hebrew poem on Rebecca's grave is an epitaph in Portuguese:

> Grave
> of the virtuous Lady Mrs Rebecca,
> wife of Benjamin Henriquez da Costa
> died while a Bride of Genesis
> on the eve of the sabbath day
> on 26 Tishrei of the year 5532
> corresponding to 4 October 1771
> May her soul delight in eternal glory.[9]

The use of Portuguese indicates the cultural, if not sacred, status that the language retained among the Sephardi Jews in Suriname. Giving the date of death according to both Hebrew and Gregorian calendars reveals the dual Jewish and Christian heritage of Suriname's Sephardim. The prevalence of Hebrew and Portuguese or Hebrew and Spanish epitaphs on the inventoried gravestones of Cassipora Creek, Jodensavanne,

[8] Ben-Ur and Frankel, *Remnant Stones*, vol. i: *Epitaphs*, 89.   [9] Ibid.

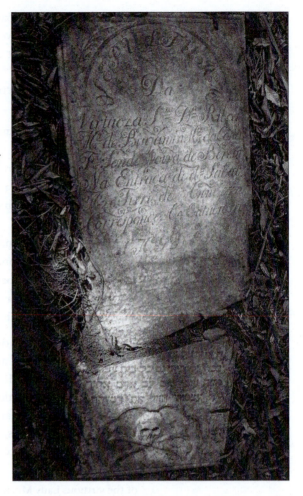

Figure 8.2 Tombstone of Rebecca, wife of Benjamin Henriquez da Costa, with image of skull and crossbones. Cassipora Creek cemetery, Suriname

Photo: Rachel Frankel, 1998; first published in Ben-Ur and Frankel, *Remnant Stones*, vol. i: *Epitaphs*, 89–90

Hunt's Bay, and Paramaribo's old Sephardi cemeteries suggests that mourners sought to affirm Jewish tradition as well as their Iberian heritage. The absence of trilingual epitaphs—Hebrew, Portuguese (or Spanish), and Dutch—at Jodensavanne and Cassipora Creek suggests that Jodensavanne's Jews preferred and hoped to perpetuate their cultural isolation. In fact, no Dutch epitaphs appeared in either cemetery until the nineteenth century (there are three nineteenth-century Dutch epitaphs at Cassipora and eleven at Jodensavanne). By then, the Jews had long abandoned Jodensavanne. In Suriname's later Jewish cemeteries in Paramaribo, there are no surviving trilingual epitaphs either. Yet of the nineteenth-century epitaphs at the old Sephardi cemetery, about 25 per cent of the inscriptions are in Dutch and a few are bilingual (Dutch and Hebrew). At the old Ashkenazi cemetery in Paramaribo almost 20 per cent of the epitaphs are in Dutch and 15 per cent are bilingual, some as early as the late eighteenth century. Hunt's Bay cemetery, unlike its contemporaries Cassipora Creek and Jodensavanne, contains at least twenty-eight trilingual (Hebrew, Portuguese/Spanish, and English) epitaphs from between 1686 and 1787. This trilingualism suggests that the Jamaican Jewish community was in the process of absorbing new cultural traits and perhaps anticipating future generations of English-speaking progeny who would visit the cemetery to mourn their ancestors and commemorate their deaths.

The image of a skull and crossbones at the bottom of Rebecca's gravestone is not unusual on the graves of western Sephardim and is also found on gravestones in Christian cemeteries throughout the western world. In Suriname, this image appears on graves from the eighteenth century in Cassipora Creek, Jodensavanne, and the old Sephardi cemetery of Paramaribo. Skull-and-crossbones imagery also appears on the eighteenth- and early nineteenth-century graves in the old Ashkenazi cemetery of Paramaribo. The source for the imagery is perhaps the book of Ezekiel.

And while I was prophesying, suddenly there was a sound of rattling, and the bones came together. . . . The breath entered them, and they came to life. . . . Thus said the Lord God: I am going to open your graves and lift you out, O My people, and bring you to the land of Israel. (Ezek. 12: 7, 12)

It is not surprising that Ezekiel 12 was incorporated into the entrance gates of the Amsterdam community's Ouderkerk cemetery (1616) and that the biblical message of national revivification is displayed inside Ouderkerk's House of Circlings (1705).[10] In Suriname, themes of deliverance find expression in the name and site design of the community's synagogue (1685), Beraha Vesalom (Blessings and Peace), at Jodensavanne. The synagogue building was positioned within a rectangular plaza surrounded by a fence. Each side of the plaza had a gate at its midpoint, corresponding to the four cardinal points.[11] Thus, upon each holy day the Jewish community's procession through the north, south, east, and west gates onto the synagogue grounds 'gathered the exiles from the four corners of the earth'.[12] The plan of the synagogue site may have expressed the plantation settlers' belief that they resided in a redemptive land, a glorious haven of freedom in which they could practise their faith, prosper, and multiply. The community made a large and ongoing investment in clearing the land, constructing and maintaining the village square, and building in brick and terracotta:

[10] A bas-relief that includes skull-and-crossbones imagery exists on the interior wall of the restored House of Circlings. The same bas-relief appears in the etching, 'Les acafoth ou les sept tours, autor du cercueil' by Bernard Picard (*Ceremonies et coutumes religieuses de tous les peuples du monde* (Amsterdam 1723)). This small building, also called Casa De Rodeamentos by Portuguese Jews, is more generally known as the Metaher House or Cleansing House. The first name refers to the seven circuits that mourners make around the bier of a deceased male. The second name reflects its function as the house where the ritual washing of the body took place. See L. Alvares Vega, *The Beth Haim of Ouderkerk aan de Amstel* (Ouderkerk aan de Amstel, 1994).

[11] The extant remains of Jodensavanne, as surveyed by CVE in 1997 under my leadership, are corroborated by descriptions of the site from various historical accounts including the *Essai historique sur la colonie de Suriname* (Paramaribo, 1788) (see *Historical Essay on the Colony of Surinam, 1788*, trans. Simon Cohen, ed. Jacob Rader Marcus and Stanley F. Chyet (Cincinnati, 1974), 149).

[12] From the 'Shemonah esreh', a central prayer of the Jewish liturgy.

materials probably imported and certainly demanding skilled labour (the latter was in short supply in the young colony). Such durable institutional (as opposed to residential) construction would not occur elsewhere in the Caribbean until the eighteenth century. In 1704 Neve Shalom Synagogue was constructed in brick in Spanish Town, Jamaica; in 1730 Mikvé Israel Synagogue was constructed in limestone in Willemstad, Curaçao; and in 1737 (but possibly not until 1772) Honen Dalim Synagogue was built in yellow brick in Orangestad, St Eustatius. The design and construction of the seventeenth-century Nidhe Israel Synagogue in Barbados are yet to be confirmed, and the first synagogue in New York was not built until 1728. Interestingly, in Jamaica and Curaçao, tombstones precede permanent synagogues by several generations, whereas at Jodensavanne, a span of less than twenty years exists between the earliest known gravestone and the construction of the 'brick' synagogue.

At Jamaica's Hunt's Bay cemetery, the Jewish cemetery for well over a hundred years, seven examples of skull-and-crossbones imagery were identified in 2008, yet none post-date the calamitous earthquake of 1692, which killed an estimated one-third of the Jewish population, destroyed their synagogue, and scattered the survivors.[13] The absence of skull-and-crossbones imagery after the earthquake may suggest a loss of messianic faith as the Jews of Port Royal viewed their homeland as less of a harbour of deliverance.

In 1767 Aron, probably the son of the aforementioned Rebecca and Benjamin da Costa, died at the age of 2 years. His gravestone is located in the south-western corner of the Cassipora Creek cemetery among other da Costa family burials. Four years after Aron's death Rebecca and her unnamed newborn were buried, with Aron now at his mother's feet. Eighteen years later, in 1789, Rebecca's husband Benjamin died and was buried beside her and thus adjacent to Aron, his toddler son.

In examining cemeteries, one must bear in mind that shifting soils mean grave markers may move within the cemetery grounds or even beyond them. Also, archival documents refer to 'notations of sepulchres, without stones . . . where stakes stand',[14] suggesting that wooden markers once stood among those of stone, the wooden ones probably used for children, those of lesser means, or lower-status community members such as Jewish mulattoes.

The Cohen Nassys were Jewish Suriname's founding family, and it is therefore not surprising that they, like the da Costa family, are well represented in the Cassipora Creek cemetery. However, unlike other extant family plots at this cemetery, the blue-

---

[13] At the request of the United Congregation of Israelites of Jamaica, the CVE team under my leadership performed a site-condition survey and gravestone inventory at the Hunt's Bay cemetery in January 2008 and March 2009.

[14] Inventories of papers kept by the *parnasim* of SVS [Sedek Vesalom] (1794), Nationaal Archief Nederland (NAN), Nederlands–Portugees–Israelitische Gemeente in Suriname (NPIGS), 132; register of burials, NAN, NPIGS, 423.

blooded Cohen Nassys are not all grouped together. Rather, their gravestones are found in a few small, separate clusters throughout the cemetery. One such cluster is on the northern edge and includes a gravestone belonging to Simha, wife of Jacob Cohen Nassy, who died in 1745. Beside her is Jacob Cohen Nassy, probably her spouse, who died three years later. In Suriname, the name Simha usually belonged to a Eurafrican Jew. In the earliest days of Jewish settlement in Suriname, the governing body drafted a by-law that defined two subdivisions of the Sephardi community: *jahid*, a full member of the Jewish community by virtue of one's European descent, and *congregante*, someone who was either a Eurafrican Jew,[15] typically the progeny of a Sephardi father and an African mother, or a European Jew demoted to a lower social status as a penalty for marrying a Jewish female of African descent. Among other things, *congregante* status for a European male Jew meant marginal seating in the synagogue. In 1750 Eurafrican members of the Pelengrino family were interred near the edges of the Jodensavanne cemetery. Their gravestones and corroborating information from the community archives provide evidence that by the mid-eighteenth century the two-class system of the community also prevailed in death.[16] At the Cassipora Creek cemetery, the location of the graves of Simha and Jacob, contemporaries of the Pelengrinos, suggests that Simha Cohen Nassy was Eurafrican and her husband Jacob Cohen Nassy a demoted *congregante*. Interestingly, two generations earlier, in 1700, Simha, wife of Abraham de Pina, was buried not at the edge of the Cassipora Creek cemetery but rather at its apparent centre. In contrast, at Hunt's Bay, no evidence has yet emerged to suggest that the community recognized a second class of Jews who were buried at the edges of the cemetery.

Burial registers and the mention of wooden markers, long since decomposed, confirm that there were many more burials than there are known gravestones at Suriname's Jewish cemeteries. Additionally, most of the names collected from epitaphs are not in the burial registers. Communal ordinances prohibited burying a body in a grave in which a body was already interred, which suggests that burial locations were not well recorded over the centuries and gravediggers sometimes encountered a corpse when digging a new grave. Another reason for the discrepancies is that some community members may not have merited mention in burial registers on account of their deeds or status. Notwithstanding the lack of corroboration from the burial registers and the probable existence of hundreds of unmarked graves, there is evidence of an orderly plan at the Cassipora Creek cemetery. In addition to spouses buried side by side and family plots, an overall pattern of rows is apparent, and within the rows burials are

[15] This term is first used in Aviva Ben-Ur, 'Still Life: Sephardi, Ashkenazi, and West African Art and Form in Suriname's Jewish Cemeteries', *American Jewish History*, 92/1 (Mar. 2004), 31–79.

[16] Aviva Ben-Ur, 'Peripheral Inclusion: Communal Belonging in Suriname's Sephardic Community', in Alexandra Cuffel and Brian Britt (eds.), *Religion, Gender, and Culture in the Pre-Modern World* (New York, 2007), 185–210.

somewhat chronological. The 1819 minutes of the meetings of the Gentlemen of the Mahamad and the Junta notes an initiative to record the names and rows of the individuals and families buried at the Cassipora Creek cemetery.[17] In addition to the arrangement of graves in rows, almost all the graves are orientated with the feet to the south-east. Exceptions are the graves of children, whose deaths would not have been anticipated, and so they are squeezed in any which way between their kin.

Four family names dominate the Cassipora Creek cemetery. The de Mezas are the most numerous. Fifty de Meza gravestones spanning the years from 1692 to 1873 cover the north-western ground of the cemetery. The da Costas are also strongly represented and include twenty-four gravestones, dating from 1692 to 1838, concentrated in the south-western area of the cemetery. The Uziel de Avilars' twelve gravestones date from between 1689 and 1782 and are close to the cemetery's oldest gravestones, which date from the 1660s. The Cohen Nassy name is found on thirty gravestones in four areas of the cemetery.

In 1788 the author of *Essai historique sur la colonie de Surinam* explained that Cassipora Creek cemetery was the old cemetery of the community, used for the interment of old families.[18] Indeed, Jodensavanne cemetery was earmarked for the burial of new families and now contains 462 gravestones, more than twice the number found at Cassipora Creek. Among Jodensavanne's sepulchres there are only one or two de Mezas, da Costas, or Uziel de Avilars. Cohen Nassy gravestones, while not as numerous in the Jodensavanne cemetery as they are in Cassipora, include twelve from 1740 to 1803. At the Jodensavanne cemetery Arria, de la Parra, and Robles de Medina are the predominant family names, but, in contrast to the Cassipora Creek cemetery, there is little evidence of family plots. Rather, there is a chronological burial sequence from one end of the cemetery to the other.

Hunt's Bay cemetery in Jamaica resembles its contemporary at Cassipora Creek. In both, almost all the graves are arranged with the feet pointing to the south-east. Also, as in the Cassipora Creek and Jodensavanne cemeteries, Hunt's Bay adheres to a pattern of rows. Hunt's Bay cemetery diverges from Cassipora Creek and looks more like Jodensavanne in its chronological layout and relative absence of family plots.

At Jodensavanne, the first generation of burials have their feet to the south-east as at Cassipora Creek and Hunt's Bay. However, some of the second generation of burials have their feet to the north-east, and by the mid-eighteenth century the north-east orientation dominates.

Two main customs exist in Judaism regarding burial orientation: one is with the feet towards the gates of the cemetery, the other is with the feet towards the Land of Israel. Both indicate a belief in resurrection. However, orientation towards the Land

---

[17] Ben-Ur with Frankel, *Remnant Stones*, vol. ii: *The Jewish Cemeteries and Synagogues of Suriname: Essays* (Cincinnati, 2012), 55 n. 43.   [18] *Historical Essay on the Colony of Surinam*, 1788, 30.

of Israel reflects a belief in the primacy of the Land.[19] The south-east orientation of burials at Hunt's Bay, Cassipora Creek, and Jodensavanne is not in the direction of Israel, and no gates or fences remain at any of the three cemeteries, so we cannot be sure if the burials were orientated towards the gates. No records survive to explain the design intent of the cemeteries. One can only speculate on the criteria of site selection and the reasons for burial orientation and organizational structure. Nonetheless, by envisioning the procession of the corpse and mourners to the cemetery, an understanding of the design and site planning of the cemeteries begins to unfold.

In Suriname, the deceased were taken along the Suriname River from riverside plantations and from Paramaribo to the Cassipora Creek and Jodensavanne cemeteries. From the eastern banks of the Suriname River, bodies would have been carried east to either cemetery. On its way to the Cassipora Creek cemetery, the procession probably passed the community's first modest wooden synagogue; on its way to the Jodensavanne cemetery, it would have passed Beraha Vesalom Synagogue. Gates on the south-east side of either cemetery would have been farthest from the river. However, it is possible that on the south-east side of each cemetery, the side farthest from each of the synagogues, existed a House of Circlings and, adjacent to the House of Circlings, the cemetery gate.

Natural disasters, such as the 1692 earthquake, and man-made landfill and development have reconfigured the harbour and shoreline adjacent to the Hunt's Bay cemetery. Nonetheless it is known that funeral processions from Port Royal crossed the harbour and approached the mainland cemetery grounds from the south and it is possible that a landing dock and cemetery gate existed on the south-east side of the cemetery, and that the feet of those buried there pointed towards this.

Whether burial orientation at Hunt's Bay and in early Suriname is with the feet pointing towards the cemetery gate or not, it is undeniable that in the Cassipora Creek and Hunt's Bay cemeteries, the colonies' first and most ancient burial grounds, graves are oriented to the south-east with feet pointing in the direction of something other than the Land of Israel: seemingly something of the Jews' own creation in their plantation setting or port town milieu. Interestingly by the early 1700s, burial orientation at the Jodensavanne cemetery began to shift from the established south-east orientation to a north-east one, presumably towards the Land of Israel. What caused the change of burial orientation? An increased belief in the primacy of the Land of Israel? And why does the change in burial orientation not occur at Cassipora Creek? Did Cassipora Creek's status as the first cemetery of the colony mean its layout had to be preserved whereas that of the second cemetery at Jodensavanne did not? Unfortunately, Hunt's Bay's successors, the Jewish cemeteries of Kingston and Spanish Town, no longer exist, and nothing is known of the orientation of their graves.

[19]   Adam Mintz, email to Rachel Frankel (29 Dec. 2009). See *Pitḥei teshuvah* 262: 2; *Gesher haḥayim*.

Documentation and analysis of Suriname's and Jamaica's cemeteries beg comparison with contemporary cemeteries in other places in the New World, such as Curaçao and Barbados. New technologies are needed to learn more about extant cemeteries and those of which little remains.[20] Nonetheless the historic cemeteries of the New World, while not necessarily well preserved, whole, or undisturbed, testify to the importation of antecedents from the Old World; yet, more interestingly, they suggest that the Caribbean enabled and inspired its port and plantation Jews to create something new. The cemeteries of Suriname and Jamaica are expressive of the ideals and status of Jews residing in an environment full of possibility: places that were fervently religious yet distant from rabbinical authority. The cemeteries also show that, among these settlers, a radical altering of kinship relationships and tolerance of mercurial and marginal identities existed.

[20] To remedy this problem, the International Survey of Jewish Monuments (<www.isjm.org>) announced the creation of a regional inventory and assessment of Jewish sites in the Caribbean on the occasion of the 'Jewish Diaspora of the Caribbean' international conference, at which an earlier version of this chapter was presented.

CHAPTER NINE

COUNTING THE 'SACRED LIGHTS OF ISRAEL'

Synagogue Construction and Architecture in the British Caribbean

BARRY L. STIEFEL

IN 1688 DANIEL LEVI DE BARRIOS (1635–1701) gave in verse one of the earliest known surveys of Jews in the English empire:

Now, in six English cities, are known six sacred lights of Israel: three in Nevis, London, Jamaica; the fourth and fifth in two parts of Barbados; [and] the sixth is verified in Madras Patân.[1]

De Barrios's concise survey testifies to the remarkably broad geographical distribution of Jews in the English-speaking world during the late seventeenth century. His survey is extraordinarily global in its perspective, with the Caribbean, not the British Isles, as the central representation of English Jewry. The synagogues of the Caribbean are a rich historical resource, which can offer new perspectives on British Jewry. Synagogues, as physical structures of cultural heritage, can serve as an indicator of the place of Jews within society at large. Such analysis raises questions about the socio-political and economic influences on the Jewish communities in the English Caribbean compared to those in Great Britain. For instance, what informed the planning and architectural design of synagogues in the British empire during the colonial period? Did architectural influence come from Jews, non-Jews, or the environment? Did the mercantile wealth of the Jewish communities have an impact upon the construction of synagogues and their architectural evolution? If so, how? How did the distribution of English (and later British) synagogues compare with those in other Atlantic empires tolerant to Jews, such as the Dutch, the Danish, and (to a lesser extent) the French? I take as my starting point an observation made by Cardozo de Bethencourt in 1925: 'I don't think this extract

---

[1] 'Ya, en seis ciudades anglas, se publica luz de seis juntas de Israël sagradas: tres en Nieves, London, Iamaica; Quarta y quinta en does partes de Barbadas; Sexta en Madras Patân se vérifica' (Daniel Levi de Barrios, *Historia real de Gran Bretaña* (Amsterdam, 1688); quoted in Cardoza de Bethencourt, 'Notes on the Spanish and Portuguese Jews in the United States, Guiana, and the Dutch and British West Indies during the Seventeenth and Eighteenth Centuries', *American Jewish Historical Society Journal*, 29 (1925), 38; my translation).

[de Barrios's poem] has been sufficiently considered by historians.'[2] In the tradition of de Barrios, I will address this lacuna by means of a survey.[3]

Distinct parameters are a necessity for a methodologically sound survey. First, the 'sacred lights of Israel' in this study will be the synagogues, in contrast to de Barrios's focus on congregations. In fact, de Barrios did not compile a comprehensive register of congregations for English Jewry. There were congregations, such as the one in Dublin, Ireland, founded around 1660, which disbanded before building a synagogue and whose name has been forgotten. Others, such as Shearith Israel of New York, did not erect its first synagogue until well after 1688.[4]

Second, the buildings to be included in this study are those intentionally built as houses of worship. Makeshift accommodations where a *minyan* (a group of ten Jewish males over the age of 13) gathered in a pre-existing building modified for the purpose of communal worship are excluded. My emphasis will be on Jewish houses of worship 'purpose-built' as synagogues. Synagogues found within the colonies built by 'indigenous Jews', such as those in India, are also excluded since these Jewish communities were very different in historical and cultural background from English Jewry.[5]

The years between 1701 and 1783 were significant in the construction of synagogues in England and the British empire. The era began with the completion of Bevis Marks Synagogue in London and concluded with the fracturing of the first British empire by the Treaty of Paris at the end of the American War of Independence. The year 1783 separates the first imperial period (1583–1783) from the second (1784–1914), when Jewish life and synagogue architecture became very different. During the second imperial period, improvements in construction and engineering and a larger population from which to gather resources allowed synagogue designers to produce substantially larger edifices. British Jewry had also become predominantly Ashkenazi and so did its synagogues.

---

[2] De Bethencourt, 'Notes on the Spanish and Portuguese Jews', 38.

[3] The model for this survey is Sharman Kadish, *Jewish Heritage in England: An Architectural Guide* (Swindon, Wilts., 2006). Kadish's monumental work marked the 350th anniversary of Jewish settlement in England. Her study is not only local in scope but also focused on Ashkenazim, the current majority of English Jewry.

[4] Shearith Israel congregation built its first synagogue in 1730 (Jonathan D. Sarna, *American Judaism: A History* (New Haven, 2004), 11–12; Louis Hyman, *The Jews of Ireland, from Earliest Times to the Year 1910* (Shannon, 1972), 13).

[5] The synagogue in the colony of Madras Patân was included in de Barrios's survey since Jewish colonists from England built it. However, Madras Patân was not the only settlement in India with Jews. Judaism in India is ancient and the Madras synagogue of 1695 was hardly the first. The oldest synagogue within the (British) Commonwealth of Nations today is the Paradesi Synagogue in Cochin. First constructed in 1568, it was rebuilt in the 1660s after the Portuguese vandalized it when they withdrew from the invading Dutch. Not until 1795, in response to Napoleon Bonaparte's invasion of the Netherlands, did Cochin and the Malabar Coast become part of the British empire (see Nathan Katz and Ellen S. Goldberg, *The Last Jews of Cochin: Jewish Identity in Hindu India* (Columbia, SC, 1993)).

The First Post-Readmission Synagogues in the English Commonwealth

As a result of the Edict of Expulsion promulgated by King Edward I (1239–1307) in 1290, England was officially devoid of Jews from the end of the thirteenth century. Following a conference held at Whitehall in December 1655, presided over by Oliver Cromwell (1599–1658), the Lord Protector unilaterally decided to stop enforcing the edict. After his restoration to the throne in 1664, Charles II (1630–85) continued Cromwell's policy of permitting Jews to settle in England. This permission was reiterated in another declaration in 1674 that officially granted Jewish residents the privilege to assemble for worship. Nonetheless, the precarious position of Jews in English society was not resolved until the ascent of King William III (1650–1702) and Queen Mary II (1662–94), when Parliament passed the Toleration Act of 1689. The Blasphemy Act of 1698, making it illegal to openly deny the Christian Trinity, served to reinforce the Jews' sense of security since it included a clause specifically exempting them from the legal penalties.[6]

It is believed that, in response to these legal developments, London's Jews conducted services in a small building in or around Aldgate during the 1660s. This place of gathering, of which very little is known, may have been used clandestinely before 1655 by the city's crypto-Jews.[7] Nonetheless, this site and the one that succeeded it on Creechurch Lane (c.1674) may represent English versions of the secret houses of worship found in the Netherlands, known as *schuilkerken*, a possibility suggested by the close economic and ethnic ties between the Jews of the two empires.[8] England also had its own type of clandestine houses of worship that emerged during the religious upheavals of the English Reformation.[9] These locations became official places of Jewish worship when King Charles II made his decrees granting privileges to the Jews in 1664 and 1674. In both instances the 'synagogues' were rented, with the landlord of the Creechurch Lane property being the local parish of the Anglican Church. Internal rifts became visible within London's Jewish community after the Toleration Act of 1689, when the Ashkenazim left the Sephardi Sha'ar Hashamayim to form their own congregation

---

[6] Jacob Rader Marcus, *The Colonial American Jew, 1492–1776*, 3 vols. (Detroit, 1970), i. 500; M. Wilensky, 'The Royalist Position Concerning the Readmission of Jews to England', *Jewish Quarterly Review*, NS 41 (Apr. 1951), 397–409.

[7] See Wilfred S. Samuel, *The First London Synagogue of the Resettlement* (London, 1924); Todd M. Endelman, *The Jews of Britain, 1656 to 2000* (Berkeley, Calif., 2002).

[8] *Schuilkerken* were popular from the late fifteenth to the early nineteenth centuries. Besides Jews, Protestants and Catholics also used them depending on their location and the prevailing political attitude towards the minority religions.

[9] See Thomas M. McCoog, *The Reckoned Expense: Edmund Campion and the Early English Jesuits. Essays in Celebration of the First Centenary of Campion Hall, Oxford (1896–1996)* (Woodbridge, Suff., 1996).

called the Great Synagogue. In 1692 members of the Great Synagogue began renting
their own quarters in an area of London called Duke's Place.[10]

Not until 1699 did Sha'ar Hashamayim congregation begin work on its first
purpose-built synagogue, located at the edge of the City on an inconspicuous plot off
an alley called Bevis Marks. The structure took two years to complete. The congregation had to rent the land on which the synagogue was erected since Jews were considered aliens and forbidden to own land.[11] The synagogue's out-of-the-way location was
ideal for both the Jews and the Anglican authorities, who initially wanted the edifice
to attract as little attention as possible. This project appears to have begun shortly after
the promulgation of the Blasphemy Act of 1698.[12] At this time, Jews were categorized
as one of several tolerated 'dissenting' groups in England, which also included Congre-
gationalists, Puritans, and Quakers.

Sha'ar Hashamayim congregation contracted master builder Joseph Avis, assisted by the joiner Henry Ramsay, to construct what would be England's first post-
readmission synagogue.[13] Avis was a Quaker—thus a fellow dissenter—and therefore
more approachable than an Anglican. Before the Jews recruited him, he had worked
under the architect Robert Hooke (1635–1703), a close associate of the great English
architect Christopher Wren (1632–1723). All three had participated in rebuilding London after the Great Fire of 1666. Their projects included such monumental works as
St Paul's Cathedral and the Royal Observatory at Greenwich, which profoundly influenced the development of English architecture, religion, and science during the
eighteenth century.[14] Joseph Avis is also said to have worked on St Bride's Church in
Fleet Street, which was designed personally by Wren.

Besides Christopher Wren and Robert Hooke, England's other renowned architects of the time included Nicholas Hawksmoor (1661–1736) and John Vanbrugh (1664–
1726);[15] however, they would all have been out of reach economically and socially for
Jews. The anticipated synagogue was too small and its constituents too insignificant to

---

[10]   David S. Katz, *The Jews in the History of England, 1485–1850* (Oxford, 1994), 182–3.

[11]   Sharman Kadish, *Bevis Marks Synagogue, 1701–2001* (London, 2001), 1–5.

[12]   The Blasphemy Act of 1698 declared 'that if any person, educated in or having made profession of the
Christian religion, should by writing, preaching, teaching or advised speaking, deny that the members of the
Holy Trinity were God . . . [for the first offence, he shall] be rendered incapable of holding any office or place
of trust, and for the second incapable of bringing any action, of being guardian or executor, or of taking a
legacy or deed of gift, and should suffer three years imprisonment without bail'. Special provisions were made
for Jews and other minority Protestant groups regarding their civil status in English society, relegating them to
second-class status below Anglicans (see H. S. Q. Henriques, 'The Jews and the English Law, II', *Jewish
Quarterly Review*, 13 (1901), 275–95).   [13]   See Kadish, *Bevis Marks Synagogue*, 1–5.

[14]   Henry William Robinson, 'Robert Hooke as a Surveyor and Architect', *Notes and Records of the Royal
Society of London*, 6/1 (Dec. 1948), 48–55.

[15]   See Bruce Allsopp and Ursula Clark, *English Architecture: An Introduction to the Architectural History of
England from the Bronze Age to the Present Day* (Stocksfield, Northumb., 1979).

warrant the attention of these giants in architecture, and they would probably have charged more than the congregation could afford. The experience, social stature, and fees of Joseph Avis, however, were an excellent fit. Avis's religious background is mani-fest in Bevis Marks's design, which is similar to other dissenting meetinghouses (in England and its colonies only an Anglican house of worship could be called a 'church' at this time). Because of the 'dissenters' second-class status, the architectural orna-mentation (if any) on the exterior of meetinghouses could not visually compete with Anglican churches.[16] Sha'ar Hashamayim's close relationship with Amsterdam Jewry is also apparent in the design elements borrowed from Amsterdam's Portuguese Syn-agogue, especially its interior furnishings and floor plan.[17] The design of England's first post-readmission synagogue can be seen as a product of the position and expecta-tions of its congregation in keeping with its status as a tolerated dissenting minority (see Figure 9.1).

Looking beyond Great Britain's shores at the time of Bevis Marks's completion in 1701, we find that this synagogue was not the only Jewish house of worship in the realm. As in England, crypto-Jews had trickled into the colony of Barbados and are believed to have settled there as early as the late 1620s.[18] In 1654 Jewish settlement in Barbados swelled following the Portuguese reconquest of Dutch Brazil, and Nidhe Israel con-gregation was formally established around 1656. Jews are identified in the historical record on the island before Cromwell permitted their readmission in December 1655. Almost a full year before the Whitehall Conference, the Barbados Assembly declared:

On the petition of several Jews, it is ordered that, behaving themselves civilly and doing nothing to disturb the peace, they shall enjoy the privileges and laws of the Island relating to foreigners and strangers.[19]

Cromwell also specifically permitted two Jews, Abraham and Raphael de Mercado, to settle on Barbados in April 1655, eight months before his decision on the rest of the English empire.[20] Like London's Sha'ar Hashamayim, Nidhe Israel may also have been

---

[16] See Anne C. Loveland and Otis B. Wheeler, *From Meetinghouse to Megachurch: A Material and Cultural History* (Columbia, Mo., 2003).

[17] Harold A. Meek, *The Synagogue* (New York, 2003), 146–7; for an in-depth description of the architectural history of the Bevis Marks and Portuguese synagogues, see Barry L. Stiefel, *Jewish Sanctuary in the Atlantic World: A Social and Architectural History* (Columbia, SC, 2013).

[18] Unlike Spanish Jamaica, where crypto-Jews are believed to have resided prior to the English conquest in 1655. When the English began colonizing Barbados in 1625, they found the island uninhabited (Kenneth R. Andrews, *Trade, Plunder, and Settlement: Maritime Enterprise and the Genesis of the British Empire, 1480–1630* (Cambridge, 1984), 301–2).

[19] J. Graham Cruickshank, 'Mention of the Jews in the Records of Barbados', in N. Darnell Davis, 'Notes on the History of the Jews in Barbados', *Publications of the American Jewish Historical Society*, 18 (1909), 146.

[20] Menasseh ben Israel and Lucien Wolf, *Menasseh ben Israel's Mission to Oliver Cromwell: Being a reprint of the pamphlets published by Menasseh ben Israel to promote the re-admission of the Jews to England, 1649–1656* (London, 1901), pp. xxxvi–xxxvii.

Figure 9.1 Front elevation of Bevis Marks Synagogue, London (built 1701)

Photo: Kathy Stiefel and Gilbert Stiefel; personal collection of Barry Stiefel

a continuation of a clandestine society of crypto-Jews, though how discreet they were during the years preceding 1655 is a matter of debate. For a good part of the English Civil War (1642–51), colonial Barbados trod a fine line of neutrality between the Parliamentarians and the Royalists. Refugees from the conflict sought asylum on the island. Neutrality allowed the colony to maintain a degree of political and economic autonomy and to admit Jews without consent from London. Trade with Dutch ships and merchants, which included Sephardi Jews, strengthened Barbados's independence.[21] Through these social and economic ties, seventeenth-century Barbadian Jewry established a closer relationship with the Jews of Amsterdam and the Dutch empire than with London. In fact, Amsterdam provided the island's first Torah scrolls in 1657 along with its first rabbi, Eliahu Lopez (b. 1648) in 1679.[22]

[21] Carla Gardina Pestana, *The English Atlantic in an Age of Revolution, 1640–1661* (Cambridge, Mass., 2004), 37.

[22] Yda Schreuder, 'A True Global Community: Sephardic Jews, the Sugar Trade, and Barbados in the Seventeenth Century', *Journal of the Barbados Museum and Historical Society*, 50 (2004), 166–94; Mordechai Arbell, *The Jewish Nation of the Caribbean: The Spanish-Portuguese Jewish Settlements in the Caribbean and the Guianas* (Jerusalem, 2002), 210.

Exactly when Nidhe Israel built its first house of worship is unknown. The earliest account is a surveyor's record from 1664, mentioning a synagogue already in existence in Bridgetown.[23] It was destroyed by a hurricane in 1831, and the only known surviving image of the building is in the background of a painting called *Governor Robinson Going to Church* depicting Bridgetown in about 1740 (see Figure 9.2). The island's two extant buildings from the 1650s, St Nicholas's Abbey and Drax Hall, are examples of structures built by Barbados's upper class and do not necessarily reflect the condition of Barbadian Jewry at the time. Based on the few surviving buildings and portraits of the period, however, it can be surmised that the synagogue used vernacular architectural elements of the late medieval English or Jacobean styles.[24]

In the mid-seventeenth century, Barbados's economy boomed with the expansion of sugar-cane cultivation. Other experimental crops, such as tobacco, cotton, ginger, and indigo, had all been economic failures. As sugar cane emerged as the sole cash crop, planters preferred to import African slaves as a labour force rather than use indentured servants. Jewish refugees from Dutch Brazil, which was now under Portuguese control, came to Barbados with much-needed experience in the sugar-cane trade. The Jews, in turn, were eager to continue the lifestyle they had known in Brazil.[25] By 1660 the Brazilian refugees made up a significant percentage of Barbadian Jewry. One thing they had been accustomed to in their former home was a synagogue. Indeed, Dutch Brazil had had two synagogue buildings, Tsur Israel, built in 1640, and Magen Abraham, built in 1648. At this time, Swan Street, nicknamed Jew Street, was both the Jewish neighbourhood in Bridgetown and a commercial centre for the colony as a whole. In the mid-seventeenth century rentable building stock in the colonies was in relatively short supply; however, land and materials tended to be cheaper. In England the situation was reversed. These factors caused many second sons of England's aristocracy, who did not stand to inherit property, to seek their fortune in the New World. The colonies, in need of entrepreneurs, also attracted itinerant Jews who sought a place to settle down and pursue economic advancement.[26]

---

[23] Arbell, *The Jewish Nation of the Caribbean*, 191–2, 198, 210; Wilfred S. Samuel. 'A Review of the Jewish Colonists in Barbados in the Year 1680', *The Jewish Historical Society of England Transactions*, 13 (1932–5), 95.

[24] On Barbadian architectural history, see David Button and Keith Miller, *Architecture and Design in Barbados* (Edgehill, St Thomas, 2001). Karl Watson, a professor of history at the University of the West Indies, conducted research on Nidhe Israel in 2008–10 (Karl Watson, email to Barry L. Stiefel (26 Mar. 2010)). See also Therese Hadchity, *'Of Bridges, Berths, and Hawkers': Paintings of Bridgetown from the National Art Collection of Barbados, the Barbados Gallery of Art and the Barbados Museum and Historical Society at the Zemicon Gallery* (Barbados, 2003).

[25] Pieter Emmer, 'The Jewish Moment and the Two Expansion Systems in the Atlantic, 1580–1650', in Paolo Bernardini and Norman Fiering (eds.), *The Jews and the Expansion of Europe to the West, 1450–1800* (New York, 2001), 501–18; David Eltis, 'The Total Product of Barbados, 1664–1701', *Journal of Economic History*, 55/2 (June 1995), 321–38.

[26] For a detailed case study of Daniel Lascelles (1714–84), second son of Henry Lascelles (1690–1753), see Simon David Smith, *Slavery, Family, and Gentry Capitalism in the British Atlantic: The World of the Lascelles, 1648–*

Figure 9.2 Detail of *Governor Robinson Going to Church*, showing the city of Bridgetown, Barbados. In the centre is what is believed to be Nidhe Israel Synagogue. Unknown artist, *c.*1740

Courtesy of the Barbados Museum and Historical Society Collection

Clearing for sugar-cane plantations and new construction had depleted Barbados's forests, and timber was already being imported from other islands, such as Tobago.[27] Stone and brick were readily available locally and were also imported as ballast on ships from Europe. The identity of the synagogue's builder has long been forgotten. Indeed, no renowned architects are recorded as practising in Barbados during the seventeenth century. Like many of the buildings on the island, Nidhe Israel Synagogue would have used a vernacular architectural vocabulary; however, architectural pattern books may have also been consulted for its design.[28] Archaeological excavations on Nidhe Israel's grounds have unearthed iron nails, implying the use of wood. Fragments of slate roof tile, brick, and window glass dating from the mid 1600s were also found. While it has not been established that these fragments are from the synagogue, they are at least from contemporary buildings in the vicinity. Typically, synagogues use the same

1834 (Cambridge, 2006); see also David Cesarani, *Port Jews: Jewish Communities in Cosmopolitan Maritime Trading Centres, 1550–1950* (London, 2002).

[27] See William Beinart and Lotte Hughes, *Environment and Empire* (Oxford, 2007).

[28] Frederick H. Smith and Karl Watson, 'Urbanity, Sociability, and Commercial Exchange in the Barbados Sugar Trade: A Comparative Colonial Archaeological Perspective on Bridgetown, Barbados in the Seventeenth Century', *International Journal of Historical Archaeology*, 13/1 (Mar. 2009), 63–79.

materials as neighbouring structures. It is likely that Nidhe Israel Synagogue was built of wood and brick, with a slate roof, and glass panes in its windows.[29]

Popular belief has it that the Nidhe Israel congregation built its first synagogue in 1654 or 1655.[30] This was probably not the case. Barbadian Jewry might have leased a building, or used a room in a private dwelling in 1655, or met earlier as a secret society like their co-religionists in London, but they probably did not erect an edifice until several years later. The reasons for this conjecture are many. In 1659 and 1668 fires ravaged Bridgetown, with as much as 80 per cent of the town being destroyed in the two conflagrations.[31] Indeed, it is plausible that the synagogue mentioned in the 1664 survey was not the one lost in 1831 but a later structure built in the same location.[32] Following the two fires, little remained of Bridgetown, and a building boom ensued shortly thereafter. Because Bridgetown's Jews lost their premises in one of the fires, they constructed a purpose-built synagogue shortly afterwards. This also coincided with the economic success of the nascent sugar-cane trade. While an even larger surge in construction was occurring in London as a consequence of its Great Fire of 1666, the neighbourhood where the Jews rented space for worship had been spared the devastation. Hence London Jewry had no need for a new sanctuary and continued to lease the facility they were already in.[33]

The logic of the situation indicates that the probable construction date of the first synagogue in Bridgetown was the 1660s or 1670s. As mentioned previously, the first re-corded Torah scrolls on the island were brought from Amsterdam in 1657. According to Jewish tradition obtaining a Torah scroll takes priority over erecting a synagogue. It is also easier to accomplish. Establishment of a cemetery and a *mikveh* also supersede construction of a house of worship. The oldest Jewish tombstone on Barbados dates from 1658. While this does not necessarily indicate when the cemetery was created, acquiring a Torah scroll, a cemetery, and constructing a synagogue by 1658 would have been a Herculean task for a Jewish community established less than four years earlier. Considering that the cemetery and the synagogue are on the same plot of land, it is likely that land for both was acquired at the same time, possibly around 1656. Archae-ological excavations have revealed that the *mikveh* at Nidhe Israel was probably built at

---

[29] Derek Miller, 'Report for the Synagogue Pathway Project (Site 1 BM 4), Bridgetown, Barbados' (unpublished archaeological report, College of William and Mary, 2010).

[30] e.g. Christina P. Colón et al., *Frommer's Caribbean, 2010* (Hoboken, 2009), 144, a traveller's guide for tourists in the Caribbean states that the first synagogue on the site was built in 1654. This is also reiterated in publications like Karl Watson, 'The Iconography of Tombstones in the Jewish Graveyard, Bridgetown, Barbados', *Journal of the Barbados Museum and Historical Society*, 50 (2004), 196.

[31] Smith and Watson, 'Urbanity, Sociability, and Commercial Exchange in the Barbados Sugar Trade'.

[32] For a similar set of circumstances at Beracha Veshalom Vegemiluth Hasadim, St Thomas at the end of the eighteenth and the beginning of the nineteenth centuries, see Judah M. Cohen, *Through the Sands of Time: A History of the Jewish Community of St. Thomas, U.S. Virgin Island* (Hanover, NH, 2004); see also Eli Faber, *Jews, Slaves, and the Slave Trade: Setting the Record Straight* (New York, 1998), 91.

[33] Cecil Roth, *A History of the Jews in England* (Oxford, 1941), 174.

around the same time as the synagogue.[34] Unless hard evidence is found proving the
contrary, we can assume that Barbados's first purpose-built synagogue was erected
after the Torah scrolls had been obtained, the cemetery founded, and a *mikveh* planned.

Although fires again devastated parts of Bridgetown in 1756, 1758, and 1766, research
has not uncovered any evidence of the building of, or significant repair to, a synagogue following these disasters. Archaeological excavations of the site suggest a mid-
to late seventeenth-century construction date since no burn layers were found in the
eighteenth-century deposits. Indeed, the synagogue's surroundings may offer clues as
to how the building escaped the fires. Unlike most synagogues built during this period,
Nidhe Israel has its associated cemetery located in close proximity and there was more
open space around it that was used as a common. A wall also enclosed the property.
This arrangement may have served as a firebreak, protecting the building. Indeed, in
1832, a year after Nidhe Israel was ruined by a hurricane, the predominantly Jewish
town of Jodensavanne in Dutch Suriname was almost completely destroyed by fire.
Located in the heart of the town, the brick synagogue from 1685, Beraha Vesalom,
survived. Surrounding the synagogue and acting as a firebreak was an enclosed courtyard. With their homes destroyed, the town's inhabitants moved back to the capital,
Paramaribo, abandoning the synagogue to the elements.[35]

While Barbadian Jewry was centred in Bridgetown, it was by no means confined to
it. So substantial was the settlement of Jews in Speightstown that a second synagogue,
Semah David, was built in the late seventeenth century. Again, due to lack of surviving
records little is known about the structure. Semah David was not a separate congregation from Nidhe Israel but merely a satellite facility to accommodate Jews residing
in Speightstown ten miles away—too far to walk on the sabbath. The arrangement
between Bridgetown's and Speightstown's Jews had parallels to the arrangement in
Dutch Brazil between Tsur Israel in the town of Recife and Magen Abraham in
Mauricia, and could be seen as another influence of the Brazilian refugees.[36]

Between the construction of the two synagogues on Barbados and London's Bevis
Marks, three additional synagogues came into existence in the English empire. Two
were built by the mid 1680s, one in Charlestown, Nevis, and the other in Port Royal,
Jamaica; however, as with Barbados, records with more specific information on these
synagogues are lacking.[37] Among the early Jewish colonists in Jamaica was one Jacob

[34] Miller, *Report for the Synagogue Pathway Project*.

[35] Het dorp Jodensavanne aan de Surinamrivier (The village Jodensavanne on the Suriname River),
Nationaal Archief Surinam, miscellaneous documents; Coenraad Liebrecht Temminck Groll, *De Architecture
Van Surinam, 1667–1930* (Zutphen, 1973), 90–8.

[36] In 1739 Semah David was destroyed by an antisemitic mob after a dispute between a Jew and a non-Jew
(see Eustace M. Shilstone, *Monumental Inscriptions in the Jewish Synagogue at Bridgetown, Barbados: With
Historical Notes from 1630* (London, 1988); Samuel Oppenheim, 'The Jews in Barbados in 1739. An Attack Upon
their Synagogue: Their Long Oath', *Publications of the American Jewish Historical Society*, 22 (1914), 197–8).

[37] Arbell, *The Jewish Nation of the Caribbean*, 224, 235; Peter Wiernik, *History of the Jews in America from the*

Jeosua Bueno Enriques. In 1661 Bueno Enriques petitioned King Charles II for permission to explore the island's copper deposits, promising the Crown a percentage of the profits. He also requested the king 'to naturalize myself and my brothers, Josef and Moise Enriques, so we can practise our [Jewish] law and have synagogues confirmed by Parliament'.[38] Based on this petition, it is possible that Bueno Enriques or one of his brothers was involved in the development of Port Royal's Jewish community and its first synagogue. Port Royal's synagogue, Neve Zedek, was destroyed in the earthquake of 1692, before the completion of Bevis Marks. Nevis's synagogue, whose congregational name has been forgotten, was lost in a hurricane that struck the island in 1772. For both Charleston and Port Royal no images or descriptions of the synagogues have been found; however, their economies and the circumstances of Jewish settlement in each of these locations paralleled Barbados. It can thus be surmised that the synagogues of Nevis and Jamaica developed in a like manner, with similarities in architectural design, size, and building materials.

Five out of six of de Barrios's 'sacred lights of Israel' have now been examined. The sixth, Madras Patân (*Madarasapatinam* in Tamil), was a settlement next to Fort St George, founded in 1639 by the East India Company. Here, the English established a beachhead on the Indian subcontinent for the purposes of trade and colonization. Despite the Edict of Expulsion banishing Jews from England and her territories between 1290 and 1655, English explorers did not hesitate to use the services of Jewish translators and businessmen abroad.[39] Commerce soon developed at Madras, attracting a small number of Jewish merchants to settle there by the 1680s. By 1700 Madras was a major centre for the diamond trade along with London and Amsterdam, a trade in which the Jews of all three localities were intensively involved. Madras's Jewish community was made up mainly of Dutch and English Sephardim, but the colony's location also attracted Jewish merchants from elsewhere, including Cochin and Baghdad. Nonetheless, there is no evidence of a synagogue in Madras before 1695, corresponding to a period of development in the town and nearly seven years after de Barrios wrote his poem about the six 'sacred lights of Israel'.[40]

Period of the Discovery of the New World to the Present Day (New York, 1914), 60; Michelle M. Terrell, *The Jewish Community of Early Colonial Nevis: A Historical Archaeological Study* (Gainesville, Fla., 2004), 48; Marilyn Delevante and Anthony Alberga, *The Island of One People: An Account of the History of the Jews of Jamaica* (Kingston, Jamaica, 2005), 65–75, all indicate that synagogues had been built in Charlestown and Port Royal prior to 1690; however, based on surviving documents surveyed no precise dates were found.

   [38] Jacob Jeosua Bueno Enriques to King Charles II (1661), facsimile, American Jewish Archives, Small Collections, SC-3232; my translation.

   [39] B. Lionel Abrahams, 'A Jew in the Services of the East India Company in 1601', *Jewish Quarterly Review*, 9 (1896), 173–5.

   [40] Walter J. Fischel, 'The Jewish Merchant-Colony in Madras (Fort St. George) during the 17th and 18th Centuries: A Contribution to the Economic and Social History of the Jews in India (Concluded)', *Journal of the*

Figure 9.3 Front elevation of Neve Shalom
Synagogue, Spanish Town, Jamaica (built
c.1704)

From the Library of the American Sephardi
Federation, with the assistance of the ASF staff,
courtesy of the United Congregation of Israelites,
Kingston, Jamaica

Synagogues of the British Empire, 1704–83

Approximately three years after Bevis Marks was completed the next synagogue in the British empire, Neve Shalom of Spanish Town, Jamaica was erected. Photographs of Neve Shalom from the early twentieth century show striking architectural similarities with Bevis Marks (see Figures 9.1, 9.3). Though the Jamaican synagogue was smaller, the similarities reveal the strong cultural, religious, and economic ties among British Jews in the Americas and Europe. With the development of Jamaica's sugar-cane economy, the island experienced a significant increase in both population, including Jews, and capital. After the completion of Neve Shalom, it was not long before Neve Zedek Synagogue, destroyed in the 1692 earthquake, was rebuilt in Port Royal. A congregation also emerged in Kingston, named Sha'ar Hashamayim after the Sephardi congregation in London. It is believed that two synagogues were built for this congregation: the first in the early eighteenth century and its larger successor between 1744 and 1750 (see Figure 9.4).[41]

Parallel synagogue development was taking place elsewhere in the British empire. In 1722 London's Ashkenazi Great Synagogue constructed its first building, funded by Moses Hart, one of the city's wealthiest Jews. This was followed four years later by another Ashkenazi synagogue in London, called the Hambro.[42] Thus from the 1730s

Economic and Social History of the Orient, 3/2 (Aug. 1960), 175–95. A new fort house, expanded fortifications, and the creation of Fort Square, among other projects, were undertaken in Madras between 1692 and 1711.

[41] Mordechai Arbell, *The Portuguese Jews of Jamaica* (Kingston, Jamaica, 2000), 29.
[42] Peter Renton, *The Lost Synagogues of London* (London, 2000), 30, 39.

Figure 9.4 Sha'ar Hashamayim Synagogue, Kingston, Jamaica. *Above*: the first building (early eighteenth century); *left*: the second synagogue (built 1744–50)

From the Library of the American Sephardi Federation, with the assistance of the ASF staff; courtesy of the United Congregation of Israelites, Kingston, Jamaica

to the 1750s the islands of Great Britain and Jamaica each hosted three purpose-built synagogues. However, two of the three synagogues in England were Ashkenazi whereas all three in Jamaica were Sephardi.

Compared to other British colonial synagogues, much more is known about the origins of New York's Shearith Israel of about 1730. Land for the synagogue was purchased in 1728 at a cost of £100, plus a loaf of sugar and a pound of Bohea tea. Luxury

Figure 9.5 Thumbnail sketch of Shearith Israel Synagogue (built *c*.1730), from David Grim, *A Plan of the City and Environs of New York* (New York, 1813)

William A. Rosenthall Judaica Collection, College of Charleston, Special Collections

goods such as sugar (most likely from the Caribbean), tea, and other commodities were often used as barter in an empire where liquid cash was in short supply. Shearith Israel congregation contracted Stanley Holmes, a local bricklayer, who obtained his free-manship in New York on 20 February 1728.[43] The synagogue is the only known building attributed to him. It appears in an 1813 illustration entitled *A Plan of the City and Environs of New York*, by cartographer David Grim (see Figure 9.5).[44] Significant in this illustration is the structure's vernacular architecture. It was approximately 35 feet square and 21 feet in height.[45] Given the sizes of Shearith Israel and Nidhe Israel, they may have been representative of smaller, colonial-era Jewish communities in the Americas, including the Dutch empire. The use of cash and barter to finance synagogue development; contracts with local, ordinary builders trained in carpentry or masonry; obtaining Torah scrolls, cantors, and substantial Jewish communal resources from the mother communities in Amsterdam and London perhaps attests to the modest socio-economic circumstances of these early congregations.

The year 1740 marks a watershed for Nonconformist Protestants and Jews in the British colonies. Designed to promote economic and territorial expansion, the Naturalization Act promised naturalization after seven years of residence. Before 1740 individual Jews had to petition the monarch, colonial government, or Parliament for some degree of citizenship, variously described as endenization, freemanship, or burgher's

[43] Jacques J. Lyons, Naphtali Phillips, and Mordechai M. Noah, 'Items Relating to the Newport Synagogue', *Lyons Collection 2, Publications of the American Jewish Historical Society*, 27 (1920), 194–5; New York Historical Society, *Collections of the New York Historical Society* (New York, 1886), 110.

[44] David Grim, *A Plan of the City and Environs of New York, 1813* (repr. New York, n.d.), College of Charleston Library, Special Collections, William A. Rosenthall Judaica Collection.

[45] Lyons, Phillips, and Noah, 'Items Relating to the Newport Synagogue', 194–5.

rights, depending on the location. This usually entailed a long, tedious, and expensive process, and the resulting rights were not necessarily recognized across the empire.[46] The Naturalization Act had a significant impact on synagogue development not only in the British colonies but also in Dutch possessions. The fact that Great Britain and its colonies were waxing in prosperity in contrast to the Netherlands and her colonies, also influenced the destinations that Jewish emigrants chose. Synagogues continued to proliferate in the British colonies as they had before;[47] however, their development in the Dutch Americas came almost to a halt. Between 1740 and 1783 only three syn-agogues were built in the Dutch colonies, whereas at least thirteen were constructed in the century before (compare Tables 9.1 and 9.2).[48]

British Jews in Europe were by no means confined to the British homeland. During the War of the Spanish Succession (1701–14), the British conquered Gibraltar in 1704, enabling Jews to return to a corner of the Iberian peninsula more than 200 years after their expulsion by Spain and Portugal. Under the British, Gibraltar grew as a centre of mercantile trade with Europe, Africa, and the Americas. In many ways its economy and society functioned more like a fortified Caribbean island with a commercial port strategically located for trade than a provincial town in continental Europe. In 1749 Rabbi Isaac Nieto of London founded Sha'ar Hashamayim congregation of Gibraltar, and a synagogue was built shortly thereafter. This synagogue was Iberia's first since the expulsions of 1492–8 and greatly perturbed the Spanish overlooking the British enclave. The structure was destroyed in 1766, and another was built two years later.[49]

Until the completion of Gibraltar's Sha'ar Hashamayim Synagogue in around 1749, synagogue construction had proceeded at a steady rate across the British empire. This changed after 1750. During the following decade no new synagogues were built, as building projects were hampered by the Seven Years War (1756–63). In the case of

[46] In 1753 Parliament passed the Jewish Naturalization Bill, which was intended to extend full natural-ization to the Jews of Great Britain and Ireland. However, due to widespread antisemitism the Bill was repealed several months later (Edward A. Hoyt, 'Naturalization Under the American Colonies: Signs of a New Community', *Political Science Quarterly*, 67/2 (June 1952), 248–66; Sheldon Godfrey and Judy Godfrey, *Search Out the Land: The Jews and the Growth of Equality in British Colonial America, 1740–1867* (Montreal, 1995), 54–6).

[47] By the mid-eighteenth century, Ashkenazim had become a numerical majority in North America and a significant minority in Jamaica, though the Ashkenazim continued to follow the established Sephardi *minhag* in the synagogues.

[48] The three Dutch colonial synagogues built after 1740 were Neve Shalom, Curaçao (1746); Darkhe Yesharim, Suriname (1779); and a congregation on St Maarten whose name has been lost (1783). The second Neve Shalom synagogue of Suriname, built between 1833 and 1835 (outside the period of this study), was the fourth after 1740.

[49] Isaac Nieto, son of R. David Nieto (1654–1728) of Bevis Marks, returned to London in 1751 to take over his father's position (Lionel D. Barnett, *Bevis Marks Records: Being Contributions to the History of the Spanish and Portuguese Congregation of London*, pt 1: *The Early History of the Congregation from the Beginning until 1800* (Oxford, 1940), 33; Lawrence A. Shawchuck and Doris Ann Herring, 'Historic Marriage Patterns in the Sephardim of Gibraltar, 1704 to 1939', *Jewish Social Studies*, 50/3–4 (1988–1993), 177–200).

Table 9.1 Synagogues in English colonies of the first imperial period (1583–1783)

Synagogue	Dates	Location	Notes
Nidhe Israel	1660s–1831	Bridgetown, Barbados	Destroyed by hurricane
Semah David	1660s/70s–1739	Speightstown, Barbados	Destroyed in pogrom
Neve Zedek (I)	c.1684–92	Port Royal, Jamaica	Destroyed by earthquake
Unknown	c.1684–1772	Charlestown, Nevis	Destroyed by hurricane
1688: Daniel Levi de Barrios wrote *Historia real de Gran Bretaña*			
Unknown	c.1695–	Madras, India	
Sha'ar Hashamayim/ Bevis Marks	1701–present	London, England	
Neve Shalom	1704–1907	Spanish Town, Jamaica	
Neve Zedek (II)	after 1704–1815	Port Royal, Jamaica	
Sha'ar Hashamayim (I)	after 1704–44	Kingston, Jamaica	
Great Synagogue / Duke's Place	1722–90	London, England	Ashkenazi; enlarged 1766
The Hambro	1726–1893	London, England	Ashkenazi
Shearith Israel	1730–1818	New York	
1740: British Naturalization Act			
Sha'ar Hashamayim (II)	c.1744–1882	Kingston, Jamaica	
Sha'ar Hashamayim (I)	1749–66	Gibraltar	Destroyed
Plymouth Synagogue	1762–present	Plymouth, England	Ashkenazi
Jeshuat Israel / Touro	1763–present	Newport, RI	
Exeter Synagogue	1763–present	Exeter, England	
Sha'ar Hashamayim (II)	1768–81	Gibraltar	Destroyed in a Spanish bombardment
Shearith Israel	1777–1824	Montreal, Quebec	
Sha'ar Hashamayim (III) / Great Synagogue	1781–present	Gibraltar	
Mikveh Israel	1782–1825	Philadelphia, Pa.	First synagogue built in the USA
Ets Haim	1783–present	Gibraltar	

Only Madras is listed from India as it is mentioned by de Barrios. All the synagogues followed the Sephardi tradition unless otherwise noted, even though several in the Americas had Ashkenazi majorities in their congregations.

Jeshuat Israel of Newport, Rhode Island, for example, construction of its (Touro) synagogue began in 1759, but completion was delayed until 1763 (see Figure 9.6).[50] Ply-

[50] Jeshuat Israel's synagogue did not acquire the name Touro until after 1822 (see US National Park Service, *Touro Synagogue National Historic Site*, 'Frequently Asked Questions' (2011), <http://www.nps.gov/tosy/faqs.htm>).

Table 9.2 Sephardi synagogues built in the Dutch empire before the Patriot Revolt of 1787–89

Synagogue	Dates	Location	Notes
Talmud Torah/Portuguese Synagogue (I)	1636–1931	Amsterdam, Netherlands	Used as the primary synagogue until 1675, then as an auxiliary building until 1931
Tsur Israel	1640–1900s	Recife, Brazil	Used as a synagogue until 1654
Magen Abraham	1648–53	Mauricia, Brazil	Satellite of Tsur Israel
Unknown	1661–7	Cayenne, (French) Guiana	
Unknown	1671–after 1685	Thorarica, Suriname	
Mikvé Israel (I)	1674–92	Willemstad, Curaçao	
Talmud Torah (II)/The Esnoga	1675–present	Amsterdam, Netherlands	
Beraha Vesalom	1685–after 1832	Jodensavanne, Suriname	
Mikvé Israel (II)	1692–1703	Willemstad, Curaçao	
Mikvé Israel (III)	1703–30	Willemstad, Curaçao	
Santa Irmandad	1710s–20	Tucacas, Venezuela	
Neve Shalom	1719–1835	Paramaribo, Suriname	Ashkenazi satellite of Beraha Vesalom
Neve Shalom	1720–1839	Maarssen, Netherlands	
Honen Dal / The Snoge	1726–present	The Hague, Netherlands	
Mikvé Israel (IV) / The Snoa	1732–present	Willemstad, Curaçao	
Sedek Vesalom	1735–present	Paramaribo, Suriname	Sephardi satellite of Beraha Vesalom
Honen Dalim	1739–after 1800	Oranjestad, St Eustatius	
Neve Shalom	1746–after 1864	Willemstad, Curaçao	Satellite of Mikvé Israel
Portuguese Synagogue	1759–1935	Naarden, Netherlands	
Darkhe Yesharim	1779–1800	Paramaribo, Suriname	Mulatto satellite of Beraha Vesalom
Unknown	1783–before 1828	Philipsburg, St Maarten	

All the synagogues followed the Sephardi tradition unless otherwise noted.

mouth Synagogue (1762) and Exeter Synagogue (1763), in England, were also completed towards the end of the war. These were the first two synagogues built in Great Britain outside London: the former being Ashkenazi and the latter Sephardi. In 1766, a renovation of London's Great Synagogue by architect George Dance the Elder was completed, providing more room for the growing congregation.[51] All four synagogues were built in the Georgian style, though only Newport, Plymouth, and Exeter are

[51] Renton, *The Lost Synagogues of London*, 32.

Figure 9.6 Front elevation of Jeshuat Israel's Touro Synagogue, Newport, RI (built 1759–63)
Photo: Lori H. Stiefel; personal collection of Barry Stiefel

extant. The replacement for Gibraltar's Sha'ar Hashamayim Synagogue was also completed in 1768.[52]

The architect for Jeshuat Israel's Touro Synagogue was Peter Harrison (1716–75). Like his contemporary Joseph Avis, Harrison was born into a Quaker family. In 1740 Harrison migrated from England to New England. In Rhode Island he became a successful merchant and converted to Anglicanism. As a merchant, Harrison's travels took him back to England from 1743 to 1745, where he studied architecture under Richard Boyle, third earl of Burlington (1694–1753). Lord Burlington was a gentleman scholar who developed an interest in architecture during a series of grand tours in the 1710s. He collected architectural drawings and publications by architects such as Inigo Jones (1573–1652) and Andrea Palladio (1508–80), and used them as inspirational resources for designing buildings in the Palladian style.[53] Harrison did the same, using

---

[52] See Barry L. Stiefel, 'Jeshuat Israel (Touro) Synagogue's Place within the British Empire Prior to 1776', *Rhode Island Jewish Historical Association: Notes*, 39 (2008), 191–207; see also Kadish, *Jewish Heritage in England*; Sharman Kadish, *Jewish Heritage in Gibraltar: An Architectural Guide* (Reading, Berks, 2007).

[53] 'Lord Burlington', *Architecture Week: Great Buildings Collection*, <http://www.greatbuildings.com/architects/Lord_Burlington.html>.

books by Inigo Jones, John Webb (1611–72), and James Gibbs (1682–1754).[54] Lord Burlington always worked with a building contractor as he was an artist of architecture and unskilled in engineering. Harrison practised architecture in the same way, deciding what the buildings should look like but needing someone else to make them work. For Touro Synagogue, Harrison worked with Joseph Hammond, the builder.[55]

With pattern books by Jones, Webb, and Gibbs available to part-time architects like Peter Harrison, the Georgian–Palladian style spread across the British empire. During this period there were no full-time professional architects in the British Americas, and those who practised architecture did so while pursuing other economic endeavours. Harrison's known accomplishments include the Redwood Library (1747–49) and Brick Market Building (1762–72) in Newport, Rhode Island; King's Chapel in Boston (1749); Christ Church in Cambridge, Massachusetts (1759–60); and Antigua's courthouse (1747–50).[56] While engaged primarily in trade, Harrison used his travels—such as to Massachusetts or the Caribbean—to pursue architectural projects. He worked simultaneously on projects in Newport, Boston, and Antigua, for example, and turned a profit at both commerce and construction. Unfortunately, the breadth of Harrison's architectural career is difficult to ascertain, especially outside New England. At the onset of the American War of Independence, Harrison sided with the Loyalists and his papers were destroyed by a mob of Patriots shortly after his death.[57]

Founded in 1768, Shearith Israel was the first non-Catholic congregation in Quebec, besides being the first Jewish one. The congregation followed the Sephardi *minhag* even though the majority of its members were Ashkenazim. During the American War of Independence, many Loyalist Jews displaced by the conflict sought asylum in Canada, swelling the congregation's numbers. In 1777–8 Montreal's Jews built their first synagogue, which was used until 1824.[58] Unfortunately, no known description or image of the edifice survives. The synagogue was, most likely, a modest vernacular building.

The American War of Independence also directly affected Gibraltar's Jews half a world away. Spain, a close ally of the religiously tolerant United States, launched a direct offensive on the British stronghold in Gibraltar (1779–83). Though nearly 300 years had passed since the Edict of Expulsion, Spain was still officially intent on keeping the Jews out of Iberia. The Gibraltar synagogue of 1768 was destroyed during a bombardment. It was replaced by a newer building in 1781–3. What is seen today is the result of a renovation in 1812 (see Figure 9.7). A new congregation, Ets Haim, built a second

---

[54] Nancy Halverson Schless, 'Peter Harrison, the Touro Synagogue, and the Wren City Church', *Winterthur Portfolio*, 8 (1973), 187–200; Carl Bridenbaugh, *Peter Harrison, First American Architect* (Chapel Hill, NC, 1949).

[55] Susan R. Slade, *Touro Synagogue, Congregation Jeshuat Israel*, Historic American Building Survey, No. RI–278 (Washington, DC, 1972); Marcus, *The Colonial American Jew*, ii. 684.

[56] Edward E. Crain, *Historic Architecture in the Caribbean Islands* (Gainesville, Fla., 1994), 162.

[57] See Bridenbaugh, *Peter Harrison, First American Architect*.

[58] Shearith Israel congregation minutes (1778–79), American Jewish Archives, Small Collections, SC-8355.

Figure 9.7 Front elevation of the Great
Synagogue, Gibraltar. The Hebrew year
5528 on the pediment corresponds with
1768—the date the previous synagogue
was completed

Drawing by Lori H. Stiefel

synagogue at this time. Before 1783 Ets Haim Synagogue apparently also functioned as a
yeshiva.[59] Both synagogues survive and are still in use.

In 1782 Philadelphia's Mikveh Israel congregation erected the first synagogue under
the Stars and Stripes. The edifice was designed and built by John Donohue, a carpenter,
and Edward McKegan, a bricklayer.[60] However, since it was built in the United States
and not Pennsylvania colony, this synagogue falls outside the purview of this study
(see Table 9.1).

Synagogues of Other Atlantic World Empires

Besides the British, the Dutch were the only Atlantic power to have had sufficient
Jewish participation in its empire to result in the development of synagogues. A small
number of Jews also lived in the Danish and French empires. The Dutch golden age of
the seventeenth and eighteenth centuries ushered in a renaissance of synagogue architecture in the Atlantic world. When the crypto-Jews of Amsterdam obtained permission from the Dutch authorities to practise Judaism in 1603, Jewish immigration to the
Netherlands rapidly increased.[61] The immigrants included Sephardim from Iberia and

[59] Kadish, *Jewish Heritage in Gibraltar*, 11–64.
[60] William Pencak, *Jews and Gentiles in Early America, 1654–1800* (Ann Arbor, Mich., 2005), 208, 212, 227, 263.
[61] See Gérard Nahon, 'The Portuguese Jewish Nation of Amsterdam as Reflected in the Memoirs of
Abraham Haim Lopes, 1752', in Chaya Brasz and Yosef Kaplan (eds.), *Dutch Jews as Perceived by Themselves and*

Ashkenazim from central and eastern Europe. By 1618 three Sephardi congregations existed in Amsterdam—Beth Jacob (founded 1604), Neve Shalom (founded 1608), and Beth Israel (founded 1618)—all using *schuilkerken* as houses of worship. In 1612 Neve Shalom congregation attempted to build a synagogue but the project failed because of opposition from the Dutch populace. Beth Israel congregation purchased a plot of land in 1632 for what became the city's first non-clandestine synagogue, constructed between 1636 and 1639. During these same years the three Sephardi congregations were unified into a single community called Talmud Torah, and the synagogue, called the Portuguese Synagogue, became its home.[62]

In contrast to the case in the English empire, the earliest Dutch synagogue was built in the mother country; however, construction in the colonies soon followed. Half a world away, the Dutch West India Company (WIC), with Jewish participation, was carving out an empire at the expense of the Spanish and Portuguese. By 1636 the Jews of Dutch Brazil had established Tsur Israel congregation, and they completed its synagogue by 1640. A *mikveh* and yeshiva were also built. Isaac Aboab da Fonseca (1605–93) travelled from Amsterdam to Brazil in 1642 to officiate at Tsur Israel, becoming the first rabbi in the New World. The community grew and a satellite building was constructed in 1648 at Mauricia, a settlement opposite the Capibaribe River from Recife, called Magen Abraham.[63] Though Dutch Brazil was lost to a Portuguese reinvasion in 1654, it set the precedent for organized Jewish life and synagogue development in the other colonies of the WIC, including Cayenne, Suriname, Curaçao, Tucacas, St Eustatius, and St Maarten (See Table 9.2).

As in English-controlled territories, Sephardi synagogues proliferated to a far greater extent in the Dutch colonies than in the Netherlands. Following the first Portuguese synagogue in Amsterdam, and its successor, the Esnoga, built in 1671–75 by architect Elias Bouman, only three more Sephardi synagogues were erected in the Netherlands before the Patriot Revolt of 1787–9, the defining event in late eighteenth-century Dutch history. These were Neve Shalom of Maarssen (1720); Honen Dal (or the Snoge) of The Hague (1726); and the Portuguese Synagogue of Naarden (1759). The other significant Dutch Sephardi communities, such as Rotterdam, Middleburg, and Nijkerk, had only developed *schuilkerken*.[64] In contrast, Ashkenazim, constituting the

by Others: Proceedings of the Eighth International Symposium on the History of the Jews in the Netherlands (Leiden, 2001), 59–78; Judith C. E. Belinfante, 'The Sephardis, the Jews of Spain', in Martine Stroo and Ernest Kupershoek (eds.), *The Esnoga: A Monument to Portuguese-Jewish Culture* (Amsterdam, 2001), 11–33.

[62]   David P. Cohen Paraira, 'A Jewel in the City: The Architectural History of the Portuguese-Jewish Synagogue', in Stroo and Kupershoek, *The Esnoga*, 41–68; Steven M. Nadler, *Rembrandt's Jews* (Chicago, 2003), 149.

[63]   Arnold Wiznitzer, 'The Synagogue and Cemetery of the Jewish Community of Recife, Brazil (1630–1654)', *American Jewish History*, 94 (1953), 129; Bruno Feitler, 'Jews and New Christians in Dutch Brazil, 1630–1654', in Richard L. Kagan and Philip D. Morgan (eds.), *Atlantic Diasporas: Jews, Conversos, and Crypto-Jews in the Age of Mercantilism, 1500–1800* (Baltimore, 2009), 123–52.

[64]   Organized Sephardi settlement took place in Amsterdam, The Hague, Rotterdam, Middleburg,

majority of Dutch Jewry, built scores of synagogues that dotted the towns and villages of the Netherlands. The Dutch Americas counted sixteen purpose-built synagogues, of which almost all were Sephardi. The exception was the Ashkenazi satellite building Neve Shalom of Sephardi congregation Beraha Vesalom in Suriname. With the exception of Curaçao's Mikvé Israel (the Snoa), the Sephardi synagogues of the Netherlands were often architecturally more substantial than those in the colonies.[65]

While not on the same scale as the British and Dutch, the Danes also permitted synagogue construction in their American colonies. From 1619 onwards King Christian IV (1577–1648) invited Sephardi Jews from Hamburg and Amsterdam to settle in Denmark. Ashkenazi Jews were also invited to Denmark from Germany. This marks the earliest record of Jewish settlement in the country. Christian IV's successor, King Frederick III (1609–70), formally opened Denmark to Jewish settlement in 1657. Jewish communities were established throughout the major commercial centres of Denmark, the most important being Copenhagen. The Danish Sephardi Jewish communities had strong social, economic, and religious ties to their brethren in England and the Netherlands where they originated. Congregations in Denmark during this early period, such as the one founded in 1684 in Copenhagen, used vernacular buildings that were conceptually similar to Dutch *schuilkerken*.[66] The first purpose-built synagogue in Denmark was the Great Synagogue in Copenhagen, completed in 1766.[67]

In 1671 the Danish West India Company established Denmark's first permanent Caribbean colony on the island of St Thomas. Jews from Denmark, as well as from the Dutch, British, and French empires, settled on St Thomas in the 1670s and 1680s. Colonies were also established on St John in 1717 and St Croix in 1733. While St John never had a significant Jewish presence, Jews settled in St Croix shortly after the Danes purchased the island from France. In 1764 they built a synagogue; however, it burned down two years later and was never replaced. Though its name is long forgotten, St Croix's synagogue was the first purpose-built synagogue under the Danish Crown, predating the Great Synagogue of Copenhagen by two years. The Jewish presence on St Thomas remained small until the eighteenth century, when the community grew large enough to build its first synagogue, Beracha Veshalom Vegemiluth Hasadim, in 1796. This building was lost in a fire in 1804.[68]

Maarssen, Nijkerk, and Naarden (Jonathan I. Israel, *The Dutch Republic: Its Rise, Greatness and Fall, 1477–1806* (Oxford, 1995), 1025. This was collated with the database at the Joods Historisch Museum, *Four Hundred Years of Dutch Jewry*, <http://www.jhm.nl/culture-and-history/the-netherlands>; see also Paraira, 'A Jewel in the City').

[65] See Israel, *The Dutch Republic*.

[66] Conrad Kisch, 'The Jewish Community in Denmark: History and Present Status', *Judaism*, 47 (1998), 214–31.

[67] Tatjana Lichtenstein, 'Jews in Denmark', in Melvin Ember, Carol R. Ember, and Ian A. Skoggard (eds.), *Encyclopedia of Diasporas* (New York, 2004), 935.

[68] Frederik C. Gjessing, 'National Historic Landmark Nomination: St. Thomas Synagogue', prepared for

Though the Code Noir officially expelled Jews in 1685, France had a short-lived Jewish presence in its American colonies before then. In the small Jewish communities of the French Caribbean colonies of Martinique, Guadeloupe, and Saint-Domingue, no synagogues have been identified.[69] Religious worship was most likely conducted in clandestine locations. Nonetheless, in what is now French Guiana there was an exception. In 1643 France made its first attempt at colonizing Cayenne, but abandoned it a few years later. The Dutch found the deserted settlement and commenced recolonization in 1656. Jews were invited to the colony, and a number of Sephardim from the Netherlands and Livorno settled in a newly constructed town called Remire. Around 1660 a synagogue was built in Remire. In 1664 the French returned to reclaim their colony and the Dutch surrendered Cayenne with little resistance. As part of the capitulation agreement it was stipulated that the Jews could continue the free exercise of their religion under the French regime.[70] French Guiana's Jews thus obtained official recognition fifty-nine years before their co-religionists in France, who were legally referred to as New Christians until 1723, though they were often open about their Judaism in *schuilkerk*-like synagogues.[71] In 1667 the Remire synagogue was destroyed when the English sacked the colony in the second Anglo-Dutch War.[72]

Conclusion

Using Daniel Levi de Barrios's metaphor of counting the 'sacred lights of Israel' we find that during the first British empire not only were synagogues more widespread in the colonies than in the mother country, but were concentrated in the Caribbean until the end of the Seven Years War. Following the war, English Jewry progressively shifted from an imperial diaspora, based in the Caribbean, to Great Britain, centred in London. New World congregational customs also reflected the changes in Jewish demographics of the British Isles, from chiefly Sephardi to primarily Ashkenazi. De Barrios's late seventeenth-century survey of English Jewry should cause contemporary scholars to reconsider the way the historiography of Jews is approached. The traditional method of studying American, English, and Caribbean Jewish histories independently of one

---

the US Department of the Interior, National Park Service, 1997; Cohen, *Through the Sands of Time*, 3, 28, 35; Arbell, *The Jewish Nation of the Caribbean*, 285.

[69] John D. Garrigus, '"New Christians," "New Whites," Sephardic Jews, Free People of Color and Citizenship in French Saint Domingue, 1760–1789', in Bernardini and Fiering (eds.), *The Jews and the Expansion of Europe to the West*, 314–27; Elliott Ashkenazi, *The Business of Jews in Louisiana, 1840–1875* (Tuscaloosa, 1988), 5.

[70] Arbell, *The Jewish Nation of the Caribbean*, 45–9.

[71] See Esther Benbassa, *The Jews of France: A History from Antiquity to the Present* (Princeton, 1999); see also Zosa Szajkowski, 'Population Problems of Marranos and Sephardim in France, from the 16th to the 20th Centuries', *Proceedings of the American Academy for Jewish Research*, 27 (1958), 83–105. The Ashkenazim in Alsace-Lorraine had received permission from the French Crown to remain and practise Judaism following the Thirty Years War (*c*.1648).   [72] Arbell, *The Jewish Nation of the Caribbean*, 45–9.

another is an artificial paradigm created by contemporary historians.[73] Nevis, Jamaica, Barbados, and India (Madras Patân) are four modern independent countries that did not exist when de Barrios's poem was composed in 1688.[74] Furthermore, North American congregations like New York's Shearith Israel and Rhode Island's Jeshuat Israel also considered themselves loyal subjects of the British monarch until 1776.

Expanding this analysis to include the Dutch Caribbean, we find a similar phenomenon. There were more Sephardi synagogues in the Dutch West Indies than in the Netherlands. As was the case in the British empire, the first synagogue in the Danish empire was in a Caribbean colony, not in Denmark. A similar dynamic typified the French empire as well. Prior to their official expulsion in 1685, Sephardim in the colony of French Guiana obtained greater recognition and privileges than their co-religionists in France. While, to some degree, England, the Netherlands, and Denmark were havens for Iberia's displaced Jews during the seventeenth and eighteenth centuries, it was primarily their overseas empires—most importantly their holdings in the Caribbean—that served as the cradle of western Sephardi synagogue development. Many of these first purpose-built synagogues were simple, vernacular, and quaint compared to those constructed in Europe and North America during the nineteenth century. Understanding the context in which these synagogues were built is essential for appreciating not only their architectural history but also the changing roles and status of early modern Jews.

[73] Examples include Delevante and Alberga, *The Island of One People*; Sarna, *American Judaism*; Terrell, *The Jewish Community of Early Colonial Nevis*; Gerald J. Tulchinsky, *Canada's Jews: A People's Journey* (Toronto, 2008); Todd M. Endelman, *The Jews of Georgian England, 1714–1830: Tradition and Change in a Liberal Society* (Philadelphia, 1979).   [74] Nevis is part of the Federation of St Christopher and Nevis.

ACKNOWLEDGEMENTS

I am very grateful to Derek Miller at the College of William and Mary for sharing with me his findings from the excavations at the Nidhe Israel Synagogue site in Bridgetown, Barbados. Michael Stoner and Karl Watson at the University of the West Indies, Cave Hill, Barbados, and Randy Belinfante at the Library of the American Sephardi Federation in New York also provided valuable research assistance. I am also indebted to Dale Rosengarten at the College of Charleston for her assistance at the Jewish Diaspora of the Caribbean Conference as well as her and Laura Moses's editorial assistance in preparing this article for publication. Finally, special thanks are in order to Jane Gerber and Stanley Mirvis at CUNY's Graduate Center, Ainsley Cohen Henriques, and the United Congregation of Israelites, Kingston, Jamaica for their excellent planning and execution of the conference on the Jewish Diaspora of the Caribbean, Jan. 2010.

PART IV

JEWS AND
SLAVE SOCIETY

THE CULTURAL HERITAGE OF EURAFRICAN SEPHARDI JEWS IN SURINAME

AVIVA BEN-UR

Introduction

Earlier scholars and researchers have argued that Caribbean Jewish society generally discouraged the conversion of people of African origins to Judaism and that the number of Eurafrican Jews, whether enslaved or free, was either nil or negligible.[1] However, ongoing archival research is steadily disproving these assertions for Suriname. Most recently, Natalie Zemon Davis has ascertained that the Surinamese physician, *philosophe*, and diplomat David Cohen Nassy (1747–1806) circumcised at least three of his mulatto slaves (Moses, Ishmael, and Isaac) and instructed them in the Jewish religion.[2] My own research shows that Nassy's infirm daughter Sara owned at least one Jewish slave, who appears in the records in 1790 as the manumitted mulattress Simha de Pina.[3] Judging from his last name, the mulatto Joseph de David Cohen Nassy, accused of convening an illegal Eurafrican Jewish prayer gathering that same year, may have been the illicit son of David Cohen Nassy.[4] Whether the senior Nassy's tendency to convert his slaves to Judaism was representative of Surinamese Jews in general or was symptomatic of local elite privilege remains to be explored. What may be said with certainty is

[1] Jonathan Schorsch, *Jews and Blacks in the Early Modern World* (Cambridge, 2004), 224; Nicolaas Hendrik Swellengrebel and Edwin van der Kuyp, *Health of White Settlers in Surinam* (Amsterdam, 1940), 31; *Surinaamsche almanak voor het jaar 1821* (Paramaribo, Suriname, 1821), 30.

[2] Natalie Zemon Davis, 'David Nassy's "Furlough" and the Slave Mattheus', in Pamela S. Nadell, Jonathan D. Sarna, and Jonathan Sussman (eds.), *New Essays in American Jewish History: To Commemorate the 60th Anniversary of the American Jewish Archives Journal and the 10th Anniversary of the American Jewish Archives under the Direction of Dr. Gary P. Zola* (New York, 2010), 85.

[3] Minuut-notulen van vergaderingen van de Senhores do Mahamad (Minutes of the Mahamad) (25 Aug. 1790), Nationaal Archief Nederland (NAN), Nederland–Portugees–Israëlitische Gemeente in Suriname (NPIGS) 3. This example and the one in n. 4 are extracted from a database of enslaved and manumitted Eurafrican Jews I am currently compiling based, at this stage of my research, on a exhaustive study of the Minutes of the Mahamad until 1863.

[4] Minuut-notulen van vergaderingen van de Senhores do Mahamad (21 Apr. 1790), NAN, NPIGS 2. Joseph de David Cohen Nassy may have been the husband of Pumba d'Avilar, who inherited and served as executor of his estate (Minuut-notulen van vergaderingen van de Senhores do Mahamad (17 Sept. 1790), NAN, NPIGS 3).

that many—and probably most—cases of conversion of slaves to Judaism remain buried in the archives. Most importantly, arguments that seek to minimize the size of Suriname's Eurafrican Jewish population disregard alternative forms of communal membership. The autonomy of Suriname's Jews and their unprecedented New World environment allowed for the development of conversion practices and communal inclusion that often defied halakhah.

This chapter explores the religious and cultural identities of a number of enslaved and manumitted Eurafrican Jews who lived in or on the fringes of Suriname's Jewish community. Once their existence and sometimes liminal status as Jews have been verified, we can begin to ask thematic, substantive questions. Why is it valuable to study this group? What can they tell us about the Jewish community that members of the mainstream Jewish community cannot? What can they tell us about other slaves and free people that members of these populations cannot? It is too early to answer these broad questions diachronically for the whole of Suriname's Eurafrican Jewish population. But some headway can be made by focusing on a few dozen Jewish Eurafricans who lived in the Dutch colony over the course of the eighteenth century. Appraising the religious and cultural heritage of Eurafrican Jews is a start to answering some of these questions.

Culture is an evanescent concept, here defined as the tastes, attitudes, and manners of a social group, transmitted through generations, and manifested in language, name-giving practices, religion, and ancestral consciousness. As free-floating as culture may be, its concrete components tie it down to meaningful and assessable data. Culture, so defined, is a useful concept for understanding identity.[5] A methodological parallel is found in Michael Gomez's treatment of ethnic identity among slaves of the southern USA. In his attempt to identify Muslim (or Muslim-influenced) slaves in North America, Gomez applied similar criteria, including names (which sometimes appeared in Anglicized form, such as Hammett for Hamid) and religious practices (for example, turning eastwards for prayer).[6] Finally, David Biale has urged scholars to replace the concept of 'Judaism' with 'Jewish culture', because, among other reasons, the former focuses on one component of Jewish civilization, while the latter considers them all together.[7] This paradigm makes particular sense for Suriname, where Jewishness was an ethno-religious, rather than a religious, identity.

[5] For the challenges of defining and identifying culture, see Ann Swidler, *Talk of Love: How Culture Matters* (Chicago, 2001); Clifford Geertz, *The Interpretation of Cultures* (New York, 1973); William H. Sewell Jr., 'The Concept(s) of Culture', in V. E. Bonnell and L. Hunt (eds.), *Beyond the Cultural Turn: New Directions in the Study of Society and Culture* (Berkeley, Calif., 1999), 35–61. I would like to thank Amy Schalet for these sources.

[6] Michael Gomez, *Exchanging our Country Marks: The Transformation of African Identities in the Colonial and Antebellum South* (Chapel Hill, NC, 1998), esp. ch. 4. As the latter example suggests, not all cultural manifestations are exclusive to a particular ethno-religious group. Culturally ambiguous traits (ambiguous because they are shared by more than one group), therefore, cannot serve as definite examples.

[7] David Biale, 'Confessions of an Historian of Jewish Culture', *Jewish Social Studies*, NS 1/1 (1994), 40–51

Tracking Eurafrican Jews: The Sources

There are three major sources for identifying Eurafrican Jews and their cultural orientations: burial grounds, conventional archival documents, and oral testimony (including genealogical research carried out by their descendants).

Jews in early modern Suriname established four cemeteries, two located inland, near or within the riverside settlement of Jodensavanne, and two in the capital city of Paramaribo. As recently demonstrated, these cemeteries reserved a section, usually situated along one of the fences, for Eurafrican Jews.[8] Thanks to the surviving stones and archival descriptions of their location, the names and some biographical details of dozens of Eurafrican Jews have been preserved. One example is the individuals known to be buried in the Jodensavanne cemetery. Their identity and the whereabouts of their remains were verified through a combination of on-site research and burial records. Next to each other in the extreme north-east corner of the cemetery, from north-west to south-east, were buried: Miriam Nassy;[9] Luna, daughter of David Haim del Monte;[10] Abigail, daughter of the mestiza Simha de Meza;[11] the mulatto Ismahel Judeo;[12] the mulatto Matatia de Robles;[13] Moses Rodrigues del Prado;[14] Jacob Peregrino, a 'negro', 'molato', or 'karboeger';[15] Joseph Pelengrino;[16] the 'mulattresses' Simha[17] and her

(43); id. (ed.), *Cultures of the Jews: A New History* (New York, 2002). The Eurafricans mentioned here obviously also embodied Creole or African cultures. The evidence I have amassed in this direction goes beyond the parameters of this chapter and will be discussed in my book on Eurafrican Jews in Suriname. On the historiographical trend towards exploring cultural mutuality in the Atlantic world, see Tobias Green, 'Equal Partners? Proselytising by Africans and Jews in the 17th Century Atlantic Diaspora', *Melilah: Manchester Journal of Jewish Studies*, 12/1 (2008), 1–12, esp. the sources on p. 2.

[8] Epitaphs of Jacob Peregrino (J [Jodensavanne cemetery] 460, d. 1750); Joseph Pelengrino (J461, d. 1751); Joseph, son of Gabriel de Mattos (J462, d. 1751), in Aviva Ben-Ur and Rachel Frankel, *Remnant Stones*, vol. i: *The Jewish Cemeteries of Suriname: Epitaphs* (Cincinnati, 2009), 277; Aviva Ben-Ur with Rachel Frankel, *Remnant Stones*, vol. ii: *The Jewish Cemeteries and Synagogues of Suriname: Essays* (Cincinnati, 2012), 66.

[9] Mirjam Nassy (*congreganta*) (d. 15 Sept. 1811), Register van begravenen op de kerkhoven van de Savanne (Register of graves in the cemetery of the Savanna) (1777–1833), NAN, NPIGS 423, p. 37.

[10] Luna fa. de Dd. Hm del Monte (*congregante*) (d. 21 Sept. 1816), ibid., p. 41.

[11] Hua Criatura Abigail fa d[illeg.] Simha de Meza [illeg.] (d. 13 Feb. 1788), ibid., p. 14; Simha de Meza is identified as a 'mustiça' in the entry for Miriam Nassy.

[12] Ismahel Judeo (*molato congregante*) (d. 1 Dec. 1791), ibid., p. 19.

[13] Matha. de Robles (*molato congregante*) (d. 2 Nov 1793), ibid., p. 21.

[14] Mosseh Rodrigues del Prado (*congregante*) (d. 3 Oct. 1797), ibid., p. 25.

[15] Epitaph of Jacob Peregrino (J460, d. 1750), in Ben-Ur and Frankel, *Remnant Stones*, vol. i: *Epitaphs*, 277 (Hebrew and Portuguese); Wieke Vink, *Creole Jews: Negotiating Community in Colonial Surinam* (Leiden, 2010), 225; Jean Jacques Vrij to Aviva Ben-Ur (15 Aug. 2003), without archival attribution.

[16] Epitaph of Joseph Pelengrino (J461, d. 1751), in Ben-Ur and Frankel, *Remnant Stones*, vol. i: *Epitaphs*, 277 (Portuguese).

[17] 'Hua molata livre chamada Simha . . . que foy escrava de Jos. Gabay Farro' (d. 1 May 1791), Register van begravenen op de kerkhoven van de Savanne (1777–1833), NAN, NPIGS 423, p. 19.

sister Jahel,[18] both former slaves of Joseph Gabay Farro and both formally manumitted in 1767;[19] and Joseph, son of Gabriel de Mattos.[20]

Data from the cemetery provide in shorthand what the archival documents describe more fully. These documents, housed in the Dutch National Archives in The Hague, represent the richest and least mined source of information about Eurafrican Jews. The two major collections that inform the present chapter consist of records maintained by the Surinamese Jewish community and those kept by the colonial government.[21] A collation of these sources suggests that by the second half of the eighteenth century, there were around 100 Jewish Eurafricans in each generation.[22] References to Eurafrican Jews are scattered, usually unpredictably, throughout these records. Their identification, therefore, involves the careful scanning of each surviving will and court case, every page of communal minutes, and marriage, birth, and death records. They are recorded most often in Dutch and Portuguese, but Spanish, Hebrew, and French also make appearances.

Genealogical data collated by descendants of Eurafrican Jews and their extended families are crucial to the historian. Marriage patterns and family formation among Suriname's Eurafrican populations are exceedingly complex, and ancestry is often traceable or verifiable only through oral traditions combined with genealogical research. Family researchers and professional historians thus share the quest for information, and the resulting knowledge is the fruit of that relationship.[23]

Names

As the Eurafrican section of the Jodensavanne cemetery illustrates, the first and last names of Eurafrican Jews, whether born enslaved or free, were usually Portuguese Jewish or Hebrew. Typically, first names were drawn from the Hebrew Bible and were usually no different from those bestowed upon legally white Jews. Luna, Abigail, Moses, or Joseph would not be identifiable as Eurafricans had they not been buried in the 'coloured' section of the Jodensavanne cemetery.

[18] 'Hua molata livre, chamada Jahel, q foy escrava de Jos. Gabay Farro' (d. 19 June 1791), Register van begravenen op de kerkhoven van de Savanne (1777–1833), NAN, NPIGS 423, p. 19.

[19] Three other Eurafricans are buried in unspecified parts of the cemetery: Jahacob Garcia (congregante), his brother Isaac (ibid., p. 41), and 'hum morito, fo. De Ishak Naar Meza' (ibid., p. 49). Many other Jews lie in the Eurafrican row, as the burial register attests, but I have not yet ascertained their social status. For the manumission document of Jael and Simha, see the undated will of Joseph Gabay Farro (NAN, NPIGS, microfilm reel 67a, n. 785, n.p. (following the 1767 will of Moses C. Nassy and Sarah Rodrigues Monsanto, p. 89)).

[20] Josseph de g[illeg.] de Mattos (n.d.), ibid., p. 25; epitaph of Joseph, son of Gabriel de Mattos (J461, d. 1751), in Ben-Ur and Frankel, Remnant Stones, vol. i: Epitaphs, 277 (Portuguese).

[21] In this chapter I refer especially to NAN, Suriname Oud Notarieel Archief (SONA) and NAN, NPIGS.

[22] Aviva Ben-Ur, 'A Matriarchal Matter: Slavery, Conversion, and Upward Mobility in Colonial Suriname', in Richard L. Kagan and Philip D. Morgan (eds.), Atlantic Diasporas: Jews, Conversos, and Crypto-Jews in the Age of Mercantilism, 1500–1800 (Baltimore, 2009), 152–69, 270–9, 161.

[23] I would like to thank Wadily Wijnhard for sharing with me information about his Surinamese ancestors.

However, a few Eurafrican Jews bore distinctive forenames. Of these, the most common for females was Simha, meaning 'happiness' in Hebrew. Simha is especially peculiar since it is not used as a personal name in the Bible. The name is not unique to early modern Suriname: it was also found among Jewish women living in eighteenth-century Amsterdam.[24] But in Suriname it appears to have been given exclusively to Eurafrican Jewish females. Only 10 per cent of the personal names recorded in the Hebrew Bible are female, and this paucity probably played a role in stimulating the invention of personal names for Jewish females. Moreover, there must have been a desire on the part of Suriname's Jewish ruling elite to distinguish between legally white and legally black or Eurafrican Jews. Those who bestowed the name Simha in Suriname must have understood its meaning. Perhaps 'joy' was ironically ascribed to a baby born into bondage, or perhaps calling a slave the Hebrew equivalent of 'happiness' under-scored the sentiments of the master or mistress who wished to stress the bounty and gladness that slave labour could bring the owner.[25]

In terms of frequency, the male counterpart of Simha among Surinamese Jews seems to have been Ismael or Ismahel, the name of Abraham's son through his con-cubine Hagar. Ismael was understood to be the progenitor of the Muslims and high-lighted both the patrilineality of the child's Jewish descent and the status of the mother as a non-Jewish, subservient concubine. As we shall see, the name Ismael was some-times coupled with the middle name Abraham, the first patriarch of the Jewish people. Simha and Ismael are among the earliest names in Surinamese Jewish culture repre-senting a break from Portuguese Jewish tradition, where name-giving practices were strictly enshrined. Generally, the firstborn son was named after his paternal grand-father, the second after his maternal grandfather, and subsequent sons named after either great-uncles or great-grandfathers.[26] A similar rule applied to daughters and their senior female relatives. This meant that, among white Portuguese Jews, perhaps a dozen names, the vast majority biblical, were recycled until the late eighteenth century, when non-biblical names increasingly became a norm. Simha and Ismael, the two most

[24] Simcha, daughter of Israel Gompert, year of birth unknown, registered 1724, married Asser Levie; Simcha, daughter of Jonas, b. 1720, married Abraham Sacutto, registered 1742 (Dave Verdooner and Harmen Snel, *Trouwen in Mokum: Jewish Marriage in Amsterdam, 1598–1811*, 2 vols. (The Hague, 1992), ii. 185, 194. Simcha was also a female name in the Ottoman Jewish community (see José M. Estrugo, *Los Sefardíes* (Seville, 1958; repr. 2002), 56) and Iraq (see Sasson Somekh, *Baghdad Yesterday: The Making of an Arab Jew* (Jerusalem, 2007), 158). In contemporary Ashkenazi communities it is typically a male name.

[25] This latter is a tentative idea inspired by Hagar Salamon's ethnographic research, carried out in the 1980s and 1990s, showing that Ethiopian polytheists converted by their Beta Israel masters were ceremoniously given names denoting gratitude to God for bestowing a gift, or joy at having a slave to work in the owner's place (Hagar Salamon, 'Slavery among the "Beta-Israel" in Ethiopia', *Slavery and Abolition*, 15/1 (April 1994), 87).

[26] Daniel M. Swetschinski, *Reluctant Cosmopolitans: The Portuguese Jews of Seventeenth-Century Amsterdam* (London, 2000), 284.

common, distinctively Eurafrican Jewish names, set their bearers apart from main-stream Portuguese Jews even as they connected them to the broader Sephardi com-munity.

Eurafricans with only a slight connection to Jewishness are a different matter. Some of their names, like those of non-Jewish slaves of non-Jewish masters, were drawn from Greek and Latin antiquity, Christian Europe, or Creole traditions. A small-scale, sys-tematic survey of name-giving practices in Suriname's eighteenth-century Jewish com-munity illuminates this trend. The survey examined the names of testators and legatees in all available wills filed by the colonial government between 1716 and 1805,[27] and found twenty-one testators who were either Eurafrican Jews or who had some connection to Judaism, as suggested by their contribution to a synagogue or their possession of Jewish names and close relatives who were Jews. About half of them had what were at that time conventional Portuguese Jewish names (Abigail, Blanka, Daniel, Dina, Gabriel, Hana, Joseph, and Sipora).[28] Two with distinctive Eurafrican Jewish forenames were Ismael and Simcha. Others, especially those with slight connections to the Jewish com-munity, bore names that were either European Christian or Creole (Ammerentie, five Marias or Mariannas, Diana, Jaberie, Isabelle, and Loco).

Eurafrican Jews also possessed bynames, which were only coincidentally and in-termittently recorded in archival sources. Whether or not all Eurafrican Jews had bynames (and how many they possessed) remains conjectural. These unofficial nick-names tended to be of Surinamese Creole rather than West African origin. One ex-ample is a housemaid belonging to her own aunt, the Eurafrican Jew Roza Judia (1705–71),[29] alias Roza Mendes Meza. The housemaid's official name, Ajaja, was Creole, and her byname, Luna, was Portuguese Jewish.[30]

By comparison, the personal names inscribed in Suriname's rural Jewish ceme-teries (Cassipora Creek and Jodensavanne), where most decedents were not, presum-ably, of African origin, are overwhelmingly biblical, running the gamut from Aaron to Solomon and Abigail to Yael.[31] In the Cassipora Creek cemetery, whose stones date

---

[27]   NAN, SONA. When I began my examination of these wills in 2002, the following eight registers were not available to the public: 1, 2 (before 1716), 10 (1729–32), 16–27 (1736–40), 33 (1763–5), 47–53 (1781–5), 71 (1794–5).

[28]   However, Siporah, the name of Moses's wife, may be a distinctly Eurafrican Jewish name in Suriname, since she is described in the Torah as a 'Cushite' (Ethiopian) (Num. 12: 1), and Surinamese Jews may have been influenced by a variety of medieval Jewish exegetes, who identify her as 'dark' or 'black' (see Abraham Melamed, *The Image of the Black in Jewish Culture: A History of the Other* (London, 2003), 176–8, 187, 191. It is also possible that Dina is a distinctly Eurafrican Jewish name, since I have not identified any who were white.

[29]   The year of her birth is based on my conjecture that she was Moses da Costa's son (will of Isaac, son of Moses da Costa (8 May 1725), NAN, SONA 13, p. 245).   [30]   Book of inventories, NAN, SONA 234, pp. 442–3.

[31]   Separate interment of Eurafrican Jews in the Jewish cemeteries at Cassipora Creek, Jodensavanne, and the old Sephardi cemetery of Paramaribo was officially abolished in 1820 (Minuut-notulen van vergaderingen van de Senhores de Mahamad (Parnassijns) en van de Junta (Parnassijns en ouderlingen) (Minutes of the Mahamad (*parnasim*) and the Junta (*parnasim* and elders)) (30 Oct. 1820), NAN, NPIGS 11, p. 13). In the Ashkenazi community, a Eurafrican section existed since at least 1775 (Wink, 'Creole Jews', 157, 166–7).

from 1666 to 1873, no men and only five women (5 per cent) have vernacular names. Even these vernacular names, Luna and Branca or Blanca, are Portuguese and Spanish translations of Levanah, a Hebrew name meaning 'moon' or 'white'. Among males, David is the most popular name (17 per cent), followed by Isaac (15 per cent), Jacob (13 per cent), Samuel (12 per cent), Abraham (12 per cent), and Joseph (11 per cent). Among women, Sarah is the most popular (22 per cent), followed by Esther (16 per cent), Rachel (16 per cent), Abigail (15 per cent), and Rebecca (12 per cent). At the Jodensavanne cemetery, where ledgers date from 1685 to 1873, Abraham is the most popular among males (19 per cent), while among female decedents the most commonly recorded names are Rachel (10 per cent), Rebecca (9 per cent), and Sarah (8 per cent). Only females bear non-Jewish names (a fraction of 1 per cent). While some of these vernacular names are again translations of Hebrew words (Gracia for Hannah, Reina for Malkah, Blanka for Levanah), and were recognizably and distinctively Jewish, others have no early modern counterpart (Roza, Bemvenida, Mariana).[32]

In the old Sephardi cemetery of Paramaribo (where stones date from 1734 to 1904), non-Jewish forenames are more prevalent, reflecting a cultural shift beginning in the late eighteenth century. Three non-Jewish names for males are recorded: Rudolph, Isam Isam, and Samuel George. Non-Jewish female names occur in greater variety, though they are still rare (4.5 per cent): the more traditional Gracia, Luna, Reyna, and Blanca are joined by the uncompromisingly non-Jewish Anna (possibly a vernacular interpretation of Hanna), Selly, Violeta, Roza, Rosette, Esperane (possibly an error for Esperance), Sol, Clara, Louisa, Josephine, Mariana, Julia, and Maria Elisabeth Sophia, most likely a convert. By the second half of the nineteenth century, names had become a completely unpredictable gauge of communal membership, as evidenced by Adjuba Sara Wolff (1877) and Hendrick Christiaan Nassy (1890).[33]

The predilection for the forenames Abraham and Sarah, regarded in rabbinical tradition as the first patriarch and matriarch of the Jewish people and, loosely, as the first Jews, was reinforced by a legacy of formal conversion to Judaism by both New Christians returning to their ancestral religion and slaves or former slaves. In the seventeenth century and the first half of the eighteenth, the names Abraham and Sarah suggest the shedding of a crypto-Jewish identity for a professing Jewish one and may indicate the Iberian peninsula as the birthplace of the deceased.[34] Abraham Gabay Izidro, who married Sara Oxeda and served as Suriname's ḥakham in the 1730s and who

[32] Marianna was sometimes used as an equivalent of Miriam.

[33] Ongeïnventariseerd archief van de Nederlandse Portugees Israëlitische gemeente te Suriname (Uninventoried archives of the Dutch Portuguese Israelite community in Suriname), NAN, NPIGS 537. For a discussion of names in the early modern Jewish communities of the Caribbean, largely based on cemetery epitaphs and plantation inventories that enumerate slaves, see Schorsch, *Jews and Blacks in the Early Modern World*, 332–48.

[34] This trend is also evident in New York's oldest Jewish burial site (see David de Sola Pool, *Portraits Etched in Stone: Early Jewish Settlers, 1682–1831* (New York, 1952), 196).

had fled Spain and returned to Judaism in London, is one example.[35] These names may
have also held special appeal for manumitted slaves who embraced Judaism either
during slavery or after their liberation. One possible example is Sarah Roldão, a Jewish
slave (*escrava Judia*) who died in 1822 and was buried in the old Sephardi cemetery of
Paramaribo.[36] From the late eighteenth century onwards the names Abraham and
Sarah appear to have become more common among free Eurafrican Jews.[37]

Languages

From its colonial beginnings, Suriname was a multi-ethnic and multi-lingual colony.
Dutch people did not form a majority of the European population until the nineteenth
century.[38] Besides the Ashkenazi and Portuguese Jewish communities, the colony's
white population included non-Jews of British, Dutch, French Huguenot, and German
descent. The vast majority of Suriname's population (96 per cent by the late eighteenth
century) were both enslaved and of African origin.[39] Ewe was the major West African
language spoken by slaves brought to Suriname,[40] but African languages ultimately
gave way to Creoles, particularly Sranan Tongo, which was an autonomous language
by the mid-eighteenth century,[41] spoken by the majority native-born enslaved population.[42] Sranan Tongo was variously, and probably polemically, known as the 'Negro
English Language' or 'Negro English Speech' and very rarely, if ever, appears in wills or
communal records.[43] Documents in the municipal archives are typically recorded in

[35] Abraham Gabay Izidro, *Sermon predicado neste K.K. de T.T. por Ribi Abraham Gabay Izidro. En Sabat Vaikrà
en R.H. Nisàn del Año 5484 En Amsterdam* (Amsterdam, 1724), 9–11; Cecil Roth, 'The Remarkable Career of
Haham Abraham Gabay Izidro', *The Jewish Historical Society of England Transactions*, 24 (1974), 211–13.

[36] Registro mortuorio (Register of deaths), NAN, NPIGS 418, p. 113.

[37] See e.g. Abraham, son of Hana de Prado (d. 20 Oct. 1794); Abraham del Castilho (d. 29 May 1806);
Abraham Abenacar (d. 3 July 1812); Abraham Haim, son of Hana Marcus Samson (d. 9 Sept. 1820); Isaac, son of
Sarah Rodriguez del Prado (d. 14 Aug. 1800); Solomon de la Parra, son of Sarah Rodriguez del Prado (d. 3 Nov.
1799); Sarah, widow of Isaac Nunes Ferro (d. 18 Oct. 1785); Sarah d'Oliveira (d. 17 Aug. 1811); Sarah de Vries,
daughter of Ribca Henriquez (d. 7 Sept. 1813); and Sarah, wife of Isaac de la Parra Junior (d. 3 Mar. 1822)
(Alfabetische staat van overledenen (Alphabetical record of deaths) (1777–1812), NAN, NPIGS 418, pp. 3, 5–7, 55,
89, 95, 98–99, 113).

[38] Jacques Arends, 'The History of the Surinamese Creoles I: A Sociohistorical Survey', in Eithne B. Carlin
and Jacques Arends (eds.), *Atlas of the Languages of Suriname* (Leiden, 2002), 115–30.

[39] Aviva Ben-Ur, 'Peripheral Inclusion: Communal Belonging in Suriname's Sephardic Community', in
Alexandra Cuffel and Brian Britt (eds.), *Religion, Gender, and Culture in the Pre-Modern World* (New York, 2007),
186.

[40] Jacques Arends, 'Young Languages, Old Texts: Early Documents in the Surinamese Creoles', in Carlin
and Arends (eds.), *Atlas of the Languages of Suriname*, 193.

[41] Arends, 'The History of the Surinamese Creoles I', 124–5.

[42] Arends, 'Young Languages, Old Texts', 204; Norval Smith, 'The History of Surinamese Creoles II:
Origin and Differentiation', in Carlin and Arends (eds.), *Atlas of the Languages of Suriname*, 132.

[43] The terms are *negerder gelschtie*, *Neger Engelsche Taal*, and *Neger Engelsche Spraak* (see will of the free Diana
van Adam (1788), NAN, SONA 59, pp. 154–6).

Dutch, with a few, such as wills, in English, French, and German. Colonial government records refer to Dutch as either the 'Lower German language' or as 'Hollandish'.[44] Records of the Portuguese Jewish community appear in Portuguese and, more rarely, in Spanish and Hebrew, while the Ashkenazi community favoured Dutch.

The main language of Sephardi Jews was called simply 'the Portuguese language'. In one case, the phrase 'the Portuguese Jewish language'[45] appears, either reflecting a colonial equation of Jews with early modern Portuguese or suggesting a Jewish dialect of Portuguese developed in Suriname. A distinctive Portuguese spoken by Sephardi Jews and heavily influenced by early modern Spanish seems to have been common among western Sephardim in their lands of exile. One scholar, who observed this dialect on the epitaphs of New York's western Sephardim, called it a 'Spaniolic mixture'.[46] Isaac Samuel Emmanuel, who documented the Sephardi epitaphs of Curaçao, concluded that the Portuguese spoken by the island's Jews was 'far from being pure', being substantially mixed with Spanish.[47] In the oldest New Christian cemetery of southern France, most epitaphs are in Spanish, but a number bear traces of Portuguese.[48]

The overwhelming majority of Iberian New Christians who settled in the New World were of Lusitanian origin.[49] In Suriname, Portuguese was the dominant language among Sephardi Jews in both rural areas and the capital city well into the nineteenth century. This is readily apparent in Suriname's Sephardi cemeteries. In the two rainforest burial sites (Cassipora Creek and Jodensavanne), Portuguese appears on about three quarters of all tombstones, most of which date to the eighteenth century.[50] At the old Sephardi cemetery of Paramaribo nearly 60 per cent of epitaphs include Portuguese.[51] Portuguese epitaphs in Suriname's Sephardi cemeteries began to peter out in the 1840s and had almost entirely disappeared by the 1870s.

[44] The terms are *neederduitsche taal* and *Hollandsche* (see wills of the free Ammerentie van Hartog Jacobs (1 Nov. 1799), NAN, SONA 76, will no. 29; the free Amimba van Casper (14 Aug. 1799), ibid., will no. 10).

[45] The terms are *de Portugeesche taal* and *Portugeesche Joodsche taal* (see will of Sarah Nahar, separated from Isaac Lopes Telles (24 Jan. 1803), NAN, SONA 82, p. 10).

[46] De Sola Pool, *Portraits Etched in Stone*, 167; David de Sola Pool, 'The Use of Portuguese and Spanish in the Historic Shearith Israel Congregation in New York', in Izaak A. Langnas and Barton Sholod (eds.), *Studies in Honor of M. J. Benardete (Essays in Hispanic and Sephardic Culture)* (New York, 1965), 360.

[47] Isaac S. Emmanuel, 'El Portugues [sic] en la Sinagoga "Mikve Israel" de Curaçao', *A Treasury of the Jews of Spain: Towards a Study of the History of the Jews of Spain and Their Culture* [Otsar yehudei sefarad: leḥeker toledot yehudei sefarad vetarbutam], 1 (1959), 31.

[48] Gérard Nahon, 'Inscriptions funéraires Hébraiques et Juives a Bidache Labastide-Clairence (Basses-Pyrénées) et Peyrehorade (Landes): Rapport de mission', *Revue des Études Juives*, 127 (1968), 351.

[49] Nathan Wachtel, 'Marrano Religiosity in Hispanic America in the Seventeenth Century', in Paolo Bernardini and Norman Fiering (eds.), *The Jews and the Expansion of Europe to the West, 1450–1800* (New York, 2001), 149–71: 150.

[50] 75.5 and 72.3 per cent respectively (Ben-Ur with Frankel, *Remnant Stones*, vol. ii: *Essays*, 37 n. 160).

[51] Ibid. Precisely 58.7 per cent of the stones contain Portuguese.

But epitaph language, particularly when carved on stones, may be the result of linguistic prestige rather than a reflection of the deceased's fluency. A more convincing way to gauge the extent of spoken language is by considering legal and communal documents, where the mode of communication was practical rather than aesthetic. Wills and communal records suggest that perhaps the majority of Suriname's Sephardim spoke or at least understood Portuguese until the early 1800s. Of nearly 200 wills filed by Jews and dating from 1716 to 1805, the bulk (some 54 per cent) were written in Dutch, however Portuguese was the next language in terms of frequency (29 per cent). The content of these wills clearly indicates that for many Portuguese Jews—both men and women—Portuguese was their strongest or only language. Abraham Gabay Izidro (b. 1736) recorded his last will in Portuguese on his deathbed in 1785.[52] Rebecca Jessurun (née de Pina, 1742), required a Portuguese translator when she and her husband, Aron Jessurun, wrote a joint will in 1777.[53] In 1780 Esther Baruh Louzada (b. 1760) claimed to know Portuguese, but not Dutch. Although her husband (b. 1751) knew Dutch, he nevertheless wrote a joint will with her in Portuguese.[54] The wills suggests that it was not solely or mainly Jewish women who preserved Portuguese as their strongest language. Rachel (1766–1803), wife of Isaac Fernandes Junior, required a Portuguese interpreter when she wrote her will in 1801 at the age of nearly 37.[55] But Joseph del Castilho, born around 1779, also recorded his will in Portuguese in 1802, two years before his death at the age of 25.[56] Several others wrote their wills in Portuguese around the end of the century, including Mordachai Fernandes in 1801.[57] Other Jews requiring a Portuguese interpreter around that time were Joshua de Abraham Hisquia Arrias, who was living at Jodensavanne in 1801,[58] and Sarah Nahar in 1803.[59] Even at the end of the century, there was a new generation of Portuguese-speaking testators, albeit much smaller than earlier ones. Judith Jessurun Lobo, probably in her late teens or early

---

[52] Will of Abraham Gabay Izidro (23 Nov. 1785), NAN, SONA 55, p. 20.

[53] Will of Aaron Jessurun and Rebecca Jessurun, née Pinto (18 Feb. 1777), NAN, SONA 66; epitaph of Rebecca Jessurun (J372, d. 1812), in Ben-Ur and Frankel, *Remnant Stones*, vol. i: *Epitaphs*, 245 (Hebrew and Portuguese).

[54] Will of Joseph Hayim Baruh Louzada and Esther Jessurun (24 Nov. 1780), NAN, SONA 62, p. 459; epitaphs of Esther Jessurun, widow of Joseph Hayim Baruh Louzada, and Joseph Hayim Baruh Louzada (OS [old Sephardi cemetery] 191, d. 1813; OS571, d. 1789), in Ben-Ur and Frankel, *Remnant Stones*, vol. i: *Epitaphs*, 333, 436 (both in Hebrew and Portuguese).

[55] Will of Isaac Fernandes Junior and Rachel Gabay Fonseca (11 Mar. 1801), NAN, SONA 79, will no. 30; epitaph of Rachel, wife of Isaac Fernandes Junior (OS127, d. 1803), in Ben-Ur and Frankel, *Remnant Stones*, vol. i: *Epitaphs*, 317 (Hebrew and Portuguese).

[56] Will of Joseph del Castilho (27 Dec. 1802), NAN, SONA 84, will no. 6; epitaph of Joseph del Castilho (OS646, d. 1804), in Ben-Ur and Frankel, *Remnant Stones*, vol. i: *Epitaphs*, 456 (Hebrew and Portuguese).

[57] Will of Mordachai Fernandes (19 Nov. 1801), NAN, SONA 80, will no. 58.

[58] Will of Josuah de Abraham Hisquia Arrias (18 Dec. 1801), NAN, SONA 80, will no. 73.

[59] Will of Sarah Nahar, separated from Isaac Lopes Telles (24 Jan. 1803), NAN, SONA 82, will no. 10.

twenties, required an interpreter when she wrote her will in 1801. Her husband, David Jessurun Lobo Junior, son of Joseph Abarbanel, had died in 1800 at the age of 20.[60]

The death knell for 'Jewish Portuguese' came in 1837, when the colony's Mahamad decided to abandon Portuguese as the official language of communal minutes.[61] This pattern of use and decline closely parallels what transpired in Curaçao, whose Jewish population numerically rivalled that of Suriname during the last half of the eighteenth century. On Curaçao, Portuguese was the dominant language among the Sephardim until the mid-nineteenth century, when it ceded to Dutch. The last rabbi to preach there and correspond in Portuguese, Aron Mendes Chumaceiro, served from 1856 to 1868, and the last Portuguese epitaph in the old cemetery dates to 1865.[62]

Throughout the generations, a small minority of Suriname's Jews spoke Spanish as their only or strongest language. Their linguistic preference (or the literary prestige of the language) is faintly reflected in death monuments: less than 10 per cent of epitaphs in the three oldest burial grounds (Cassipora Creek, Jodensavanne, and the old Sephardi cemetery of Paramaribo) are recorded in Spanish.[63] Samuel Cohen Nassy, the founder of Suriname's Sephardi community, composed his military journal in Spanish while serving as a captain during the French attack on Suriname in 1689.[64] The presence of Hispanophone Jews was important enough to merit notice in mid-eighteenth-century *ascamot*, the earliest complete copy that survives. There, they are acknowledged as a component of the Sephardi community.[65] As late as 1788, David Cohen Nassy still identified his community's native languages as both Portuguese and Spanish.[66] Around the same time Suriname's Jewish communities included several official translators of Dutch, French, Portuguese, as well as Spanish.[67] Literary interest, if not ability, in these languages was partly influenced by Nassy, who in 1785 established a college of litera-ture, Docendo Docemur (We are Taught by Teaching). There, students of both Christian and Jewish backgrounds would gather in the evenings to study a variety of topics, including literature. The languages of discourse included French and Dutch, and, in

[60] Will of Judith Jessurun Lobo, widow of David Jessurun Lobo Junior (9 Mar. 1801), NAN, SONA 79, will no. 29; epitaph of David Jessurun Lobo Junior (OS544, d. 1 June 1800), in Ben-Ur and Frankel, *Remnant Stones*, vol. i: *Epitaphs*, 426 (Hebrew and Portuguese).

[61] Minuut-notulen van vergaderingen van de Senhores de Mahamad (Parnassijns) en van de Junta (Parnas-sijns en ouderlingen) (Minutes of the Mahamad (*parnasim*) and the Junta (*parnasim* and elders)), (15 Nov. 1837), NAN, NPIGS 13.   [62] Emmanuel, 'El Portugues [*sic*] en la Sinagoga "Mikve Israel" de Curaçao', 25.

[63] Spanish appears on less than 1 per cent of tombstones in the cemeteries of Cassipora and Jodensavanne, and on only 6.8 per cent of those found in the old Sephardi cemetery of Paramaribo.

[64] David Cohen Nassy, *Essai historique sur la colonie de Surinam* (Paramaribo, 1788; repr. Amsterdam, 1968), pt. 1, 50.   [65] Ascamot (1754), tractate 25, article 1, NAN, NPIGS 105.

[66] 'Elle [notre langue] est la Portuguaise & l'Espagnole' (Nassy, *Essai historique*, pt. 1, p. vii); 'La langue qu'on parle généralement dans le païs, est la Hollandoise, & parmi les Juifs Portuguais on y ajoute la Portuguaise & l'Espagnole' (ibid., pt. 2, 82).

[67] *Surinaamsche Almanach op het jaar onzes heere jesu christi anno 1789* (Paramaribo, 1789), 13.

deference to Sephardim ignorant of these tongues, also Spanish and Portuguese.[68] Like Portuguese, Spanish was to endure into the nineteenth century. When Esther de Leon (née Monsanto, 1770–1817) died at the age of nearly 47 years, she required a Spanish interpreter. Her gravestone bears a Hebrew biblical verse, followed by a Spanish epitaph, including a poem.[69] Sarah d'Anavia (née de Miranda, 1750–1803) also required a Spanish interpreter. For unknown reasons, her epitaph bears a Hebrew caption with a Portuguese, rather than Spanish, text.[70]

Finally, a tiny minority of Sephardi Jews spoke English or French as their primary language. Some Francophone Jews may have originated in the New Christian settlements of France (such as Bayonne), which may help to explain the single Surinamese Jewish epitaph in French.[71] Anglophone Jews may have arrived in the colony when it briefly came under British rule at the beginning of the nineteenth century. Among them may have been Luna Robles de Medina, née Monsanto (1746–1842), who died at the age of 96 and required an English interpreter to read her final will, which was recorded in Dutch.[72]

By contrast, Ashkenazi Jews generally recorded their wills with the municipal authorities in Dutch, not Yiddish. The similarity of Yiddish and the other Germanic dialects they spoke to Dutch may partly explain why they so easily adapted to the colony's official vernacular. There are also indications that recent Ashkenazi immigrants to Suriname could understand Dutch even if they could not write it. Joseph Jacob Levy, whose siblings still lived in his native Bohemia, is one such example. The clerk recorded

[68] Robert Cohen, *Jews in Another Environment: Surinam in the Second Half of the Eighteenth Century* (Leiden, 1991), 99, 101.

[69] Will of Abraham de Leon and Esther Nunes Monsanto (15 Feb. 1803), NAN, SONA 82, will no. 19; epitaph of Esther Monsanto, wife of Abraham de Leon (OS61, d. 1817), in Ben-Ur and Frankel, *Remnant Stones*, vol. i: *Epitaphs*, 299.

[70] Will of Sarah de Miranda, wife of Emanuel d'Anavia (4 Apr. 1803), NAN, SONA 82, will no. 34; epitaph of Sarah de Miranda (OS52, d. 1803), in Ben-Ur and Frankel, *Remnant Stones*, vol. i: *Epitaphs*, 295.

[71] One author surmises that Jewish immigration from Bayonne to Suriname partially explains the 'surprising linguistic choice' of the author of the *Essai historique* (see Gérard Nahon, 'The Portuguese Jewish Nation of Saint-Esprit-Lès-Bayonne: The American Dimension', in Bernardini and Fiering (eds), *The Jews and the Expansion of Europe to the West*, 262). However, only one tombstone bears a French epitaph (David Gabriel d'Anavia (OS610, d. 1781), in Ben-Ur and Frankel, *Remnant Stones*, vol. i: *Epitaphs*, 447), and the only epitaph that mentions Bayonne is in Spanish (Abraham, son of Isaac Valery (OS554, d. 1803), in Ben-Ur and Frankel, *Remnant Stones*, vol. i: *Epitaphs*, 431). David Cohen Nassy also wrote a political treatise and a medical tract in French, by no means unusual for an Enlightenment figure (see David Cohen Nassy, *Mémoire sur les moyens d'améliorer la colonie de Surinam* (Philadelphia, 1795); id., *Observations sur la cause, la nautre, et le traitement de la maladie epidemique, qui regne a Philadelphia*, a bilingual work translated as *Observations on the Cause, Nature, and Treatment of the Epidemic Disorder, Prevalent in Philadelphia* (Philadelphia, 1793)).

[72] Will of Isaac Robles de Medina and Luna Robles de Medina, née Monsanto (10 Dec. 1790), NAN, SONA 64, p. 347 (only she needed an English translation); epitaph of Luna, widow of Isaac Robles de Medina (OS280, d. 1842), in Ben-Ur and Frankel, *Remnant Stones*, vol. i: *Epitaphs*, 355 (Dutch). For the three Anglophone epitaphs, see Ben-Ur and Frankel, *Remnant Stones*, vol. i: *Epitaphs*, 662.

Levy's last will in 1798 in Dutch, which the testator could understand. But Levy signed his name in Hebrew, the only alphabet he knew how to write.[73]

Most Eurafrican Jews who filed wills favoured European languages. The four examples of Portuguese-speaking Eurafrican Jews who recorded their testaments are Hana Pelengrino, Daniel Pelengrino (probably her brother), the free mulattress Maria or Mariana del Prado, who was not in full command of Dutch, and Simcha Judia, all of whom wrote their wills in the 1780s and 1790s. Other Eurafrican Jews, or non-Jews whose close relatives were Eurafrican Jews, spoke Dutch and did not need a 'Negro English' translator, unlike most of their Eurafrican contemporaries. One of these Jews, Mariana van Musaphia, raised her children in the Dutch Reform religion.[74] Another, Abigail Abenacar, despite being illiterate, was in full command of Dutch when she filed her three wills, the last in 1803.[75] Only Simcha Pinto, who left a nominal bequest to the Eurafrican Jewish society Darhe Jessarim, spoke Negro English and no Dutch.[76] This evidence would seem to contradict the findings of historian Wieke Vink, who has argued that by the last quarter of the eighteenth century most of the colony's Jews were Sranan Tongo speakers.[77] As no systematic survey is cited, this statement is probably an inference based on the handful of examples cited in her study, but the implication is that Eurafrican Jews would have been in the vanguard of a linguistic shift from Portuguese (or Spanish) to Sranan Tongo. In fact, in my systematic survey of eighteenth-century wills, a narrow majority of Eurafrican Jews preferred either Dutch or Portuguese. In other words, Dutch and Portuguese were the strongest languages among precisely those Jews whom one might expect to be most creolized: Eurafricans.[78] The Pelegrinos, Maria del Prado, and Simcha Judia may have been exceptional in their Portuguese fluency, but, as the survey has shown, it is incorrect to assume

[73] Will of Joseph Jacob Levy (26 July 1798), NAN, SONA 75, p. 51.

[74] Will of Marianna van Musaphia (27 Sept. 1788), NAN, SONA 60, pp. 135–40.

[75] Will of Abigail Abenacar (Eurafrican Jew) (22 Oct. 1803), NAN, SONA 83, no. 190.

[76] Will of Simcha Pinto (17 Dec. 1790), NAN, SONA 64, pp. 376–7.   [77] Vink, *Creole Jews*, 63–4.

[78] The following six Eurafrican Jews or Eurafricans with some connections to the Jewish community filed their wills in Dutch: the free mulattress Dina Mussaphia or Musafia (17 Nov. 1780), NAN, SONA 44, pp. 237–9 (14 Aug. 1787), NAN, SONA 58, pp. 205–9; Gabriel Davilar (possibly the byname of Gabriel Judeu) (29 July 1788), NAN, SONA 60, pp. 42–3; Marianna van Musaphia (closely related to Eurafrican Sephardim) (27 Sept. 1788), NAN, SONA 60, pp. 135–40; Abraham Ismael Judeo (14 Mar. 1780), NAN, SONA 61, pp. 297–308; the free Isabelle van Polak (with perhaps familial Portuguese Jewish connections) (18 Nov. 1790), NAN, SONA 64, pp. 338–42; the free Abigael Abenacar (19 Aug. 1779), NAN, SONA 42, p. 307 (4 May 1792), NAN, SONA 67, p. 25 (22 Oct. 1803), NAN, SONA 83, p. 190. The following four filed their wills in Portuguese: Hana Pelengrino (23 Feb. 1786), NAN, SONA 57, p. 148; the free mulattress Maria or Mariana del Prado (not in full command of Dutch) (12 June 1787), NAN, SONA 57, p. 463; Daniel Pelengrino (17 Nov. 1787), NAN, SONA 58, p. 497; Simcha Judia (10 May 1790), NAN, SONA 75, p. 39. The following nine or ten filed in Sranan Tongo: the free Mariana van D'acosta (name and charitable bequest suggest Jewish identity) (21 June 1787), NAN, SONA 57, p. 430 (1 Nov. 1788), NAN, SONA 60, p. 224; the free Diana van Adam (apparent links to Jewish community or identity) (1788), NAN, SONA 59, pp. 154–6; the free Loco van de Britto (name and charitable bequest suggest Jewish identity) (28 Oct. 1789), NAN, SONA 62, p. 351; Sipora van Mercado (name and some social networks suggest

that all or most Eurafrican or white Jews spoke Sranan Tongo during the eighteenth or early nineteenth centuries. In fact, only 6 per cent of all wills studied in this survey were filed in that language.

Of course, one might argue that Jewish Eurafricans (and, for that matter, whites) wealthy and informed enough to leave their last wishes in writing were a select group with a tendency towards fluency in one or more European languages. For Eurafricans generally, especially former slaves, the use of a European language may have been a badge of pride and incontrovertible evidence of their association with white society (and, in some cases, their white Sephardi fathers). That is indeed my impression of a great number of wills filed by freed non-Jews fluent enough in Dutch not to require a Sranan Tongo interpreter.[79] But coupled with the earlier discussion of Dutch and Portuguese use among the colony's Jews, there is persuasive evidence that Surinamese Jews, whether Eurafrican or not, were generally slow to creolize. This does not necessarily mean that Portuguese Jews—Jewish Eurafricans included—were ignorant of Sranan Tongo. In fact, it may point to the possibility of bi- or multi-lingualism, since a polyglot testator might prefer to claim fluency in a prestigious language (Dutch, Portuguese, or Spanish) rather than Sranan Tongo. Modern sociologists claim that in multicultural environments, natal language is central to identity formation.[80] The foregoing discussion suggests that Eurafrican Jews may have grown up hearing more than one language spoken in their homes and communities. This may mean that ethnic identification through language use was a matter of option rather than a foregone conclusion.

The linguistic complexities of Suriname's Jewish community have not yet been fully appreciated. What defines Jewish languages as opposed to languages used by Jews, where these languages were spoken, and the importance of hard data to document the actual extent of language use are vital matters ignored by some scholars who have attempted linguistic analyses of Suriname's population. For example, a fairly recent volume on the dissemination of Atlantic Creoles includes various assertions

Jewish identity) (5 Feb. 1790), NAN, SONA 63, pp. 77–80; Simcha Pinto (17 Dec. 1790), NAN, SONA 64, pp. 376–7; the free Blanka van Abigael de Britto (name and charitable bequest suggest Jewish identity) (15 Apr. 1786), NAN, SONA 68, p. 10; the free Jaberie van Polak (connections to both the Ashkenazi and Portuguese Jewish communities) (27 Oct. 1799), NAN, SONA 76, p. 27; the free Ammerentie van Hartog Jacobs (Ashkenazi Eurafrican Jew) (1 Nov. 1799), NAN, SONA 76, p. 29; possibly Judith Carrilho de Mattos, who filed with her Dutch-speaking husband David Pereyra but was not completely fluent in Dutch (3 June 1800), NAN, SONA 77, p. 40; the free mulattress Marianna Pinto (26 May 1803), NAN, SONA 82, p. 58.

[79] See e.g. the free Frans van India (15 Nov. 1803), NAN, SONA 83, p. 240; the free Simon Petrus Adam van de weduwe van de Lande (15 Nov. 1803), NAN, SONA 83, p. 248; the free Joseph Hendrik van Schuyt (15 Nov. 1803), NAN, SONA 83, p. 252; the free Cornelis van [the free] Dafina van Rocheteau (16 Nov. 1803), NAN, SONA 83, p. 292.

[80] Raymond L. M. Lee, 'The Paradox of Belonging: Sino-Indian Marginality in Malaysia', Ethnic Groups, 8 (1990), 119–21.

that Ladino was spoken among Suriname's Jews.[81] Nowhere in the collected articles is Ladino defined, and it is probable that the authors were unaware that Ladino was the vernacular of Ottoman Sephardim, not of Iberian Jews who remained in the western hemisphere and therefore continued to speak the Portuguese and Spanish vernaculars of the Iberian peninsula.[82] Moreover, none of the discussions of Jewish languages are based on systematic surveys of actual language use as verifiable through, for example, epitaphs, wills, and communal minutes.[83] The importance of such surveys for Jewish history is self-evident. However, systematic surveys may also have implications for the origins of Surinamese Creole languages, which contain Portuguese and sometimes Hebrew vocabulary. The enduring vitality of Portuguese among Suriname's Jews— especially Eurafricans—may help to explain the survival of Portuguese in these Creole languages (an estimated 4 per cent of Sranan Tongo and 35 per cent of Saramaccan).[84]

Conversion to Judaism

The earliest known case of a Surinamese master officially converting his children to Judaism is Isaac da Costa (d. 1734),[85] owner of the Wayenrebo plantation on the Caxewinica (Cassewinica) Creek, just north-east of Jodensavanne. With an unnamed mother (or mothers), he produced Roza (1705–71),[86] Ismael (1707–91),[87] Simha (1716–98),[88] David (b. 1719), and Hana (b. 1721). A 'muleca' (young black girl) named Aquariba, daughter of his late 'negress, Assiba', was also probably his child. In his 1725 will, recorded in Spanish, da Costa declared that all six merited manumission by virtue of being 'born in my house and from my female slaves, and [by virtue of] the good service and loyalty that I had from their mothers, and [by virtue of] the inclination of said mulattoes to be observant of our Holy Law and having received it willingly and with love'. The males had already been circumcised and the females ritually immersed according to the Jewish rite.[89] The locution of the will ('inclination', 'received it willingly') suggests that, at least from their master's point of view, these enslaved chil-

---

[81] Magnus Huber and Mikael Parkvall (eds.), *Spreading the Word: The Issue of Diffusion Among the Atlantic Creoles* (London, 1999).

[82] On languages among western and eastern Sephardi Jews, see Yosef Hayim Yerushalmi, 'Castilian, Portuguese, Ladino: The Non-Hebrew Literatures of Sephardi Jewry' (Heb.), in Tsvi Ankori (ed.), *From Then Until Now* [Me'az ve'ad atah] (Tel Aviv, 1984), 35–53.   [83] Huber and Parkvall, *Spreading the Word*.

[84] Statistics from Arends, 'The History of the Surinamese Creoles I', 115–130, 118.

[85] Epitaph of Isaac da Costa (J387, d. 1734), in Ben-Ur and Frankel, *Remnant Stones*, vol. i: *Epitaphs*, 251 (Hebrew and Portuguese).

[86] The year of her death is recorded in the inventory of her possessions (1771), NAN, SONA 234, pp. 442–3.

[87] Grave register of Ismahel Judeo (*molato congregante*) (d. 1 Dec. 1791), Registro dos Sepultados no Bethahaim na Povoaçao da Savana, do k:k: B:V:S: (Register of Graves in the Cemetery in the Village of the Savanne of the Holy Congregation Beraha Vesalom), NAN, NPIGS 423, p. 19.

[88] Official reading of Simha Judia's will (31 Oct. 1798), NAN, SONA 75, p. 39.

[89] Will of Issac, son of Moses da Costa (8 May 1725), NAN, SONA 13, p. 245.

dren possessed some degree of agency; that is, if they did not initiate the conversion process, they theoretically had the prerogative to reject or accept it.

Da Costa seems to have been at odds with the Surinamese Mahamad the year he wrote his will. His request for the customary prayer to be recited in the synagogue eleven months after his death for the spiritual elevation of his soul was accompanied by an elaborate justification. He reminded the board that he was a veteran regent of Jodensavanne's Mahamad and thus entitled to such a post-mortem honour, as were other former *jehidim* and benefactors. Moreover, he had also been a *jahid* and bene-factor much earlier than most veteran members of the congregation.[90] This apolo-getic approach was unusual, since all it took to secure such an honour was a charitable contribution, and da Costa had already offered the considerable sum of 200 guilders. Why would da Costa have felt compelled to remind the Portuguese Jewish regents of his veteran status? In forming a Jewish family, he had broken no laws. Neither Portu-guese Jewish communal ordinances nor colonial decrees prohibited white males from procreating with enslaved women. Furthermore, the Jewish community recognized converted Eurafrican children as Jews, albeit of a lower status (they were *congregantes* as opposed to *jehidim*). Perhaps da Costa, legally married to his childless first cousin, had violated a rule of decorum by publicly recognizing the paternity of his enslaved children and bequeathing the bulk of his property to his progeny. If my hunch is cor-rect, flaunting the conversion and manumission of enslaved children and treating them as rightful heirs was seen as scandalous in 1725.

A similar case was that of Joseph Pelegrino, a Jew of ambiguous ancestry, who in 1720 petitioned the Surinamese authorities to recognize the manumission of his chil-dren. (The family name appears as Peregrino, Perengrino, Pelegrino, and Pelengrino.) Simha, Jacob, and Mariana, he declared, were all conceived outside legal marriage and had all been converted to the Jewish religion through the Portuguese rabbinical teacher (*leraar*). Moreover, these children had been properly manumitted according to the rules of the Jewish 'nation'. What prompted the senior Pelegrino to approach the govern-ment was his concern that their status and right to inheritance would not be accepted outside Jewish circles, whose laws were sometimes at variance with those of the Dutch colonial government. The court granted Pelegrino's request, declaring these children 'free of all slavery' and legitimized as his true descendants.[91]

While this petition and Jewish communal sources lack references to the racial status of Joseph Pelegrino,[92] the legal position of his descendants suggest that he was either a mulatto or a black. According to historian Jean Jacque Vrij, Joseph's son Jacob was clas-

---

[90] NAN, SONA 13, p. 245   [91] Ben-Ur, 'A Matriarchal Matter'; ead., 'Peripheral Inclusion'.

[92] When he pledged a nominal sum to the Beraha Vesalom Synagogue in 1690, his racial status was also unspecified (Bijlagen tot de notulen van mahamad en Junta: Mem das promesas que Prometeraõ os Sres nomeados Abaixo (Appendices of the minutes of the Mahamad and the Junta: Memorandum of pledges promised by the below-mentioned people) (1690), NAN, NPIGS 25).

sified as a *karboeger* (a child of a mulatto and a black) and his grandson Daniel Pelegrino as a negro.[93] My own search for Jacob Pelegrino's racial status has proven largely unfruitful, since the Jewish birth records do not mention it.[94] However, Jacob Peregrino was laid to rest in the *congregante* row of the Jodensavanne cemetery in 1750, as we have seen, confirming his second-class position in Suriname's Jewish community. Moreover, Eurafrican Jewish activists in the 1790s remembered Joseph Pelegrino's son Jacob Pelengrino as a *karboeger* who 'enjoyed similar rights and privileges' to full members of the Jewish congregation.[95]

It is not now possible to reconstruct Joseph Pelegrino's family tree. But his last name—unusual in Suriname—and the naming patterns in his family suggest a New Christian ancestor who had settled on Africa's west coast during the previous century. The story begins with Jacob Peregrino (or Pelegrino), alias Jerónimo Rodrigues Freire, a Portuguese New Christian born in the Portuguese town of Tancos. Peregrino laboured in his native town as a farmer before moving to Lisbon, where he became a salesman. At some point thereafter, he fled to Amsterdam, where he publicly embraced his ancestral faith. His wife also escaped the peninsula for the United Provinces, where she died. In 1611 the widowed Peregrino once again took up the pilgrim's staff, departing for Joal, on the Petite Côte in present-day Senegal.[96] Peregrino intended to combine mercantile goals with religious endeavours. When he departed for the Guinean coast he took not only merchandise for trading,[97] but also a Torah scroll, twelve Bibles, and circumcision tools.[98] Amsterdam's Portuguese Jewish authorities had allegedly dispatched Peregrino to serve as 'the rabbi' (religious teacher) in Guinea's burgeoning New Christian communities, concentrated in Joal and Porto de Ale. His son Manuel Peregrino subsequently followed and functioned as the community's ritual slaughterer.[99] Father and son joined a group of New Christians and reconverted Jews, entirely male or nearly so, who had already settled there, trading iron for ivory, wax, and gold.[100]

[93] Jean Jacques Vrij to Aviva Ben-Ur (15 Aug. 2003), without archival attribution.

[94] In 1732 the birth of Jacob's daughter Hana was recorded in the birth register, but her racial classification is not mentioned ('Hana fa de Jb Pelengrino' (21 Apr. 1732), NAN, Oud Archief Burgerlijke Stand (OABS) 44, p. 27). Two years later, Jacob sired a son named Gabriel, oddly listed in the girls' column, with no circumciser mentioned ('Gabriel f[ilh]o de Jacob Pelengrino' (21 Jan. 1734), NAN, OABS 44, p. 25). The following year, the birth and circumcision register records the arrival of Daniel, son of Jacob Perengrino, but omits any mention of racial classification ('Daniel fo. De Jb. Perengrino', circumcised by David Mendes (20 Oct. 1735), NAN, OABS 44, p. 6). The silences regarding racial status seem to suggest upward mobility at that time.

[95] Vink, *Creole Jews*, 225.

[96] Peter Mark and José da Silva Horta, 'Two Early Seventeenth-Century Sephardic Communities on Senegal's Petite Côte', *History in Africa*, 31 (2004), 238; Tobias Green, 'Further Considerations on the Sephardim of the Petite Côte', *History in Africa*, 32 (2005), 172.

[97] Green, 'Further Considerations on the Sephardim of the Petite Côte', 172.

[98] Mark and Horta, 'Two Early Seventeenth-Century Sephardic Communities', 240–2, 247.

[99] Ibid. 247.   [100] Ibid. 245–6.

About a generation before Peregrino's arrival, some Jewish traders on the western African coast had chosen as their consorts and mothers of their children native-born women, either daughters of local political leaders or affluent merchants. This practice was widespread among immigrant men in the area.[101] As we have seen, Jacob Peregrino had already married and procreated in Portugal. But one of his sons, Manuel Pelegrino, reportedly engaged in sexual intercourse with the daughter of the king of the Wolofs.[102] Whether or not they produced children is unknown, but other inter-cultural couples definitely did. Around 1612 the Jewish communities of Joal and Porto de Ale counted among their members four mulattoes, three of whom were 'identified by their Portuguese city of origin'.[103] This suggests that the community determined Jewishness through patrilineal descent and that some New Christians regularly returned to Europe with their new families. The year before, one Portuguese Jew, a native of Zeeland, related that he had overheard three blacks standing in front of the Portuguese Synagogue in Amsterdam, lamenting the conversion of their African companion to Judaism.[104] Peter Mark and José da Silva Horta, who together unearthed this remarkable material from inquisitorial archives, suggest that such conversions to Judaism 'may have been part of a broader strategy by Dutch Jews to recruit Africans to assist them in their mercantile endeavours on the Guinea coast'.[105]

Other sources also point to the continuing presence of Eurafrican Jews in both Portugal and the Jewish colony of Brazil, founded around 1630. A 'mulatto New Christian', named Manoel Lopes Seixada and born in Lisbon in the first half of the seventeenth century, converted to Judaism in Pernambuco and married a Jewish woman in Brazil. For a time Seixada was the beadle of Recife's synagogue, which may indicate a second-class status, considering that in Amsterdam this role was frequently assigned to Ashkenazi Jews.[106] Francisco de Faria, an Old Christian mulatto (amulatado) with 'woolly hair' converted to Judaism apparently in order to marry his fiancée, a scion of the respected Amsterdam Jewish family Leão. The acceptance by such a highborn family of someone who was both Old Christian and 'mixed race', historian Bruno Feitler surmises, may indicate lack of prejudice in the Recife community. Faria is known to have frequented the Portuguese Synagogue in Amsterdam and signed the registers of Tsur Israel as a jahid.[107] One Salomão Pacheco, also described as mixed race (pardo), was married to a daughter of Moisés Monsanto by 1646. Whether any of these individuals were once slaves is uncertain. What we do know is that Brazil's Mahamad did its

---

[101] Mark and Horta, 'Two Early Seventeenth-Century Sephardic Communities', 252–3; Peter Mark and José da Silva Horta, 'Catholics, Jews, and Muslims in Early Seventeenth-Century Guiné', in Kagan and Morgan (eds.), Atlantic Diasporas, 290.

[102] Green, 'Further Considerations on the Sephardim of the Petite Côte', 177.

[103] Mark and Horta, 'Catholics, Jews, and Muslims', 290.   [104] Ibid. 292.   [105] Ibid. 293.

[106] Bruno Feitler, Inquisition, juifs et nouveaux-chrétiens au Brésil: Le Nordeste XVIIe et XVIIIe siècles (Leuven, 2003), 158.   [107] Ibid.

best to prevent the existence of Jewish slaves. The 1648 *ascamot* of Tsur Israel forbade the conversion of male slaves to Judaism, but implicitly allowed their conversion after manumission.[108] Similarly, a Surinamese ordinance of 1662–3 prohibited 'any *jahid*, under pain of excommunication, to circumcise the sons of those demoted from *jahid* status'. This ordinance discouraged the circumcision of what we may assume were 'coloured' sons, though it does not indicate their status as free or enslaved. It is also unclear from this ordinance what act the *jahid* might have committed in order to be demoted. A later source, an *ascama* from the mid-eighteenth century, cited marriage with a Eurafrican Jew as grounds for such a demotion. But for such a marriage to take place, the woman would have had to be both free and Jewish. The ordinances are probably deliberately opaque, in order to mask public secrets. The euphemisms and lack of detail also suggest that racial policies were both dynamic and hotly contested. The ordinances foreshadow an uneven trajectory that sought unsuccessfully to exclude individuals of African ancestry from the Jewish community or ascribe them a second-class status.

Behaviour

The foregoing evidence indicates that conversion was for some individuals a critical rite of passage into the Jewish community. It does not, however, shed light on the cultural and religious experiences of Eurafricans as Jews. Arnold Eisen, a scholar of American Jewish sociology, suggests that Jewishness can be gauged not by stated or implied religious beliefs, but rather actions: ritual, communal, political, and professional. In other words, what Jews did, rather than what they allegedly believed, is most important.[109] Recorded behaviour indicates that Jewish identity among Africans and Eurafricans was not merely a legal status in the community. One example is a 'Jewish negro' belonging to a Jew by the last name of de la Parra. This unnamed slave had absconded into the woods in 1759, taking his master's scroll of Esther. The scroll was found in one of the Maroon huts by a military expedition charged with capturing runaway slaves.[110] The master may have been the lieutenant of the Jewish military division, Joseph de Abraham de la Parra, who reported the flight and recapture of runaway slaves.[111] The slave's religious identity or formal belonging in the Jewish community are ambiguous. Was he a 'Joode Neeger' because he was owned by a Jew? Or had he undergone a circumcision and immersion ritual that accorded him Jewish status or status as the slave of a Jew? Since a biblical scroll was not a practical object to steal or to ensure survival in

---

[108] Ascamot (5409) [1648–49], Stadsarchief Amsterdam (Amsterdam Municipal Archives) 334, 1304. Literally, no slave may 'be circumcised without first having been freed by his master, so that the master shall not be able to sell him from the moment the slave will have bound himself [to Judaism]'.

[109] Arnold M. Eisen, 'Rethinking Jewish Modernity', *Jewish Social Studies*, NS 1 (1994), 18.

[110] Gouvernements Journaal, 411 (10 Aug. 1759), NAN, Archief West Indie Surinam.

[111] Gouvernements Journaal, 411 (29 Feb. 1756; 27 May 1759), NAN, Archief West Indie Surinam.

the woods, he may have been fully aware of the religious significance of his booty. Given the centrality of the book of Esther to New Christian identity, he may have also realized the sentimental value of biblical scrolls as precious relics passed down through the generations or perhaps he regarded the roll of parchment as a talisman to protect him from capture.

The Jewish holiday of Purim, during which the scroll of Esther is publicly read twice, was a time of raucous, uncontrollable agitation in Suriname. In 1777 the Mahamad complained about the great disorder that always occurred during the ritual recitation of Esther, both in Beraha Vesalom, Jodensavanne's synagogue, and in Sedek Vesalom, the Sephardi house of prayer in Paramaribo. Those present would beat the benches with hammers, clubs, and other hard objects, not only causing damage to the furniture (and hence expense to the community), but also preventing worshippers from hearing the reading of the cantor as required by Jewish law. The Mahamad forbade everyone—including teachers, fathers, and children's tutors—from 'beating Haman' with hard instruments and permitted only clappers or similar implements.[112] The tradition of masquerading at Purim was also perceived as a threat by the colonial authorities. Governor General J. F. Friderici prohibited the wearing of masks or costumes or dressing children up in 'strange dress'. This would ensure the 'good order and tranquillity' of the Jews and would also stop the assembly of slaves, commotion in the streets, and 'indecency' by body servants (*moleques*), who circled the masqueraders with shouts and meandered through the streets singing.[113] The agitation was evidently a male phenomenon, tied in with a long tradition of Jewish violence erupting during the festive observance of that holiday.[114] Despite the Mahamad's efforts to subdue the festivities, Purim was eagerly anticipated by Surinamese Jews each year. An advertisement for Purim masks in 1793 appeared in November, some four months before the holiday, illustrating Roger Caillois's observation that members of traditional societies lived 'in remembrance of one festival and in expectation of the next'.[115]

Purim, which celebrates the overturning of a royal decree to wipe out the Jews of ancient Persia, was arguably the most boisterous Jewish holiday. It was especially attractive to judaizing New Christians, who identified with Queen Esther, the young Jewess who deliberately passed as a non-Jew in order to reverse the king's edict and save her people from annihilation. Because most privately owned biblical scrolls were the property of men, it is telling that a number of Surinamese women owned scrolls of Esther. Being both female and of crypto-Jewish ancestry perhaps led them to identify more closely than their male counterparts with the 'closet' Jewess of the Bible. One

---

[112] Minuut-notulen van vergaderingen van de Senhores do Mahamad (26 Feb. 1777), NAN, NPIGS 1.

[113] Minuut-notulen van vergaderingen van de Senhores do Mahamad (28 Feb. 1800), NAN, NPIGS 4.

[114] Elliott S. Horowitz, *Reckless Rites: Purim and the Legacy of Jewish Violence* (Princeton, 2006).

[115] *Weeklysche Surinaamsche Courant*, 20 (14 Nov. 1793), 6; Roger Caillois, *L'Homme et le sacré* (Paris, 1963), 125; trans in Peter Burke, *Popular Culture in Early Modern Europe*, 3rd edn. (Farnham, Surrey, 2009), 256.

cannot help but speculate about this when considering Sarah de Miranda, wife of Emanuel d'Anavia, who in 1803 left her daughter Rachel a 'meguila or the History of Ahasuerus',[116] or the aforementioned Roza Judia, who also owned a scroll of Esther, which is listed in the 1771 inventory of her possessions.[117]

The 'Jewish negro' who ran away in 1759 may have also prized as his own the historical narrative of his master's scroll. There is indirect evidence suggesting that Jewish identity or practice among slaves owned by the de la Parra clan was not particular to him or his generation. The Creole cemetery in Jodensavanne, where former slaves and their freeborn descendants were interred, preserves several epitaphs from the Wijngaard (or Wijngaarde) family.[118] According to Surinamese custom, many manumitted slaves adopted the family name of their former masters or mistresses, but in a translated or otherwise altered form.[119] This was encoded in law in 1832, when slaves were forbidden to carry the family name of their owners or any white family in the colony.[120] Following this tradition or regulation, one branch of the Eurafrican de la Parra clan became Wijngaard, meaning 'vineyard' in Dutch (and a wink at Parra, 'grapevine' in Spanish).[121] Annaatje van la Parra had been owned by Jeosua de la Parra. Her (common-law?) husband, Abraham Garsia Junior, was director of the Rijks Steen-springerij plantation and the De Worsteling Jacob timber estate and is buried in the Jodensavanne cemetery, with a bilingual Hebrew/Portuguese epitaph covering his grave. In 1831 Annaatje gave birth at Jodensavanne to a daughter named Salij Garsia Junior, and in 1860 was buried in the Creole cemetery in Jodensavanne.[122] Three years

---

[116] Will of Sarah de Miranda, wife of Emanuel d'Anavia (4 Apr. 1803), NAN, SONA 82, will no. 34.

[117] Will of the free mulattress Roza Mendes Meza (23 Feb. 1802), NAN, SONA 81, will no. 17.

[118] Legible epitaphs from this family identify the following individuals: Annatje van la Parra (d. 3 Oct. 1860); Abraham Garcia Wijngaarde (1823–1915); Jacobus Jacques Wijngaarde (1854–1943), evidently a Christian, judging from the cross in the first line of his epitaph; F. R. Wijngaarde (1810–88); J. G. Wijngaarde (1821–95); Naatje-E. Wijngaarde (1868–1937); Marius Wijngaarde (1896–1943); Rosalina Helena Selina Wijngaarde Colin (1880–1947); Jachevs H. Wijngaarde (1858–1948); Francina Elizabeth Wijngaarde (1863–[illeg.]); Gertruida Anna Wijngaard (19[illeg.], at the age of 40); Maria A. Wijngaarde, dates of birth and death illegible. Wadily Wijnhard believes that Abraham of [meaning either 'son of' or 'slave of', or both] Jeos. de la Parra, manumitted in 1827, is the aforementioned Abraham Garcia Wijngaarde. Wijnhard located the manumission request in *Surinaamsche Courant* (24 Jan. 1827).

[119] See e.g. the will of the free mulatto Joseph Nassy (25 Feb. 1790), which mentions Anna Jacoba Yssan, probably the daughter of the testator and his manumitted concubine (NAN, SONA 63, will no. 98).

[120] Okke ten Hove and Frank Dragtenstein, *Manumissies in Suriname, 1832–1863* (Utrecht, 1997), 62.

[121] Wadily Wijnhard, email to Rachel Frankel (11 Mar. 2010).

[122] Wijnhard discovered this information in a request for a manumission certificate for Antonia Wijngaard. The request was registered by the widow of Jeosua de la Parra, as heir of her deceased husband (Wadily Wijnhard, emails to Rachel Frankel (11, 13 Mar. 2010)). For Annaatje van la Parra's epitaph, see Ben-Ur and Frankel, *Remnant Stones*, vol. i: *Epitaphs*, 153; for that of Abraham Garcia Junior, see ibid. 181 (the correlation of the man buried in Jodensavanne and Annaatje's husband is tentative). See also births and acknowledgements (Paramaribo), NAN 2.10.61, 4, fiche no. 5, fo. 239/2. I thank Wadily Wijnhard for this source. On the Wijn-gaarde family, see also H. A. Oron, 'No aksi mi fu libi yu: A View on the History of the Congregation "Sivah Darkhey Y'sharim"—the Judeo-Creole Jews of Suriname' (M.A. thesis, Leiden University, 2009).

after her death, Annaatje's four heirs (Judith Grasiana Wijngaard, Abraham Garsia Wijngaard, Elias Garsia Wijngaard, and Salij Garsia Wijngaard) were all living at Joden-savanne.[123]

The religious or ethnic identities of Annaatje and other decedents buried in the Creole cemetery are unclear, and, as Wieke Vink notes, the Sephardi last names some bear are not definitive indications of Jewish identity.[124] However, other Eurafricans with similar family names (and first names that suggest conversion to Judaism) were definitely part of Suriname's Sephardi community. One was Abraham van Wyngarde, active in the Portuguese Jewish burial society in the 1790s and a former slave, as indicated by the 'van' in his last name.[125] Another, Abraham Wyngaarde, purchased a large coffin from the Portuguese Jewish burial society Liviat Hen in 1803.[126]

Material possessions demonstrate other ways in which Eurafricans identified with Judaism and its rituals. Roza Judia owned several timber estates in the 1760s and 1770s, a few dozen slaves, and real estate in Paramaribo; she also possessed various Hebrew books, a prayer book in Spanish, a Hanukah candelabrum, and a sabbath lamp (in addition to the scroll of Esther mentioned earlier).[127] Roza Judia's library marks her as the member of an elite not only in her Jewish community, but also in the colony in general. Rosemary Brana-Shute has noted that 'colonial Suriname was a profoundly alliterate society' that placed a 'relatively low value' on literature.[128] To reinforce her assertion, consider that even among Jews, the proverbial 'people of the book', reading material was rare, or at least rarely passed down in wills. Of several hundred Jewish testaments and codicils passed from 1716 to 1805, only nineteen Jewish legators, most of them Portuguese Jews, mentioned books or sacred scrolls. Roza's library was all the more exceptional given her gender. As a rule, secular and sacred books mentioned in Jewish wills were owned and legated by men to other males. This rule applies equally to Sephardi and Ashkenazi Jews.

Roza Judia's nephew Abraham (or Abram) Ismael Judeo (d. 1789) also showed a strong European Jewish orientation. A former slave, Abraham could sign his name and had his will recorded in Dutch, rather than Sranan Tongo. In his 1780 will, he clearly

---

[123] Wadily Wijnhard, emails to Rachel Frankel with transcribed documents (11, 13 Mar. 2010). Judith, described as a 'mustice' and a child, was owned by Jeosua de la Parra and manumitted in 1824 (Humphrey Ewald Lamur and Heinrich E. Helstone, *Namen van Vrijgemaakte Slaven, 1816–1827* (Amsterdam, 2002), no. 482).

[124] Vink, *Creole Jews*, 157–8. Besides variations of de la Parra, one may also observe Lobles, an alteration of Robles, and Cotin, an abbreviation of Cotino.

[125] Records of freewill offerings (July 1794; 24 Mar. 1797), NAN, NPIGS 439.

[126] Liviat Hen account books and receipts (27 May 1803), NAN, NPIGS 440, pp. 5, 10.

[127] Will of Roza Judia, NAN, SONA 218, p. 625; inventory of Roza Judia (1771), NAN, SONA 234, pp. 442–3; will of the free Abram Ismael Judeo (15 Mar. 1780), NAN, SONA 61, p. 302.

[128] Rosemary Brana-Shute, 'Legal Resistance to Slavery in Eighteenth Century Suriname', in Gary Brana-Shute (ed.), *Resistance and Rebellion in Suriname: Old and New* (Williamsburg, Va., 1990), 119–36, 132.

stated his desire to be buried in the Jewish fashion, requesting, as did so many white Jewish testators throughout the century, a blue sark stone. Abraham bequeathed the poor of the Dutch Protestant Reform community a perfunctory 5 guilders, with a more symbolic 10 guilders going to the Beraha Vesalom Synagogue of Jodensavanne.[129]

A final example is the free mulattress Maria or Mariana del Prado (alias de Prado), with roots on the Caxewinica Creek. Her family had owned property on the creek since at least 1737, when a plantation belonging to E. R. R. de Prado was listed at 2,300 acres.[130] Maria owned land near the Quapibo timber estate on the Caxewinica Creek that had, by 1780, been left to her children.[131] When she dictated her will in Paramaribo in 1787, she required a Portuguese interpreter, not being in full command of Dutch. She gave 5 guilders each to the Dutch Protestant Reform and Portuguese Jewish congregations. Although no instructions regarding last rites are indicated, Maria's children all bore Hebrew names: David, Abram, Moses, Hana or Gana, and Ribca. As is typical of Eurafricans in general, Maria named no father in her will, suggesting she bore the children out of wedlock.[132]

Additional examples, recorded in the minutes of the Portuguese Jewish community, also point to Eurafrican identification with religious Jewishness. In 1783 the 'mulatto Simon Mendes' approached the first *parnas* of the Mahamad with a confession of religious transgression. Having been unaware that it was the first day of the Festival of Shavuot, he had travelled aboard a ship to carry out his work. Realizing that he had violated the holy day, even though inadvertently, he humbly submitted himself before the Jewish governing board for punishment. Given his own initiative in coming forward, his great repentance, and the fact that the infraction was involuntary, the Mahamad sentenced him to fast for five consecutive Thursdays, ordered him to worship three times in the synagogue every sabbath, and, finally, required a donation of 10 guilders to the charity chest. Mendes received the spiritual correction (*tesuba*) very willingly and promised to observe it solemnly and to tend to his obligations better henceforth. It would be tempting to speculate from this that Eurafrican Jews were more isolated from mainstream Judaism than their legally white co-religionists. However, Mendes's profession as some kind of travelling merchant may have been the cause of his calendrical ignorance.[133] Religious conscientiousness also prompted David Judeo to seek special permission to shave his beard during the High Holy intermediary days, using a loophole in a seventeenth-century ordinance that forbade hair removal during holiday weeks. In 1788 he was one of seventeen Portuguese Jews on the

---

[129] Will of Abraham Ismael Judeo (15 Mar. 1780), NAN, SONA 61, p. 302; death register, Abm. Ismahel Júdeó (*congregante*), died on 'Caxewinica no Plante. Cúpij' (31 May 1789), NAN, NPIGS 420, p. 2.

[130] Ana Crespo Solana, *América Desde Otra Frontera: La Guayana Holandesa (Surinam), 1680–1795* (Madrid, 2006), 231. [131] Inventory of the Quapibo plantation (22–3 Jan. 1782), NAN, SONA 790, pp. 17–29.

[132] Will of the free mulattress Maria de Prado (12 June 1787), NAN, SONA 57, pp. 460–5.

[133] Minuut-notulen van vergaderingen van de Senhores do Mahamad (4 June 1783), NAN, NPIGS 2.

savannah—and the only verifiable Eurafrican—who submitted a physician's notice declaring his medical necessity to shave.[134]

Conclusion: Religious Conversion or Cultural Bequest?

Recent scholarly attention has focused on enslaved and freed people in the Atlantic world and their identification with various denominations of Christianity and Islam.[135] But little thought has been given to their relationship to what is arguably the world's first monotheistic religion. Suriname should be the first place to explore this question. In no other Caribbean colony is the record of Eurafrican Jews so rich, varied, and long. Even as scholars seek to include Judaism in the recognized array of Atlantic religions embraced by slaves and their manumitted or freeborn descendants, we must contend with the reality that Jewishness among this population in Suriname and perhaps elsewhere more approximated an ethnic, rather than a religious, identity. Herein lie the perils of the term 'Jewish' and its comparison to 'Muslim' and 'Christian'.

All of the foregoing evidence suggests that to assess Jewishness and Jewish identity among Eurafricans by determining their ritual conversion (circumcision and immersion for males, just immersion for females) distorts the picture of what many Jewish slave masters attempted to do when they included slaves in their household and what belonging in a Jewish community may have meant to Eurafricans. Conversion was but a small part of a bequest of an entire culture that included—besides 'religion'—language, name-giving practices, historical consciousness, and identification with the Jewish people, both locally and remotely. This discussion suggests the limits of focusing on conversion as an expression of Jewishness or Jewish identity among Surinamese Eurafricans. The cultural patrimony of Suriname's Jews, whether legally white or Eurafrican, was multidimensional, including, but not limited to, religion. During the second half of the eighteenth century, moreover, it is perhaps more proper to speak of a 'cultural matrimony', since Eurafrican Jews were increasingly not converts, but rather born Jews, often the progeny of a Eurafrican Jewish mother and unnamed father. For all these reasons, we would do better to consider the conversion ritual as just one—and probably not the most central—component of Jewishness and Jewish belonging among Eurafrican Jews.

---

[134] Minuut-notulen van vergaderingen van de Senhores do Mahamad (18 Oct. 1788), NAN, NPIGS 2. The earliest known use of this loophole is from 1778, when Samuel Uziel D'avilar complained to the Mahamad that his beard caused him sickness and was greatly bothersome; he asked permission to shave it during the High Holy intermediary days (Minuut-notulen van vergaderingen van de Senhores do Mahamad (8 Oct. 1778), NAN, NPIGS 1).

[135] See e.g. Gomez, *Exchanging our Country Marks*; Sylvia R. Frey and Betty Wood, *Come Shouting to Zion: African American Protestantism in the American South and British Caribbean to 1830* (Chapel Hill, NC, 1998); Jon F. Sensbach, *A Separate Canaan: The Making of an Afro-Moravian World in North Carolina, 1763–1840* (Chapel Hill, NC, 1998); *Rebecca's Revival: Creating Black Christianity in the Atlantic World* (Cambridge, Mass., 2005).

Perhaps because of their novelty, a quest for enslaved and manumitted Jews in Suriname is sufficiently interesting in and of itself. These individuals are an anomaly in broader Jewish history and, as Wieke Vink has noted, offer a counter-narrative to the equation of Jews with both whiteness and eliteness.[136] But far more than a collective 'curiosity', Jewish slaves and their free descendants shed light upon the majority societies in which they lived. After identifying as many Eurafrican Jews as possible, it may be possible to discover the uneven, transgenerational process by which they were rejected or marginalized and then gradually accepted by the mainstream Jewish community as social equals to whites. The means by which this subgroup became integrated and achieved legal equality may tell a larger story about social change in the Caribbean. Their complex ethno-religious identity and the initiatives they took to assert and preserve it also invite scholars to shift the focus from black Atlantic religions to black ethnicities. Jewishness is historically a civilization, not a religion, as the history of Eurafrican Jews constantly reminds us.

[136] See Vink, *Creole Jews*, 267.

ACKNOWLEDGEMENTS
I would like to thank the American Council of Learned Societies for an ACLS/SSRC/NEH International and Area Studies Fellowship and the Memorial Foundation for Jewish Culture for its fellowship, both granted for the 2008 calendar year. These grants were awarded to advance my work on Suriname's Eurafrican Jews and it is a pleasure to present some early gleanings in this chapter. The archivists at the Nationaal Archief Nederland have my gratitude for the assistance they have offered me since my first research trip there in 2001.

CHAPTER ELEVEN

SHIFTING IDENTITIES

Religion, Race, and Creolization among the Sephardi Jews of Barbados, 1654–1900

KARL WATSON

RELIGION, historical associations, language, and geographical origin all combined to give the Jews of Barbados a distinct identity which marked them as a separate category within seventeenth- and eighteenth-century Barbadian society. These markers of identity, as Tajfel and Turner point out in their theory of social identity, are integral factors which provide that degree of distinctiveness on which group comparisons are based.[1] First and foremost, they were Jews in a Christian society, notwithstanding the fact that, as a number of scholars have pointed out, when they arrived on the island in the 1650s, there was no religious cohesion in Barbados, with splinter groups, particularly the Quakers, providing a challenge to the established state religion, Anglicanism. Jews were sufficiently distinct in religious practice and sufficiently burdened with the stereotypes ingrained in the European psyche, to be labelled 'Other'.[2]

However, the Barbadian Jewish community was not simply a group of Jews. They were Sephardim, whose origins lay essentially in Spain and Portugal. This was an extremely important marker that singled them out as a distinct category. They had a clear understanding of their identity as a group, one that was positive, despite the shock of the Expulsion from the Iberian peninsula and their subsequent diaspora.[3] Wherever the Sephardim went, they took with them specific rituals which distinguished them from the Ashkenazim. In the seventeenth century, the development of an Atlantic economic system presented new opportunities, which the Sephardim were well placed to exploit. The Atlantic, the North Sea, the Baltic, the Mediterranean, and the Indian Ocean were all convenient highways which linked the nodal points of an extensive Sephardi trading network.[4]

[1] Henri Tajfel and John C. Turner, 'The Social Identity Theory of Intergroup Behaviour', in S. Worchel and W. G. Austin (eds.), *Pyschology of Intergroup Relations* (Chicago, 1986), 7–24.

[2] See L. Brett Brinegar, 'Radical Politics and Civil Disobedience: Quaker Resistance in Seventeenth Century Bridgetown', *Journal of the Barbados Museum and Historical Society*, 49 (2003), 150–66.

[3] Gordon Merrill, 'The Role of Sephardic Jews in the British Caribbean Area during the Seventeenth Century', *Caribbean Studies*, 4/3 (1964), 32–49.

[4] David Cesarani, 'Port Jews: Concepts, Cases and Questions', in id. (ed.), *Port Jews: Jewish Communities in Cosmopolitan Maritime Trading Centres, 1550–1950* (London, 2002), 1.

Initially, the Dutch conquest of Pernambuco and the growth of Recife as a Dutch entrepôt linked to Amsterdam and Hamburg, provided the opportunity for several Jewish families from Antwerp and Amsterdam to re-establish themselves in Brazil. Their numbers were enlarged by New Christians already in Brazil. So numerous did the Jewish population of Pernambuco become that two synagogues were established there, Magen Abraham in Mauricia and Tsur Israel in Recife.[5] During the relatively short period that the Dutch occupied Pernambuco (1630–54), the Sephardi families became a formidable and indispensable force in the economy. Not only did they play their traditional role as financiers and middlemen in trade matters, they also actively entered the production process. Growing sugar cane and processing the juice into crystals for export formed the backbone of the Pernambucan economy. Many Sephardim moved beyond the stage of intermediary merchants in Recife and acquired land for growing sugar cane. This thrust them into another area of economic activity: supplying and managing workers to meet the needs of the labour-intensive sugar business. Even though some labour was supplied by the local Amerindian population, the majority of it came from enslaved West Africans. Although the ex-Iberian Sephardim had been exposed to enslaved Africans in Spain and Portugal, it did not prepare them for the extent to which slavery dominated every aspect of life in Brazil. Slavery acted as a powerful agent in the shaping of a new identity for this New World Sephardi group.

Barbados

Dutch notarial records make it clear that there were commercial contacts between Pernambuco and Barbados in the 1630s and that some involved Sephardi Jews.[6] Although the records do not enable us to say with certainty when a Sephardi population first established itself in Barbados, it is clear that by the 1640s, Jewish individuals or families were starting to move to the island. The source of this migration was most likely either Amsterdam, which by then dominated the western Sephardi diaspora, or Brazil. The minutes of the Council of Barbados for 8 November 1654 include a request from the existing Jewish community of Barbados to allow Jews from Brazil entry to the island.[7] We have no idea of the size of this community, but the fact that a group of

[5] See Arnold Wiznitzer, 'The Minute Book of Congregations Zur Israel of Recife and Magen Abraham of Mauricia, Brazil', in Martin A. Cohen (ed.), *The Jewish Experience in Latin America*, 2 vols. (New York: Ktav, 1971), ii. 227–303; see also Albert Dines et al., *A Fênix, ou, o eterno retorno: 460 anos da presença judaica em Pernambuco* (Brasilia, Brazil, 2001).

[6] Yda Schreuder, 'Evidence from the Notarial Protocols in the Amsterdam Municipal Archives about Trade Relationships between Amsterdam and Barbados in the Seventeenth Century', *Journal of the Barbados Museum and Historical Society*, 52 (2006), 54–82.

[7] Yda Schreuder, 'A True Global Community: Sephardic Jews, the Sugar Trade and Barbados in the Seventeenth Century', *Journal of the Barbados Museum and Historical Society*, 50 (2004), 166–94.

Jews had sufficient coherence and sense of community to allow them to make a formal petition to the island's council would indicate a certain level of rootedness. In its response two months later, the council, in granting the request, used the word 'several' to describe the petitioners. Schreuder points out that at the same time, the 'Jewish nation' of Barbados made a similar request to the Dutch West India Company.

Other evidence, both monumental and archaeological, points to Jews in Barbados having a solid footing early on. The earliest documented reference to a synagogue comes from a plot survey by Andrew Norwood from 1664 which shows as a 'bounder', 'The Jewes Synagogue & Burying Place'.[8] A marble tablet inscribed with the date 1752 unearthed in the synagogue yard some years ago commemorates the centennial anniversary of an event that occurred in 1652, although we do not know exactly what. Speculation associates it with the establishment of the *mikveh* excavated in March 2008 (Figure 11.1). The ceramics and clay pipes removed from uncontaminated levels 4 and 5 of the Nidhe Israel Synagogue compound, certainly confirm a median date of 1660, plus or minus ten years.[9] The level of activity revealed by the archaeological record and the permanence implied by the substantial structures of the seventeenth-century synagogue and *mikveh* would certainly indicate a community with a sense of purpose and permanence (Figure 11.2).

Many Sephardim fleeing the Portuguese reconquest of Dutch Brazil sought refuge in Barbados, attracted by its potential for economic growth and its political independence during the Commonwealth of England (1649–60). It also allowed them to maintain their foothold in the tropical Americas while using their extended family networks in Europe to further their economic well-being.

The historian Arnold Wiznitzer has published lists of the congregations of the two Brazilian synagogues that have been correlated with the subsequent Sephardi community established in Barbados. The number of individuals making the transition to Barbados is remarkable. Fourteen of the twenty-one Mahamad members listed in Wiznitzer's record, as well as all five members honoured by inclusion in the ritual reading known as the 'Hatan bereshit', emigrated to Barbados.[10] Tracing surnames in the Barbadian and Brazilian records shows that some 30 per cent of the remaining Sephardi families of Recife chose Barbados as their destination.

The name the group chose for their Barbadian synagogue, Nidhe Israel (The Dispersed of Israel), is also significant, reflecting the aspirations and messianic outlook

---

[8] This plot is reproduced in *Journal of the Barbados Museum and Historical Society*, 15 (1948), 82.

[9] The University of the West Indies conducted excavations in the compound of the synagogue from February to April 2008. In the course of the excavations, the seventeenth-century *bano* or *mikveh* was revealed. An initial report by Michael Stoner and Karl Watson is in preparation. In the surviving documents of the Nidhe Israel Synagogue, which are on deposit in the London Metropolitan Archives, the Spanish/Portuguese term *bano* is always used and the female caretaker is listed in the minutes and accounts as the *banadeira*.

[10] Arnold Wiznitzer, 'The Members of the Brazilian Jewish Community (1648–1653)', in Cohen (ed.), *The Jewish Experience in Latin America*, ii. 218–26; see also Schreuder, 'A True Global Community', 178.

which informed their world-view. Menasseh ben Israel's tract 'Hope of Israel' (1650), which was influential at this time, stressed the point that the dispersion of Jews around the world was a portent of the pending messianic age and represented the 'hope of Israel'. Even as late as 1800 evidence of hope and deliverance persisted. The wealthiest and most influential Barbadian Jew of the time, Abraham Rodrigues Brandon, named his plantation 'Hopeland'.

Demographic Patterns

In 1679 the governor of the island, Jonathan Atkins, responding to a request from the Board of Trade and Plantations, carried out a detailed census. The perceived 'Otherness' of Barbadian Jews is revealed by the fact that they were included in the island's white population but listed separately. Fifty-four Sephardi families were counted in Bridgetown; six in St Peter, almost certainly inhabitants of Speightstown; and a single individual, David Nemias, was listed for Christ Church. He is singled out as 'a Jew',

Figure 11.1 *Mikveh*, Nidhe Israel Synagogue, Bridgetown, Barbados

Celso Brewster, Manager Nidhe Israel Museum

Figure 11.2 Front elevation of Nidhe Israel Synagogue, Bridgetown, Barbados (rebuilt)
Courtesy of the collection of the Barbados Museum and Historical Society

owning 20 acres of land and twelve slaves. He may well have been counted twice and be the same David Nemias who is listed as a resident of Bridgetown. Another individual, David Acosta is listed as a landowner in the parish of St Thomas. All told, there were 317 Jews in Barbados in 1679.[11]

The 1715 census of the white population did not single out Jews. Using surnames to distinguish members of the Sephardi community, an estimated 411 people were counted, 91 adult males, 122 adult females, 103 boys, and 95 girls. All of these totals are almost certainly inaccurate. Male members of families were often travelling, and other evidence such as wills and deeds reveals that some names were omitted from the censuses. However, for all their flaws, the censuses do point us in the right direction. By the mid-eighteenth century, contemporary estimates put the Jewish population at between 600 and 800 people, though this figure may be slightly inflated. By the mid-nineteenth century, this number had dropped to less than 100. Emigration increased,

---

[11] The census material for 1679/80 was reproduced in John Camden Hotten, *Original Lists of Persons of Quality 1600–1700* (Baltimore, 1968), 449–50. There is a transcribed copy of the 1715 census in the Barbados Department of Archives (BDA). This material has also been reproduced in David L. Kent, *Barbados and America* (Arlington, Va., 1980). Material relating to the Jewish population of Barbados was extracted from this census and used by Wilfred S. Samuel, *Review of the Jewish Colonists of Barbados in 1680* (London, 1936).

Table 11.1 Jewish wills registered in Barbados

Date	Male	Female	Total
1650–1700	16	1	17
1701–1750	51	15	66
1751–1800	50	28	78
1801–1850	47	35	82
1851–1900	28	15	43
Total	**192**	**94**	**286**

Source: Will books, BDA

especially to destinations such as New York, London, and Philadelphia; marriages decreased; and entire families died out or became assimilated into the Christian population.

The Massiah family illustrates the extent of Jewish assimilation into Barbadian Christian society. By the end of the eighteenth century some members had already become planters in St John.[12] By the end of the nineteenth all the Massiahs had joined the white planter elite. By the 1860s there are very few wills bearing the names of the families who had established themselves in the seventeenth century. Between 1880 and 1884 the last Barbadian representatives of the Belinfante, Carvallo, and Nunes families wrote their wills. The last of the Pinheiros wrote her will in 1895, the last Lindo in 1904, the last Lealtad in 1909, and the last Valverde in 1910. New surnames such as Elkins, Daniels, Lobo, Finzi, and Baeza appear briefly and by the twentieth century they too disappear, though they all have descendants on the island today (see Table 11.1).

The Sephardim largely practised endogamy. Marriage among cousins was also quite frequent, and Sephardi males clearly shielded their women from the amorous attentions of non-Jews. Casual sexual relations between Jews and Christian whites generally involved Jewish males. There are only three records in the Anglican baptismal registers of the children of a Jewish woman and a Christian man. In 1770 Dean, 'a bastard' son of Sarah Delaplane (De la Penha), was baptized at St Michael's parish church, as was Moses Aboab, the son of Esther Aboab, seven years later. In 1784 Rebecca Lopez and Samuel Goodridge had their two illegitimate children, Felix and Sarah, baptized at St Peter's parish church.[13] Interreligious marriages occurred very infrequently: the island's marriage registers for the period 1643–1800 record only fifteen

---

[12]   The name of Massiah Street in the parish of St John derives from the settlement of a branch of that family in the district in the eighteenth century.

[13]   Baptism records of Dean Delaplane (De la Penha) (24 July 1770), BDA, RL 1/5, p. 40b; Moses Aboab (28 Dec. 1777), BDA, RL 1/5, p. 149; Felix and Sarah Lopez (8 Feb. 1784), BDA, RL 1/39, p. 20.

marriages between Jews and Christians. By the late nineteenth century, however, this pattern was changing, as the number of Jews plummeted dramatically. One such family is that of Edward S. Daniels (see Figure 11.3). Daniels was a descendant of the D'Azevedo, Lindo, and DePaz families. He married into an elite white Barbadian Christian family, the Bonyuns. Their descendants in Barbados today are the Parravicinos, whose Italian links mask their Sephardi heritage.

Apart from their use in reconstructing family histories, wills give an indication of income levels among the Jewish population and demonstrate that a number of Jews were so poor that they left no wills. From the ninety-eight eighteenth-century wills that included specific bequests, the following statistics emerge:

Requests to be 'buried with the Jewish nation' or 'among my brethren the Jews'	45
Bequests of the Five Books of Moses	10
Bequests of cash to relatives	50
Bequests of cash to the synagogue	30
Bequests of cash to 'the poor of the Jewish nation'	15
Bequests of slaves as property	51
Bequests of houses or land	32
Bequests of personal items	23
Manumission of slaves	3
Bequests to family in Barbados	28
Bequests to family overseas	12
Mention of property overseas	3

The high rate of poverty is confirmed by the number of bequests to the Jewish poor. These bequests also show the testators' attachment to their faith, which stressed the importance of charitable deeds. The wills show that slaves and cash constituted the two main pillars of Jewish disposable wealth in Barbados. Initially, Sephardi wills exhibit a level of concern for all their relatives. Over time, however, concern for the extended family declines and vanishes. Until the last decades of the eighteenth century, bequests were made to aunts, uncles, and cousins living outside Barbados, and it is apparent that family contacts and family networks were highly valued and maintained. The situation changed during the nineteenth century, when bequests were almost always confined to the immediate family. Contacts with scattered family members in Amsterdam, Curaçao, and other points ceased. None of the known nineteenth-century wills include bequests for overseas relatives, now removed by two or three generations. This breakdown of the extended family can be traced through an examination of the wills of the Lindo family. After first looking after the interests of their Barbadian relatives in all degrees, they turned their attention to relatives living overseas. Thus, in 1759 David

Figure 11.3 The Daniels family, descendants of the DePaz, Lindo, and D'Azevedo families photographed outside their residence Galba Lodge, *c*.1890

Courtesy of Mrs Noreen Patterson

Lindo made bequests to his three sisters and various nieces who were living in Amsterdam.[14] In 1784 his brother-in-law Abraham Lindo Junior continued the practice, leaving bequests to relatives in Amsterdam, Curaçao, and London. He even remembered in his will two second cousins, Abraham and Jacob Arzulay, 'sons of my cousin Solomon Arzulay dec'd at the Hague in Holland'.[15] Isaac Lindo left money in his will, proved in 1780, to his Amsterdam-based aunt Rebecca Mocatto Nunez and another sum to his cousin Esther Mocatto Nunez of London.[16] In contrast, in 1827 David Lindo, grandson of the first David Lindo, bequeathed all his possessions to 'my dear wife Rachael Lindo'. After her death, the residue was to go to his daughter Sarah Lindo Elkin.[17]

Even in death, a duality existed. Their wills indicate that the Sephardim wished to be 'buried with their brethren the Jews'. At the same time, their tombstones reflect a blending of Jewish and Christian iconography which underscores their adaptability and adoption of other cultural symbols.[18]

[14]   Will of David Lindo (8 June 1759), BDA, RB 6/5, pp. 39–41.
[15]   Will of Abraham Lindo Junior (1784), BDA, RB 6/28, p. 250.
[16]   Will of Isaac Lindo (10 Nov. 1780), BDA, RB 6/23, p. 346.
[17]   Will of David Lindo (11 June 1827), BDA, original wills.
[18]   Karl Watson, 'The Iconography of Tombstones in the Jewish Graveyard', *Journal of the Barbados Museum and Historical Society*, 50 (2004), 195–212.

Role-Switching: Sephardi Jews as Barbadian Whites

Barbadian Jews were bound by laws and halakhic principles, and refusal to adhere to these could result in expulsion from the community. There are several examples of *ascamot* relating to correct behaviour issued by the Barbadian Mahamad in the minute books. As in England, 'the Mahamad kept a firm hand on the Yehidim'.[19] The laws included dietary proscriptions, attendance at synagogue and participation in and respect for the High Holy Days and other Jewish festivals, payment of financial contributions such as the *finta* (poll tax), adherence to Jewish educational norms for the young, and overall adherence to moral and cultural principles. There were sanctions against marrying outside the community and getting too close to Christians. The Mahamad oversaw the management of the synagogue's funds, employed and managed the *ḥazan* and other officers of the synagogue, paid for the physical upkeep of the synagogue, provided educational services for Jewish children and pensions and medical services for the aged and destitute, maintained transient Jews, and paid the passage of those who wished to leave Barbados. They also functioned as a quasi-legal body, arbitrating civil cases and imposing penalties. The Mahamad, in some cases more so than the religious functionaries, were the final arbiters of Orthodoxy and the maintainers of the spirit of Sephardi identity. When seeking to obtain the services of a *ḥazan*, the Mahamad invariably stressed the need for a married individual with a good voice, who read Hebrew well and understood 'the Spanish so as to be able to teach our children to Ladinar'.[20]

There were difficulties. Sobriety was valued among the Sephardim, yet time and time again, the minutes address concerns over inebriation among the synagogue's officers. The *ḥazan*, David Sarfatti de Pinna was described as having 'an attachment to strong drink and a natural slothfulness of disposition'.[21] Six years later, the Mahamad forced the *shamash*, David Carvalho, to resign on the grounds that he was always 'drunk and incapable of performing his duties'.[22] In 1836 the *shamash*, De Meza, was found 'at various periods in a State of Intemperance & of late it has become a complete Nuisance and disgrace upon the Nation'. At the same time, the *ḥazan*, E. R. Miranda, was often 'in such a state of intemperance as not to be able to do the duty of his office'.[23]

[19] Albert M. Hyamson, *The Sephardim of England: A History of the Spanish and Portuguese Jewish Community 1492–1951* (London, 1951), 65.

[20] Phineas Nunes to Jacob Barrow, Minutes of meetings of the Mahamad and Adjuntos (31 [*sic*] Apr. 1797), p. 33, London Metropolitan Archives (LMA)/4521/D/01/01/002. The reference to Ladinar is significant as this underscores the strong desire to maintain cultural continuity in the face of 'our now very much reduced congregation'. Ladino was, and still is, a linguistically binding force for the Sephardim, akin to Yiddish for the Ashkenazim.   [21] Ibid.

[22] Minutes of meetings of the Mahamad and Adjuntos (27 Sept. 1803).

[23] Letterbook (13 Oct. 1836), p. 101, Minutes of meetings of Yehidim, Vestry, etc., LMA/4521/D/01/01/005.

As often happens, illicit sex also caused problems. In 1806 the Mahamad struck Rebecca Ramos off the pension list 'for her suffering herself to be debauched'.[24] In 1811 the widow Gomez, who had just given birth to a son, was castigated for her behaviour which 'brought disgrace on the community'. Ḥazan Abendana testified that on a March night he, Mr Castillo, and others were congregated at Mrs Burgess's front door when 'Mrs Gomez came up and behaved in a most vindictive and indecent manner & declared Mr Castillo had kept her nine months & that if he left her, she would go on the Town'.[25] In response, the Mahamad decreed that no officer of the synagogue should attend the circumcision of the child nor would any offerings by Mrs Gomez to the synagogue be accepted. One year later, it was the ḥazan's turn to fall from grace, this time in spectacular fashion. A rumour had been circulating for some time among the slaves of the neighbourhood that Abendana had impregnated the enslaved nurse of his three children. Worse, from the Mahamad's point of view, 'there was a report that he had a venereal disease'. Doctor Richards, who had examined Abendana, was questioned and confirmed that 'it was that disease & that he had directed medicine for him, in conformity to that Belief'. It seems that Abendana, wishing to retain his anonymity, had sent a young man to the pharmacist to have the prescription filled. The Mahamad decided on a full investigation, based 'on an Internal conviction that he has been with women & disgraced the sacredness of that office'. Various inhabitants of the synagogue yard were called in and offered mostly circumstantial evidence. Thus Sarah Massiah, the *banadeira*, 'deposed that from the Negro woman constantly following him about the yard as well as conversation that took place among Negroes, she entertained no doubt that a connection existed between Mr Abendana and the woman'. The *shoḥet*, Mr Belasco, also said that he 'had heard the same talk among Negroes of such improper connection'. However, the most damning testimony came from the ex-*shamash*, Judah Massiah, who declared that 'he had been an eye witness to such instances of Familiarity as left no doubt in his mind that a connection existed'. Moreover, he had 'heard this woman disputing with another, in jealousy of Mr Abendana', that she 'had owned to him she was with child for Mr Abendana & that a white woman had told this Witness that she was compelled to leave Mr Abendana's service in consequence of his attempting to take improper liberties with her'.[26] Protesting his innocence, Abendana was told to pack his bags and return to England with his family. Of note in this case and others of similar nature which occurred in the synagogue yard, was the degree to which slaves were informed about and discussed the private lives of the whites of Bridgetown.

The Mahamad attempted to stem the tide of assimilation while also ensuring that the community maintained a low profile. In a meeting of the Mahamad on 14 October 1814, Mr DaCosta advised that decorations and lighting of the synagogue on festive

---

[24]   Minutes of meetings of the Mahamad and Adjuntos (15 Sept. 1806).
[25]   Minutes of meetings of Mahamad and Adjuntos and of Yehidim (17 Mar. 1811), LMA/4521/D/01/01/003.   [26] Ibid. (4 Sept. 1812; 11 Oct. 1812), pp. 40–3.

occasions should be toned down, as these were attracting inquisitive crowds. The members also decided at that meeting 'that no part of the prayers shall in future be sung in English tunes'.[27] Ensuring that food was kosher was also part of the Mahamad's mandate, as the earliest surviving minutes, dating from 1769, make clear. The Mahamad passed a regulation that 'the Kaal [community] may eat Kassher meat according to our most sacred law'. It was unanimously agreed that there should be 'a Bodeh [ritual slaughterer] saliriated [salaried] from the sedaca [charity box] & the sedaca should find stamps and lead to mark the meat'. Further, 'when the Bodeh kills a Beef he is not to leave it in the possession of the Goim all night unless it be marked with a stamp Kassher made for such uses, also all sheep & Goats, etc.'. Also, it was noted that 'all kind of Poultry killed by the Samaz [sexton] should be marked Kassher the same manner as the meat is marked to prevent the tricks of the Negroes'. This is the second reference to the 'tricks and stratagems of the Negroes',[28] suggesting they knew of Jewish dietary restrictions and were involved in supplying food to the free inhabitants of Bridgetown.[29] Slaves sold food of all types, either in their own slave market or carried from house to house. Thus, as the Mahamad pointed out, Jews might, through necessity or carelessness, buy 'treso' (*treif*, non-kosher) meat. This was also the case with the bread used in religious ceremonies, especially Passover: 'As a result, it was decided that a certain number of men be paid from the communal charitable funds' to make the 'Simurim Bispora de Pesah [*shemurah matsah* for the Eve of Passover] in order that no Negro or Goy may bake the Simurim'.

The Sephardim of Barbados were also whites in a society that valued whiteness, which was synonymous in many ways with privilege, though this tends to ignore the very real tensions generated by class differences among whites. Mid- and late seventeenth-century Barbadian society experienced profound changes characterized by rapid economic growth and demographic shifts. In the early years of settlement the majority of the population was white, albeit with ethnic and political differences. With the expansion of the sugar industry, labour needs mounted, bringing massive influxes of African slaves to the island: there were twice as many blacks as whites by 1680 and four times as many by 1780. As a result of this demographic shift, group identification based on race manifested itself ever more strongly. The white elite, dominated by a powerful, entrenched planter class, sought initially, but unsuccessfully, to maintain the

---

[27] Ibid. (9 Oct. 1814).   [28] Minutes of Adjuntos (28 Oct. 1776), LMA/4521/D/01/01/001.

[29] For an eyewitness account of the Bridgetown slave market, see Karl Watson (ed.), 'Robert Poole, The Beneficent Bee or Traveller's Companion', *Journal of the Barbados Museum and Historical Society*, 46 (2000), 174–239; see also Hilary Beckles and Karl Watson, 'Social Protest and Labour Bargaining: The Changing Nature of Slaves' Responses to Plantation Life in Eighteenth-Century Barbados', *Slavery and Abolition*, 8/3 (1987), 272–93; Frederick Smith and Karl Watson, 'Western Bridgetown and the Butchers Shambles in the Seventeenth–Nineteenth Centuries: New Insights from the Jubilee Garden Archaeological Investigations', *Journal of the Barbados Museum and Historical Society*, 52 (2007), 185–98.

proportion of whites in the population by passing deficiency laws, which required there
be a minimum number of whites on each plantation, and to keep control through a
militia tenant system, which required each plantation to support a number of white
families, whose adult males would serve in the militia when required. Its apparent
cohesiveness, disarmingly presented as the idea of 'kith and kin', was undercut by
competition within white Barbadian society, already divided by class and religion, for
the finite arable land of the small island. The 'sugar revolution' may have arrived, but
the myth of a society of rich white planters and poor black slaves ignored the reality
that most Barbadian whites were poor and existed on the peripheries of plantation
society.

By the beginning of the eighteenth century, the glory days of Barbadian Quakerism
were over, resulting in greater attention being paid to the Jewish minority. Jews were a
convenient economic target, although they were spared overt persecution because
there were too few of them to pose a threat to the Christian whites. Jews or their surro-
gates were readily accepted into the militia, whilst being consistently denied civil rights
until 1831. They were also taxed at higher rates than their Christian counterparts. Initial
efforts were made to restrict the number of slaves that Jews could own, but such
restrictions proved totally unworkable in a burgeoning slave society.[30] Jews also experienced difficulties serving as witnesses in legal matters. A few changes were made to
their legal status, such as the acceptance in 1674 of Jewish testimony sworn on the Five
Books of Moses in the island's courts. Jews were granted, in this manner, a juridical
persona denied to free coloureds, free blacks, and slaves. In this respect, whiteness took
precedence over religion. Ernst Pijning's observation about Brazil is equally applic-
able to Barbados: 'conveniently, legal concepts such as "race" and "Jewishness" were
negotiable'.[31]

That some social interaction took place between the two groups can be seen in
Jewish wills, a great many of which were witnessed by white Christian neighbours or
acquaintances. Jews often referred to non-Jews in their wills as 'good friends'. For
example, Daniel Ulloa on his deathbed, conscious that he was leaving behind a young
wife and children, requested my 'well beloved friends, the Hon. Thomas Maycock &
William Barnett to be aiding and ascribing my said wife with their advice as and when
she shall require it'.[32] In 1796 Isaac Pinheiro left £10 to his friend Alexander Sandiford
Kinch to buy mourning garments. This bequest implies a very close friendship, as
wearing mourning garments was usually restricted to family members.[33]

---

[30] Act for the Governing of Negroes (1688). This is discussed in greater detail below.
[31] Ernst Pijning, 'New Christians as Sugar Cultivators and Traders in the Portuguese Atlantic, 1450–1899',
in Paolo Bernardini and Norman Fiering (eds.), The Jews and the Expansion of Europe to the West, 1450–1800 (New
York, 2001), 498.
[32] Will of Daniel Ulloa (14 Jan. 1713), BDA, RB 6/37, p. 249.
[33] Will of Isaac Pinheiro (8 Dec. 1796), BDA, RB 6/38, p. 314.

Another area where some male social interaction between Jews and Christians seems to have taken place was cockfighting, a popular amusement in eighteenth-century Bridgetown. Moses Lopez sold cockspurs, and his accounts show that among his customers for that particular item was his brother Isaac, who bought four pairs on 25 January 1788.[34] Interestingly, among the artefacts recovered from the excavation at the rabbi's house in Bridgetown is a cockspur.

Interaction among various groups is also implied by housing patterns. A decided clustering of Jewish houses existed on Swan Street, which at one time was called Jew Street, but Jewish families could be found living all over the centre of Bridgetown. The restored levy books for Bridgetown from 1686 to 1844 list, on an annual basis, the taxpayers street by street, thereby permitting reconstruction of housing patterns for the seventeenth to early nineteenth centuries. They reveal a sometimes surprising mix of class, religion, and race (see Tables 11.2 and 11.3). Furthermore, by the late eighteenth century some Jewish families were establishing 'country seats' and moving out of Bridgetown, indicating a rise in social aspirations. Moses Lopez bought his house in the country in 1787.[35] On a visit to Barbados, young Moses Montefiore Ancona records having dinner at the 'country seat' of his uncle Eliezer Montefiore in 'the village of Fonte Belle'.[36]

Commenting on relationships between Sephardi communities and state officials, Jonathan Sarna observed that 'in Sephardic communities as diverse as those at Bayonne, France, Curaçao and the Virgin Islands, synagogue leaders looked to government to buttress their authority'.[37] From an early period, Barbadian Jews exhibited the tendency to turn to the government to resolve their internal disputes. In 1693 Nidhe Israel congregation was rocked by religious controversy. So strong were the divisions that a group sought to establish a separate synagogue in Bridgetown using tactics that challenged the authority of the Mahamad. They invaded the synagogue during sabbath services and were reportedly 'troublesome and disorderly'. Apparently not wanting to deal with the issue themselves, the Mahamad petitioned Governor James Kendal, pointing out that 'some hot spirited persons amongst us have maliciously assembled themselves together to disturb and make another synagogue'. They asked the governor to prohibit the erection of another synagogue within a two-mile radius of Bridgetown. Kendal assented to the request and ruled that 'any further disturbances will be met by imprisonment and enforced appearance before me to answer charges brought by the Jewish Churchwardens'.[38]

[34] Account book of Moses Lopez (1779–89), p. 219, New York Historical Society, MSS Collection BV Barbadoes, WI. This is listed in the NYHS library catalogue as Account book, 1779–1789 Mathias Lopez Sr. 1779.   [35] Ibid., p. 199.

[36] Diary of Moses Montefiore Ancona (in the possession of his descendant Sara A. Straub).

[37] Jonathan D. Sarna, 'The Jews in British America', in Bernardini and Fiering (eds.), *The Jews and the Expansion of Europe to the West*, 523.

[38] Eustace M. Shilstone, 'Records of Jews in Barbados C' (n.d.), Barbados Museum, Shilstone MS IX, p. 88.

Table 11.2 Jewish residential patterns, Bridgetown, Barbados, 1749

Street	Property Owners	Properties owned	Renters / house-tax payers
Cheapside	5	11	2
High Street	3	3	7
Swan Street	18	29	46
Middle Street	2	3	0
James Street	2	3	3
Marle Hill	1	1	0
Church Street	0	0	2
Back Church Street	4	4	1
George Street	1	1	0
Maiden Lane	1	1	2
Tudor Street	6	7	7
Reed Street	1	1	0

Source: Bridgetown levy book (1749), BDA.

The duality between Jewishness and whiteness persisted. On the accession of Queen Anne on 1 May 1707, the Jewish community issued its own congratulatory proclamation. Incoming governors were traditionally met and presented with a 'Jewish pie' a collection of gold coins masked by a piecrust. This unabashed attempt at bribery may or may not have succeeded in swaying governors in time of need, but it certainly became a traditional gift and was expected.[39] Yet, in the controversy of 1711 surrounding William Sharpe, a prominent Barbadian planter and one of three members of the Council of Barbados suspended by Governor Mitford Crowe over questions relating to the governor's alleged corruption, eighteen prominent Sephardim signed a petition supporting Sharpe. Ordinarily one would have expected members of the Jewish community not to draw attention to themselves or at least to have appeared neutral. However, as Gabbay and Levy point out, 'traditional Sephardic attitudes of accommodation and tolerance did not inhibit their ability to play a proper part in the affairs of their host countries'.[40] Thus in 1745, when Governor Thomas Robinson was attacked by members of the House of Assembly, Sephardi Jews felt confident enough in their social status to defend him. Elite Barbadian whites also included Jews in their public ceremonial events. Upon the proclamation of the reign of King George III in 1760, ten male members of the most prominent Sephardi families were invited to join the island's white elite in the

[39] Cecil Roth, *A History of the Jews in England* (Oxford, 1941), ch. 8, n. 54; see also Stephen A. Fortune, *Merchants and Jews: The Struggle for British West Indian Commerce, 1650–1750* (Gainesville, Fla., 1984), 77.

[40] Lucien Gabbay and Abraham Levy, *The Sephardim: Their Glorious Tradition from the Babylonian Exile to the Present Day* (New York, 1992), 9.

Table 11.3	Racial/religious profiles of house owners/occupants, Bridgetown, Barbados, 1804		
	Swan Street	Part of Church Yard and Church Street	Tudor Street
Sephardi Jew	39	3	19
Christian white	20	20	136
Free mulatto	2	8	11
Free Negro	0	3	9
Slave	0	0	2

Source: St Michael's levy book (1804), BDA.

official ceremony on Broad Street. Yet for all the seeming accommodation, anti-Jewish feeling could easily erupt into violence. In Speightstown in 1739 an enraged white mob destroyed Semah David Synagogue following a physical altercation between a Jew and a Christian. However, even that provocation resulted from the drunkenness of a Christian guest at a Jewish wedding.[41]

Other instances of the Jewish community's civic consciousness can be seen in their contribution of one-tenth of the cost of establishing the Barbados General Dispensary for the relief of the sick poor.[42] This was lauded in the *Barbados Mercury* on 28 October 1786. Nor was this the only occasion on which Christian white officialdom took notice of the responsible way in which Jews contributed to the broader civic well-being. Even after emancipation and with a rapidly dwindling community, Jewish philanthropy continued. Following the cholera outbreak of 1854, the Jewish businessman John Montefiore donated a water fountain to Bridgetown. Moreover, despite their limited means, the Jewish community also assisted Jewish congregations in other parts of the world, until it was no longer possible due to dwindling numbers. The following list, taken from the minute books of the Mahamad, shows the nature of local Jewish contributions to other communities.

1772 Letter from St Eustatius requesting help in rebuilding their synagogue: granted.

1791 £20 sent for assistance of distressed Jews in Tetouan.

1792 Assistance asked for and £25 granted for building a synagogue in Charleston, South Carolina.

1801 £25 sent for 'distressed Brethren in Tiberia'.

[41] Samuel Oppenheim, 'The Jews in Barbados in 1739. An Attack Upon their Synagogue: Their Long Oath', *Publications of the American Jewish Historical Society*, 22 (1914), 197–8; quoted in Jerome Handler, *A Guide to Source Materials for the Study of Barbados History 1627–1834* (Carbondale, Ill., 1971), 100.

[42] Karl Watson, 'The Sephardic Jews of Bridgetown', in Woodville Marshall and Pedro Welch (eds.), *Beyond the Bridge: Lectures Commemorating Bridgetown's 375th Anniversary* (St Michael, Barbados, 2005), 55.

1819 $500 granted to Philadelphia for building a synagogue.

1838   Requests from Edinburgh and Charleston for rebuilding their synagogues denied
        as so much money had been spent rebuilding the Bridgetown synagogue.

1840   £50 sent for 'our suffering brethren in Damascus and Rhodes'.

When the new synagogue was consecrated, after the old one had been destroyed in a hurricane in 1831, all the principal members of the island's governing and mercantile elite were in attendance.[43] As the *Barbados Globe* reported on 1 April 1833, 'the people of the Hebrew nation were joined by a number of the most respectable inhabitants and ladies of grace, fashion and beauty'.[44] In fact, on that occasion, there were probably more Christians present than Jews, who only numbered ninety-one. Yet the mere act of rebuilding the synagogue with a capacity of 300, when it was clear that the community was dwindling through the twin processes of migration and assimilation, speaks of their continued attachment to Judaism and presages the days in the early twentieth century when the last warden would continue to open the synagogue even though there was no Jew left to come to worship.

One institution of the broader white community which Sephardim joined from its inception was Freemasonry, which was introduced into Barbados in 1740. One of the first Jewish Freemasons on the island was Abraham Valverde. The iconography of his 1746 tombstone, which includes a set square, attests to his masonic affiliation. In 1797 Abraham Rodrigues Brandon was named Worshipful Master of Hiberian Lodge number 622. Other Sephardi members of masonic lodges included another Abraham Valverde (a descendant of the Abraham Valverde mentioned above), Abraham Baruh Lousada, and David Nunes Carvalho. A Jewish lodge, Mount Horeb, was established in 1804 and lasted until 1829. As the historian Aviston Downes points out, 'while Jews were often despised by the Christian majority, their membership in local lodges facilitated their acceptance by the white Creole population'.[45]

Sephardim as Creoles

The Sephardim of Barbados were influenced by their experiences and interactions with people of African descent, much as other whites were. The reality of life in a slave society was that everyone interacted with their slaves at all levels, and a distinguishing

[43] It had previously been thought that the hurricane had completely demolished the synagogue. However, careful reading of the minutes of the rebuilding committee make it clear that the shingled roof was lost, leaving the walls standing. These were partially pulled down and rebuilt to accommodate the weight of the new copper roof. The marble tiled floor of the present synagogue was installed in 1810, when some other renovations were carried out.

[44] Eustace M. Shilstone, *Monumental Inscriptions in the Jewish Synagogue at Bridgetown, Barbados: With Historical Notes from 1630* (London, 1988), p. xix.

[45] Aviston Downes, 'Freemasonry in Barbados, 1740 to 1900: Issues of Ethnicity and Class in a Colonial Polity', *Journal of the Barbados Museum and Historical Society*, 53 (2007), 54–5.

mark of Creole society was that whites changed the cultural orientation of their slaves but, at the same time, were changed in various ways by the slaves who were an indispensable part of their lives. While resistant to assimilation, Sephardi Jews were becoming involved in the broader Barbadian society by the early eighteenth century, as shown by references to visiting or transient Jews as 'strangers' or 'foreigners'. However, it was in their racial attitudes that the Barbadian Jews showed themselves to be true Creoles. The official position of the white Christian population was racial separation and denial of power to non-whites. Barbadian Jews came to share this world-view. In the preamble to the Hebrew Vestry Act it was pronounced that 'no person whose original extraction shall be proved to have been from a Negro shall be deemed or allowed to choose or be chosen a Vestry-man under this Act'.[46] Unofficially, the principle of absolute segregation was softened by the realities of life on a small island. The twin forces of sex and economics undermined any efforts to enforce racial separation. As much as the collective will might aspire to separation, individuals often found ways to make exceptions or bridge the yawning racial gulf.

The initial Sephardi settlement in Barbados, coming largely as it did from Brazil, brought people to the island who were personally acquainted with slavery. It is not known whether the Brazilian émigrés brought slaves with them, but it is certain that they acquired them very soon after arriving in Barbados. The 1679 census of Bridgetown shows that of the fifty-four families listed, only five did not own slaves, and four of these five were headed by women. Furthermore, only five families had no children. Children are important in the process of creolization. Jonathan Schorsch has observed that black enslaved women acted as conduits of creolization for their white charges.[47] Jewish children in Bridgetown and Speightstown learnt the Creole variant of English from their black nurses, just as Jewish children spoke Sranan Tongo in Suriname, and Papiamiento in Curaçao, and Jamaican Creole in Jamaica. Other aspects of expressive culture were also transmitted. Folk tales, 'duppy' or 'Anancy' stories, circulated among Jews, and food tastes (within, or more likely circumventing, kosher restrictions) changed. Among the food items distributed to poor Barbadian Jewish families were two tropical staples: rice and yams.[48] Music and concepts of rhythm were imparted in the songs nannies sang to the children in their care.

---

[46] An Act Concerning the Vestry of the Hebrew Nation Resident within this Island (1820), Duties of the Public Officers of Kaal Kadesh Nidhe Israel, Byelaws as passed on 19 April 1821, and Ketubot (in English) from 1834 to 1843, LMA/4521/D/01/01/009.

[47] Jonathan Schorsch, Jews and Blacks in the Early Modern World (Cambridge, 2004), 264.

[48] Minutes of meetings of Mahamad and Adjuntos (4 Mar. 1804). The Jewish settlement of Suriname, with which Barbadian Jews had frequent contact, provides a useful comparison, showing that in areas such as language and cuisine, Jews were fully creolized. The Surinamese historical novel by Cynthia McLeod Hoe duur was de suiker [The Cost of Sugar] (Paramaribo, 2010) is not only entertaining reading but also speaks of the creolization of the Surinamese Jewish population. One could make similar statements about the Jewish populations of Curaçao and Jamaica.

The 1688 Act for the Governing of Negroes was a determined effort by the British authorities to restrict slave ownership among Jews. In one clause, 'town' Jews were accused of keeping large numbers of slaves to 'hire out' to plantations. As a consequence, it was decreed that 'no person of the Hebrew nation . . . shall keep or employ any Negro or other Slave more than one Negro or other slave, Man or Boy, to be allowed to each person of the said Nation'. The only exception to this ruling was 'such as are denizened by His Majesty's Letter Patent'.[49] However, in 1706 this clause was repealed, since:

> The said Nation inhabiting here are become considerable Traders, and in order to carry on the same to advantage, as well of the Public as of themselves, are obliged to employ a greater number of Negroes and Slaves, than were at the time of making the said Law thought necessary . . . the said Clause is hereby repealed, annulled and declared void . . . it shall be lawful for every person of the said Nation to employ as many Negroes and other Slaves, as they might legally have done, if no such clause had ever been in force.[50]

In one exceptional case from the early nineteenth century, Abraham Rodrigues Brandon had 216 slaves to run his plantation.

Although the Sephardim were urban dwellers, slave ownership was widespread among them. Slaves were one of the most commonly bequeathed items followed by cash and real estate. The Lopez family, who by the 1780s were fourth-generation Barbadians, had a series of complicated relationships with their slaves. Their wills provide some useful insights into the variety of these relationships: at times cruel and exploitative or, conversely, caring at best, paternalistic at worst, and often sexual in nature. In 1680 the first members of the Lopez family to establish themselves on Barbados were slave owners. Abraham Lopez owned one, Eliah Lopez two, and Rachel Lopez one. Various Lopez males fathered children outside their marriages. Sometimes the evidence for these liaisons is clear; on other occasions, it is circumstantial. Their female partners could be white non-Jews but were mostly black or mulatto women, enslaved or free. The baptismal records for St Michael and All Angels provides this interesting entry for 17 March 1761: 'This day baptized in church a female child named Mary Ann ye mother of whom said she was the daughter of Rob: Scott and Eliz; Scott his wife, but ye mother of it was a wife to one Morton who ran off ye island for murder & now a whore to R. Scott & was a whore to Moses Lopez a Jew who got ye sd: child, her maiden name was Eliz; Barrow'.[51] The Moses Lopez mentioned in the registry was probably either the grandfather or uncle of the Moses Lopez discussed above since the latter was too young in 1761 to father children. There is no mention of any illegitimate children of Moses, but his brother Isaac fathered several by enslaved or free coloured women. His favourite partner was a free coloured woman (described as a mulatto) by

---

[49] Richard Hall, *Acts Passed in the island of Barbados: From 1643 to 1762* (Barbados, 1764), no. 82.

[50] Ibid., no. 108.   [51] Baptism record of Mary Ann Scott (17 Mar. 1761), BDA, RL 1/4, p. 152.

the name of Martha Blackman. Prior to her liaison with Isaac Lopez, Martha had children by various fathers. The baptismal records show that in 1774 she had a daughter, Willey Aimey, baptized at St Michael's, and in 1777 her son John Whittaker was also baptized.[52] She seems to have borne Isaac at least four children, one son William, who was given the surname Lopez, and three girls, Christian, Rebecca, and Rachel. It is possible that of the girls, only Christian survived, since she is the only one mentioned in Isaac's will of 16 January 1804, which states: 'I do give to Christian Lopez the daughter of Martha Blackman a free coloured woman £50 to be paid to her or her assigns when she attains her age of 21 years'.[53] Christian may also have been his favourite since in the baptismal records of St Michael's, he is recorded as the father whereas this is not stated for the other children.[54] But it is telling that Christian is identified by Isaac not as 'my daughter' but as 'the daughter of Martha Blackman'. He also seems to have fathered another child by one of his household slaves since in his will he also directed that 'my mulatto slave girl be manumitted in England and I do give and bequeath to the said mulatto Loretta the sum of fifty pounds currency to be paid to her or her assigns four years after my death'.[55]

The fate of most of the racially mixed children of Jewish fathers is unknown, as the records are often missing. From wills we can occasionally glimpse the complexities of interracial family relationships. In 1779 David DaCosta drew up his will, in which he left a sum of £20 to the synagogue. To his 'reputed daughter Hester DaCosta' he also left the sum of £20.[56] The rest of his estate went to Susanna Jacobs, a free mulatto. Susanna's birth was recorded in the parish of St Philip in 1747. She was the child of Thomas and Thomasin Jacobs, both mulattoes.[57] She seems to have moved to the parish of St Lucy as a young adult, where in 1771 she is recorded as having borne a child to James Whitehead. The infant was christened William and given the surname Jacobs.[58] Later, we hear of her in St Michael, where it is apparent that she has become the mistress and confidante of David DaCosta. She may very well have borne him a son in 1777, as the baptismal records for St Michael's show that a male infant of Susanna Jacobs was baptized and given the name Jacob.[59] In his will, David DaCosta gave:

Susanna Jacobs free mulatto . . . for her many true and valuable services to me done and performed, all the rest residue and remainder of my Estate both real and personal either in this island or elsewhere, she maintaining my honoured mother Lunah DaCosta during her natural life after complying with my bequests to her and her heirs forever and decently interring her at her death.[60]

[52] Baptism records of Willey Aimey (1774), BDA, RL 1/5, p. 41; John Whittaker (1777), BDA, RL 1/5, p. 134.
[53] Will of Isaac Lopez (16 Jan. 1804), BDA, RL 1/6, p. 122.
[54] Baptism record of Christian Lopez (20 Jan. 1796), BDA, RL 1/6, p. 40.
[55] Will of Isaac Lopez (16 Jan. 1804).   [56] Will of David DaCosta (1779), BDA, RB 6/23, p. 286.
[57] Baptism record of Susanna Jacobs (20 Apr. 1747), BDA, RL 1/22, p. 140.
[58] Baptism record of William Jacobs (5 May 1771), BDA, RL 1/36, p. 97.
[59] Baptism record of Jacob Jacobs (6 Jan. 1777), BDA, RL 1/5, p. 37.   [60] Will of David DaCosta (5 May 1779).

The sole executrix named was Susanna Jacobs, the first time a free coloured person was empowered to administer the affairs of a member of the Sephardi community and underscoring the very intimate relationship between the two people.

The will of Isaac Pinheiro revealed his intimate and caring relationship with Vinello Pinheiro, a free black woman. He left everything to her and her heirs: two slaves, Sammy—a mulatto man—and James—a Negro boy, as well as his household furniture, cattle and stock, and the sum of £50. He also gave her 'during the term of her natural life a Negro woman slave named Diah'.[61] After Vinello's death, ownership of Diah was to pass to his niece Leah Pinheiro. His concern for the well-being of Vinello led him to direct that she be paid half yearly 'during her natural life', the interest on the sum of £1,200 which he had loaned to Joseph a Cohen Belinfante. He further charged his estate with paying the sum of £25 to cover the funeral expenses of Vinello, 'when that event shall happen'.

The will of the widow Rachel Baruh Lousada makes a number of bequests.[62] The first was to a daughter of the prominent Sephardi family Nunes to whom she left £200 and a slave by the name of Princess Amelia. A silver lamp was left to Deborah Nunes, the daughter of Abraham Israel Nunes, who had migrated to the USA. Deborah was underage and the interest from the bequest was 'to be applied to her maintenance and education'. Rachel left bequests to a number of free mulattoes. Special beneficiaries were Amelia Baruh and two young mulatto individuals, John Meik and his sister Judith Annesly. Meik was left the sum of £50 and 'a certain boy slave named Cuffy'. In the event of John's death without issue: 'I give and devise the said slave unto his sister Judith Annesly (free mulatto)'. Judith was also bequeathed 'a certain Mulatto woman slave named Dutchess'. Rachel further directed that Ann Jordan, a free mulatto, should inherit 'a certain Mulatto slave named Nanny'. She also left £10 each to five children: William, John Isaac, Robert, Mary Amelia, and Ward, who are all described as 'freed mulattoes, sons and Daughters of Henrietta Smith Bovell'; and a black girl, Hester, to Rachel Bovell (free mulatto) with a proviso:

In case the said Rachel Bovell should depart this life without attaining the Age of twenty one years, or without leaving such child or children, then I give and devise the said slave with her future issue and increase unto Amelia Baruh of the Parish of Saint Michael and Island aforesaid, free mulatto and her heirs and assigns forever.[63]

Not all of Rachel Lousada's slaves were condemned to remain in servitude:

[61] Will of Isaac Pinheiro (8 Dec. 1796), BDA, RB 6/38, p. 314. Whether Vinello Pinheiro ever got this money is debatable. Joseph A. Cohen Belinfante does not seem to have been a trustworthy character. He is discussed in the minutes of meetings of Mahamad and Adjuntos of 18 Mar. 1792 as being guilty 'of many vile and vilanous acts of Forgery'. He was forced 'to quit this country in a Clandestine manner', though he later did return to Barbados.   [62] Rachel Baruh Lousada (2 May 1810), BDA, original wills.   [63] Ibid.

I do hereby authorize and impower my Executor and Executrix herein after named or either of them who shall qualify to sell and convey my mulatto boy slave named George to any Person or Persons resident in Great Britain or in any of the other Islands for the purpose of being liberated from slavery, but I direct that my Estate be not liable for the payment of any sum of money required by the Law of this Island to be paid on the Manumission of Slaves.[64]

Amelia Baruh was named the principal beneficiary of 'all the rest residue and remainder of my estate of whatever nature, kind or quality soever'. This left her a wealthy woman, since Rachel Baruh Lousada had inherited her husband's fortune. The executors named were John Meik, who was not yet 21, and Amelia Baruh. This is the second of only three known cases where a member of the Sephardi community nominated free coloured individuals as executors. The witnesses to the will included the powerful John Spooner, president of the Council of Barbados and acting governor of the island. It is clear that a very special relationship existed between Rachel, Amelia, John, and Judith, a relationship that exceeded the bounds of social friendship, a blood relationship. This relationship probably extended to the Bovells, though their links do not seem to be as close. Amelia Baruh was in all likelihood the illegitimate daughter of Emanuel Baruh Lousada and thus the step-daughter of the childless Rachel Lousada. The two siblings, John and Judith were probably the children of Amelia Baruh. The parentage of John Meik can be ascertained through his unusual surname. There was only one Meik on the island at the time, a merchant in Bridgetown identified in the Bridgetown levy book of 1790. Judith Annesly was probably a half-sister to John Meik. The surname Annesly is also unusual and does not appear in the census or baptisms records for the island. John Meik died in 1836, leaving the bulk of his estate to his sister Judith.[65] He also left 'all my wearing apparel unto William Bovell'. This is the same William Bovell who inherited £10 from Rachel Baruh in 1809. In the 1830 slave registration returns, Judith Annesley is recorded as the owner of seven slaves, two males and five females. William Bovell (free mulatto) owned one male slave. The third case of a Sephardi entrusting the administration of his estate to a non-white is confirmed by the will of Moses DePiza, who appointed his mistress Susanna DePiza (free mulatto) executrix and guardian of their two children, Sarah and Rachael. DePiza left his two girls, six slaves and prime land on Broad Street, the main street of Bridgetown.[66]

Another series of relationships can be discerned in the will of Princess Castello, a free mulatto.[67] She first directed that two of her slaves be manumitted. She then went on to bequeath small sums of money and items of furniture to three Jewish women, Sarah Hester Barrow, Mary Barrow, and Sarah Elkin. She referred to all three women as

[64] Ibid.   [65] Will of John Meik (19 Mar. 1836), BDA, original wills.
[66] Will of Moses DePiza (13 Jan. 1802), BDA, RB 4/60, p. 142.
[67] Will of Princess Castello (1 June 1833), BDA, RB 4/67, p. 113.

her friends. Sarah Elkin was the daughter of David and Rachel Lindo, a cousin of the Nunes Castello family, and, in all probability, also a cousin of Princess Castello. The will also establishes a relationship with another Afro-Sephardi family, the Carvallos, who had their origins in Speightstown. Princess Castello bequeathed three slaves to her great-niece and nephews: Isaac Carvallo, the younger; John Carvallo; and Christian Ann Carvallo. These were the children of Isaac Carvallo, the elder, a prominent but conservative civil-rights campaigner, the son of Dutchess Carvallo a free mulatto of Speightstown. The latter had her two sons, Isaac and Abraham, baptized at St Peter's parish church in 1781 and 1786 respectively.[68] Further evidence of the close relationships between many Sephardi Jews and their mixed blood relatives can be seen in the will of Rachel Carvallo, who at her death in 1791, left for 'Ann Carvallo, free mulatto, a mulatto boy slave named Benny'.[69] Princess Castello owned a substantial property in Bridge-town, confirmed by the levy books of the period. The building was located at the corner of Lucas Alley and James Street. She did not personally occupy the building but rented it to a prominent white Barbadian, Robert Boucher Clarke. She directed that this property should be sold and the proceeds given to her great-niece and nephews.

The case of Philly Judy Lindo is even more interesting. In Isaac Lindo's will of 1780 (he was the father of Rachel, wife of Moses Lopez) he bequeathed 'several Negro slaves following, Phillias, Flora and Pamela (women) Judy (a girl)' to his wife Judith and, after her death, to his son David.[70] Twenty-one years later Philly Judy, described as a mulatto woman (obviously the daughter of Phillias and almost certainly fathered by Isaac Lindo), was manumitted by David Lindo.[71] Philly Judy Lindo died in 1858 at the approx-imate age of 88. Her half-brother David, half-sister Rachel (Lopez), and several of her other Lindo relatives had predeceased her. David Lindo's will makes no mention of her. Yet Rachel Lindo's will of 1847 leaves $160 to 'my faithful servant Philly Judy to be paid her by monthly payments of three dollars until the same be paid'.[72] Her white family therefore had employed Philly Judy and maintained a paternalistic relationship with her, though it is doubtful that the family relationship was acknowledged. Yet Philly Judy's will, dated 26 February 1858, betrays no rancour. Its terms make it clear that she had over the course of her life valued her close, albeit subordinate, relationship with the Jewish community and especially her Lindo relatives. She lived next to the synagogue in a 'wooden tenement or house situate in Magazine Lane in the city of Bridgetown at the corner of Synagogue Lane'. She left £30 to Belle Myers, wife of Abraham Myers, and £7. 10s. od. to their son, Lindo Samuel Myers. Katherine Isaacs, wife of Michael Baber Isaacs, was left the sum of £10 and, as 'a token of my sincere respect and esteem for him', Edward Aaron Moses was bequeathed £3. 6s. 6d. She gave 'divers articles of plate'

---

[68] Baptism records of Isaac Carvallo (28 Nov. 1781), BDA, RL 1/39, p. 10; Abraham Carvallo (23 Apr. 1786), BDA, RL 1/39, p. 30.   [69] Will of Rachel Carvallo (1 Apr. 1791), BDA, RB 6/19, p. 378.

[70] Will of Isaac Lindo (10 Nov. 1780).   [71] St Michael Vestry Minutes (26 Mar. 1801), p. 205, BDA.

[72] Will of Rachel Lindo (24 July 1847), BDA, original wills.

to Elizabeth Margaret Shannon, wife of Samson Shannon, 'for her sole and separate use and benefit independent of her husband the said Samson Shannon. . . . I declare that the said E. M. Shannon shall be at full liberty to sell and dispose of the said articles of plate and apply the money arising from the sale thereof in such manner as she alone shall think fit.' After leaving her house to her friend Christian Malloney and a plot of land she owned to her relative Mary Letts, 'all the rest, residue of her estate was left to her friend Michael Baber Isaacs'.[73] There must have been some sort of reciprocal affectionate and caring relationship between Philly Judy and the Jewish beneficiaries of her will who outnumbered all other beneficiaries. In 1858 £30 was not a modest bequest. That Belle Myers gave her son the first name Lindo indicates some relationship with the Lindo family and thus with Philly Judy.

The Jewish marriage records of the nineteenth century do much to clear up the connections and clearly show that Philly Judy and the Lindo family were indeed close.[74] Michael Baber Isaac's wife Katherine (Kate is noted on the marriage entry) was the daughter of Mozley and Sarah Elkin (the beneficiary of a bequest by Princess Castello discussed above). Sarah Elkin, in turn, was the daughter of Philly Judy's half-brother, David, and Rachel Lindo (Rachel's maiden name was Massiah). So Philly Judy left bequests to her niece Katherine and her cousins (on the Massiah side) Belle Myers (formerly Esther Massiah) and Lindo Samuel Myers. No evidence has been discovered to establish family connections with the other two parties mentioned in the will, Edward Aaron Moses and Elizabeth Margaret Shannon. However, it is quite likely that Elizabeth Margaret Shannon had some links to the Lindo family. The Shannons were early nineteenth-century additions to Barbados's Jewish community. It is noteworthy that Philly Judy remembered the women of the Lindo family in her will. The emphatic directive that Elizabeth Margaret Shannon was to have 'sole' control over the proceeds of the sale of plate 'as she alone shall think fit' is an interesting comment on Philly Judy's empowered outlook.

Yet another intimate connection with the Lindo family is revealed in the will of the free coloured woman, Philly O'Neal.[75] Philly directed that her executors, two prominent Jewish men, Walker Jacob Levi and Mozley Elkin, should at her death, sell her 'stock in trade', specified household items, and her 'slaves, hereditaments, tenements, houses, land etc.' The proceeds were to be 'placed out at interest', after the payment of her debts, including those incurred as a result of her illness. The will specified that her 'medical attendants [were] to be paid the amount of their respective demands as far as correct for their attendance of [her] present illness'. The interest was for the benefit of her two sons, Isaac Massiah Lindo and Jacob Lindo. In the event of their early death, the remainder of her estate was left to 'my beloved friend Mr Jacob Lindo'. In the event of

[73] Will of Philly Judy Lindo (26 Feb. 1858), BDA, RB 4/76, pp. 494–7.
[74] Jewish marriage records, Barbados (1830–85), BDA, RL 1/74.
[75] Will of Philly O'Neal (19 Jan. 1824), BDA, RB 4/63, p. 45.

his death, Philly asked that the residue of her estate should go to 'Miss Sarah Lindo daughter of Mr David Lindo'. Jacob Lindo was Philly's lover, the 27-year-old son of David and Rachel Lindo and brother of Sarah. Jacob did not long survive Philly, dying on 17 July 1824. Of Jacob and Philly's two children, we can only be sure of the survival of one. In the slave register for 1830, Isaac Massiah Lindo (free mulatto) (named Massiah after his grandmother, Rachel Massiah who married David Lindo) is listed as the owner of two slaves.

The case of Nancy Daniels provides a useful comparison. Primary material evidence and oral tradition exists on Daniels, preserved by the white Barbadian descendants of the Jewish family who owned her. Now separated by at least three generations from their Jewish roots, this family still has in its possession a photograph of the aged Nancy Daniels, taken in the middle of the nineteenth century. The family tradition states that Nancy was an African-born slave of their D'Azevedo ancestors who died in 1871 at the age of 116.[76] The Slave Compensation Register for Barbados shows that in 1834 Moses D'Azevedo owned four slaves, among whom was Nancy. It confirms she was born in Africa, but it estimated her date of birth as 1777, making her 94 at the time of her death.[77] After emancipation in 1834, Nancy Daniels was cared for by the children of her ex-owner until her death and assumed the status of valued and beloved family retainer. Like Philly Judy, whom she must have known, Nancy lived near the synagogue. Her photograph shows a well-dressed woman looking at the camera with a considerable degree of composure and equanimity (Figure 11.4).

The will of Hannah Ester Lopez, mother of Isaac and Moses Lopez, also demonstrates that the boundaries of colour were blurred and the harshness of slavery often softened by the tacit recognition of family relationships. A shared white world-view did not encourage open declaration of these family connections, even though they would be common knowledge in a small society like Barbados's Jewish community. Privately, both whites and non-whites tended to acknowledge these connections and to be influenced by them. When, for instance, Hannah Ester Lopez composed her will in 1807, she was getting on in years: she had seen her immediate family dissolve; her daughters-in-law both died in childbirth in their thirties; one of her sons, Isaac, had died three years earlier, and her grandson Matthias, Isaac's son, died when he was 10 years old; her surviving son, Moses, and his two boys had left the island for New York. She was alone in Barbados except for her Brandon connections, both white and non-white. Her relative Abraham Rodrigues Brandon was the wealthiest and most influential member of the Sephardi community in the early nineteenth century. He was also one of a handful of Jewish plantation owners of the period.

[76]   Death Certificate of Nancy Daniels (24 Sept. 1871), BDA, RL 3/14b, LIII, p. 739.

[77]   Return of M. C. D'Azevedo of Slaves his own Property (19 Feb. 1834), Slave Compensation Register, University of the West Indies Library, West Indies Collection, microfilm.

Figure 11.4 Nancy Daniels, ex-slave of the D'Azevedo family and housekeeper of the Daniels family, *c.*1860

Courtesy of Mrs Noreen Patterson

Hannah Ester left Ester Gill (free mulatto) a mulatto slave girl by the name of Rachel and various household items.[78] To Isaac Brandon (free mulatto), she left a large desk, two small desks, and a Dutch case. To his sister, Sarah Brandon (free mulatto), she left three trunks, a cedar chest, all her chairs, and a pitch-pine chest. Then, to both of the children she left 'their grandmother, a mulatto woman slave named Deborah and I do also give & bequeath to the said Isaac and Sarah Brandon, a bedstead and four beds'. She then directed that 'all [her] apparel whatsoever shall be equally divided' and given to Sarah Brandon and the 'said slave girl Rachel'. All her other slaves and the rest of her estate were to be sold and the proceeds sent to her son Moses Lopez in New York. The sole executor she named was 'my friend Abraham Rodriguez Brandon'. We can unravel some of the complexities of these relationships but, unfortunately, not all of them. We do not know who Ester Gill was, nor the nature of her relationship with Hannah Ester, but internal evidence and corroborating material from other sources enable us to make reasonable assumptions. She is the first named in Hannah Ester's

---

[78] Will of Hannah Ester Lopez (23 Oct. 1815), BDA, RL 1/6.

will, and the bequest of the mulatto slave girl Rachel would indicate that she had very close links with Hannah Ester's household. A clue to a possible relationship with Abraham Rodrigues Brandon may lie in a reference in his 1831 will to his slave, Sally Gill, to whom he gave 'her time so she may be at liberty to work for herself'.[79] Ester and Sally Gill may have been related. It is possible that she may originally have been the Ester Lindo identified in Moses Lopez's account book as a mulatto woman who was one of his clients. This would help to explain the connection, as Hannah Ester would have entered the Lopez household as one of the slaves of Moses's wife, Rachel Lindo, and may very well have later married a Gill. The surname Gill occurs in the levy books throughout the eighteenth and nineteenth centuries as house owners in Back Church Street (later Suttle Street) and they were therefore neighbours of the Lopez's. (At the present time, mixed-race descendants of the Gills still own property in Suttle Street.)

Brandon was a close and trusted associate of the Lopez household. He had various powers to represent the financial assets of Moses Lopez, who, as noted, had migrated to the USA. He visited the Lopez household frequently, and it is apparent that he had sexual relations with various slaves owned by Hannah Ester Lopez. Isaac and Sarah Brandon were his children, and they were manumitted by him on 7 May 1801, already bearing his surname.[80] The identity of their mother has not been established, but it is quite likely that it was Ester Gill and that she had been freed previously by Hannah Ester, who chose to retain the grandmother, Deborah, in her service. In the will, Deborah is described as a mulatto. Assuming that her daughter was fathered by a white man, Isaac and Sarah Brandon would be very fair-skinned. In other jurisdictions, they would have been classified as octoroons or may even have passed for white. Surmounting various difficulties, Isaac Lopez Brandon converted to Judaism.

The complex Jewish attitudes towards race reveal themselves in the struggle over the Hebrew Vestry Act of 1820.[81] Jews who opposed it used Abraham Rodrigues Brandon's mulatto children to stir up Christian opposition to it, by spreading the rumour that the increased taxation which the Mahamad would levy on the Jews would be used to 'send money to America to build a synagogue for Mr Brandon's coloured connexions'.[82] The Mahamad's denial of these accusations contains some interesting details on its members' attitudes to race. They stressed that religion (underlined in the original document) was no grounds for distinction.

---

[79]   Will of Abraham Rodrigues Brandon (7 Apr. 1831), BDA, original wills.

[80]   St Michael Vestry Minutes (7 May 1801), p. 414, BDA.

[81]   The Hebrew Vestry Act envisaged a restructuring of the operations of the Jewish community with greater power being given to the Mahamad. The Jewish community was split on the question of increased taxation, and petitions and counter-petitions were filed, which were quite acrimonious. Though passed by the Barbados legislature, the bill was refused royal assent.

[82]   Minutes of meetings of Vestry, Mahamad and Adjuntos, and Yehidim (13 Sept. 1820), p. 45, LMA/4521/D/01/01/004.

It is proper to explain that in a religious point of view we make no distinction between Mr Brandon's son (who is a man of colour) and any other member of our community. It might truly be said of this young man that he is a Jew from inclination as he chose the religion of his father at a time of life when capable of judging for himself, for he was of age when he went to Surinam in order to be admitted within the pale of Judaism. His conduct is most exemplary and he is assessed as much as any person out of the Vestry except two and the synagogue is likely to benefit considerably by him as he intends to pay £17 10 a year during his life tho' absent from the Island as above explained.'[83]

As the minutes make clear, Isaac Lopez Brandon, regardless of whatever prejudices individual members of the Jewish community may have had against him, continued to pay his *finta* dues and on those occasions when he was on the island, played a role in the affairs of the community. As death approached, Abraham Brandon made handsome provisions for his various children. Isaac, then residing in the USA, was left £5,000, and bequests were made to the children of his deceased daughter Sarah, who in 1817, with a dowry of £5,000 from her father, had married Joshua Moses and gone to live in New York. In his later years Brandon had started yet another family, this time with a Sarah Simpson Wood. He made provisions to leave her his house on Chapel Street in Bridgetown, which was to be 'put in good repair for her use', and she was given the choice of any of his furniture. Brandon also left three slaves to her—Dennis, Sopley, and Beckey—as well as a bequest of £2,500. The five children he had with Sarah Wood were also treated well. All of them—Julia, Esther, Lavinia, Joseph, and Alfred—were given his name and left £2,500 as well as the proceeds of 200 shares which he held in the American Insurance Company in New York. Alfred died and was buried in the graveyard of the synagogue on 1 June 1831, six days before his father passed away.

In 1834 Abraham Rodrigues Brandon owned 216 slaves, who worked his sugar plantation.[84] In his will, he directed his attention to his household slaves. Sally Gill, as we noted, was to be allowed to work for herself. 'James a coloured boy & Tom Gittens a coloured boy' were to be manumitted. These manumissions were effected.[85] He then directed that his mulatto slaves—Beck, John, and William Francis—were to be freed 'on payment by them or any person on their behalf' the arrears owed to him from the estate of John Gilbert Birkett deceased as well as the manumission costs. The latter provision was not taken up, as the compensation records for 1834 list the last three individuals as slaves of the estate of A. R. Brandon. Brandon may have had good intentions, but the financial costs of securing their own freedom were obviously too high and benefactors were not forthcoming. They thus continued as slaves until the abolition act was passed three years later.

---

[83] Fair copies of petitions to the Speaker and General Assembly of Barbados . . . (1820), pp. 33–4, LMA/4521/D/01/01/008.

[84] These slaves are listed individually by name in the Slave Compensation Registers (University of the West Indies Library, West Indies Collection, microfilm).   [85] Will of Abraham Rodrigues Brandon.

Conclusion

The Sephardi Jews who migrated to Barbados in the late seventeenth century brought with them a strong sense of cultural identity and shared familial background, which united them and created a sense of community. As long as they maintained a certain numerical strength, they could maintain this cultural identity. However, as internal demographics shifted and the tensions inherent in the slave society in which they lived became internalized, change was inevitable. As a result of the twin forces of emigration and assimilation, the Sephardim were unable to sustain their population into the late nineteenth century. Nevertheless, for the duration of their sojourn in Barbados, irrespective of their multiple identities, they remained a distinct community, at once connected to the wider community through marriages, liaisons, and offspring and retaining their sense of identity with each other and their past.

ACKNOWLEDGEMENTS
I would like to thank Mr Paul Altman and the Barbadian Jewish Community for their support and the Spanish and Portuguese Jews' Congregation of London for permission to examine the documents of the Nidhe Israel Synagogue now in their possession.

CHAPTER TWELVE

SEXUALITY AND SENTIMENT

Concubinage and the Sephardi Family in Late Eighteenth-Century Jamaica

STANLEY MIRVIS

O N 25 MARCH 1795 Moses Gomes Fonseca travelled from Kingston to Spanish Town to manumit Nancy, Sally, and Nelly James, the daughters of a 'free black woman' named Eleanor Minol Thomas.[1] Moses, who does not mention a wife or legitimate children in his will, manumitted his daughters out of 'the natural love and affection which I have and bear towards my three mulatto children'.[2] After paying the manumission fee and the cost of the administrative stamp, Moses arranged the mandatory security bond: a £5 life annuity for each of his enfranchised children. Five years later, an ailing Moses drafted his last will and testament. After allocating funds for his funeral expenses and providing an endowment for the Portuguese synagogue in Kingston, he bequeathed the remainder of his estate to his concubine,[3] Eleanor, and their three children.[4]

---

[1] Manumission of Nancy, Sally, and Nelly James (13 Aug. 1797), Jamaica Archives and Records Department, Spanish Town, Jamaica (JA), Manumissions 1B/11/6/21, fos. 125–6.

[2] It is possible that Moses Gomes Fonseca was the resident of St Eustatius listed in the 1790 census as married with two children. If indeed these are the same person then Moses was born in Bayonne and in 1787 married Sara de David Rodriques da Costa with whom he had two children. Sometime after 1790 he moved to Jamaica where he died around 1800. Since he does not mention a wife or children in his will, it is possible that they died sometime before 1795, at which point he had children with Eleanor Thomas, or that he abandoned his original family (see Isaac S. Emmanuel and Suzanne A. Emmanuel, *A History of the Jews of the Netherlands Antilles*, 2 vols. (Cincinnati, 1970), ii. 1050, 1066).

[3] I use the term 'concubine' to refer to women in relationships that are not legally recognized. Therefore, 'concubine' is used to refer to women even when they may have been living in what has been referred to as a 'marriage Suriname-style' meaning a long-term, even monogamous, relationship between a white man and a woman of colour. This was almost certainly the case with Moses Gomes Fonseca and Eleanor M. Thomas. On 'marriage Suriname-style', see Rudolf Asveer Jacob Van Lier, *Frontier Society: A Social Analysis of the History of Surinam* (The Hague, 1971), 77–8; with regard to the Jews, see Robert Cohen, *Jews in Another Environment: Surinam in the Second Half of the Eighteenth Century* (Leiden, 1991), 158; see also Jonathan Schorsch, *Jews and Blacks in the Early Modern World* (Cambridge, 2004), 228. Schorsch provides examples in which it appears that some couples had an actual marriage under Jewish law with a *ketubah*. This could also be the case in Jamaica, but in the absence of hard evidence we can only speculate.

[4] Will of Moses Gomes Fonseca (19 July 1800), Island Record Office, Twickenham, Jamaica (IRO), Wills, lib. 67, fo. 58.

This chapter examines the emotional bonds that developed between Sephardi men, women of colour, and their children in late eighteenth-century Jamaica. Whereas previous scholarship has focused on the absorption of people of colour into Atlantic Jewish communities, this study of sentiment offers an alternative mode of enquiry by focusing on families. Though there is little concrete evidence to suggest the nature of Jewish identity possessed by mulatto children of Jewish men in Jamaica, manumission records and wills are explored here as measures of devotion on the part of Sephardi men to their illegitimate children and their mistresses, regardless of Jewish identity. The evidence points to the incorporation of people of colour into the Sephardi family, though not without some of the same racial tensions found in other places on a communal level, and raises new questions about the role of ethnic continuity as a determinant of familial belonging for late eighteenth-century western Sephardim.

Communal 'Absorption' in Jamaica

Questions of concubinage and ethnic fluidity in Jamaican Jewish society have not been comprehensively studied. With the exception of a short paragraph in Jacob Rader Marcus's *The Colonial American Jew*, the literature on concubinage among Jews in the colonial Atlantic world has focused predominantly on the Dutch colonies of Suriname and Curaçao.[5] This somewhat skewed focus is not surprising given the relative surfeit of internal Jewish records from the larger Dutch communities, which stands in sharp contrast to the paucity of similar documentation from colonial Jamaica.[6] The greater scholarly attention devoted to the Dutch colonies has also helped to shape a perception of the English West Indies as settlements of peripheral importance in the western Sephardi diaspora. However, Jamaica was not only home to the largest Jewish community in the British empire outside London during the late eighteenth century, it also had a comparable Jewish population to Suriname.[7] Furthermore, as one of the largest plantation economies dependent on slave labour in the Caribbean during the eighteenth century—far more so than Dutch Curaçao—Jamaica is a particularly fruitful location for investigating questions of concubinage and ethnic fluidity.

[5] Jacob Rader Marcus, *The Colonial American Jew, 1492–1776*, 3 vols. (Detroit, 1970), 121–2; see also Thomas G. August, 'Family Structure and Jewish Continuity in Jamaica since 1655', *American Jewish Archives*, 41/1 (1989), 37–9.

[6] The scarcity of internal records from the early Jewish settlement of Jamaica is most likely due to repeated natural disasters, such as the devastating earthquake of 1907 which flattened the island's synagogues and destroyed their records. The earliest known Jamaican Jewish birth and death records are from 1789 (Ashkenazi) and 1807 (Sephardi), and the earliest known communal minutes book from Jamaica dates from 1907 (Archives of the United Congregation of Israelites, Kingston, Jamaica).

[7] See Cohen, *Jews in Another Environment*, 64. Whereas Cohen describes a dramatic population decline in Suriname during the late eighteenth century, the Jamaican Jewish population continued to rise throughout the nineteenth century (see Eli Faber, *Jews, Slaves, and the Slave Trade: Setting the Record Straight* (New York, 1998), 58; see also Mordechai Arbell, *The Portuguese Jews of Jamaica* (Kingston, Jamaica, 2000), 36.

Marcus collected evidence of concubinage among Jamaican Jews from eight eighteenth-century wills of Jewish male testators where slaves were manumitted or otherwise provided for, only five of which are convincing examples of concubinage. One is from a will of 1765, in which the testator explicitly 'leaves a bequest to his quadroon daughter'. However, Marcus also included cases that are more doubtful. For example, he cites a will of 1752, in which 'a man who has a wife living out of the country manumits a Negro woman', who may or may not have been his mistress, and a will from 1722, in which 'three slaves are manumitted' without reference to relationship or even gender.[8] To expand upon the groundbreaking work of Marcus and better understand the scope and nature of concubinage among Jews in colonial Jamaica, it is therefore necessary to assess a wider range of sources and apply a more selective set of definitional criteria.

Since there is little question that concubinage between Jewish men and women of colour was a pervasive social reality throughout the Atlantic world, as it was for non-Jewish men, scholars who have studied concubinage among Jews in the Dutch Atlantic have been mainly interested in the question of communal 'absorption' or the Jewishness of people of colour and to what extent mulatto children of Jewish men were integrated into the Jewish community. Were mulatto children circumcised, encouraged to convert, or buried in Jewish cemeteries? Or were children of Jewish fathers perhaps considered Jewish by virtue of their patrilineal descent?

The Surinamese Mahamad made explicit attempts to define the social status of mulatto Jews.[9] Like its mother community in Amsterdam, the Surinamese Mahamad, between 1777 and the end of the century, enacted legislation intended to stigmatize mulatto Jews as second-class citizens by making it impossible for them to become *jehidim* and restricting their communal involvement, such as where they could sit in the synagogue and where they could be buried.[10] According to the historian Robert Cohen there was, nevertheless, little question of their actual Jewishness, and there was a strong communal imperative to convert mulatto descendants of Jewish men to Judaism. Cohen cites a letter from three leaders of the Paramaribo community to the local governor in 1794 which states: 'Several among the Portuguese Jewish Nation, out of private affection begot children with some of their female slaves or mulattos. Out of particular love for the Jewish religion the boys were properly circumcised and the girls instructed by a teacher.'[11]

---

[8] Marcus, *The Colonial American Jew*, i. 121–2 n. 48; iii. 1408–9.

[9] Cohen, *Jews in Another Environment*, 156–72; Aviva Ben-Ur, 'Peripheral Inclusion: Communal Belonging in Suriname's Sephardic Community', in Alexandra Cuffel and Brian Britt (eds.), *Religion, Gender, and Culture in the Pre-Modern World* (New York, 2007), 185–210.

[10] On the Jewish community in Amsterdam, see Yosef Kaplan, 'The Self-Definition of the Sephardi Jews of Western Europe and their Relation to the Alien and the Stranger', in id., *An Alternative Path to Modernity: The Sephardi Diaspora in Western Europe* (Leiden, 2000), 51–77.   [11] Cohen, *Jews in Another Environment*, 159.

Subsequent scholarship sought to further qualify the place of mulatto Jews in the community and their relationship to powerful Jewish slave owners. On the one hand, Jonathan Schorsch has suggested that, as a result of the formation of the new identity of western Sephardim as 'white' during the seventeenth century, there developed a racialized aversion to the absorption of people of colour into their communities, especially in the English Caribbean.[12] Schorsch further asserts that Jewish slave owners displayed no distinctiveness in their manner of slave owning. On the other hand, Aviva Ben-Ur has argued that Eurafricans who embraced Judaism culturally, if not fully halakhically, played a decisive role in the continuity of Jewish life in Suriname.[13] Over time, the discourse of communal legitimacy became increasingly deracialized as Eurafricans became more integrated into communal life.[14] According to Ben-Ur, Jews were not unique in converting their slaves to the household religion, but they did seem to have taken a lead among the Surinamese planter class.[15]

Given the ethnic solidarity of Spanish-Portuguese Jews, which transcended national boundaries, it is likely that what was true for the Sephardi community in Dutch Suriname was equally true for the Sephardi community in English Jamaica. The scarcity of internal Jewish documentation from Jamaica, however, prevents firm conclusions about the communal place of mulatto Jews. Some circumstantial evidence illustrates the complexity of the issue in Jamaica. Several known people of colour appear in the manumission record and wills with clearly Jewish names, but there is no surviving record of them being buried in Jamaican Jewish cemeteries.[16] Whereas burial patterns at the Surinamese cemetery at Jodensavanne reflect the social marginality of mulatto Jews, no such burial patterns are evident at Hunt's Bay cemetery in Kingston, making it impossible to speculate on the presence of people of colour there.[17] Alternatively, the lack of an apparent marginal section for people of colour at Hunt's Bay cemetery may indicate their complete lack of social distinctiveness. In several wills, as will be discussed, free people of colour are bequeathed properties within Jewish residential

---

[12]   Schorsch, *Jews and Blacks in the Early Modern World*; see also id., 'Transformations in the Manumission of Slaves by Jews from East to West: Pressures from the Atlantic Slave Trade', in Rosemary Brana-Shute and Randy J. Sparks (eds.), *Paths to Freedom: Manumission in the Atlantic World* (Columbia, SC, 2009), 68–95.

[13]   Aviva Ben-Ur, 'A Matriarchal Matter: Slavery, Conversion, and Upward Mobility in Suriname's Jewish Community', in Richard L. Kagan and Philip D. Morgan (eds.), *Atlantic Diasporas: Jews, Conversos, and Crypto-Jews in the Age of Mercantilism, 1500–1800* (Baltimore, 2009), 152–69; see also Chapter 10 above.

[14]   Ben-Ur, 'A Matriarchal Matter', 164–5.   [15]   Ibid. 158.

[16]   See n. 34 below for some examples of people of colour who appear with Jewish names in the manumission record.

[17]   See Ben-Ur, 'Peripheral Inclusion', 191–3; see also Rachel Frankel, 'Antecedents and Remnants of Joden-savanne: The Synagogues and Cemeteries of the First Permanent Plantation Settlement of New World Jews', in Paolo Bernardini and Norman Fiering (eds.), *The Jews and the Expansion of Europe to the West, 1450–1800* (New York, 2001), 422–3; see also Chapter 8 above.

enclaves, suggesting at least some level of social integration. In one explicit case from 1767, the testator Michael Levy, a German Jew, stipulates a legacy for his illegitimate children of colour, from his mistress and housekeeper Frances Warren, on condition that 'they [are] educated and brought up in the Jewish faith', a sentiment reminiscent of the letter from the leaders of the Paramaribo community mentioned earlier.[18]

However, conversion, marriage, burial, and belonging to the community are not the only measures of absorption. Absorption could and did take place to varying degrees in Jamaica through the incorporation of mulatto children into Jewish families, even when there is no evidence of active conversion. The place of people of colour in the Jewish family was certainly not unambiguous and reflects many of the same anxieties about race, class, and status found in Suriname or Amsterdam on a communal level. But in Jamaica, the question of absorption must be explored on personal, familial, and emotional levels rather than on the communal one.

Sentiment in a Slave Society

The sentiment discussed here is the emotional attachment between Jewish men, women of colour, and their children expressed through manumission or inheritance. But before discussing the presence of people of colour in Sephardi families, the complex role of sentiment in a slave society must be further defined. Colonial Atlantic slave societies have, quite rightly, been characterized as dominated by an ethos of accumulation, which included the exploitative treatment of slaves as human commodities. This is especially important with regards to the attitude of white men towards enslaved women, who were not only the chief victims of their sexual exploitation, adventurism, and violence, but were also commodified through long-term investment in their 'increase' or offspring.[19]

That is not to say that enslaved women were nothing more than passive victims. Recent scholarship has challenged the dominant narrative of the submissive role of enslaved women in the colonial West Indies by focusing on their reproductive agency and their resistance to enslavement.[20] Furthermore, enslaved women were more likely than enslaved men to serve as household labour, a position often synonymous with concubinage. As housekeepers, cooks, and nursemaids, enslaved women were not only more integrated into the routine of the white household than men—sometimes even serving as wet nurses for white children—they tended to live longer, healthier lives, assume leadership roles among the enslaved community, and, at times, even manage to

---

[18] See August, 'Family Structure and Jewish Continuity in Jamaica since 1655', 37; see will of Michael Levy (24 June 1767), IRO, Wills lib. 36, fo. 187.

[19] See Jennifer Morgan, *Laboring Women: Reproduction and Gender in New World Slavery* (Philadelphia, 2004).

[20] See Barbara Bush, *Slave Women in Caribbean Society, 1650–1838* (Kingston, Jamaica, 1990).

take advantage of their sexually exploited positions to improve their own and their children's stations.[21]

Quotidian interpersonal interactions between slaves and their owners were not always hostile despite their exploitative foundations. The paradoxical nature of sentiment within a slave society is illustrated by the Jamaican slave manager Thomas Thistlewood, who, despite his now infamous, though not unusual, obsessive sexual abuse of enslaved women, also seemed to have formed an emotional bond with an enslaved woman named Phibbah.[22] The sources available to us are too limited to give an accurate picture of the extent to which emotional bonds between a white master and an enslaved woman such as Thistlewood and Phibbah developed out of true affection or out of a mutually beneficial companionship ultimately rooted in the white male's prerogative. This paradoxical sentiment is especially evident with regard to paternity. Though affectionate relationships between white masters and enslaved children certainly was not limited to paternity,[23] paternity most often translated into concrete financial and material support, even at the expense of the white male father and his legitimate family.

The role of sentiment among Jewish slave owners comes with its own set of contentious implications. Jewish slave ownership in the West has been apologetically portrayed as guided by a religiously informed humanitarianism. Isaac Emmanuel and Suzanne Emmanuel, for instance, write in their pioneering *History of the Jews of the Netherlands Antilles* that 'the slaves employed by Jews were generally treated more humanely'.[24] Similarly, in his sweeping history of Jewish slave ownership in the Americas, Saul Friedman claims that 'in the West Indies, it was customary for Jews to emancipate several blacks in their wills'.[25]

---

[21] See Hilary Beckles, 'Black Female Slaves and White Households in Barbados', in David Barry Gaspar and Darlene Clark Hine (eds.), *More than Chattel: Black Women and Slavery in the Americas* (Bloomington, 1996); see also Trevor Burnard, '"Do Thou in Gentle Phibia Smile": Scenes from an Interracial Marriage, Jamaica, 1754–86', in David Barry Gaspar and Darlene Clark Hine (eds.), *Beyond Bondage: Free Women of Color in the Americas* (Urbana, Ill., 2004).

[22] Trevor Burnard, *Mastery, Tyranny and Desire: Thomas Thistlewood and His Slaves in the Anglo-Jamaican World* (Kingston, Jamaica, 2004); Burnard, '"Do Thou in Gentle Phibia Smile"', 93; see also Bush, *Slave Women in Caribbean Society*, 114.

[23] See Natalie Zemon Davis, 'David Nassy's "Furlough" and the Slave Mattheus', in Pamela S. Nadell, Jonathan D. Sarna, and Jonathan Sussman (eds.), *New Essays in American Jewish History: To Commemorate the 60th Anniversary of the American Jewish Archives Journal and the 10th Anniversary of the American Jewish Archives under the Direction of Dr. Gary P. Zola* (New York, 2010), 79–93. David Nassy sustained a paternal relationship with the enslaved boy Mattheus though he was not his father. A similar case is found in the 1796 will of Rachel Nunes who refers to the offspring of her household slaves as her own and ensures their future security by bequeathing them to the wardens of the synagogue in Kingston (will of Rachel Nunes (10 Nov. 1796), IRO, Wills, lib. 63, fo. 78).   [24] Emmanuel and Emmanuel, *A History of the Jews of the Netherlands Antilles*, i. 79.

[25] Saul Friedman, *Jews and the American Slave Trade* (New Brunswick, 1998), 68; see also Schorsch, 'Transformations in the Manumission of Slaves by Jews from East to West', 94 n. 82.

However, it is not difficult to demonstrate that a clear ethos of accumulation existed and, unsurprisingly, even dominated among Jews in colonial Jamaica. I found that in Jewish wills from late eighteenth-century Jamaica, slaves, along with the 'increase' of the females, are bequeathed within families and sold off for the 'highest and best price' with much greater frequency than they are 'emancipated'. Out of 248 Jamaican Jewish wills recorded between 1673 and 1814, the manumission of slaves was stipulated in only twenty-nine—under 12 per cent.[26] It is also clear that sexual liaisons did not always produce affective bonds between Jewish men, their concubines, and their illegitimate children, as can be illustrated in the case of the Kingston merchant Jacob Bravo.

Jacob Bravo, along with his wife Sarah and their three children, built a large estate in Jamaica. Included in Jacob's ample assets was a small farm called Lucy Lawn where he, 'did dwell together with [his] Negro woman slave named Betty and her two daughters named Abba and Pheba'.[27] Though Jacob most likely had a sexual relationship with Betty—based on the unusual expression 'dwell together'—he wills that she along with her two daughters, who are presumably also his daughters,[28] 'be immediately after [his] decease sold for the highest and best price that can be gotten for the same by [his] executors'. If indeed the relationship between Jacob Bravo and Betty was a sexual one and one that produced children, their relationship produced in Jacob no apparent sense of devotion or financial obligation towards his mistress or his children.

Another indication of the complex negotiation between sentiment and accumulation among Jewish slave owners is found in the manumission record for the twenty-one years between 1779 and 1799. Out of a total of 219 slaves manumitted by Jews in those years, 95 were children. The vast majority of these freed children, 77 individuals (81 per cent of the total number of children), are classified as other than Negro. The disparity between the manumission of black children and those identified as other than Negro suggests an important correlation between the manumission of children and white biological paternity.[29] It would have been unlikely for children to be manumitted as a reward for their 'faithful service', and manumission motivated by biological paternity is just as likely as manumission as a reward to the mothers received through their children. Therefore, it seems that biological paternity was most likely the dominant motivation behind the manumission of children among Jamaican Jews, though it should be made clear that the Jewish manumitter associated with the enfranchised

[26] These 248 wills consist of the 208 available Jamaican wills of known Jews in the collection of the American Jewish Archives in Cincinnati and 40 collected from the IRO through cross-referencing with the available manumission records between 1779 and 1799 (IRO, Wills, libs. 46–135).

[27] Will of Jacob Bravo (16 Mar. 1780), IRO, Wills, lib. 46, fo. 81.

[28] Though the will refers to them as *her* daughters, the probable sexual relationship between Jacob and their mother is suggestive of his paternity.

[29] For the relationship between manumission and illegitimacy in Jamaica, see Burnard, '"Do Thou in Gentle Phibia Smile"', 83 n. 10.

child was not necessarily always the white parent in question. The great infrequency with which black children were manumitted, however, points to long-term invest- ment and accumulation through slave 'increase'. Children of mixed ancestry occupied a decisively more favourable social position among colonial Jamaican Jews, who, echo- ing colonial patterns more generally, treated their black slaves with the same accumu- lative ethos as non-Jews.

Manumission as an Indication of Sentiment

Manumission was certainly perceived as an act of charity by some slave owners, a reward for faithful service, and perhaps even an act of parental or sexual affection. Manumission records are, however, notoriously misleading. In most cases, they are frustratingly inarticulate about motivation. Moreover, as the historian John F. Camp- bell has recently suggested, manumission in the colonial West Indies may have been used by slave owners as a method of manipulation: dangling the promise of freedom to ensure loyalty and hard work among their enslaved labourers.[30] Given the general infrequency of manumission in Jamaica this was without doubt often true. Neverthe- less, the nature of the act of manumission itself is revealing. Manumission was highly expensive in late eighteenth-century Jamaica, as shown by the case of Moses Gomes Fonseca above. Owners were required to pay a manumission fee in addition to the cost of the administrative stamp.[31] The security bond, made law by an Act of the Jamaican Assembly in 1774, was the greatest cost to the owner, requiring a £5 life annuity for the freed person.[32] Therefore, if not an act of charity, manumission in Jamaica after 1774 was deliberate, calculated, and certainly not an act of cruelty.

Manumission in general occurred infrequently throughout the Atlantic world.[33] In Jamaica, the prohibitive cost seems to have been but one factor preventing many Jews, as well as non-Jews, from manumitting slaves. Therefore, to whatever extent manumission is revealing about concubinage it is, at best, only a limited measure of the pervasiveness of concubinage among Jews in colonial Jamaica. In the twenty-one years between 1779 and 1799 Jews appear in the manumission record in only 161 cases,

[30] John F. Campbell, 'How Free is Free? The Limits of Manumission for Enslaved Africans in Eighteenth- Century British West Indian Sugar Society', in Brana-Shute and Sparks (eds.), *Paths to Freedom*, 143–59.

[31] See JA, 1B/11/Laws of Jamaica, 1792–99. The Act states: 'Over and above the stamp to which deeds of manumission are liable by this act, a further duty of 10*l* is hereby set thereon: in cases where manumission is made by will, an additional stamp of 20*s* is to be imposed on the security-bond required by 15 *Geo*. III *cap*. XVIII [1774]; which bonds must be recorded in the secretary's office before they can be admitted in evidence: Proviso, manumissions by or at the instance of any public or parochial body not contemplated hereby.'

[32] JA, 1B/11/Laws of Jamaica, 1760–92. The assembly was compelled to pass this legislation as a remedy to the apparently pervasive problem of slave owners dumping enfeebled or rebellious slaves on the public coffers through manumission. The assembly viewed these manumitted slaves as a 'nuisance to the community through frequent thefts'.

[33] Robin Blackburn, 'Introduction', in Brana-Shute and Sparks (eds.), *Paths to Freedom*, 2–3.

representing a total of 150 individual Jews.[34] If we conservatively estimate the total Jewish population of Jamaica to be around 1,000 individuals by the end of the eighteenth century, then no more than 13 per cent is represented in the manumission records.

Among the 161 cases of Jewish slave owners manumitting slaves between 1779 and 1799, I have identified 53 cases (33 per cent) where parental affection is the most likely motivation.[35] Though the historian Rosemary Brana-Shute has cautioned against using the manumission of women or children of colour to draw conclusions about white paternity, concubinage, or affection in general, in these 53 cases the children are classified as other than Negro and are mentioned along with, or in proximity to, either the manumission of a specific woman or with an explicit reference to a mother.[36] Some cases among the 161, though exhibiting these criteria, contain indications of other motivations and are therefore not included as possible cases of concubinage. For instance, in some manumissions the recognized owner does not pay the fee. In such cases it is suspected that the manumitted adult female or child with mixed ancestry was the mistress or offspring of another white man—though this may also have been another Jew—or alternatively, that the freed slaves themselves purchased their freedom.

From among these 53 cases some representative examples are instructive. Only two instances of manumission between 1779 and 1799 state explicitly that paternity was in fact the motivation. The first, as has already been shown, was Moses Gomes Fonseca's manumission of his three children through 'the natural love and affection which I have and bear towards my three mulatto children'—a formulation that, though conventional in other contexts appears only in this manumission, suggesting that Fonseca insisted upon it. Four months later, Daniel Almeyda manumitted his 'reputed daughter', a mulatto girl named Abigail Almeyda.[37] Other less explicit examples include the manumission by shopkeeper David Gomes Rabello in 1782 of a Negro woman named Affey along with her five mulatto children: Mary, Alexander, Lydia, Sarah, and Sophia Reallo (a name which is possibly a clerical error or a variation of Rabello).[38] In 1786

---

[34] I have disqualified some cases, mostly those of free black or mulatto owners with clearly Jewish names because of the difficulty of determining the Jewishness of freed slaves. For instance, Lea Ferro, a free 'mulatto woman' (Manumission of Sally (4 Sept. 1796), JA, Manumissions 1B/11/6/15, fos. 219–20) and Joseph Silvera, a 'mulatto bricklayer' (Manumission of Jane Williams and Nathaniel Benson (1 June 1796), JA, Manumissions 1B/11/6/16, fos. 58–9).

[35] Sole male owners, and the executors of deceased sole males, constitute the majority of Jewish owners, seventy-two cases (45%). I do not include cases where Jews manumitted slaves in groups. Among the groups are twenty-four married couples (15%) and eighteen groups with unknown associations (11%).

[36] Rosemary Brana-Shute, 'Sex and Gender in Surinamese Manumissions', in Brana-Shute and Sparks (eds.), Paths to Freedom, 185–9.

[37] Manumission of Abigail Almeyda (21 Dec. 1797), JA, Manumissions 1B/11/6/23, fo. 103. Illegitimate children were referred to as 'reputed' by notarial convention.

[38] Manumission of Affey and Mary, Alexander, Lydia, Sarah, and Sophia Reallo (23 Dec. 1782), JA, Manumissions 1B/11/6/15, fos. 49–50. For the practice of altering names, see also Chapter 10 above.

Isaac de Castro manumitted a mulatto woman named Sarah Winters along with Isaac, her infant quadroon son.[39] Hananel de Aguilar manumitted a mulatto infant named Allan M. Leon de Aguilar in 1788, who is identified as the son of a Negro woman named Nancy M. Leon.[40] On 9 August 1799 Abraham Alexander Lindo manumitted a mulatto child named James, the son of a Negro woman named Sally.[41] On the next day, Abraham manumitted Sally.[42]

Cases of individual Jewish female slave owners manumitting slaves have not been discounted as potential cases of manumission through parental devotion. Most women who manumit slaves do so shortly after the deaths of their husbands. Seventy-two per cent of Jewish women in the manumission records are identified as widows and are probably settling their husband's estates.[43] For example, in 1781 the widow Grace Lopes Torres manumitted a mulatto boy named Richard, the son of a Negro woman named Eve, a year after her husband's death.[44] This may even suggest that Jewish wives in Jamaica, as with Jewish wives in Curaçao and throughout Atlantic slave societies, tacitly countenanced the public secret of concubinage.[45]

Given that a third of cases of manumission among Jewish owners can be shown to reasonably suggest paternity as the most likely motivation, it can be concluded that manumission may in some cases represent an expression of affection between white men, their mistresses, and their children. Biological parental affection was, therefore, a major, though certainly not the only or even dominant, motivation behind manumissions for Jewish slave owners.

Voluntary Support of Reputed Children Within Sephardi Families

Unlike the early non-Jewish white settlers of colonial Jamaica, who largely settled as single men, Sephardim in early eighteenth-century Jamaica tended to settle as families and build their community as much through procreation as through immigration.[46]

---

[39] Manumission of Sarah Winters and Isaac (19 Nov. 1786), JA, Manumissions 1B/11/6/16, fo. 139.

[40] Manumission of Allan M. Leon de Aguilar (10 May 1788), JA, Manumissions 1B/11/6/16, fo. 175.

[41] Manumission of James (9 Aug. 1799), JA, Manumissions 1B/11/6/24, fo. 17.

[42] Manumission of Sally (10 Aug. 1799), JA, Manumissions 1B/11/6/22, fos. 212–13.

[43] Ten women (21% of women) appear in the record as deceased and their estates are being settled and only three women (7% of women) are identified as 'spinsters', who are probably manumitting slaves of their own accord.

[44] Manumission of Richard (9 Aug. 1781), JA, Manumissions 1B/11/6/21, fos. 120–1. Grace is identified as the wife of David Lopes Torres in his will recorded in 1780 (will of David Lopes Torres (22 Aug. 1780), IRO, Wills, lib. 46, fo. 133). Though David L. Torres does make provisions for several slaves in his will he does not mention Eve or Richard explicitly.

[45] See Eva Abraham-Van der Mark, 'Marriage and Concubinage Among the Sephardic Merchant Elite of Curaçao', in Janet Momsen (ed.), *Women and Change in the Caribbean: A Pan-Caribbean Perspective* (Kingston, Jamaica, 1993), 38–49; see also Ben-Ur, 'Peripheral Inclusion', 200–1.

[46] See Trevor Burnard, 'Inheritance and Independence: Women's Status in Early Colonial Jamaica',

This more comprehensive family life did not, however, prevent Sephardi men from embracing the libertine nature of West Indian slave society. Male sexual exploitation could have affective consequences. The voluntary support of concubines and their children apart from manumission reveals some of the implications of these affective bonds on colonial Sephardi families. Incorporation into Jewish families is measured here by the support given to mistresses and reputed children along with legitimate members of the family through inheritance.

Most wills of Jamaican Sephardim from the late eighteenth century reveal a sustained commitment to Sephardi communal institutions to the exclusion of both non-Jewish and Ashkenazi interests. I have included some examples here to help illustrate the nature of ethnic and religious identity among Jamaican Sephardim. The continuity of Sephardi ethnic identity also helps to contextualize some of the resistance to incorporating reputed children of colour, who may or may not have been considered Jewish, into the family, though this is in itself certainly not the full explanation. Voluntary support of mistresses along with reputed children suggests the growing importance and legitimacy of affective bonds among Sephardi Jews in Jamaica as a determining factor of familial belonging, while the role of ethnicity, a hallmark of Sephardi identity throughout the early modern period, started to become less relevant throughout the eighteenth century.

Judah Cohen Henriques was a married Kingston merchant with no known surviving legitimate children, who issued his last will and testament in 1808.[47] In his will he specified that he was to be buried 'according to the rights and ceremonies of the Hebrew religion' and left money for all three Jamaican synagogues—Kingston, Port Royal, and Spanish Town—and financial support for sixteen indigent Jews, from among whom men were to be chosen to carry his body to the cemetery. Judah not only left an endowment to the Jewish orphanage society, the Aby Yetomim (Father of the Orphans), he also bequeathed his Hebrew books to the institution—a rare display of hope for Jewish intellectual continuity on the island.[48] Judah supported his wife, Rebecca, with an annuity of £50 along with the entire monetary residuum of his estate, although with the significant exception of the proceeds of his stable and the attached residence located in West Street, Kingston.

William and Mary Quarterly, 3rd ser. 48/1 (1991), 93–114. Very few Jamaican Jewish wills do not mention local family, and there are also a disproportionate number of female testators among the Jews.

[47] Will of Judah Cohen Henriques (23 Mar. 1808), IRO, Wills, lib. 79, fo. 30.

[48] Though there was certainly an active Jewish intellectual culture in colonial Jamaica, the dominantly mercantile interests of the community and the lack of internal records conspire to silence this aspect of Jewish life on the island. On the Aby Yetomim, see Marcus, *The Colonial American Jew*, i. 129–30. I suspect that the Aby Yetomim may have offered an alternative to the manumission of reputed children by providing an alternative home. Yet without surviving records there is no way to know to what extent the orphanage sheltered reputed children.

After supporting his wife, he stipulated that a one-time sum of £20 be allotted to each of his reputed children: a 'mustee' daughter named Clara and two 'mustee' sons named Gerald and Isaac. To 'Perina Maria Garcia a free Black Woman and unto such reputed child or children Male or Female as may happen to leave me surviving', Judah left a portion of the proceeds from his stable, which he charged his executors to continue operating, along with its associated residence. The proceeds of his business were intended specifically to pay Perina's rent and medical expenses: 'the Doctors Bill for medicines furnished and attendance on the said Perina Maria Garcia'. It is likely that Perina was pregnant at the time Judah drafted his will.

Judah's will thus offers a clear case of concubinage along with the explicit desire to voluntarily support both his mistress and his reputed children through housing and medical care, as much as through financial legacies. His will also reveals the extent to which Jewish wives were aware of and even complacent about the realities of concubinage in Jamaican slave society.

Judah's three reputed children are mentioned in his will alongside members of his extended Sephardi family network which included his two cousins, Jacob of David de Castro and David of Isaac de Castro, along with his two nieces, Sarah of Moses Aboab and Sarah Gomez. Judah's cousins are allotted the same sum as his reputed children—£20 each—but are given no additional portion of the estate. Though monetary value alone is admittedly not a fully representative reflection of familial affection, it does provide at least some sense of how reputed children of colour shared an estate with legitimate members of a western Sephardi family. Whether or not his three reputed children became integrated members of the Jewish community or considered themselves (or were considered) Jews, Judah Cohen Henriques certainly considered them members of his family.

Isaac Depass, who died around 1831, was apparently a bachelor who lived just north of Kingston in St Andrew Parish and who left all his possessions to two beneficiaries: the Jamaican Jewish community and his four reputed children.[49] In return for the recital of an *escava* (*hashkavah*), a memorial prayer, on the eve of Yom Kippur, as well as the recital of Kaddish for eleven months after his death, he made bequests to the Portuguese synagogue of Kingston, the poor Jews of the 'Hebrew Nation', and 'two discreet orphan boys' under the care of the Aby Yetomim, conceivably a reference to his own children. Before mentioning his reputed children, who seem to be from different mothers, he supported his extended Jewish kinship network. Isaac makes provisions for two nephews with nothing more than monetary bequests though to a greater extent than he supported any one of the previously mentioned Jewish communal institutions.

Isaac appears to have had a sexual relationship with a 'black woman' named Elizabeth Laing, the housekeeper of his residence on his farm in St Andrew Parish called Happy Retreat. Isaac bequeathed Happy Retreat along with its livestock to Elizabeth

---

[49] Will of Isaac Depass (2 Dec. 1831), IRO, Wills, lib. 112, fo. 135.

and his reputed son Edward Moore.[50] Though the identity of Edward's mother is not stated explicitly, he is always mentioned together with Elizabeth. To Edward, Isaac left his messuages (dwelling houses) and tenements on White Street in Kingston. Additionally, Isaac bequeathed to Elizabeth, Edward, and James White, seemingly a much younger reputed child, several 'Negro' slaves along with the increase of the females and a supplementary sum of £70. Isaac later mentions an older reputed daughter Emily Almeyda, the wife of one Robert Almeyda, to whom he willed his house in the Jewish enclave of Orange Street, Kingston. Towards the end of his will, Isaac refers to yet a fourth reputed child named George Robinson to whom he left a modest allotment of £10. Despite Isaac's apparent sexual opportunism, he clearly continued to support at least one of his mistresses along with several of his reputed children through bequests of a number of valuable assets.

Though the cases of Judah Cohen Henriques and Isaac Depass provide evidence of affective attachments to mistresses and their children, they are cases of men with no apparent surviving legitimate children. It may therefore seem that devotion to reputed children developed only when there were no surviving legitimate children to inherit an estate. However, the will of Joseph Cohen Deleon, a Spanish Town merchant, provides a case where reputed children are supported with legacies alongside legitimate children, and it is here that some of the tensions of familial absorption become apparent.

Joseph Cohen Deleon, who died in 1825, may have entered into a sexual relationship with Johanna Marin Devereaux, a 'black woman', after the death of his wife with whom he had two children, Abraham and Judith.[51] Joseph bequeathed the vast majority of his estate to Abraham, Judith, and his mother as well as to his nephew and godson David Lyon. After making the customary gesture of support for the Spanish Town synagogue, Joseph bequeathed the sum of £25 to each of his reputed daughters, Ellen and Louisa Deleon, who were 'begotten on the body of Johanna Marin Devereaux'.

---

[50] All of Isaac's reputed children have different surnames, none of which are his own. Though I do not know why this is, I can suggest several possibilities. It is possible that the children became the slaves of other men and took their other master's name. Likewise, their mothers may have belonged to other masters or the children took their mother's name. This, in fact, may have been preferred by Isaac in order to distance himself from his illegitimate children. It is also possible that they were self-emancipated and that they gave themselves new names to remove the stigma of enslavement. Emily Almeyda appears to have taken the name of Robert, who was probably the freed slave of a Jewish household and who may have identified himself as Jewish. Whatever the reason, it should be taken as a cautionary note that the absence of Jewish names is not evidence against illegitimacy and, vice-versa, the presence of the same family name as an owner should not be taken as evidence in and of itself of illegitimacy. On slave-naming patterns in Jamaica, see Trevor Burnard, 'Slave Naming Patterns: Onomastics and the Taxonomy of Race in Eighteenth-Century Jamaica', *Journal of Interdisciplinary History*, 31/3 (2001), 325–46; see also Schorsch's discussion of slave-naming patterns among Jewish owners in Schorsch, *Jews and Blacks in the Early Modern World*, 238–47.

[51] Will of Joseph Cohen Deleon (2 Nov. 1825), IRO, Wills, lib. 106, fo. 79. This would be in sharp contrast to Thomas August's supposition that concubinage with women of colour most frequently occurred among young unmarried Jewish men (August, 'Family Structure and Jewish Continuity in Jamaica', 38).

Joseph thus supported his reputed children of colour alongside his legitimate heirs, although to a far lesser extent. While he provided for the education of his legitimate children, for instance, he makes no such provisions for his reputed children. This stands in sharp contrast to Judah Cohen Henriques's generous support of his reputed children in the absence of surviving or suitable heirs. It appears that, although Joseph Cohen Deleon felt some obligation towards his reputed children, he did not see them as equal heirs. In cases such as these, where legitimate children were supported alongside reputed children, there is little doubt that considerable tension arose within the family. This tension is dramatically apparent in the case of Aaron Baruh Lousada, the reputed son of Emanuel Baruh Lousada.

Emanuel Baruh Lousada, quite possibly the most distinguished Jewish legal expert in Kingston in the late eighteenth century, drafted his will two years before his death in 1795.[52] Emanuel made bequests to his wife Esther and his four sons Jacob, Daniel, Aaron, and Isaac Baruh Lousada along with his daughter, granddaughter, son-in-law, and three nieces. To his four sons he left an equal annuity of £140, each later amended to £200, for clothing and education. Furthermore, individual lump sums for each of his sons are mentioned as having been established as a legacy entrusted to him by his cousin Grace Lopes Torres, who had died only a day before Emanuel drafted his will.[53] By far the largest portion of Grace's legacy is bequeathed to Aaron Baruh Lousada, who is allotted the substantial sum of £1,000.

Although in the original draft of the will, Emanuel made no distinction between his sons, eight days later he attached a codicil stipulating that though Aaron was only his reputed son, anyone who contested Aaron's due share would in turn forfeit his or her own inheritance, which would be given instead to Aaron:

Whereas Aaron Baruh Lousada who is in my Will named as one of my sons is in fact only my reputed child now for preventing all possible controversy I do hereby declare that the person intended to be benefited in my said Will by the description of Aaron Baruh Lousada one of my sons is my reputed Son Aaron Baruh Lousada and it is my Will that if any person or persons whosoever shall in any wise controvert or call in question the right or capacity of my said reputed son Aaron Baruh Lousada to take all or any of the Benefits intended for him by my said Will such person or persons so controverting or calling in question such right or capacity shall forfeit and lose all benefits whatsoever to which he she or they might or would otherwise be entitled under my said Will.

Emanuel clearly anticipated that some of his beneficiaries, possibly even his wife, would challenge Aaron's right of inheritance. There are also other elements in Aaron's

---

[52] Will of Emanuel Baruh Lousada (25 Oct. 1797), IRO, Wills, lib. 62, fo. 185. For the year of his death, see Richard D. Barnett and Philip Wright, *The Jews of Jamaica: Tombstone Inscriptions, 1663–1880* (Jerusalem, 1997), 52–3 no. 299. Emanuel B. Lousada's legal expertise is clear, as he appears six times as an executor for other Jews in the manumission record—always mentioned as 'esquire'—and his name appears on the list of subscribers to the 1786 edition of the *Laws of Jamaica* (see Herbert Friedenwald, 'Material for the History of the Jews in the British West Indies', *Publications of the American Jewish Historical Society*, 5 (1897), 57).

life story that suggest his peripheral place in the family. Perhaps because of his illegitimacy, Aaron lived apart from the Lousada household, raised under the care of his aunt,
Grace Lopes Torres, who referred to him as her 'adopted son'.[54] Despite his familial
marginality it appears that Aaron Baruh Lousada was considered sufficiently part of
the Jewish community to be buried in the Spanish Town Jewish cemetery upon his
death in 1808 at the age of 25.[55]

The qualifier 'reputed' only indicates illegitimacy in general and is not used
exclusively to describe illegitimate children of colour. The identity of Aaron's mother is
never stated in Emanuel's will, nor is any hint given as to his appearance. One possible,
though highly circumstantial, clue to his racial identity is Aaron's proximity to people
of colour in the will of his aunt and adopted mother Grace. Aaron's inheritance and the
provision for his upkeep are mentioned between a list of slaves to be manumitted and a
list of slaves bequeathed to Emanuel, whose cumulative value, after being sold, is
intended exclusively for Aaron's benefit. Aaron's proximity to people of colour and his
financial stake in them in Grace's will may suggest that he was perceived as somehow
connected to them. One other circumstantial clue about Aaron's racial identity is that
Grace appointed an enslaved female named Amelia to 'attend upon and be for the
Service of my adopted son Aaron Baruh Lousada Son of my Cousin Emanuel Baruh
Lousada'.[56] Grace further mandated that Amelia was to be manumitted after Aaron
reached the age of majority or in the event of his premature death. Given that Amelia's
fate was so connected to Aaron's, it is attractive, though highly speculative, to suggest
that she may have in fact been his biological mother. If Aaron was the son of a white
woman, however, his place in the Lousada family still reveals much about the nature of
illegitimacy and paternal affectivity.

If Aaron was of mixed ancestry then his life serves as a compelling model of the full
extent to which people of colour could be absorbed into both the Jamaican Sephardi
family and community despite some clear evidence of acrimony. Even though he lived
apart from the Lousada household, and there were those in the family who clearly
questioned his right to inherit, he was undoubtedly dear to his father and aunt, listed
without distinction among his brothers, given an unaltered family name (indeed the
name of Emanuel's father), and buried among Jews in a Jewish cemetery. Perhaps most
importantly, neither Aaron's father nor his adopted mother felt in any way compelled

[53] Barnett and Wright, *The Jews of Jamaica*, 94 no. 1066. Emanuel's will was most likely drafted on that date
to accommodate the estate of Grace Lopes Torres.

[54] Will of Grace Lopes Torres (19 Mar. 1795), IRO, Wills, lib. 61, fo. 105.

[55] Barnett and Wright, *The Jews of Jamaica*, 109 no. 1161. The dates on this tombstone reasonably correspond with the life of Aaron B. Lousada. I could not confirm definitively that this tombstone was indeed that
of the reputed son of Emanuel Baruh Lousada and not another member of the community with the same
name.

[56] Amelia was left to Grace by her husband David Lopes Torres six years earlier in 1780. She is described in
his will as 'a Negroe girl' (will of David Lopes Torres (22 Aug. 1780), IRO, Wills, lib. 46, fo. 133).

to define him as a person of colour, which may indicate either a complete lack of racial stigma or the desire to prevent such a stigma from developing. If Aaron was the illegitimate son of a white mistress, possibly even someone who was herself Jewish, then his case would offer an important control to the other evidence presented here, where the racial identity of reputed children is stated clearly. In the cases where the racial identity of reputed children is certain, there are very few indications of complete familial integration such as that enjoyed by Aaron. Similarly, some of the tensions evident in the incorporation of Aaron into the family might reflect tensions of illegitimacy in general and should be considered as nothing more than this and as revealing little about racial stigma. If the tensions apparent in the wills of Joseph Cohen Deleon and Emanuel Baruh Lousada are indeed tied to issues of race, then many of the same conflicts which are apparent on a communal level with regard to the place of 'mulatto Jews' in Suriname and Amsterdam are seen to be manifest on a familial level as well.

Conclusion: An Affective Revolution

Ethnicity played a critical role in the maintenance of Spanish-Portuguese Jewish identity and familial belonging throughout the early modern period.[57] Not only did endogamous family networks protect the wealth generated from colonial trade, but they provided a bulwark for a shared sense of ethnic solidarity and even supremacy as Members of a Portuguese nation.[58] By defining familial membership as essentially determined by ethnicity above all else, including religion, western Sephardi families incorporated Converso kin remaining in Iberia or southern France while shunning the integration of Ashkenazim. As the Sephardi population of the British Atlantic declined, along with its wealth, during the eighteenth century, the frequency of marriages between Sephardim and Ashkenazim, as well as with non-Jews, increased. Though this change in Sephardi families was unavoidable, it took place in the context of a more general social trend: the rise of 'affective individualism' in Great Britain, which stressed

[57] On the definitions of 'ethnicity' within the context of early modern western Sephardim, see David Graizbord, 'Religion and Ethnicity Among "Men of the Nation": Toward a Realistic Interpretation', *Jewish Social Studies*, NS 15/1 (2008), 32–65.

[58] On the role of ethnic identity in the formation of the western Sephardi diaspora, see Yosef Kaplan, 'Familia, matrimonio y sociedad: los casamientos clandestinos en la diáspora sefaradí occidental (siglos XVII–XVIII)', *Espacio, tiempo y forma*, 4/6 (1993), 129–54; Daniel Swetschinski, 'Kinship and Commerce: The Foundation of Portuguese Jewish Life in Seventeenth-Century Holland', *Studia Rosenthaliana*, 15 (1981), 52–74; Daviken Studnicki-Gizbert, *A Nation Upon the Ocean Sea: Portugal's Atlantic Diaspora and the Crises of the Spanish Empire, 1492–1640* (Oxford, 2007). For a recent study which corrects and expands upon earlier work on the economic importance of kinship in the western Sephardi diaspora, see Francesca Trivellato, *The Familiarity of Strangers: The Sephardic Diaspora, Livorno and Cross-Cultural Trade in the Early Modern Period* (New Haven, 2009). For an interesting anthropological investigation of the Sephardi family as it relates to concubinage in the Caribbean, see Abraham-Van der Mark, 'Marriage and Concubinage Among the Sephardic Merchant Elite of Curaçao'.

the importance of companionate love and emotional attachment as the ideal determin-
ants of family.[59] The absorption of people of colour into Sephardi families offers but
one measure of the declining centrality of ethnicity among western Sephardim during
the late eighteenth century.

The absorption, albeit limited, of illegitimate children into Sephardi families may
seem to reinforce the centrality of ethnicity as opposed to either religion or physical
appearance in the construction of Spanish-Portuguese identity. The absorption of
reputed children into Sephardi families may have been encouraged by the fact that, as
the sons and daughters of Sephardi fathers, they could be considered to be within the
ethnic boundaries of 'the nation'. Ethnic identity alone, however, does not account for
the desire among some Sephardi men to provide for their concubines as well as their
children. There are many cases in the manumission record in which probable children
of Jewish men were manumitted alongside their probable mothers, such as David
Gomes Rabello's manumission of Affey; and, in the wills, mistresses, such as Eleanor M.
Thomas and Perina M. Garcia, are also supported with legacies from the family estate.

When we examine western Sephardi families in colonial Jamaica during this period,
it is important to consider the role played by affectivity, sexual attraction, companionship, and romantic interest in the formation and definition of family among the
will-making elite in Great Britain whose economic profile was similar to the Sephardi
merchant class in Jamaica. Despite the fact that, to a certain extent, Sephardi families
were still being defined along ethnic lines in the late eighteenth century—as is evidenced by the persistent centrality of kinship in the division of estates[60]—it also seems
to have been a period of transition when more emphasis began to be placed on expressions of affectivity throughout the western Sephardi diaspora.[61] Though a comprehensive and comparative study of Jewish wills throughout the colonial period would
offer confirmation of or correction to this theory, there is little doubt that by the late
eighteenth century many of the same revolutionary developments in the companionate family that were seen in Great Britain began to occur within 'legitimate' Jewish
families of colonial Jamaica, as is indicated for instance in the surviving tombstone
records.

Whereas tombstone epitaphs for women between the 1670s and 1780s included

[59] For a classic examination of sentiment and the rise of 'affective individualism' in Great Britain during
the eighteenth century, see Lawrence Stone, *The Family, Sex and Marriage in England, 1500–1800* (New York,
1977). For a general survey of the literature devoted to modern developments in the 'western family', see
Michael Anderson, *Approaches to the History of the Western Family, 1500–1914* (Cambridge, 1995).

[60] This attention to kinship among Sephardi testators in Jamaica does seem to be particularly Jewish. Not
only was conjugal family life relatively rare among the white planter class, compared to the Jews, those who
had families seemed to have attached very little importance to kinship in their wills (see Trevor Burnard,
'Inheritance and Independence', 103).

[61] Yosef Kaplan, 'The Threat of Eros in Eighteenth-Century Sephardi Amsterdam', in id., *An Alternative
Path to Modernity*, 280–300.

only formulaic and traditional qualifiers in Hebrew and Spanish, such as 'modest', 'virtuous', 'righteous', and 'charitable', in the 1780s some epitaphs for women began to include phrases in their English passages such as 'tender mother' and 'affectionate daughter'.[62] These phrases suggest that companionship was becoming as important as religious piety among the attributes for which people were remembered, or at least that it was considered significant enough for people to alter the epitaphic conventions to include a more articulate expression of emotional content. Furthermore, although there are many tombstones for infants in Jamaican Jewish cemeteries throughout the late seventeenth and early eighteenth centuries, it was not until the first decade of the nineteenth century when the first known tombstones of infants were embellished with the panegyric poetry that was customary for adults. This is not to say that before the nineteenth century Jamaican Sephardim had no emotional attachment to their infants or felt no sense of loss when they died, only that an unprecedented trend to individualize infants and publicly express a sense of loss had become part of the vocabulary of family life.[63]

Though changes in the expression of familial affectivity are apparent within the nuclear Jewish family during the late eighteenth century, what is surprising is the extent to which expressions of companionate affection extended to women of colour and their children even in the absence of formal marriage. It seems that, especially for men with no legitimate children or wives, such as Moses Gomes Fonseca, concubines, such as Eleanor M. Thomas, and their children formed a type of conjugal nuclear family. Moses Gomes Fonseca was indeed an emotional revolutionary when he chose, in manumitting his three daughters, to incorporate the conventional, but highly uncommon, phrase 'the natural love and affection which I have and bear towards my three mulatto children'.

[62] Barnet and Wright, *The Jews of Jamaica*, [in chronological order of date on tombstone] 89 no. 1030, 87 no. 1017, 84 no. 996, 95 no. 1072, 103 no. 1122 (n.d.).

[63] See ibid. [in chronological order of date on tombstone] 86 n. 1016, 47 n. 264.

ACKNOWLEDGEMENTS
I would like to thank Professors Jane S. Gerber, Jonathan Schorsch, and Aviva Ben-Ur for their critical comments on earlier drafts. Thank you to Marsha Vassell at the Jamaican Archives and Records Center and Stephen Campbell at the Island Records Office. I would also like to extend a special thank you to Ainsley Henriques for his friendship and continual support of my research.

CHAPTER THIRTEEN

THE 'CONFESSION MADE BY CYRUS' RECONSIDERED

Maroons and Jews during Jamaica's First Maroon War
1728–1738/9

JAMES ROBERTSON

JEWS were far more prominent in eighteenth-century Jamaica than in Britain or in any of Britain's other colonies. During the 1760s in Spanish Town, the island's seat of government, Jews comprised a third of the town's white population, at least when the assembly and law courts, with all the visitors they brought, were not in session.[1] Their presence was widely recognized, both on the island and abroad, as a benefit and a scourge. One testament to this ambivalence comes from the 1770s, when the French polymath Abbé Raynal, in his *History of the Two Indies*, expressed the pious hope that one day the Jews might 'collect their children' together 'to live free, unmolested, and happy, in some corner of the world'. He thought that this might be attained by their gaining 'the possession of Jamaica, or some other rich island'.[2] But immediately after expressing these opinions, Raynal proceeded to observe that debt repayments were swallowing two-thirds of the profits from Jamaican sugar planting. Even as an inadvertent juxtaposition, his second statement highlighted the persistent potential for resentment between creditors and debtors in a colonial society where all the plantations' prosperity rested on access to credit.[3] The planters' ingrained suspicion of the merchants in Kingston fuelled the political rivalries that divided the colonial assembly until the mid-nineteenth century.[4] Jamaica's Jewish merchants and traders were viewed with similar suspicion by the planters and as rivals by other merchants.

[1] Aubrey N. Newman, 'The Sephardim of the Caribbean', in Richard D. Barnett and Walter M. Schwab (eds.), *The Sephardi Heritage: Essays on the History and Cultural Contribution of the Jews of Spain and Portugal*, vol. ii: *The Western Sephardim* (Grendon, Northants, 1989), 456–7.

[2] Guillaume-Thomas-François Raynal, *A Philosophical and Political History of the Settlements and Trade of the Europeans in the East and West Indies*, 5 vols., trans. J. Justamond, 3rd rev. edn. (London, 1777), iv. 345–6.

[3] See Richard B. Sheridan, *Sugar and Slavery: An Economic History of the British West Indies, 1623–1775* (Eagle Hall, Barbados, 1974), 269–81; Richard Pares, *Merchants and Planters*, Economic History Review Supplement, 4 (Cambridge, 1960), 43–8.

[4] See James Robertson, *Gone is the Ancient Glory: Spanish Town, Jamaica, 1534–2000* (Kingston, Jamaica, 2005), 79–81, 89–97.

Some of these jealousies were demonstrated in the successive questioning of Jewish settlers' loyalty to the colonial state. The most explicit expression was offered by Edward Long, author of a three-volume *History of Jamaica* published in 1774, whose data and presuppositions still underpin many discussions of Jamaican history. Long included a speech that he located in the aftermath of Tacky's Rebellion, a major slave revolt by the African-born, Akan-speaking Coromantee that swept across much of the island in 1760. A Jewish militiaman is guarding one of the captured rebel leaders. In the depths of the night the prisoner tries to persuade his guard to allow his escape, arguing:

> You Jews . . . and our nation (meaning the Coromantins), ought to consider ourselves as one people. You differ from the rest of the Whites, and they hate you. Surely then it is best for us to join in one common interest, drive them out of the country, and hold possession of it to ourselves. We will have (continued he) a fair division of the estates, and we will make sugar and rum, and bring them to market. As for the sailors, you see they do not oppose us, they care not who is in possession of the country, Black or White, it is the same to them that after we are become masters of it, you need not fear but they will come cap in hand to us (as they now do to the Whites) to trade with us . . . and be glad to take our goods in payment.

These claims were succeeded by a further promise to lead the guard to a hoard of gold coins.[5]

Neither argument proved sufficiently persuasive. The prisoner went to his execution, while the militiaman reported the conversation to his officers. Retelling this anecdote offered Long an opportunity not only to articulate the deep divisions within white society in Jamaica, an island where Jews did serve in the colonial militia, but also to suggest that first-generation enslaved Africans were aware of these divisions and might seek to turn them to advantage.

Listening to the stories that people tell or were prepared to believe offers opportunities to explore contemporary assumptions about the boundaries of the possible. Long's readers might well acknowledge the readiness of European sea captains to trade with any regime that would deliver cargoes of sugar and rum, but that still left unanswered this enslaved rebel's assumptions about Jamaican Jews' ambivalent loyalties to an unequal colonial society. This paper examines another incident from thirty years earlier, during Jamaica's First Maroon War (1728–38/9), a campaign waged by the colonial government against the island's long-established communities of African ex-slaves and their descendants, who had found refuge in Jamaica's mountainous interior. The name 'Maroons' is an anglicized form of the Spanish *cimmarrones*, a word for feral

[5] Edward Long, *History of Jamaica*, 3 vols. (London, 1774), ii. 460. On the Coromantee as a distinct group among the enslaved Africans in the British colonies, see John Thornton, 'The Coromantees: An African Cultural Group in Colonial North America and the Caribbean', *Journal of Caribbean History*, 32 (1998), 161–78; id., 'War, the State, and Religious Norms in "Coromantee" Thought: The Ideology of an African American Nation', in Robert Blair St George (ed.), *Possible Pasts: Becoming Colonial in Early America* (Ithaca, NY, 2000), 181–200.

cattle, variants of which were employed across the Caribbean to describe communities of escaped slaves.[6]

The text of the interrogation of a captured Maroon agent enclosed with the governor's dispatch of 25 August 1733 includes a statement that Maroon insurgents were purchasing gunpowder from a Jewish merchant in Kingston (see Appendix 1). This claim reinforced preconceptions that had been demonstrated in 1731, when a well-connected West India merchant responded to a query from the Board of Trade in London about whether the Spaniards were supplying the Maroons with munitions by stating that they were not and that the Jews 'had always supplied them with arms', a comment which probably reflected other white settlers' assumptions too.[7] In default of harder evidence the assertions included in this captured Maroon's testimony have been invoked—and, indeed, expanded, with the Maroons described as purchasing gunpowder from 'Jewish merchants'—in several modern discussions of Jewish dealings with the African Jamaican Maroons.[8]

By 1733 sixty years of skirmishing had escalated into a sustained campaign. During the 1720s, clashes between the African Jamaican groups living in the mountainous interior and the slave-holding white society established on the island's coastal plains increased as a result of several local issues.[9] British attempts to settle the north-eastern coast of the island increased in the 1720s, marked by the formal establishment of the parish of Portland in 1723 and plans to develop a major naval base at Port Antonio (see Maps 13.1, 13.2). These efforts put increasing pressure on the neighbouring Maroon groups' hunting grounds and on the trails they used to get to the sea to collect salt, which prompted raids on newly established plantations and, for the enslaved Africans

[6] Jean-Pierre Tardieu, 'Cimarrón-Maroon-Marron: Note épistémologique', *Outre-Mers Revue d'Histoire*, 94 (2006), 236–47; Jane Landers, 'Leadership and Authority in Maroon Settlements in Spanish America and Brazil', in José C. Curto and Renée Souloudre-La France (eds.), *Africa and the Americas: Interconnections During the Slave Trade* (Trenton, NJ, 2005), 173–84; E. Kofi Agorsah, 'Freedom, Geography and Maroon Military Strategies', in E. Kofi Agorsah and G. Tucker Childs (eds.), *Africa and the African Diaspora: Cultural Adaptation and Resistance* (Bloomington, 2006), 175–203.

[7] Evidence of Mr Richard Harris (3 June 1731), *Journal of the Commissioners for Trade and Plantations from January 1728–9 to December 1734* (London, 1928), 206. Harris was a London-based merchant frequently consulted by the commissioners for information on Jamaican, eastern Caribbean, Irish, and African trades. He had recently been proposed as Jamaica's agent in London, demonstrating his strong colonial contacts, but the assembly had rejected the governor's suggestion (*Journals of the Assembly of Jamaica*, vol. iii: *1731–45* (Spanish Town, Jamaica, 1811), 5, 7 May 1731).

[8] Eli Faber, *Jews, Slaves, and the Slave Trade: Setting the Record Straight* (New York, 1998), 63; for extending the claim from an individual Jew to Jewish shopkeepers, see Mavis Campbell, *The Maroons of Jamaica 1655–1796: A History of Resistance, Collaboration & Betrayal* (Boston, Mass., 1988), 73; Bev Carey, *The Maroon Story: The Authentic and Original History of the Maroons in the History of Jamaica, 1490–1880* (Gordon Town, Jamaica, 1997), 242. One modern scholar has queried using testimony acquired by torture, Werner Zips, *Nanny's Asafo Warriors: The Jamaican Maroons' African Experiences* (Vienna, 2003; Eng. trans. Kingston, 2011), 34.

[9] Orlando Patterson, 'Slavery and Slave Revolts: A Socio-Historical Analysis of the First Maroon War, 1655–1740', *Social and Economic Studies*, 19/3 (1970), 289–325.

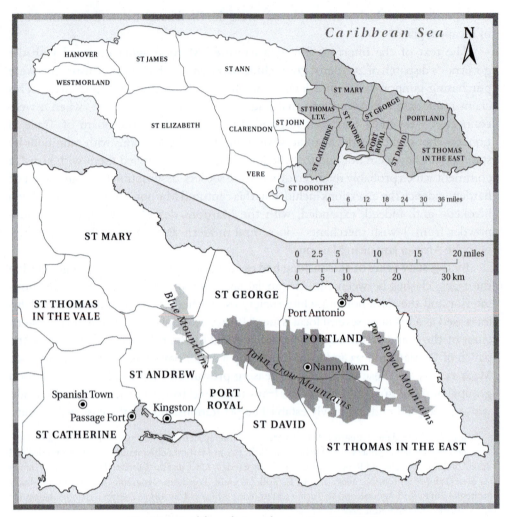

Map 13.1 Parish boundaries and eastern Jamaica, 1723–69

toiling to hack the plantations out of the tropical forest, to hopes of finding a refuge if they escaped. External forces contributed as well. Growing threats from Spain in the late 1720s exposed the vulnerability of Jamaica's northern shore to raids and invasion.[10] Military criteria not only prompted efforts to establish a defensible base on the island's northern shore, but also the appointment of an energetic governor, General Robert Hunter, who arrived in January 1728. Hunter was a successful former governor of New

[10] For warning of a planned Spanish invasion, see Council of War at St Jago de la Vega (7 Apr. 1729), Jamaica Archives and Records Department, Spanish Town, Jamaica (JA), 11B/5/18/1, unfol.; for the governor's precautions, see Cecil Headlam (ed.), *Calendar of State Papers, Colonial Series, America and West Indies, 1728–1729* (London, 1937), 362–3.

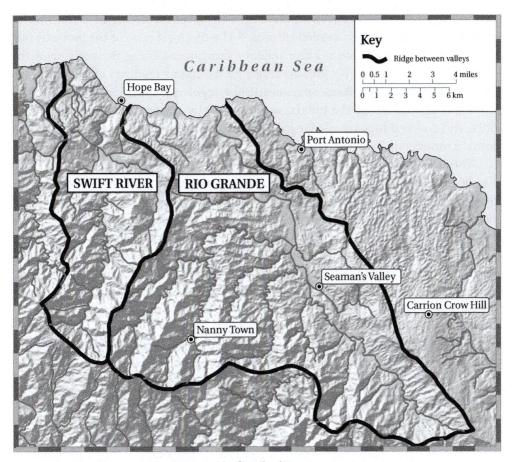

Map 13.2 Parish of Portland, Jamaica, 1723–69

York and before that one of the duke of Marlborough's staff officers, who had begun his career in the 1690s as a junior officer in William of Orange's bloody campaigns to suppress rebel clans in the Scottish highlands.[11] Even after Britain's war with Spain ended, Hunter was prepared to turn to military solutions to settle intransigent local problems.

The Maroons had participated in the preliminary escalation too. Interrogations of prisoners suggested that the Windward Maroons, the community established in the Blue Mountains, which rise behind Port Antonio, had sent delegates to Cuba to

[11] Mary Lou Lustig, *Robert Hunter, 1666–1734: New York's Augustan Statesman* (Syracuse, NY, 1983); on Hunter's political agility as governor in New York, see Alison Gilbert Olson, 'Governor Robert Hunter and the Anglican Church in New York', in Anne Whiteman, J. S. Bromley, and P. G. M. Dickson (eds.), *Statesmen, Scholars and Merchants: Essays in Eighteenth-Century History presented to Dame Lucy Sutherland* (Oxford, 1973), 44–64; on Hunter's more heavy-handed approach in his dealings with Native Americans, see Eric Hinderaker, *The Two Hendricks: Unraveling a Mohawk Mystery* (Cambridge, Mass., 2010), 115–16.

investigate the possibility of reviving older ties with Spain, expressing an 'inclination' to assist the Spaniards if they invaded Jamaica.[12] The tit-for-tat raids of the previous two generations developed into a bitter military campaign. During the early 1730s the Windward Maroons were the primary target for the colony's military efforts, with successive patrols by independent companies, British regulars in the colony's pay, or parties of whites drafted out of the militia, accompanied by armed slaves, known as Black Shot, and enslaved baggage carriers, all pursuing elusive Maroon raiding parties deep into the mountains.[13]

The colonists achieved a few successes, particularly once the African-born Captain Sambo located the Windward Maroons' primary settlement at Nanny Town near the Stony River in 1728 and an African slave fled captivity among the Maroons and provided descriptions of their paths and plans.[14] Afterwards a succession of attacks targeted the town, trying to reach it directly from Port Antonio or indirectly from the north-east or even from the south of the island across the rugged Blue Mountains.[15] Although individual patrols could get through, and some managed to burn the houses in its lower part, even remaining long enough to construct a 'defensible house or Barrack' of stone large enough to house fifty men, by 1733 none of the efforts by the colonial government to establish a permanent garrison had succeeded.[16]

Even these limited achievements came at considerable cost, with prolonged campaigning stretching the colony's resources. The repeated assaults on Nanny Town could only be mounted by reducing patrols elsewhere on the island, which, over the previous decade, had proved fairly effective against Maroon settlements at the western end. Meanwhile the Windward Maroons repulsed a succession of columns that aimed to take Nanny Town, defeating two in carefully co-ordinated ambushes, and also under-

---

[12] An Extract of Colonel Campbell's Letter Concerning the Examination of Some Rebellious Negros lately taken, enclosed in General Robert Hunter to Thomas Pelham Hollis, duke of Newcastle (23 Jan. 1730/1), National Archives, Kew (TNA), Colonial Office (CO) 137/47, fo. 91^r. For the prolonged Spanish resistance after the English invasion in 1655 and the key role that the Spanish settlers' alliance with African Jamaican groups played in sustaining it, see Francisco Morales Padrón, *Spanish Jamaica*, trans. Patrick Bryan (Kingston, Jamaica, 2003), 185–216; James Robertson, 'The Battle at Rio Nuevo, 15–17 June 1658', in Jonathan Greenland (ed.), *Rio Nuevo Battlefield Site* (Kingston, Jamaica, 2009), 10–24; sketching the survivors' subsequent activities, Barbara Klamon Kopytoff, 'The Early Political Development of Jamaican Maroon Societies', *William and Mary Quarterly*, 3rd ser. 35/2 (1978), 287–307.

[13] For the act establishing these patrols, see An Act for Raising Parties to Suppress Rebellious and Runaway Negroes (1699), *Acts of Assembly Passed in the Island of Jamaica; from 1681, to 1754, Inclusive* (London, 1756), 66.

[14] For Sambo's locating of Nanny Town, see Beverly Carey, *Portland and the Rio Grande Valley* (Montego Bay, Jamaica, 1970), 13; for 'Mr. Brereton's Cork a Negro that formerly was Prisoner in the Rebells Town' and the information he gave, see Soaper's Account of a Battle with Rebell Negroes (12 June 1730), TNA, Admiralty (ADM) 1/231, pt 1, fo. 103^v.

[15] See Christopher Allen, 'A Journal of my Travels in the Country's Service Commencing Sunday 27th of February, 1731/2', National Library of Jamaica, Kingston, Jamaica (NLJ), MS 440.

[16] See Robert Hunter to Board of Trade (20 Sept. 1732), JA, 1B/5/18/1 (unfol.).

took a succession of counter-raids on the main plantations of the area.[17] Successive
reverses undermined settlers' morale to such an extent that a dispiriting prophecy
circulated among the island's whites, which claimed that it had been foretold fifty years
before that in 1732 'this Island, would be in the possession of the Negros'.[18] Even after
the colony got through 1732 without collapsing, the Speaker of the House of Assembly,
himself a planter with estates just outside Port Antonio, continued to express 'fears of a
General Insurrection of the Negroes there'.[19]

In late August 1733 the naval base at Navy Island, Port Antonio and the small
mainland settlement at Titchfield, the new parish's administrative centre, buzzed with
efforts to prepare the largest and most ambitious assault on Nanny Town yet—'the
most promising Effort for the Reduction of the Slaves in Rebellion that has hitherto
been made'.[20] In a three-pronged attack, one column under Captain Sambo, the experienced free African Jamaican patrol leader, would approach from the west up the Swift
River, while a second column, made up of white militiamen and Black Shot, would take
a trail up the Back Rio Grande and a third, consisting of 200 naval ratings on loan from
Sir Challoner Ogle, the commanding admiral in Jamaica, would approach through the
mountains.[21] This elaborate plan was never put into effect. The militiamen refused to
take the trail along the Back Rio Grande where two earlier parties had been mauled by
Maroon ambushes. They only marched under the guns of the naval contingent—and
then only in the sailors' company.[22]

Governor Hunter had involved himself in all these plans, recommending the three-
pronged attack and dictating orders for the unit commanders. Officers who failed faced
interrogations before the governor and his council. However, all his exhortations still
proved insufficient to overcome the realities of campaigning in the Blue Mountains.
Ambushed patrols broke and ran, while successive local officers had withdrawn from
Nanny Town when they ran short of supplies or ammunition. In such an atmosphere,
when there were any local-level successes to report, the news went straight to the
governor in Spanish Town.

One such nugget was the capture of a Maroon agent, described in the colonial
records as Cyrus the slave of a Mr George Taylor of St Catherine Parish, on the south

[17]   See Charles Stewart to Josiah Burchett (Mon. 15 Feb. 1729/30), enclosed in 16 Mar. 1729/30, TNA, ADM
1/232, pt 1, fo. 59ᵛ; on the Maroons' defensive tactics, see Agorsah, 'Freedom, Geography and Maroon Military
Strategies', 191.   [18] Charles Stewart to Josiah Burchett (9 Jan. 1731/2), TNA, ADM 1/232, pt 2, fo. 313ᵛ.
[19]   William Nedham to Sir Challoner Ogle (6 July 1733), JA, 1B/5/18 (unfol.).
[20]   Robert Hunter to the duke of Newcastle (8 Sept. 1733), JA, 1B/5/18 (unfol.).
[21]   Orders and Instructions for Captain John Brooke Commanding of the Parties Sent out against the Slaves
in rebellion on the North East of the Island (5 Sept. 1730), JA, 1B/5/18 (unfol.); for further instances, see Orders
and instructions to Lieutenant Thomas Allan Commanding the Detachments from the Independent
Companys and the Party rais'd by the Act of the Assembly for the Reduction of the Slaves in Rebellion (n.d.
[Aug. 1733]), JA, 1B/5/18 (unfol.); orders to Lieutenant Thomas Swanton or the Officer Commanding the two
hundred Seamen detach'd by Sir Challoner Ogle (n.d. [Aug. 1733]), JA, 1B/5/18 (unfol.).
[22]   Lustig, Robert Hunter, 213.

side of the island, who was arrested by the navy at Port Antonio in late August 1733, days before the scheduled departure of the latest expedition. Cyrus was first interrogated by Captain Charles Knowles, a naval officer seconded to oversee the construction work for the new base at Navy Island, and later by Jasper Ashworth, a colonist and militia officer, who combined the posts of chief magistrate and government commissary at Port Antonio. To induce co-operation the prisoner was tortured with his thumbs squeezed in a vice. Copies of both of Cyrus's interrogations were sent to Governor Hunter, who enclosed copies of Captain Knowles's, the first he received, in his regular dispatches to the secretary of state, the duke of Newcastle, with copies to the Board of Trade in London.[23] Six weeks later, when another wounded Maroon captive, Sara, alias Ned, was interrogated by Hunter, the vaunted naval column had fallen into an ambush at what became known as Seaman's Valley. At that battle not only were the combined contingent of sailors and conscripted white militiamen routed, but they were jeered by the Maroon attackers saying that the column had arrived at the ambush site a day too early to rendezvous with Captain Sambo's party, demonstrating that the Maroons knew all about the plans for the attacks.[24]

Cyrus's and Sara's depositions remain intriguing documents. Cyrus's interrogation focused on current operational intelligence, while the bulk of the information that Sara revealed in October was background information about the Maroon society which survived at Nanny Town, but it also covered some issues raised during Cyrus's interrogation. The texts reveal as much about the interrogators' expectations as about Maroon strategy. Much of the information that Cyrus gave appears to have been shaped by the questions he received. These queries sought confirmation for the local militia officers' current assumptions: they knew that the Maroons had just looted Hobby's plantation and apparently suspected that they were preparing elaborate ambushes there. Cyrus's 'very particular Account' of an ambush being constructed 'on a Ridge a back the Plantain Walk at Hobby's' corroborated reports already received from local militia patrols. Fears of a potential ambush—be it at the Stony River, where an earlier party had been stopped in 1731, or elsewhere—helped to prompt the refusal a few days later by the white militiamen to advance along that route as the third prong in the attack on Nanny Town. For the rest, his revelations sounded persuasive, because so many confirmed what his interrogators already assumed, such as the claim that an enslaved

---

[23] Robert Hunter to Board of Trade (25 Aug. 1733), TNA, CO 137/20, fo. 178ʳ (a copy is in CO 137/47, fo. 170ʳ). In his cover letter Hunter describes the interrogation as having been made by Captain Charles Knowles RN, who had captured Cyrus, and then forwarded the report of the interrogation to Hunter via the Naval Commander. Hunter also says that there had been a further interrogation by Jasper Ashworth, which at that juncture he had yet to receive. He repeated the same information in Robert Hunter to the duke of Newcastle (25 Aug. 1733), TNA, CO 137/54, fo. 338ʳ. George Taylor is described as 'of St Catherine's parish' (Letters Testamentary, 1747–1749 (21 July 1748), JA, 1B/11/18/10, fo. 154ᵛ).

[24] James Draper to Robert Hunter (4 Sept. 1733), JA, 1B/5/18 (unfol.); see also Jasper Ashworth to Robert Hunter (4 Sept. 1733), JA, 1B/5/18 (unfol.).

Madagascan Indian, who had run away from some guards a few days before, had been living with the Maroons. Intermixed with such information, Cyrus also slipped in more daunting threats. His statement that the Maroons would attack Titchfield itself, if the town was left undefended, offered a justification for reducing the force to be sent out on the forthcoming attack. He also added disquieting details that could prompt local officers to question the loyalty of the Crown slaves, enslaved Africans trained as specialist craftsmen who lived on Navy Island where the dockyard was.[25] As these were themselves recently acquired slaves and included Coromantee, their loyalty might well appear suspect. Cyrus's description of Sam, a Crown slave, visiting his 'wife' at Hobby's plantation and chatting with the Maroons when they occupied the plantation would be disquieting, even if at this juncture Cyrus proceeded to tell his interrogators just what they wanted to hear: that Sam had said that the parish's slaves would not join the rebellion so long as the whites did not maltreat them. The incident would appear all the more plausible because there was indeed a 'Sam' listed among the enslaved labourers on Navy Island.[26] Yet however loyal the comments attributed to Sam might be, such discussions still compounded Cyrus's white interrogators' uncertainty about how far they could trust slaves who had had any contact with the Maroon insurgents. Two months later, interrogators asked another prisoner if the Maroons' agents had lodged with Sam when they stayed in Titchfield—though the answer they received implicated another 'Sam'. To fearful whites even a whisper of fraternization could appear as an indicator of potential disloyalty. Cyrus's claims would cause division and suspicion among the white officers in Titchfield, as much as, if not more than, providing his interrogators with useful current information.

There were certainly some snippets of general information included in his deposition that were later substantiated, particularly Cyrus's claim that the Maroon combatants were organized into three gangs of a hundred men, with each gang including some women in support roles. Valuable as the report appeared when this interrogation was first transcribed, subsequent events might well have—but in the event did not—cast doubt on its individual details. Most conspicuously there remained a very striking silence about the elaborate ambush that the Maroons were busy preparing for the naval contingent in Seaman's Valley as Cyrus was being forced to talk.

A further set of revelations indicates that Cyrus was then pressured to elaborate on the Maroons' sources of munitions. A stock of musket parts that an earlier militia party found as they searched deserted houses at Nanny Town suggested that the Maroons

---

[25] See Charles Stewart to Josiah Burchett (29 Dec. 1730), TNA, ADM 1/232, pt 1, fos. 147^v–148^r. Stewart advised obtaining adolescent Coromantee for this purpose: they were purchased in 1731. (Charles Stewart to Josiah Burchett (6 May 1731), TNA, ADM 1/232, pt 1, fo. 206^r).

[26] A slave named Sam is among the 'Labouring Negroes' in A List of His Majesties Negroes at Port Antonio, enclosed with Charles Knowles to Josiah Burchett (25 July 1735), TNA, ADM 1/2006, Captains' Letters, K, 1713–1743 (unfol.).

had the capability to repair their muskets, while any scrap lead or even pewter cutlery captured in attacks on plantations could be melted down for bullets. Later recollections of Maroon raids commented 'that when they plundered the first thing lookt for were shot or pewter plates to make Balls'.[27] Gunpowder remained the Maroons' Achilles heel as they could not manufacture it themselves. Muskets could be repaired, but 'gunpowder was an expendable and perishable commodity which only Europeans could supply'. Hence, in commenting on an earlier ambush at the Snake River, where a volley of an estimated 200 shots shredded the advance guard of a colonial patrol and forced its survivors to retreat, one of the few positive points that white officers noted in analysing this defeat lay in offering an explanation for the Maroons' not continuing their initial withering volleys: 'they were Scarce of Ammunition'.[28] Even the powder captured when patrols were ambushed or the stocks seized during raids on outlying plantations would hardly sustain prolonged fire fights. This was a current issue. Only a month before, after a white patrol had seized Nanny Town and was besieged there, 'the wild Negroes Surrounded them and fir'd very briskly upon them'. One Maroon sniper even called across to the soldiers 'and ask'd them if they wanted any Powder or balls, if they did, they would let them have some', a piece of bravado that proved highly effective in undermining the troops' morale.[29] The patrol's commanders had already requested a resupply, but it had yet to arrive. Meanwhile the Maroons fired on the garrison from 8 a.m. to 3 p.m., 'so thick' that the troops 'could not possibly stay any longer'. Afterwards the explanation offered by the patrol's officers for ordering a retreat was that they were short of ammunition and only had enough left to fight their way through any Maroon ambushes on the way back.[30]

The Jamaican Assembly had recognized the need to control access to gunpowder and ammunition in 1730, when it passed an Act to Prevent the Selling of Powder to

[27] Extract of Lamb's Journal, included in Gen:l Hunter's Duplicate (18 Nov. 1732), JA, 1B/5/18/1 (unfol.), noting: 'Bags of old Irons belonging to Old Guns, Such as, Old Cocks, Skrew Pins, broken Gun Barrells & the like'. Gun parts were also recovered in archaeological excavations at Nanny Town in 1973 (Michelle Topping, 'The Nanny Town Excavations after 37 Years: An Insight into the Material Culture', Paper delivered to the Eighth Archaeological Society of Jamaica Symposium, Kingston, Jamaica (6 May 2010)); for the raiders' preferences while looting, see An Account of the Origin & Progress of the Revolted Negroes [1740s], Papers & Original Letters Relating to Affairs in Jamaica (c.1733–99), British Library, London, Additional MS 12,431, fo. 76ᵛ.

[28] For similar gunpowder shortages in North American Amerindian societies, see Armstrong Starkey, *European and Native American Warfare, 1675–1815* (Norman, Okla., 1998), 23; for the skirmish, see Jasper Ashworth to General Robert Hunter (7 Dec. 1731), JA, 1B/5/18/1 (unfol.).

[29] This incident, or one like it, has also been recalled among the Maroons, where the offer is attributed to one Opong, but it is now interpreted as an actual offer to supply bullets to the English. It is therefore seen as either an instance where the British could get a loan of someone who never loaned anything to his neighbours or else as rank treachery on Opong's part (Kenneth M. Bilby, *True-Born Maroons* (Gainesville, Fla., 2006), 270–1).

[30] James Draper to Governor Hunter (27 June 1733), TNA, CO 137/20, fos. 150–1; for the request for supplies, see Henry Williams and Ebenezer Lamb to Lieutenant Draper, Port Antonio (June 1733), JA, 1B/5/18/1 (unfol.).

Rebellious, or any Other Negroes Whatsoever, which aimed to restrict the persistent trickle of gunpowder to the Maroons. According to the Act retail outlets for gun-powder were to be restricted to one or two shops in each town whose proprietors were to take out substantial compliance bonds. Oaths backed up with the threat of heavy fines were intended to stop any sales of less than fifty pounds weight of gunpowder—and those purchasers would have to produce a licence with the governor's signature, which in turn required a certificate from the parish vestry.[31] Despite such complicated administrative procedures, the Maroons continued to fire from their ambushes.

How were they managing this? The final section of Cyrus's deposition offered several answers. One, which described how all the whites' legislative precautions were being bypassed, was his report that the Windward Maroons were harbouring two runaway servants, white youths who were busily writing passes which would allow individual Maroons to get through militia patrols by claiming to be slaves from one of the major landowners in the parish's estates. This was hardly new information. The discovery of 'pen, Ink and paper' at Nanny Town two years before had already prompted discussion of their use by 'two white Men (who are amongst [the Maroons]) to make Ticketts as if they were Negroe[s] belonging to some of the Plantations that they might not be detected when they come to any Town'.[32] Whites already suspected that Maroon agents buying supplies could carry passes identifying them as law-abiding slaves going about their masters' business. Cyrus's latest details would resonate with white planters' existing fears about the loyalty of poorer whites, which had already led the assembly to first pass—and then repeal—the Protestant Act, which sought to restrict the admission of Roman Catholic indentured labourers who might prove disloyal to the island's Protestant regime.[33] It would also help to explain the ineffective-ness of a further law that the assembly passed in March 1730 to restrain the ability of free people of colour to attend markets, aimed at preventing Maroons from trading. The bill passed the House of Assembly and received Hunter's assent, but was then vetoed by the Board of Trade in London.[34] Any allegations about these pass-scribbling white renegades added to the interrogators' fears.

The next part of Cyrus's testimony has been invoked by a succession of historians of Jamaica, in part because it includes such intriguing claims of betrayal. This is the claim that Maroon agents were obtaining gunpowder from a Jewish merchant in Kingston. The testimony came with convincing details. The Maroon who crossed the mountains with one of the forged passes to buy two powder horns full of powder was called Quashee. Then there was a name and address: 'one Jacob a Jew in Church Street'.

---

[31] An Act to Prevent the Selling of Powder to Rebellious, or any Other Negroes Whatsoever (1730), *Acts of Assembly*, 168.   [32] Charles Stewart to Josiah Burchett (14 Mar. 1730/1), TNA, ADM 1/232, pt 1, fo. 191^{v}.

[33] I have used an early twentieth-century set of transcripts of the Jamaica Council Minutes (Oct. 1730–Sept. 1732), NLJ, MS 60/22, fo. 180^{r}; Robert Hunter to Lords Commissioners of Trade (Nov. 1731), JA, 1B/5/18 (unfol.).   [34] Charles Delafay to Alured Popple (17 July 1731), TNA, CO 137/19, fo. 73^{r}.

For Cyrus's interrogators this information far outweighed a further comment about 'an Indian' who had brought a barrel of gunpowder to Hobby's plantation which the raiders had then sent up to Nanny Town.

Should we take any of this detail at face value? The island's governor did, and subsequent historians have continued to line up behind him. Early in October Sara was also questioned about the matter. After providing a long description of the relations between the residents of Nanny Town and those of a nearby settlement, Guy's Town, the interrogation reverted to the sources of gunpowder described in Cyrus's testimony (see Appendix 2).[35] Investigations had found no Jewish shopkeeper called Jacob on Kingston's Church Street. Another round of leading questions produced answers which apparently satisfied Sara's interrogators. Perhaps this elusive shopkeeper was trading on Jews Alley (Peters Lane[36]). Meanwhile the elusive 'wild Negro' sneaking into Kingston with a false pass to purchase gunpowder was not Quashee but Cuffee—both very common day names among the island's Akan-speaking slaves.[37] At the same time, while further details were offered on 'the Indian' whom Cyrus had described delivering a cask of gunpowder to the Maroons—his 'Master is Jaco', and he was a crew member on a sloop—the transactions were also changed. Now the Maroons were obtaining a whole keg of powder and 'a Crowns Bagg' of musket balls from the mercenary Jewish shopkeeper, while the Amerindian crewman only brought in 'a large Horn of Powder' and a smaller bag of musket balls. The interrogator's revisiting of these questions during Sara's questioning highlights which aspects of Cyrus's testimony appealed to Hunter.

Reappraising what Cyrus told his captors suggests a different story. He may have told them what they expected to hear, but his description of the Maroons' activities in late August 1733 still bore very little relation to the elaborate ambushes in Seaman's Valley that the colony's militia men and the Royal Navy's sailors walked into on 2 September. Even so, Cyrus's interrogators continued to judge him a valuable source. The colonists had few other Maroon prisoners, and he had been 'at their Settlements & at Hobbie's', while 'the description he gave of their Ambushes' conformed to what patrols were reporting. This last claim sounds as though Ashworth, at least, wanted to believe, not just in the value of the captive they had secured but also that a body of testimony which appeared to confirm the interrogators' preconceptions was highly significant. Though, even here, he admitted some reservations about Cyrus's accusa-

---

[35] Bilby, *True-Born Maroons*, 221; also cited in Kopytoff, 'Early Political Development', 298–300, 303–4; Barbara Klamon Kopytoff, 'Jamaican Maroon Political Organization: The Effects of the Treaties', *Social and Economic Studies*, 25/2 (1976), 89.   [36] I owe this identification to Holly Snyder.

[37] Kwashi for a Sunday-born boy, Cuffee for a Friday-born boy (Maureen Warner-Lewis, 'The Character of African-Jamaican Culture', in Kathleen E. A. Monteith and Glen Richards (eds.), *Jamaica in Slavery and Freedom: History, Heritage and Culture* (Kingston, Jamaica, 2002), 90; on their frequent use, see Trevor Burnard, 'Slave Naming Patterns: Onomastics and the Taxonomy of Race in Eighteenth-Century Jamaica', *Journal of Interdisciplinary History*, 31 (2001), 337 table 3.

tions against individual slaves in Port Antonio—where his stories could be cross-checked—commenting that 'it was Observ'd that he prevaricated as he was punish'd and Alter'd his information for & against the Negroes he mentioned'. Despite this caveat, it still seemed worth sending him across to the governor on the other side of the island.[38]

If Cyrus was telling seductive lies that his captors were willing to listen to, then we can perhaps take his logic further. Constructing plausible allegations about a shop-keeper on the south side of the island would make clear sense. When torture forced him to say something, he delivered stories about a venal Kingston shopkeeper 'Jacob' that his interrogators were receptive to. Naming a remote source that would involve crossing Jamaica to check could extend Cyrus's life, though it ultimately failed to prevent his execution. When the captive Sara was interrogated the following October, telling his captors what they wanted to hear kept him alive and even in receipt of medical treatment for at least another month.[39]

A further incident may suggest that, besides seeking as distant a plausible venue for purchasing ammunition as he could find, Cyrus's tale may well have been protect-ing a far closer source of supplies for the Maroons. In April 1734 another patrol from Port Antonio reached Nanny Town and once again endeavoured to hold it. The Ma-roons' initial response was 'pretty easie', but their subsequent assaults were prolonged 'so Smart till they came Muzzle to Muzzle'. The party had arrived on a Monday and the desperate counter-attacks continued through Tuesday and Wednesday, with the Maroons firing improvised pewter bullets. By Thursday the character of the struggle changed, and the British commander suspected that:

They had a fresh Supply of Ammunition from where I cannot tell unless from Port Antonio, for they fir'd new Swan Shott [a heavy-gauge buckshot] and Ball of the same Cast of Ours, and their Powder was the same. Their departing so soon on Wednesday Evening and not returning till late on Thursday causes me to Imagine they went for Ammunition, for the several days before they fir'd mostly with Pewter balls, but on Thursday nothing but Leaden Balls and new Swan Shott.[40]

Elaborate tales about a mercenary Jewish shopkeeper in Kingston or an Amerindian crew member on an anonymous sloop, could help to conceal the Maroons' access to far

[38] Jasper Ashworth to Robert Hunter (4 Sept. 1733), JA, 1B/5/18/1 (unfol.).

[39] Some scholars who have used these texts have assumed that Sara/Sarra was another alias for Cyrus, and therefore he was the source of both depositions. It would be nice to think so. However, Cyrus was tortured on his thumbs. A bill from Drs Charles Rose and Robert Cooke described different injuries, they 'administering Physick and Curing several wounds in the head and other parts of a Rebellious Negro Man named Sarra in the Gaol of St. Jago de la Vega'. This covers Sarra's treatment between 10 Sept. 1733 and 'the 8th November following' (Jamaica Council Minutes, Nov. 1732–Feb. 1736 (2 Dec. 1735), NLJ, MS 60/23, fo. 332ʳ); for treating the two names as aliases for a single captive, see Kopytoff, 'Early Political Development', 299; Bilby, *True-Born Maroons*, 229. Carey states that Cyrus was executed in Kingston along with the black guide from the Seaman's Valley debacle (*Maroon Story*, 253). She offers no source for this, but it seems all too plausible.

[40] Jamaica Council Minutes, Nov. 1732–Feb. 1736 (6 May 1734), fo. 141ʳ.

closer sources of munitions: out of the back door of the same armoury that supplied the patrols. This source lay under the immediate control of Commissary Ashworth, who undertook Cyrus's second interrogation and then sent him to Governor Hunter. If this was indeed the case, the tales succeeded. Two years later there was still 'no [dedicated] Storehouse for the Provisions provided by the Public' in the town of Port Antonio, a situation likely to facilitate the continued leakage of gunpowder and ammunition from improvised warehouses.[41]

Despite the sparseness of the evidence, the claim that Jews had sold ammunition to the Maroons remained tenacious. When James Knight, a leading Kingston merchant, compiled a history of Jamaica in the 1740s, he repeated the story, adding arms to the other materials Jews had allegedly supplied to the rebels. However, testifying to wider white interest in this question, once the war was over, surviving Maroon leaders were asked directly whether they had received munitions and arms from the island's Jewish population, and they denied it. Knight later showed his draft to a friend, one of whose comments was: 'Since their coming in, Capt. Cajo [Cudjo] and all the rest of the Wild Neg[roe]s have been Strictly Examined upon that Head, & all declar'd, that [they] never had any Corispondance with the Jews upon any head wh[at]soever'. Afterwards Knight, at least, struck out the paragraph in his unpublished history which repeated the Jewish arms-sales claim.[42] Among the rest of the island's Christian population the familiar negative veranda gossip would have been harder to stop.

Reconsidering the testimony extorted from Cyrus in 1733 may allow us to go further than giving belated credit to what appears to have been considerable courage and ingenuity on his part when interrogated under torture. These elaborate stories justified sending him south to be questioned by the governor, giving him another few days reprieve and offering opportunities to try to escape in a part of the island near where his former owner lived. His testimony may also have helped to direct his interrogators' attention away from sources of supply at Port Antonio that the Maroons were using. Reconsidering the stories that Cyrus chose to tell can also illuminate his expectations about what his white interrogators would be prepared to believe. His assertions reinforced long-established antisemitic prejudices in Jamaica—which for European-trained military officers like Hunter may also have drawn on seventeenth-century reports of Amsterdam's Jewish merchants supplying armaments to Morocco's Sallee pirates.[43]

However, the information in Cyrus's interrogation hardly offers hard and fast evidence of the readiness of any Jewish merchants to trade with the Maroons. They

---

[41] Jamaica Council Minutes, Feb. 1736/7–1739 (6 May 1736), NLJ, MS 60/24, fo. 386ʳ.

[42] Faber, *Jews, Slaves, and the Slave Trade*, 63, 287 n. 20.

[43] I owe this suggestion to Jonathan Israel, see Jonathan I. Israel, 'Piracy, Trade, and Religion: The Jewish Role in the Rise of the Muslim Corsair Republic of Saleh (1624–1666)', in id., *Diasporas Within a Diaspora: Jews, Crypto Jews and the World Maritime Empires (1540–1740)* (Leiden, 2002), 291–311.

appear to be being made scapegoats. His captors' readiness to believe such stories—being turned away from promising lines of investigation in the process—not only highlights contrasts between the British commanders' foggy knowledge of Maroon society and a more nuanced appraisal of British preconceptions by a Maroon spy, it also suggests that Cyrus was quite right when it came to recognizing the potential divisions within Jamaica's white society.

Looking back across the social advances achieved during the nineteenth-century, it has been tempting to commend the openness of colonial societies to Jewish settlers, with claims that 'the Jews arriving in Britain's North American colonies were usually treated like other Europeans without special reference to religion' and as 'their settlement had made no impression upon their contemporaries [it] elicited no special legislation'.[44] Jews in Jamaica could obtain naturalization, and they were obliged to turn out for service in the colonial militia. But eighteenth-century Jamaica still saw successive efforts by the island's assembly to exploit the colony's substantial Jewish population. From the late seventeenth century extra taxes were imposed on the colony's Jewish residents, which appeals to the monarch in London failed to suppress.[45] In the 1730s, when the cash-strapped Jamaican Assembly sought funds to sustain the Maroon War, the assemblymen tried to lay additional taxes on the island's Jewish community. The new levy was justified by invoking the Jews' religious exemption 'from many Expensive Offices and services to which the rest of the Inhabitants thereof are Subject'. The act also asserted both that 'several' Jews had pursued 'indirect or underhand Dealings or correspondence with the Spaniards' while, by 'spreading false Accounts', some Jewish merchants had hindered 'the Sale of Goods carried thither to the great loss and Damage of the English Inhabitants of the Island'. These claims demonstrated the range of rationales that prejudice adopted in the 1730s—though it did not add specific charges of supplying munitions to the rebel Maroons. In this instance the assemblymen's volley backfired, as a further long petition to King George II not only included flat denials of each of these claims, but the protest was also signed by several Christian merchants in Kingston and London. This petition was successful, and, when a new governor arrived from London in 1738, it was one of the first items he read into the island council's official journal.[46] Tensions certainly remained with attempts in 1750 and again in 1820 by individual Jews who owned sufficient property to vote in

[44] Salo W. Baron, 'Newer Approaches to Jewish Emancipation', *Diogenes*, 29 (1960), 61.

[45] Samuel J. Hurwitz and Edith Hurwitz, 'The New World Sets an Example to the Old: The Jews of Jamaica and Political Rights 1661–1831', *American Jewish Historical Quarterly*, 55/1 (1965), 37–56; on the extra taxes, see Mordechai Arbell, *The Portuguese Jews of Jamaica* (Kingston, Jamaica, 2000), 16–19.

[46] Jamaica Council Minutes, 1736/7–1739 (12 Jan. 1737/8), NLJ, MS 60/24, fo. 104ʳ. The 'Petition and Representation to His Majesty of Several Traders to Jamaica and others in behalf of the Jews who are Inhabitants of that Island' is transcribed on fos. 105–9.

assembly elections, arousing even fiercer opposition.[47] The strength of these local prejudices reflected the opposite reaction to the Jewish prominence that prompted the Abbé Raynal's optimistic hopes that they might 'collect their children' together 'to live free, unmolested, and happy, in some corner of the world'.

APPENDICES

1 Copy of the Negro's Confession before Capt: Knowles[48]

Copy of the Confession made by Scyrus a Negro belonging to Mr. Geo: Taylor

He Says he came from the Negroe Town 4 weeks agoe to see what Partys were fitting out, that the Rebels told him of their Design in robbing Sparks & Hobbys Plantations, & which last place he left them at on Thursday the 9th Instant, that afterwards if he found the Partys in Titchfield Town not too Strong, on his return to them they would come & take it; that on Saturday last the 11th Instant he went from this place to Hobbys (in Company with 3 rebellious Negroes more, who had been in this town near a week making their Remarks undiscover'd, their Names were Cuffey, Cudjoe & Quamina,[49] which last belongs to Canker or Cock of Guanaboa) where they found the rebels just going off with their Plunder; They told them that there was Men of War, Soldiers & Party Men enough come; that the rebels answer'd let them come; he says that there were at Hobbys 2 Gangs of Men a 100 in each Gang & Several Women Which they had brought to help Carry of the Spoil: that they left one Gang in the

---

[47] On the contested elections, see Holly Snyder, 'Rules, Rights and Redemption: The Negotiation of Jewish Status in British Atlantic Port Towns, 1740–1831', *Jewish History*, 20 (2006), 147–70.

[48] Several copies of this deposition survive. They were all transcribed as enclosures for Hunter's regular dispatches to the Secretary of State and the Board of Trade. As a safety precaution duplicate copies of each dispatch were sent on different London-bound ships. Although there are minor variants in transcription between the individual copies, no single copy appears to have provided the base text or seems more authoritative. Individual variations in spelling, capitalization, and punctuation have not been noted. For convenience, I have used the copy that is now in the Jamaica Archives and Records Department, Spanish Town, as my base text (Robert Hunter to the duke of Newcastle (enclosure in 25 Aug. 1733), JA, 1B/5/18/1; Dispatches, Governor of Jamaica to Secretary of State, Oct. 1725–Oct. 1735 (unfol.) (original copies, returned from Public Records Office as duplicates)). Further copies were sent to the Board of Trade (TNA, CO 137/20, fo. 179; CO 137/47, fo. 172), as well as to the duke of Newcastle as Secretary of State (TNA, CO 137/54, fo. 340).

[49] Quamina is the name for a Tuesday-born boy (Warner-Lewis, 'Character of African-Jamaican Culture', 90).

Negro Town to Guard the rest of the women & children, the names of those who Commanded at Hobbys were Pompey & Coll Needham's Cudjoe, that the Wednesday before he left Hobbys (the first time) in the morning he Saw the Kings Negro Sam come there in his Way to town, but he Says he does not know whither he came to See the Rebels or his Wife (he having one there) but So soon as Pompy & Cudjoe Saw him they went & asked him how he did and how all the Negroes on the Kay did, if they lived well, & why they would not come to them, at which Sam Answered & Say'd Master uses us goodee yet, but when him use us ugly wee'l come; that what pass'd more he heard not, but Says Sam Stay'd with them most part of the day, & that on Thursday Morning an Indian brought a Cagg of Powder to the Rebels, Which they Sent up to their Town, he gives also a very particular Account of an Ambush just built by the Rebels on a Ridge a back the Plantain Walk at Hobby's, & Several Circumstances which Corroborates with what the Militia Gentry Says who went there in pursuit of the rebels. He Says that the way they got Powder is, they have with them 2 white boys one named Jn:o Dove or Deen, who belonged to blind Fletcher of Passage Fort, the other Charles (his other name he knows not) that these 2 boys writes Passes in Coll. Needham's Name & one Quashee goes to Kingstown with it to one Jacob a Jew in Church Street, that he went once last month & brought with him two large horns full, that they have now he believes 200 horns full, but very little Shott, tho' Guns & Launces [ᵛ] Enough. That the Madagascar Indian who run away from the Guard the other day, has also been some time with the Rebels, And that they had determined, on hearing of these[50] Partys coming, to ambush them at the River Course, that a Gang of 100 was to lay on Carrion Crow Hill[51] & 100 more on Hobbys Way. That a Drum was to be placed on the ridge over the town to View the Partys & the Women in the town to burn the Houses in case the Party should be too strong, if not the three Gangs to Surround them on the beat of Drum, All under the command of Scipio.

2   The further Examination of Sara alias Ned taken by Order of His Excellency, October 1st 1733[52]

He Says that the Old Town formerly taken by the Soldiers goes now by the Name of Nanny Town, that there are now, or were when he was there three hundred men, all armed with Guns or Launces, that they have more fire arms than they use, that the

---

[50]   'of these': 'the' in TNA, CO 137/20, fo. 179ᵛ; CO 137/54, fo. 340ᵛ.

[51]   Now known as John Crow Mountain.

[52]   Enclosed with Hunter's dispatch (13 Oct. 1733), JA, 1B/5/18/1 (unfol.); a further copy is in TNA, CO 137/54, fo. 354.

number of the Women and Children far exceed those of the Men, that the Rebels have one head man who Orders every thing, and if a Man Committs any Crime he is instantly Shott to Death, but there is hardly any thing Esteem'd a Crime with them but the lying with one anothers Wives, the Women are whip'd for most of the Crimes they Committ, and they and such of the Men as are least noted for their Courage perform all Such Work as is necessary for the raising Provisions, making it a Custom to work one day and play the next; And if the head man should be Guilty of any great Crime, his Soldiers (as they are call'd) shoot him, and appoint another in his place. Their present head Man is call'd Cuffee, and he is distinguish'd by wearing a Silver lac'd Hatt, and a Small Sword, no other daring to wear the like.

He further Says that the Rebels have another Town at the back or rather on the top of Carrion Crow Hill, called Gay's or Guy's Town from the Name of the head Man Commanding there, that there is a Great Deal of Open Ground about it in which is plenty of Cow, Sugar Canes, Plantains, Melons, Yams, Corn, Hog and Poultry; that the number of the Men in that Town is about two hundred, and a greater Number of Women, that the Men choose to arm themselves with Launces and Cutlashes rather than Guns, and never go to meet the Partys unless to defend the Paths which leads to their own Town, and then they are joyn'd by those of Nanny Town who are Esteem'd the best fighting Men.

He further Says that the Rebels when they were first beat from Nanny's Town went to Gay's or Guy's Town, and remain'd there 'till the Provisions began to be Scarce, and then they return'd and made themselves Masters of their old Town again, and that they [the Rebels] upon hearing that there were Stronger Partys to be sent against them, Sent and search'd the Woods for about Seven or Eight Miles round to see for other Settlements, that they might Unite their Strength, but could find none, that there is no Town at Long Bay, but that they have all their Salt from thence, and have made a Convenient place for boiling it. [ˠ] They give Encouragement for all Sorts of Negroes to joyn them, and Oblidge the Men to be true to them by an Oath which is held very Sacred among the Negroes, and those who refuse to take that Oath, whether they go to them of their own accord or are made Prisoners, are instantly put to Death, and they have a Guard Night and Day over the Women who for their Defence carry about them each two or three Knives.

He says the name of the wild Negro that goes to Kingston for Powder is Cuffee, and not Quashee as mention'd in the Examination taken by Mr. Ashworth, and by the Description of the Place where the Jew lives that sold the Powder it must be Jew Ally and not Church Street; He says also that it was a Cag of Powder and a Crowns Bagg of Ball that the said Cuffee had from the Jew, and that it was Quashee and Cudjo who were the Spys at Port Antonio; He further Says that the Indian Carry'd with him a large Horn of Powder, and Ball in a Bagg, and that the name of the Indian's Master is Jaco and belongs to some Sloop, and that Quashee and Cudjo above mention'd were mostly entertain'd while at Port Antonio by Coll. Needham's Negroes, particularly by one nam'd Sam.[53]

[53] In 1731 William Nedham, a leading local planter, undertook to complete Fort George 'Furnishing materials for the Carrying on of that Work', and his slaves were 'Employ'd in getting Materials', including stone, sand, and lime (Jamaica Council Minutes, Oct. 1730–Sept. 1732 (27 Nov. 1731), NLJ, MS 60/22, fo. 197ʳ). This Sam would be a different individual from the labourer of the same name listed among the Crown Negroes on Navy Island.

ACKNOWLEDGEMENTS
I am grateful to Aviva Ben-Ur, Thera Edwards, Holly Snyder, and Linda Sturtz for reading and commenting on drafts of this essay. The maps were compiled by Thera Edwards.

CHAPTER FOURTEEN

JEWISH POLITICIANS IN POST-SLAVERY JAMAICA

Electoral Politics in the Parish of St Dorothy, 1849–1860

SWITHIN WILMOT

DURING much of the period of slavery in Jamaica, the governing class of white Protestants regarded the Jews as a 'distinct alien minority', despite their sharing a common white phenotype. Because of their religion, Jews were denied the political privileges and social status that otherwise came with white skin and until 1831 were barred from public office. Indeed, even highly successful Jewish merchants were assigned an 'off-white' status in Jamaica's slave society and considered socially inferior to non-Jewish whites of very modest means, such as artisans and settlers. Clearly, antisemitism flourished alongside other racist attitudes in Jamaican slave society.[1]

However, the Haitian Revolution and the establishment of the first black republic in 1804 underscored the demographic threat to the white population from the blacks and coloureds, free and enslaved.[2] The planters now placed a higher premium on white skin than on religious conformity and reassessed their attitude towards Jews, the only other group in the slave society that could offer racial solidarity. Strategically, Jamaica's ruling white Protestant community made common cause with other slave owners, notably the increasingly affluent Jewish merchant class and wealthy free coloureds. Accordingly, Jews were granted full civil rights in 1831, six months after the free blacks and the free coloureds received theirs and three years before the abolition of slavery in 1834. This strategic retreat from anti-Jewish legislation by the white Protestant ruling

---

[1] Robert Brock Le Page, *Jamaican Creole: An Historical Introduction to Jamaican Creole* (London, 1960), 111–12; Thomas August, 'Jewish Assimilation and the Plural Society in Jamaica', *Social and Economic Studies*, 36/2 (1987), 109–12; Carol S. Holzberg, *Minorities and Power in a Black Society: The Jewish Community of Jamaica* (Lanham, Md., 1987), pp. xiv, 16–19.

[2] Free coloureds were of mixed African and European ancestry, as distinct from blacks, who were mostly enslaved and were exclusively of African ancestry. In Jamaican slave society, free blacks and free coloureds faced social and political discrimination because they were non-white, although a very select number of wealthy free coloureds were granted special privileges that afforded them the status of being 'white by law'. Social discrimination and tensions also existed between free blacks and free coloureds. For a study of the free coloureds, see G. Heuman, *Between Black and White: Race, Politics, and the Free Coloureds in Jamaica, 1792–1865* (Westport, Conn., 1981).

class explains why Jamaican Jews became the first British subjects of their faith to gain full political equality, twenty-seven years before their brethren in England received similar status.[3] After 1831 the gradual process of Jewish assimilation into Jamaican white society began and accelerated after 1865 when the Morant Bay Rebellion buried traditional Creole social divisions, founded on wealth and Protestant culture. Thereafter, the 'Jamaican white' segment unreservedly embraced the Jews as racial allies against the 'teeming hordes' of blacks.[4] In the interim, the story of Jewish participation in politics between 1831 and 1865 underscored the dynamics of Jamaica's Creole society, where significant class differences within the respective cultural sections of black, coloured, and white profoundly influenced how the society adjusted in the transition from slavery to freedom.

With their political emancipation in 1831, Jews qualified for election to the Jamaican Assembly, which guarded its legislative privileges very closely. In the immediate post-slavery period, the assembly consisted of forty-seven members, two from each of the island's twenty-two parishes and an additional one each from the urban areas of Kingston, Spanish Town, and Port Royal. All members of the assembly were elected and each assembly sat for seven years, though the governor could dissolve it and call elections at any time. Prior to 1831, when the male free blacks, free coloureds, and then the Jews were granted political rights, the assembly had been the exclusive preserve of male propertied whites. After 1838 the former male enslaved population also attained some modicum of political rights, although membership in the assembly and the exercise of the franchise remained severely limited by restrictive property qualifications. The qualifications for assembly membership required that a man have an income of £180 from land, real property worth £1,800, or both real and personal property worth £3,000. A man could qualify to vote in any one of three ways: ownership and payment of taxes on land worth £6, payment of £30 rent annually on real estate, or payment of at least £3 in direct taxes.[5] Clearly, most of the former enslaved were excluded by these requirements. Nonetheless, those who met the requirements to vote were as passionate about politics as other free groups before them, and there is clear evidence that by the 1840s some members of the assembly owed their election to the support that they received from small rural landholders, many of whom had been enslaved.

By 1837 two Jews, Daniel Hart and Jacob Jacob Sanguinetti, had been elected to the assembly, the former in Kingston and the latter in Spanish Town, reflecting the influ-

---

[3] Jacob A. Andrade, *A Record of the Jews in Jamaica: From the English Conquest to the Present Time* (Kingston, Jamaica, 1941), 30; Samuel J. Hurwitz and Edith Hurwitz, *Jamaica: A Historical Portrait* (New York, 1971), 142; Holzberg, *Minorities and Power in a Black Society*, 26–8.

[4] August, 'Jewish Assimilation', 116–17; Glen O. I. Phillips, 'The Changing Role of the Merchant Class in the British West Indies, 1834–1867' (Ph.D. thesis, Howard University, 1976), 90, 120; Holzberg, *Minorities and Power in a Black Society*, 120.

[5] James M. Phillippo, *Jamaica: Its Past and Present State* (London, 1843), 110–12; Douglas Hall, *Free Jamaica, 1838–1865: An Economic History* (Barbados, 1970), 2–3.

ence of the Jews in the island's most significant urban areas. Jewish membership of the assembly grew in proportion to their increasing social and political influence, and a total of twenty-seven Jews were elected to the Jamaican Assembly before its abolition in 1866. Whereas in 1838 the Jews formed a mere 4 per cent of the assembly's membership, by 1849 this had increased to 17 per cent, and in 1866, when the assembly surrendered its legislative powers and made way for the introduction of Crown colony government, the Jews accounted for 28 per cent of its membership.[6] Several of the Jews who sat in the assembly before 1866 were part of the growing mercantile plantocracy, who conducted extensive import–export businesses and were also connected with agricultural interests as attorneys or mortgagees, or were planters or pen-keepers (livestock farmers) in their own right. Samuel Magnus and George Lyons Phillips, merchants in Falmouth and Montego Bay, two significant port towns that serviced the extensive network of sugar plantations in Jamaica's western hinterland, demonstrate the political ties between the white planting interests and Jewish merchants. Magnus and Phillips were first elected to the assembly in 1844 for the parishes of Trelawny and St James, respectively, with the solid support of the planters who welcomed them as counterweights to the political challenge mounted by the new voters in free villages under the pastoral care of William Knibb and Thomas Burchell, the island's most influential Baptist missionaries. Significantly, Magnus's and Phillips's electoral successes represented the first time that the influential sugar interests in the parishes of Trelawny and St James were represented in the assembly by men who were not white or well-to-do coloured Protestants.[7] George Lyons Phillips invested extensively in sugar and pen properties in the parishes of St James, Hanover, and Westmoreland in the 1850s and held his seat in the assembly until 1861, when he was promoted to the Legislative Council. In 1862 Governor Eyre described Phillips as a 'personal friend and political supporter' and appointed him to the executive committee that assisted the governor in the administration of the island. Samuel Magnus, a 'considerable landed proprietor' had a shorter and less spectacular political career, serving in the assembly until 1850 when he resigned, apparently a victim of the economic situation following the removal of protective sugar duties in 1846. In 1855 Magnus migrated to Australia with other white Jamaicans seeking new fortunes in the gold rushes there.[8] In the period up to 1865 George Lyons Phillips and Samuel

[6] Andrade, *A Record of the Jews in Jamaica*, 29–30, 223; Glory Robertson, *Members of the Assembly of Jamaica from the General Election of 1830 to the Final Session January 1866* (Kingston, Jamaica, 1965), 11, 13–14, 16–18, 22, 26, 28, 33, 35–7, 40, 42, 45, 48. Since individuals with Jewish surnames in Creole society could be black, coloured, or white Christians, the Jewish status of the assemblymen were verified in the Jewish records (see register of births, English and German Synagogue (1788–1820), Jamaica Archives and Records Department, Spanish Town, Jamaica (JA), 5/4/5; register of births, marriages, and deaths, KKSA (Spanish and Portuguese Synagogue) (1809–1902), JA, 5/4/8.

[7] Elgin to Stanley (7 Sept. 1844), National Archives, Kew (TNA), Colonial Office (CO) 137/280, no. 108; *Baptist Herald* (25 June 1844); *Falmouth Post* (3 Sept. 1844).

[8] Eyre to Newcastle, confidential (8 Apr. 1863), TNA, CO 137/371; Eyre to Newcastle (8 July 1863), TNA, CO 137/375, no. 107; Eyre to Newcastle (26 Dec. 1863), TNA, CO 137/376, no. 304; land deeds, lib. 912, fo. 20; lib.

Magnus, as well as four other Jewish merchants who invariably supported the planting interests in the assembly, Alexander Lindo, Robert Nunes, Jacob Jacob Sanguinetti, and George Solomon, were all appointed *custos rotulorum* or senior magistrate for their respective parishes, thereby unambiguously confirming their social journey from the counting house to magisterial authority among the rural 'gentry'.[9] Clearly, commercial wealth and extensive investments in landed property had sufficiently 'whitened' these Jewish merchants, despite their ethnicity, and they laid the foundations for the Jewish assimilation into Jamaica's Protestant 'white caste' after 1865.[10] By then, the political alliance between the traditional white planting interests and the new Jewish mercantile plantocracy had countered the political impact of the extension of civil rights to the free blacks and the free coloureds after 1830 and after 1838 to the freedmen.[11]

In contrast, seven other Jewish assemblymen, who were mainly provisions, dry-goods, and liquor retailers and produce dealers, built electoral alliances with blacks and coloureds, including former enslaved men, who owned the £6 worth of land which qualified them to vote. This alliance enabled the Jewish retailers to defeat white planters, coloured professionals, and even other Jewish candidates who were high-profile members of the mercantile plantocracy.[12]

The Jewish provisions and dry-goods retailers were located in the traditional market towns and the new trading centres that flourished after 1838, when retail trade expanded as the better-off freed people rejected food and clothing that symbolized their enslavement and hankered after consumer goods and industrial products that befitted their new status. As Jamaica's retail trade in imported goods and local produce expanded after 1838, so too did the fortunes of the Jewish retailers who were central to the expanding post-slavery commercial ethos of 'markets, traders and the rum shops'.[13] The commercial relationship between the freed people and the Jews had its foundations during slavery, when the Jews, who were the chief purveyors of imported goods in the island's port towns, also developed commercial links with free blacks, free

925, fo. 142; lib. 926, fo. 132; lib. 930, fo. 101; lib. 935, fo. 18; lib. 939, fo. 165; lib. 940, fo. 64; lib. 942, fo. 22 (Island Record Office, Twickenham, Jamaica (IRO)); Andrade, *A Record of the Jews in Jamaica*, 155, 167; *Falmouth Post* (7 Apr. 1854; 17 Apr. 1855). Andrade was unaware of Magnus's emigration and incorrectly assumed that he had died when another *custos* was appointed in 1857. For a discussion of Jamaican migration to Australia in this period, see Barry Higman, 'Jamaicans in the Australian Gold Rushes', *Jamaica Journal*, 10 (1976), 38–45.

[9]   Andrade, *A Record of the Jews in Jamaica*, 155, 157, 166–7.

[10]   Philip Curtin, *Two Jamaicas: The Role of Ideas in a Tropical Colony, 1830–1865* (Cambridge, Mass., 1955), 50; Hurwitz and Hurwitz, *Jamaica: A Historical Portrait*, 142; August, 'Jewish Assimilation', 109–12.

[11]   Darling to Newcastle, private (24 Nov. 1860), TNA, CO 137/351; Thomas Holt, *The Problem of Freedom: Race, Labor and Politics in Jamaica and Britain, 1832–1938* (Baltimore, 1992), 223; *Morning Journal* (24 Apr. 1862).

[12]   House of Assembly poll book (1803–43), JA, 1B/11/23/18, fos. 150–2, 207–8; House of Assembly poll book (1844–66), JA, 1B/11/23/19, fos. 19–21, 52–3, 71–4, 115–16, 120–1, 127–9, 149–50, 184, 199–202; Robertson, *Members of the Assembly of Jamaica*, 16, 26.

[13]   Hall, *Free Jamaica*, 23–6, 209–12, 234–5; Glen O. I. Phillips, 'The Stirrings of the Mercantile Community in the British West Indies Immediately After Emancipation', *Journal of Caribbean History*, 23/1 (1989), 75, 88.

coloureds, and slaves. Besides food, slaves also produced a variety of goods, including gums, arrowroot, castor oil, and oil nuts, that were exported by local entrepreneurs. With the proceeds, the slaves purchased clothes, household wares, and other articles not supplied by their owners, and this trading nexus was largely responsible for the growth of the 'negro' or Sunday markets in Kingston and the smaller towns, where Jewish traders were very active.[14] For example, at the beginning of the nineteenth century the 'negro' market in Kingston attracted up to 10,000 people from the surrounding areas who sought provisions and dry goods or to barter their surplus products. In 1819 Reverend Bicknell described the rhythms of the market in the heart of downtown Kingston and highlighted the stalls from which the Jews, who were not constrained by the dictates of the Christian sabbath, conducted a thriving business 'selling old and new clothes, trinkets and small wares at cent per cent to adorn the Negro person'. Clearly, the Jewish traders and the enslaved market sellers formed important links that facilitated the internal marketing system and were closely associated economically.[15] After 1838 these commercial connections were consolidated and political links between the Jewish retailers in the market towns and the freed people residing in the new settlements in the countryside serviced by the markets were nurtured. The Jewish retailers' political careers followed a different path to those of their brethren who were connected with planters or the free coloureds. Indeed, the Jewish retailers looked to the freed people with property of sufficient value to exercise the franchise to achieve their political ambitions. The political activities of Jewish shopkeepers underscore the overarching social connections that cut across racial and ethnic groupings in post-slavery Jamaica and challenge the assumption that, after 1831, the Jewish fraternity was quickly absorbed into Jamaica's monolithic 'white caste'. Instead, it will be demonstrated that in post-slavery Jamaica, class factors influenced the politics pursued by different segments of the Jewish community, which was much more than just the 'prosperous' merchants with ties to the plantocracy.[16]

The following discussion of the political alliance between the Jewish retailers and the mainly black small landholders in the parish of St Dorothy between 1849 and 1860 underscores how the Jewish retailers translated their commercial relationship with black and coloured artisans and small settlers into a solid electoral base. Together, the retailers and the small settlers shared a vision of post-slavery Jamaica that offered some

---

[14] Lowell Ragatz, *The Fall of the Planter Class in the British Caribbean 1763–1833* (New York, 1928; repr. 1963), 16; Sidney Mintz, *Caribbean Transformations* (Baltimore, 1974), 182–3, 198–201.

[15] Robert Renny, *An History of Jamaica with Observations on the Climate* (London, 1807), 328; Colin G. Clarke, *Kingston, Jamaica: Urban Development and Social Change, 1692–1962* (Berkeley, Calif., 1975), 16.

[16] Assumptions that Jews were readily absorbed into the 'white caste' in the post-slavery period neglect the Jewish shopkeepers whose commercial activities tied them to the freed people (see Curtin, *Two Jamaicas*, 49–50). For a critique of M. G. Smith's assumptions that the elite position and role of the Jews in Jamaican society by 1960 reflected their history, thereby failing to appreciate the heterogeneity among the Jewish population in the nineteenth century, see Holzberg, *Minorities and Power in a Black Society*, p. xxiii.

modicum of social justice by providing more schools, improved roads, lower taxation, equitable wages and working conditions, and the extension of suffrage.

The parish of St Dorothy was located to the west of Spanish Town, and its lowlands formed part of the island's important southern sugar belt. Livestock pens were also operated in support of the plantation economy, and coffee properties dominated its northern, more mountainous, region.[17] In the early post-slavery period the livestock pens and sugar plantations generally managed to continue, but the larger coffee properties in the mountainous regions of St Dorothy were abandoned, and a new class of small settlers, former slaves, rapidly established themselves, cultivating provision crops, such as corn, yams, peas, and plantains, which they sold by the 'cartload, hamper or head-load'. Also, using very rudimentary mills, some of the settlers manufactured sugar for local consumption and sold coffee and pimento to produce dealers. Indeed, it was the 'mountain Negroes' of St Dorothy and the adjoining parish of St John who supplied the food traded at the village known as Old Harbour Market, about 2 miles inland from Old Harbour Bay, an important trading port for plantation produce and supplies during the slavery period. Old Harbour Market was located 10 miles to the west of Spanish Town, along the main southern road linking the island's capital with the parishes of Vere, Clarendon, and Manchester. It emerged as a thriving trading centre after 1838 driven by the enterprise of the freed people, as did Four Paths and Porus, two other important market towns along the road.[18] Members of Spanish Town Jewry responded to these increased trading opportunities in the new market towns, and eight retailers conducted dry-goods stores or ran liquor shops at Old Harbour Market. Three also had branch stores at Bartons and Bellas Gate, thereby extending the retailers' commercial network into settlements in the mountainous interior to the north of Old Harbour Market, trading dry goods for coffee and pimento grown by the small freeholders, who also received credit from the retailers (see Map 14.1).[19]

It would appear that none of the Jewish retailers in St Dorothy enjoyed sufficient wealth to represent the parish in the assembly. However, within a decade of emancipation, the retailers, the black and coloured artisans, and the small settlers developed an electoral alliance that undercut the traditional political dominance of St Dorothy's mainly white sugar planters and owners of livestock pens. In the early post-slavery period, the combined political influence of the Jewish retailers and the new class of

[17] Report of S. M. Bell enclosed in Barkly to Newcastle (26 May 1854), TNA, CO 137/322, no. 73; Higman, *Slave Population and Economy*, 25, 29–30; Verene A. Shepherd, *Livestock, Sugar and Slavery: Contested Terrain in Colonial Jamaica* (Kingston, Jamaica, 2009), 25, 29, 31.

[18] Report of S. M. Bell (Jan. 1841), cited in Hall, *Free Jamaica*, 25–6; *Morning Journal* (24 Mar. 1849).

[19] Report of S. M. Bell enclosed in Elgin to Stanley (2 Sept. 1845), TNA, CO 137/284, no. 79. Henry Benjamin, Joseph Deleon, Isaac Dolphy, George Hasten, Abraham and Benjamin Melhado, David Peixotto and Henry Soares were the Jewish retailers in Old Harbour in the 1840s and 1850s. Both the Melhados and Soares had outlets at Bartons and Bellas Gate (see land deeds, lib. 915, fo. 28 (IRO); *Jamaica Gazette* (27 Jan. 1848; 22 Dec. 1853; 26 Jan. 1854; 5 Apr., 7 June 1855; 3 Apr. 1856; 4 Apr. 1861)).

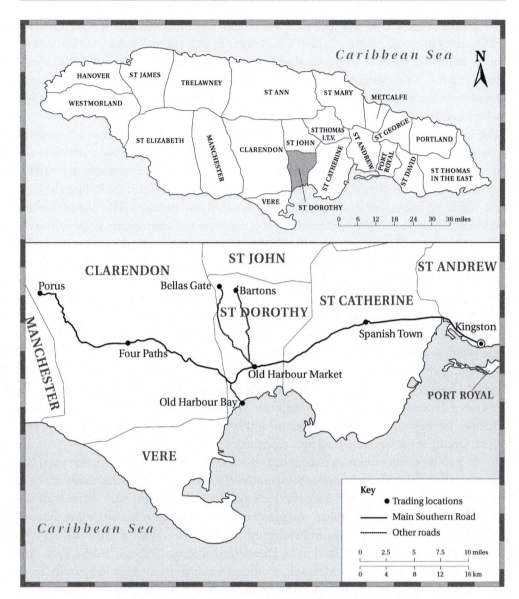

Map 14.1 Jewish trading networks, St Dorothy, Jamaica, 1841–65

small landholders in St Dorothy ensured that three Jews, Moses Lyon (1849–54), David Brandon (1850–6, 1860–2), and Solomon Rodriques (1854–9), who resided outside the parish but had ethnic and business ties with St Dorothy's Jewish retailers, defeated white planters and a coloured shopkeeper in elections for the two seats that St Dorothy had in the island's assembly.[20]

[20] Report of S. M. Bell enclosed in Darling to Lytton (25 Oct. 1858), TNA, CO 137/339, no. 134; report of

Moses Lyon, a tavern-keeper in Spanish Town, became the first Jew to represent
St Dorothy in the assembly when, in the 1849 general elections, he defeated the incumbent, Peter Harrison, a coloured shopkeeper at Old Harbour Bay who was also a
pen-keeper.[21] The elections followed two years of protracted battles in the island's
legislature between the planter-dominated assembly and the Legislative Council,
which consisted of senior government officials and others nominated by the governor.
The council could reject or amend the assembly's bills and quite often reflected the
position of the governor, who had the power to confirm or disallow enactments of
the assembly and the council. Between 1847 and 1849 the council steadfastly rejected the
assembly's extreme measures to arbitrarily reduce public salaries, including those of
the judiciary, and other drastic reductions in public expenditure. The planters in the
assembly insisted that their retrenchment plans were the appropriate response to declining revenues. These reflected the depressed state of the island's sugar and coffee
properties after 1846, when Britain's adoption of free trade gradually removed all the
protective tariffs that favoured West Indian produce and exposed it to competition from
cheaper sugar and coffee from Cuba and Brazil where slave labour continued to be
used.[22] This political contest took on additional significance in 1848, when absentee
planters in Britain encouraged their representatives in Jamaica to orchestrate chaos in
the island's finances in order to pressure the British government to abandon its free
trade policy.[23] Clearly, political compromise was impossible, and, when in June 1849 the
council rejected the assembly's revenue bills with appropriations that restricted government expenditure, the planter majority in the assembly resolved to abstain from
'further exercise of legislative functions' until the 'people' pronounced on their conduct, forcing the governor to call new elections.[24]

In a more moderate and conciliatory political climate in 1844, Peter Harrison had
been elected as the first coloured representative for St Dorothy in the assembly with the
support of planters and pen-keepers. However, since Harrison had voted with the
minority in the assembly against the planters' retrenchment schemes, some planters
withdrew their support in 1849 and endorsed Stephen Hannaford, a sugar planter who
owned over 13,000 acres of land in St Dorothy, including Colbeck, Bushy Park, and
Whim sugar estates. Francis McCook, the other incumbent, resided in Spanish Town
but was connected to sugar and livestock properties in St Dorothy. He received the

S. M. Bell enclosed in Darling to Newcastle (8 Sept. 1859), TNA, CO 137/346, no. 144; *Jamaica Tribune* (7 July
1860); Robertson, *Members of the Assembly*, 16.

[21] Land deeds, lib. 840, fo. 78; lib. 916, fo. 211 (IRO); *Jamaica Gazette* (28 June 1849); *Falmouth Post* (18, 24 July
1849). Gad Heuman suggests that Peter Harrison was white, but marriage records confirm his coloured status
(see Heuman, *Between Black and White*, 140; register of marriages, St Dorothy (1826–1843), JA, 1B/11/8/3/35, fo.
3; *Falmouth Post* (18, 24 July 1849)).   [22] Hall, *Free Jamaica*, 3–4, 81–98.

[23] Charles Grey to Earl Grey (19 Feb. 1849), TNA, CO 137/301, no. 21; *Morning Journal* (13 Sept. 1848).

[24] Charles Grey to Earl Grey (7 July 1849), TNA, CO 137/303, no. 70; *Falmouth Post* (17 July 1849).

Table 14.1 Landholding of voters for Moses Lyon and Peter Harrison, St Dorothy, Jamaica, 1849

Voters' landholding (acres)	Number of votes	
	Moses Lyon	Peter Harrison
<4	13	4
4–15	5	7
15–50	5	5
>50	2	4
Unknown	10	8
Total	**35**	**28**

Source: House of Assembly poll book, 1844–66; land deeds; Jamaica Almanac, 1845.

undivided support of the planters, since he had endorsed their retrenchment measures. Moses Lyon specifically targeted Harrison by campaigning on a platform of 'public economy' and 'lower taxation' and topped the poll with 35 votes. McCook was placed second with 31 votes: Harrison with 28 votes and Hannaford with 10 votes were defeated.[25]

These results indicate an important development in a rural constituency in the post-slavery period: a Jewish tavern-keeper had ousted a coloured incumbent, out-performed the other incumbent, and defeated another planter through the strong support of small settlers who endorsed his call for reductions in taxation and official salaries. The land-holding patterns of the respective groups of voters for Moses Lyons and Peter Harrison underscore the importance of the small settlers' support to Lyon's historic triumph (see Table 14.1).

There were two seats to be filled, and each voter had two votes. Of those with less than 4 acres, John Harrison—a shop- and tavern-keeper at Old Harbour Bay and brother of Peter Harrison—was the only one to withhold support from Lyon. John Harrison's social status and economic activities certainly differentiated him from the other voters in this category, as in 1854 he purchased 180 acres at New Market Pen.[26] Three men with less than 4 acres divided their votes between Lyon and Harrison: they were also from the Old Harbour Bay area where Peter Harrison's commercial activities were concentrated, which could explain their voting pattern. Furthermore, the occupation data for all thirteen artisans or small settlers with under 4 acres who supported Lyon confirm the importance of the humbler class of voters to the outcome of the election. Two, including William Bayley, a mason, were from the village of Old Harbour Market, and five were from the post-slavery settlement at Logwood Valley Pen,

[25] House of Assembly poll book (1844–66), JA, 1B/11/23/19, fos. 11–13; *Falmouth Post* (18, 24 July 1849); returns of proprietors, *Jamaica Almanac 1845*, 4, 5, 18, 19.   [26] See land deeds, lib. 916, fo. 211 (IRO).

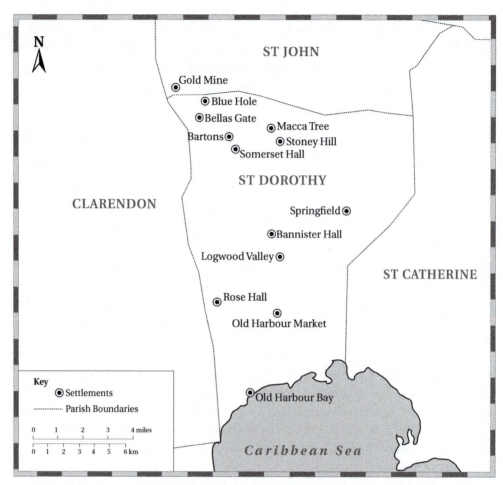

Map 14.2 Settlements, St Dorothy, Jamaica, 1841–65

2 miles north of Old Harbour Market on the road to the St Dorothy mountains. Another of these artisans, Joseph Woodhouse, a carpenter, owned 2 acres at Macca Tree in the mountainous interior near the border with St John. Significantly, Woodhouse was one of thirteen freedmen who voted for the first time in the 1849 elections. Five of these freedmen, including three from the Old Harbour Bay area where Harrison's shop was located, supported him, while eight voted for Lyon. Five of the freedmen who supported Lyon were described as 'small settlers' from Bartons, Macca Tree, Orange Hall, Somerset, and Stoney Hill in St Dorothy's mountainous area that produced provisions and minor export crops which were most likely traded with Jewish retailers through their branch stores at Bartons and Bellas Gate in the vicinity of these post-slavery settlements (see Map 14.2).[27]

[27] Report of S. M. Bell enclosed in Barkly to Newcastle (26 May 1854), TNA, CO 137/322, no. 73; register of

Table 14.2 Regional distribution of voters, St Dorothy, Jamaica, 1850

Voters' location	Number of votes	
	David Brandon	Peter Harrison
Old Harbour Bay	6	13
Old Harbour Market	8	3
Rural settlements	17	9
Unknown	13	11
Total	44	36

Source: House of Assembly poll book, 1844–66; land deeds; registers of baptisms and marriages, St Dorothy, 1826–73.

Moses Lyon's victory in 1849 was the first in a chain of political successes for Jewish retailers in St Dorothy. Francis McCook's death precipitated a by-election in December 1850, and Peter Harrison leapt at the opportunity to recover his seat. However, David Brandon, a Jewish wholesaler and retailer of dry goods in Kingston with a network of stores at Annotto Bay, Linstead, and Port Antonio, stood against him. Although it is unclear whether Brandon had commercial links with the Jewish traders in Old Harbour Market, it is possible that they could have been part of his dry-goods distribution network.[28] Brandon was clearly ambitious for higher office: when he set his sights on the assembly seat in St Dorothy he had served for less than twelve months in local government as a member of the Kingston Common Council. In a keen contest, Brandon polled 44 votes to Harrison's 36 votes, and the local coloured shopkeeper experienced his second defeat in eighteen months to yet another Jewish retailer from outside the parish (see Table 14.2).[29]

The geographical distribution of the voters for David Brandon in the 1850 election repeated the pattern of Lyon's success in 1849. Despite Peter Harrison's receiving 68 per cent of the votes from the Old Harbour Bay area, David Brandon's victory was built on his enjoying the support of 73 per cent of the voters from the village at Old Harbour Market and 65 per cent of those in the rural settlements. Clearly the majority of small settlers, including former slaves, preferred the candidate from Kingston with ethnic and

baptisms and marriages, St Dorothy (1826–35), JA, 1B/11/8/3/22, 29, 35; House of Assembly poll book (1844–66), JA, 1B/11/23/19, fos. 52–3; land deeds, lib. 827, fo. 19; lib. 838, fo. 109; lib. 840, fos. 74–5, 78; lib. 844, fo. 165; lib. 854, fos. 47, 48, 113, 114, 115; lib. 856, fo. 213; lib. 864, fo. 153; lib. 888, fo. 211; lib. 889, fo. 67; lib. 907, fo. 9; lib. 916, fo. 211 (IRO); *Jamaica Gazette* (28 June 1849; 17 Feb. 1859).

[28] Land deeds, lib. 931, fo. 78 (IRO); *Morning Journal* (16 Aug. 1848; 3 Dec. 1849; 10 Jan. 1850); *Daily Advertiser* (10 Aug. 1854).

[29] House of Assembly poll book (1844–66), JA, 1B/11/23/19, fos. 105–6; *Morning Journal* (11 Dec. 1850); *Falmouth Post* (26 Nov. 1850).

business ties to the local Jewish shopkeepers over the local coloured businessman.
Indeed, the political choices of the four former slaves who voted for the first time in
1850 reflected the regional influence of the competing shopkeepers. William Caddell
and Peter Ricketts, both fishermen from Old Harbour Bay, voted for Harrison, while
George Irwin and William McDonald, who were from Bannister and Springfield, new
settlements in the northern mountainous region of St Dorothy, endorsed Brandon.[30]
After the election Harrison complained that Brandon had corrupted the electoral
process by bribing voters with dry goods that had 'flooded' Old Harbour Market on
election day. The practice of providing incentives to prospective voters was not uncommon in the island's elections. Neither for that matter was intimidating voters to
dissuade them from supporting another candidate. Nonetheless, it is possible that
Harrison confused standard trading between Jewish retailers and small settlers with the
corrupt exchange of dry goods for votes. Also, no doubt, Harrison reaped political
benefits from the commercial influence he wielded in lower parts of the parish, especially in the Old Harbour Bay area where his commercial activities were located.[31]

   Moses Lyon's and David Brandon's victories underscored the combined political
influence of the Jewish retailers at Old Harbour Market and the new class of small
settlers in the vicinity of Old Harbour Market and in the new settlements in St
Dorothy's mountains. This alliance ensured that for the first time, in 1850, two Jewish
retailers represented the parish in the assembly, a distinction that had been reserved
for white Protestant planters and pen-keepers up until 1844. Peter Harrison added a
coloured dimension with his electoral success in 1844, only to be defeated in successive
elections by Moses Lyon and David Brandon.

   The sugar planters and pen-keepers refused to surrender St Dorothy's politics to
the Jewish retailers, and, in the 1854 general election, they made a determined challenge
to take back one of the seats, as Moses Lyon's declining health forced his retirement.
For this election, David Smith, the manager of the Jamaica Railway Company and a co-
founder of Smith's Agricultural Society for Jamaica, which invested in sugar properties
in the island, came forward as the standard bearer for the planters of St Dorothy.
Although it is unclear whether Smith owned property or was linked to estates in St
Dorothy at the time of the 1854 election, he certainly later invested in the parish,
acquiring Hayes Pen in 1859 and the former coffee plantation at Blue Hole in 1861.[32]
Undaunted by Smith's impressive credentials, the Jewish retailers were also determined
to maintain their recent monopoly over St Dorothy's political representation in the

[30] House of Assembly poll book (1844–66), JA, 1B/11/23/19, fos. 105–6; register of baptisms of slaves and
free people, St Dorothy (1818–32), JA, 1B/11/8/3/22, fos. 80, 96, 111; register of baptisms, St Dorothy (1843–71),
JA, 1B/11/8/3/29, fo. 237; register of marriages, St Dorothy (1826–43), JA, 1B/11/8/3/35, fo. 5; *Jamaica Gazette* (2
June 1859).
[31] Report of S. M. Bell enclosed in Elgin to Stanley (2 Sept. 1845), TNA, CO 137/284, no. 79; *Jamaica Gazette*
(28 June 1849; 3 Apr. 1856; 4 Apr. 1861); *Morning Journal* (22 Feb. 1851).
[32] Land deeds, lib. 936, fos. 94, 107 (IRO). Hall, *Free Jamaica*, 35, 92–3; *Falmouth Post* (19 Sept. 1854).

assembly and brought forward Solomon Rodriques, who was also from the Spanish Town Jewish community. Like David Brandon, Rodriques was part of a network of commercial interests beyond the town where he resided, owning, with his father-in-law, dry-goods and liquor shops in Four Paths. Solomon Rodriques was also related to Joseph Rodriquez Deleon, a retailer at the Old Harbour Market and in the neighbouring parish of Vere.[33]

In 1854 St Dorothy's planters and pen-keepers were prepared to share the two seats with the Jewish politicians, and they supported David Brandon's re-election but opposed Solomon Rodriques. Initially, the planters queried whether Rodriques had attained the legal age for the office, even though he was 28 and eligible. The opposition persisted, however: as the canvassing became more spirited, his opponents extended their objections to include his ethnic background, and various antisemitic sentiments were aired.[34] Solomon Rodriques countered his opponents' propaganda by appealing to the interests of the small settlers. He emphasized his opposition to the immigration schemes that David Smith and St Dorothy's planters endorsed in order to drive down wages and provide employers with greater control over the sugar plantations and pens. Rodriques also promised the small freeholders that if they sent him to the assembly they could rely on him to demand increased grants for education and to support lower taxation on the imported dry goods and food staples that they consumed. These issues were especially topical, because the assembly had reduced grants for education in the face of declining revenues after the Sugar Duties Act had sparked the retrenchment crisis. This was particularly detrimental to the freed people, since the Negro Education Grant, the other main source of funds for their education, had expired in 1845. Indeed, the small settlers were particularly concerned about their children's access to schools, which they hoped would broaden their social opportunities beyond agricultural labour. In addition, the cutbacks in social expenditure had coincided with increased taxation on imported provisions and dry goods, and this affected the small settlers who consumed these goods as well as the Jewish retailers who were their chief distributors. Clearly, Rodriques's campaign strategy linked his business and political interests with those of the small settlers, and his endorsement of the popular view that immigrants lowered wages and restored the planters' control over labour earned him further support among small settlers and those who may have worked as artisans on sugar or livestock properties.[35]

---

[33] *Jamaica Gazette* (27 Jan. 1848; 19 Apr. 1855); Andrade, *A Record of Jews in Jamaica*, 46; *Morning Journal* (14, 25 Sept. 1854).

[34] *Morning Journal* (25, 27 Sept. 1854). Antisemitic sentiments were also used to oppose Jewish candidates, without success, in elections in St Catherine, Kingston, and Port Royal during this period.

[35] Hall, *Free Jamaica*, 176–7, 281; Carl Campbell, 'Social and Economic Obstacles to the Development of Popular Education in Jamaica', in H. Beckles and V. Shepherd (eds.), *Caribbean Freedom: Society and Economy From Emancipation to the Present* (Kingston, Jamaica, 1993), 262–7; *Morning Journal* (25 Sept. 1854).

Table 14.3 Occupation of voters for Solomon Rodriques and David Smith, St Dorothy, Jamaica, 1854

Voters' occupation	Number of votes	
	Solomon Rodriques	David Smith
Artisan	3	2
Businessman	3	1
Planter/Pen-keeper	0	4
Small Farmer	14	3
Not Known	5	3
Total	**25**	**14**

Source: House of Assembly poll book, 1844–1866; land deeds; registers of baptisms and marriages, St Dorothy, 1826–73.

The slurs against Rodriques's ethnicity failed to sway the electorate, who responded to his promises to promote their interests. David Brandon, the incumbent, topped the poll with 28 votes and Solomon Rodriques with 25 votes comfortably defeated David Smith, who received only 14. Two other candidates, James Dollar and Moses Lyon, received 13 and 3 votes respectively. Table 14.3 clearly underscores the nature of the class support for Rodriques and Smith.

Significantly, the four voters in Table 14. 3 associated with the ownership or management of sugar estates and livestock pens exclusively supported Smith, as did Francis Moxy, the wharfinger and rum trader at Old Harbour Bay, the only businessman to do so. In contrast, the three businessmen who voted for Rodriques were Jewish retailers, and, most importantly, Rodriques received three times as many votes from artisans and small farmers, including former slaves, as Smith. The planters' efforts to recapture the seat failed because the small landholders from Old Harbour Market, Bartons, Bellas Gate, Blue Hole, Goldmine, Rose Hall, and Somerset kept faith with the Jewish retailer who associated himself with issues that determined the quality of their lives, such as education, labour relations, and taxation.[36] Clearly, as long as the Jewish retailers retained the confidence of the small settlers in both the lowlands and the mountainous regions of St Dorothy, their opponents' antisemitic propaganda would prove ineffective.

David Brandon and Solomon Rodriques served in the assembly until reversals in their businesses precipitated their resignations, as they no longer had the requisite

[36] House of Assembly poll book (1844–66), JA, 1B/11/23/19, fos. 120–1; register of baptisms, St Dorothy (1843–71), JA, 1B/11/8/3/29, fos. 85, 89, 189, 252; register of baptisms, St Dorothy (1826–43), JA, 1B/11/8/3/37, fo. 34; register of marriages, St Dorothy (1826–43), JA, 1B/11/8/3/35, fo. 9; land deeds, lib. 813, fo. 122; lib. 838, fo. 153; lib. 888, fo. 38; lib. 894, fo. 14; lib. 940, fo. 148 (IRO); *Jamaica Gazette* (3 Apr. 1856; 2 June 1859); returns of proprietors, *Jamaica Almanac 1845*, 7–8.

income for public office. In 1856 Moses Bravo, whose family had extensive landholdings in St Dorothy and who had converted to Christianity in 1833, replaced Brandon, unopposed. In 1859 Bravo resigned his seat, and Robert Pearson, a white solicitor and penkeeper in Manchester, was elected unopposed. In the same year, Andrew Henry Lewis, a Jewish pen-keeper from Spanish Town, was elected unopposed to replace Solomon Rodriques. So, between 1856 and the general election in 1860, the representation for St Dorothy in the assembly changed hands without electoral contests and was shared between Jews and Christians, including a convert from Judaism.[37]

In the absence of contested elections for the assembly, the Jewish retailers in St Dorothy maintained their political involvement in the annual elections for the parish vestry, the institution of local government. Established in Jamaica in 1677, each vestry had twelve elected members—ten vestrymen and two churchwardens—and the *custos rotulorum*. The other magistrates and the Anglican rector served as *ex officio* members. The vestries administered the local markets, roads, animal pounds, parochial education, and appointed individuals to salaried posts such as constables, clerks of the peace, offices of the Established Church, and pound-keepers, which were financed by parish rates.[38] The composition of the vestries in the post-slavery period mirrored the changing fortunes of the plantation economy; and, in parishes where a vibrant black peasantry emerged, artisans, retailers, and small settlers from the newly enfranchised social groups—free coloureds, Jews, and blacks—entered the vestry, since freeholders with £6 worth of land qualified for election as a vestryman.[39] By 1860 the composition of St Dorothy's vestry reflected similar social changes: two Jewish retailers at the Old Harbour Market, Henry Soares and Isaac Melhado, were vestrymen, as were at least four black or coloured artisans, including George Richards and James H. Bailey, who had been enslaved; and L. D. Clark, a free coloured carpenter, was one of the two elected churchwardens.[40] This was the context in which the stipendiary magistrate in St Dorothy lamented that the dwindling number of the 'upper classes' in the parish made it difficult to find 'highly respectable parties to fill the magistracy and Parochial

[37]   Robertson, *Members of the Assembly*, 16; Andrade, *A Record of Jews in Jamaica*, 30, 152; *Falmouth Post* (2 Dec. 1856). Despite the Bravo family's conversion in 1833, a recent publication incorrectly lists Alexandre Bravo, Moses's father, as the first Jew to be elected to the House of Assembly when he won a seat for St Dorothy in 1835 (see Mordechai Arbell, *The Portuguese Jews of Jamaica* (Kingston, Jamaica, 2000), 47).

[38]   Edward Brathwaite, *The Development of Creole Society in Jamaica 1770–1820* (London, 1971), 20–3; Hedley Powell Jacobs, *Sixty Years of Change, 1806–1866: Progress and Reaction in Kingston and the Countryside* (Kingston, Jamaica, 1972), 13; *Morning Journal* (27 Apr. 1839).

[39]   For two examples of this, see Swithin Wilmot, '"The Old Order Changeth": Vestry Politics in Two of Jamaica's Parishes, Portland and Metcalfe, 1838–65', in Brian Moore and Swithin Wilmot (eds.), *Before and After 1865: Education, Politics and Regionalism in the Caribbean* (Kingston, Jamaica, 1998), 101–11.

[40]   Register of baptisms of slaves and free people, St Dorothy (1818–32), JA, 1B/11/8/3/22; register of baptisms, St Dorothy (1843–71), JA, 1B/11/8/3/29; register of marriages, St Dorothy (1826–43), JA, 1B/11/8/3/35; *Jamaica Gazette* (24 July 1845; 2 June 1859); *Jamaica Tribune* (7 July 1860).

Offices', which were no longer occupied by 'people from Great Britain'. Indeed, he complained that 'the great Bulk of Electors' were 'low, ignorant people', who were 'manipulated' by the Jews and who were replacing the 'upper classes' in parochial politics.[41]

Reverend Benjamin Kingdom, the Anglican rector for St Dorothy, also resented the fact that Jewish retailers and small freeholders were deciding the outcome of elections for the vestry. In 1858, when the Jewish retailers' candidate for the post of churchwarden for St Dorothy defeated the rector's 'anointed', who also had the backing of the so-called 'respectable portion of the Members of the Church of England', the clergyman accused the Jews of improperly interfering in the Anglican Church's internal affairs. Reverend Kingdom's complaint had no legal standing, since the churchwarden was chosen by the electors of the parish, regardless of their religious persuasion, and any elector who was a member of the Church of England was entitled to stand for the post. The crux of the matter was that the contest had underscored the social cleavages within the Anglican Church in St Dorothy, with the Jewish retailers backing the candidate who enjoyed the support of the majority of the small settlers.[42]

The 1860 general elections for the assembly took place against this background of political feuding between the Anglican rector and the Jewish retailers and presented another opportunity for the contending political groups in St Dorothy to demonstrate their influence. Andrew Henry Lewis, a member of the Spanish Town Jewish community, who had succeeded Solomon Rodriques in 1859, sought re-election, but William Pearson, the other incumbent, declined to stand, and, since David Brandon's economic fortunes had recovered sufficiently for him to qualify again for membership of the assembly, he offered himself to the electorate in St Dorothy. Given his electoral successes in 1850 and 1854 and the political influence of the Jewish retailers, Brandon's return seemed assured. However, Reverend Kingdom was determined to curb the influence of the local Jewish retailers and their supporters, and he brought forward James Harvey, a white planter and pen-keeper in St Dorothy, as well as the attorney for important sugar plantations in the neighbouring parish of Vere. Harvey also enjoyed some support in the local community, as he was one of the elected churchwardens for St Dorothy. In 1860 James Harvey, like David Smith before him in 1854, entered the contest as the candidate of those who were determined to resurrect the rector's and the planters' social influence in the parish and defeat the political alliance of Jewish retailers and small freeholders.[43]

---

[41]   Report of S. M. Bell to Austin (1 July 1858) enclosed in Darling to Lytton (25 Oct. 1858), TNA, CO 137/339, no. 134; report of S. M. Bell enclosed in Darling to Newcastle (8 Sept. 1859), TNA, CO 137/346, no. 144.

[42]   Report of S. M. Bell enclosed in Darling to Newcastle (8 Sept. 1859), TNA, CO 137/346, no. 144; *Jamaica Tribune* (27 July 1860). A related case embittered the social relations in St Thomas in the east at the time of the Morant Bay Rebellion in 1865 when the *custos* and the rector successfully removed George William Gordon from his post as churchwarden, despite his election by the freeholders, on the grounds that he was not a communicant of the Anglican Church (see Holt, *The Problem of Freedom*, 293).

[43]   Darling to Newcastle, private (24 Nov. 1860), TNA, CO 137/351; *Jamaica Tribune* (7, 27 July 1860).

In this context of competing class interests, David Brandon strategically pinned his political ambitions on the support of the new class of small settlers. He addressed issues that mattered to them, such as educational facilities for their children, the entitlement to vote, and the burdens of taxation. As far as the first was concerned, months before the election, he had provided a very tangible demonstration of his commitment to broadening the opportunities for the education of the small settlers' children when he donated land for a school at Bartons that would serve mountainous parts of the parish far from the Old Harbour area. By the time of the election, the small settlers in Bartons, in a commendable demonstration of self-help and of the importance that they attached to education, had pooled their labour and constructed a building in which forty pupils attended school. Further, skilfully manipulating the class divisions in the parish, Brandon denounced the assembly's recent imposition of a 10-shilling poll tax on all voters, as an 'obnoxious electoral tax', because it was 'unjust to call on the poor man of one acre to pay ten shillings for recording his vote, while he who owned hundreds, thousands of acres, and a mansion should only pay the same amount for the like privilege'. He also promised to agitate for the removal of the licence on animal carts, which the small settlers used to transport their produce, because it was 'oppressive on the lower classes', who also had to pay the land tax, the election tax, and the greater portion of duties on imports. Brandon also reminded the small landholders that the 'aristocracy' of St Dorothy were opposed to his election because he wanted 'not only to protect the rich but the poor'.[44]

Like Solomon Rodriques in 1854, when faced with a concerted challenge from the planters, Brandon concentrated on the concerns of the new class of small freeholders, and they rewarded his efforts in education and accepted his promises to promote their interests in the assembly. On the day of the election, James Harvey withdrew from the contest three hours after polling commenced, when it was clear that his 16 votes were incapable of stopping Brandon, who by then had accumulated 30, with more of his black supporters from distant country districts still to reach the polling station. The voters for the respective candidates underscored the divisions between the social groups in St Dorothy, as the so-called 'respectable portion' of the electorate sided with Harvey, while Brandon's impressive performance confirmed the electoral strength of the Jewish retailers whenever they were backed by the small settlers. The rector and John Walker, the schoolmaster and clerk to St Phillip's Anglican chapel at Old Harbour Bay, voted for Harvey, as did Stephen Hannaford, the sugar planter who had lost to Brandon in 1850. Augustus and David Morais, two coloured pen-keepers; George Willet, a wharfinger at Old Harbour Bay; and Francis Robert Lynch, a white solicitor who represented St Catherine in the assembly and who also had close links to the island's leading coloured politicians, also voted for Harvey. In contrast, six Jews—Henry

[44] *Jamaica Tribune* (27 July 1860).

Wolfe Benjamin, Joseph Rodriquez Deleon, Isaac Dolphy, Abraham Melhado, Benjamin Melhado, and Henry Soares—who were linked with four retail establishments in Old Harbour Market, two of which had branches in the mountain settlements at Bartons and Bellas Gate, voted for Brandon. Significantly, at least fifteen, or 63 per cent, of the other twenty-four of Brandon's supporters, were small settlers, including eight from Bartons where Brandon had donated land for the school.[45] Accordingly, in his victory speech, Brandon promised never to 'forget the small settlers, for it was to them he was indebted for his election. Had he depended on the Aristocracy he never would have been one of the members for St Dorothy.'[46]

Moses Lyon, Solomon Rodriques, and David Brandon were politically indebted to the mainly black small settlers in St Dorothy who between 1849 and 1860 elected them over white planters and pen-keepers and a free coloured shopkeeper. Clearly, in this period Jewish retailers from Kingston and Spanish Town enjoyed a near monopoly of St Dorothy's seats in the assembly, because they cultivated the support of the newly enfranchised 'mountain Negroes', who used the ballot to articulate their passion for inclusion in Jamaica's political arrangements in the immediate post-slavery period. Together with the Jewish retailers, they were navigating their way and seeking a place in an emerging Creole society that had complex issues of class, ethnicity, and colour inherited from slave society.

This discussion of Jewish politics in the immediate post-slavery period in Jamaica underscores the significant class differences that profoundly influenced how society adjusted itself in the transition from slavery to freedom. There were Jews who, 'whitened' by wealth and commercial links to the planters, allied themselves with the white and coloured propertied classes, and there were Jewish retailers who championed the interests of the freed people with whom they had a well-established tradition of doing business. Finally, the discussion reiterates the work of the late Professor Carl Stone, who emphasized the relevance of a class analysis of social division in nineteenth-century Jamaican politics, in contrast to the emphasis on cultural perspectives associated with Philip Curtin's pioneering work on Jamaica's post-slavery society.[47]

[45] House of Assembly poll book (1844–66), JA, 1B/11/23/19, fos. 149–50; register of baptisms, St Dorothy (1843–71), JA, 1B/11/8/3/29, fos. 89, 118, 139, 186; register of marriages, St Dorothy (1826–43), JA, 1B/11/8/3/35, fos. 9, 22, 37, 44; land deeds, lib. 826, fo. 222; lib. 845, fo. 5; lib. 888, fo. 36; lib. 914, fo. 66; lib. 916, fo. 159; lib. 915, fo. 28; lib. 920, fo. 127; lib. 935, fo. 190; lib. 921, fo. 23 (IRO); returns of proprietors, *Jamaica Almanac 1845*, 18–19; *Jamaica Gazette* (27 Jan. 1848; 22 Dec. 1853; 26 Jan. 1854; 7 June 1855; 3 Apr. 1856; 24 Mar., 2 June 1859; 4 Apr. 1861).

[46] *Jamaica Tribune* (27 July 1860).

[47] Carl Stone, *Class, Race and Political Behaviour in Urban Jamaica* (Kingston, Jamaica, 1973), 14. Curtin adopted the 'plural society' model in his analysis (see Curtin, *Two Jamaicas*).

PART V

REASSESSING THE GEOGRAPHICAL BOUNDARIES OF CARIBBEAN JEWRY

CHAPTER FIFTEEN

THE BORDERS OF EARLY AMERICAN JEWISH HISTORY

ELI FABER

IN ALMOST ANY WORK on early American Jewish history during the seventeenth and eighteenth centuries, American Jewry is limited to five congregations on the North American mainland—New York, Newport, Philadelphia, Charleston, and Savannah—as well as a handful of settlers in the interior, and, later, joining the original five in the late eighteenth century, Richmond and Baltimore. But if we were to transport ourselves back to London in the middle of the eighteenth century and eavesdrop upon a meeting of the Mahamad of the Sephardi congregation worriedly appraising an apparently inexorable increase in the number of poor Jews in the community, many of whom relied upon the congregation for assistance, and wondering what additional assistance could be asked for from communities elsewhere, we would be treated to a far more expansive definition of what comprised the borders of colonial American Jewry.[1] Instead of limiting their scope to the North American mainland, London's Jewish leaders undoubtedly viewed the contemporary Jewish settlements in the Caribbean, the metropolitan centres of London and Amsterdam, and the North American mainland congregations as one seamless entity.

Though this might be obvious to some, not too long ago, when I wrote a chapter entitled 'The Atlantic World of Colonial Jewry', the editor of the book in which it was to appear, one of the senior figures in the field of American Jewish history, wrote in his assessment: 'I wonder why nobody ever noticed it before'. Happily, he accepted the perspective as valid and approved the chapter for publication, but I daresay that for

---

[1] Such a meeting is in no way fanciful. Facing shortfalls because of the increasing numbers of those who were dependent upon Bevis Marks—London's Sephardi congregation—the officers launched a Jewish settlement in Georgia during the early 1730s and later briefly planned for another in South Carolina (see Todd M. Endelman, *The Jews of Georgian England 1714–1830: Tradition and Change in a Liberal Society* (Philadelphia, 1979), 31–2; Richard D. Barnett, 'Dr. Samuel Nunes Ribeiro and the Settlement of Georgia', in Aubrey Newman (ed.), *Migration and Settlement: Proceedings of the Anglo-American Jewish Historical Conference Held in London Jointly by the Jewish Historical Society of England and the American Jewish Historical Society, July 1970* (London, 1971), 82–3; Barnett A. Elzas, *The Jews of South Carolina from the Earliest Times to the Present Day* (Philadelphia, 1905), 31–2; Richard D. Barnett, 'The Correspondence of the Mahamad of the Spanish and Portuguese Congregation of London during the Seventeenth and Eighteenth Centuries', *The Jewish Historical Society of England Transactions*, 20 (1959–61), 4, 16).

many scholars the map of early American Jewry continues to be defined by an old historiography, which by now ought to be replaced. We need a new historiography, one that paints a far broader picture of early American Jewish history. I dare to predict that we will indeed have one: first, because of gatherings and conferences devoted to the history of the Jewish people in the Caribbean; second, because many historians of the colonial period of American history have become cognizant of the colonies' position in a broader Atlantic community; and third, most significant perhaps, because of the growing field of global history, which integrates different nations, regions, and civilizations in an all-encompassing approach to their histories, stressing the interchanges and similarities between and among them, rather than the differences that distinguish them. A shift among historians of American Jewish history away from their traditional isolationist perspective to viewing and analysing the settlements in North America, the Caribbean, the eastern Atlantic (the Canaries and Madeira), the north-eastern coast of South America (Suriname), and western Europe as an integrated entity spanning the Atlantic region is a logical extension of the more general development of global history. Perhaps the best examples to date of the latter are studies of the Indian Ocean basin as a central driving force in the history of the last millennium, before the Atlantic emerged to play a similar role, and the fascinating history of central Asia and its links to the east and west along the Silk Road. There is every reason to think of colonial American Jewry in similarly expansive and cosmopolitan terms.

Evidence for the Atlantic-wide context of colonial Jewry comes from the economic, religious, and social histories, especially family histories, of the early American Jewish population. However, before examining examples of such evidence, let us note that the first two North American Jewish communities, New York and Newport, derived from earlier communities in the Caribbean and their need for overseas commercial outlets and trading posts: the fundamental reason for Jewish settlement in the Atlantic world in the first place. I do not include in this the allegedly first permanent Jewish settlement in North America in 1654 in New Amsterdam, as it lasted only a few years, collapsing and disappearing by the early or mid-1660s.[2] In retrospect, it may perhaps best be compared to the ill-fated colony of Roanoke, planted by the English off the coast of North Carolina in the mid-1580s, only to have mysteriously disappeared by 1592. No one counts Roanoke as the first colony in what ultimately became the United States of America; that distinction is reserved for Virginia in 1607. The Jewish presence at New Amsterdam ought to be acknowledged for what it was: a similarly ill-fated effort, with a second attempt at establishing a Jewish presence in New York not occurring for another twenty-five to thirty years in the early 1680s.

[2] Samuel Oppenheim, *The Early History of the Jews in New York, 1654–1664: Some New Matter on the Subject* (New York, 1909), 23, 59–60, 63–4, 67. Oppenheim observed that by 1663 'there is little evidence' for the presence of Jews 'in any numbers' in New Amsterdam. Most of the few who do appear in the records are mentioned once in court documents.

In the interim a Jewish presence arose in Newport, Rhode Island, beginning in 1658, spearheaded most likely by emigrants from Barbados. The latter was England's first colony in the Caribbean, dating from the mid-1620s, and Jews were present there by the 1650s.[3] Establishing themselves primarily as Atlantic merchants and local traders, they no doubt recognized from the start that, in an era that lacked credit agencies, international fairs and expositions, and professional organizations, an extended ethnic and religious network that reached across the Atlantic was of great value for commercial success. Sephardim who resided in London, Amsterdam, Bordeaux, and Hamburg had ties not only with each other but also with New Christians in Spain, Portugal, and the Canaries. The ethno-religious factor in business was not peculiar to Jews: the Huguenots, Quakers, and Scots who settled in the colonies during the seventeenth and eighteenth centuries depended similarly upon one another, though never exclusively.

It was no doubt this cosmopolitan perspective that impelled Jews to migrate from Barbados to Newport, which was destined to become an important seaport and, although much later, the largest single port engaged in the slave trade in the North American colonies. They chose not to go to New Amsterdam and join the small Jewish presence there, probably because merchants on Manhattan Island—Jewish, Dutch, or otherwise—could not break the hold of four major Amsterdam trading firms—all non-Jewish—on commerce in New Netherland.[4] Consequently, the advantages of membership of an Atlantic-wide religious group did not apply in New Amsterdam, and it failed to attract new Jewish immigrants, hastening the demise of the 'Jewish Roanoke'. Newport's Caribbean connections were reinforced thirty-five years later, when in 1693 ninety new Jewish settlers arrived from Curaçao. The newcomers were not driven by commerce but by an epidemic on the island. Again, however, they chose not to go to Manhattan Island, despite the fact that by then a small Jewish presence existed in what was now New York.

The new Jewish community in New York had begun to form in the early 1680s, and this time it was successful, and once again its origins were to a considerable extent in the Caribbean, this time not only in Barbados but also in Jamaica, where Jews had begun to settle in the mid-1660s. Indeed, the first burial in New York's Jewish cemetery, the second-oldest surviving Jewish burial place on the North American mainland, was in 1683, of Benjamin Bueno de Mesquito, a merchant who appears to have come from Jamaica.[5] By 1690 Luis Gomez had arrived from Jamaica and settled in New York, where

---

[3] Ibid. 16–17; Morris A. Gutstein, *The Story of the Jews of Newport: Two and a Half Centuries of Judaism, 1658–1908* (New York, 1936), 28, 340–1.

[4] Oliver A. Rink, *Holland on the Hudson: An Economic and Social History of Dutch New York* (Ithaca, NY, 1986), 175–206, 212–13.

[5] David de Sola Pool, *Portraits Etched in Stone: Early Jewish Settlers, 1682–1831* (New York, 1952), 187–9. The oldest surviving Jewish cemetery, in Newport, dates to 1677 (Gutstein, *Story of the Jews of Newport*, 36–9). The Jews of New Amsterdam established a cemetery during the 1650s, but its location is unknown.

he became one of the fledgling Jewish community's leaders and founder of New York's foremost Sephardi family of the colonial era.[6] What drew men such as these from the Caribbean to New York was the islands' need for North American wheat, corn, meat, and fish, which North American merchants (non-Jewish as well as Jewish) distributed through their co-religious counterparts and connections in Port Royal and Bridgetown, even shipping as far afield as Curaçao and Suriname.

With the passage of time, the prosperity of Newport's and New York's Jewish populations, and later Savannah's, Charleston's, and Philadelphia's, continued to depend to a large extent upon the network that connected Jewish merchants in the mainland colonies with their counterparts in the Caribbean and Suriname, as well as in London, Amsterdam, and the eastern Atlantic, though the latter to a lesser degree. This also meant that the Atlantic-wide network provided an important foundation for the establishment of Jewish religious life and institutions among colonial America's Jews. When, for example, it undertook to build its first permanent synagogue in 1728, New York's congregation wrote to Jamaica's to request funds. It also received donations from individual benefactors in Jamaica and Barbados, in Boston and London, as well as a substantial sum from Curaçao's congregation. Several years later a woman in Barbados supplied the means to construct a wall around the cemetery in New York, a requirement according to Jewish law for burial sites.[7] Newport's congregation received financial assistance to construct and furnish its house of worship (later named the Touro Synagogue) not only from New York but also from the communities in London, Suriname, Jamaica, and Curaçao, while Torah scrolls came from congregations in London and Amsterdam.[8]

The Atlantic connection also provided such religious functionaries as cantors, who not only chanted the synagogue service but also read the Torah on sabbaths and festivals; ritual slaughterers; and teachers, who were recruited not only from London and Amsterdam but also from the Caribbean islands. Isaac Touro, for example, Newport's cantor during the 1760s and 1770s, was born in Amsterdam and came to Rhode Island from the West Indies, where he returned in the wake of the American War of Independence, settling in Jamaica, after having supported the British side in the conflict.[9] In general, the islands were far ahead of the mainland congregations when it

---

[6] De Sola Pool, *Portraits Etched in Stone*, 218–19.

[7] 'The Earliest Extant Minute Books of the Spanish and Portuguese Congregation Shearith Israel in New York (1728–1786)', *Publications of the American Jewish Historical Society*, 21 (1913), 19–24, 37.

[8] Stanley F. Chyet, *Lopez of Newport, Colonial American Merchant Prince* (Detroit, 1970), 54–5; Gutstein, *Story of the Jews of Newport*, 88, 95–7, 105–6.

[9] For Touro, see Gutstein, *Story of the Jews of Newport*, 72, 94, 188–9; Samuel Rezneck, *Unrecognized Patriots: The Jews in the American Revolution* (Westport, Conn., 1975), 17, 137. For an example of a cantor recruited from London, albeit, once in New York, a disgruntled one, see Barnett, 'Correspondence of the Mahamad', 15–16. Cantor Pinto protested to the New York congregation that he had left his 'native place, the great city of Amsterdam, and come to a very populous city, more highly praised and more glorious than all

came to knowledgeable, trained, and authoritative leadership. Curaçao, Jamaica, and Barbados could boast of rabbinic leadership long before the mainland could. The first rabbi did not appear in North America until 1840, whereas Port Royal and Bridgetown had *ḥakhamim* by the beginning of the 1680s and Curaçao in 1674.[10] Curaçao even attempted to assert religious leadership over the mainland colonies, as we may deduce from a letter written by the *ḥakham* of Curaçao to the congregation in New York in 1729, in which he exhorted the New Yorkers to beware of the influence of their Ashkenazi members, who were in the majority. When the Curaçao community sent funds that year to help construct New York's first synagogue, he wrote saying:

I must tell you that the Members of this Holy Congregation Whom devoutly Contributed to Wards this Benefaction, as they know that the (asquenazum) or Germans, are more in Number than Wee there, they desire of you not to Consent, not Withstanding they are the most, to Let them have any More Votes nor Authority then they have had hitherto and for the performance of which you are to Get them to Signe and agreement of the Same by all of them, and that one Copy Of the Sayd agreement Remain in the Hands of Mr. Luis Gomez as the Eldest Member, and Another to be Sent to me for the Treasurer of this Congregation to Keep in his Books; and as this request is funded in Solesiting the Peace and Unety of that Holy Congregation, I hope that you as Well as the Asquinazim, Whom all I wish God may bless Will Comply With this my Petition.[11]

However, the outnumbered Sephardim in New York disregarded the instructions of the Curaçaoan *ḥakham*, and the hostility that generally characterized relations between Sephardim and Ashkenazim in London, Amsterdam, the Caribbean, and Suriname was not allowed to undermine the congregations in the mainland colonies.[12] This is one significant example—but perhaps the only one—of a distinct divergence in the Atlantic Sephardi community.

others, London, where [he] began to find rest for [his] feet', only later to 'come hither [to New York] across the dangerous seas' (Jacques J. Lyons, Naphtali Phillips, and Mordechai M. Noah, 'Items Relating to the Newport Synagogue', *Lyons Collection 2, Publications of the American Jewish Historical Society*, 27 (1920), 15–16). For other instances of recruitment abroad, see 'The Earliest Extant Minute Books', 73, 75, 92. In the latter instance, in 1765, the congregation resolved that 'Notices thereof may be given to Foreign Parts'.

[10] For the first mainland rabbi, see Leon A. Jick, *The Americanization of the Synagogue, 1820–1870* (Hanover, NH, 1976), 70; for Barbados, Jamaica, and Curaçao, see Wilfred S. Samuel, 'A Review of the Jewish Colonists in Barbados in the Year 1680', *The Jewish Historical Society of England Transactions*, 13 (1932–35), 6–7; M. Kayserling, 'The Jews in Jamaica and Daniel Israel Lopez Laguna', *Jewish Quarterly Review*, 12 (1900), 711; Isaac S. Emmanuel and Suzanne A. Emmanuel, *History of the Jews of the Netherlands Antilles*, 2 vols. (Cincinnati, 1970), i. 53–61; Isaac S. Emmanuel, *Precious Stones of the Jews of Curaçao: Curaçaon Jewry, 1656–1957* (New York, 1957), 6, 218.

[11] David de Sola Pool, *The Mill Street Synagogue (1730–1817) of the Congregation Shearith Israel* (New York, 1930), 49.

[12] For conflicts between Sephardim and Ashkenazim in the Atlantic world, see the discussion, with examples, in Eli Faber, *A Time for Planting: The First Migration, 1654–1820* (Baltimore, 1992), 60–2. The only known exception in North America occurred in Georgia in the mid-1730s, but it proved short-lived: the small congregation there had disappeared through emigration by the beginning of the 1740s.

The connections based on a common religion operated both ways. The Jewish inhabitants of North America supplied kosher meat to the Caribbean. Newport merchants exported it to Suriname, Barbados, and Jamaica; Philadelphia supplied it to Barbados and Curaçao; and New York supplied it to Jamaica and Curaçao. Indeed, in 1752 the New York congregation had to deny rumours on both islands that meat from Manhattan was not kosher, forcing the New Yorkers to exercise greater vigilance over their ritual slaughterer.[13]

As well as its impact upon religious life, the cosmopolitan orientation to the Atlantic world also profoundly affected family life. In order to establish and maintain trading connections, colonial Jewish merchants had to travel far and wide, and the extent of their perilous journeys (they often wrote their wills before commencing a voyage) seems nothing short of extraordinary.[14] Their travels between the ports of North America, the Caribbean, London, and Amsterdam were an essential part of their life experiences and educations, and provided them with knowledge of market conditions, familiarity with the produce of other locations, and, perhaps above all else, the contacts that could lead to prosperity. Although it was the men who journeyed, women were also significantly affected, for they played a part, perhaps the central part in some instances, in minding the store and maintaining the business while their husbands and sons were abroad.

In addition to their extensive journeys, colonial Jewish merchants established family representatives as widely as possible in the Atlantic basin. That commercial success was often predicated upon dispersal of the family was an unfortunate fact of life, as one New York mother wrote in 1741 to her son who had been posted permanently to London:

I wish but for the happyness of Seeing you wich I begin to fear I never Shall. . . . I am Sure there is Little porbability of my Goeing to England. If parents would Give themselves Leave to Consider the many Difficulties that attends the bringing up of Children, there would not be such Imoderate Joy att there birtth I dont mean the Care of there infancy thats the Least but its affter they are grown Up . . . for the Cares of giting a Liveing Disperses Them Up and down the world and the Only pleassure wee injoy (and that's intermixt with Anxiety) is to hear they doe well Wich is A pleassure I hope to have.[15]

The importance to commerce of interpersonal connections based upon religion and ethnicity extended to marriage. By joining families residing in distant locations around the Atlantic, marriage solidified commercial networks, rooting them in ties

---

[13] 'The Earliest Extant Minute Books', 77–8.

[14] For wills written on the eve of overseas journeys, see Leo Hershkowitz (ed.), *Wills of Early New York Jews (1704–1799)* (New York, 1967), 8, 33, 44, 65; for examples of extensive travel, see Faber, *Time for Planting*, 42–7.

[15] Abigail Franks to Naphtali Franks (18 Oct. 1741), in *The Lee Max Friedman Collection of American Jewish Colonial Correspondence: Letters of the Franks Family (1733–1748)*, ed. Leo Hershkowitz and Isidore S. Meyer (Waltham, Mass., 1968), 93. Abigail never saw her son again.

deeper than those provided by religion. Admittedly, the limited number of eligible partners in the small North American Jewish communities, together with the commitment to marry within the faith forced families to look beyond their immediate surroundings to the larger domain of the Atlantic, but marriages also bestowed commercial advantages.

The history of New York's Luis Gomez and his family illustrates the far-flung nature of life for Atlantic Jewry. Gomez came originally from Madrid, but had to leave with his father in the 1660s to escape a resurgent Inquisition. He went first to France, then to Jamaica, and then to New York, where he remained permanently. He established a trading post on the Hudson River in 1714, the considerable remains of which are the oldest surviving above-ground building in North America associated with a Jewish settler.[16] Shortly after he arrived in New York, Luis Gomez married a woman with connections in Barbados, where her mother and brother resided. Gomez and his wife had six sons, the eldest of whom perished during a voyage to the Caribbean, probably murdered and cut into quarters by Spaniards in Cuba. Their third son married first a woman whose father and brother lived in Jamaica and later a woman from Curaçao, whose brothers became his commercial correspondents there. The sixth son married a woman in Barbados and, from there, maintained trading ties with his older siblings back in New York. The Gomez family's ties may have extended even more distantly across the Atlantic, for their commercial ledgers list transactions with a Gomez in Madeira.[17]

The third generation of the Gomez family continued in much the same manner. Four of its members married people from Newport, Jamaica, Curaçao, and London. Many more transatlantic marriages like those of the Gomez family could be cited, but suffice it to say that the impulse to marry abroad was common to all Jewish inhabitants in the North American colonies who hoped for commercial success.

In sum, there is ample evidence to support the assertion that colonial America's Jewish settlers owed much to and were deeply affected by their counterparts in the wider Atlantic basin. A thorough rewriting of early American Jewish history that locates it within the context of an ethno-religious world stretching from London and Amsterdam to the North American continent, to the Caribbean, and all the way to Suriname would be highly welcome. This would probably reveal a far greater impact by Jamaica and Barbados not only upon New York, Newport, Charleston, Philadelphia, and Savannah but also upon London. Jamaica, after all, had the largest Jewish population anywhere in the British empire outside London during the eighteenth century,[18]

[16] The Gomez Mill House in Orange County, New York. The cemetery in New York pre-dates it by thirty-two years.

[17] Malcolm Stern, *Americans of Jewish Descent: A Compendium of Genealogy* (Cincinnati, 1960), 46, 63, 133; Faber, *Time for Planting*, 47–8.

[18] Jamaica's Jewish population in Port Royal grew from 75 during 1680 to 'about seven or eight hundred' in 1736, and by 1776 to between 800 and 900 (for 1680, see National Archives, Kew (TNA), Colonial Office (CO) 1/45, 96–107; for 1736, see TNA, CO 137/22, 34; for 1776, see *The North-American and the West-Indian Gazetteer*

and it would be valuable to know more about the impact of that population upon London's Jewish population, not only economically but also through Jamaican Jews who returned to England and settled there permanently.[19] Perhaps the same impact upon Amsterdam would be found for Curaçao and Suriname. Comparisons and contrasts would also be of great interest. I mentioned the difference in relationships between Ashkenazim and Sephardim in the mainland colonies and in the other localities in the Atlantic community. But what about patterns of intermarriage with non-Jews? What about relations with Africans, for example, in manumission and concubinage practices?[20] What about degrees of adherence to religious law and practice? What about political expression, particularly during the era of the American and French Revolutions? And perhaps most elusive of all, what impact did the Spanish and Portuguese backgrounds of many early American Jews, certainly a live issue in the eighteenth-century, have in the Americas?[21]

(London, 1776), s.v. 'Jamaica'). In North America, none of the colonies that hosted the original five Jewish settlements on the mainland came close to the total for Jamaica at the time of the American War of Independence.

[19] Alexandre Lindo, the most successful of Jamaica's Jewish merchants in the late eighteenth century, relocated from Kingston to London, first in the mid-1790s, and then again permanently by 1805 (see Jackie Ranston, *The Lindo Legacy* (London, 2000), 37–42, 45–64; Eli Faber, *Jews, Slaves, and the Slave Trade: Setting the Record Straight* (New York, 1998), 40, 117–21).   [20] See Chapter 12 above.

[21] For most Jews in America during the colonial period this was not an issue, for by 1720 the majority were of Ashkenazi descent, despite the fact that the period between 1654 and 1820 is known as the Sephardi era in American Jewish history.

CHAPTER SIXTEEN

PORT JEWS AND PLANTATION JEWS

Carolina–Caribbean Connections

DALE ROSENGARTEN

W E ARE USED TO THINKING of Charleston, South Carolina, as the southern frontier of British settlement in North America, but to understand the dynamics of colonial expansion and the pattern of Jewish dispersion it may be more fruitful to view the port city as the northernmost outpost of the Caribbean plantation region. Charleston, like most Caribbean ports, served a backcountry dominated by plantations that used slave labour to grow crops for export. Throughout the colonial period and well into the nineteenth century, commercial routes, social ties, and similarities in climate, crops, and labour systems created a network that bound together Jewish families in Carolina and the West Indies.

Carolina has been called 'the colony of a colony', referring to its relationship to Barbados, the 'cultural hearth' of the British West Indies.[1] John Colleton, who, as a royalist in exile in Barbados, had witnessed first-hand the fortunes to be made in sugar, proposed that King Charles II establish a colony between Virginia and Spanish Florida on the American mainland. Chartered in 1663 and successfully settled by 1670, Carolina adopted nine of the eleven parish names used in Barbados and a Barbadian socio-economic model, including plantation slavery, a highly stratified society, and a Creole culture that was part African, part European. Indeed, West Indian influences on the houses, speech, and cuisine of both European and African settlers have been major attractions of Charleston's tourist trade for the last hundred years.

As purveyors of southern staples produced by enslaved Africans, Carolina's Jewish merchants maintained intense relationships—commercial and social—with traders in other port cities along the North American coast as well as across the Atlantic. Enterprising Jews became agents of a global trade in American goods. From the backcountry came deerskins and forest products—pitch, tar, turpentine, and wood for ship building. From plantations came rice, cattle, indigo, and later cotton, to be exchanged for

---

[1] Walter Edgar, *South Carolina: A History* (Columbia, SC, 1998), ch. 3, 'A Colony of a Colony', esp. pp. 36, 38, 40; Richard S. Dunn, 'The English Sugar Islands and the Founding of South Carolina', *South Carolina Historical Magazine*, 72 (1971), 81–93.

imported foodstuffs and a variety of manufactured products, including cloth, thread, lace, hats, shoes, ironware, tools, guns, dishes and pots, soap, candles, and medicines, and the occasional shipload of captives from Africa. Like their contemporaries in other port cities around the Atlantic basin, Charleston's early Jews served as middlemen between the producers and consumers of two worlds.[2] I would argue that their southern sensibilities gave them a special affinity, however, with white settlers in plantation economies similarly dependent on slave labour, such as those of the West Indies and South America. At the same time, their identity as North Americans set them apart from their Caribbean co-religionists and destined them to join in the revolt against the mother country—a momentous struggle with consequences for the rights and liberties that facilitated their movement across the continent.

In recent years, the study of 'port Jews' has captured the interest of historians and encouraged them to explore the influence of geography on settlement patterns and cultural change within a dynamically expanding diaspora. Inspired by the work of David Sorkin and Lois Dubin, a five-year research programme and several international symposia hosted by the universities of Southampton, England, and Cape Town, South Africa, have produced an outpouring of monographs, case studies, and critiques— enough to establish a basis for cross-cultural comparison.[3] Initially, the concept of port Jews focused on the experience of Sephardi merchants as drivers of commerce and harbingers of Jewish modernity in seventeenth- and eighteenth-century Mediterranean and Atlantic ports such as Livorno, Trieste, Bordeaux, Amsterdam, and London.[4] Extending the enquiry to colonial outposts in Asia and the Americas, scholars have raised, in historian Jonathan Sarna's words, 'the tantalizing prospect of a new Jewish history, re-imagined in global or trans-national terms'.[5]

The roles Jews played and the reception they received in Old World ports and New World colonies varied according to the European power in charge and the religious attitudes and economic agendas of non-Jewish settlers. Catholic France officially forbade Jews to settle in its American colonies, though in practice the ban was loosely enforced. Spain and Portugal prohibited Jews from their New World territories but allowed and even encouraged the immigration of New Christians. In contrast, Britain, Denmark, and the Netherlands 'recognized that Jewish merchants could be advanta-

---

[2] Dale Rosengarten, with research assistance from Barbara Karesh Stender and Judith Alexander Weil Shanks, 'Narrative of the Exhibition', in Theodore Rosengarten and Dale Rosengarten (eds.), *A Portion of the People: Three Hundred Years of Southern Jewish Life* (Columbia, SC, 2002), 61.

[3] The proceedings of the symposia were published in David Cesarani (ed.), *Port Jews: Jewish Communities in Cosmopolitan Maritime Trading Centres, 1550–1950* (London, 2002); David Cesarani and Gemma Romain (eds.), *Jews and Port Cities, 1590–1990* (London, 2006); David Cesarani, Tony Kushner, and Milton Shain (eds.), *Place and Displacement in Jewish History and Memory: Zakor v'Makor* (London, 2009); see also C. S. Monaco, 'Port Jews or a People of the Diaspora? A Critique of the Port Jew Concept', *Jewish Social Studies*, NS 15/2 (2009), 137–66.

[4] Lois Dubin, 'Port Jews in the Atlantic World', *Jewish History*, 20 (2006), 117.

[5] Jonathan D. Sarna, 'Port Jews in the Atlantic: Further Thoughts', *Jewish History*, 20 (2006), 213.

geous to imperial trade and selectively provided incentives for Jews to settle in their colonies'.[6] After seizing Brazil from the Portuguese in 1630, for example, the Dutch offered Jews unprecedented toleration and civil rights and in 1720 granted equality to Jews who agreed to settle on the small island of St Eustatius, an important centre of the shipping trade strategically situated in the Lesser Antilles, between the Leeward and Windward Islands, in the midst of Danish, English, French, and Spanish territories.[7]

The British valued Jews as commercial partners because they were experienced traders with international contacts, access to capital, and a willingness to take risks.[8] Nevertheless, within the British empire there were discrepancies in economic and political opportunities for Jewish settlers. 'Why', Sheldon Godfrey and Judith Godfrey ask, 'did Jews of the early period settle in Jamaica, Nevis, New York, Rhode Island, South Carolina, Quebec, Nova Scotia, and Pennsylvania? Why did they avoid Massachusetts, Maine, Maryland, North Carolina, Bermuda, and St. Kitts?'[9] Put another way, why did similar societies, governed by the same colonial laws, vary significantly in their reception of Jews? Why were Jews in South Carolina able to attain civil and political rights with relative ease, whereas Jamaica's Jews were burdened with special taxes, discouraged from entering the retail trade, hindered from holding office by the requirement of Christian oaths, and restricted in the numbers of slaves and indentured servants they could employ? Why did some colonies resist implementing the British Plantation Act of 1740, while others followed Parliament's intentions and allowed Jewish settlers to be naturalized after seven years' residence?

Charles Town (Plate 16.1), as it was called during the period of British rule, would seem to be a likely place to find an eighteenth-century port Jew. The settlement quickly became the South's major port and, after New York, Boston, and Philadelphia, one of the most populous towns in North America. Jews were present from as early as the 1690s and by 1749 were numerous enough to establish a congregation, Kahal Kadosh Beth Elohim. Engaged in trade and cosmopolitan in outlook, the majority of Charleston's early Jewish settlers were of Sephardi descent, though by the mid-eighteenth century Ashkenazim were becoming numerically dominant. Despite palpable tensions, the two groups united in the 1790s to build a synagogue. By 1800 the city's 500 or 600 Jews constituted the largest Jewish community in North America.[10]

---

[6] Sheldon J. Godfrey and Judith C. Godfrey, *Search Out the Land: The Jews and the Growth of Equality in British Colonial America, 1740–1867* (Montreal, 1995), 36.   [7] Ibid. 37.   [8] Ibid., pp. xxii, 52–4.

[9] Ibid., p. xix. By 1712 the provincial colony of Carolina was divided into North and South, although the same proprietors continued to control both. In 1729, after protracted efforts by the British government to buy out seven of the eight Lords Proprietor who still controlled North Carolina, both Carolinas became royal colonies. The province of Maine, originally settled in 1607, was sold to the Massachusetts Bay Colony seventy years later. It became a separate state only in 1820, as part of the Missouri Compromise.

[10] Solomon Breibart, 'Two Jewish Congregations in Charleston, S.C., before 1791: A New Conclusion', *American Jewish History*, 69 (1980), 360–3; James William Hagy, *This Happy Land: The Jews of Colonial and Antebellum Charleston* (Tuscaloosa, 1993), 64–8.

What attracted Jewish settlers to Carolina? Economic opportunity, surely, was the most powerful inducement. Intended to lure migrants from established colonies, especially Barbados, the Fundamental Constitutions of Carolina offered land grants, property rights, titles of honour, naturalized citizenship for aliens, and to every freeholder 'absolute power and authority over his negro slaves'.[11] In addition to these incentives, the constitutions' explicit provisions for religious tolerance, though never ratified, created an environment friendly to Christian dissenters and Jews. Among all the New World destinations available to European Jews, South Carolina was rightly perceived as one of the most tolerant.

Not all historians share this rosy view. Analysing Carolina's role in the 'port Jewish diaspora', Gemma Romain questions the common characterization of Charleston's Jews as 'the pre-eminent American community of the antebellum period, composed of the most educated, refined and prosperous individuals, who were accepted politically and socially into the fabric of white middle class society'.[12] She argues that antisemitic stereotypes emerged at times of crisis and that tolerance of Jews was predicated on their adherence to Charleston's 'strict racial hierarchy'.[13] Scrutinizing relations between Jewish merchants and the non-Jewish planters they serviced, she asks if their mutual dependence engendered respect or contempt. Did the 'noble' lineage of the Sephardim entitle them to a place in 'the "higher" echelons of Charleston society'?[14]

While it is true that South Carolina was not free of anti-Jewish prejudice and also true that Jews rarely reached the highest rungs of society, the degree to which Jewish Carolinians were knit into the social fabric is attested by the frequency of 'mixed' business partnerships, friendships, and even marriages. Moreover, merchants and planters were not such distinct classes as Romain maintains. Whether Jewish or Christian, some merchants became planters, and some planters made their fortunes in trade. The bottom line, as Romain correctly points out, was that in a colony and later a state with a black majority, the ruling elite welcomed white settlers, whether Jews, Quakers, Presbyterians, or French Protestants: only Catholics were discouraged.

The tendencies of port Jews towards Enlightenment ideas and educational reform 'constituted an Atlantic *haskalah*', according to Arthur Kiron.[15] This Jewish Enlightenment did not necessarily 'represent a secularizing trend' or advocate religious reform; indeed, the periodicals published in London, Philadelphia, and Kingston that Kiron cites were a reaction against both Christian proselytizing and Jewish religious reform. In 1820 Beth Elohim's *adjunta* adopted a new constitution that tightened its oligarchical control over the congregation. Chafing under the rule of the old guard and influenced

[11] Edgar, *South Carolina*, 43–4.

[12] Gemma Romain, 'Ethnicity, Identity and "Race": The Port Jews of Nineteenth-Century Charleston', in Cesarani and Romain (eds.), *Jews and Port Cities*, 123. Romain cites Hagy's *This Happy Land* as a leading example of this interpretation.   [13] Ibid. 126, 129.   [14] Ibid. 131.

[15] Arthur Kiron, 'An Atlantic Jewish Republic of Letters?', *Jewish History*, 20 (2006), 171.

by Enlightenment ideals in general, and the American Bill of Rights in particular, a contingent of young, well-educated, largely native-born Jews led what became America's first movement to reform Judaism.[16]

Charleston stands out, then, as an example of a port city with a significant Jewish population that fostered religious reform, if not among the first generation, then among their offspring. Isaac Harby, Abraham Moïse Junior, David Nunes Carvalho, and their followers grew to maturity at a time when Charleston was a commercial hub and cultural capital of Jewish America. It is interesting to note that all three belonged to families with Caribbean connections. Isaac Harby's father, Solomon, had sojourned in Jamaica for three years before sailing to Charleston in 1781 at the age of 21.[17] Abraham Moïse Junior's father came from Saint-Dominque, his mother from St Eustatius. David Carvalho's older brother, Emanuel, was cantor of the Portuguese congregation in Barbados for eight years, before moving to New York and then Charleston in 1811 to become cantor of Beth Elohim, 'the best post on the continent'.[18] Early on Emanuel may have sown seeds of reform when he taught the boys in the choir to sing the concluding psalm in the morning service 'in a very handsome manner which in a measure did away with the discordance which attends every Synagogue'.[19] It was probably during his residence in Charleston that Emanuel brought David to the United States.[20]

In 1824 the young reformers petitioned Beth Elohim's *adjunta* for changes that would produce a 'more rational means of worshipping the true God'.[21] Rebuffed, they founded the Reformed Society of Israelites and began meeting separately at Seyle's Masonic Hall. They shortened the sabbath service and introduced topical sermons, hymns, and prayers, mainly in English. Their prayer books, handwritten by the leaders of the society, contained what historian Michael Meyer described as 'the first radical liturgy produced by the Reform movement anywhere, preceding by twenty years the 1845 prayer book of the Berlin Reform Congregation' (see Plate 16.2).[22]

In 1825, the very year Isaac Harby delivered the first manifesto of Charleston's Reform movement—his *Discourse . . . before the Reformed Society of Israelites*—the city directory devoted a page to a calendar of the Jews' 'Fasts, Festivals, and other days'.

---

[16] Hagy, *This Happy Land*, 83–4, 133–44.

[17] Gary Phillip Zola, *Isaac Harby of Charleston, 1788–1828: Jewish Reformer and Intellectual* (Tuscaloosa, 1994), 5; L. C. Moïse, *Biography of Isaac Harby with an Account of the Reformed Society of Israelites of Charleston, S.C., 1824–1833* (Columbia, SC, 1931), 1.

[18] Jacob Rader Marcus, *United States Jewry, 1776–1985*, 4 vols. (Detroit, 1989), i. 276. For a discussion of Emanuel Nunes Carvalho's career in New York, Charleston, and Philadelphia, where in 1815 he proposed that Mikveh Israel establish a Jewish free school, see Kiron, 'An Atlantic Jewish Republic of Letters?', 186–8.

[19] Mordecai Manuel Noah to Napthali Phillips (10 May 1812); quoted in Hagy, *This Happy Land*, 79–80.

[20] Bertram Wallace Korn, 'Introduction', in Solomon Nunes Carvalho, *Centenary Edition of Incidents of Travel and Adventure in the Far West* (Philadelphia, 1954), 19–20.

[21] Quoted in Deborah Dash Moore, 'Freedom's Fruits: The Americanization of an Old-Time Religion', in Rosengarten and Rosengarten (eds.), *A Portion of the People*, 13.

[22] Michael Meyer, *Response to Modernity: History of the Reform Movement in Judaism* (New York, 1988), 231.

Perhaps intended to let shoppers know when the stores would be closed, the listing attests to the importance of Jewish merchants in the city (see Plate 16.3). Yet in terms of numbers, North America's Jewish communities could not rival Britain's major West Indian ports. While Charleston in the early 1800s boasted a Jewish population of upwards of 500, the Jews of Jamaica have been estimated at nearly 2,000, out of a total free white population of just over 16,000.[23] One out of every eight white people in Jamaica was Jewish, compared to one in twelve in Charleston.

Simon Valentine

South Carolina's 'first permanent Jewish settler', according to historian and genealogist Malcolm Stern, was Simon Valentine, one of four Jewish men who, with sixty French Protestants, petitioned the governor of Carolina, Joseph Blake, for naturalization in 1697.[24] Valentine's roots were probably in Vilna, Lithuania,[25] which would have made him the only Ashkenazi among the four Jews. Before coming to Carolina he had lived in New York and Jamaica. He was mobile, well connected, and litigious, and his name appears again and again in the provincial records. In January 1682 he purchased 'burgher rights' as a 'handy craftsman' in New York.[26] A month later his uncle Asser Levy died suddenly and Valentine was soon embroiled in a legal battle to acquire a portion of Levy's estate.[27]

In 1684 Valentine was party to a law suit in Albany and sometime thereafter moved to Port Royal, Jamaica, at the western end of the sand spit that protects Kingston harbour. When an earthquake struck Port Royal in 1692, destroying the harbour and paralysing commerce, he sailed to Carolina, yet it took some time for him to wrap up his Jamaican interests: on 3 July 1701 he was sued for debts owed to Jacob Mears of Jamaica. By 1696 he had settled in Charleston, where he signed his name as surety on an administrative bond and recorded the sale of a slave. Two years later, Abraham Avilah named Valentine his 'true and lawful attorney'.[28] The petition he signed in 1697

---

[23] Samuel J. Hurwitz and Edith F. Hurwitz, *Jamaica: A Historical Portrait* (New York, 1971), 57. 'The number of Jews in Jamaica, which undoubtedly housed the largest share of the Jews spread through the various Caribbean possessions of the European powers, is really not known with any precision. The estimate of Samuel and Edith Hurwitz that in the early nineteenth century the figure reached nearly 2,000 probably is the best guess available' (Ira Rosenwaike, *On the Edge of Greatness: A Portrait of American Jewry in the Early National Period* (Cincinnati, 1985), 15).

[24] Malcolm H. Stern, 'Charleston's First Jews', *Southern Jewish Historical Society Newsletter* (Oct. 1988), n.p. [4].

[25] Leo Hershkowitz, 'Asser Levy and the Inventories of Early New York Jews' (1990); repr. in Jeffrey S. Gurock (ed.), *American Jewish History*, vol. i: *The Colonial and Early National Periods 1654–1840* (New York, 1998), 239.   [26] Godfrey and Godfrey, *Search Out the Land*, 59.

[27] Malcolm H. Stern, 'Asser Levy: A New Look at Our Jewish Founding Father' (1974); repr. in Gurock (ed.), *American Jewish History*, vol. i: *The Colonial and Early National Periods*, 219–20; Stern, 'Charleston's First Jews', n.p. [3–4].   [28] Hagy, *This Happy Land*, 57, 91.

motivated the colonial assembly to pass 'an Act for the making aliens free of this part of the Province and for granting liberty of conscience to all Protestants'—legislation aimed at Quakers and French Huguenots but broadly interpreted to include Jews.[29] In 1703 he was selected as a commissioner of the town's guard and patrol, 'an unprecedented appointment for a Jew'.[30]

The first documentation of a Jew owning land in South Carolina is Valentine's purchase, in partnership with Mordecai Nathan, of a 350-acre farm, by which the two men met the property qualification to vote. In 1715 Nathan and Valentine were shipping quantities of kosher beef from Charleston[31]—evidence of a network of New World co-religionists and also of Valentine's involvement in one of Carolina's premier frontier industries.

The De Leons

Most settlers of Iberian descent arrived in South Carolina by a circuitous route. The births, marriages, and deaths inscribed in the De Leons's *Biblia Hebraica* trace one of the many paths Sephardim followed from the Old World to the New—in the case of the De Leon family, from Almeria in Spain to the Netherlands to the West Indies to New York to South Carolina.[32]

The De Leons (also spelled DeLeon) became a prominent and far-flung clan, with branches in Amsterdam, London, Hamburg, Barbados, Suriname, St Thomas, and

[29] Ibid. 31. The text of the Act is reprinted in Barnett A. Elzas, *The Jews of South Carolina from Earliest Times to the Present Day* (Philadelphia, 1905), 20–1, app. A; see also Godfrey and Godfrey, *Search Out the Land*, 46; Jacob Rader Marcus, *The Colonial American Jew, 1492–1776*, 3 vols. (Detroit, 1970), i. 463–4. Godfrey and Godfrey concur with Marcus: 'Notwithstanding this wording, there is no evidence to support the conclusion that the Jewish religion was not legally tolerated' (*Search Out the Land*, 256 n. 41). Eighty years after the passing of the Colonial Naturalization Act, in an astonishing reading of South Carolina's constitution of 1778, Reverend Gershom Mendes Seixas of New York's Shearith Israel congregation claimed that the clause restricting office-holding to Protestants 'did not intend that restriction to apply to Jews'. 'A Jew is a Protestant', he wrote to Shearith Israel's cantor, and therefore is entitled to election to all offices (*Search Out the Land*, 119). It would be a mistake, however, to extrapolate a general principle from the symbiosis of Jews and Protestants in South Carolina. In Hamburg in Germany, for example, the arrival of Huguenot merchants from south-western France after the revocation of the Edict of Nantes in 1685 'accelerated the decline of the Jewish community' (Klaus Weber, 'Were Merchants More Tolerant? "Godless Patrons of the Jews" and the Decline of the Sephardi Community in Late Seventeenth-Century Hamburg', in Cesarani and Romain (eds.), *Jews and Port Cities*, 83).

[30] Godfrey and Godfrey, *Search Out the Land*, 51, 59; Marcus, *The Colonial American Jew*, i. 464; Elzas, *The Jews of South Carolina*, 59. [31] Marcus, *The Colonial American Jew*, i. 345.

[32] See Rosengarten with Stender and Shanks, 'Narrative of the Exhibition', 62–3; Perry M. DeLeon, 'Sketch of DeLeon Family' (unpublished memoirs, n.d.), College of Charleston, Special Collections (CCSC), Tobias family papers, MS 1029; Helen Kohn Hennig, 'Edwin DeLeon' (M.A. thesis, University of South Carolina, 1927), 1–2. Perry DeLeon alleged that the family Bible was lost in 'Sherman's raid' on Columbia at the end of the Civil War, and Hennig repeated the claim. The Bible in fact remained in the hands of De Leon descendants until 2007, when it was donated to Special Collections at the College of Charleston Library.

Jamaica. Members of the family were among the earliest Jewish settlers in Jamaica. The De Leons began acquiring land in the 1670s, and during the next decade at least two were naturalized—Jacob de Leon in 1681 and Dr Jacob Rodrigues de Leon in 1684.[33] Nine years later Jacob Rodrigues was appointed, along with other Jewish leaders, to collect a special tax of £700 levied on the Jews. When he died in 1703, he was buried in the Hunt's Bay cemetery under an inscription in Hebrew, Portuguese, and English.[34]

As notable members of Jamaica's Jewish community, the De Leons were frequently involved in contention over what they considered excessive taxation. In 1714 Abraham de Moses de Leon and Moses Mendes Quixano, 'on behalf of themselves and the rest of the Jewish inhabitants of this island', petitioned for relief.[35] Though prevented from holding most offices by the requirement of swearing a Christian oath, Jews were impressed as collectors of the punitive rates and taxes. In May 1735 the minutes of the House of Assembly reported efforts of the commissioners to recover 'considerable sums' from Moses de Leon and Abraham Rezio, 'formerly two of the Constables of the parish of St. Thomas in the Vale'.[36] The commission had more luck retrieving the money from De Leon than from Rezio.

Jacob de Leon, grandfather of the South Carolina settler of the same name, apparently acquired the *Biblia Hebraica* from his father, Abraham Cohen de Leon, and gave it to his son Abraham on 12 May 1736 (see Plate 16.4). On a blank page at the front of the Bible, Abraham noted his own date of birth, 8 May 1702, and recorded the date of his marriage in 1731 in Spanish Town, Jamaica. Beginning with his eldest son, Abraham —named for himself, in the Sephardi custom—he goes on to inscribe the birth of each of his children, ending with the youngest, David, on 19 August 1751, each inscription concluding with the same blessing: 'God Give him Long Life.'

When Abraham de Jacob de Leon's eldest son, Abraham, died at the age of 52 in Spanish Town, his son Jacob Cohen de Leon (1764–1828) (Plate 16.5) duly noted the date of death in the Bible. Three years later, on 4 October 1789, Jacob recorded his marriage in New York to Hannah Hendricks, one of ten surviving children of Eve Ester Gomez and Uriah Hendricks, who had emigrated from Holland in 1755. Hannah's brother Harmon entered the family business in 1785, at the age of 14, and would make a name for himself as a merchant and manufacturer: he operated the first copper-rolling mill in America, supplying, collaborating, and competing with Paul Revere and Robert Fulton, among others.[37] In keeping with the family's wealth and reputation for philan-

[33] Jacob Andrade, *A Record of the Jews in Jamaica from the English Conquest to the Present Time* (Kingston, Jamaica, 1941), 136 *et passim*.

[34] Henry P. Silverman, 'The Hunt's Bay Jewish Cemetery, Kingston, Jamaica, British West Indies', *Publications of the American Jewish Historical Society*, 37 (1947), 332.

[35] George Fortunatus Judah, 'The Jews' Tribute in Jamaica, Extracted from the Journals of the House of Assembly', *Publications of the American Jewish Historical Society*, 18 (1909), 153.   [36] Ibid. 156–7.

[37] Maxwell Whiteman, *Copper for America: The Hendricks Family and a National Industry, 1755–1939* (New Brunswick, 1971), 4.

thropy, the Hendrickses were admitted to New York's most prestigious clubs, including the St Nicholas Society, the Union Club, the Union League Club, the Jockey Club, the New York Yacht Club, the Vaudeville Club, the Engineers Club, and the Fulton Club.[38]

Over two generations the Hendrickses had established themselves in the shipping trade, specializing in ironmongery, cutlery, and importing copper in all forms to be turned into sheathing for the hulls of ships. The De Leons were among their trading partners in the West Indies,[39] and, through the union of Jacob and Hannah, two successful New World families strengthened ties between distant outposts of the Atlantic commercial system. The couple may have returned to Jamaica for a short time after their wedding, but their first child, Abraham, was born in Philadelphia in 1790. Between 1791 and 1796 the De Leons travelled between New York, where Jacob's best customer was his father-in-law, Uriah Hendricks, and Kingston, where he introduced his brother-in-law Harmon to the island trade.[40]

The connection paid off for young Hendricks. His first shipload of goods to Kingston and Spanish Town found a ready market. He soon followed with deliveries of 'hickory canes, hair ribbons, umbrellas, watches, cheap jewelry, and barrels of New England onions, flour, or apples' in exchange for 'such produce as coffee, quince pears, pimento, Jamaica ginger, Spanish segars, and puncheons of castor oil'. Cayenne pepper, he discovered, was a 'trifling article', while rum and 'old metal' brought 'a good profit'.[41] Harmon returned the Jamaicans' hospitality when the West Indian merchants visited the Hendrickses' household in New York in 1795. 'He became so enamored of the island trade', reports historian Maxwell Whiteman, 'that he confided to [David P.] Mendez [of Kingston] his desire to settle in Jamaica for a period of four to five years'.[42]

For Jacob de Leon neither Kingston nor New York 'seemed to suit his needs or enhance his abilities. . . . Hannah became ill, business was poor, Jamaica was about to erupt in a series of slave revolts'.[43] To allay her father's worries, the dutiful daughter spiced her letters with gossip about island pedlars and sent an occasional gift of marmalade. By 1799 Hannah was writing from Charleston.[44] Jacob promptly joined Beth Elohim congregation, paid his dues, and on occasion was fined for not attending the general meeting.[45] The 1801 Charleston directory lists him as a vendue master, or auctioneer, with a dwelling house on Tradd Street. In 1802, still living on Tradd Street, he was doing business on Exchange Square. Though not a fully fledged agent of his brother-in-law, De Leon continued to purchase copper on behalf of Harmon, with 'a blanket order for old copper, scrap copper from ships, and new or old brass cannon' to supply the company's new foundry 'that could reconvert old and scrap copper'.[46]

[38] Ibid. 218, 293.   [39] Ibid. 31.   [40] Ibid. 35.   [41] Ibid. 36, 246.
[42] Ibid. 41.   [43] Ibid. 33.   [44] Ibid. 245–6.
[45] Cash book (1800–10), 5; ledger: member offerings and fines (1807), 15; petty ledger: member offerings and fines (1808–9, 1813), 21, CCSC, Kahal Kadosh Beth Elohim congregational records, MS 1047.
[46] Whiteman, *Copper for America*, 55.

Hendricks also relied on southern merchants to supply plantation crops—tobacco, cotton, corn, and molasses—to exchange for English goods. He 'had established good business connections with the brokers, commission merchants, and planters, who were as numerous in the South as his range of metal customers in the North'.[47] Between 1804 and 1806 Jacob de Leon provided Hendricks with tobacco and bales of upland cotton. To avoid reshipment from New York, Hendricks had his brother-in-law 'ship the cotton directly to England from South Carolina: 220 bales to Bristol, 250 bales to London, and 180 bales to Liverpool'. Harmon had a voracious appetite for the products of southern agriculture but no taste for the slave trade. De Leon's offer of '$70,000 in "Black Birds" [captives from the west coast of Africa] left him cold'. Likewise, another supplier's 'boastful account of a cargo of 700 Africans who had been "packaged" in three vessels' discomfited him. 'Although he handled the bills of exchange, [he] thereafter discontinued handling similar bills.'[48]

While coastal and inland commerce expanded, American trade with the West Indies waned as a consequence of slave revolts on the islands and war between France and England. Hendricks' Jamaican trading partners 'either set sail for the American mainland or else returned to England or Holland'. Harmon tried to help out the newcomers, though 'he sensed their discontent with the new environment and their failure to adapt to the brisk manner of a growing nation'. When a cousin from London, Mordecai Gomez Wagg, who came with a flair for manners but little aptitude for business, stumbled in New York, Harmon sent him to the De Leons in Charleston.[49]

The business correspondence between Hendricks and De Leon was intermingled with family news. Reports on cotton bales and hogsheads of tobacco were juxtaposed with a 'glowing account' of the barmitzvah of Jacob's son Mordecai, who 'acquitted himself with credit to himself and much satisfaction to me and his mother'.[50] By 1806 the De Leon household, now including eight children, had moved to South New Street. Four years later they were back on Tradd Street. Their eldest sons, Abraham and Mordecai, were listed at the same address, with Abraham running a medical store at 246 King Street. In 1810, while Mordecai was studying medicine in Philadelphia, he visited his New York cousins. Harmon Hendricks enjoyed seeing his nephew, but unlike Mordecai's parents, he 'had no desire to encourage his sons to enter the medical profession'. Rather, he was intent on steering them towards the copper trade.[51]

By the early 1820s the De Leons, following their sons, had left Charleston and settled in the South Carolina midlands.[52] Abraham, 'late of the Hospital Dept. of the U. S. Army', had hung out his shingle in Camden in 1816, a year after marrying Bilha

---

[47] Whiteman, *Copper for America*, 57–8, 253.   [48] Ibid. 58.   [49] Ibid. 69–70.

[50] Quoted ibid. 71, 257–8.   [51] Ibid. 104.

[52] At the time of Jacob's death in 1828 at the age of 64, his estate was described in the *Columbia Telescope* as 'four miles from Columbia, containing 100 acres more or less, with dwelling House, Out Houses, and every convenience for such an establishment' (Belinda Gergel and Richard Gergel, *In Pursuit of the Tree of Life: A History of the Early Jews of Columbia and the Tree of Life Congregation* (Columbia, SC, 1996), 9).

(Isabella or Isabel) Nones of Philadelphia.[53] Doctor De Leon's social standing was dramatically demonstrated in 1825 when General Marquis de Lafayette came to Camden to attend the laying of cornerstones for a monument to General Baron DeKalb, hero of the American War of Independence. At the ceremony welcoming Lafayette, so the story goes, De Leon—then Worshipful Master of Masonic Kershaw Lodge number 29—greeted the general in French, inspiring him to remove the Grand Master's Jewel of France from his neck and place it on 'brother' De Leon's, as a keepsake of the event.[54]

Mordecai Hendricks de Leon ran a pharmacy and general merchandise store in Camden and in 1822 returned to Charleston, where he worked briefly as an auctioneer and commission merchant. Soon after, he established himself in Columbia, where he built up a lucrative medical practice and operated a small hospital which included 'six wards for Negroes'. In 1833 Mordecai was elected Columbia's intendant, or mayor, for the first of three straight terms. Like his good friend Thomas Cooper, president of South Carolina College, Mordecai was an ardent 'nullifier', believing in a state's right to annul federal law. Both Mordecai and his wife, Rebecca Lopez de Leon, were active in civic affairs. From 1841 to 1849 he served as regent of the Columbia Lunatic Asylum; Rebecca headed Columbia's newly organized Ladies Benevolent Society, which drew its members from the capital's social elite.[55]

Among Jacob and Hannah de Leon's sons and grandsons, two served the Confederacy in civilian capacities and eight in the army or navy. Of those eight, four died in the War Between the States, as the American Civil War is still widely known in the South.[56] Mordecai and Rebecca de Leon's eldest son, David Camden, briefly held the post of assistant surgeon general. David had earned the nickname 'the fighting doctor' while serving in the US army in the Mexican War in the 1840s. 'I have loved my country', he remarked, 'I have fought under its flag and every star and stripe is dear to me.'[57] But when the time came to choose sides, he offered his services to the Confederate States of America. After the war, he went to Mexico and then to New Mexico, never to return to his home state.[58]

[53] Malcolm H. Stern, *First American Jewish Families, 1654–1977* (Cincinnati, 1978), 55, 233; also available at <http://www.americanjewisharchives.org/FAJF/intro.php>.

[54] Lafayette, a Frenchman, and DeKalb, a German, were among a dozen Europeans who came to America in 1777 to fight for the Patriots. DeKalb was wounded in the Battle of Camden and died two days later ('The Lafayette Jewel', *First Masonic District of South Carolina: Welcome to the Albert G. Mackey Library and Museum* (pamphlet, n.d.), n.p. [10–11]; Hennig, 'Edwin DeLeon', 2–3; see also Elzas, *The Jews of South Carolina*, 95–7 n. 43).

[55] Profiles of the De Leons here and below are drawn from Gergel and Gergel, *In Pursuit of the Tree of Life*, 8–11, 13, 21, 24, 26, 31–5; see also Rosengarten with Stender and Shanks, 'Narrative of the Exhibition', 116–17; Hennig, 'Edwin DeLeon', ch. 1.

[56] Perry M. DeLeon, 'Military Record of the DeLeon Family and of Captain Perry M. DeLeon', *Publications of the American Jewish Historical Society*, 1 (1961), 332.

[57] Quoted in Robert N. Rosen, *The Jewish Confederates* (Columbia, SC, 2000), 39.

[58] See Elzas, *The Jews of South Carolina*, 271–3.

David's younger brother, Edwin, was appointed by Jefferson Davis as Confederate propagandist in Europe but lost the post by antagonizing Confederate Secretary of State Judah Benjamin and his chosen candidate, John Slidell.[59] Thus, Edwin de Leon and Benjamin, two Jewish men of West Indian origins (Benjamin was most probably born on St Croix, although St Thomas is also a possibility), both married to Catholics, served in Davis's inner circle and came to loggerheads over the Confederacy's effort to win support from England and France.

The De Leons' third son, Thomas Cooper, served as a clerk in the Confederate navy and afterwards wrote two best-sellers, *Four Years in Rebel Capitals* and *Belles, Beaux, and Brains of the '60s*.[60] In 1870 he wrote a burlesque called *Hamlet ye dismal Prince*, the first American play to run for more than a hundred performances on Broadway.[61] As adults, all three brothers lapsed in their faith. To paraphrase historian Jacob Rader Marcus, after three generations in America, the De Leons proved to be more southern than Jewish.

The Moïses

Another West Indian family that took advantage of South Carolina's expanding economy and assurances of religious liberty were the Moïses, who settled in Charleston about the same time as the De Leons. Unlike the De Leons, they came under duress. Abraham Moïse (1736–1809) had been born in Strasbourg and immigrated to Saint-Dominque, then under French rule, where he established himself in trade. In St Eustatius, a commercial hub of the West Indies, he met and married Sarah, the daughter of a Jewish family whose name has been lost. She was twenty-six years younger than him. They were living on a plantation in north-western Saint-Dominque near the port of Cap Français with their four small sons when the Haitian Revolution (1791–1803) broke out. They fled to Charleston, along with hundreds of other French-speaking refugees.[62] According to family historian Harold Moïse, the couple was warned of the coming danger by a loyal servant, who later, under the name General Moïse, played 'a conspicuous part in the revolution'.[63] Escaping with a small trunk of valuables, the

[59] Charles P. Cullop, 'Edwin De Leon, Jefferson Davis' Propagandist', *Civil War History*, 8/4 (1962), 386–400.

[60] Rosen, *The Jewish Confederates*, 139; DeLeon, 'Military Record of the DeLeon Family', 332.

[61] Thomas McAdory Owen, *History of Alabama and Dictionary of Alabama Biography* (Chicago, 1921), iii. 477; Gergel and Gergel, *In Pursuit of the Tree of Life*, 35.

[62] Winston Chandler Babb, 'French Refugees from Saint Domingue to the Southern United States: 1791–1810' (Ph.D. thesis, University of Virginia, 1954), 380.

[63] Harold Moïse, *The Moïse Family of South Carolina* (Columbia, SC, 1961), 1–2. Harry Simonhoff repeats Moïse's claim: 'The faithful black ringleader of the rescue party subsequently became General Moise and distinguished himself in the revolution that established a Negro Republic of Haiti' (*Jewish Notables in America, 1776–1865: Links of an Endless Chain* (New York, 1956), 251). The implication that Abraham and Sarah's slave became the well-known rebel leader 'General Moïse' (or General Moyse, to use the spelling on his letterhead stationery) has not been substantiated. The famous general was born on the Breda estate at Haut du Cap in

Plate 16.1 *An Exact Prospect of Charles Town, the Metropolis of the Province of South Carolina* (9 June 1739). Engraving with watercolour. Original painting by Bishop Roberts; engraved by William Henry Toms (London Magazine, 31 (1762))

Collection of Robert N. Rosen

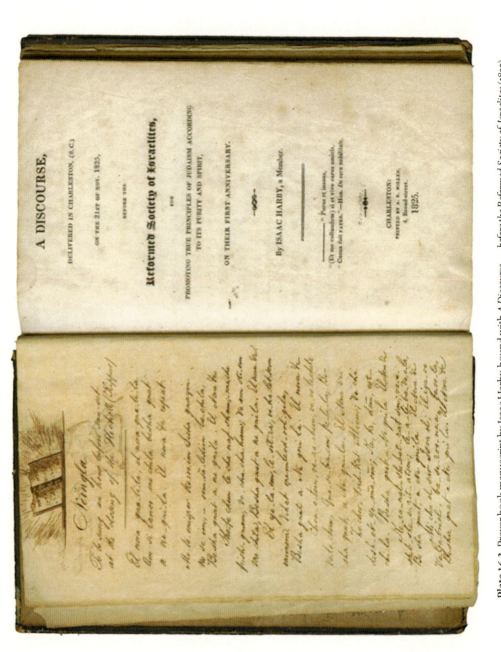

Plate 16.2 Prayer book manuscript by Isaac Harby, bound with *A Discourse . . . before the Reformed Society of Israelites* (1825)

Temple Sinai Archives, College of Charleston, Special Collections

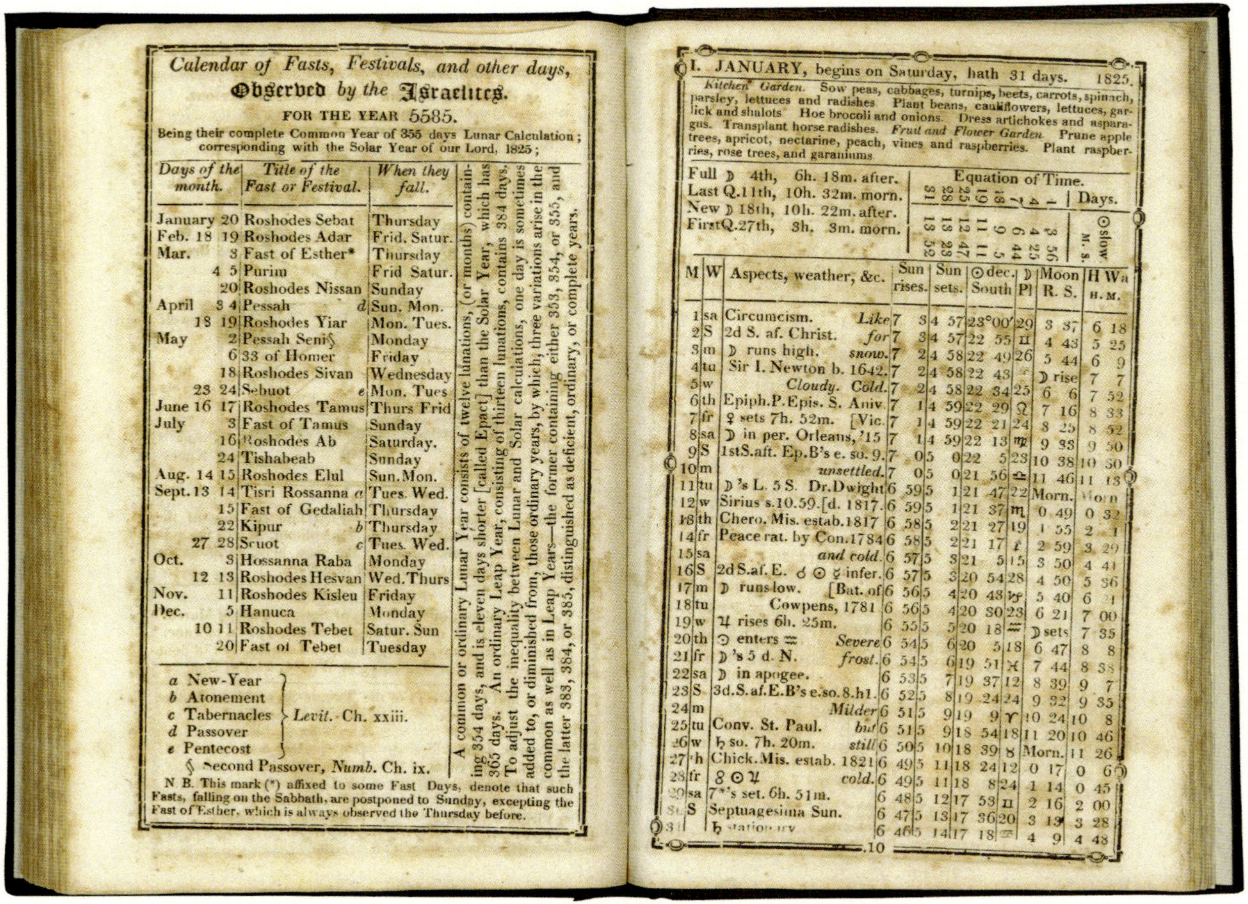

Calendar of Fasts, Festivals, and other days,
Observed by the Israelites.
FOR THE YEAR 5585.
Being their complete Common Year of 355 days Lunar Calculation; corresponding with the Solar Year of our Lord, 1825;

Days of the month.		Title of the Fast or Festival.	When they fall.
January	20	Roshodes Sebat	Thursday
Feb. 18	19	Roshodes Adar	Frid. Satur.
Mar.	3	Fast of Esther*	Thursday
4	5	Purim	Frid Satur.
	20	Roshodes Nissan	Sunday
April 3	4	Pessah *d*	Sun. Mon.
18	19	Roshodes Yiar	Mon. Tues.
May	2	Pessah Seni§	Monday
	6	33 of Homer	Friday
	18	Roshodes Sivan	Wednesday
23	24	Sebuot *e*	Mon. Tues
June 16	17	Roshodes Tamus	Thurs Frid
July	3	Fast of Tamus	Sunday
	16	Roshodes Ab	Saturday.
	24	Tishabeab	Sunday
Aug. 14	15	Roshodes Elul	Sun. Mon.
Sept. 13	14	Tisri Rossanna *a*	Tues. Wed.
	15	Fast of Gedaliah	Thursday
	22	Kipur *b*	Thursday
27	28	Scuot *c*	Tues. Wed.
Oct.	3	Hossanna Raba	Monday
12	13	Roshodes Hesvan	Wed. Thurs
Nov.	11	Roshodes Kisleu	Friday
Dec.	5	Hanuca	Monday
10	11	Roshodes Tebet	Satur. Sun
	20	Fast of Tebet	Tuesday

a New-Year
b Atonement
c Tabernacles } *Levit.* Ch. xxiii.
d Passover
e Pentecost
§ Second Passover, *Numb.* Ch. ix.

N. B. This mark (*) affixed to some Fast Days, denote that such Fasts, falling on the Sabbath, are postponed to Sunday, excepting the Fast of Esther, which is always observed the Thursday before.

A common or ordinary Lunar Year consists of twelve lunations, (or months) containing 354 days, and is eleven days shorter [called Epact] than the Solar Year, which has 365 days. An ordinary Leap Year, consisting of thirteen lunations, contains 384 days. To adjust the inequality between Lunar and Solar calculations, one day is sometimes added to, or diminished from, those ordinary years, by which, three variations arise in the common as well as in Leap Years—the former containing either 353, 354, or 355, and the latter 383, 384, or 385, distinguished as deficient, ordinary, or complete years.

I. JANUARY, begins on Saturday, hath 31 days. 1825.

Kitchen Garden. Sow peas, cabbages, turnips, beets, carrots, spinach, parsley, lettuces and radishes. Plant beans, cauliflowers, lettuces, garlick and shalots. Hoe brocoli and onions. Dress artichokes and asparagus. Transplant horse radishes. *Fruit and Flower Garden.* Prune apple trees, apricot, nectarine, peach, vines and raspberries. Plant raspberries, rose trees, and garaniums.

Full ☽ 4th, 6h. 18m. after.
Last Q. 11th, 10h. 32m. morn.
New ☽ 18th, 10h. 22m. after.
FirstQ. 27th, 3h. 3m. morn.

Equation of Time. Days.	☉ slow. M. S.
1	3 56
4	4 25
7	6 44
13	9 5
19	11 11
25	12 47
28	13 23
31	13 52

M	W	Aspects, weather, &c.	Sun rises.	Sun sets.	☉ dec. South	☽ Pl	Moon R. S.	H Wa H. M.
1	sa	Circumcism. *Like*	7 3	4 57	23°00′	29	3 37	6 18
2	S	2d S. af. Christ. *for*	7 3	4 57	22 55	♊	4 43	5 25
3	m	☽ runs high. *snow.*	7 2	4 58	22 49	26	5 44	6 9
4	tu	Sir I. Newton b. 1642.	7 2	4 58	22 43	♋	☽ rise	7 7
5	w	*Cloudy. Cold.*	7 2	4 58	22 34	25	6 6	7 52
6	th	Epiph. P. Epis. S. Aniv.	7 1	4 59	22 29	♌	7 16	8 33
7	fr	♀ sets 7h. 52m. [Vic.	7 1	4 59	22 21	24	8 25	8 52
8	sa	☽ in per. Orleans, '15	7 1	4 59	22 13	♍	9 33	9 50
9	S	1st S. aft. Ep. B's e. so. 9.	7 0	5 0	22 5	23	10 38	10 30
10	m	*unsettled.*	7 0	5 0	21 56	♎	11 46	11 13
11	tu	☽'s L. 5 S. Dr. Dwight	6 59	5 1	21 47	22	Morn.	Morn
12	w	Sirius s. 10. 59. [d. 1817.	6 59	5 1	21 37	♏	0 49	0 32
13	th	Chero. Mis. estab. 1817	6 58	5 2	21 27	19	1 55	2 1
14	fr	Peace rat. by Con. 1784	6 58	5 2	21 17	♐	2 59	3 29
15	sa	*and cold.*	6 57	5 3	21 5	15	3 50	4 41
16	S	2d S. af. E. ☌ ☉ ☿ infer.	6 57	5 3	20 54	28	4 50	5 36
17	m	☽ runs low. [Bat. of	6 56	5 4	20 48	♑	5 40	6 [illegible]
18	tu	Cowpens, 1781	6 56	5 4	20 30	23	6 21	7 00
19	w	♃ rises 6h. 25m.	6 55	5 5	20 18	♒	☽ sets	7 35
20	th	☉ enters ♒ *Severe*	6 54	5 6	20 5	18	6 47	8 8
21	fr	☽'s 5 d. N. *frost.*	6 54	5 6	19 51	♓	7 44	8 38
22	sa	☽ in apogee.	6 53	5 7	19 37	12	8 39	9 7
23	S	3d. S. af. E. B's e. so. 8. h1.	6 52	5 8	19 24	24	9 32	9 35
24	m	*Milder*	6 51	5 9	19 9	♈	10 24	10 8
25	tu	Conv. St. Paul. *but*	6 51	5 9	18 54	18	11 20	10 46
26	w	♄ so. 7h. 20m. *still*	6 50	5 10	18 39	♉	Morn.	11 26
27	th	Chick. Mis. estab. 1821	6 49	5 11	18 24	12	0 17	0 6
28	fr	☍ ☉ ♃ *cold.*	6 49	5 11	18 8	24	1 14	0 45
29	sa	7*'s set. 6h. 51m.	6 48	5 12	17 53	♊	2 16	2 00
30	S	Septuagesima Sun.	6 47	5 13	17 36	20	3 13	3 28
31		♄ stationary	6 46	5 14	17 18	♋	4 9	4 48

10

Plate 16.3 'Calendar of Fasts, Festivals, and other days, Observed by the Israelites. For the year 5585', *Directory and Stranger's Guide for the City of Charleston; Also . . . An Almanac for the Year of our Lord 1825 . . .* (Charleston, SC, 1824)

College of Charleston, Special Collections

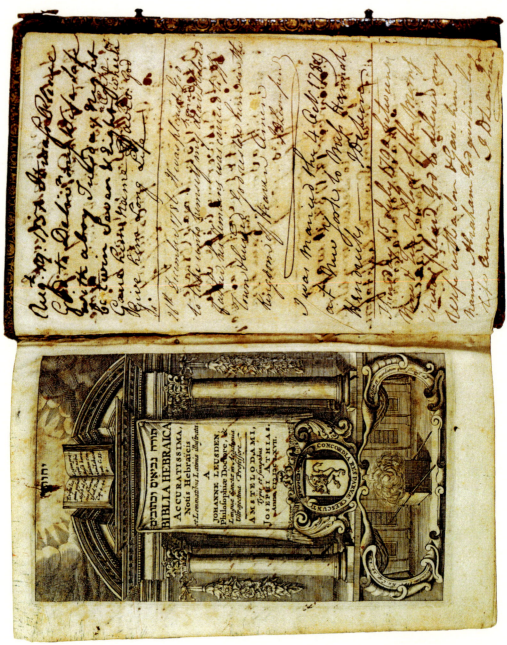

Plate 16.4 *Biblia Hebraica* (Amsterdam, 1667)

Gift of I. Harby and Harriet C. Moses; College of Charleston, Special Collections

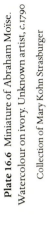

Plate 16.6 Miniature of Abraham Moïse.
Watercolour on ivory. Unknown artist, c.1790
Collection of Mary Kohn Strasburger

Plate 16.5 Miniature of Jacob de Leon.
Oil on ivory. John Ramage, 1789
American Jewish Historical Society

Plate 16.7 Portrait of Rebecca Isaiah Moses, née Phillips. Oil on canvas. C. W. Uhl, 1843

Collection of Judith Alexander Weil Shanks

Plate 16.8 Portrait of Isaiah Moses. Oil on canvas. Theodore Sidney Moïse, *c.*1835

Collection of Cecil A. Alexander

Plate 16.9 Portrait of Isabel Rebecca Lyons Mordecai. Oil on canvas. Theodore Sidney Moïse, *c.*1835

Estate of Judith Tobias Siegel

Moïses took care to pack the miniature portrait of Abraham pictured here, mounted in gold and engraved with the family monogram on the back (Plate 16.6).

In Charleston the Moïses made their living selling cloth and tea from their house on Queen Street. They never regained their wealth and prestige, but what they lacked in material assets they made up for in progeny. After her arrival in Charleston at the age of 29, Sarah bore five more children: remarkably, in an era of high infant mortality, all nine of her offspring lived to maturity. Among them perhaps the best known is the poet, hymnist, and school teacher Penina Moïse.[64] The Moïses' eighth child, Abraham Junior, was one of the founders of the Reformed Society of Israelites. Heir-apparent and biographer of his mentor, Isaac Harby, Abraham helped publish the first Reform prayer book in America and the nation's first Jewish hymnal, containing many of his sister's compositions.[65]

While the Moïses who fled Saint-Dominque described themselves as 'unfortunate sufferers from the Cape',[66] within two generations their grandchildren had married into the upper classes of southern Jewish society. In 1851, for example, Caroline Agnes Moïse, Abraham Junior's eldest daughter and the namesake of her mother, married Harmon Hendricks de Leon, son of Abraham and Rebecca de Leon and namesake of his great-uncle Harmon Hendricks.

Carolina's Jewish gentry were not all ardent secessionists, fearing perhaps that war would be bad for business, but once the South seceded they supported the Confederate cause with enthusiasm. Caroline and Abraham Moïse Junior's son Edwin Warren Moïse was a case in point. Born in Charleston in 1832, he started working as a clerk for a wholesale grocery at the age of 14 before beginning a small mercantile business of his own. In 1854 he married Esther Lyon of Petersburg, Virginia. The couple moved to Columbus, Georgia, where he operated the flour mill on the plantation of his uncle Raphael J. Moses and studied law in Moses's office. At the onset of hostilities Moïse assembled a company of irregular cavalry, officially named the Moïse Rangers, and rose to the rank of major and then commander of the regiment that became Company A of the 7th Confederate Cavalry. He fought in Virginia and North Carolina, and in 1864 led

the central North Province and lived there as a slave until the revolution. Toussaint Louverture adopted him as a nephew (he was probably Louverture's wife's nephew), and relied on him as a commander until 1801, when the general sided with rebellious black farmworkers and Louverture had him arrested, tried, and executed (David P. Geggus, personal communication (28 June, 1 July 2012)). For a brief account of the uprising that cost General Moïse his life, see Jeremy D. Popkin, *A Concise History of the Haitian Revolution* (Chichester, 2012), 112–3.

[64] Solomon Breibart, 'Penina Moïse, Southern Jewish Poetess', in Samuel Proctor and Louis Schmier with Malcolm Stern (eds.), *Jews of the South: Selected Essays from the Southern Jewish Historical Society* (Macon, Ga., 1984), 31–43; repr. in Solomon Breibart, *Explorations in Charleston's Jewish History* (Charleston, 2005), 39–50; see also Rosengarten with Stender and Shanks, 'Narrative of the Exhibition', 95–6.

[65] For admiring profiles of Abraham Moïse and his older sister Penina, see Moïse, *The Moïse Family of South Carolina*, 75–80, 61–9.   [66] *South Carolina State Gazette and Daily Advertiser* (28 Apr. 1795), quoted ibid, 2–3.

the advance guard for Major General Wade Hampton's forces in a battle that became known as the 'Great Beefsteak Raid'. After the war, Moïse practised law in Sumter, South Carolina, and worked as an editor for the local press. In the violent struggle to return the state to 'white rule', he supported Hampton and his paramilitary Red Shirts and was elected Hampton's adjutant general in the riotous 1876 election.[67] To this day Edwin Moïse is regarded as a hero by members of the family, who refer to him as 'the General'.[68]

Rebecca and Isaiah Moses

While usually associated with ports and accustomed to buying and selling, southern Jewish merchants took advantage of new opportunities, as upcountry traders, professionals, or property owners and producers of staple crops. The odyssey of Rebecca Isaiah Moses, née Phillips (1792–1872), exemplifies the permeable border between port and plantation and the peripatetic lifestyle of Caribbean and Carolinian Jews (see Plate 16.7). Rebecca was born in 1792, possibly on board her father's cargo ship en route to St Eustatius, but more likely in Martinique, as she herself claimed to have been 'born under the French flag'.[69] For five generations, Rebecca's forebears had lived or sojourned in New York, Newport, Curaçao, London, Martinique, and Jamaica. Her great-grandfather, Abraham Isaacks, was an early *parnas* of New York's Shearith Israel congregation.

Some time before 1790, Rebecca's parents acquired a plantation in the South Carolina upcountry, near a vast tract belonging to the Salvador family. Like Francis Salvador, the first Jewish casualty of the American War of Independence, Rebecca's father, Jacob Phillips, served in the Patriot militia. He had made his way to South Carolina from St Eustatius when the island's Jews were forcibly removed by the British, who had seized the Dutch port in an effort to halt its trade with the American rebels.[70] Rebecca, the Phillipses' fourth child, was not quite 6 years old when her mother died in Martinique, and only 15 in 1807, when she married 35-year-old Isaiah Moses (1772–1857), a widower who had been born in the German Kingdom of Hanover (see Plate 16.8). Moses had resided in London, where he married his first wife and fathered four sons,

[67] Moïse, *The Moïse Family of South Carolina*, 108–26; Rosengarten with Stender and Shanks, 'Narrative of the Exhibition', 138–9.

[68] Interview with Virginia Moïse Rosefield, Sumter, SC (9 Feb. 1995), CCSC, Jewish Heritage Collection Oral History Archives, MS 1035-007.

[69] See Judith Alexander Weil Shanks, *Old Family Things: An Affectionate Look Back*, ch. 1, 'Rebecca Moses (1792–1872): The Shape of a Life', available at <http://judithwshanks.com/old_family_things/RIMbook_CH1_8MAR10b.pdf>.

[70] J. Franklin Jameson, 'St. Eustatius in the American Revolution', *American Historical Review*, 8/4 (1903), 705 *et passim*; Barbara W. Tuchman, *The First Salute* (New York, 1988), 97; Shanks, *Old Family Things*, 4.

before moving to South Carolina with his brother Levi sometime before 1800. After her early marriage, Rebecca lived with Isaiah in Charleston, bore twelve children, and worked in his store on King Street. Between 1801 and 1819 Isaiah's occupation, as described in the city directory, progressed from 'grocer' to 'shopkeeper' to 'planter'. Seven years after marrying Rebecca, he bought a plantation on Goose Creek, seventeen miles from Charleston. Named The Oaks for the stately avenue of live oaks that led to the big house, the property was originally settled in 1678 by the younger sons of the Barbadian branch of the Middleton family.[71] Moses paid $6,000 for 794 acres and put as many as thirty-five 'hands' to work cultivating the grain known as 'Carolina gold' on some 60 acres of rice fields. The plantation also functioned as a timber farm and brick factory. For some if not all of the two decades they owned The Oaks, the Moses family maintained a house and business in town. In 1837, while still a plantation mistress, Rebecca Moses appears in Charleston's directory as proprietor of a dry-goods store at 248 King Street.

The Oaks served as collateral on several occasions, notably during the Panic of 1837 when Isaiah borrowed money from Beth Elohim's charity fund. The plantation house burned down in 1840, the same year the congregation split between reformers and traditionalists. In 1841 Moses, who sided with the traditionalists, sold the property for $3,750, over $2,000 less than he had for it paid, to satisfy his debt to Beth Elohim. Very possibly he sold off some of his slaves as well.[72]

The Mordecais

Shipping proved a surer route to success than planting. Moses Cohen Mordecai, Charleston's most prominent Jewish citizen of his day, made a fortune as an importer of West Indian commodities such as fruit, sugar, tobacco, and coffee. Mordecai regarded slaves as legitimate objects of commerce and owned a work force of as many as fourteen enslaved people at one time. In 1834, acting as agent for the brig *Encomium*, he shipped a cargo of slaves from Charleston to New Orleans. Though the weather was clear and the captain was on deck, the brig ran aground one night in the Bahamas. Mordecai claimed the captain 'did not care a damn for the slaves' and blamed him for the disaster. Britain had just abolished slavery in its territories, and the Bahamian authorities seized and liberated the captives. Seven of them made their way back to Charleston, where they were returned to their owner who then sued Mordecai for repayment of his commission.[73]

---

[71] Dunn, 'The English Sugar Islands', 85.

[72] For additional information about the Moses family, based on documentation in the Jewish Heritage Collection's vertical files, CCSC, see Rosengarten with Stender and Shanks, 'Narrative of the Exhibition', 100–6; Henry Aaron Alexander, *Notes on the Alexander Family of South Carolina and Georgia, and Connections* (Atlanta, Ga., 1954), 50–69.   [73] Hagy, *This Happy Land*, 94.

Mordecai's flagship, *The Isabel*, was reportedly christened 'in compliment to the reigning queen of Spain',[74] though it seems more likely that it was named after his wife, Isabel Rebecca Lyons (1804–95) (Plate 16.9). From 1848 to 1859 *The Isabel* carried the mail between Charleston and Havana, with stops at Savannah and Key West. After lapsing for a year, the federal mail contract was renewed in 1860, but service was suspended by the Civil War.[75] Mordecai had helped launch a newspaper, the *Southern Standard*, which opposed secession. Once the war began, however, he supported the Confederate cause with all the resources at his command. *The Isabel* removed Major Robert Anderson of the US Army and his troops from Fort Sumter to the safety of the Union fleet following the bombardment of the fort in April 1861. Later, painted grey, the ship became famous as a blockade runner. After the war, operating out of Baltimore, Mordecai's company brought home the bodies of soldiers from South Carolina who had been killed at Gettysburg.

Port Jews and Reform

The classic profile of the port Jew includes a tendency to Enlightenment rationalism and educational innovation. It is interesting, therefore, to consider where the Mordecai, Moïse, and Moses families fell on the spectrum between traditionalism and religious reform. Individuals from all three families were present at the flash point in the conflict between traditionalists and reformers in Beth Elohim congregation—the vote over the installation of an organ in the synagogue—which occurred sixteen years after the founding of the Reformed Society of Israelites.

When the sanctuary that burned to the ground in the Great Fire of April 1838 was replaced, thirty-eight members of the congregation petitioned the board of trustees to call a meeting 'to consider the Propriety of erecting an Organ in the Synagogue'. On 26 July 1840 Abraham Moïse Junior and Moses Cohen Mordecai steered the reformers to victory. When Reverend Gustavus Poznanski, who 'to the surprise of the old Jews . . . had joined the innovators',[76] backed the pro-organ faction, Moïse moved that the instrument should be installed but, in a conciliatory gesture, suggested that it be purchased by voluntary contributions not congregational funds. Board President Nathan Hart ruled the motion out of order, and Mordecai countered with an appeal to override

[74] 'Launch of the Steamship Isabel', *Baltimore Sun* (21 Feb. 1848).

[75] 'The Isabel', loose-leaf notebook compiled c.2006 by John Sands, containing newspaper accounts and documents concerning the ship, CCSC. For a description of the arrival of *The Isabel* in Havana with a sketch of the harbour and forts, see David Henry Mordecai, travel diary (1849), CCSC, Thomas J. Tobias papers, MS 1029. The full text of the diary with scans of each page is also available at <http://lowcountrydigital.library.cofc.edu/>.

[76] *The State ex rel. A. Ottolengui et al. vs. G. V. Ancker et al.: Report of the Evidence and Arguments of Counsel, by a Member of the Charleston Bar* (Charleston, SC, 1844), 8, quoted in Hagy, *This Happy Land*, 242.

the chair's ruling. He prevailed against Hart by 47 votes to 40, and the organ proposal was then passed, 46 votes to 40.[77]

On the other side of the protracted struggle, Isaiah Moses steadfastly opposed changes to the Sephardi customs and liturgy that had been in place for nearly a century. For many years he had sat on Beth Elohim's governing board, including the profoundly conservative board of 1820. After losing the vote over the organ, the traditionalists formed a breakaway congregation, Shearit Israel. A bitter struggle over control of the building was decided in court in favour of the reformers. The traditionalists subsequently built their own house of worship on Wentworth Street. On Friday 13 August 1847, at the consecration of the new building, Isaiah Moses carried one of the three Torah scrolls. He was followed in the procession by his son-in-law, Jacob Rosenfeld, Shearit Israel's new cantor. Yet another family member, Isaiah's son Levy, opened the door, as Reverend Rosenfeld commenced singing in Hebrew: 'Open for me the gates of righteousness.'[78]

The American War of Independence

Exactly a century before, in 1747, the three-member emigration committee of London's Bevis Marks congregation—Solomon da Costa, Joseph Salvador, and Benjamin Mendes da Costa—had surveyed British America with an eye to finding a refuge for thousands of exiled Bohemian Jews and for England's Jewish poor. 'From the point of view of legal equality for Jews', Godfrey and Godfrey conclude in their account of the committee's deliberations, 'South Carolina must have appeared . . . as the clear winner among the Thirteen Colonies'.[79] Its charter, drawn up by philosopher and physician John Locke, allowed equality—not mere toleration—for minority religions. In 1704 the province passed an Act eliminating the requirement of swearing a Christian oath. Foreign-born Jews could become citizens 'on the sole condition that they swear oaths acceptable to them according to their own religion'.[80] By 1740 South Carolina, alone among the thirteen North American colonies to have a general naturalization law, was prepared to accept a liberal interpretation of Britain's Plantation Act and do away altogether with the disability of swearing oaths on the New Testament.[81]

The emigration committee's plans foundered on the issue of who would pay to acquire land and resettle the refugees. But in 1755 Salvador himself purchased 100,000 acres, which became known as the 'Jew's Land', in the Carolina Piedmont. Eighteen years later, his nephew and son-in-law Francis Salvador sailed for Charleston with the

---

[77] Hagy, *This Happy Land*, 242–3.

[78] 'Consecration of the new Synagogue, Charleston, South Carolina', S. Valentine to Isaac Leeser, Charleston (17 Aug. 1847); a photocopy of autograph manuscript and typescript of the text are in the Jewish Heritage Collection's vertical files, CCSC; Rosengarten with Stender and Shanks, 'Narrative of the Exhibition', 103.   [79] Godfrey and Godfrey, *Search Out the Land*, 66, see also 62–9 *et passim*.

[80] Ibid. 48.   [81] Ibid. 51, 66.

intention of planting indigo on some 7,000 of those acres. Francis would become
the first professing Jew in America to represent the people in a legislative assembly.
In December 1774, at the age of 27, he was elected to the First Provincial Congress of
South Carolina as one of ten deputies from Ninety-Six, the colony's second most populous district. The young man did not live to see the outcome of the War of Independence: he was killed in an ambush by Loyalists and Indians on 1 August 1776.[82]

Ultimately it was America's rebellion against England that set South Carolina on a
different course from the West Indies. Regional affinities with the Caribbean plantation
system were trumped by a war for independence waged by the merchant class—Jews
among them—of the thirteen colonies. The revolution that provided a secure environment for Jewish traditionalists to pursue their religious beliefs also fuelled the ideology
of Jewish reformers. 'We claim', declared Abraham Moïse Junior on the first anniversary of the Reformed Society of Israelites, 'to be the advocates of a system of rational
religion; of substance, not form'. Utility, not antiquity, would be their criterion for
observance. 'We regard the free toleration of religion in this country as a bond of union
between Jew and non-Jew; and the great privileges which have been guaranteed to us
by the heroes of the Revolution, as strong evidences of national deliverance'[83]—by
which he meant that the 'nation' of Jews had found their promised land in America.

Jews who fought on the Patriots' side, and later in the War of 1812, viewed the
struggle against British rule as 'an initiation rite, an ordeal through battle', according to
Jonathan Sarna. 'Having passed the test—having shed blood for God and country—
they considered themselves due full equality.'[84] Religious liberty for Jews and for all free
people in the new country was affirmed by the Constitution of the United States in 1787
and the Bill of Rights in 1789. Whereas some state constitutions continued discriminatory provisions for another hundred years, South Carolina adopted the federal provisions for religious freedom in 1790. Jamaica remained a British colony, sealed off from
the revolutionary ardour and ideology of Britain's mainland colonies, and did not grant
Jews full political rights until forty years later. Yet its inclusion in the British empire and
increased attachment to the mother country meant that Jamaica would participate in
the 'humanitarian revolution' that culminated in the abolition of slavery in 1834.[85]

Apart from differences in the political culture of South Carolina and the West
Indies, other factors account for variations in the ways Jews fared in the two regions.
Enjoying a broad range of opportunities over a seemingly limitless terrain, South
Carolina's Jews availed themselves of the freedom to buy land and operate planta-
tions and the freedom to uphold, change, or abandon their traditional religion. Jewish

---

[82] See Rosengarten with Stender and Shanks, 'Narrative of the Exhibition', 79; Elzas, *The Jews of South Carolina*, 68–77.   [83] Moïse, *The Moïse Family of South Carolina*, 78.

[84] Jonathan D. Sarna, 'The Impact of the American Revolution on American Jews', *Modern Judaism*, 1/2 (1981), 151.

[85] Edward Brathwaite, *The Development of Creole Society in Jamaica, 1770–1820* (Oxford, 1971), pp. xiii–xiv.

Carolinians had ridden the coat-tails of French Protestant immigrants, who aggressively pursued the rights of citizens. The large number of German-speaking immigrants to South Carolina may have helped create a 'German-friendly' environment that extended to German Jews, while the status attained by Jews of Sephardi background rubbed off on all Jews in the colonial and federal periods.

Most importantly, in the only colony that specifically equated Africans with slaves, Jews found refuge on the white side of the colour line. In the ambiguous racial climate of the West Indies, where mixed-race 'people of colour' had standing, the Jews' position was more tenuous. Jamaican Jews won the vote only in 1831, when people of colour were threatening to move ahead of them in achieving civil rights.[86] Just three years later, slavery was abolished in Jamaica at the very time that South Carolina moved to the forefront of the defence of slavery and closed loopholes permitting manumission. Jews took positions on both sides of the leading issues of the day, such as a state's right to nullify federal laws and federal spending on internal infrastructure, but on the morality and necessity of racial slavery they closed ranks with their white compatriots. South Carolina's Jews served in the Confederate army and in positions of power in the rebellious government in numbers far greater than their proportion of the population, demonstrating their allegiance to the state and to its way of life, and seeking to win, as every generation of Jews feels it must, their unquestioned rights as full citizens.

[86] Samuel J. Hurwitz and Edith Hurwitz, 'The New World Sets an Example for the Old: The Jews of Jamaica and Political Rights, 1661–1831', *American Jewish Historical Quarterly*, 55/1 (1965), 45–56, esp. 53.

PART VI

PERSONAL
NARRATIVES

THE STRANGE ADVENTURES OF BENJAMIN FRANKS, AN ASHKENAZI PIONEER IN THE AMERICAS

MATT GOLDISH

ON 7 JUNE 1692 shortly before noon a certain Benjamin Franks was attending to his jewellery business in Port Royal, Jamaica. While we do not know much about Franks's life up to this point, he must have enjoyed a comfortable existence on the island. A brisk trade in the spoils of piracy brought goods of every description from around the world. And Franks, an Ashkenazi Jew, could even find a significant community of his co-religionists living with relatively little prejudice in that multicultural society. While most of the island's Jews were of Portuguese Sephardi extraction, there was also the occasional Ashkenazi. Most were apparently doing well for themselves.[1] All that, however, was about to change. An event occurred that day which would transform the fate of Mr Franks, his family, and the entire island.

It began with a low rumble, which slowly developed into a roar. The ground shook in three cataclysmic waves, each more destructive than the last. A tsunami drew the water from the harbour, then hurled it back in a wall against the defenceless city, dragging large areas down into the depths of the ocean. Thousands lost their lives. The city of Port Royal would never recover.[2] Benjamin Franks was spared his life, but he lost his entire business and livelihood. He was, in fact, left not destitute, but far worse—with debts of £12,000 and no way to repay them. Whether it was to start anew or to escape his debtors, Franks determined to leave Jamaica and seek his fortune to the north. He found a ship and headed for New York.[3]

---

[1] On Jews in seventeenth-century Jamaica, see Mordechai Arbell, *The Jewish Nation of the Caribbean* (Jerusalem, 2002), 225–60; id., *The Portuguese Jews of Jamaica* (Kingston, Jamaica, 2000); David Buisseret (ed.), *Jamaica in 1687: The Taylor Manuscript at the National Library of Jamaica* (Kingston, Jamaica, 2008), 238, 240, 250, 294; Edward Long, *The History of Jamaica*, 3 vols. (London, 1774; repr. New York, 1972), ii. 293–7; Benjamin Schlesinger, 'The Jews of Jamaica: A Historical View', *Caribbean Quarterly*, 13 (1967), 46–53; Zvi Loker, *Jews in the Caribbean: Evidence on the History of the Jews in the Caribbean Zone in Colonial Times* (Jerusalem, 1991).

[2] On the Port Royal earthquake, see William James Gardner, *A History of Jamaica* (London, 1873), 75–8; Long, *History of Jamaica*, 139–44.

[3] This information comes from the deposition given by Franks in Bombay, India, on 20 Oct. 1697

Franks was not a young man at the time of these events. Records describe him as being about 46 years of age in 1697, placing his birth about 1651. He is characterized as a Danish citizen,[4] which, for an Ashkenazi Jew, almost certainly meant he was a native of Altona in Germany, a town that was held at that time by the Danes.

New York would certainly have seemed as good a destination for a middle-aged Ashkenazi Jew as any in the New World. Portuguese Jews had first arrived there in 1654, when Recife in Brazil was wrested back from the Netherlands by Portugal—the very country they had escaped in order to practise Judaism freely. At that time the town was called New Amsterdam, and it was also a Dutch colony. The governor, Peter Stuyvesant, had been none too happy to see Jews arriving in his territory, but he was told in no uncertain terms by his employers, the Dutch West India Company, that the Jews were to be tolerated. Ten years later the Dutch lost this colony as well—in this case to the English—though they would regain it shortly afterwards. In 1674 New Amsterdam was permanently ceded to the English, who called it New York.

When Franks arrived, New York had a small but thriving Jewish community led by one Saul Brown. While the right to public worship had not been granted to non-Christians in colonial legislation, Jews were guaranteed basic privileges of safety and property, and they carried on at least a semi-public worship. A 1695 map shows a Jewish synagogue near Mill Street with a membership of about twenty families.[5]

However, even in England's American colonies, freedom of religion and enlightened views about faith were by no means the rule at that time. Full freedoms were guaranteed only to Christians, and there were limits even to these. In Massachusetts, the Salem witch trials took place the very year Franks arrived in New England. A key figure in those events was also a foreigner recently arrived from the Caribbean—the Barbadian slave Tituba.[6] Quakers were still being routinely harassed, though they were no longer having their tongues cut out or being summarily executed.[7] In short, New England in general, and New York in particular, was gradually developing a toler-

('Deposition of Benjamin Franks: October 20, 1607', in J. F. Jameson (ed.), *Privateering and Piracy in the Colonial Period: Illustrative Documents* (New York, 1923; repr. New York, 1970), 190–1). The original document is preserved in the British Library, India Office Records, Original Correspondence 6448, E/3/53 and runs to five pages.

[4] 'Governor Lorentz cites several instances [of piracy at St Thomas]. Benjamin Frank, a Jew, but a Danish subject, had his ship detained and his skipper maltreated and robbed' (Waldemar Westergaard, *The Danish West Indies Under Company Rule (1671–1754)* (New York, 1917), 110 n. 13). This is one of the very few testimonies concerning Franks outside the Kidd episode. It indicates that he was still in the Caribbean and owned a ship around 1696, shortly before his move to New York.

[5] On the Jewish community of New York at this time, see Jacob Rader Marcus, *Early American Jewry: The Jews of New York, New England, and Canada, 1649–1794*, 2 vols. (Philadelphia, 1951), vol. i, chs. 2–3.

[6] See Elaine G. Breslaw, *Tituba: Reluctant Witch of Salem* (New York, 1996).

[7] See Carla Gardina Pestana, 'Martyred by the Saints: Quaker Executions in Seventeenth-Century Massachusetts', in A. Greer and J. Bilinkoff (eds.), *Colonial Saints: Discovering the Holy in the Americas, 1500–1800* (New York, 2003), 169–92.

ant attitude towards those outside their traditional religious and cultural limits, but nothing could be assumed.

It may be for this reason that Franks chose not to remain in New York, or it may be that there was simply not sufficient economic opportunity for a jeweller there. After one or two unremarkable years, Franks sought passage to Surat, India, an English-controlled centre of the diamond trade. He clearly had some connections in the English world, because, from the first record of him in Jamaica, he always appears in British domains.

Franks must have known that Jews from Baghdad and later others from Persia and Arabia had come to work in Surat, particularly in the diamond trade. They had even built a synagogue and cemetery there. Unlike the persecuted Jews of Cochin, those of Surat were part of a tolerant metropolitan society that one author described as resembling Amsterdam. The traveller J. Frayer, over a decade before the disaster in Jamaica, spoke of the influence of Jews in the diamond trade of Surat. Franks, who clearly did not shy away from new frontiers and adventures, set his sights on India.[8]

Franks's next fateful decision, however, would plunge him into adventures far more numerous and unpleasant than he could have imagined. He must have been pleased to find a ship whose swaggering captain seemed oddly unconcerned about the nautical experience of the crew he signed on and perfectly willing to take Franks as far as Surat. The name of that captain would have meant little at the time, but within a few years it would become infamous around the world and remain that way until our own day: William Kidd.

Captain Kidd (1645–1701) has been known for centuries as one of the most notorious characters of the golden age of piracy. He was born in Scotland but moved to New York at the age of 5 after his father died. He apparently went to sea quite young and found himself privateering from a tender age.[9]

To understand why so much confusion surrounds Kidd's career to this day and to understand Franks's role in it, it is critical to know about privateers and pirates. Privateers and pirates were both in the business of attacking trading vessels, plundering the ships and their cargoes, and living a riotous life from the proceeds of this enterprise. The difference is that privateers did so under the licence or mandate of a state, with the aim of interrupting and impoverishing its enemies' trade. Privateers only attacked

---

[8] See Walter J. Fischel, *The Jews in India: Their Contribution to the Economic and Political Life* [Hayehudim behodu: ḥelkam baḥayim hakalkaliyim vehamediniyim] (Jerusalem, 1960), 40–1. On Jews in the eighteenth-century gem trade, including the Caribbean and India, see Gedalia Yogev, *Diamonds and Coral: Anglo-Dutch Jews and Eighteenth-Century Trade* (Leicester, 1978).

[9] Excellent work has been done on Kidd in recent years (see esp. Robert C. Ritchie, *Captain Kidd and the War Against the Pirates* (Cambridge, Mass., 1986); Richard Zacks, *The Pirate Hunter: The True Story of Captain Kidd* (New York, 2002)). The standard documents on Kidd's trial are in Graham Brooks (ed.), *Trial of Captain Kidd* (Edinburgh, 1930).

vessels of enemy countries' merchant marine and generally gave their spoils, or some share of them, to their government and to whoever had financed the voyage. Pirates, on the other hand, were in business for themselves. They would attack any ship in any waters and keep the booty for themselves and their crew. Pirates were often also violent and destructive, because they had no investment in the ships and passengers they captured as privateers did. This made them the enemy of all states.

Jews were involved in privateering throughout the early modern period, but only occasionally in piracy. Privateering was a legitimate business venture in which one invested like any seagoing mercantile project. Piracy was crime, but there were a few Jews among the 'Barbary pirates'.[10]

The distinction between privateers and pirates could be very subtle, as one might imagine, and it appears that Kidd played the game very close to the line.[11] Interestingly, while Kidd was commissioned as a privateer, he had another appointment as well. The governor of New York wanted him to seek out and destroy a number of notorious pirates. He was sent to England to obtain the royal privateering letter of marque and take possession of a new ship.[12]

It turned out that Kidd was desperate for additional crew members when he returned to New York, because of an event that was characteristic of his personal style. He had received his privateering commission in England in 1695 and was given a fine new ship, the *Adventure Galley*, in which to carry out his charge. As the *Adventure Galley* travelled down the Thames from the shipyard where it was built, it passed some naval vessels but failed to salute. A navy ship fired a shot across Kidd's bow to indicate it should be shown respect, but Kidd and his crew mooned the navy. As a punishment, the majority of his most experienced crew members were taken from him and pressed into naval service.[13] Thus, when Kidd arrived in New York he was desperate for hands— even a middle-aged Jewish diamond merchant. Neither Franks nor Kidd realized at the time that their fates would soon be intertwined in a most bizarre manner.

The voyage from New York began in September of 1696 and suffered setbacks from the very beginning. Many of the crew died in a cholera outbreak. Once he reached the Red Sea, Kidd could not find any pirates to attack, and his crew became mutinous. Finally, he found a rich target in the Armenian ship *Quedagh Merchant*. Unfortunately for Kidd, the captain was an Englishman with letters of passage from the French East India Company. Kidd allowed himself to be persuaded by his crew that a ship under an

[10] On Jewish privateers in the Americas, see e.g. Jacob Rader Marcus, *American Jewry: Documents, Eighteenth Century* (Cincinnati, 1959), 11–12, 321 (indicating members of the Franks family in this business), 337–40, 356–8; on a Jewish Barbary pirate, see Mercedes García-Arenal and Gerard Wiegers, *A Man of Three Worlds: Samuel Pallache, a Moroccan Jew in Catholic and Protestant Europe* (Baltimore, 2003), ch. 4.

[11] See James G. Lydon, *Pirates, Privateers, and Profits* (Hyannis, Mass., 1970). Lydon's study is focused on New York, Kidd's port of embarkation.

[12] See Ritchie, *Captain Kidd*, chs. 1–2; Zacks, *Pirate Hunter*, chs. 1–2.   [13] See Zacks, *Pirate Hunter*, 107–8.

Armenian flag with French letters of passage was a legitimate prize. The English government did not see it that way.

The incident of the *Quedagh Merchant* was typical of the problems Kidd encountered: targets whose legitimacy was ambiguous; a rebellious crew, which elicited either bad decisions or violence on his part; and the failure of his backers to rally to his defence. Kidd may have been a pirate, but it is equally likely that he carried out his commission to the best of his ability in confusing circumstances. Either way, his crew abandoned him for the pirate Robert Culliford and, upon his return to New York, Kidd was arrested and dispatched to England for trial.[14]

Franks was ill for most of the voyage, but he did witness various acts of possible piracy and Kidd's violent temper. After Kidd had hunted for pirates and legitimate booty with little success in Madagascar, Johanna, and regions of the Indian Ocean, he anchored off Carwar on the Indian coast on 3 September 1697 to take on fresh water.

Franks begged Kidd to let him disembark now that the ship had reached India, as that had been their arrangement. Kidd resolutely refused. Franks offered Kidd a beaver hat and Kidd agreed. As Richard Zacks comments, it was a 'big mistake'.[15] The entire contingent of nine sailors who rowed Franks ashore immediately deserted. Most were captured and whipped by Kidd, but Franks and a young Boston sailor named Jonathan Treadway made immediately for the East India Company headquarters and escaped. Treadway's testimony reveals the feelings of the honest crew member: he said he had been 'trapanned to be a pyrate instead of a privateer'.[16]

The East India Company in Carwar had already received various reports about Kidd's piracy and had just drafted a letter to their Bombay headquarters about the matter, when the two escaped crew members appeared. They now added a postscript containing the statements of Franks and Treadway, stating that Kidd had captured and ransacked an English ship near Bombay and that he had planned to take other vessels unlawfully. This was the last piece of evidence the company needed against Kidd.[17]

Franks and Treadway were the star witnesses against their erstwhile captain. They were immediately taken to the company's Bombay headquarters, where their testimonies were taken, and held prisoner there for months. (It is noteworthy that Franks's Bombay testimony states that he swore to the truth of his statement on 'the Old Testament'.[18]) They were sent to England in January 1698 to testify against Kidd before the Board of Trade in August of that year.[19] This was the outcome of Franks's aspiration to reach India: he made it, but it did him little good. Kidd himself was held at Newgate prison and attempted to defend himself during a lengthy trial. Treadway's and

---

[14] This story is told in greater detail in Ritchie, *Captain Kidd*; Zacks, *Pirate Hunter*.

[15] Zacks, *Pirate Hunter*, 136; 'Deposition of Benjamin Franks', 194.   [16] Zacks, *Pirate Hunter*, 136.

[17] Ibid.; 'Deposition of Benjamin Franks', 194.   [18] 'Deposition of Benjamin Franks', 105.

[19] Ritchie, *Captain Kidd*, 186–7; Zacks, *Pirate Hunter*, 136; *Calendar of State Papers, Colonial Series: America and West Indies (1697–98)* (London 1905), 399 no. 763 (22 Aug. 1698).

Franks's were just two among a number of voices raised against Kidd, who was found guilty and hanged in 1701.[20]

The fate of Benjamin Franks after the trial of William Kidd is mainly a matter of conjecture. What we do know is that within a generation the Frankses would become a leading Jewish family in colonial North America. Robert Ritchie's version of the Franks family's journey from Europe to the New World appears to be narrated out of order, and his estimation of Benjamin Franks is suspect:

> [Benjamin] was a member of an important Jewish mercantile family, the Franks, who traded to the West Indies, North America, and India. He, however, represented a failing branch of the family. . . . Burdened with losses of £12,000, he left Jamaica for North America (a notable branch of the Franks family lived in Philadelphia and another had settled in New York). . . . The London branch of the Franks family, with other Jewish families, traded inside the East India Company's monopoly; thus their activities centered on Surat and Bombay.[21]

Franks's deposition before the East India Company and a few mentions of his name in related documents are almost all the evidence we have about him. No Frankses are known to have been living in Philadelphia or New York when Benjamin arrived there: they came in the eighteenth century. The evidence points to Benjamin being the first. As Jacob R. Marcus observed: 'Benjamin Franks of New York, an uncle of Jacob Franks, was the first of the family in New York as far as the records show.'[22] It is also unclear what Ritchie means by a 'failing branch' of the family. We simply do not have enough evidence to know whether Benjamin married, raised children, recovered his fortunes, or encouraged his relatives to come to America. I am also unaware of any evidence that members of the Franks family were involved with the East India Company when Benjamin Franks sought to reach Surat. While Ritchie's assessment might be correct, all indications suggest that Benjamin Franks was an adventurous, daring, and lead-ing member of a family that had not yet emerged into a position of major wealth or greatness.

Aside from the interest of Benjamin Franks's story, he is important as the first member of one of the greatest Jewish families in colonial North America. Marcus men-tions seven important families in the New York Jewish community at the beginning of the eighteenth century, six of which were closely connected to each other. The Franks family was one of these. Jacob Franks, Benjamin's nephew, was the best-known mem-ber of the family and married a daughter of the wealthy Levy family. Marcus suggests that Jacob may have been a poor member of the Franks family in England who was sent to find his fortune in America and made good. Jacob Franks and his family were involved in lucrative shipping and trade and became official purveyors and agents for

---

[20] See Brooks, *Trial of Captain Kidd*; Ritchie, *Captain Kidd*, chs. 9–10; Zacks, *Pirate Hunter*, chs. 17–21.

[21] Ritchie, *Captain Kidd*, 65–6.

[22] Jacob Rader Marcus, *The Colonial American Jew, 1492–1776*, 3 vols. (Detroit, 1970), ii. 581.

the British Crown in the American colonies. Jacob's wife, Abigail, is the best-known Jewish woman in colonial North America because of her extensive correspondence with her son, who moved to England. Members of the Franks family fought on both sides during the American War of Independence. It is ironic that among the Franks family's many business interests in the middle and later eighteenth century were extensive trade with the West Indies and outfitting privateers to operate in the Caribbean.[23]

I would like to conclude by using the case of Benjamin Franks to highlight several trends among Jews at the end of the seventeenth century. First, Ashkenazi Jews often followed closely in the footsteps of the western Sephardim as they opened up new territories to Jewish settlement. Franks travelled to the Caribbean, New York, and London, and he tried to join the Sephardi and Iraqi Jews in Surat. In many places, including Amsterdam and London, Ashkenazim became very numerous or even outnumbered Sephardim within a century or less of their first settlement. While German and Polish Jews are often described as poor, uneducated, and uncouth, the record shows that a few of them rose to positions of wealth and influence. At the same time, there were many poor Sephardim. The Ashkenazim did not usually begin with the advantages the Sephardim had, one of which was an available Christian identity, as western Sephardim generally arrived as Portuguese New Christians. Western Sephardim also had a ramified trade network and knowledge of Romance languages. As Glikl of Hameln's memoir and other sources reveal, however, the Ashkenazim used their own kinship networks and developed skills and flexibility that could sometimes outstrip those of their Sephardi co-religionists.[24]

Benjamin Franks was also not the only Ashkenazi in the Caribbean during this period. Even before the English occupied Jamaica in 1655, a Dutch vessel fleeing the war in Recife landed there with a mixed group of Sephardi and Ashkenazi Jews on board.[25] Ashkenazi Jews from Rotterdam had joined the Sephardim in Suriname by the late seventeenth century.[26] Enough of them had arrived by the 1730s to cause strained relations between Portuguese and Ashkenazi Jews and the creation of an Ashkenazi synagogue.[27] Poor Ashkenazim were noted in Curaçao in the 1730s,[28] and the Jewish population of St Eustatius contained a considerable number of Ashkenazim.[29] Simon

[23] See Marcus, *Early American Jewry*, vol. i, chs. 3–9, esp. pp. 57–72; Max Kohler, *Rebecca Franks, an American Jewish Belle of the Last Century* (New York, 1894); L. Hershkowitz and I. S. Meyer (eds.), *Letters of the Franks Family, 1733–1748* (Waltham, Mass., 1968); *The Letters of Abigaill Levy Franks, 1733–1748*, ed. E. B. Gelles (New Haven, 2004).

[24] See e.g. Yosef Kaplan, 'Amsterdam and Ashkenazi Migration in the Seventeenth Century', in id., *An Alternative Path to Modernity* (Leiden, 2000), 78–107; Glikl of Hameln, *Zikhroynes, 1691–1713*, ed. C. Turniansky (Jerusalem, 2006); Eng. trans.: Beth-Zion Abrahams, *The Life of Glückel of Hameln 1646–1724, Written by Herself* (London, 1962); Jonathan Israel, *European Jewry in the Age of Mercantilism*, 3rd edn. (London, 1998), ch. 4 *et passim*; David S. Katz, *The Jews in the History of England* (Oxford, 1994), 180–5.

[25] Arbell, *Portuguese Jews of Jamaica*, 8; id., *Jewish Nation of the Caribbean*, 226.

[26] Arbell, *Jewish Nation of the Caribbean*, 91, 93.   [27] Ibid. 109–12.   [28] Ibid. 145.   [29] Ibid. 174.

Abrahams, almost certainly an Ashkenazi, was mining for gold and silver on the 'Wilde Kust' in Guiana around 1720, and shortly afterwards Moses Isaac de Vries, presumably also an Ashkenazi, was a militia commander in the same region.[30] A particularly interesting episode is the donation of funds by the Curaçao Portuguese community for the building of the New York Portuguese synagogue, Shearith Israel. The treasurer of Shearith Israel, whose signature appears first on the gift document, is none other than Jacob Franks, nephew of Benjamin Franks, who had married into the Sephardi elite and become an officer of the Portuguese synagogue.[31]

A second point illustrated by Benjamin and Jacob Franks is the particularly close trading relationships between Jews from the British colonies in North America and the Caribbean. This was of course a very important route for all Atlantic mercantile interests, but the Jews seem to have been especially involved in this connection. There are many cases of Jews, both Sephardi and Ashkenazi, following Franks's route from the Caribbean to New England and vice versa. Even rabbis such as the learned Hebron emissary Hayim Joseph Karrigal travelled between these areas.

Third, Benjamin Franks is an example of why we must be careful about thinking strictly in terms of an Atlantic diaspora, an Indian Ocean world, a New England Jewry, or any other overly localized framework. Recent research has even taught us to be wary of distinctions such as African and European or Jew and Christian.[32] Franks was typical of merchants around the world in the late seventeenth century who felt comfortable setting up shop or travelling almost anywhere. He was multi-lingual. He did not have a 'base of operations'. Had he not run into Captain Kidd, and thus left more than ephemeral records of his existence, Franks's history would have been swallowed up among those of the thousands of small-scale merchants—Jewish, Christian, and Muslim—whose openness to new vistas made them unknown pioneers of both physical and mental new worlds.

[30] Loker, Jews in the Caribbean, 333–4.   [31] Ibid. 80.

[32] See e.g. Margaret Jacob, Strangers Nowhere in the World: The Rise of Cosmopolitanism in Early Modern Europe (Philadelphia, 2006); Natalie Zemon Davis, Trickster Travels: A Sixteenth-Century Muslim Between Worlds (New York, 2006). On Jewish merchants crossing geographical and ideological borders in the period, see García-Arenal and Wiegers, A Man of Three Worlds; Francesca Trivellato, The Familiarity of Strangers: The Sephardic Diaspora, Livorno, and Cross-Cultural Trade in the Early Modern Period (New Haven, 2009); Yogev, Diamonds and Coral; Richard L. Kagan and Philip D. Morgan (eds.), Atlantic Diasporas: Jews, Conversos, and Crypto-Jews in the Age of Mercantilism, 1500–1800 (Baltimore, 2009), chs. 6, 9; on the porous nature of the Jewish–Christian divide, see Richard H. Popkin and Gordon M. Weiner (eds.), Jewish Christians and Christian Jews from the Renaissance to the Enlightenment (Dordrecht, 1994).

ACKNOWLEDGEMENTS
I would like to thank Jane Gerber, Stanley Mirvis, Ainsley Henriques, and all those involved in organizing the conference 'The Jewish Diaspora of the Caribbean'. I would also like to acknowledge the enormous help of Richard Zacks, through whom I discovered Benjamin Franks, both for his book on Captain Kidd and his personal communications. I am also grateful to Robert Ritchie for his book on Captain Kidd and his help locating archival sources.

CHAPTER EIGHTEEN

DANIEL ISRAEL LÓPEZ LAGUNA'S *ESPEJO FIEL DE VIDAS* AND THE GHOSTS OF MARRANO AUTOBIOGRAPHY

RONNIE PERELIS

AFTER GENERATIONS of living as Catholics in the Iberian peninsula, Spanish and Portuguese Jews went on to establish thriving, openly Jewish communities throughout western Europe and the Atlantic world. This phoenix-like re-emergence has been extensively analysed from sociological, economic, religious, and cultural perspectives by many scholars, including Yosef Kaplan and Jonathan Israel. One of the more intriguing aspects of this phenomenon is the psychological dimension: what were the psychic or intellectual processes involved in such a radical transformation? Who were the Marranos? Do their descendants, the children of former Conversos now living in Amsterdam or Hamburg like Benito Espinoza, partake of some form of Marrano mentality?[1] What are the features of this identity: duality, heterodoxy, scepticism, a heroic postmodernism *avant la lettre*? The idea of the 'Marrano as metaphor' is alluring and seductive, as is the belief that we can distil a neat phenomenology or 'psychology' of Marranism.[2] While distancing ourselves from some of the more facile excesses of this scholarly tendency, we can still ask about the possibility of exploring the interiority of crypto-Jewish life and the process of spiritual transformation implicit in the Conversos' move towards normative Judaism.

[1] Yirmiyahu Yovel uses the idea of a 'Marrano mentality' to unlock the meaning of modernity in *Spinoza and Other Heretics*, 2 vols. (Princeton, 1989) and most recently in *The Other Within. The Marranos: Split Identity and Emerging Modernity* (Princeton, 2009).

[2] I borrow this term from Elaine Marks's study of modern French literature, *Marrano as Metaphor: The Jewish Presence in French Writing* (New York, 1996). The idea of a quintessentially Converso consciousness or sensibility can be found in Américo Castro's work on the *Celestina* and Saint Teresa (*Santa Teresa y otros ensayos* (Madrid, 1929)) and in many of his other works. One of Castro's students, Stephen Gilman follows this line of analysis with great erudition in *The Spain of Fernando de Rojas: The Intellectual and Social Landscape of La Celestina* (Princeton, 1972). Paul Julian Smith offers a brilliant reassessment of this critical approach in 'La Celestina, Castro and the Jews', in id., *Representing the Other: 'Race', Text, and Gender in Spanish and Spanish American Narrative* (Oxford, 1992).

What textual records do we have of this process? Why do individuals record their individual process of transformation—for personal reflection, self-glorification, or for the edification of others? Turning to the wider European cultural context of the early modern period, we see that both Catholics and Protestants had a vibrant tradition of personal-narrative writing. Travel accounts, spiritual autobiographies, and personal histories of persecution at the hands of their respective 'infidel' oppressors were widely circulated throughout early modern Europe. However, the Iberian Conversos, who were so adept at using the cultural practices of their Christian neighbours, overwhelmingly chose to avoid direct reflection on their tumultuous past. Instead they concentrated their literary energies on volumes of ornate baroque poetry as well as drama and didactic religious works. We rarely find instances of autobiography that reflect the move towards Judaism or their former lives as crypto-Jews. The exceptions prove the rule: Luis de Carvajal, the Mexican crypto-Jew and martyr of the late sixteenth century, wrote a spiritual autobiography, but he lived his entire life in a Catholic Iberian setting; Manuel Cardozo de Macedo, a Portuguese Old Christian who converted to Judaism, also wrote a stirring autobiography of his tumultuous path to the God of Israel, and he too was the product of a thoroughly Christian upbringing;[3] Uriel da Costa wrote his *Exemplar vitae humanae* after being expelled from the *kehilah* of Amsterdam. This fascinating document was only brought to light posthumously by his friend, the Christian theologian Philipp van Limborch, as *De veritate religionis christianae: Amica collation cum erudito judaeo* (Gouda, 1687). The repackaging of da Costa's passionate *Exemplar* within an anti-Jewish/pro-Christian polemic casts doubt on the fidelity of Limborch's edition. The absence of da Costa's original manuscript complicates the issue even further. Da Costa's case points to the uneasy place of autobiographies within the Sephardi community. On the whole, only those thoroughly immersed in Christian culture followed this literary practice.[4] Family histories such as the De Pinto Manuscript and the texts relating to the life of Fernão Álvares Melo (1569–1632), both of which were collected and studied by H. P. Salomon, rarely discuss the tribulations of Jewish life in the Iberian world or the internal process involved in openly embracing Judaism.[5] This short list is

---

[3] For Carvajal's autobiography, see Alfonso Toro, *La familia Carvajal* (Mexico City, 1977), app. 1; Eng. trans.: Seymour B. Liebman, *The Enlightened: The Writings of Luis de Carvajal, el Mozo* (Coral Gables, Fla., 1967), 53–86. On Carvajal's life and times, see Martin A. Cohen, *The Martyr Luis de Carvajal: A Secret Jew in Sixteenth-Century Mexico* (Albuquerque, 1973; repr. 2001). Manuel Cardoso de Macedo's spiritual autobiography, *La vida del buenaventurado Abraham Pelengrino*, was edited with a Dutch translation and commentary by Benjamin Teensma, 'The History of Abraham Perengrino, Alias Manuel Cardoso de Macedo', *Studia Rosenthaliana*, 10 (1976), 1–36.

[4] It should be noted that Converso and post-Converso Judaism challenge the clear lines of demarcation between Christian and Jewish culture.

[5] Herman P. Salomon, 'The "De Pinto" Manuscript: A Seventeenth-Century Marrano Family History', *Studia Rosenthaliana*, 9 (1975), 1–62; id., 'Portrait of a New Christian, Fernão Álvares Melo (1569–1632)', *Fontes documentais portuguesas*, 18 (1982), 333–46.

certainly not exhaustive, and over time scholars may discover new texts, however the overwhelming impression is that the spiritual autobiography was not a robust genre among the western Sephardim. The list illustrates the paucity of autobiographies written by former Conversos and the lack of interest in these texts by the wider Spanish and Portuguese community. Whereas the Reformation and the Counter-Reformation used spiritual autobiographies as weapons in their external and internal wars of ideas, western Sephardi Jews at most allowed these works to gather dust in their archives.

In their fascinating monograph *A Man of Three Worlds*, Mercedes García-Arenal and Gerard Wiegers offer an intriguing explanation for the autobiographical silence among the ex-Conversos of Amsterdam. They describe the atmosphere of a self-imposed 'collective amnesia' within the Sephardi community:

The New Jews of sixteenth- and seventeenth-century Amsterdam had suffered pain and traumatic experiences in the Iberian Peninsula, which later led them to deny or suppress their collective memory of a 'marrano' past. This denial of memory, or 'collective amnesia,' resulted in a general refusal to acknowledge the fact that generations of Jews had ever been forcibly converted to Christianity; and this refusal clearly made it difficult to admit to the notion of a later 'return' to Judaism. The topic of past conversions was strictly taboo among the Jewish community and could not even be mentioned as a way of exalting the Inquisition victims in one's own family. The family chronicle of Isaac Pinto and the works of Miguel de Barrios himself are good examples of genealogical memoirs illustrating the extent to which Amsterdam Jews had suppressed disquieting aspects of their Iberian pasts: the theme of Jewish descent and of a return to a religion that their forebears had been forced to abandon is quite simply never broached. The reason for this silence is clear—these authors had great difficulty in accepting the Christian conversions of ancestors who had been born, and might have been brought up as, Jews. The emotional effect of this denial was kept alive by many factors, and can still be detected even in the works of some contemporary historians.[6]

At best, García-Arenal and Wiegers can offer only a partial explanation for this absence of autobiography. Perhaps, as historians, we must look at what was written with a different eye and a more nuanced understanding of the practice of autobiography in the early modern period.

Scholars of early modern autobiography, such as Natalie Zemon Davis, James Amelang, and Richard Kagan, have suggested that autobiographies during this period rarely take on the formal literary structure of the modern autobiography—what Sylvia Molloy calls 'the I that is the matter of this book'.[7] Instead, early modern

---

[6] Mercedes García-Arenal and Gerard Wiegers, *A Man of Three Worlds: Samuel Pallache, a Moroccan Jew in Catholic and Protestant Europe* (Baltimore, 2003), 3.

[7] Sylvia Molloy, *At Face Value: Autobiographical Writing in Spanish America* (Cambridge, 1991), 3; see also James S. Amelang, *The Flight of Icarus: Artisan Autobiography in Early Modern Europe* (Stanford, Calif., 1998); Natalie Zemon Davis, 'Fame and Secrecy: Leon Modena's *Life* as an Early Modern Autobiography', in Mark R. Cohen (trans. and ed.), *The Autobiography of A Seventeenth-Century Venetian Rabbi: Leon Modena's Life of Judah* (Princeton, 1988), 50–72; see Richard L. Kagan and Abigail Dyer, 'Introduction', in eid. (ed. and trans.), *Inquisitorial Inquiries: Brief Lives of Secret Jews and Other Heretics* (Baltimore, 2004).

autobiographical practices are 'embedded'—to borrow Zemon Davis's phrase—within juridical discourse—such as ledgers, correspondence between business associates, and family documents such as the tradition of writing *tsava'ot* (ethical wills) and personal inscriptions in the family Bible.

Historians have been able to gain insight into aspects of Marrano and post-Marrano religious sensibilities and the attendant psychological processes by examining these embedded moments of reflection and self-fashioning, whether they be inquisitorial testimonies, correspondence, polemical works, rabbinic responsa, sermons, or poetry.

Poetry is especially attractive to both author and reader because it at once invites self-expression and mediates that expression through a text which requires interpretation. Partially because the poet turns thought and emotion into line and verse, the poet's interiority can be expressed, while at the same time hiding behind the aesthetic packaging. Poetry conceals as it reveals. The dialectic of hiding at the heart of much baroque poetry, in particular, lends itself perfectly to the apparent discomfort of many former Conversos as they reflect upon their experience.

Jamaica was the home of one of the great poets of the Sephardi diaspora in the eighteenth century, Daniel Israel López Laguna. What could the tropical haven of Jamaica have to do with the aesthetics of concealment and the poetics of self-fashioning?

Laguna's magnum opus was his *Espejo fiel de vidas que contiene los Psalmos de David en verso* (A Faithful Mirror of Lives Contained in the Psalms of David in Verse), a poetic paraphrase of the Psalms in lyrical Spanish, published in London in 1720. The poem originated during the author's imprisonment in Spain and was brought to light after his many prosperous years in Jamaica. It never directly mentions the tropical context of its composition; however, some of Laguna's London patrons, who wrote verses praising the work, refer to its Caribbean origin, often in a comic or racist mode. For instance, the approbation by Jahacob Henriques Pimentel, alias Don Manuel de Humanes, praises the author's accomplishments, mixing his praise with a good dose of scathing humour. He tells the reader that he was initially concerned that the power of poetry would not be able to penetrate that island so heavily populated with blacks. However this doubt was resolved when he realized that:

God desired to help him with his influence for the greater glory of His name to have the dark shadows of the Blacks serve as greater contrast to the light and clarity of this Divine *Mirror* (*Espejo fiel de vidas*).[8]

Laguna's island home and its African inhabitants are at most a curiosity, a crude joke, apt to be transformed into a late baroque witticism.

---

[8] Jahacob Henriques Pimentel, 'Aprobación', in Daniel Israel López Laguna, *Espejo fiel de vidas que contiene los Psalmos de David en verso* (London, 1720), n.p.

I have found no reference to Jamaica in any of Laguna's poems, which fits neatly into the larger sketch being drawn in this chapter, whereby a central feature of the author's life experience recedes into the background or is only noticed as a passing joke by a metropolitan reader. Despite the lack of any references to the Caribbean, *Espejo fiel de vidas*, in its composition and publication, is a striking product of the Atlantic world and of the trade between metropolis and colony. Instead of sugar or tobacco, we have the work of an Iberian New Christian, born in southern France and educated in Spain, who found a haven in the British Caribbean and who returned to his own (Sephardi) nation's headquarters in London to publish his work. *Espejo fiel de vidas*, in its published form, with its elaborate graphics and pages of laudatory poems and prefatory remarks penned by the bright lights of the London Sephardim, is much like the raw materials of the Americas that were shipped to Europe to be refined, packaged, and sold. It is a 'value-added product', produced through the peculiarities and vicissitudes of the Atlantic world system.

The Psalms have long served as a medium through which the devout channelled their heartaches, fears, joys, and raptures. King David's own tumultuous life served as the inspiration of many of the most evocative of the psalms. This autobiographical (or pseudo-autobiographical) model invites the reader to follow David's path and be inspired by trials and difficulties to call out to God in desperation or praise. Laguna's poetic paraphrase offers a unique opportunity to consider post-Marrano autobiographical writing. By expanding on the original biblical verse, which is in and of itself fundamentally autobiographical, Laguna is able to 'find his own voice', express his own sentiments and reflect on his own life of tumult and salvation. In the rest of this chapter I will explore Laguna's autobiographical presence and absence in this fascinating work.

Laguna was the first Jamaican Jewish author of note. He published *Espejo fiel de vidas* after a labour of love that lasted almost twenty-three years. The publication was an event. The rabbi of the London community, the esteemed Hakham David Nieto, wrote approvingly of Laguna's poetic gifts and trustworthiness as a translator:[9]

As faithful in the translation as he is energetic in his expression, his piety and devotion shine through his verses, indicating their origin as legitimate and uncontested daughters of his Heart.[10]

Laguna's passion, sensitivity, and poetic skill are employed for the good of the community. Nieto explains who will benefit most from this edition:

[9] Laguna acknowledges his debt to a previous Spanish translation of the Psalms, Jacob Jehuda León Templo's *Las alabanzas de santidad* (Amsterdam, 1671). This edition included the original Hebrew text, a translation, and a series of apparatuses meant to clarify the grammatical sense of the biblical original, as well as a commentary explicating the literary and religious meaning of the verses.

[10] 'Tan fiel en la translación, como enérgica en la expressiva, resplandecen su devoción, y piedad, brillantes de forma, que indican ser legítimas, e incontestables hijas del Corazón, de quien emanan' (David Nieto, 'Aprobación', in Laguna, *Espejo fiel de vidas*, n.p.).

The devout of our Spanish and Portuguese Nation, not possessing the Holy Tongue, desire to share in this inexhaustible and celestial Treasure.[11]

The 1720s witnessed a new wave of anti-Converso investigations in Portugal that prompted many New Christians to leave and seek refuge in openly Jewish communities, such as Amsterdam and London. These newly arrived immigrants had almost no knowledge of Judaism and certainly did not have the command of Hebrew that would give them direct access to the prayer book.[12] Laguna's own life followed a similar path.

The first (and basically only) scholar to work on Laguna's life and poetic work was Meyer Kayserling, over a century ago.[13] Kayserling scoured *Espejo fiel de vidas* and other documents for information about Laguna's life. He found very little, except for the information contained in the prefatory remarks by his friends and a few lines by the author himself in his introduction. Laguna tells the 'zealous reader':

> To the Muses I was Inclined
> From the time of my Youth
> My adolescence in France
> Sacred schooling I was given
> In Spain I mastered the Arts
>
> .   .   .   .   .   .
>
> Eyes opening to virtue
> I escaped the Inquisition
> Today in Jamaica in Song
> The Psalms give to my harp
> The desires, first born in my prison cell
> I have now fulfilled
> Finishing this Work.[14]

We learn that he spent his youth in France, studied arts and letters in Spain, was arrested by the Inquisition, was eventually released, and found refuge in Jamaica. He refers to now being able to realize a desire that was born while in prison: to complete

[11] 'Los devotos de nuestra Nación española y portuguesa, que no posseiendo la lengua santa, desean participar deste inexhausto, y celeste Tesoro' (ibid.).

[12] For a discussion of the educational resources available to Conversos while still living in Iberian lands, see Yosef Hayim Yerushalmi, 'Marranos Returning to Judaism in the 17th Century: Their Jewish Knowledge and Psychological Readiness' (Heb.), *Proceedings of the Fifth World Congress of Jewish Studies* (Jerusalem, 1969), ii. 202.

[13] Meyer Kayserling, 'Jews in Jamaica and Daniel Israel Lopez Laguna', *Jewish Quarterly Review*, 12 (1900), 708–17.

[14] 'A las Musas Ynclinado / E sido desde mi ynfan sia / La adolecensia en la Franc ya / Sagrada escuela m E ha dado, / En España algo han limado / Las Artes mi Yoventud // Ojos abriendo i en Virtud / Sali de la Inquisicion / Oy Yamayca en can sion / Los Psalm Os da a mi Laud / En my Pricion los Deseos / Cobré, de hacer Esta obra' (Daniel Israel López Laguna, 'Introduction', in id., *Espejo fiel de vidas*, n.p.). 'Oy Yamayca en can sion' is possibly a double-entendre between *sión* which finishes *canción* (song) and an allusion to Jamaica as another Zion.

this poetic paraphrase of the Psalms. The only other information that is known about him after this point is that his children and his wife became naturalized on the island after his death.[15]

Abraham Pimentel, the son of Jahacob Pimentel, a friend of Laguna's, opens another window into the author's experience. In his preface, he writes:

The work was the product of twenty-three years of labour, marked by misfortunes, persecutions, wars, fires, and hurricanes in order to create a 'mirror' where the reader can see God, speak with God, and delight in God.[16]

Laguna might have omitted this detail out of modesty; however, it is another example of the invisibility of the past. The persecutions and sufferings mentioned are general, they rarely happen to the author, but to:

Our Brothers, those that come from Spain and Portugal, fleeing the persecutions of such tyrannical and cruel countries in order to enjoy in these [lands] the repose and quiet which allow them to meditate on our sacred and Divine Law.[17]

Pimentel's comments reveal another route by which former Conversos connected with and meditated on their past and the experience of so many of their fellow Jews: those who had suffered could 'find repose in the Psalms'. Laguna's text serves as a place of textual mediation of the individual's harrowing experiences. It is a locus of divine encounter and personal reflection patterned on the ups and downs of King David's tumultuous and exhilarating life. The traumatic and all-too-near past can be engaged through veils—through alter egos, dramatic masks that allow the devotee to speak, to cry out.

Most of *Espejo fiel de vidas* does not in any obvious way relate to the particular persecution of Iberian Jewry or to Laguna's personal experience at the hands of the inquisitors. However, there are moments when he inserts his own experiences into the verses. At times, in the space between the biblical original and Laguna's paraphrase, an act of ventriloquism is performed: Laguna pours his own sentiments into what is already a first-person poetic narrative of suffering, thanksgiving, complaint, outrage, and praise.

This mode of poetic self-fashioning is developed in a striking manner in his rendering of Psalm 10.[18]

---

[15] Kayserling, 'The Jews in Jamaica,' 717.

[16] 'Le costó a su autor veinte y tres años de trabajo, y otros tantos de desvelo, entre persecuciones de guerras incendios, y uracanes, para perfeccionar, y darte este Espejo, donde puedes a todas horas ver a Dios, hablar con Dios, y gozar de Dios' (Abraham Pimentel, 'Prefacio', in Laguna, *Espejo fiel de vidas*, n.p.).

[17] 'Nuestros hermanos los que vienen de España y Portugal, huyendo las persecuciones de tan tiranas y crueles tierras a gozar en estas el reposo y quietud que alla no les es concedido, por la prohibición de meditar en nuestra santa , y Divina Ley' (ibid.).

[18] I hope to chart Laguna's autobiographical dialectic as it plays out throughout the entire text in a monograph dedicated to the *Espejo fiel de vidas*.

1. Why Lord do you hide from afar
   o our pleading at the hour of brokenness
   Piously your shadow enlightens us

2. When in his arrogance, the wicked one causes horror
   To the poor, pursuing him with councils
   Of the tribunal, that the infidels call holy.[19]

Laguna takes a psalm decrying the impunity of the wicked—the stereotypical *rasha*—and places it within an undeniably inquisitorial context. In the second verse, Laguna elaborates on the phrase, the 'schemes' of the wicked and renders something much more direct and personal: 'the tribunal which the infidels call holy'—a clear reference to the 'Holy Office'.

In the next verse, Laguna expands on the idea of the 'wicked one' and gives the reader the vivid image of that hated Iberian figure, the *malshin*, the informer or betrayer:

3. May the *malshin* who audaciously praises himself
   Even if in faith he blesses himself, in bad faith he will meet his end

4. Perfidious and haughty
   His atrocities injure the righteous

5. With the false arguments of the Sophists
   Your judgments he tramples, when he attains
   The pomp and glory, of vain splendour.[20]

Laguna chooses in verse 3 to refer to the 'wicked one' not as the *rasha*, but by a decidedly more exact term, *malshin*. This word of Hebrew origin worked its way into Spanish usage to refer specifically to an informer, one who betrays his brothers. In the inquisitorial context the informer was given respect and protection from the inquisitors, but obviously his fellow Conversos would heap opprobrium on him. In place of the psalm's abstract evildoers and faceless persecutors of the poor, the wicked who feel invincible in the light of God's apparent disinterest in the affairs of humanity are identified with the agents of the inquisitorial apparatus, from the tribunals to the informers (often fellow Conversos) that act with impunity and arrogance against the 'pious'. They twist God's laws with false, sophistical arguments, pumped-up by their own success and illustrious (yet hollow) reputation.

---

[19] '1. Por que Señor te encumbres a lo lexos / A nuestro ruego en horas del quebranto: / Piadosos nos alumbren tus reflexos. 2. Quando soberbio el Malo, causa espanto / Al pobre persiguindole en consejos, / Del tribunal, que infieles llaman santo.'

[20] '3. Preso sea el Malsin que audaz se alava, / Pues aun que en fe bendize en mal fe acaba. / 4. Por pérfido, y altivo no requiere, / El pertinaz a Dios en sus intentos, / Su atrocidad al Justo ofende, y hiere, / 5. Con sofisticos falsos argumentos, / Tus juizios atropella, quando adquiere / Próspera pompa, en vanos luzimientos.'

The inquisitors trample on God's law as they persecute the Conversos, but their particular sin is presenting themselves as God's representatives and the enforcers of his law, which they pervert and twist to justify their oppression. They act with impunity because they are buoyed by their apparent success and honour. The arrogance and sense of righteousness is a dangerous combination. Laguna is reflecting on the absurdity, from the point of view of a Converso, of the Inquisition seeing itself as the 'Holy Office' and the inquisitors seeing their work as God's will. The psalm begins by calling out in bafflement and in protest to God for his hiddenness: how can you allow *this* to be the world order?

Laguna describes the predatory tactics of the wicked, likening them to lions and bears on the prowl. He locates their destructive power in their speech:

> 7. His lying lips are
> full of falsehood, craftiness and intrepidity.
> His tongue is a viper that kills.
>
> .   .   .   .
>
> 10. He tramples [the innocent] as he sings hypocritical praise
> He traps in his net the flock of the afflicted.[21]

They trap the persecuted through trickery, hypocrisy, and manipulating words. As used by the inquisitors, basic religious terms such as righteousness, holiness, and salvation are twisted beyond recognition, transforming the sacrifice and dedication of the crypto-Jew into perfidy.

The horrors of the Inquisition echoed in this poem serve as the evidence Laguna places before God in his protest. The inquisitors can act with such impunity because God has allowed them to.

> 11. He says in his heart, He has already forgotten
> And the Eternal God has hidden His benevolence
> The world, to the stars He has abandoned
> And to the planets His Governance.[22]

Laguna takes a classic trope of the Psalms—the demand that God reveal his ways in the world, that the afflicted be redeemed and their oppressor be brought low—and uses it to express his own anguish and possibly make sense of his own experience and the experience of his wider community.

---

[21] '7. De maldición su labio fementido / Lleno con falsedad, arte, y denuedo, / Siendo su lengua bivora que mata. // ... 10. Pues lisongeando ipocrita abatidos, / Coje en su red rebaños de afligidos.'

[22] '11. Dize en su coraçón ya se ha olvidado, / Y encubierto su agrado el Dios eterno; / Ya del mundo a los Astros a dexado, / Y a los planetas el total Govierno.'

14. You saw him, my Lord, in the ashes
    Of the downtrodden, that the inhuman one has reduced
    He awaits the vengeance of Your hand
    For You have always been the guardian of the orphan.[23]

Expanding upon the first phrase of the biblical verse, *ra'itah*, 'you saw', Laguna retains the basic meaning but expands it to meet the needs of his particular historical experience. Laguna, echoing the psalm and a long tradition of biblical cries for justice, reminds God that he always defends the orphans and he should do so again, meting out his wrath on those who burn his people *al kidush hashem*.

The next verse follows the biblical original closely. However, considering it within the wider context of the previous verses the reader cannot help but hear a more personal and contemporary request:

15. Break the arms of the malignant infidel,
    Enquire after his evil.[24]

He calls on God to break the arms of the *brazo seglar*—the 'secular arm' dedicated to meting out the physical punishments at the auto-da-fé. Laguna asks that the tables be turned, that instead of the inquisitors persecuting the innocent, it is the inquisitors who must be enquired into and called to account for their violence.

There is much more to consider and explore in Laguna's rich and complex text, but it is clear from this one example that Laguna's personal experience and the collective experience of his community find expression in this poem. That said, it is one step removed from his own experience, it is left in the abstract, in the third person. Perhaps, in the shuttling back and forth of Laguna's paraphrase we encounter a unique mode of autobiographical reflection that can help us reconsider the ghosts of Marrano autobiography.

[23] '14. Tu lo viste Señor, en la cenisa, / A que reduxo al Pobre; el inhumano / Su Vengança esperando de tu mano, / Pues del Huerfano siempre fuiste ampáro.'
[24] '15. Quebranta brasos del infiel maligno, / Ynquiere su maldad.'

CHAPTER NINETEEN

'MY HEART IS GRIEVED'

Grace Cardoze—A Life Revealed through Letters

JOSETTE CAPRILES GOLDISH

THE CARIBBEAN and American Sephardim of the nineteenth century are often remembered as enterprising and wealthy merchants, many of whom ended up being part of the elite societies of the cities and towns they called home. It is always misleading, however, to focus only on those individuals whose activities cause them to be written about, admired, and emulated when discussing a population or culture. By doing so, historians have often overlooked the sick, the poor, the oppressed, and the women who were all part of the same society. The story of Grace Cardoze reveals these less-discussed elements of Sephardi life as they affected one unfortunate individual.

Grace Cardoze was born on 2 June 1857 in St Thomas, Danish Virgin Islands, to David Cardoze and Rachel de Meza.[1] At the age of 16, Grace's father had migrated from the Dutch island of Curaçao to St Thomas in search of greater economic opportunities.[2] In 1840 when he arrived on the island, St Thomas's harbour at Charlotte Amalie was a busy stop-over for ships travelling from Europe to the Americas and back. The island's tax-free status and welcoming pluralistic society appealed to Jewish merchants and brokers in the import/export business, and David was one of many who came to St Thomas to take advantage of these conditions. Over time he became a well-respected merchant in Charlotte Amalie,[3] and by 1850 he was earning enough to start a family. That year he married St Thomas-born Rachel de Meza.[4]

Grace, the couple's second daughter, was named for her maternal grandmother and grew up in a family where religion was important. David Cardoze was the son of a cantor and well schooled in Jewish traditions.[5] After his arrival in St Thomas, he frequently served as reader in the synagogue, assisting the many rabbis that came to and left the island over the years. Grace appears to have received both a secular and a Jewish

---

[1] Sandra R. De Marchena, Genealogy of Curaçao's Sephardic Jews. Sandra R. de Marchena's genealogical data on more than 18,000 Sephardim and their descendants are contained in a digital database to which the author had access in 2010. It is constantly updated with births and deaths, as well as other information. See <www.demarchena.org>.   [2] Grace Cardoze Delvalle to David Simonsen (28 Nov. 1907).

[3] Judah M. Cohen, *Through the Sands of Time: A History of the Jewish Community of St. Thomas, U.S. Virgin Islands* (Hanover, NH, 2004), 109.

[4] De Marchena, Genealogy of Curaçao's Sephardic Jews.   [5] Cohen, *Through the Sands of Time*, 109.

education. The former is evident from her well-written letters, and the latter is likely in view of the importance of Judaism to her parents as well as the availability of Jewish schooling for the young in St Thomas. During key years of her childhood, Reverend Moses Nathan Nathan was the religious leader of St Thomas's Beracha Veshalom Vegemiluth Hasadim Synagogue. During Nathan's first period in St Thomas (1845–50), he had instituted a confirmation ceremony for the Jewish girls and boys of St Thomas, the first of which took place in 1846.[6] During his second stay on the island (1863–71), which coincided with Grace's school years, he continued his efforts to educate children. These classes, coupled with her Jewish home life, ensured that Grace Cardoze grew up to be a pious daughter of Israel.

In the late 1860s the economy of the Virgin Islands collapsed, and the Jewish community of St Thomas began to decline. The decrease in the number of Jews on the island, together with the secession of several Beracha Veshalom families to form a new Reform community in 1867, made it unlikely that the synagogue would be able to afford a full-time rabbi after Reverend Nathan's departure. With great foresight, Nathan made a conscious attempt to prepare David Cardoze to follow in his footsteps as leader of the congregation. In 1869, when David's eldest daughter, Bertha, was married, her father co-officiated with Reverend Nathan at the ceremony. When Reverend Nathan left in 1871, David accepted the responsibility—a commitment that he upheld for many decades.[7]

In 1871 Grace's youngest sister, Esther Consuelo, was born.[8] With the eldest daughter, Bertha, running her own household on the island, Rachel and David Cardoze's household now consisted of the 13-year-old Grace, her brothers Isidore and Moses, who were 12 and 10 respectively, and the newly arrived baby.

On 3 July 1873, shortly after her sixteenth birthday, Grace married David Delvalle, the youngest son of respected St Thomas businessman Benjamin Delvalle. Like his father and brothers, David was a dry-goods merchant in St Thomas, and it seems likely that the Cardozes thought him a good match for their daughter.[9] Benjamin Delvalle, who had been a leader of St Thomas's Jewish community, must have been pleased as well to see his youngest son marry into the pious Cardoze family. However, David's mind appears to have been elsewhere. Although he was twelve years older than Grace, he did not seem to be ready to settle down. During the first year of their marriage, he had an affair that resulted in the birth on 14 March 1875 of Henry H. Delvalle. The child was born to Henrietta Lucas, an Episcopalian woman, and was baptized in the Catholic Church on 28 April 1875. It was not uncommon for Sephardi men of those days to have children out of wedlock,[10] but for this to have occurred so soon after the marriage was

---

[6] Cohen, *Through the Sands of Time*, 83.

[7] Ibid. 130.   [8] De Marchena, Genealogy of Curaçao's Sephardic Jews.

[9] *St. Thomas Times Almanac* (Charlotte Amalie, St Thomas, 1877).

[10] Eva Abraham-Van der Mark, 'Marriage and Concubinage among the Sephardic Merchant Elite of Curaçao', in Janet Momsen (ed.), *Women and Change in the Caribbean* (Bloomington, 1993), 43.

somewhat unusual. Yet the possibility of divorce does not seem to have crossed the minds of the Cardoze family. One can imagine, however, that David's infidelity must have been a blow to his young bride and that this publicly known incident must have caused her great unhappiness. Nevertheless, all appeared to be forgiven.[11]

A year later, Grace gave birth to her first child, which they named Benjamin after David's father. At the age of 5 months, the child died of unknown causes, just a few months before the death of the elder Benjamin Delvalle. Two other sons died in infancy in 1879. Of Grace and David's nine children, only six lived to adulthood.[12]

In the mid 1880s David Delvalle decided to try his luck in Panama. Many of St Thomas's Jews had preceded him there during the speculative years when the Panama Canal was being built. It is unlikely that Grace accompanied him on this venture, as she later wrote: 'My Husband went to Panama in the time of the French Canal and lost his money.'[13] For an unknown period she lived in St Thomas with her six young children, presumably supported by her parents and siblings while David was away.

So far, her married life appears to have been a trial. But more trouble awaited her. At home her daughter Deborah Viola, who had been born on 20 June 1883, began to display increasingly odd behaviour. In the small town of Charlotte Amalie, where everyone knew everyone else's business, it was a terrible burden to have a child who was a social misfit and, worse, one who might be mentally unstable. For this to be happening in a 'respectable family' during the time David Cardoze was the leader of the St Thomas Jewish congregation was a source of shame to Grace.

The older Viola became, the harder it was to control her. To her family's distress, she would run away several times a day, wandering the streets of Charlotte Amalie in an agitated state. The doctors on the island had no idea what was wrong with her and were unable to offer much help. The island had no suitable hospital or asylum, and Viola was labelled 'mentally deranged' and became an ever-increasing problem to her mother and the rest of the family.[14]

One can imagine Grace at home with this difficult, handicapped child and her five other children, trying to make ends meet, while David was losing money in Panama. It must have been a very trying time. Eventually David returned to St Thomas, but by 1902, at the age of 57, he was paralysed, most likely from a stroke. Except for his brother, Jacob Delvalle, who had moved to Curaçao, all his siblings had died, and thus no help was forthcoming from his side of the family. Instead, David became totally dependent on his wife and in-laws. Grace wrote in 1905:

I am really desolate as my Husband has been an Invalid for the past three years, and I have to work hard to support him, my six children and self. My struggles are great.[15]

[11] Cohen, *Through the Sands of Time*, 147.   [12] De Marchena, Genealogy of Curaçao's Sephardic Jews.
[13] Grace Cardoze Delvalle to David Simonsen (28 Nov. 1907).
[14] Grace Cardoze Delvalle to David Simonsen (14 Jan. 1907).
[15] Grace Cardoze Delvalle to David Simonsen (18 Aug. 1905).

In the same year, in consultation with her elderly father, Grace decided to send Viola, then aged 22, to Denmark and have her hospitalized there.

The Cardozes appealed to the former chief rabbi of Denmark, Dr David Simonsen of Copenhagen.[16] Neither Grace nor her father knew him, but his scholarly reputation and good name were recognized throughout the Jewish world at the time. David Cardoze's introductory letter began by attempting to establish a bond on the grounds of their common religion.

Respected Sir!

Your highly respectable name, glad am I to say, is quite familiar to me, having heard it very often mentioned. My name, perhaps, is not known to you, but when I tell you that we are from the same stock, you will, I am sure, understand that, in faith, we are not strangers to one another.[17]

He then proceeded to explain exactly who he was and provided Dr Simonsen with the name of 'Mr. S. Wulff, partner of the highly respectable firm of Messrs. Moses Melchoir & Co. of your city' as a character reference. Finally he got to the point of his letter and requested that Dr Simonsen procure a place for his granddaughter, Viola Delvalle, in an institution in Denmark where her 'nervousness and weakness of the brain' might be treated.[18] A week later, not waiting for a response to her father's letter, Grace Cardoze Delvalle wrote to Dr Simonsen herself in what was to be the first of many letters to the unknown Danish scholar who would become her friend.

Reverend Sir,

My Father Revd. David Cardoze the Minister of our Holy Congregation having addressed himself to you in behalf of my Daughter who is suffering from some mental derangement and who I intend sending on under the charge of a trustworthy Servant by the Danish Steamer Sto. Domingo which will be leaving on or about next month, I take the liberty of addressing you, and hope am not encroaching on your valued time, if you will kindly look after her and see her placed in the Hospital and get all information from the Doctor what is really the matter with her.[19]

In this day and age, it is hard to imagine approaching a stranger in this manner with the expectation of a positive response. It must have been equally difficult for Grace and her father to do so 100 years ago. But Grace must have been at her wits' end. With the encouragement of her father, she put her daughter in the hands of someone she did not know, thousands of miles away on the other side of the Atlantic, and prayed that she had made the right decision. Her husband's views of the matter are never mentioned in any of her letters.

---

[16]   David Simonsen was chief rabbi of Denmark from 1892 to 1902.
[17]   David Cardoze to David Simonsen (10 Aug. 1905).   [18] Ibid.
[19]   Grace Cardoze Delvalle to David Simonsen (18 Aug. 1905).

On 3 or 4 September 1905 the ship carrying Viola and her caretaker left for Denmark, and by 27 October 1905 the anxious mother had received notification of their arrival in Copenhagen. She immediately wrote back to Dr Simonsen:

Respected Sir,

Your valued and welcome lines addressed to my Father were perused with great attention announcing the arrival of my poor unfortunate child in your city. I cannot sufficiently thank you and your good Wife for the kindness and attention you have shown to my poor child and trust that the great God will pour down his blessings on you for your good and noble act. I took note of all you write that she would not speak to the Doctor and Nurses and would not eat except what your good Wife so kindly gave her. Oh, my friend as I can term you that name, you can picture what distress I am in to know my dear girl is in such a bad state. I kindly ask of you to enquire from the doctor if her malady is curable or not and let me know all particulars.[20]

Grace Cardoze Delvalle was clearly devastated that she had to send her daughter away.

Viola appears to have stayed in Copenhagen for some time, but was soon placed in Sindssygeanstalten ved Vordingborg—an asylum for the insane located in Vordingborg, about 50 miles from the Danish capital. For a while yet, Grace would not know if sending her daughter into the unknown would lead to a cure for the 'poor unfortunate child', as Viola was henceforth referred to, but already in her early letters the issue of money arose.

About the charges: [from] what I understand the money will not suffice. I have to place my position to you, as my Husband is lying in a helpless condition and I have to support my children and Self. I had to make a great sacrifice to get my girl away, as here in this Country there are no places to cure such patients, so was obliged to sacrifice all for her. I again beg of you to try and secure a free Ward after the time of three months as really am unable to do anything, the country['s economy] is so bad that one can hardly make expenses.[21]

At the end of December she heard from Dr Simonsen that Viola had become incontinent, but was eating and sleeping well. In her response, Grace wrote that she was 'sorry to learn she is not clean'. Apparently, Viola had been incontinent before, but had improved for the two years prior to her departure. Grace also informed the Simonsens that her eldest daughter Judith was getting married in Panama in January and that her youngest daughter Rebecca had gone to Panama to take over Judith's job as a telephone operator for the company that was building the canal. The Delvalle women were enterprising enough to make sure that this particular job stayed in the family once Judith was forced to retire.

After Viola had been in Denmark for almost a year, it became clear that there would be no cure for her mental disabilities. Grace was deeply saddened by this news and wrote to Dr Simonsen:

[20] Grace Cardoze Delvalle to David Simonsen (27 Oct. 1905).   [21] Ibid.

My heart is grieved when I think of the condition of my poor unfortunate child. Took note dear and respected Sir that the chief Physician does not think she can be cured, and she showed sign of that dreadful malady Consumption. Your letter received today wherein you stated that you returned from Germany and went to see her, and that the second leading Physician said that the signs have already gone away, but that the other Physician had little hopes of her being cured, although you write she eats and sleeps well and much cleaner than before, but now she will not go in the garden or speak to the Doctor, also she would not speak to you. What must I do but put my trust in God and He will help me.[22]

Occasionally Viola wrote to her mother, but her letters were often confused and saddened Grace even more.[23] Yet she continued to write to her ailing daughter in Denmark and also continued her correspondence with Dr and Mrs Simonsen.

The Simonsens were childless and travelled frequently throughout Europe and the Middle East. Whenever they returned to Copenhagen, they would enquire after Viola Delvalle's well-being and occasionally visit her despite the substantial distance between Copenhagen and Vordingborg. Many of their reports to St Thomas contain information they had received from the medical staff at the asylum. Had it not been for the Simonsens' constant involvement in her care, Viola may not have been as well looked after as she was. The Cardozes were fortunate to have found this kind and compassionate couple, and Grace was well aware of this. She thanked them profusely in all her letters: 'God bless you for your kindness to a poor strange girl'; '[I] pray to Almighty God to pour down his choicest gifts and blessings for your befriending a Stranger and acting the part of a true Messenger of God'.

By January 1909 a photograph of the Danish couple had been placed in a 'conspicuous part of [the Cardoze–Delvalle] Drawing Room', and, from the letter acknowledging receipt of the picture, it may be inferred that David and Grace Delvalle and their single children had moved into Grace's father's home.[24]

On 5 April 1909, during the festival of Passover, David died and was buried in the Jewish cemetery of St Thomas. Although he had caused Grace much sorrow during his lifetime, Grace chose to forget those slights and wrote to her Danish friend: 'As you can imagine my spirit is grieved on the loss I have sustained as he was a devoted companion of 35 years. May his Soul rest in peace. Amen.'[25]

Money continued to be an issue. At the end of 1909 Grace incurred unexpected additional expenses, when she had to travel to Puerto Rico for another daughter's unspecified surgery. Fortunately the surgery was successful, and this daughter's illness did not present her with a new source of worry. It did, however, set her back financially.[26]

---

[22] Grace Cardoze Delvalle to David Simonsen (1 Aug. 1906).
[23] Grace Cardoze Delvalle to David Simonsen (7 Mar. 1907).
[24] Grace Cardoze Delvalle to David Simonsen (26 Jan. 1909).
[25] Grace Cardoze Delvalle to David Simonsen (10 May 1909).
[26] Grace Cardoze Delvalle to David Simonsen (13 Jan. 1910).

Until her husband's death, Grace signed her letters 'Mrs. David B. Delvalle' or 'Mrs. Delvalle'. On 10 May 1909, when she first informed the Simonsens of her husband's demise, she signed herself G. C. Delvalle. Subsequently, this is the signature she seemed to prefer, occasionally appearing liberated enough to sign her first name as well.

Grace's sadness permeates her letters. In 1911 she wrote: 'some days my great sorrow comes before me that it makes me sick, but I place my trust in the God of Israel who will never forsake us'.[27] Seven years after Viola's departure from St Thomas, it was clear that Grace continued to feel terrible about her fate, as she wrote to Dr Simonsen: 'Oh how my heart bleeds when I think of her wrecked life, but it is only my faith in God that keeps me safe.'[28]

The tragedies in Grace's life did not cease. On 15 August 1912 she wrote:

Sorrow entered my home and heart. My daughter came from Panama to see me and brought the two grandchildren, the little girl was suddenly taken from us after two days illness—a promising child of five years. We are plunged into great grief and only God in Heaven can comfort the bereaved Parents and other dear Ones.[29]

When this letter was written, Reverend David Cardoze, Grace's father, was 88 years old and starting to show his age. Three years earlier, he had fasted all day on Yom Kippur and had read the whole service without any aid.[30] As he approached 90, however, he began to tire more easily, and Grace clearly started to worry about him too.

Reverend David Cardoze's ninetieth birthday was celebrated with much fanfare in St Thomas on 31 December 1913.[31] Businessmen, government officials, and members of the Jewish community feted him and expressed their appreciation for this man who had made a name for himself in St Thomas as a merchant and a tireless spokesman of the Jewish congregation.[32] Shortly before her father's birthday, Grace wrote to the Simonsens that her father was about to turn 90: 'He is very strong for that age and goes about and does all he has to do. I pray he will live for some years more.' The Simonsens sent a congratulatory cable for the occasion, and Grace thanked them for this kindness in a letter dated 9 January 1914.

Despite a display of vigour at his ninetieth birthday celebration, Cardoze is reported to be quite feeble in Grace's letter to the Simonsens dated 13 May 1914. She recounts that he was very worried as well, since Grace's sister, Esther Consuelo, who had been living in Costa Rica, was expected to arrive in St Thomas, accompanied by her

27 Grace Cardoze Delvalle to David Simonsen (10 Oct. 1911).
28 Grace Cardoze Delvalle to David Simonsen (3 July 1912).
29 Grace Cardoze Delvalle to David Simonsen (15 Aug. 1912).
30 Grace Cardoze Delvalle to David Simonsen (28 Oct. 1909).
31 His actual date of birth was 1 Jan. 1824.
32 Cohen, *Through the Sands of Time*, 161–2.

husband Joseph Athias Robles and their seven children. Esther's husband was in poor health and out of work, and David Cardoze must have been wondering how he was going to feed this large penniless family.[33] Grace also mentioned in this letter that she had not been well for a few months either and that she was still under a doctor's care.

Grace Cardoze's life had been a vale of tears. The youthful and romantic illusions she may have had as a 16-year-old when she married David Delvalle had been quickly shattered by his unfaithfulness. Although the couple had arrived at a modus vivendi after this episode, David's subsequent failure in Panama plunged the family into a life of poverty. It is not clear what would have become of them, if they had not been able to move into Reverend Cardoze's home. To make matters worse, illness and death had been Grace's constant companions. Her life was repeatedly diminished by the death of three children, a mentally ill daughter who had been sent to Denmark, a paralysed husband, the death of a granddaughter, and her own depression and guilt. Yet she never wavered in her faith. In her second to last letter to Dr Simonsen she wrote:

It is only God who keeps me safe, otherwise I would sink under this great sorrow. The only light I see is that [Viola] is well treated. Tears are blinding me, so must conclude.[34]

In early July of 1914, a year that had started with the happy celebration of David Cardoze's ninetieth birthday, the Simonsens were stunned to receive a letter from St Thomas that read:

Dear Sir

You will think it strange to see another writing but I am sorry to inform you of the death of my Mother who died on the 14th of June & my Grandfather Revd Cardoze two days after. I am the daughter of Mrs. Delvalle & you may suppose what a house of mourning ours are [sic]. When next you address your letters
Miss Idalia Delvalle
St Thomas

Let me know how Viola is getting on & if she understood the letters and postal sent to her last mail. I remain respectfully yours,
Idalia Delvalle[35]

That June, Grace was laid to rest in the Altona Jewish cemetery of St Thomas without ever laying eyes on her beloved Viola again. She was 57 years old.

Later that year Grace's brother-in-law, recently arrived from Costa Rica, also passed away, and the following year Grace's daughter Idalia explained to the Simonsens that she was in dire financial straits and that she and her sister Illia now depended on a brother in Panama for their very small income.[36] She continued to correspond with

33 Grace Cardoze Delvalle to David Simonsen (13 May 1914).
34 Grace Cardoze Delvalle to David Simonsen (9 Jan. 1914).
35 Idalia Delvalle to David Simonsen (28 June 1914).
36 Idalia Delvalle to David Simonsen (22 Sept. 1916).

Dr Simonsen in Copenhagen, faithfully remitting whatever funds she could afford for Viola's care. In late 1919, five years after her mother's death, Idalia moved to Panama to live with her sister Judith Delvalle Halman. As she explained to Dr Simonsen, she decided to be closer to her brother and sisters who lived there, since 'all my other relatives are dead'.[37]

Viola Delvalle died in Denmark on 2 December 1927, twenty-two years after she left St Thomas. She was given a Jewish funeral and buried in Copenhagen's Mosaic western cemetery.[38] Idalia responded to this news on 16 January 1928 in almost illegible handwriting. In her letter she mentioned that she had been quite sick. She expressed her sadness at her sister's demise and, like her mother, did not forget to add 'May God bless you and grant you everything good.'[39] It was to be her last letter to Dr Simonsen. Idalia Delvalle died in Panama on 28 April 1929.[40]

Although Viola is always described as poor and unfortunate, she actually received the best care available to emotionally disturbed Danish citizens at the time. In spite of the monetary constraints within which the Delvalles had to function, they had placed her in a special hospital for the mentally ill, where it appears that she was well cared for, fed, clothed, attended by doctors, and visited by the Simonsens and their extended family. Until the end of 1917 the money sent from St Thomas had been enough for Viola to remain in the asylum's first-class ward. On 1 January 1918, however, she was downgraded to third-class, although she was allowed to continue occupying the room where she had lived for quite some time.[41] At the time Dr Simonsen wrote to Idalia:

> She is, hélas, so unconcerned in all matters that we think she will perhaps not know at all, that her conditions are altered. In these days I had again a letter from the physician, and he tells me that she is sitting longtime without taking part in any thing, she does not speak at all and does not show any interest and has no possibility to work in any direction. A seldom time she is not quiet but does not tell anything what he does not like, but the most time she is quiet smiling, eating well and sleeping well.[42]

A few years later, in 1921, it became clear that the money Idalia was able to remit from Panama had slowed to a trickle. But Dr Simonsen assured Idalia that 'if it is not possible to send money, it shall be no pain for you; we will continue to look after the little patient so long as it will be possible for us'.[43] It is quite likely that the Simonsens covered most of the expenses associated with Viola's care in the last decade of her life and that the rabbi made all the arrangements for her funeral as well.

[37] Ibid.   [38] De Marchena, Genealogy of Curaçao's Sephardic Jews.
[39] Idalia Delvalle to David Simonsen (16 Jan. 1928).
[40] De Marchena, Genealogy of Curaçao's Sephardic Jews.
[41] David Simonsen to Idalia Delvalle (13 Nov. 1917).   [42] Ibid.
[43] David Simonsen to Idalia Delvalle (13 Oct. 1921).

Of Grace's six children who lived to adulthood, Viola, Idalia, and Illia remained single; Judith, Rebecca, and Moses married within the Jewish faith and lived out their lives in Panama, where many of their descendants still reside.[44]

The correspondence between the Cardoze–Delvalle family of St Thomas and Dr Simonsen of Denmark forces us to consider some aspects of the lives of Caribbean Sephardim beyond the usual success stories of the time. Clearly the stresses caused by ill health, premature death, and economic uncertainty were not unique to this family. But historians rarely get to see the personal hardships affecting individual members of a society that is mostly remembered for its achievements. The letters preserved in the David Simonsen Archives in Copenhagen offer a window into the everyday worries and hardship that people like Grace Cardoze Delvalle endured, while others in the same community went from success to success.

Throughout the twentieth century, Viola's grave remained unmarked in Copenhagen's Mosaic western cemetery. Shortly after the discovery in the early twenty-first century of the correspondence between Grace Delvalle and Dr Simonsen, however, Grace's surviving descendants and wider family in Holland, the United States, and Panama collected the necessary funds to erect a tombstone for their Caribbean cousin buried so far away from the tropical shores where she had been born. In an e-mail written on 25 February 2009, René van Wijngaarden of the Netherlands, who is a distant relative of the St Thomas Delvalle family, described to Deborah Viola's relatives around the world this act of loving kindness as follows:

Dear cousins,

This weekend our family returned from Copenhagen where we attended the unveiling of the headstone of cousin Deborah Viola Delvalle. Sunday morning—10 o'clock—we met with Chief Rabbi of Denmark Bent Lexner. Everything went as planned. When we arrived at the cemetery our Rabbi stepped out of his car the very same moment as we did and after shaking hands we walked to the designated place and there we saw Deborah's gravestone.

.   .   .   .

The Rabbi recited a special prayer for Deborah in Hebrew, and, of course, our thoughts lingered back in time to the very days she was hospitalized in Vordingborg Oringe in 1905. After having thanked Rabbi Bent Lexner on behalf of our families, the ceremony ended. Bent told us he had never experienced this before and appreciated it tremendously. We said goodbye and stayed for a while on the graveyard to look around and enjoy the serenity of this peaceful environment.

After an hour we had already left Copenhagen behind us and drove home to the Netherlands. We had a wonderful feeling for, after all, our mission was accomplished and we are convinced that our cousin will be looking down with a big smile on her face. Now her name is engraved in granite as well and she will no longer lie anonymously in that far away cemetery in Copenhagen.

Although the synagogue in Charlotte Amalie where David Cardoze presided over services for so many years remains in operation, offering religious services on the

---

[44] De Marchena, Genealogy of Curaçao's Sephardic Jews.

sabbath and Jewish festivals, there are no Sephardi Jews left in St Thomas. The descendants of the Sephardim who once called this island home are scattered across the globe, but their sense of history and dedication to the memory of their ancestors is abundantly clear from this final homage to Deborah Viola Delvalle and her long-suffering mother, Grace Cardoze Delvalle.

ACKNOWLEDGEMENTS
This chapter is based on the 1905–28 correspondence between the Cardoze–Delvalle family of St Thomas and Rabbi David Simonsen of Copenhagen (Det Kongelige Bibliotek, Copenhagen, Oriental and Judaica Collections, David Simonsen Archives). The author is grateful for the use of these letters, which were made available to her by René van Wijngaarden of the Netherlands. Part of this chapter was presented at the American Comparative Literature Association conference in Puebla, Mexico, April 2007.

PART VII

THE FORMATION OF
CONTEMPORARY
CARIBBEAN JEWRY

CHAPTER TWENTY

REFUGEES FROM NAZISM IN THE BRITISH CARIBBEAN

JOANNA NEWMAN

W HEN the Spanish-Portuguese poet Daniel Israel López Laguna proclaimed his freedom in Jamaica, he may have been aware of the paradox that the British colony that tolerated his freedom was based on a slave economy that denied thousands theirs. During the height of the slave trade, a small but significant number of Jews of Spanish and Portuguese origin were able to escape persecution and find a niche for themselves in Caribbean colonies, making good use of family networks along the trade routes between Amsterdam, London, Iberia, and the New World.[1]

Unlike those Jews who went there during the seventeenth and eighteenth centuries, those fleeing persecution in the 1930s and 1940s were not on the whole seeking economic opportunity but viewed the Caribbean as an accidental destination, a way-station, en route to the barred new worlds of North and South America. In a context of world recession, protectionist immigration policies, antisemitic regimes in eastern Europe and Nazi Germany, and a global refugee crisis, the movement of Jewish refugees to the Caribbean is a largely hidden history which throws into sharp relief themes which still have relevance today, such as the role of international relief agencies and the politics of refuge and rescue.

It is a history that became visible when public anger and frustration forced the Western democracies to focus on issues such as the plight of refugees in the 1930s and the rescue of Jews during the Holocaust. The Caribbean, and other destinations, featured as a potential refuge only when it became clear that the main emigration channels would remain closed.[2]

[1] See e.g. Eli Faber, *Jews, Slaves, and the Slave Trade: Setting the Record Straight* (New York, 1998); Stephen Alexander Fortune, *Merchants and Jews: The Struggle for British West Indian Commerce, 1650–1750* (Gainesville, Fla., 1984).

[2] For a full historiographical account of how the Caribbean fits into the general context of refuge in the 1930s and rescue in the 1940s, see Joanna Newman, 'Nearly the New World: Refugees and the British West Indies, 1933–1945' (Ph.D. thesis, University of Southampton, 1998); on US responses to refuge and rescue, see Arthur Morse, *While Six Million Died: A Chronicle of American Apathy* (New York, 1968); David Wyman, *The Abandonment of the Jews: America and the Holocaust, 1941–1945* (New York, 1984); Henry Feingold, *The Politics of*

At the conference held in the French spa town of Evian-les-Bains convened by President Roosevelt in July 1938 to discuss the mounting refugee crisis, it quickly became clear that no country would be required to alter its existing immigration policy or use exceptional legislation to enable the admittance of refugees. The underlying reasons for this had less to do with the problems of assimilating what was a relatively small German Jewish refugee population and more to do with the fear that, by relaxing immigration restrictions for some, the floodgates would open and antisemitic eastern European regimes would make their own Jewish populations stateless. At Evian little was achieved, except for an offer from the Dominican Republic to allow a refugee settlement at Sosua.[3] Like the British Guiana plan offered by the British in 1939, shortly after the publication of the Palestine White Paper that drastically limited Jewish emigration to Palestine, resettlement schemes were always intended for a small proportion of able-bodied Jews willing to engage in physical work. They were not suitable for mass refugee settlement. President Roosevelt's Advisory Committee on Political Refugees, for example, investigated potential settlements in the Dominican Republic, British Guiana, Cyprus, the Philippines, the Belgian Congo, Ecuador, Mexico, Haiti, and Suriname. Refugee bodies had serious reservations about the role that 'exotic' places could play in solving the refugee crisis but were often called on to fund investigations while their policy remained focused on persuading the Allied powers to enable refugee migration to mainstream countries of immigration. A memorandum from Cecilia Razovksy of the National Coordinating Committee summed up their attitude:

There isn't a day that we don't get letters from committees in all parts of the country insisting that we put Jews on the land and they are very indignant because we seem to pass over these suggestions, as though we never heard of them and write a cold reply to their enthusiasm. . . . It seems to

Rescue: The Roosevelt Administration and the Holocaust 1938–1945 (New Brunswick, 1970); on British responses, see Ari Joshua Sherman, Island Refuge: Britain and Refugees from the Third Reich 1933–1939 (Berkeley, Calif., 1973); Bernard Wasserstein, Britain and the Jews of Europe, 1939–1945 (London, 1979); Louise London, Whitehall and the Jews, 1933–1948: British Immigration Policy, Jewish Refugees and the Holocaust (New York, 2000); on the historiography of Allied responses to the Holocaust, see Tony Kushner, The Holocaust and the Liberal Imagination: A Social and Cultural History (Oxford, 1994); Michael R. Marrus, The Holocaust in History (Hanover, NH, 1987); id., The Unwanted: European Refugees in the Twentieth Century (New York, 1985); on Canada's response, see Irving Abella and Harold Troper, None is Too Many: Canada and the Jews of Europe 1933–1948 (Toronto, 1982); on Australia's response, see Michael Blakeney, Australia and the Jewish Refugees, 1933–1948 (Sydney, 1985); on Brazil's response, see Jeffrey Lesser, Welcoming the Undesirables: Brazil and the Jewish Question (Berkeley, Calif., 1995); on Cuba's response, see Robert Levine, Tropical Diaspora: The Jewish Experience in Cuba (Gainesville, Fla., 1993); on India's response, see Anil Bhatti and Johannes H. Voigt (eds.), Jewish Exile in India 1933–1945 (New Delhi, 1999); on responses of the British empire, focusing on the dominion states, see Paul Bartrop, False Havens: The British Empire and the Holocaust (Lanham, Md., 1995).

[3] For an eyewitness account of the Evian Conference, see Shalom Adler-Rudel, 'The Evian Conference on the Refugee Question', Leo Baeck Institute Year Book, 13 (1968), 235–73; on Sosua, see Marion A. Kaplan, Dominican Haven: The Jewish Refugee Settlement in Sosúa, 1940–1945 (New York, 2008). Kaplan notes that thousands were able to leave Germany on visas for the Dominican Republic.

me that a statement worked out by the JDC, emphasising exactly what Dr. Rosen has said today, would be very helpful in educating the Jewish population in the United States. They say they don't want them in the cities. Put them on the land.[4]

By 1 September 1939 some concessions had been introduced in Britain and America: in Britain's case, these resulted in some 40,000 refugees being admitted between November 1938 and the outbreak of war. But immigration regulations were not changed and most refugees escaped to countries of refuge by virtue of their compliance with existing immigration regulations. In some cases refugees migrated using illegal means such as purchasing false travel documents (in many cases unknowingly) or through finding loopholes, for example in Trinidad, which allowed entry on production of landing money and did not require visas.[5]

Once war broke out, the imperative to find homes for European Jews was replaced by Allied wartime imperatives that placed rescue second to winning the war, a stance generally supported by a public now suspicious of refugees with 'enemy alien' nationalities. However, in December 1942, once the Allies had broadcast the news of the mass extermination of European Jewry, there were again concerted efforts from a broad consortium of religious, lay, and political groups in the UK and the USA calling for the Allies to 'do something'. These efforts culminated in the Bermuda Conference of April 1943. This time the conference was held in a remote location inaccessible to the media, where its deliberations could be kept secret.

As with the Evian conference, detailed proposals were submitted in Bermuda by expert witnesses and refugee organizations. By 1943 these proposals centred on removing restrictions from immigration to Palestine, finding ways to send emergency food and medical supplies to occupied areas, encouraging neutral countries to admit refugees, and creating temporary havens in Africa and the Caribbean that would enable refugees to reach neutral territory.[6] By April 1943 it was already too late for the majority

---

[4] Typescript of meeting of the Subcommittee for Central and South America (13 Apr. 1939), Joint Distribution Committee (JDC) Archives, New York (JDCA), file 112.

[5] In 1939 the USA enabled a full quota of visas for Austrian and German immigrants to be used. In Britain, following the events of Kristallnacht in November 1938, the Home Office allowed the issue of block visas which enabled some 10,000 refugee children entry to Britain. This arrangement also allowed several thousand young men temporary admittance to the UK from German concentration camps (see Sherman, *Island Refuge*, 231; London, *Whitehall and the Jews*, 11–12).

[6] In Britain, the National Committee for Rescue from Nazi Terror put forward a twelve-point rescue programme, which included the suggestion that refugees be housed in Gibraltar Camp. From the USA, the Emergency Committee for European Jewish Affairs also submitted a twelve-point plan suggesting that possibilities in Africa and the Caribbean be explored without delay (see Eleanor Rathbone, *Rescue the Perishing: A Summary of the Position Regarding the Nazi Massacres of Jewish and Other Victims and of Proposals for their Rescue: An Appeal, a Programme and a Challenge* (London, 1943); see also Kushner, *The Holocaust and the Liberal Imagination*, 179; for a reprint of the demands, see William D. Rubinstein, *The Myth of Rescue: Why the Democracies Could Not have Saved More Jews from the Nazis* (London, 1997), 132–5; for a discussion of British concerns at Bermuda, see Newman, 'Nearly the New World', 76–80).

of European Jewry, who had been murdered in camps and massacres across Nazi-occupied Europe. The conference spent much time referring to what had already been achieved and spent little time debating what could be done, using the exigencies of war as sufficient reason to veto most of the suggestions.[7] Despite one of the recommendations of the 1943 Bermuda Conference report for the 'admission of a limited group to Jamaica', it would seem that objections from the governor, reduced space in the camp, and perhaps the exigencies of war prevented their removal there.

Therefore at times of increased pressure during the 1930s and 1940s, the Caribbean became involved as a potential and actual place of refuge for Jews escaping Nazi Europe. Here I will give a brief overview of how the West Indies became involved with Jewish refugees before concentrating on two British West Indian colonies, Jamaica and Trinidad. In Trinidad, the majority of Jewish refugees arrived before the outbreak of war as a result of forced migration, their journeys often aided by refugee charities. In Jamaica, most refugees arrived during the war, as the British government relocated them there. Both examples highlight the tensions that existed between British immigration policy, West Indian and colonial concerns, and the pressures of refugee resettlement.

The American Jewish Joint Distribution Committee estimated that it supported approximately 125,000 refugees in central and southern American republics as well as in British and Dutch colonies. Between 1936 and 1943, its expenditure on these refugees amounted to over $2 million, with about 8 per cent of its budget spent on aid to refugees in the British West Indies, principally Trinidad and Jamaica.[8] This relatively high figure reflects how dependent refugees in the British West Indies were on aid from the JDC and other agencies and emphasizes how few economic opportunities were open to them.

From the 1920s new immigration regulations were enacted and existing ones strengthened in most colonies to protect West Indian labour. In Jamaica, visas were introduced specifically to prevent Chinese and Syrian immigrants from entering the country.[9] In the early 1930s most people concerned with refugee migration felt that

---

[7] Concessions granted at Bermuda included allowing further movement of refugees from Spain and Portugal to Gibraltar Camp in Jamaica, but the conference was mainly perceived by refugee bodies as a failure (see *Report to the Governments of the United States and the United Kingdom from their Delegates to the Conference on the Refugee Problem held at Bermuda (19–29 Apr. 1943)* (London, 1943), National Archives, Kew (TNA), Colonial Office (CO) 733/449). During 1944 further concessions were made by the War Refugee Board, a body that finally had more power to act than any refugee agencies had previously. This included granting passage to approximately 1,000 refugees who were allowed entry to Oswego, a disused army camp in New York State for the duration of the war (see Ruth Gruber, *The Haven: The Dramatic Story of 1,000 World War II Refugees and How They Came to America* (New York, 1983; repr. 2000)).

[8] Committee on Refugee Aid in Central and South America (7 Mar. 1943), JDC Work in Central and South America (1936–43), JDCA, file 114.

[9] 'Change to Immigration, Jamaica' (5 Nov. 1931), press cuttings left by the Chinese chargé d'affaires

Palestine, the United States, and neighbouring European countries would play the largest role in receiving refugees from Nazi Germany. However, from 1933 onwards a series of circulars asked colonial governors to report whether opportunities existed for entrepreneurs and skilled chemists, engineers, doctors, and dentists in their territories.[10] The circulars were phrased in such a way as to imply that the British government was eager to help solve the refugee problem and that if there were vacancies in the colonial empire, the government would be in favour of allowing refugee admittance. However, in practice, despite some exceptions (in British Honduras, the governor encouraged an initiative to establish a handbag factory), the main responses to these requests were unenthusiastic, reflecting protectionist attitudes towards local labour and local prejudices. For example, the governor of the Bahamas stated that an 'anti-Semitic bias' existed in the colony and that as a consequence there were 'very few Jews in the Bahamas'.[11]

Responses from the West Indian colonies were also negative. In the 1930s economic conditions were harsh, with seasonal unemployment, overpopulation, and serious poverty. Strikes spread throughout the West Indies as a new political leadership was born, demanding change from the Crown colony system, accountability, and increased suffrage. Britain reacted by forming a royal commission on the West Indies which issued a far-reaching set of recommendations in 1938. But while the Colonial Office sought to review legislation, it believed that the existing entry quotas in place in most colonies, although relatively low, would continue to act as a deterrent to seasonal migrants and destitute immigrants.[12]

While there were good reasons why the Caribbean was not expected to play any significant role in refugee placement, by 1939 hundreds had found their way to Caribbean colonies, and a government scheme for mass refuge in British Guiana was being discussed in the House of Commons. This change reflected the increasingly desperate tenor of the refugee crisis. In 1938, with the annexation of Austria, Nazi policy entered a fiercer and more chaotic phase as ideologues took over from pragmatists in the Nazi hierarchy. Thousands of Jews were arrested: their release dependent upon their leaving Germany; their possessions and money surrendered to the state. Refugees and aid agencies found loopholes in entry regulations and scanned the globe for places without

regarding the restriction of immigration into Jamaica, TNA, CO 351/86135/31 (file not available); Acting Governor to Secretary of State for the Colonies (27 Apr. 1934), TNA, CO 351/36431/34 (destroyed).

[10] See Newman 'Nearly the New World', 52–3.

[11] Governor of the Bahamas to Sir John Maffey (20 Apr. 1934), TNA, CO 323/1271/1.

[12] Immigration legislation varied between West Indian colonies where laws were the result of discussions between local legislature and the Colonial Office. Once the Secretary of State for the Colonies had approved the format, the bill could become law. In 1931 only Jamaica, the Leeward Islands, Trinidad, and the Windward Islands demanded passports, and no colonies asked for visas. By 1933 passports were required in all British West Indian colonies with the exception of the Bahamas, and only Jamaica and British Honduras demanded visas (see Newman, 'Nearly the New World', 33–4).

visa requirements. Ironically, the research departments of the Gestapo and refugee aid organizations were aligned in this as Nazi policy dictated a mass exodus of Jews.[13] The more places that refused admittance, the more their anti-Jewish policies were seen to be supported by other countries. Those British colonial dependencies, including Trinidad, that did not require visas began to receive refugees daily from Germany and Austria. By December 1938 Port of Spain in Trinidad had a refugee population of 600 Jews.

Most of the refugees had come as a result of advice and information from Jewish aid organizations. The National Coordinating Committee in New York, the JDC, and other organizations sent regular information on immigration requirements to their European counterparts who processed refugee migration through their offices. Information regarding Trinidad had been sent to the National Coordinating Committee by Edgar Pereira, a Trinidadian who set up a refugee aid organization in Trinidad to help co-ordinate refugee arrivals.[14] In a communiqué to aid committees in Europe, Cecilia Razovsky of the National Coordinating Committee gave further details:

Cooperating agencies had to notify the National Coordinating Committee of details of the refugees. The National Coordinating Committee would then notify the Harbour Master in Trinidad and obtain landing certificates. These certificates would be forwarded to the passenger, who would present it to the steamship company at the port of embarkation. The cash deposit of $256 should be paid at the port of embarkation but in cases where American relatives were supplying the money, other arrangements could be made.[15]

While the number of destitute refugees increased, most countries remained unwilling to let refugees in and instead focused on ill-conceived plans for mass resettlement in far-flung places, including Madagascar, the Kimberley in Western Australia, the US Virgin Islands, and Alaska. The British Guiana scheme did have possibilities according to Sir Walter Citrine, General Secretary of the TUC and member of the West India Royal Commission, and Roger Makin of the Foreign Office. Both felt the experiment would be justified, but for a small group of skilled Jewish migrants, not as a mass refuge for thousands who had no other place to go.[16]

In Trinidad, the local paper, the *Trinidad Guardian*, began to reflect a siege mentality, campaigning for restrictive measures to be taken. In a series of articles under the

[13] See e.g. Arthur Prinz, 'The Role of the Gestapo in Obstructing and Promoting Jewish Emigration', *Yad Vashem Studies*, 2 (1958), 214–18; Herbert Strauss, 'Jewish Emigration from Germany: Nazi Policies and Jewish Responses (II)', *Leo Baeck Institute Yearbook*, 26 (1981), 367.

[14] Pereira informed the Coordinating Committee that 'landing permits of $250 are issued in Trinidad bearing the name of the intended passenger. The permits must be paid to the steamship company at the port of embarkation' (Edgar Pereira to Cecilia Razovsky, National Coordinating Committee (19 Dec. 1938), JDCA, file 1047).

[15] National Coordinating Committee Memorandum to All Cooperating Agencies from Cecilia Razovsky (29 Dec. 1938), JDCA, file 1047.

[16] See Walter Citrine to Malcolm MacDonald (8 May 1939), TNA, CO 950/248; Makins, Minute (1 Dec. 1938), cited in Sherman, *Island Refuge*, 189.

heading 'Jewish Influx', the public was informed of the impending immigration changes the government was about to make.[17] Justifying its campaign, the paper concentrated on highlighting the economic problems that penniless Jewish refugees would pose to the colony, illustrating this with the example of a refugee who had to pay the German authorities £2,000 in order to bring £1,000 with him. It reported that he had also brought gold fountain pens, cameras, and other valuables in the hope of selling them in Trinidad, but the article emphasized (in bold) that this refugee was the exception, and that most 'land with only about ten shillings'.[18]

Calypsonians also joined the debate, suggesting that Jewish refugees would overrun the colony, a sentiment clearly stated in a calypso composed by Charlie 'Gorilla' Grant in December 1938:

> Since Jews coming to this Colony
> They are marrying and raising a family
> In a couple of years, believe it's true
> Trinidad children will be only Jews.[19]

But some calypsos were more sympathetic. For example, one by Atilla the Hun (Raymond Quevedo), called 'The Persecuted Jews', welcomed Jewish immigration, stating that West Indians should remember the suffering of their slave ancestors and extend a welcome to another persecuted group:

> Let's give serious contemplation,
> To the question of Jewish immigration
> Just like our forefathers in slavery
> From the brutality of tyrants they have to fell
> So it's nothing but Christian charity
> To give these oppressed people sanctuary.
>
> . . . .
>
> Negroes, our slave fathers long ago
> Suffered all kinds of tribulation and woe
> With yokes round their necks beaten day and night
> Their only salvation remained in flight
> So in remembrance of their agony
> And gratitude to those who showed them sympathy
> We shall extend to the Jews hospitality
> As a monument to our ancestors' memory.[20]

[17] For example, the *Sunday Guardian* reported on the Emergency Session of the Executive Council, who were meeting to discuss how to prevent the *Caribia* from docking in Trinidad (*Sunday Guardian* (8 Jan. 1939)). On 10 January 1939 a front-page headline proclaimed 'Government to Check Jew Influx', reporting on the new measures taken to ban European refugees (*Trinidad Guardian* (10 Jan. 1939)).

[18] *Trinidad Guardian* (10 Jan. 1939).

[19] Charlie 'Gorilla' Grant, 'Jews in the West Indies', in Gordon Rohlehr, *Calypso and Society in Pre-Independence Trinidad* (Port of Spain, Trinidad, 1990), 313.

[20] Atilla the Hun, 'The Persecuted Jews' (19 Dec. 1938), ibid. 314.

Pressure from the local legislature led to the closing of Trinidad's borders in January 1939, and during the campaign a spotlight was thrown on Jewish refugees in Trinidad as the debate about immigration continued.[21] Focusing on the effect of Jews on housing and employment in the colony, many reports spoke of overcrowding in Jewish houses and the health risk that this posed to the general population.[22] Many refugees did arrive penniless, having spent what they had on the voyage and the deposit securing their entry. The Jewish Association of Trinidad rented a number of houses in which they could stay upon arrival. The situation was described in January by an American Jewish organization advising other agencies that the following situation had created a ban on immigration:

A Committee of Jews is renting housing accommodation and has seriously accentuated the already acute housing situation. Certain local inhabitants have been dispossessed. There is a serious overcrowding among the refugees and the director of Medical services states that the conditions under which they are living constitute a grave danger to the public health.[23]

Although it is true that the presence of Jewish refugees did exacerbate a housing shortage, the language in which the debate about overcrowding took place suggests that the issue was also used to stir up anti-refugee sentiment. In June 1939 a report from the Chief Medical Officer to the Port of Spain City Council found that no serious overcrowding occurred in Jewish homes. He described how 'there would be six or eight or ten people coming off the boat and staying at the house for two days or so and then going to another place. I could not satisfy myself that there was any overcrowding.'[24]

The *Trinidad Guardian* started regular features on who the refugees were and where they had come from. In an article entitled 'The Strangers Within Our Gates' the correspondent from the *Sunday Guardian* commented that:

At the outset I must say I have been struck by their general appearance, the evident high standard of education and knowledge shown on all matters on which we conversed. I think it will interest those who have not had the opportunity of meeting the new comers to know that these recent

---

[21] The Colonial Office was not in favour of wholesale restriction because of sensitivity to Britain's stated aim of helping refugees. It introduced new legislation that gave the governor further powers to prohibit the entry of any alien while avoiding specifically naming refugees as prohibited immigrants. New ordinances were introduced to this effect in British Guiana in February, Barbados in May, and British Honduras in June and September (see Newman, 'Nearly the New World', 46).

[22] For example, this was the reason used to seek permission from the Secretary of State for the Colonies to prohibit further emigration to Trinidad. On 6 January the Executive Council met to discuss the situation and submitted the report which advised the closing of immigration, in part in response to the effect of refugees on 'housing accommodation, employment and health conditions' (Meeting of Executive Council Trinidad (6 Jan. 1939), TNA, CO 298/178).

[23] 'Recent Developments Regarding Emigration to Trinidad', JDCA, file 1049 (19 Jan. 1939).

[24] Report of meeting of Port of Spain City Council, 'No Crowding in Jewish Homes', *Trinidad Guardian* (23 June 1939).

arrivals comprise professional men, such as, doctors, dentists, engineers, lawyers, dairy men, farmers and so on.[25]

Ernst Fischer, a journalist who arrived in Trinidad in 1938 with his wife, wrote in the *Trinidad Guardian*: 'the more I see of this beautiful island the more I am enchanted. Before arrival here I was very much afraid I would not be able to settle down in Trinidad. . . . We feel that we have come to a home which will be to us a haven of rest and peace, not only for our travel worn bodies but also for our wounded souls.'[26]

Not all of the Jewish refugees came under the spotlight. Those who had come from eastern Europe earlier, during the 1920s and early 1930s, had, on the whole, more success in integrating into the West Indian community. They followed in the footsteps of a number of Jewish migrants who came to the Caribbean from the Middle East. In Jamaica, a number of Lebanese immigrants became influential members of both the Jewish community and Jamaican society.[27] Using case studies, Robin Cohen has shown the general pattern of mobility of Syrian immigrants, with the majority initially establishing themselves as pedlars and traders. He cites the following as typical:

To the end of his life old Elias Issa, who had arrived in Jamaica in 1894, could show the mark on his back made by the box he carried as a pedlar. After some years he was able to buy a donkey and then set up shop in Princess Street, later moving to Orange Street.[28]

Those eastern European Jews who had arrived shortly after the First World War en route to destinations in South America were young and more able to adapt to their circumstances than those who came as refugees in the late 1930s. For example, in 1932 a young electrician from Lublin, Henry Altman, arrived in Barbados with his family and began peddling before moving on to owning a store. When I was in Trinidad in 2002 I interviewed Arthur Ince, a former editor of the *Trinidad Guardian*, who remembered that his mother talked about the Jewish pedlar who came every Friday to his house. He travelled around the island. Ince recalls that the Jewish pedlars were the first to extend credit to their customers.

Whereas most east European refugees, even those arriving as late as 1938, continued to be successful in the dry-goods trade and peddling, refugees from Germany and

[25] *Sunday Guardian* (25 Dec. 1938).

[26] Ernst D. Fischer, 'An Austrian Jew in Trinidad Writes About Changing Europe', *Trinidad Guardian* (11 Dec. 1938).

[27] For example, the Matalon family in Jamaica achieved economic and political power in Jamaica after the Second World War. Joseph Matalon arrived from Syria in the 1920s and entered the dry-goods business (see Carol Holzberg, *Minorities and Power in a Black Society: The Jewish Community of Jamaica* (Lanham, Md., 1987), 203–5). In Jamaica, there was co-operation between Chinese, Syrians, and Jews involved in trading. Holzberg states that some Jews and Syrians worked together but, by the 1920s, Syrians had monopolized the retail dry-goods trade while Jews concentrated more on wholesaling (ibid. 127).

[28] See Robin Cohen, *Global Diasporas* (London, 1997), 96–7.

Austria found it much harder to adjust to their new surroundings. They placed advertisements in the *Trinidad Guardian*'s 'Situations Wanted' section:

A first Class European Dressmaker, just arrived from Europe, looking for employment.

European lady seeks work as secretary or stenotypist. English, French and German translated.

Young Viennese Gentleman seeks work of any kind.

Piano lessons by expert European musician.[29]

Many of the refugees were at first reliant on help from local and international aid organizations. A Jewish Loan Fund Committee was established by the JDC, and several tailors, watchmakers, milliners, shoemakers, and hat makers started small businesses with its loans.[30] The money went towards the purchase of machinery for the manufacture of upholstered furniture and of shirts and pyjamas, for the payment of merchandise for retail, for the establishment of a boarding house and a restaurant, for the manufacture of sausages, and for the expansion of a photographic business.[31] Successful businesses included Siegel and Karlsbad's ladies' hat factory and Stecher's jewellery and watch business, both in Port of Spain.

By the middle of 1939 two separate communities were established: one of east European Jews, the other of Jews from Germany and Austria. They were divided by language, culture, and religious practice, and the divisions were exacerbated once war broke out and enemy alien refugees were interned. Both communities applied for JDC funding for community activities and religious schools, and both made contact with Jewish communities in Britain, the United States, and other Caribbean colonies for help in obtaining religious material and to engage the services of a rabbi.[32] In October 1939, 250 graves were reserved for Jewish burial in a special section of the cemetery at Mucurapo.[33] On 31 May 1940 the first Jewish death was consecrated at the Jewish cemetery.

With the outbreak of war, the Caribbean was used as a transit and detention station. Between February 1939 and May 1942, refugee traffic between Europe and the

---

[29] *Trinidad Guardian* (17 Jan. 1939).   [30] Pereira to Razovsky (16 Jan. 1939), JDCA, file 1047.

[31] JDC report on loan fund, meeting of subcommittee on refugee aid in Central and South America (17 May 1940), JDCA, file 113. This report was issued a month before mass internment took place. The loans had been secured with the $250 landing money deposits, and the meeting noted that, if successful, it would be possible to decrease the monthly subsidy sent by the JDC to Trinidad.

[32] Since there were insufficient funds and a lack of agreement about securing a minister, it was not until American troops entered the colony that a rabbi was found to officiate over services. With the presence of American bases in Trinidad, some 200 American Jewish soldiers entered the colony, and the Jewish community gained the services of an American army chaplain, Rabbi Sydney Ungar. The rabbi took services in the synagogue of the Jewish Association, which were attended by the refugees and American soldiers present in the colony (see report from M. W. Beckelman to JDC, New York (19 Oct. 1941), JDCA, file 1048).

[33] Town Clerk to Girion, Secretary, Jewish Association of Trinidad (27 Oct. 1939), Max Markreich Collection, Leo Baeck Institute Archive.

western hemisphere resulted in a continual stream of Jewish refugees temporarily admitted to British West Indian colonies. Those without valid travel documents remained in the Caribbean for long periods, and those suspected of enemy activity were inspected and either interned or allowed to proceed with their journey.

In 1940 enemy alien refugees were interned throughout the Caribbean (sometimes for longer periods than in the UK), and new businesses were abandoned as their owners were moved to internment camps. The roots that many refugees had begun to put down were now severed, leading them to feel a renewed desire to leave Trinidad when the war was over and move to the United States, Canada, or Palestine.

Throughout the war calls continued to be made for the colonial empire and the West Indies to provide sanctuary for refugees. The difference now was that the British deemed winning the war more important than being generous to refugees. At times, when British interests dictated a change in policy, refugees were moved to parts of the colonial empire, where they were housed in refugee camps. For instance, refugees who reached Palestine were turned back by the British authorities and interned in Mauritius, and those in Portugal hampered the entry of more refugees and allied servicemen escaping occupied Europe. Until they were found places, the Portuguese authorities were unwilling to admit more into Portugal and through Lisbon to the west. The British sent some of them to Jamaica.

The situation in Jamaica, a British West Indian colony 1,000 miles from Trinidad, was very different. Few refugees had been able to satisfy Jamaica's immigration regulations, and it was not until 1941 that Jewish refugees came to the island in any number.[34] The decision to build a refugee camp in Jamaica resulted from the perceived military importance that the allies placed on Gibraltar, considered throughout the war to be a key military and strategic point guarding the entry to the Mediterranean.[35]

In April 1940 the British government agreed to evacuate the civilian population of Gibraltar to French Morocco.[36] During May and June some 13,000 Gibraltarians were evacuated, but after the fall of France discussions took place over where the evacuees

[34] In Jamaica, there were a number of Jewish refugees who, on the outbreak of war, were interned. Jamaica had three camps during the war: an internment camp (Up Park Camp), a prisoner of war camp, and the evacuee camp.

[35] During September and October 1940 Hitler considered plans to send troops through Spain to Gibraltar but, after meeting with Franco on 23 October, dropped the idea. A further reason for British sensitivity has been suggested by Fitz Baptiste, who states that in retaliation for the Anglo-American Bases Agreement, Hitler was advised by Grand Admiral Raeder, chief of the German Navy, to seize Gibraltar, French North West and West Africa, and the Spanish and Portuguese Atlantic Islands off the African coast (see Fitzroy A. Baptiste, *War, Cooperation, and Conflict: The European Possessions in the Caribbean, 1939–1945* (New York, 1988), 59).

[36] The governor of Gibraltar was given compulsory powers to evacuate the civil population on 30 Apr. 1940 (see Colonial Office, note for the War Office on the evacuees from Gibraltar in Jamaica (30 Apr. 1940), TNA, CO 91/518/14)).

could be re-housed. Investigations were made in South Africa, the West Indies, and other parts of the colonial empire. A note from the Colonial Office confirms that, for the British government, a major objective was to avoid the admittance of refugees to Britain.[37]

In 1940 the governor of Jamaica received instructions to build a camp to house 9,000 evacuees (the figure was later revised down to 7,000). It was called Gibraltar Camp because its original purpose was to house the evacuated civilian population of Gibraltar. Despite the original plan, only 1,700 Gibraltarians came to Jamaica; of the rest, 12,000 remained in Britain and 2,000 in Malta. Throughout the rest of that year and the next, the camp, with its capacity of 7,000, housed only the 1,700 Gibraltarians. The cost to the British government was high. In a note to the Treasury Department, a Colonial Office official estimated it at £330,000 or £66 per head. In justifying this to the Treasury, he explained:

The camp was constructed at very great speed under strong pressure from this end to use the utmost expedition, and that may well have increased the cost. In the circumstances, it is little short of lamentable that we should only have been able so far, to arrange for some 1,500 evacuees to occupy the camp. It may be that the proposal to send some of the evacuees from this country to the West Indies will be revived. We can only hope that by these or other means the vacant accommodation will, sooner or later, be turned to practical advantage.[38]

That practical advantage became clear in December 1941 when the British government, the Polish government-in-exile, and the JDC decided on an initial arrangement to send Polish Jewish refugees from Lisbon to Jamaica. The entry of these refugees into Jamaica rested on the British imperative of clearing Lisbon of a surfeit of refugees and a promise to the Jamaican legislature that none would seek employment or citizenship and that the JDC would take financial responsibility for the Polish Jews.[39]

With wartime shipping problems, lack of suitable destinations, and restrictions on visas and immigration, large numbers of refugees became 'stuck' in Spain and Lisbon. While ways could be found to transport those refugees able to fight for the Allies, the Jewish refugees in Lisbon had nowhere to go. By allowing them entry into Jamaica the Allies were able to offer a partial solution to the need for a suitable refuge and thereby persuade Spanish and Portuguese officials to allow further immigration. During 1942 and 1943 additional small groups of Jewish refugees were dispatched from Lisbon to Gibraltar Camp, their maintenance undertaken by Allied governments and Jewish organizations.[40]

[37] Colonial Office, note for the War Office (n.d.), TNA, CO 91/518/14.
[38] A. B. Acheson, Colonial Office to C. G. Syers, Treasury (1 Apr. 1941), TNA, CO 91/515/12.
[39] The JDC initially issued a twelve-month guarantee (see Jan Ciechanowski, Polish Ambassador, Washington, to Joseph Hyman, Executive Vice Chairman JDC (3 Jan. 1942), JDCA, file 884).
[40] The Polish request for further evacuations of Polish Jews to Jamaica did not happen, because the Polish government-in-exile could not provide funding and the governor was disposed against admitting

It is unlikely that refugee organizations knew about Gibraltar Camp before December 1941, as they would certainly have pressed for it to be used for refugees. By 1942 knowledge of the camp was widespread among refugee organizations, partly because of their participation in maintaining refugees at the camp. However, by then accommodation had been drastically reduced, and the Colonial Office was no longer disposed to facilitate refugee entry. In December 1942 the Foreign Office approached the Colonial Office about a request from the High Commissioner:

> The High Commissioner for Refugees Sir Herbert Emerson is now faced with the problem of finding asylum for refugees escaped and escaping from France into Spain and Portugal. The President of Hicem, Max Gottschalk, has asked whether room can be found for them in British colonies. Emerson has enquired whether we can let him know the position particularly in regard to Jamaica where a statement has been made to him that there is room in existing barracks for about 4,000 persons. . . . In view of the unfavourable insinuations about Jamaica which certain Jewish ex-internees have been spreading on reaching the United States it may seem odd that the Jewish organisations should appear to want more accommodation in the Colony, but if we can truthfully tell Sir Herbert Emerson that the island's accommodation is entirely used up, so much the better.[41]

Complaints by refugees over the restrictions in Gibraltar Camp, and the effect that these complaints had on the governor of Jamaica, dissuaded the Colonial Office from any further admission of refugees to the camp. One official noted:

> I am getting tired of these Jewish refugees. In Jamaica we have a letter from some of them expressing gratitude for good treatment in Jamaica: now we have complaints such as those described [in the above correspondence]. If these people really think that conditions in Jamaica are no better than in concentration camps in Germany, it is a pity they didn't remain there.'[42]

During December 1942 the Colonial Office approved the removal of twelve accommodation units from the camp to serve as barracks for local forces. Replying to the Foreign Office, the Colonial Office stated that some six units remained available, capable of housing up to 500 refugees. The letter related the governor's reluctance to admit further refugees and stated that only if a case were made that the removal of refugees to Jamaica was in the national interest would a further proposal be put to him.[43]

Polish refugees because of the complaints made by some already in Gibraltar Camp. Groups of Dutch, Czech, and Luxembourger refugees were evacuated from Lisbon to Gibraltar Camp, their maintenance being shared between their governments and the JDC. Some eight sailings from Lisbon to Jamaica took place between January 1942 and December 1943. Most of the Dutch refugees were men of military age who spent brief spells in Gibraltar Camp before being sent to Suriname.

[41] A. W. G. Randall, Foreign Office to P. Rogers, Colonial Office, (4 Dec. 1942), TNA, CO 323/1846/7. HICEM was the result of the merger of three refugee agencies: HIAS (Hebrew Immigrant Aid Society); ICA (Jewish Colonization Association), and EmigDirect.

[42] J. Emmens, memorandum (17 Dec. 1942), TNA, CO 323/1846/7.

[43] H. Sidebothom, Colonial Office, to A. W. G. Randall, Foreign Office (19 Dec. 1942), TNA, CO

On 19 May 1943 the House of Commons again debated the refugee question and issued a statement giving an account of the emergency conference held in Bermuda. Although the recommendations of the conference remained secret, Mr Peake, Under-Secretary of State for the Home Office, stressed the contribution already made by the colonial empire to solving the refugee problem, stating that:

We must, I think, recognise that the United Nations can do little or nothing in the immediate present for the vast numbers now under Hitler's control. He is determined not to let those people go. The rate of extermination is such that no measures of rescue or relief on however large a scale could be commensurate with the problem. . . . Any slackening of our war effort or any delay to shipping in the attempted rescue of refugees could only delay the day of victory and result in the infliction of greater suffering on the subjugated peoples of Europe.[44]

Gibraltar Camp was not a concentration camp, but the refugees felt trapped, particularly the young, and, as news of the war in Europe increased, frustrated that they were unable to contribute to the war effort. While the JDC and other relief agencies celebrated their rescue (and made much of it for fundraising purposes), refugees in the camp felt otherwise. On 11 August they wrote to the JDC, reminding it that 'it is exactly one and a half years since by your action we arrived here. You will not be surprised to hear that our group remembers this jubilee with rather mixed feelings.' The letter concluded:

If the Joint took it upon them to 'rescue' us they ought to complete their 'rescue work' and not leave us halfway to our sad fate. What we desire is to be 'rehabilitated' just as so many others have been, and as this is impossible in this country under the hospitality conditions accepted by you for us, we must insist that we should be sent to another country where we will be allowed to be free, law abiding, useful citizens, earning our living and where we will not be obliged to live in barracks and spend our life in idleness.[45]

Camp life was spartan, with little privacy. Refugees could leave the camp, but had to return each evening. Once a month, they were granted seventy-two hours' leave. In the camp, various clubs and societies provided entertainment, films were shown three times a week, and a library was at their disposal. Magazines and books in Yiddish or

---

323/1846/7. See also the correspondence between the Secretary of State for the Colonies and the governor of Jamaica over this request by the High Commissioner. On 15 January 1943 the Secretary of State for the Colonies asked the governor to confirm that no accommodation was available to house Jewish refugees from European countries, on guarantee of maintenance and removal at the end of the war. On 18 January 1943 the governor replied that room for 500 existed, but was 'being reserved for emergencies such as a sudden influx by refugee ships. It might be inconvenient if it were given up permanently' (see Secretary of State for the Colonies to governor of Jamaica (15 Jan. 1943); governor of Jamaica to the Secretary of State for the Colonies (18 Jan. 1943), TNA, CO 323/1846/6).

[44] See Charles Jordan report for JDC of Gibraltar Camp (17 Dec. 1942), XIII–8, Jamaica, Yivo Archives, NY.

[45] Boruch Eksztajn and Samuel Schipper to JDC, New York (11 Aug. 1943), XIII–7, Jamaica, Yivo Archives, NY.

German were regularly sent from Jewish organizations. The Polish group established a synagogue and were joined by some thirty-eight Orthodox Jews from the Gibraltarian evacuees for services. The camp had a separate kosher kitchen, but the camp commandant, Mr Rae, had been unable to arrange for kosher meat to be delivered.[46]

Although generally favourable in his report, Charles Jordan, the JDC representative for the Caribbean, described several problems for the inhabitants of Gibraltar Camp. The most serious were the restrictions of camp life and the lack of opportunities to remigrate, which created serious frustration among the refugees.[47] A Gibraltarian evacuee wrote the following account to his wife, who had been evacuated to London, of the boredom and futility of camp life:

Here I am getting more and more bored, it is no life at all, the majority of us men are just desperate. One cannot make any request or protest, we have some very severe laws in the camp, here we have to say that black is white, indeed sometimes various women have been put in prison because they made riots in the canteens to protest about the food and in regard to food I could tell you many things, but we have to be silent. So no wonder I am longing for this to be ended, so that I can be with you and see the last of this place called Gibraltar Camp, which has nothing good about it. . . . At last we shall leave it.[48]

For Jewish refugees taken from Lisbon, Gibraltar Camp was hard to bear for reasons that went beyond food rationing. Many felt that once in Jamaica they would be at liberty and able to play an active role by enlisting in the Allied forces. Pinning their hopes on entry into Canada, Polish refugees in Gibraltar Camp wrote to Winston Churchill in August 1942, asking that he intervene with the Canadian authorities to allow them entry, where they could enlist for active service. They wrote that:

While a world war rages and hecatombs of victims fall, we young people, wanting to fight and to work and able to be useful through our technical and branch knowledges are here in complete spirit- and health-killing inactivity, in Gibraltar Camp. After three years, fleeing from the terrors of the flaming Europe, trying to save ourselves and ours from Nazis and Fascist concentration camps

[46] The lack of kosher meat was an issue which the Polish group repeatedly attempted to redress. See e.g. Polish Group to JDC (20 Apr. 1942), XIII–3, Jamaica, Yivo Archives, NY. In a report on Gibraltar Camp in November 1942, Sylvain Hayum noted that, in the separate kosher kitchen, fish or eggs were served daily. A rabbi among the refugees, Uscher (a representative of the Polish group), refused to become a *shoḥet*: 'Il y a au camp une cuisine kocher, et une autre. La cuisine kocher ne sert jamais de viande, mais un plat de poisson et un plat d'oeufs par jour. On pourrait avoir de la volaille, mais le rabbin Uscher refuse de remplire les fonctions de shoichet, sous pretexte qu'il n'en a plus l'habitude' (There are two kitchens, one kosher. The kosher kitchen does not serve meat, it serves a fish dish and an egg dish daily. One could have chicken, but Rabbi Uscher refuses to carry out the function of *shoḥet* (ritual slaughterer) under the pretext that he isn't used to doing it anymore) (see report by Sylvain Hayum (10 Nov. 1942), XIII–5, Jamaica, Yivo Archives, NY).

[47] Joseph L. Cruz, Hut 16, Gibraltar Camp, to Herminia Cruz, London (9 July 1941), TNA, CO 91/515/12. As this letter was found in the Colonial Office file at the Public Records Office, it is not known whether it was received by Herminia Cruz in London.

[48] Group of Polish Refugees, Gibraltar Camp, to Prime Minister Winston Churchill (24 Aug. 1942), TNA, CO 323/1846/6.

we are now on the English territory, where we wish to give all our possible efforts of our technical and branch knowledges for our common cause. We would have considered ourselves as parasitical individuals if we were not conscious that we are leading these camp-lifes absolutely against our own will. But our conscience do not leave us in peace; others fight and die; others work and help, and we live in uselessness. We feel very very depressed, particularly now as the war seems to reach crisis point and when useful strength is more and more necessary. In our despair and helplessness, we decided to address ourselves to you and through your excellency to the Canadian Government, to deliver us and our families Canadian visas.[49]

Given the circumstances under which most refugees came to be in Jamaica, it was not surprising that few decided to stay and put down roots. Those released from intern-ment were able to integrate into Jamaican society, but for those in Gibraltar Camp there was limited contact with Jamaicans and therefore limited possibilities to interact so-cially or become part of the economic life of Jamaican towns. This was partly because of the distance from the camp to Kingston and partly because kerosene shortages dur-ing the war made transport difficult, so their contact was mainly limited to Jamaicans working in the camp, although some inmates made use of daily passes and did spend time with members of the Jamaican Jewish community. Entry to Gibraltar Camp was granted to the refugees on the condition that they would not seek employment or remain after the war. By the end of 1944 the majority of Gibraltarian evacuees had left Jamaica, but seventeen Polish and Czech Jews, who were unable to find onward destinations and who refused to return to Europe, remained in the camp until 1947. These refugees had few relatives in countries of migration, no money for travelling expenses or to procure visas, and suffered from ill health. But in other Caribbean islands a sizeable number decided to stay. In a 1989 interview, Henry Altman described the process by which he became a Barbadian:

When we first came to Barbados it happened that most of us had blue eyes and the original Jews had black eyes, the ones who came from the Mediterranean, the Spanish and Portuguese, and they were suspicious, they [West Indians] thought that we were Germans. It is a fact, and people called us Germans until the war broke out. Then slowly they realised that we were not. We are Polish Jews. Most of us are Polish Jews. We always thought that we would leave the Island and go somewhere else, like to New York, America, Canada. But somehow we loved it here and we are Barbadians.[50]

Many also decided to stay in Trinidad, despite the experience of internment. In June 1945, of an estimated 320 refugees remaining in Trinidad, the majority, some 250, were self-sustaining, including 187 refugees from Poland and Rumania and 128 from Ger-many, Austria, and Czechoslovakia.[51]

[49] Report of House of Commons Debate on the Refugee Problem (19 May 1943), TNA, CO 733/449.
[50] Henry Altman, interview by Joanna Newman, Barbados (Aug. 1989).
[51] Newman, 'Nearly the New World', 208.

Today, most of the descendants of those who stayed in the West Indies have either emigrated or assimilated. The clue to their presence remains in the phone books, with Aubs, Lobbenbergs, and Fagenbaums listed alongside Pereiras and Henriques. As interest in the history of Jewish immigration to the West Indies grows, this episode is explored and retold as part of the rich cultural diversity of West Indian heritage. The site of Gibraltar Camp is now part of the University of the West Indies. Few people knew why it had its name until 1990 when the *Sunday Gleaner* serialized the memoirs of Miriam Stanton, a former refugee at the camp who had corresponded with Father William H. Fenney, the camp chaplain.[52] In Trinidad, an article in the *Sunday Guardian* in December 1989 was captioned, 'Visitors baffled by some street names in New Yalta', and a photograph of 'Dr. Theo Hertzel [*sic*] Avenue' was shown. That area of Trinidad had been developed by Jewish immigrants, hence the street names, but the majority had left. In Barbados in the 1950s the Jewish community bought back from the government and restored the ancient Sephardi synagogue, now a point of pride for the remaining community and a tourist attraction mentioned in most guide books and Jewish travel guides.[53] Jewish heritage in the West Indies is often used to attract tourists (a recent example being the report of the 2010 conference in the *Wall Street Journal*: 'Jamaica's New Tourism Spiel, Beaches and Reggae and Jews').[54]

The story of Jewish immigration has been integrated into a history of the West Indies which emphasizes tolerance and acceptance and the role of the West Indies as a haven. But in these accounts little is made of the facts that it was by accident rather than by design that Jews ended up in the Caribbean in the 1930s and 1940s, and that they did so in order to find refuge during the critical Holocaust period.

[52]   Five articles serialized in the *Sunday Gleaner* (Mar. 1990).

[53]   In 1990 the Barbados community received a Jewish Commonwealth Award for its work in restoring the synagogue. It is one of a variety of places pointed out in tourist guide books on Jewish heritage in the West Indies. See e.g. Malcolm Stern and Bernard Postal's guide for American Airlines, *Jews in the West Indies*, which provides a history of Jewish immigration to the West Indies, lists colonies with a current Jewish population, colonies of 'Jewish historical interest', and Jewish synagogues, graveyards, and other points of interest for the American tourist.

[54]   Tamara Audi, 'Jamaica's New Tourism Spiel: Beaches and Reggae and Jews', *Wall Street Journal* (9 Mar. 2010), <http://online.wsj.com/article/SB10001424052748703382904575059113221038280.html>.

CHAPTER TWENTY-ONE

INSCRIBING OURSELVES WITH HISTORY

The Production of Heritage in Today's Caribbean Jewish Diaspora

JUDAH M. COHEN

In St Thomas, Jewish living is a unique combination of Caribbean history and tradition, as well as fun in the sun and a more casual lifestyle. From the spirituality of worship at our historic synagogue, to *havdalah* at sea, we enjoy the best of two worlds. And so it goes, somewhere in paradise, between her coconut palms, her crystal blue waters, her balmy nights, and her sun-drenched days lies an amazing Jewish treasure, unparalleled in the Western world. In St Thomas, you will fall in love with a congregation which has stood the test of time: a synagogue whose sand-covered floor proclaims the message of the hours. Through the sands of time, *am yisrael chai*: the Jewish people live.

Hebrew Congregation of St Thomas, bicentennial promotional video, 1995

SINCE THE MID-TWENTIETH CENTURY, Jewish communities living in the Caribbean have found themselves balancing a complex combination of archaeology and curatorship. While leading largely liberal religious lives, they have had to co-ordinate their standard complement of communal activities with efforts to present their islands' historical Jewish presence—even when they have little in common with their religious forebears. Such issues of historicism have characterized the Caribbean region in general over the past century, as local peoples and governments, as well as the international leisure industry, looked to the past to cultivate cultural sites and grow tourism economies.[1] For Jews this process involved engagement with the developing field of American Jewish history. Jacob Rader Marcus's efforts, starting in the 1940s, to turn the field into a meeting ground between large-scale scholarly ideas and local congregational narratives helped raise interest in Caribbean Jewish communities among scholars and gave the Caribbean a new significance for Jewish American lay populations.[2] Likewise,

---

[1] See Polly Pattullo, 'The Lock and the Key: History and Power', in ead., *Last Resorts: The Cost of Tourism in the Caribbean* (Kingston, Jamaica, 1996), 2–27.

[2] See e.g. Jacob Rader Marcus, 'The Program of the American Jewish Archives', in id., *The Dynamics of American Jewish History: Jacob Rader Marcus's Essays on American Jewry*, ed. Gary P. Zola (Hanover, NH, 2004), 108–15.

the 1954 tercentenary celebration of the Jewish presence in the USA brought the Caribbean into discussions of North American Judaism's origins. The rise of tensions between African American and Jewish communities in the 1990s highlighted the Caribbean-based slave trade as a key arena for scholarly arguments and counter-arguments in both the public and academic spheres.[3] More recently, developments in the fields of Sephardi studies and Latin American and Caribbean Jewish studies opened the door for scholars to reassess the Caribbean's place between European and American Jewish histories; and the celebration of the 350th anniversary of Jews in the USA in 2004 re-energized American interest in the hemisphere's oldest Jewish communities.[4] The popular and scholarly attention these and other events have generated led Jews living in the Caribbean to understand the value of cultivating public connections with the islands' pasts—including the showcasing of their old synagogues, cemeteries, artefacts, and (sometimes inherited) memories—while exploring how to bring their islands' Jewish legacies into their contemporary identities.

Jewish Caribbean populations have consequently brought history to bear upon their own senses of collectivity, particularly to celebrate their communities publicly as stable and continuous over centuries. Their pronouncements often conflicted with the islands' actual histories of hurricanes, earthquakes, tsunamis, fires, volcanoes, epidemics, drastic economic fluctuations, uprisings, wars (often conducted from afar), political corruption, ethnic conflict, and scarce natural resources. Yet in maintaining a continuous view of the past, they revealed nuanced understanding of the meaning of history in a contemporary Caribbean context. Caribbean Jewish communities have frequently needed to distinguish themselves within the Jewish world, and they have done so by writing and rewriting their own histories and co-ordinating with prevailing scholarship. At the same time, these communities tacitly recognized the importance of history in ensuring communal survival. Their maintenance of a delicate rhetorical balance between past and future ensured scholarly interest, helped establish their place in island politics, and created a moral imperative for preserving, commemorating, and ensuring the future of Caribbean Jewish life.

Addressing how these communities develop the layers of their own historical narratives—what David Glassberg calls a 'sense of history'[5]—offers insights into the nature of Caribbean Jewish studies. Through the eyes of the contemporary communities themselves, which are often overlooked in both historical and tourist-based

---

[3] Nation of Islam, *The Secret Relationship Between the Blacks and the Jews*, vol. i (Chicago, 1991); Saul S. Friedman, *Jews and the American Slave Trade* (New Brunswick, 1998); Eli Faber, *Jews, Slaves, and the Slave Trade: Setting the Record Straight* (New York, 1998).

[4] See e.g. Jane S. Gerber (ed.), *Sephardic Studies in the University* (Madison, NJ, 1995).

[5] David Glassberg, *Sense of History: The Place of the Past in American Life* (Amherst, Mass., 2001); David Lowenthal has also addressed this history somewhat more parochially in *The Heritage Crusade and the Spoils of History* (New York, 1998).

accounts of the region, complex questions emerge about what a Caribbean Jewish diaspora really entails. I explore these questions here by considering how public image production and local forms of commemoration factor into the identity discourses of one such population—the Jewish community of St Thomas, in the US Virgin Islands—as it seeks to reconcile its current practices with its self-described 'Sephardi' past. The current congregation's communal expressions of 'sephardiness' may not reflect the customs or culture of its island forebears with great accuracy, and the themes it uses to exhibit its adopted communal heritage publicly may often seem to emphasize popular and exotic imagery. Nonetheless, the community's planning and presentation of the synagogue's bicentennial celebration in 1995–7, which highlighted the island's centuries-old Jewish sites and included a 'Sephardi' rededication ceremony, infused the Reform congregation with a 'usable' (to use David Roskies's term) sense of Sephardi identity.[6] In connecting to its past, moreover, the island's Jewish population created what Francio Guadeloupe describes as 'bridges of commonality' with the rest of the population, fashioning an image of Jewish identity that would reinforce the community's identity as Virgin Islanders committed to the island's economic and spiritual livelihood.[7]

Developing a Caribbean Jewish History

Starting in the late nineteenth century, as steam power reduced the Caribbean's importance to the trade circuit between Europe and the Americas, Jews on islands such St Thomas, Jamaica, and Barbados employed a number of strategies to improve their lives in a transfigured economic and cultural landscape. Many left for places with greater commercial potential, such as Panama (from the 1870s to 1914), Costa Rica, and the United States (particularly New York and Miami). Those who stayed on attempted to increase commerce and enhance the status of their islands by, among other things, promoting their history. Articles that highlighted the area's past prominence began to circulate through the international media, taking advantage of the advances in travel that had shifted resources away from the islands in the first place. Ultimately, however, these accounts appeared to do little to improve the islands' fortunes besides buoying self-esteem in hard times.

Such efforts also, however, helped shape the form of Caribbean Jewish history. Through the twentieth century, historical accounts of Caribbean Jewish communities generally took three popular forms: writings by businessmen and professionals, who viewed their work as a meaningful hobby that also promoted their islands;[8] scholars

---

[6] David Roskies, *The Jewish Search for a Usable Past* (New Haven, 1999); see also Roy Rosenzweig and David Thelen, *The Presence of the Past: Popular Uses of History in American Life* (New York, 2008).

[7] Francio Guadeloupe, *Chanting Down the New Jerusalem: Calypso, Christianity, and Capitalism in the Caribbean* (Berkeley, Calif., 2009), 217.

[8] Particularly prominent in this regard was Isaac S. Emmanuel, who wrote his monumental books on

who largely specialized in other areas;[9] and visiting (photo-)journalists looking for good stories on far-off Jewish communities, especially as middle class leisure time increased after the Second World War. Each island, moreover, had a different history, and the forces at play in a given era or region influenced how its story was told. The resulting melange of narratives left Caribbean Jewish history marginal to both American and European Jewish historical studies, yet increasingly prominent in the public imagination.

These issues arose with particular clarity during events of the Hebrew Congregation of St Thomas's bicentennial between 1995 and 1997. While relatively recent and small by Jamaican or Curaçaoan historical standards, the congregation by the end of the twentieth century prided itself on its central role in Caribbean Jewish life, particularly during the nineteenth century, and highlighted its religious and familial ties to nearly all of the region's Jewish communities, as well as various major European and American port cities. Yet the congregation also faced many of the challenges experienced by Jewish communities across the Caribbean: highly unstable climatic, financial, and political conditions; the twentieth-century desire to ensure itself a place in the tourist economy as a site of Jewish interest; and the desire to establish its residents as both deeply grounded islanders and seasoned travellers. These contrasting perspectives gained physical form in 1995, when the congregation chose different modes of display for two of its cherished ritual candelabra. One came to the synagogue as a gift in the early 1970s from a prominent Ashkenazi family on the island (Figure 21.1). Presented under the impression that it was an authentic menorah from eleventh-century Cordoba, it was eventually mounted behind the reader's desk in the synagogue sanctuary. Guided tours and the synagogue's literature highlighted it as a symbol of the congregation's Sephardi heritage. The other object, a ḥanukiyah (Hanukah menorah) less prominently displayed in the synagogue's adjacent museum area, had probably been created in Amsterdam in the early 1760s and sent to St Eustatius[10] and arrived in St Thomas with a family of merchants in the early 1800s (Figure 21.2). Handed down from

Curaçaoan Jewry (and Jewish life in Coro, Venezuela) while rabbi of the congregation (Isaac S. Emmanuel, *Precious Stones of the Jews of Curaçao: Curaçaon Jewry, 1656–1957* (New York, 1957); Isaac S. Emmanuel and Suzanne A. Emmanuel, *History of the Jews of the Netherlands Antilles*, 2 vols. (Cincinnati, 1970)). See also Mordechai Arbell, *The Jewish Nation of the Caribbean: The Spanish-Portuguese Settlements in the Caribbean and the Guianas* (Jerusalem, 2002); Harry Ezratty, *500 Years in the Jewish Caribbean* (Baltimore, 2002); Zvi Loker, *Jews in the Caribbean: Evidence on the History of Jews in the Caribbean Zone in Colonial Times* (Jerusalem, 1991); Eustace M. Shilstone, *Monumental Inscriptions in the Burial Ground of the Jewish Synagogue in Bridgetown, Barbados* (New York, 1956).

[9] Johannes Hartog, *The Jews of St. Eustatius: The Eighteenth Century Jewish Congregation Honen Dalim and Description of the Old Cemetery* (St. Maarten, 1976).

[10] A similar ḥanukiyah (presumably the original) is on display in Amsterdam's Jewish Historical Museum: its image appears on greeting cards in the synagogue's gift shop. The copy is engraved with the Hebrew date 5522 (1761/2).

Figure 21.1 'Cordovan' menorah.
Hebrew Congregation of St Thomas
Photo: Ella Ogden. Used with permission

one religious leader to the next, it eventually faded from view until 1995, when the local island history museum retrieved it from storage during a search for artefacts for the congregation's history museum created for the bicentennial. Seen together, these two objects reflected the way the congregation—which has been affiliated with the Union for Reform Judaism since 1967—viewed its own identity in the late twentieth century: on the one hand, publicly situated as a spiritual heir to a distant and exoticized Sephardi past, and on the other, connected directly to a history of island-based Jewish practice.[11] For Jews in St Thomas, history became a mediation between these two narratives, forming a particularly rich landscape through which to integrate numerous worlds—Sephardi and Ashkenazi, Caribbean and American, insider and tourist—into a coherent corporate body.[12]

---

[11] Lee Shai Weissbach has highlighted similar patterns of immigration and emigration within communities in 'small-town America', noting that the pattern can also be seen outside the Jewish community (Lee Shai Weissbach, *Jewish Life in Small-Town America: A History* (New Haven, 2005), 92–3). The Caribbean represents a somewhat different paradigm, since the islands themselves, relatively speaking, retain historical urban landscapes (at least when it comes to Jewish population distributions). Their small populations, nonetheless, compare more effectively with small towns than with cities in analogous issues in socio-cultural dynamics.

[12] Elsewhere I have referred to this phenomenon as a 'cumulative identity' (Judah M. Cohen, *Through the Sands of Time: A History of the Jewish Community of St. Thomas, U.S. Virgin Islands* (Hanover, NH, 2004), 225).

Figure 21.2 St Eustatius Hanukah menorah. Hebrew Congregation of St Thomas
Photo: Ella Ogden. Used with permission

St Thomas and its Historical Legacy

Founded in 1796 by both Sephardi and Ashkenazi Jewish merchants from the Caribbean
and western Europe, St Thomas's Beracha Veshalom Vegemiluth Hasadim congregation thrived under the island's Danish colonial rule. By 1802 the island's Jews had
erected their first synagogue.[13] Fires destroyed the building three times (1804, 1806,
1831), but in 1833 the congregation consecrated a thick-walled structure of brick and
rubble masonry that remains in use today. Regional and world events helped determine
the make-up and health of the community. In the 1850s civil unrest in Venezuela caused
many Jews to flee to St Thomas from the coastal towns of Coro and Barcelona. An
economic decline, and hurricanes in 1867 and 1871, caused many young family members
to leave St Thomas seeking greener pastures, only to be replaced by a small but active

---

[13] For a fuller discussion, see Cohen, *Through the Sands of Time*.

wave of east European immigrants. When the first generations of east European Jews began to pass away after the Second World War, a new wave of American Jews from New York City and New England revived the congregation as part of a general reinvention of the island as a tourist centre. In the 1990s Israeli desalinization technology and the establishment of a branch of Coral World Ocean Park led several Israeli families to call the island home, often rotating through for a few years apiece. And in the late 1990s Chabad Lubavitch established a small outpost on the island as well. Never numbering more than a few hundred in total, the Jewish population periodically seemed on the verge of extinction, regularly renewing itself due in large part to the major Jewish and secular migration patterns of the modern era.

The congregation's worship patterns reflected the make-up of the population. From the synagogue's founding until the Second World War, congregants officially worshipped using a Sephardi rite. Starting in the 1950s however, the practice slowly changed, with members describing a hybrid 'Reform/Sephardi' ritual by the early 1960s. Stateside, American Jewish families increasingly dominated the synagogue population by this time, leading the congregation to affiliate with American Reform Judaism in 1967. Since then, the congregation has exclusively employed rabbis trained at the Hebrew Union College (and for a while in the mid-2000s also employed a Reform Jewish cantorial student); has developed many of the corporate structural components of a Reform synagogue, such as a sisterhood, a youth group, and membership in the New York region of the Union for Reform Judaism; and has adopted the Reform movement's liturgy. Regardless of these changes, however, the congregation's self-identified Sephardi legacy provided its members with a sense of curatorship: leading them to care for the 1833 sanctuary, maintain the island's two Jewish cemeteries, express pride in the abundance of Jewish surnames among the local (non-Jewish) population, and preserve their extant congregational documents.

Thus, although an American Reform congregation by institutional affiliation, at the end of the twentieth century the members of Beracha Veshalom saw themselves as guardians and recipients of a long-standing island tradition of Jewish life, symbolized most dramatically by the historical, sand-covered floor and Sephardi layout of the sanctuary in which they prayed. Many collectively found this past to be a compelling facet of the synagogue's identity in the post-war period and readily expressed interest in activities that promoted the continual maintenance of that Sephardi heritage. Perhaps no event in recent memory, however, illustrated these discourses more vibrantly than the congregation's bicentennial celebration. Underscoring numerous events meant to appeal to the broad, world Jewish community, including presentations by Elie Wiesel and Yitzhak Perlman, the congregation's claims on its Sephardi heritage effectively framed the celebration period and served as a symbol of the St Thomas synagogue's longevity. Three central aspects of the celebration emphasized both the inherited identity the congregation attempted to showcase and the complexity of the congrega-tion's relationship with that identity: its use of 'sephardiness' to enhance its public image, its self-imposed need to preserve the physical remnants of its Sephardi past, and its attempts to re-enact the Sephardi past within a local ritual setting.

St Thomas Jewry's Auto-Historiography

Historiography tends to focus heavily on the writings of scholars, with much less atten-tion paid to lay historians. In St Thomas, however, a relative lack of scholarly interest and access, combined with the island's international reputation as a shipping entrepôt in the nineteenth century and its periodic attempts to claim attention as a tourist attrac-tion ever since, have opened an important doorway for understanding the meaning of history to the lay population; especially, in this case, the Jewish population. In order to parallel local interest in Jewish history that dated from at least the early 1830s,[14] Jews on St Thomas needed to produce history on their own in ways that would interest the readers of Jewish (and non-Jewish) periodicals of the time.

Starting in about the mid-nineteenth century, the president of the synagogue sup-plied periodicals and interested historians around the world with a relatively standard statement of synagogue facts and figures.[15] In this narrative, the first Jewish birth on the island took place in 1757 and the community became viable with arrivals from St Eustatius 'after the sacking of [the island] by [British admiral George] Rodney, in 1781'. The account ended with numerical details of the island's growing Jewish popu-lation, along with an assertion of 'the most kindly feelings exist[ing] between them and the rest of the community'. Portraying St Thomas Jewry as a thriving and respected population, this historical statement served to put the island on the map of the Jewish world of the time.

By the 1880s, as shipping decreased and the island started to slip into obscurity, the synagogue's historical narrative shifted to one of magnification. In place of a pro-gressive history, local newspapers instead published a series of portraits of famous nineteenth-century Jewish residents, including David Levy Yulee and Judah P. Ben-jamin.[16] This new style of presentation maximized the impact of the island's Jewish community upon the rest of the world: the profiled figures, though claimed as mem-bers of the Virgin Islands Jewish community, had all made their names and homes

[14] The *Sanct Thomae Tidende* of 6 July 1833 advertised that Henry Hart Milman's three-volume *History of the Jews* (London, 1830) was for sale in its bookshop. It may not be coincidental that this advertisement was inserted a little more than two months before the congregation consecrated its newest synagogue on the Jewish New Year 1833.

[15] Most of the time this statement was a slight variation of the account in John P. Knox, *A Historical Account of St. Thomas, W. I.* (New York, 1852), 162–3.

[16] 'Judge David Naar', *St. Thomas Times* (1 May 1880), 4; 'David Yulee', *St. Thomas Times* (23 Apr. 1881); 'Judah Benjamin', *St. Thomas Herald* (28 July 1883), 2–3.

outside the territory. Faced with a shrinking population, Jewish residents seemed to prefer measuring their community's significance in the broader scale rather than recounting the uncertain future of their own current members.

In 1940 'social minded photographer' Alexander Alland[17] wrote a history and portrait of the St Thomas Jewish community in a series of four articles commissioned by *American Hebrew*.[18] Accompanying portraits of the synagogue and the island population, Alland's account situated St Thomas's Jews within a Jacob Riis-like cauldron of ethnic vibrancy and poverty, as government workers, clerks, and a recently arrived activist. His experiences on the island led to detailed and colourful descriptions of the Jews' records, artefacts, and prominent figures on an island that 'has lost its past glory'.[19] While it did mention the group's history, however, the series as a whole seemed to be more a paean to the Jewish worker: the magazine's description of the community as a 'unique subject, [that] should be of great interest to our readers' gave the impression of an interesting ethnic population with a wondrous if marginal role in American Jewish life.[20]

By the 1950s Caribbean Jewish history once again began to play a part in the American Jewish story. Spurred on by an American Jewish tercentenary project that aimed to celebrate Jews' long and peaceful existence in American life and culture,[21] American Jewish Archives founder Jacob Rader Marcus led an 'expedition' to various communities in the Caribbean. 'Jews in this land [the USA] are becoming increasingly conscious of their historic background; they are interested in their origins', he noted. 'It is only natural . . . that [American Jews] should seek to secure material which will throw light on their early days.'[22] The expedition, which included a stop in St Thomas,[23] yielded a substantial amount of photocopied material on colonial Jewish life in the region, which was deposited in the American Jewish Archives and renewed Marcus's interest in seventeenth- and eighteenth-century American Judaism. Those communities from which he collected material, meanwhile, began to reassess the value and meaning of their own pasts, eventually repackaging them for an American Jewish audience.[24]

[17] Bonnie Yochelson, *The Committed Eye: Alexander Alland's Photographs* (New York, 1991), 2.

[18] Alexander Alland, 'The Jews of the Virgin Islands: A History of the Islands and Candid Biographies of Outstanding Jews Born There', *American Hebrew* (29 Mar. 1940), 5, 12, 13, 16; (5 Apr. 1940), 6–7; (26 Apr. 1940), 5, 12, 13; (17 May 1940), 5, 12.   [19] Alland, 'The Jews of the Virgin Islands' (29 Mar. 1940), 5.

[20] Ibid. Alland's later projects on gypsies and the Hebrew Congregation of Commandment Keepers in New York, reinforced this project of humanizing exoticized ethnic communities (see Yochelson, *The Committed Eye*, 8–10).

[21] On the US tercentennial, see Arthur A. Goren, *The Politics and Public Culture of American Jews* (Bloomington, 1999), 195–204.

[22] Jacob Rader Marcus, 'The West India and South America Expedition of the American Jewish Archives', *American Jewish Archives*, 5 (1953), 6–7.   [23] Marcus, 'The West India and South America Expedition', 20–1.

[24] Perhaps the best early example of this new consciousness was Emmanuel, *Precious Stones of the Jews of Curaçao*, which examined the lives of Curaçao's Jewish communities through their tombstones and

For St Thomas in particular, this renewed sense of historical significance coincided with a sharp rise in tourism to the island in the 1950s and early 1960s. By the mid-1950s the island's Jewish house of worship was being regularly described as a 'historic synagogue', and, in direct consultation with American Secretary of the Interior Fred A. Seaton, synagogue members attempted to have the sanctuary named a National Historic Site. Exaggerated historical claims were made for the synagogue at this time in an attempt to market it internationally. According to an article in the local Virgin Islands paper, the synagogue members claimed the building to be 'the oldest under the Stars and Stripes', dating 'back to the 1803–04 era', and that the congregation itself 'goes back over 300 years to its founding'.[25] This kind of rhetoric, promoted by prominent island residents enthusiastic about their emerging role as amateur historians, connected with the earlier language of the tercentennial and served as a means for the community to capitalize on its recently delineated role in American Judaism.[26]

This new historical consciousness also led to the first two local efforts to present a written version of St Thomas Jewry's history to a wider audience—both created by members of the committee charged with having the sanctuary named a historical site. In 1958 synagogue president and lawyer Harry Dreis created a trifold pamphlet entitled *Jewish Historical Development in the Virgin Islands*. Clearly intended to engage visitors with his tour-guide style, Dreis presented a timeline of the territory's Jewish history. The generally accurate recounting of highlights from the nineteenth and twentieth centuries, however, was overshadowed by overzealous efforts to conflate the community's past with late fifteenth-century Sephardi narratives, and Dreis's conflation of St Thomas with the West African island of São Tomé led to some far-fetched claims that effectively doubled the congregation's age.[27] Due to these flaws, the pamphlet was

contributed to the new push for American Jewish genealogical work perhaps best represented by Malcolm Stern, *Americans of Jewish Descent* (Cincinnati, 1960).

[25] 'Synagogue May Become Historic Site', *Virgin Islands Daily News* (4 Feb. 1957), 1, 4. The article includes the claim 'that important leaders of our yesteryears who went on to fame and fortune were of Jewish ancestry of background—Judah P. Benjamin, Alexander Hamilton, and the artist, Pissaro [sic]. They came to this territory during one of the many religious pogroms in Europe'. This inaccurate account seems more likely to be a misunderstanding on the reporter's part, though it is possible that the people interviewed for the article linked these figures to the east European Jewish migration narrative prevalent at the time.

[26] See also 'Jewish Congregation Here is Among Oldest in America', *Virgin Islands Daily News* (11 Feb. 1956), 2; 'Colorful History of Jews Told Here in Survey', *Virgin Islands Daily News* (13 June 1957), 2.

[27] At its most overreaching (and historically inaccurate), the pamphlet included a paragraph apparently based on information about the Portuguese island of São Tomé, but grafted into the Caribbean context: 'Our memories . . . must go back to 1493 to get a glimpse of the historical background of Judaism in St. Thomas, when several young Jewish sons and daughters of Portuguese parents were sent by King John II to settle there under an infamous decree which forcibly baptized them (Marranos) with an attempt to make them face the hardships of the recently discovered island as settlers for Portugal. They struggled for a time with the hardships and rigors of an unbearable existence and finally perished from starvation and slaughter at the hands of the Carib Indians' (Harry Dreis, *Jewish Historical Development in the Virgin Islands* (St Thomas, 1958), n.p.).

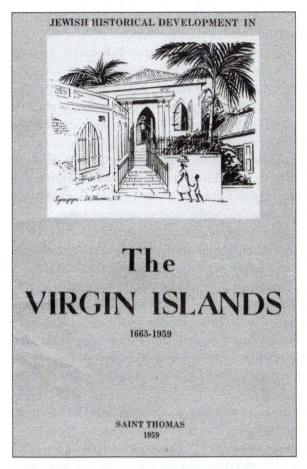

Figure 21.3 Cover of Isidor Paiewonsky, *Jewish Historical Development in the Virgin Islands, 1665–1959*

Used with permission of the St Thomas Hebrew Congregation

only sold for a short time. The following year, it was replaced by an equally tourist centred, but more accurate, publication by island merchant Isidor Paiewonsky. Paiewonsky's text, with the slightly more focused title *Jewish Historical Development in the Virgin Islands, 1665–1959* (Figure 21.3), continued Dreis's timeline-based approach, but dispensed with the earliest historical claims and incorporated more rigorous archival research.[28] Significantly longer at twenty-four pages and elegantly produced with professional typesetting and a proper cover, the work became the centrepiece of the synagogue's public narrative (and a good seller among visitors) for the rest of the century. The work's success gained Paiewonsky a reputation as a de facto historian of the island and a respected doyen of the Jewish community's heritage: he subsequently produced three more books on St Thomas's history, each recounting extraordinary

---

[28] Paiewonsky may have conducted some of the research for this pamphlet on his own, but, based on our conversations, it appears that he relied heavily on archivists and paid researchers to provide him with historical materials.

events in extraordinary language. Synagogue docents, meanwhile, would later use the anecdote-filled narrative as a basis for their tours of the sanctuary.

In the following decades, the synagogue increasingly relied on its history as a reason for celebration, preservation, and publicity; and the community promoted it within an island tourist culture where superlatives became increasingly necessary for generating attention and reputation. In 1974, while in the final phases of a year-long renovation that restored the sanctuary's pews and other wooden structures and revealed 'the original Danish brick walls' (the plaster was stripped from the walls for aesthetic effect), the congregation celebrated a weekend-long 'rededication' that was advertised in the American Jewish press and attended by four of the five rabbis who had ministered to the congregation still living.[29] Former territory chief librarian Enid M. Baa, who had spent years compiling card files of congregants' births, deaths, and marriages, wrote a new essay for the rededication programme highlighting the history of the congregation, and called for a 'chair of Caribbean Jewish studies to be established at the College of the Virgin Islands . . . for the study of Sephardic Judaism in the Caribbean'.[30] The commemorative pamphlet marking the occasion repeatedly connected the congregation's longevity with its dedication to maintaining Jewish ritual life in the synagogue—particularly in its current lack of an active rabbi. The weekend thus enacted a historical pageant of sorts—with Sunday-morning dedication services held progressively at the congregation's old cemetery, new cemetery, and sanctuary—even as it also served as a display of the synagogue's continued vitality despite the challenges of island life.

Beneath its public face, however, the synagogue was struggling to maintain its physical plant. The old cemetery in particular had fallen into an increasing state of disrepair, exacerbated by its location in an underserved part of town and the frank reality that few current members had ancestors buried there. By the late 1970s, following several failed efforts, the synagogue leadership looked into selling the land as a public recreation area and moving the extant stones to a 'wall of remembrance' in the new cemetery. The proposal sparked an international outcry, with even Jacob Rader Marcus weighing in to stop the sale. Synagogue leaders consequently found themselves wedged uncomfortably between heritage responsibility and fiscal strain, as they sought a solution that would satisfy all parties.[31]

[29] 'Synagogue Renovation to be Aired in US Media', *Virgin Islands Daily News* (20 Dec. 1973), 3. Since the synagogue did not employ a rabbi at the time of its rededication, the presence of its former rabbinic leaders proved quite significant for maintaining a sense of religious authority.

[30] 'Synagogue to be Rededicated Sun.', *Virgin Islands Daily News* (6 Sept. 1974), 8, 13; see also Enid M. Baa, 'Notes from the Sephardic Past', *Rededication, Hebrew Congregation Blessing and Peace, and Acts of Piety* (programme pamphlet, 6–8 Sept. 1974), 6–7, Hebrew Congregation of St Thomas Archives, St Thomas, box 22: Series Events, folder B: Rededication, 1974.

[31] Discussions about the sale of the Savan ('old') cemetery can be found in the Hebrew Congregation of St Thomas Archives, box 15: folder 2.

With the sanctuary's 150th anniversary in 1983, the cemetery matter appeared to dissipate. A similar weekend-long series of events, including a religious service, prominent speakers, and a gala ball, reasserted St Thomas's long-standing Jewish presence. This time, however, in addition to issuing a revised and updated version of Paiewonsky's pamphlet in a larger format with colour photographs, the synagogue devoted a good portion of its celebration to its connection with the island's history of black liberation. Through invitations to scholars Hollis R. Lynch and Edward Wilmot Blyden III, the congregation celebrated the life of 'father of pan-Africanism' Edward Wilmot Blyden (1832–1912), who had written favourably about his childhood interactions with the St Thomas Jewish community and later supported the Zionist cause.[32] While celebrating its own religious history, the synagogue thus opened up a public space for a narrative of black nationalism within its commemoration and, in doing so, attempted to assert a common cause with the island's majority population. While the lectures themselves caused a little discomfort to some congregants, they seemed at least to acknowledge the celebration could benefit from a twinning of historical narratives. In contrast, the island's rabbi compared the celebration favourably to a somewhat more unappreciative visit by Beit Hatfutsot a couple of years earlier, which 'refer[red] to St Thomas and the Jews who live here [today] as a remnant community' and showed little interest in the actual goings-on of contemporary Jewish life.[33]

As the synagogue approached its bicentennial—on the heels of the well-publicized quincentenary observance in 1992 of the Spanish Expulsion of Jews—its leadership continued to recast its approach to St Thomas's Jewish history. While the congregation, which claimed a Sephardi heritage but few Sephardi members by this point, continued to worship according to the American Reform rite, they also saw the advantage of emphasizing Sephardi identity during the bicentennial year. The Jewish community's fashioning of its past, which had moved from factual reporting, to forging paradigms of self-importance, and then to incorporating both island needs and a tourist audience, moved further to engage a history both ethnically and temporally removed from the present day.

The Challenges of History in the Mid-1990s

The historical narrative of St Thomas's Jewry emerged in the planning stages of its bicentennial as part of a matrix of intertwined local claims to history, each of which framed Judaism in a different manner. As the synagogue prepared to celebrate, it attempted to incorporate this broader set of historical strategies to respond to specific cultural needs.

[32] Hollis Lynch, *Edward Wilmot Blyden: Pan-Negro Patriot, 1832–1912* (New York, 1967).

[33] Stanley T. Relkin, 'Between Us . . .', *Hebrew Congregation Blessing and Peace, and Acts of Piety Newsletter*, 12/7 (May 1983), 1.

The primary scholarly history of the territory, Isaac Dookhan's 1974 *History of the Virgin Islands of the United States*, had been written in part for use by students at the College of the Virgin Islands (founded in 1963).[34] Created in the context of a broader movement among West Indians to take responsibility for their own self-improvement —and intellectually centred at the University of the West Indies—the book traced a narrative from Native American to colonial rule and finally to the trials of self-actualization. 'No longer is Virgin Islands history written from the standpoint of Denmark and the United States', wrote historian Richard B. Sheridan in the introduction, 'instead, attention is focused on slave resistance and rebellion, laborers' revolts, the rise of trade unions and political parties, and the progress that has been made towards self-government, material betterment, and cultural exchange'.[35] In 1994, four years after Dookhan's death, the Canoe Press of the University of the West Indies re-issued the book, reinforcing its place as the territory's predominant historical account.[36]

Contemporary production of academic history in the territory itself took place in the discussions of the Society of Virgin Islands Historians, a group of professional and lay historians headed by Arnold Highfield, George F. Tyson, and Marilyn Krigger from the University of the Virgin Islands. Holding annual conferences in St Croix, the group encouraged new work from promising researchers, maintained active relationships and exchange with Danish historians and archivists, welcomed visiting scholars, and helped publish essay collections and editions of primary materials through grants from the Virgin Islands Humanities Council and other organizations. The society's focus on St Croix tended to help even out coverage of the Virgin Islands, where the smaller island of St Thomas often received more government attention, because of its larger tourism industry. At the same time, the society also served as a place for the island's amateur historians to present their own work within a supportive environment: these projects were regularly published in private or semi-private editions.[37]

While the Society of Virgin Islands Historians largely catered to the island's middle and upper classes, others in the territory's majority black population explored a different historical trajectory, one which emphasized black empowerment. Although groups advocating black national identity had been active on the island for decades, the early

[34] Isaac Dookhan, *A History of the Virgin Islands of the United States* (St Thomas, 1974). On the history of the University of the Virgin Islands, see Isaac Dookhan, 'The Expansion of Higher Education Opportunities in the United States Virgin Islands', *Journal of Negro Education*, 50/1 (1981), 15–25; Ralph M. Paiewonsky with Isaac Dookhan, *Memoirs of a Governor: A Man for the People* (New York, 1990), 353–85. The college officially became a university in 1986.

[35] Richard B. Sheridan, 'Introduction', in Dookhan, *A History of the Virgin Islands*, p. xiii.

[36] The Canoe Press reissued Dookhan's book in 1995 and again in 2002.

[37] See e.g. Edith deJongh Woods, *The Three Quarters of the Town of Charlotte Amalie* (St Thomas, 1989); David K. Knight (ed.), *The 1688 Census of the Danish West Indies (Portrait of a Colony in Crisis)* (St Thomas, 1998); David K. Knight and Laurette de T. Prime (eds.), *St. Thomas 1803: Crossroads of the Diaspora (The 1803 Proceedings and Register of the Free Colored)* (St Thomas, 1999).

1990s saw an international resurgence of black nationalist rhetoric: particularly through incendiary remarks by Louis Farrakhan, the publication of the Nation of Islam's *Secret Relationship between the Blacks and the Jews*,[38] and, locally, through controversial comments by two Virgin Islands senators that alarmed white and Jewish populations.[39] One of the three bookstores on St Thomas in the early 1990s, the Education Station, sold philosophical and historical tracts promoting black pride and nationalism. Within this environment, Harold W. L. Willocks, a lawyer and native of St Croix, published *The Umbilical Cord*, a history of the territory that he hoped would ameliorate 'the problem [of] the lack of native writers of Virgin Islands history'. Willocks argued in his introduction that the existing historical narratives of the territory had been 'written by scholars unfamiliar with the culture and the people, [which] produces a certain degree of alienation between the writer and the history'.[40] His response detailed a story of Africans violently ripped from their native homeland and culture, humiliated by European colonists in the Virgin Islands, and then forced to endure a difficult, centuries-long struggle to regain their culture, build self-respect, and achieve self-governance in their new home. Earnestly written, and diligently if idiosyncratically footnoted, the book offered 'a fresh perspective, which may be labeled Afrocentric', according to the foreword by Charles A. Emanuel, a writer for the local St Croix *Avis*, while 'revealing connections between apparently discrete events' that reinforced the need for this new perspective.[41] *The Umbilical Cord* was originally sold by Afrocentric bookstores in the Virgin Islands. However, its rapid adoption in many of the territory's schools reinforced a broader governmental desire to assert itself in the face of decades of perceived outside exploitation and mismanagement.[42]

Tourists encountered a more general form of history production that ambiguously emphasized the island's past in order to enhance visitors' experiences. The 'historic' towns of Charlotte Amalie (St Thomas), Fredricksted, and Christiansted (St Croix) used their existing structures to reposition a distant past of labour, hardship, and war within a framework of safe, peacetime consumerism. The complexes of nineteenth-

---

[38] Nation of Islam, *The Secret Relationship between the Blacks and the Jews*.

[39] The two senators, Celestino White and Adelbert Bryan, responded to the execution-style murders of two recently arrived white island residents with racial comments widely interpreted as insensitive (see '2 Men Killed in Ambush in St. Thomas', *New York Times* (10 Mar. 1996)).

[40] Harold W. L. Willocks, *The Umbilical Cord: The History of the United States Virgin Islands from the Pre-Colombian Era to the Present* (Christiansted, St Croix, 1995), p. xxiii.   [41] Willocks, *The Umbilical Cord*, p. xxi.

[42] *The Umbilical Cord* remained the standard text at many of these schools until at least 2010 (see Christian Simescu, 'Harold Willocks Sworn In as Superior Court Judge', *Virgin Islands Daily News* (13 Mar. 2010)). Afrocentrism was only one strategy for expressing displeasure with US management of the Virgin Islands. Professor William W. Boyer of the University of Delaware offered a similar critique from the perspective of political science and international relations in his publications (William W. Boyer, *Civil Liberties in the US Virgin Islands* (St Croix, 1982); id., *America's Virgin Islands: A History of Human Rights and Wrongs* (Durham, NC, 1983; 2nd edn., 2010)).

century stone masonry warehouses lining the shore had been converted into shops and boutiques by the late twentieth century and were seen as central to the island's commercial ambitions. Colonial cannons were conspicuously cemented into the pavement on busy thoroughfares, picturesquely highlighting the island's military past. Entrepreneurs built hotels around centuries-old watchtowers and named them after the pirates Blackbeard and Bluebeard. Two of the Virgin Islands' main museums were housed in converted seventeenth-century Danish forts. The most prominent houses of worship on the island touted their nineteenth-century construction, and the ruins of sugar mills on St Thomas, St Croix, and St John served as quaint landmarks for visitors to encounter on their hikes and tours around the island. In this manner, visitors could experience the Virgin Islands as a casual historical encounter as well as a tropical destination.

Judaism was included in these narratives in various ways: as a long-standing group on the island that deserved its own historical research, as a counter-narrative within an Afrocentric history that challenged mainstream concepts of Judaism, as an ambiguously 'ancient' form of religious life, and as a non-Christian religious identity. Members of the Hebrew Congregation of St Thomas regularly engaged with these and other narratives through various local institutions, such as the island's ecumenical council, newspaper articles, anti-discrimination programmes, synagogue open-door policies (including tours for island youth), a gift shop for visitors, and regular interactions with island politicians. In preparing to celebrate its bicentennial, the Jewish community of St Thomas consequently sought ways to write itself into this matrix of simultaneous narratives, articulating a local sense of identity, while cultivating a Jewish mystique that added to the attractiveness and prestige of the synagogue, both on and off the island.

The Bicentennial

As advertised in the official tourist brochure created and distributed by Missouri-based Brentwood Travel, the St Thomas synagogue's celebration appealed to several external demographics, with a focus on American Jews. The brochure noted that the 'extraordinary Bicentennial Celebration will capture the hearts and attention of world Jewry, making St. Thomas and the synagogue a sought-after destination and international focal point'. Beyond the Jewish narrative, however, the brochure attempted to establish a second narrative of multicultural Caribbean harmony as a model for multicultural society in general. The celebration, noted the advertisement, presented 'an opportunity to bring together all components of society to learn more about their heritage, ethnic backgrounds and the beauty of cultural diversity while enjoying the pleasures of the Caribbean'.[43] The list of planned events in the back of the brochure aimed to

---

[43] Brentwood Travel, *Celebrating 200 Years of Jewish Life in St. Thomas* (promotional brochure, 1995), 1.

support both of these agendas, including the opening of a museum of Virgin Islands Jewry, two 'play[s] of Jewish interest' to be performed in four-week runs, an exhibit by St Thomas-born Jewish painter Camille Pissarro, and lectures by world personalities such as supreme court justice Ruth Bader Ginsburg, poet Maya Angelou, and 'Ethiopian born Jew [and professor at Harvard University] Dr. Ephraim Isaac'.[44] These events, planned both as attractions for tourists and as gifts to the community, emphasized Jews as a model historical community whose concerns held relevance within Jewish history, as well as a sub-population that wanted to bring its expertise to larger historical matters of ethnic interaction.

The synagogue trained facilitators to introduce the Anti-Defamation League's anti-bias curriculum 'A World of Difference' to the island's schools. This part of the commemoration reflected a substantially different congregational self-image than the advertised version, as the Jewish population hoped an appeal to communal values and ethnic sensitivity might ease historical cycles of racial, cultural, and economic tension on the island. In doing so, it acknowledged the fraught position Jews held among different island factions as freedom fighters, impostors, oppressors, and long-standing civic contributors.[45] Ever-present in contemporary island politics and social interactions, these issues regularly led the Jewish community to offer public clarifications in word and deed.[46] By bringing 'A World of Difference' to the island, the Jewish community intended to reclaim a sense of Jewish history amid a general call for tolerance, particularly given the contemporary events on the island.

In celebrating its 200th anniversary, the Hebrew Congregation of St Thomas set to work enacting a multiply mediated and multi-layered heritage that responded to the cultural landscape of life on an American-owned Caribbean island at the end of the twentieth century. Using the strategies discussed in the next section, they developed an approach to history that brought together ethnic pride, commercialization, religious ideology, and anxiety about the future.

[44] Ibid. 25. Isaac, notably, was not a member of the Beta Israel (popularly called 'Ethiopian Jews'), but the Ethiopian-born son of a Yemenite Jewish father and an Ethiopian mother who converted to Judaism—an ancestry somewhat obscured by the formulation used in the brochure.

[45] Senator Adelbert Bryan, for example, protested against a territory senate statement honouring the Hebrew Congregation of St Thomas on its bicentennial by claiming that Jews were particularly cruel slave traders and owners; that they were not truly descendants of the 'real Israelites'; and that on an island that was 85 per cent black, such an action would be similar to the Jews establishing a holiday to honour Hitler. These comments, recorded in the senate chamber, were later circulated on a cassette tape to which I had access.

[46] See e.g. Judah M. Cohen, editorial, *Virgin Islands Daily News* (15 Sept. 1995). I wrote this editorial in response to an earlier newspaper editorial faulting the Jews for not taking care of their old cemetery. Written by a representative of the Hebrew Congregation of St Thomas, it was vetted by several members of the leadership before being sent out.

The Jewish Community of St Thomas: The Film

In the early stages of its publicity campaign to attract visitors to St Thomas to partake in the synagogue's bicentennial events, the congregation distributed a six-minute video co-created with a local production company.[47] Produced with particular attention to attracting liberal American Jews to the island, the video attempted to project an image of beauty and exoticism to potential tourists, while also appealing to an abstract yet universalized sense of Jewish 'heritage'. 'Sephardiness' played a significant part in invoking a Jewish otherness that mirrored the beguiling Caribbean setting, while also asserting a sense of history and long-term presence. At the same time, the events promoted by the video focused primarily on the opportunity for visitors to enjoy world-class accommodation within a meaningful Caribbean Jewish context.

To accomplish its goal, the video set up an evocative equation of exoticism and historical presence. An opening shofar blast, followed by the narrator's voice reciting a strategic adaptation of Genesis 22: 17—'I will bestow my blessings upon you, and make your descendants as numerous as the sands on the seashore'—served as ageless indicators of Judaism and general Judaeo-Christian spirituality. To generic Caribbean music, the narrator continued by linking the history of the island to Caribbean leisure activities:

The Virgin Islands became a paradise home for Sephardic Jews, who made the first Jewish imprint in the Western Hemisphere when they came to the sun-soaked, sand-lined beaches of the Caribbean. Two hundred years later, the Jewish community of St. Thomas is preparing to celebrate its bicentennial in 1995–1996. Through the sands of time: the Holy Congregation of Blessing, and Peace, and Loving Deeds was established with a sand-covered floor.

Numerous images and sounds of the 'exotic' Caribbean accompanied this narration, from the light reggae at the start, to the idyllic images of water and beaches that accompanied the first lines, to the re-envisioning of the Sephardi founders of the congregation in touristic terms as living in a 'paradise home', to a dramatic dissolve from the sand on a beach to the iconic sandy floor of the St Thomas synagogue. An on-camera statement from Isidor Paiewonsky reinforced a perception of historical persistence: after describing how a 'top [but nameless] French architect was brought out from Paris' to design the 1833 synagogue, he noted that the building 'has changed little since my bar mitzvah in 1922'.

The rest of the film presented a series of scenes that placed contemporary Jewish life within a similarly exotic setting. Current members of the community performed openly syncretic versions of three Jewish rituals that emphasized the interaction of Jewish tradition and Caribbean Jewish life: a Torah service conducted in the sandy

[47] The production company, Flicks Productions Inc., was run by Eric Zucker, a local Jewish author and film producer.

floored sanctuary; a *tashlikh* service dramatizing the casting away of sins into a moving body of water, enacted on a beach; and the end-of-sabbath *havdalah* service, celebrated on a yacht in the Caribbean Sea.[48] Both music and dress specifically emphasized an experience associated with Reform Judaism. Congregants dressed in contemporary clothing and sang melodies used throughout liberal Jewish prayer settings.[49] Music added two additional layers: generic Caribbean music provided a soundscape consistent with perceptions of the area and a version of 'Shalom aleikhem' with guitar and sung English interpolation, taken from an album of Reform Jewish summer-camp music, reflected the congregation's contemporary practices. The overall effect portrayed the St Thomas congregation as both familiar and exotic, a part of the world and a vacation destination, and a place for liberal Jews everywhere to feel comfortable. The film also offered potential tourists a vision of Judaism that the congregants themselves embraced as presenting a uniquely Caribbean experience.

Through its aural and visual imagery, the video juxtaposed a fantasy version of island Jewry—where the notion of 'sephardiness' served to raise the prestige of St Thomas as a site for heritage tourism—with familiar images of liberal Jewish practice. Together they signalled both an important symbolic notion of what the congregation saw as making it special and actively contributed to the pan-religious atmosphere of a site where tourism dominated the economy. Displaying such an exotic heritage reflected the sensibility of the synagogue towards tourists in general: members of the congregation, while giving tours of the sanctuary, overwhelmingly highlighted the time of the building's construction in their narratives. The congregation knew little about its history other than Paiewonsky's select anecdotes. Yet the very sparseness of such knowledge added a mystique to the synagogue and provided depth to its mission in daily life. That significance, in turn, contributed to the island's viability as a tourist destination.

Protecting an Exotic Heritage

While the Hebrew Congregation of St Thomas projected an image of its Sephardi heritage, its congregants in the mid-1990s also found themselves guardians of that heritage through the identification and preservation of sites considered important reminders of Sephardi life on the island. The congregation's two cemeteries, one of which was full by the 1830s, constituted an important part of the Jewish landscape, even

[48] This ritual would also be an option for tourists wishing to visit the island: for an extra fee, visitors could participate in a 'Havdallah Harbor Cruise' led by the congregation's rabbi 'or a representative from the Hebrew Congregation' (Brentwood Travel, *Celebrating 200 Years of Jewish Life in St. Thomas*, i, 11).

[49] The music used in the video included 'Torah orah' (described as a hasidic folk song) and 'Al sheloshah devarim' (by Chaim Zur) during the Torah service, 'Oseh shalom' (by Nurit Hirsh) during the *tashlikh* service, and a cantorial rendering of the *havdalah* blessings and Debbie Friedman's 1976 'Birchot havdalah' during the *havdalah* service.

though by the end of the twentieth century relatively few congregants had ancestors buried there. More central was the synagogue building itself, which the congregation proclaimed 'The Oldest Synagogue Building in Continuous Use Under the American Flag' in its promotional materials and which remained an important connection between the congregation and its Sephardi forebears. During the year of the bicentennial celebration, the synagogue mounted a successful campaign to have the sanctuary building declared a National Historic Landmark. In an application written by a local architect and revised by the congregation's rabbi, an archaeologist with the National Parks Service, and Stanley Hordes—a scholar of New World crypto-Jewry—the synagogue sanctuary's 'period of significance' was described as '1833–ca. 1850', effectively excluding any reference to Jewish life outside the Sephardi sphere.

To emphasize the connection between the Jewish community and its Sephardi past, the authors devoted fifteen of the application's thirty-two pages to an extensively referenced, single-spaced history of the synagogue, contextualized within a general history of the Jewish people that highlighted the Sephardi narrative:[50]

The Sephardic Jewish Synagogue and Congregation of St Thomas may trace its roots through some two thousand years of the Hebrew Diaspora, starting with the destruction of the Jewish nation and the Great Temple in Jerusalem by the Romans in the first century AD. Some of these displaced Hebrew peoples ended up in the Iberian peninsula, where over some 1500 years under Roman, Visigothic, Muslim, and Christian rulers they worshiped in their synagogues, attended to their businesses, and raised their families according to religious tenets that over time came to identify them as Sephardic (Spanish and Portuguese) Jewish peoples.[51]

Two pages were devoted to the Expulsion from Spain, three and a half to Jews during Caribbean colonization, and more than eight pages to the history of St Thomas. Within this last section, however, the writers dedicated only fourteen lines to Jewish life on the island after 1867, none of which noted any subsequent demographic change. Judging by the application, which the National Parks Service approved on 25 September 1997, the congregation defined its ethnic background by the physical vessel that contained it. While the description admittedly aimed to convince officials at the National Parks Service that the building was 'a religious property that derives its primary national significance from its historic importance', it also showcased the community's efforts to present a dear object of heritage as a public icon of the synagogue's longevity and legacy.

[50] 'National Historic Landmark Nomination' (1997), Hebrew Congregation of St Thomas Archives, box 8, folder 5. A modified version of the application document (mainly lacking photographs) can be found at <http://pdfhost.focus.nps.gov/docs/NHLS/Text/97001270.pdf>; the accepted version of the application can be found at <http://www.nps.gov/nhl/designations/samples/vi/St._Thomas_Syn_II.pdf>.
[51] 'National Historic Landmark Nomination'.

Enacting Sephardi History

The influence of the congregation's Sephardi structures and past also extended strategically into contemporary synagogue life. Congregants made brief references to Sephardi Jewry during regular sabbath services throughout the bicentennial year, mainly through announcements mentioning the 'historic synagogue' or events such as weekly grave washings in the new (Altona) cemetery. Yet their celebration also included a special project: to transform the Friday night service of 22 December 1995, coinciding with the festival of Hanukah, into an 'Authentic 1796 Sephardic Service and Chanukah celebration'. While liturgists describe sacred services as public presentations of religious lineage and belief, this particular service included an opportunity to display—and in the process comment upon—the synagogue's cultural heritage.

Years went into organizing the event. More than two and a half years before the service, the congregation's rabbi, Bradd Boxman, contacted the American Jewish Archives for information on Sephardi liturgy; and soon afterwards he began conversations with the Spanish-Portuguese synagogues Shearith Israel in New York City and Mikveh Israel in Philadelphia. Within a few months, the St Thomas congregation had hired retired cantor Reverend Abraham Lopes Cardoso to come from New York and lead the service and arranged for dozens of Sephardi prayer books to be imported from Israel. Boxman also conducted research locally and recorded liturgical melodies from one of the only remaining (and no longer practising) Sephardi Jews on the island, with hopes of using them in the service.[52] A congregant researched appropriate dress for the event and recommended formal wear and top hats for the men and empire-waist dresses and stylish hats for the women. Invitations were created and sent out to the congregation as well as to a guest list of island dignitaries. Congregants seemed genuinely excited about the opportunity to access what they saw as a long-lost part of their synagogue's history.

In the months leading up to the event, however, Cardoso had to cancel his appearance, leaving the community to its own devices to create the service and its music. The resulting event reinvigorated the congregation with a symbolic sense of self, as it modelled Sephardi identity through the eyes of modern-day American Reform Jews. Greeters at the entrance to the sanctuary handed the men top hats and directed worshippers to their seats in candle-lit, gender-separated pews. The service began with a creative re-enactment of the synagogue's 1833 consecration ceremony.[53] Several prominent synagogue members processed around the sanctuary with the congregation's

---

[52] The melodies recorded from this congregant were assumed to be Sephardi. However, Ira Rohde, the cantor of New York City's Shearith Israel congregation, did not recognize any of the tunes; Rohde also noted that the liturgy described by the congregant differed from the Sephardi liturgy with which he was familiar (personal communication). It is perhaps more likely that the congregant remembered melodies from classical Reform Judaism—that have been largely replaced (and forgotten) by contemporary Reform Judaism.

[53] *Sanct Thomae Tidende* (14 Sept. 1833), 2–3.

Torah scrolls, led by one of the oldest and one of the youngest members who together held the flame that would eventually light the eternal lamp at the front. Upon completion of the circuit and the lighting of the lamp, the assemblage read a newly created synagogue mission statement and recited several psalms, thus symbolically reconsecrating both the sanctuary and its current congregation. Then the Friday night service commenced, read from a Sephardi prayer book and accompanied at least part of the time by a professional vocalist who sang prayer texts to romancero-based Sephardi melodies. (The liturgical selection 'Mi khamokha', however, was sung to the more conventional tune of 'Ma'oz tsur' to mark the holiday of Hanukah.) An American-style Hanukah candle-lighting ceremony followed, and before the service concluded American Reform Rabbi Murray Blackman, who had served the Hebrew Congregation in the late 1960s and come in as a last minute replacement for Cardoso, gave an address entitled 'Our Sephardic Heritage'.[54] The authenticity of the evening might have been questionable, and those assembled expressed no little bemusement at their part in the re-enactment. Nonetheless, the event played an important part in the bicentennial celebration, authenticating the group's connection to the congregation's history. Their Sephardi heritage, grafted onto them through membership of the congregation, emerged for public acknowledgement as an important, yet sometimes more subtly indicated, part of their communal lives.

Connecting with Scholarship

The synagogue also hoped to commission a 'scholarly history' of St Thomas Jewry from a 'professional historian' to accompany the celebration. A congregant who had been on the board of the American Jewish Historical Society oversaw the project, and the territory's head librarian (who was also a long-time member of the synagogue) expressed interest as well. The project aimed to bring St Thomas more firmly into the American Jewish historical narrative, using rigorous scholarly methods to produce an account that would supersede the existing 'anecdotal' history. This strategy, increasingly pursued by small Jewish communities to commemorate significant events and anniversaries during the 1990s,[55] reflected the congregation's self-assessment as history-worthy.

In taking these steps, the congregation once again had to reckon with the purpose of history. As in many other projects on Caribbean Jewry, the community's dual role as producer and main consumer of the history meant that rabbinical and lay leadership had the potential to control the choice of researcher as well as the final product. Such

---

[54] See Hebrew Congregation of St Thomas Archives, box 24, Series Events (1980–97). While a video recording was made of the event as well (which I saw in the late 1990s), it has since been misplaced.

[55] See e.g. Jonathan D. Sarna, 'Jewish Community Histories: Non-Academic Contributions', *Journal of American Ethnic History*, 6/1 (1986), 62–70.

considerations facilitated my scholarly entry into St Thomas: unaware of the synagogue's plan, I had approached Rabbi Boxman in early 1994 with a request to conduct
research in the community as part of my undergraduate senior thesis. The fact that my
family had spent two years on the island when I was a young child and had been
involved with the synagogue's Hebrew school eased me through the initial approval
process and allowed me access to the synagogue's research materials and personnel. At
the time the congregants viewed me as a possible assistant to the professional historian.[56] Yet my presence also helped further the history. Upon hearing of my work
on the project, a local merchant with an interest in the synagogue offered to put up part
of the funding. After some discussion, in which the donor took specific interest in me,
and the synagogue came to understand the complications involved in attracting the
kind of scholar they sought, I eventually assumed the historian's role, as a marginal
member of the community with a connection to the desired academic standards
through my college affiliation and my aspiration to attend graduate school. Ultimately,
I had to learn how to mediate between a community's expectations and my best
understanding of scholarly methods, as I took on what would become my first book
project.

Living and researching with the community for several two-month stints over six
years, I began to experience the historical fabric of the island myself. Working in my
two on-island operational bases of the synagogue office and the municipal library's
microfilm reading room required me to face the tensions between academic and popular history, which were highlighted by the island's pervasive tourist culture I encountered walking down Main Street or while giving sanctuary tours. In the synagogue
office and in the home of my host, I learned of the latest religious and communal
matters on the island. On the streets, my queries about the Jews of the island sometimes led residents to reveal their own Jewish ancestry, enquire about the nature of
Judaism from a Christian Caribbean perspective, or offer hints about clandestine Jewish
historical sites (such as hidden graves or a neglected alternative sanctuary) purported to
exist on the island. I also encountered cautious interest from historian Isidor Paiewonsky, who gradually accepted my project as a companion to his own, rather than a
replacement. In conjunction with preparations for other bicentennial events, my ex-

---

[56] In contradistinction to more academic historical research norms, family connection has been a key to
historical and anthropological research among Caribbean Jewish communities. Alan Benjamin has written of
the stultifying complexity of conducting research among Jews in Curaçao, where he had no familial
connections (Alan F. Benjamin, *Jews of the Dutch Caribbean: Exploring Ethnic Identity on Curaçao* (New York,
2002), 22–34). Josette Goldish, in comparison, had far less trouble accessing archives and conducting
interviews due to her numerous family ties with the community (Josette Capriles Goldish, *Once Jews: Stories
of Caribbean Sephardim* (Princeton, 2009), p. xiv). See also Frances P. Karner, *The Sephardics of Curaçao: A Study
of Socio-Cultural Patterns in Flux* (Assen, 1969), which presents a form of family research within the context of
a published master's thesis.

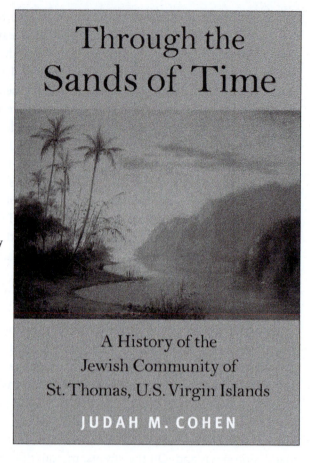

Figure 21.4 Cover of Judah M. Cohen, *Through the Sands of Time*

Cover © University Press of New England, Lebanon, NH. Reprinted with permission, featuring Camille Pissarro, *A Creek in St Thomas (Virgin Islands)*, Collection of Mr and Mrs Paul Mellon. Image Courtesy of the National Gallery of Art, Washington, DC. Reprinted with permission.

periences informed the history I would write, helping me to understand the past both in its own right and as an important function of the present.

The change in the book's publisher from the intended island press to Brandeis University Press, under the mentorship of American Jewish historian Jonathan Sarna, helped alleviate the problems of local editorial control while contributing to Sarna's broader programme (following that of Marcus) of encouraging the writing of high-quality local Jewish histories. Although the Hebrew Congregation board ultimately made no editorial suggestions about the manuscript, even as it generously gave me a publication grant, the off-island publisher ensured editorial scrutiny within a broader academic arena, and exposure to a larger scholarly community. I subsequently felt comfortable giving the book the same title as the synagogue's bicentennial campaign slogan ('Through the Sands of Time'), since it reflected our mutual quest for a historical framework, while acknowledging its origins from within the congregation's multi-faceted historical project. The press itself, meanwhile, offered its own historical gloss on the volume, by eschewing my own photos of the synagogue in favour of a painting by Camille Pissarro as the cover image (see Figure 21.4).

The book's publication in 2004 thus allowed 'scholarly history' to claim its place in the synagogue's historical discourse. It soon became regular reading for congregants and earned a spot in the synagogue's gift shop alongside Paiewonsky's pamphlet and several memoirs by prominent congregants. It complements (but has not replaced) the somewhat more sensational script presented in regular docent tours of the sanctuary.[57]

History for Survival

The congregation's constructions of historical narrative also became a force for continuity during times of crisis. On 15 September 1995, the night set for the gala opening of the synagogue's Jewish history museum that would launch the entire bicentennial, the island was devastated by Hurricane Marilyn. Wreaking over US$2 billion in damage (mostly on St Thomas) and damaging or destroying an estimated 80 per cent of the island's buildings[58]—including the back office of the synagogue—the hurricane forced the congregation to scale back its plans, cancel some events, and postpone others for months.[59] Over the next couple of years, moreover, the island's devastation took a toll on the synagogue's ability to function. A year after losing his apartment in the hurricane, Rabbi Boxman left the island with his family. The synagogue members debated the merits of hiring another rabbi for the next two years, while a local congregant and retired rabbi assumed liturgical duties, just as he had during previous interstices in rabbinical leadership. Difficulties in living on the island in the months following Marilyn also caused the congregation to lose about 40 per cent of its membership. These changes, which took place in parallel with the island's bicentennial events, emphasized the community's historical duality. By publicly promoting the narrative of the synagogue's continuity, particularly in the immediate face of adversity, congregants could continue their lives in an environment of continuous challenge and sometimes violent disruption.

The Hebrew Congregation of St Thomas and its sanctuary thus became major sources for its members' senses of personal and local significance, particularly when faced with the relentless march of the region's natural history. In one sense,

---

[57] Paiewonsky with Dookhan, *Memoirs of a Governor*; Mark Newman, *A Survivor's Memories: A Test of Everlasting Survival* (St Thomas, 1983); Henry L. Kimelman, *Living the American Dream: The Life and Times of Henry L. Kimelman* (New York, 1997).

[58] Donald Wernly et al., *Hurricane Marilyn: September 15–16, 1995* (Silver Spring, Md., 1996), 1.

[59] The Jewish history museum, originally scheduled to open on the night of the hurricane, had its dedication on 17 November, two months later; and the Camille Pissarro exhibit, originally scheduled to open on 21 January 1996, had to be pushed back nearly eleven months to 16 December 1996, in part because of significant structural damage to the synagogue's Lilienfeld House across the street, where the exhibition was to take place.

congregants became heirs to a tradition and institution that called on them for active commemoration and preservation, even though their own Jewish frames of reference differed from their forebears. In another sense, however, the members of the congregation used the scholarly and religious tools at their disposal to perform and re-enact a tradition that provided them with a sense of communal value, resolve, and historical depth.

Conclusion: The Uses of Caribbean Jewish History

Barbara Kirshenblatt-Gimblett, in her 1995 article 'Theorizing Heritage', noted that the act of simply identifying cultural items or practices as heritage may only present part of the picture. It is more significant, she suggests, to explore the means by which those claiming a given cultural heritage prepare and present it to the public, using 'the instruments for producing heritage'.[60] In St Thomas, as with much of the contemporary Caribbean, such instruments serve as important mechanisms for the island's Jewish residents to situate themselves within history. Through an acknowledgement of the simultaneous and multi-layered nature of heritage production, its tendency to intrude regularly into the realm of personal and communal identity formation, and its curiously parallel (and under-theorized) relationship with scholarly historical discourses, we can gain a more textured knowledge of the motivations surrounding the production of Caribbean Jewish history. Enacted both from within Caribbean Jewish communities and from without, the variety of representations creates bonds between current residents and their island forebears, brings islands today viewed as marginal back to their colonial prominence, and offers a sense of the exotic in sites valued by tourists for precisely that quality.

This account of the Hebrew Congregation of St Thomas's bicentennial celebration, moreover, has broader implications for a historical literature that must often juxtapose local and scholarly concerns. For centuries the Caribbean has served as home to a highly mobile and changing population, which has shifted according to variations in local and world economics, nature, politics, and culture. To try to understand history in the light of such events illuminates our own attempts to distinguish stable, continuous, and tradition-based communities existing in one place, from those that migrate en masse, and from those that converge barely long enough for us to label them. These categorizations, after all, are constructions as well. For historians, the search for a Jewish diasporic presence in Caribbean history may consequently represent only part of the equation, since such efforts tend to overlook how Jewish populations themselves have sought to stabilize matters of identity, ancestry, culture, and geographical origins in their day-to-day lives. Constantly needing to strategize their forms of self-presentation amid changing conditions, to respond to others on the islands, and to

---

[60] Barbara Kirshenblatt-Gimblett, 'Theorizing Heritage', *Ethnomusicology*, 39/3 (1995), 379.

relate to their co-religionists around the world, these communities have mediated their own ideas of what Caribbean Jewry represents. In the process, they have developed their own meaningful modes of understanding and theorizing their senses of heritage. Bringing these communities' own historically oriented activities into our scholarly discussions, thereby allows us to realize more fully the rich, complex, continuing, and profoundly wide-ranging implications that Caribbean Jewish history has to offer to our visions of the past.

NOTES ON THE CONTRIBUTORS

Aviva Ben-Ur is an associate professor in the Department of Judaic and Near Eastern Studies at the University of Massachusetts-Amherst, where she teaches Jewish history, the medieval world, comparative slavery, and American ethnic history. She is the author of *Sephardic Jews in America: A Diasporic History* and co-author, with Rachel Frankel, of *Remnant Stones*, vol. i: *The Jewish Cemeteries of Suriname: Epitaphs* (Cincinnati, 2009); vol. ii: *The Jewish Cemeteries and Synagogues of Suriname: Essays* (Cincinnati, 2012). Her current book project is entitled 'Jewish Identity in a Slave Society: Suriname, 1651–1863'.

Miriam Bodian is Professor of History at the University of Texas at Austin. She has published numerous articles on the Conversos and Portuguese Jews of Europe, as well as two books, *Hebrews of the Portuguese Nation: Conversos and Community in Early Modern Amsterdam* (Bloomington, 1997) and *Dying in the Law of Moses: Crypto-Jewish Martyrdom in the Iberian World* (Bloomington, 2007). She is currently working on a book dealing with ideas about freedom of conscience among seventeenth-century Conversos and Portuguese Jews.

Ainsley Cohen Henriques is a former president and currently a director, honorary secretary, as well as editor and publisher of the newsletter, of the United Congregation of Israelites in Kingston, Jamaica, where his family has lived since 1745. In 2006 he led the development and opening of the Jewish Heritage Center to celebrate the 350th anniversary of the Jews in Jamaica. He has represented Jamaica at the Union of Latin American and Caribbean Congregations (UJCL) Convention. A former president of the B'nai Brith (BB) Jamaica Lodge and a vice president of BB District XXIII, he currently represents Jamaica on the Commonwealth Jewish Council. He is the founding president of the Jamaican Jewish Genealogical Society.

Judah M. Cohen is the Lou and Sybil Mervis Professor of Jewish Culture and associate professor of folklore and ethnomusicology at Indiana University. He has authored *Through the Sands of Time: A History of the Jewish Community of St. Thomas, U.S. Virgin Islands* (Hanover, NH, 2004); *The Making of a Reform Jewish Cantor: Musical Authority, Cultural Investment* (Bloomington, 2009); *Sounding Jewish Culture: The Music of Central Synagogue* (New York, 2011); and co-edited, with Gregory Barz, *The Culture of AIDS in Africa: Hope and Healing Through Music and the Arts* (Oxford, 2011).

Eli Faber is Professor Emeritus of History at John Jay College of Criminal Justice (City University of New York). He is the author of *A Time for Planting*, the first in a five-volume series entitled *The Jewish People in America*, and of *Jews, Slaves, and the Slave Trade: Setting* *the Record Straight*. He has also contributed chapters to works devoted to the history of the Jewish people in America.

Rachel Frankel is the principal of Rachel Frankel AIA Architecture in New York City. She is the co-author, with Aviva Ben-Ur, of *Remnant Stones*, vol. i: *The Jewish Cemeteries of Suriname: Epitaphs* (Cincinnati, 2009); vol. ii: *The Jewish Cemeteries and Synagogues of Suriname: Essays* (Cincinnati, 2012). Her essay 'Antecedents and Remnants of Jodensavanne: The Synagogues and Cemeteries of the First Permanent Plantation Settlement of New World Jews', appeared in *The Jews and the Expansion of Europe to the West, 1450–1800*, edited by Paolo Bernardini and Norman Fiering (New York, 2001). Her Master in Architecture is from Harvard University and her Bachelor of Arts is from Duke University.

Noah L. Gelfand has a Ph.D. in Atlantic history and United States history to 1877 from New York University. He teaches American history at the University of Connecticut at Stam-ford and Hunter College and is currently working on a book about Jewish communities and networks in the early modern Atlantic world.

Jane S. Gerber is Professor of History and director of the Institute for Sephardic Studies at the Graduate Center of the City University of New York. She is past president of the Association for Jewish Studies. She is the author of *Jewish Society in Fez: 1450–1700* (Leiden, 1980); *The Jews of Spain: A History of the Sephardic Experience* (New York, 1992), which won the National Jewish Book Award; *Sephardic Studies in the University* (Cranbury, NJ, 1995); and the forthcoming *Cities of Splendor in the Shaping of Sephardic History*. She has been a visiting professor at Harvard, Yale, Columbia, the Hebrew University of Jerusalem, the University of Pennsylvania, and the Jewish Theological Seminary and has lectured widely in the United States and abroad. She heads the Advisory Board of the American Sephardi Federation and serves on the Academic Advisory Council of the Center for Jewish History.

Josette Capriles Goldish was born and raised on the island of Curaçao. She is the author of *Once Jews: Stories of Caribbean Sephardim* (Princeton, 2009), which describes the lives of nineteenth-century Caribbean Jews. In the past decade she has written several journal articles about Jewish life in the Caribbean and Latin America and has presented papers on this topic at various academic conferences. She is currently a research associate at the Hadassah-Brandeis Institute and is a graduate of the Massachusetts Institute of Technology and the MIT Sloan School of Management.

Matt Goldish is currently the Samuel M. and Esther Melton Professor of Jewish History and director of the Melton Center for Jewish Studies at Ohio State University. He received his Ph.D. from the Hebrew University of Jerusalem. He is the author of *Jewish Questions: Responsa on Sephardic Life in the Early Modern Period* (Princeton, 2008); *The Sabbatean Prophets* (Cambridge, Mass., 2004); *Judaism in the Theology of Sir Isaac Newton* (Dordrecht, 1998).

Jonathan Israel is Professor of Modern History at the Institute for Advanced Study, Princeton, where he has been since 2001. Previously, he was Professor of Dutch History at University College London (1984–2000). His two main works on Jewish History are *European Jewry in the Age of Mercantilism, 1550–1750* (Oxford, 1985) and *Diasporas within a Diaspora: Jews, Crypto-Jews and the World Maritime Empires (1540–1740)* (Leiden, 2002), and he has published several volumes on Dutch history.

Stanley Mirvis received his Ph.D. in history from the Graduate Center of the City University of New York in 2013. His dissertation, entitled 'Sephardic Family Life in the Eighteenth-Century British West Indies', explores the ways in which a persistent Iberian heritage continued to inform Sephardi family life in the West Indies well into the eighteenth century. He also teaches Jewish history at Hunter College and is the managing editor of the *AJS Review*.

Gérard Nahon is Directeur d'Études (emeritus) in medieval and modern Judaism at the École Pratique des Hautes Études (Sorbonne, Paris). A former president of the Society des Études Juives, he served from 1980 to 1996 as editor of the *Revue des Études Juives*. He is director of the Collection de la Revue des Études Juives (52 volumes published from 1980). He is the author, co-author, and editor of numerous books including *Inscriptions hébraï-ques et juives de France médiévale* (Paris, 1986); Menasseh ben Israel, *The Hope of Israel: The English Translation by Moses Wall, 1652* (Oxford: 1987); *Rashi et la culture juive en France du Nord au Moyen Âge* (Paris, 1997); *La Terre sainte au temps des kabbalistes 1492–1592* (Paris, 1997); *Métropoles et périphéries séfarades d'Occident: Kairouan, Amsterdam, Bayonne, Bordeaux, Jérusalem* (Paris, 1993); *Mémorial I.-S. Révah: Études sur le marranisme, l'hétérodoxie juive et Spinoza* (Leuven, 2001); *Juifs et judaïsme à Bordeaux* (Bordeaux, 2003).

Joanna Newman is director of the UK International Unit and formally Head of Higher Education at the British Library. Her doctorate from the University of Southampton 'Nearly the New World: Refugees and the British West Indies, 1933–1945', examined the British Caribbean, British Government, and refugees during the Second World War. The thesis was turned into a documentary for BBC Radio 4: 'A Caribbean Jerusalem'. She is co-editor of *The Holocaust and the Moving Image: Representations in Film and Television since 1933* (New York, 1995). She has worked as a journalist, researcher, and producer for television, print, and radio and has lectured at the University of Warwick and University College London. She is an honorary research fellow at the University of Southampton and a fellow of the Royal Society of Arts.

Ronnie Perelis is the Chief Rabbi Dr Isaac Abraham and Jelena (Rachel) Alcalay Assistant Professor of Sephardic Studies at the Bernard Revel Graduate School of Jewish Studies of Yeshiva University. His research explores the connections between Iberian and Jewish culture during the medieval and early modern periods. He completed his doctoral thesis, 'Marrano Autobiography in its Transatlantic Context: Exile, Exploration and Spiritual Discovery', in the Department of Spanish and Portuguese at New York University. His essays on Sephardic history investigate the dynamics of religious transformation within the context of the crypto-Jewish experience. He is currently writing a study of family and identity in the Sephardic Atlantic world.

Jackie Ranston is a researcher/writer specializing in Jamaican historical biography. She has written for both scholarly and popular audiences, and her published works range from the biographies of a street, a house, a barrister and governor-general, to the Sephardic Jewish family of Lindo and the Jamaican-born Jewish artist, Isaac Mendes Belisario. Her research on Belisario is part of an on-going project, tracing the lives of the Mendes Belisario and Lindo families from pre-Inquisition times to the present day. Born in London, England, Jackie has resided in Jamaica since 1970. Together with her husband, she runs a publishing company, focusing on Early Childhood Education and Jamaica's cultural heritage.

James Robertson joined the Department of History and Archaeology at the University of the West Indies, Mona, in 1995, where he is now a senior lecturer in history. He is the author of *Gone is the Ancient Glory: Spanish Town, Jamaica, 1534–2000* (Kingston, Jamaica, 2005) and co-editor of *Caribbean Archaeology and Material Culture*, a special issue of *Caribbean Quarterly*, 55/2 (2009). He is currently working on *The First English Century in Jamaica, 1655–c.1770*. In 2011–12 he was acting president of the Jamaican Historical Society.

Jessica Roitman received an M.A. in Latin American studies from Vanderbilt University and a Ph.D. in history from the University of Leiden in 2009 with a dissertation on intercultural trade and the Sephardim in early seventeenth-century Amsterdam. She was a fellow at the Katz Center for Advanced Judaic Studies at the University of Pennsylvania and the recipient of a Dutch Research Council-funded Rubicon post-doctoral fellowship to do a comparative study of the reception of immigrant Jews in eighteenth-century London and Amsterdam at Birkbeck College, University of London. She has published on Atlantic colonial trade, migration, identity, and intercultural interactions. She is currently a researcher at the Royal Netherlands Institute for Southeast Asian and Caribbean Studies where she is part of the 'Dutch Atlantic Connections, 1680–1795' project.

Dale Rosengarten is founding director of the Jewish Heritage Collection at the College of Charleston Library. She earned her B.A. and Ph.D. from Harvard University. Working with McKissick Museum at the University of South Carolina, she developed the travelling exhibition 'A Portion of the People: Three Hundred Years of Southern Jewish Life' (2002–3) and co-edited the accompanying volume. Most recently, in partnership with the Museum for African Art in New York, she co-curated an exhibition entitled 'Grass Roots: African Origins of an American Art', which had a six-month run at the Smithsonian Institution, Washington, DC, and co-authored the accompanying volume.

Barry L. Stiefel is an assistant professor in the joint programme in historic preservation of the College of Charleston and Clemson University. He received his Ph.D. in historic preservation from Tulane University in 2008. His forthcoming book is entitled *Jewish*

Sanctuary in the Atlantic World: A Social and Architectural History. Stiefel's research focuses on the preservation of Jewish heritage.

Hilit Surowitz-Israel received her Ph.D. from the Department of Religion, University of Florida, in 2012. Her dissertation '"May God Enlarge Japheth": Portuguese Jews in the Early Modern Atlantic World', explores the role of diaspora identity, and the complicated intersection of race, religion, and nation for Portuguese Jews in the early modern Atlantic world. Her research interests include religion in the Americas, the Jewish communities of the Atlantic world, diaspora theory, and Atlantic history. She is currently an instructor in the Department of Jewish Sudies and the Department of Religion at Rutgers, the State University of New Jersey.

Karl Watson was born in Barbados in 1944. He obtained his M.A. and Ph.D. from the University of Florida with a specialization in Latin American history. In 1974 he entered the Barbadian Foreign Service and was posted to Caracas and subsequently to Frankfurt, Germany. In 2009 he retired from the Cave Hill Campus of the University of the West Indies as senior lecturer in the Department of History. Karl is the author of several books and articles, including *Barbados, the Civilised Island: A Social History 1750–1816* (Bridgetown, Barbados, 1979); *Barbados First: The Years of Change 1920 to 1970* (Cave Hill, Barbados, 2003); *Not For Wages Alone: Eyewitness Summaries of the 1938 Labour Rebellion in Jamaica* (Mona, Jamaica, 2003; co-edited with Patrick Bryan); *The White Minority in the Caribbean* (Kingston, Jamaica, 1998; co-edited with Howard Johnson); *A Kind of Right to be Idle: Old Doll, Matriarch of Newton Plantation* (Cave Hill, Barbados, 2000). He is the president of the Barbados National Trust, and editor of the *Journal of the Barbados Museum and Historical Society*. He is also a consultant to the Bridgetown Synagogue Restoration Committee. He was recently awarded the Gold Crown of Merit in recognition of his contribution to education in Barbados.

Swithin Wilmot is Dean of the Faculty of Humanities and Education and senior lecturer in history at the University of the West Indies, Mona Campus. A graduate of the University of the West Indies, he received his Ph.D. from the University of Oxford. His main research interests are post-emancipation politics and society in Jamaica. Among his several publications are *Plantation Economy, Land Reform and the Peasantry in Historical Perspective: Jamaica 1838–1980* (Kingston, Jamaica, 1992; co-edited with Claus Fullberg-Stolberg); *Before and After 1865: Education, Politics and Regionalism in the Caribbean* (Kingston, Jamaica, 1999; co-edited with Brian Moore); *Freedom: Retrospective and Prospective* (Kingston, Jamaica, 2009).

INDEX

A

Abenacar, Abigail 181
Abendana (ḥazan) 204
Aboab, David 90
abolition of slavery, Jewish views
   on 126
abolitionists 127
Abraham, as Sephardi first name
   175
Abrahams, Simon 317–18
Aby Yetomim orphanage society
   (Jamaica) 233 n. 48
d'Acosta de Andrade, Benjamin
   70, 74
adjudication of Jewish communal
   conflicts:
   in Barbados 207
   in Curaçao 86, 90–1, 92, 96–101,
      103–5, 114–15, 117–18
Adventure Galley (ship) 314
Aerssen van Sommelsdijck,
   Cornelis 58
affectivity, familial 239–40
Africa, West, Sephardi
   communities in 185–6
African culture, in Jamaica 9
Africans, de-exoticizing of 107
   see also Eurafrican Jews
Afrocentrism 375
de Aguilar, Hananel 232
aid organizations, for Jewish
   refugees from Nazism 344–5,
      348, 352, 354, 356
Aldgate (London), synagogue 145
Aldridge, Ira 125
Alland, Alexander 369
Almeyda, Daniel 231
Almeyda, Emily 235
Altman, Henry 351, 358
Alvares Correa, Mordechay 70, 97,
   100
American Hebrew (journal) 369

American Jewish Archives 369
American Jewry, *see* North
   America, Jewish
   communities in
Amsterdam:
   Jewish Historical Museum 364
      n. 10
   Sephardi community 2, 5, 8,
      22–3, 25, 48–9, 71–2, 163;
      cemetery 137; and Curaçao
      Sephardi community 8, 91
      n. 26, 94, 96, 97, 101, 104, 105,
      108, 111–12, 113, 114–15, 117; and
      Dutch trading system 7, 29;
      excommunications 96 n. 54;
      ex-Converso psychology of
      321; French language use by
      76; leadership of western
      Sephardi diaspora 8, 23, 49,
      68–9, 70–1, 73–8, 109–10,
      115–18, 148; migration to
      Caribbean 61, 72, 87–8 n. 12,
      109; rabbinic Judaism of 24
   synagogues in 48–9, 76, 147, 163,
      164
d'Anavia, Sarah 180
Anglican Church, in Jamaica 276
Anglo-Dutch Wars:
   second (1665–7) 56
   third (1672–4) 33
Anglo-Spanish War (1655–60),
   Dutch trade profiting from
   34–5, 37
Angola, slave trade from 41–2
Annesly, Judith 214, 215
anti-Jewish violence:
   in Barbados 209
   in Portugal 19
   in Spain 17–18
antisemitism, in Jamaica 241–2,
   254–5, 261, 273
Arbell, Mordechai 54 n. 43

architecture, in North America
   161
art, *see* visual art
ascamot:
   of Amsterdam 114–15
   of Barbados 203
   of Brazil 187
   of Curaçao 111, 113–14 n. 23, 115
   of Suriname 118, 179, 187
Ashkenazi Jewry:
   in Curaçao 317
   in Dutch Republic 163–4
   in England 145–6, 154–5
   in Jamaica 12, 157 n. 47, 311
   merchants 46 n. 3, 317
   in North America 157 n. 47, 285,
      288 n. 21, 294
   in Suriname 132, 136, 137, 180, 317
Ashworth, Jasper 248, 252–3, 254
Atilla the Hun (Raymond
   Quevedo) 349
Atkins, Jonathan 198
Atlantic studies 1–2, 11
Atlantic trade:
   Ashkenazi merchants involved
      in 46 n. 3
   Curaçao's participation in 7–8,
      29–31
   Jewish networks of 318
   Sephardi merchants involved in
      2, 5, 45–7, 63, 87, 289–90
   see also colonial trade
autobiographies 321–2
   Converso 12, 320–1, 323, 324–5
   and poetry 325–7
auto-historiography, of St Thomas
   Jewish community 368–73,
      376, 377–9, 382–5
autonomy, *see* self-government
Avis, Joseph 146–7
D'Azevedo, Moses 218
Azulai, Hayim Yosef David 24

B
Baa, Enid M. 372
bankers, *see* financing
Baptiste, Fitz 353 n. 35
Barbados:
 admission of Jewish refugees to
  148, 351, 358, 359
 and Charleston's colonization
  289
 Christian–Jewish relations
  200–1, 206–9, 210
 economic development of 149,
  205
 Sephardi community 2, 53,
  147–52; conflicts in 207, 220;
  creolization 10, 211–21;
  emergence 196–8; identities
  195, 203–4, 205, 222; and other
  Sephardi communities 74,
  148, 209–10, 283; rabbis 75;
  size 198–201; wealth 201–2
 slave–Jew relationships 204,
  210–18
Barbados Globe (newspaper) 210
de Barrios, Daniel Levi (Miguel)
 143, 144, 153, 165, 321
Baruh, Amelia 214, 215
Baruh Lousada, Aaron 236–8
Baruh Lousada, Emanuel 215,
 236–7, 238
Baruh Louzada, Esther 178
Baruh Louzada, Rachel 214–15
Bayonne, migration of Jews from
 180 n. 71
Beck, Balthazar 94, 111
Beck, Matthias 38, 39, 61 n. 84
Beeston, William 71
Belisario, Abraham Mendes 124,
 126
Belisario, Isaac Mendes 9, 121–2,
 123, 124–9
Bell, S. M. 275–6
de Belmonte, Andrés 42
de Belmonte, Manuel (Isaac
 Nuñes) 35–6, 59, 71, 78–9, 95
Ben Israel, Menasseh 26, 52–3, 198
Ben-Ur, Aviva 10, 131, 133 n. 2, 135,
 226
Benjamin, Alan 383 n. 56
Benjamin, Judah 300

Beracha Veshalom Vegemiluth
 Hasadim Synagogue/
 congregation (St Thomas)
 14, 164, 330, 338, 364–5, 366, 367,
 370, 372–3, 378, 379, 380
 bicentennial celebrations of 363,
  364, 367–8, 373, 376–7, 381–2
Beraha Vesalom Synagogue
 (Blessings of Peace,
 Jodensavanne) 133, 137–8, 152
Bermuda Conference on Jewish
 refugees from Nazism (1943)
 345–6, 356
Bernal, David Israel 77
Beta Israel Jews (Ethiopia) 173 n. 25
Beth Elohim congregation
 (Charleston) 291, 292–3, 297,
 304
de Bethencourt, Cardozo 143–4
Bevis Marks Synagogue/
 congregation (London) 125,
 144, 146, 147, 148, 305
Biale, David 170
*Black Atlantic: Modernity and
 Double-Consciousness* (Gilroy)
 107
black identities 107
black–Jewish relationships:
 in Jamaica 11, 264–5, 266–72,
  273–4, 276, 277–8
 in Virgin Islands 375
 see also slave–Jew relationships
black nationalism, in Virgin Islands
 373, 374–5
Blackman, Martha 213
Blackman, Murray 382
blacks, free 261 n. 2
Bloom, Herbert 60 n. 83
Blyden, Edward Wilmot 373
Bodian, Miriam 7, 89
books, women's possession of 190
Bouman, Elias 164
Bovell, Rachel 214
Bovell, William 215
Boxman, Bradd 381, 383, 385
Boxter, C. R. 92
Boyer, William W. 375 n. 42
Boyle, Richard (third earl of
 Burlington) 160–1

Brana-Shute, Rosemary 190, 231
Brandon, Abraham Rodrigues
 198, 210, 212, 218, 220, 221
Brandon, David 267, 271–2, 274–5,
 276, 277–8
Brandon, Isaac (Lopez) 220, 221
Brandon, Ribca 80
Brandon, Sarah 220, 221
Bravo, Jacob 229
Bravo, Moses 275
Brazil:
 Dutch rule of 4, 50–1
 Jews in 4, 25, 51–2; Conversos
  25–6, 50, 51, 196; Eurafrican
  186; rights and privileges of
  291; synagogues 149, 163
 migration of Jews from 4–5, 52,
  149; to Caribbean 34, 53–4, 60
  n. 82
 Portuguese reconquest of 26, 34
 see also Recife
Breda, Peace of (1667) 56 n. 58
Bridgetown (Barbados):
 Jewish community in 207–8, 209
 synagogue in 149–52, 210
Britain:
 admission of Jewish refugees
  from Nazism to 345
 Blasphemy Act (1698) in 146
  n. 12
 colonial empire of 2, 347;
  admission of Jewish refugees
  from Nazism to 343, 348–59;
  Charleston as part of 289;
  and rights granted to Jews 2,
  54–6, 291; synagogues in
  143–4, 152–8, 165–6
 Jews in 26, 46 n. 4, 55, 145;
  Ashkenazi 145–6, 154–5;
  readmission of 26, 52–3;
  synagogues 146–7, 159
 Naturalization Act (1740) 156–7
British Guiana, schemes for Jewish
 refugees from Nazism in 347,
 348
Browne, Howe Peter (governor of
 Jamaica) 127
Bryan, Adelbert 375 n. 39, 377 n. 45
Bueno Enriques, Jacob Jeosua
 152–3

Bueno de Mesquito, Benjamin 283
Burchell, Thomas 263
burial practices, *see* funeral
practices
burial registers, from Suriname
131, 139
Byam, William 55

C
Caillois, Roger 188
calypsos, on Jewish refugees 349
Campbell, John F. 230
Campeche wood, trade in 35–6
Canada, synagogues in 161
Canny, Nicholas 107
cantors, of North American
communities 284, 293
Cardoze, David 329, 330, 332, 335–6
Cardoze, Esther Consuelo 335–6
Cardoze, Grace 12, 329–39
Cardozo de Macedo, Manuel 320
Carilho, Isaac 85
Caro, Joseph 117
Carrigal, Rafael Haim Ishac 74
de Carvajal, Luis 320
Carvalho, David 203, 293
Carvalho, Emanuel 293
Carvallo, Isaac 216
Carvallo, Rachel 216
Carvallo family 216
Carwar (India), East India
Company (British) in 315
Cassipora Creek Jewish cemetery
(Suriname) 9, 53, 133, 134–6,
137, 138–40, 141, 174–5, 177
Castello, Princess 215–16
del Castilho, Joseph 178
Castro, Américo 319 n. 2
de Castro, Isaac 232
Cayenne (French Guiana),
Sephardi community in 54,
165
*Celebrating 200 Years of Jewish Life in
St. Thomas* (Brentwood
Travel) 376–7
cemeteries, Jewish 131
of Amsterdam 137
in Jamaica 9, 131, 132, 133, 136–7,
138, 140, 141, 142, 226, 240
in New York 283

in St Thomas 372–3, 379–80
in Suriname 9, 53, 131, 132–3,
134–6, 137, 138–40, 141, 142,
171–2, 174–5, 177, 185, 189–90
in Trinidad 352
Chabad Lubavitch hasidim, in
St Thomas 367
Charles II (king of Great Britain
and Ireland) 145
Charleston (Nevis), synagogue at
153
Charleston (South Carolina):
British colonization of 289
Christian–Jewish relations in
292
Jewish community in 291–3,
305–7; Ashkenazi 294;
conflicts in 304; merchants
289–90, 294–304
Charlotte Amalie (St Thomas),
Jewish community of 329
Chartered Society of Suriname 58
chocolate-manufacturing, Dutch
5 n. 5
Christian IV (king of Denmark
and Norway) 164
Christian–Jewish relations:
on Barbados 200–1, 206–9, 210
in Charleston 292
Christianity:
excommunications in 99–100
n. 73
forced conversion of Jews to
2–3, 17, 19
Citrine, Walter 348
civil rights, *see* rights and privileges
of Jews
Cochin (India), synagogues in 144
n. 5
cockfighting, on Barbados 207
Code Noir (France, 1685) 46 n. 6,
69, 165
Cohen, Judah 14, 377 n. 46, 383–5
Cohen, Robert 118, 224 n. 7, 225
Cohen, Robin 351
Cohen Belinfante, Joseph A. 214
n. 61
Cohen Deleon, Joseph 235–6, 238
Cohen Henriques, Judah 233–4,
236

Cohen Nassy, David 169, 179, 180
n. 71, 228 n. 23
Cohen Nassy, David (Joseph
Nunes de Fonseca) 53–4, 55
n. 51, 59
Cohen Nassy, Jacob 139
Cohen Nassy, Joseph de David 169
Cohen Nassy, Samuel 55, 56, 59,
179
Cohen Nassy, Simha 139
Cohen Nassy family 138–9, 140
Coheno, Samuel 109
collective amnesia, of ex-
Conversos 321
Colleton, John 289
The Colonial American Jew (Marcus)
224
colonial history 107
colonial trade, Dutch system of
29–31, 32–3, 34–5, 36
Sephardi role in 2, 4, 29, 31, 34,
36–7, 63, 87
see also Atlantic trade
coloureds, free 261 n. 2
see also Eurafrican Jews; mulatto
Jews
commercial networks of
merchants 318
Sephardi 5, 6, 7, 21, 22, 29, 63, 70,
283, 284, 286–7
communal conflicts:
in Barbados Jewry 207, 220
in Charleston Jewry 304
in Curaçao Christian
communities 102
in Curaçao Jewry 8–9, 73, 85,
88–92, 95, 102, 112–14;
adjudication of 86, 90–1, 92,
96–101, 103–5, 114–15, 117–18
in Suriname Jewry 85
communication, transatlantic 71
concubinage among Caribbean
colonial Jewry 224, 225
in Jamaica 233, 239
and manumission records 230–1
and paternity 228, 231, 232
see also Eurafrican Jews; slave–
Jew relationships
concubines 223 n. 3
financial support of 233–8

conflicts, *see* communal conflicts
congregante status 139, 185
Consolação as tribulações de Israel (Usque) 20
conversion to Christianity, forced:
   in Portugal 2–4, 19
   in Spain 17
conversion to Judaism, of Eurafricans/slaves 10, 169–70, 176, 183–7, 192
Conversos 3
   autobiographies of 12, 320–1, 323, 324–5
   in Brazil 25–6, 50, 51, 196
   in Dutch Republic 48
   in Portugal 4, 20–1, 22, 23
   psychological transformations of 319–20, 321, 322, 325
   return to Judaism 17–18, 23–4, 319–20, 321
Copenhagen, Jewish community in 164
Copiador de Cartas 8, 68, 78–83
de Cordoba, Joshua (rabbi) 102
de Cordova, Joshua 128
Cordovan menorah (St Thomas) 364, 365
da Costa, Aron 138
da Costa, Benjamin 138
da Costa, Isaac (Curaçao) 60, 61, 87, 109
da Costa, Isaac (Suriname) 183–4
da Costa, Rebecca Henriquez 134–6
da Costa, Uriel 60 n. 82, 320
da Costa family 140
Cotinho, Ishack Henriquez 71
Creechurch Lane (London), synagogue at 145
Creole languages of Suriname 176, 181, 182, 183
creolization:
   of Barbadian Jews 10, 211–21
   in Jamaica 262, 278
   of Suriname Jews 211 n. 48
Crijnsen, Abraham 56
Cromwell, Oliver, and readmission of Jews to England 26, 52–3, 145, 147
Crowe, Mitford 208

crypto-Judaism:
   in Barbados 147, 148
   in Jamaica 123–4, 147 n. 18
   in Portugal 3–4, 19, 21–2
   psychology of 319–20
Curaçao:
   Ashkenazi Jews in 317
   as Dutch Atlantic trade centre 29–31, 32–3, 34–5, 36, 42–3; Sephardi role in 7–8, 34, 37, 63, 87
   Dutch colonial rule of 31–2, 86, 93–5, 111
   judicial systems of 86, 113
   Sephardi community of 5, 7–8, 29, 31, 56 n. 57, 76; and Amsterdam Sephardi community 8, 91 n. 26, 94, 96, 97, 104, 105, 108, 111–12, 113, 114–15, 117; class divisions in 87–8, 103–4, 113–14; conflicts in 8–9, 73, 85, 88–92, 95–102, 103–5, 112–15, 117–18; emergence 36, 37, 43, 54, 69, 87, 109; and emergence of North American Jewish communities 68, 75, 283, 285; flourishing 39, 64; language use 177, 179; leadership/organizational structure 37, 89–90, 104, 109–11; merchants 7, 36, 62–3, 64; rabbis 74, 75, 90, 102; rights and privileges 36–7, 59–61, 64, 86–7, 103, 109; size 61–2, 63, 87
   slave trade on 37–9, 40–1, 42
Curiel, Ephraim de Solomon 111
Curiel, Moses, *see* Nunes da Costa, Jeronimo
Curtin, Philip 278
'Cyrus the slave', testimony of 10–11, 247–52, 253, 254, 256–7

D
DaCosta, David 213
Daniels, Edward S. 201
Daniels, Nancy 218, 219
Daniels family 202
David Nassy and Company 54
DeKalb, General Baron 299 n. 54

Delvalle, Benjamin 330
Delvalle, David 330–1, 334, 336
Delvalle, Henry H. 330
Delvalle, Idalia 336–7
Delvalle, Jacob 331
Delvalle, Viola 331, 332–4, 337, 338
Denmark:
   Jews in 164
   synagogues in colonial empire of 164, 166, 338
Depass, Isaac 234–5
DePiza, Moses 215
DePiza, Susanna 215
Devereaux, Johanna Marin 235
diamond trade, Jewish involvement in 153, 313
diasporas:
   Ashkenazi 12
   Sephardi 2, 7, 46
   see also western Sephardi diaspora
Docendo Docemur (literary college, Suriname) 179–80
Dominican Republic, schemes for Jewish refugees from Nazism in 344
Donohue, John 162
Dookhan, Isaac 374
Dotar (Sephardi dowry society, Amsterdam) 23, 49, 74
Downes, Aviston 210
Dreis, Harry 370–1
Dubin, Lois 5, 290
Duperly, Adolphe 128
Dutch language, Jewish use of 6, 9, 136, 177, 178, 180–1
Dutch Republic:
   Ashkenazi Jews in 163–4
   colonial empire: Brazil 4, 25, 51–2; Curaçao 31–2, 86, 93–5, 111; and rights granted to Jews 291; Suriname 56, 58, 188; synagogues in 157, 159, 162–4, 166
   colonial trade system 29–31, 32–3, 34–5, 36; Sephardi role in 4, 7, 29, 34, 36–7, 63, 87
   religious freedom in 5, 48–9, 86
   Sephardi Jews in, *see under* Amsterdam

slave trade 37–9
synagogues in 159, 163–4

E
earthquakes in Jamaica (1692) 138,
    311
East India Company (British), in
    Carwar (India) 315
education:
    funding, in Jamaica 273, 277
    Jewish, in St Thomas 330
Eisen, Arnold 187
Eksztajn, Boruch 356
elites:
    of Barbados 205–6, 208–9
    Jamaican, Jews as part of 264–5
Elkin, Mozley 217
Elkin, Sarah 216
emancipation of Jews 2
    in Caribbean 6–7
    in Dutch Republic 49
    in Jamaica 11, 128, 261–2
    see also rights and privileges of
        Jews
emancipation of slaves, in Jamaica
    11
Emanuel, Charles A. 375
Emerson, Herbert 355
emissaries of Holy Land, in
    Caribbean 74
Emmanuel, Isaac Samuel 98, 131,
    177, 228, 369–70 n. 24
Emmanuel, Suzanne 98, 228
Emmens, J. 355
endogamy, Sephardi practice of
    200
England, *see* Britain
English language, Jewish use of
    180
Enlightenment, Jewish, in North
    America 292–3
entrepôt trading system, Dutch
    introduction of 30–1, 33, 34–5,
    36, 37, 42–3
epitaphs 135, 136, 180, 239–40
Esnoga (Sephardi synagogue,
    Amsterdam) 76, 147, 164
*Espejo fiel de vidas que contiene los
    Psalmos de David en verso*
    (Laguna) 12, 73, 322, 323–8

*Essai historique sur la colonie de
    Surinam* 77, 140
Esther (biblical book), and New
    Christian identity 188
ethnicity 238
Ets Haim Synagogue (Gibraltar)
    161–2
Eurafrican Jews:
    in Brazil 186
    in Suriname 10, 139, 169–72,
        192–3; Jewish identity 187–92,
        193, 226; language use 181–3;
        names 172–6, 189, 190
    in West Africa 185–6
Europeanization, of Conversos 23
Evian Conference on Jewish
    refugees from Nazism 344
exclusivism, of Portuguese Jews
    20, 24
excommunications 9, 89, 99, 100
    n. 74
    in Amsterdam 96 n. 54
    in Christianity 99–100 n. 73
    in Curaçao 90, 91–2, 96–7, 98,
        99, 101
Exemplar vitae humanae (Uriel da
    Costa) 320
Exeter, synagogue in 159
Eyre, Edward John 263
Ezekiel (biblical book) 137

F
Faber, Eli 11, 89
Faesch, Isaac 85, 89, 90–1, 96–7,
    98–9, 100, 101, 102, 104
families, Sephardi 232–3, 238–9
    absorption of mulatto children
        in 227, 233–8, 239
family names, of Eurafricans 189,
    190, 235 n. 50
family networks:
    Ashkenazi 317
    kinship, decreasing role of 239
    Sephardi 63, 201–2, 234, 286–7
    see also networks; paternity
de Faria, Francisco 186
Farrakhan, Louis 375
Feitler, Bruno 186
Fenney, William H. 359
Fernandes, Isaac 178

Fernandes, Mordachai 178
Ferrara (Italy), Jewish community
    in 20
financial support:
    for concubines 233–8
    for synagogue construction 156,
        284, 318
financing, Amsterdam Sephardi
    community's role in 70–1,
    80–3
First Maroon War (1728–38 / 9,
    Jamaica) 242–3, 244–51, 252–4,
    256–9
    Jewish 'treason' in 10–11, 243,
        251–2, 253, 254–5, 257, 258
Fischer, Ernst 351
da Fonseca, Isaac (merchant) 62
da Fonseca, Isaac Aboab (rabbi)
    163
Fonseca, Moses Gomes 223, 231,
    240
Fonseca, Rachel Gabay 178
d Fonseca Meza, Abraham
    Chyllon 133 n. 2
Ford, Bessie 121 n. 2
France:
    colonial empire, synagogues in
        165
    Converso / Sephardi migration
        to 23, 25
    Jews in 24 n. 25
    Jews expelled from Caribbean
        possessions of 47, 69, 165
Frances, Joseph 37
Franco Mendes, David 76
Frankel, Rachel 9, 131
Franks, Abigail 286, 317
Franks, Benjamin 12, 311–16
Franks, Jacob 316–17, 318
Franks family 316–17
Frayer, J. 313
Frederick III (king of Denmark
    and Norway) 164
Freemasonry, Jewish participation
    in 210, 299
French Guiana 318, 165
French language, Jewish use of 76,
    77, 180
Friderici, J. F. 188
Friedman, Saul 228

funeral practices:
　burial orientation 140–1
　for Eurafrican Jews 139
　messianic traditions in 9
　Sephardi 77, 202
　see also tombstone inscriptions

G

Gabay, Abraham 133 n. 5
Gabbay, Lucien 208
García-Arenal, Mercedes 321
Gelfand, Noah 8
Gibbs, James 161
Gibraltar:
　evacuation of civilian
　　population from (1940) 353–4
　synagogues in 157, 160, 161–2
Gibraltar Camp (Jamaica) 13, 354,
　359
　Jewish refugees from Nazism
　　interned at 13, 345 n. 6, 346
　　n. 7, 354–8
Gill, Ester 219–20
Gill, Sally 220, 221
Gilman, Stephen 319 n. 2
Gilroy, Paul 107, 118
Glassberg, David 362
Gleaner (journal) 128
Godfrey, Sheldon and Judith 291,
　305
Goldish, Josette 12, 383 n. 56
Goldish, Matt 12
Gomes, Mordechai 67–8, 75
Gomez, Daniel 63
Gomez, Luis 283–4, 285, 287
Gomez, Michael 170
Gomez, Mrs 204
Gomez family 287
Gordon, George William 276 n. 42
Goslinga, Cornelis 32, 93, 102
Gottschalk, Max 355
Governor Robinson Going to Church
　(painting) 149, 150
Gradis, Abraham 24
Grant, Charlie 'Gorilla' 349
Great Synagogue (Copenhagen)
　164
Great Synagogue (London) 145–6,
　159
Grim, David 156

Grotius, Hugo 100 n. 74
Guadeloupe, Francio 363
Guiana, *see* British Guiana; French
　Guiana
Guinea (Africa), New
　Christian/Sephardi
　communities in 185–6

H

Haiti, revolution (1791–1803) 300–1
　n. 63
halakhic rulings on slaves/slavery
　116–17
Hamburg, Jewish community in
　24
Hannaford, Stephen 268, 269
Hanukah menorah (St Thomas)
　364–5, 366
Harby, Isaac 293, 301
Harby, Solomon 293
Harris, Richard 243 n. 7
Harrison, John 269
Harrison, Peter (architect, New
　England) 160–1
Harrison, Peter (retailer and
　politician, Jamaica) 268, 269,
　271–2
Hart, Daniel 262–3
Hart, Moses 154
Hart, Nathan 304–5
Harvey, James 276, 277
Haskalah, *see* Enlightenment,
　Jewish
Havdallah Harbor Cruises
　(St Thomas) 379 n. 48
Hayum, Sylvain 357 n. 46
Hebrew poetry, on Jewish
　gravestones 135
Hendricks, Hannah 296–7
Hendricks, Harmon 296–8
Hendricks family 296–7
Henriques, Jeudit 70, 81–2
Henriques, Moses Quixano 122
Henriquez, Mordachay and Joshua
　62
Henriquez Moron, Esther 77
ḥerem, *see* excommunications
heritage, Jewish:
　in Caribbean 359, 361, 363

　in St Thomas 361, 363, 364–5,
　　367, 377–87
Hills, Robert 125
historiography, of St Thomas
　Jewish community 368–73,
　376, 377–9, 382–5
history:
　academic versus popular 383
　colonial 107
　global 282
　Jewish Caribbean 2, 362–4, 369,
　　386–7
　of Virgin Islands 374–6
History of Jamaica (Long) 242
*History of the Jews of the Netherlands
　Antilles* (Emmanuel and
　Emmanuel) 228
History of the Two Indies (Raynal)
　241
*History of the Virgin Islands of the
　United States* (Dookhan) 374
Hobby's plantation (Jamaica) 248,
　249
Hodge, Arthur 126
Hoe duur was de suiker (McLeod)
　211 n. 48
Holland, *see* Dutch Republic
Holmes, Stanley 156
Holzberg, Carol 351 n. 27
Hooke, Robert 146
'Hope of Israel' (Menasseh ben
　Israel) 198
Hordes, Stanley 380
House of Circlings (Ouderkerk
　cemetery) 137
houses of worship, secret
　(*schuilkerken*) 145, 163
Hunter, Robert 244–5, 247, 248
Hunt's Bay Jewish cemetery
　(Jamaica) 9, 131, 132, 133,
　136–7, 138, 140, 141, 226, 296
Hurricane Marilyn, St Thomas
　(1995) 385–6
Hurwitz, Samuel J. and Edith F.
　294 n. 23

I

identities 170
　black 107
　Caribbean 365 n. 11

Eurafrican/mulatto Jewish 187–92, 193, 225, 226–7, 238
masquerade used to guard 123
Sephardi 10, 14, 46, 188, 238, 319; in Barbados 195, 203–4, 205, 222; in Jamaica 233; in St Thomas 363, 364–5, 367, 378, 379–82
white, of western Sephardim 205, 226, 262, 307
Ince, Arthur 351
Inquisition 124
    Laguna's poetic references to 326–7
    Portuguese 3, 21
    Spanish 18
internment of Jewish refugees in Caribbean 353
    see also Gibraltar Camp
Isaac, Ephraim 377 n. 44
Isaacks, Abraham 302
Isaacs, Katherine 217
Isabel (ship) 304
Ismael, as first name for Eurafrican Jews 173
Israel, Jonathan 7, 46, 47, 72
Italy, Sephardi migration to 20
Izidro, Abraham Gabay 175–6, 178

J
Jacobs, Susanna 213–14
Jamaica:
    abolition of slavery in 126
    antisemitism in 241–2, 254–5, 261, 273
    class divisions in 265, 278
    immigration regulations in 346
    Jews in 5–6, 71, 133–4, 152–3, 224 n. 6, 232, 255, 296; Ashkenazi 12, 157 n. 47, 311; black–Jewish relationships 11, 264–5, 266–72, 273–4, 276, 277–8; cemeteries 9, 131, 132, 136–7, 138, 140, 141, 142, 226, 240; emancipation 11, 128, 261–2; funeral practices 77; migrants from Middle East 351; mulatto Jews 223, 226–7; and other Jewish communities 68, 75, 283–4,

287–8; poetry 12, 73, 322–8; political participation 11, 262–4, 265, 266–8, 269–75, 276–8; population size 224, 241, 294; refugees from Nazism 13, 346, 353, 354–8; rights and privileges 11, 78–9, 262, 291, 306; slave–Jew relationships 10, 122, 126, 223, 229–30, 233–8, 239, 264–5; synagogues 153, 154, 155; visual art of 9, 121–2, 123, 124–9
Jonkonnu (Christmas masquerade) 9, 121–3
slave revolts 127, 242–3, 243–51, 252–4, 256–9; and Jewish 'treason' 10–11, 243, 251–2, 253, 254–5, 257, 258
slave society 227–8, 261 n. 2, 343
Jamaica Despatch (newspaper) 121
JDC, see Jewish Joint Distribution Committee
Jeshuat Israel congregation (Newport) 160–1
Jessurun, Aron and Rebecca 178
Jesurun, Raphael 90, 112
Jewish Historical Development in the Virgin Islands (Dreis) 370–1
Jewish Historical Development in the Virgin Islands, 1665–1959 (Paiewonsky) 371
Jewish Historical Museum (Amsterdam) 364 n. 10
Jewish History Museum (St Thomas) 385 n. 59
Jewish Joint Distribution Committee (JDC, United States) 346, 352, 354, 356
Jews in the West Indies (Stern and Postal) 359 n. 53
Joal (West Africa), Jewish community of 186
Jodensavanne (Suriname) Jewish community 53, 57–8, 133, 134 cemetery 135–6, 137, 139, 140, 141, 171–2, 175, 177, 185, 189–90 destruction by fire (1832) 152 synagogue 137–8, 152

Jones, Inigo 161
Jonkonnu (Jamaican Christmas masquerade) 9, 121–3
    characters: Actor Boys 122; House-Keepers 122; Jaw-Bone (House of John-Canoe) 121–2; Set Girls 122
    customs 121–9
Jordan, Charles 357
Judaism:
    conversion to, by slaves/Eurafricans 10, 169–70, 176, 183–7, 192
    Converso loss of 22
    Converso return to 17–18, 23–4, 319–20, 321
    in Dutch Republic 48–9
    in India 144 n. 5
Judeo, Abraham Ismael 190–1
Judeo, David 191–2
Judia, Roza 190

K
Kadish, Sharman 144 n. 3
Kaplan, Yosef 9, 96 n. 54, 111
karboegers (mulatto–black children) 185
Karrigal, Hayim Joseph 318
kashrut, Barbadian Jewish adherence to 205
Kayserling, Meyer 324
Kendal, James 207
ketubot (marriage contracts) 90 n. 24, 112
Kidd, Captain William 12, 313, 314–16
Kingdom, Benjamin 276
Kingston (Jamaica):
    Jewish community 133, 154, 155
    Sunday ('negro') markets in 265
Kingston Chronicle (newspaper) 123
kinship, see family networks
Kiron, Arthur 292
Kirshenblatt-Gimblett, Barbara 386
Klooster, Wim 32, 33, 34, 63
Knibb, William 263
Knight, James 254
Knowles, Charles 248

L

Ladino 203 n. 20
  use in Suriname 183
Lafayette, Marie Joseph, Marquis
    de 299
Laguna, Daniel Israel López 12, 73,
    322–8, 343
language use:
  in Suriname 176–83
  on tombstones 135–7
  see also individual languages
Las alabanzas de santidad (León
    Templo) 323 n. 9
Leão, Samuel Jeudah 112
Leão family 91, 92, 112–13, 186
Ledesma, Aron 112 n. 19
de Leon, Abraham 296
de Leon, Abraham de Jacob Cohen
    298–9
de Leon, Abraham de Moses 296
de Leon, David Camden 299
de Leon, Edwin 300
de Leon, Esther 180
de Leon, Harmon Hendricks 301
de Leon, Jacob 296
de Leon, Jacob Cohen 296–8
de Leon, Jacob Rodrigues 296
de Leon, Mordecai 298, 299
de Leon, Moses 296
de Leon, Perry 295 n. 32
de Leon, Rebecca Lopez 299
de Leon, Thomas Cooper 300
de Leon family 295–300
León Templo, Jacob Jehuda 323
    n. 9
letters, transatlantic exchanges of
    71, 78–83
  see also *Copiador de Cartas*
Levi, Jacob 217
Levy, Abraham 208
Levy, Joseph Jacob 180–1
Levy, Michael 227
Lewis, Andrew Henry 275, 276
Lindo, Abraham Alexander 232
Lindo, Abraham Junior 202
Lindo, Alexander 264
Lindo, Alexandre 121 n. 2, 124,
    288 n. 19
Lindo, David 201–2
Lindo, David 202, 216

Lindo, Ester 220
Lindo, Isaac 202, 216
Lindo, Isaac Massiah 217–18
Lindo, Jacob 217–18
Lindo, Moses 219, 220
Lindo, Philly Judy 216–17
Lindo, Rachel 216, 220
Lindo, Sarah 218
Lindo family 123–4, 217
literacy, in Suriname 190
literary salons, in Suriname 76
liturgy, Sephardi 381
Livorno, Jewish community in 20
Locke, John 305
Loker, Zvi 68
London:
  Ashkenazi Jewish community in
    145–6, 154–5
  Sephardi Jewish community in
    26, 53, 145, 146; Laguna's
    poetry published by 323–4;
    and poverty issues 281, 305;
    synagogues 125, 144, 146–7,
    148
Long, Edward 242
Lopes Cardoso, Abraham 381
Lopes Suasso, Manuel 97
Lopes Torres, Grace 232, 236, 237
Lopez, Aaron 45
Lopez, Christian 213
Lopez, Eliahu 75, 148
Lopez, Hannah Ester 218–20
Lopez, Isaac (Barbados) 207
Lopez, Isaac (Barbados) 212–13
Lopez, Isaac (Jamaica) 128
Lopez, Moses 207
Lopez, Moses 212
Lopez family 212
Lucas, Henrietta 330
de Lucena, Jacob 63
lulav custom 117
Luria, Isaac 117 n. 30
Lyon, Esther 301
Lyon, Moses 267, 268, 269, 271,
    272, 278

M

McCook, Francis 268–9, 271
McGeachy, Edward 126–7 n. 31
McKegan, Edward 162

McLeod, Cynthia 211 n. 48
Madden, Richard R. 127
Madras Patân Synagogue (India)
    144 n. 5, 153
Magnus, Samuel 263–4
Mahamad:
  of Amsterdam 8, 70, 72, 114
  of Barbados 203–5, 220–1
  of Brazil 52, 186–7
  of Curaçao 89–90, 110–11, 113–14
  powers of 75–6, 89
  of Suriname 118, 184, 188, 191–2,
    225
  see also *parnasim*
Makin, Roger 348
Manuel I (king of Portugal) 2–3
manumission of slaves 187, 201,
    225, 229, 237
  costs 221, 230
manumitted slaves, mulatto/
    Eurafrican children of 183,
    184, 221, 223, 229–32, 239
de Marchena, Sandra R. 329 n. 1
Marcus, Jacob Rader 224, 225, 300,
    316, 361, 369, 372
Mark, Peter 186
Marks, Elaine 319 n. 2
Maroons (Jamaican escaped
    slaves) 242–3, 245–6
  see also First Maroon War
Marranos, see Conversos
masquerade, and identity 123
  see also Jonkonnu
Massiah, Judah 204
Massiah family 200
Matalon family 351 n. 27
Mauricia (Brazil), Sephardi
    community in 52, 163
Méchoulan, Henri 99
Meik, John 214, 215
Melo, Ferñao Álvares 320
Memorias Curiel (Ephraim de
    Solomon Curiel) 111
Memorias Senior (Jacob de David
    Senior) 111
memory:
  construction of 14
  denial of 321
Mendes, Francisco 21

Mendes, Simon 191
Mendes Belisario, *see* Belisario
Mendes Chumaceiro, Aron 179
Mendes Quixano, Moses 296
Mendes Seixas, Gershom 295 n. 29
de Mercado, Abraham and
    Raphael 147
merchants:
    Ashkenazi 46 n. 3, 317
    global travel of 318
    Jamaican Jewish: non-Jewish
        distrust of 241, 243, 251, 255;
        and white planter interests
        263, 264
    North American Jewish 286,
        289–90, 294–304
    Sephardi 290–1; in Brazil 51;
        commercial networks of 5, 6,
        7, 21, 22, 29, 63, 70, 283, 284,
        286–7; in Curaçao 7, 36, 62–3,
        64; rights and privileges
        granted to 31, 36, 47–8, 51–2,
        53–6, 58–61, 64; in St Thomas
        329, 331; in slave trade 39,
        41–2, 54, 298, 303; success
        46–7; in transatlantic trade 2,
        5, 36–7, 45–7, 63, 87, 289–90
Meyer, Michael 293
de Meza (*shamash*) 203
de Meza, Rachel 329
de Meza family 140
Middle East, Jewish migration to
    Caribbean from 351
migration of Jews:
    to/from Barbados 196, 197,
        199–200, 283
    from Bayonne 180 n. 71
    to/from Brazil 4–5, 34, 52, 53–4,
        60 n. 82, 149, 196, 197
    to/within/from Caribbean 4–5,
        7, 343, 351, 363; of Amsterdam
        Jews 61, 72, 87–8 n. 12, 109
    to/from Curaçao 56 n. 57, 60,
        69, 109, 283
    to France 23, 25
    to Italy 20
    from Jamaica 283–4, 288, 311
    to North America 283–4, 300,
        305, 312
    from Portugal 19–20, 22, 23, 324

to/from St Thomas 366–7
    see also refugees, Jewish
Mikvé Israel congregation (Hope
    of Israel, Curaçao) 76, 88, 109
    Amsterdam congregation as
        model for 109–10, 111
    judicial system of 90
Mikveh Israel Synagogue/
    congregation (Philadelphia)
    162
minority status of Jews 46
    see also emancipation of Jews
Miranda, E. R. 203
de Miranda, Sarah 189
Mirvis, Stanley 10
Moerbeeck, Jan Andries 50, 51
Moïse, Abraham 300–1
Moïse, Abraham Junior 293, 301,
    304, 306
Moïse, Caroline Agnes 301
Moïse, Edwin Warren 301–2
Moïse, 'General' 300–1 n. 63
Moïse, Harold 300
Moïse, Penina 301
Moïse, Sarah 300–1
Moïse family 300–2
Molloy, Sylvia 321
Montefiore, John 209
Montefiore Ancona, Moses 207
Montreal, synagogues in 161
Moore, Edward 235
Mordecai, Moses Cohen 303–5
Morning Journal (newspaper,
    Jamaica) 123
Moses, Isaiah 302–3, 305
Moses, Levy 305
Moses, Raphael J. 301
Moses, Rebecca 302–3
Moxy, Francis 274
mulatto Jews:
    in Barbados 213–21
    in Jamaica 223, 226–7, 229–32,
        234
    in Suriname 10, 139, 169–70
    in West Africa 186
    see also Eurafrican Jews
music, of St Thomas Jewish
    community video 379
Myers, Belle 217

Myers, Lindo Samuel 217

N
Nahon, Gérard 8
naming practices, for Eurafrican
    Jews 172–6, 189, 190, 235 n. 50
Nanny Town (Jamaica) 246, 247,
    253
Nassy, *see* Cohen Nassy
Nathan, Mordecai 295
Nathan, Moses Nathan 330
National Coordinating
    Committee (New York)
    344–5, 348
nationalism, black, in Virgin
    Islands 373, 374–5
nations, Portuguese Jewish 46
Nazism, Jewish refugees from
    344–6, 347–8
    in Caribbean 13, 343, 346–7,
        348–59
Nedham, William 259 n. 53
Nemias, David 198–9
Netherlands, *see* Dutch Republic
Nettleford, Rex 128–9
networks:
    commercial 318; of Sephardi
        merchants 5, 6, 7, 21, 22, 29,
        63, 70, 283, 284, 286–7
    family: Ashkenazi 317; Sephardi
        63, 201–2, 234, 286–7
    of Sephardi communities 69
Neve Shalom congregation
    (Amsterdam) 163
Neve Shalom Synagogue (Spanish
    Town, Jamaica) 154
Neve Shalom Synagogue
    (Suriname) 157 n. 48
Neve Shalom Synagogue/
    congregation (Curaçao) 88,
    114
Neve Zedek Synagogue (Port
    Royal, Jamaica) 153, 154
Nevis, synagogue on 153
New Amsterdam, Jewish
    community in 282, 283, 312
New Christians, *see* Conversos
New York:
    granted to England in Peace of
        Breda 56 n. 58

New York (*cont.*):
Jewish communities in 312;
cantors 284–5 n. 9; Caribbean
roots 75, 282, 283–4; Franks
family 316–17; merchants
286; Sephardi–Ashkenazi
relations 285; synagogues
144, 155–6, 318
Sephardi merchants trading
with 63
Newman, Joanna 13
Newport Jewish communities:
Caribbean roots of 75, 282, 283
synagogues of 160–1
wealth of 45 n. 1
nicknames, of Eurafrican Jews 174
Nidhe Israel Synagogue /
congregation (Barbados)
147–52, 197, 198–9, 207
Nieto, David 323–4
Nieto, Isaac 157
North America, Jewish
communities in 11, 166, 281
Ashkenazi 157 n. 47, 285, 288
n. 21, 294
Caribbean roots of 75, 281–2,
283–4, 362, 369
and Enlightenment 292–3
merchants 286, 289–90, 294–304
synagogues 160–1, 162
see also United States
Norwood, Andrew 197
Nunes, Deborah 214
Nunes, Rachel 228 n. 23
Nunes, Robert 264
Nunes da Costa, Alexander 95
Nunes da Costa, Jeronimo (Moses
Curiel) 41, 42, 94
Nunes de Fonseca, *see* Cohen
Nassy, David

O
Ogle, Challoner 247
Old Harbour Market (Jamaica)
266, 271–2
O'Neal, Philly 217–18
Oppenheim, Samuel 282 n. 2
orphans, care of 94 n. 46, 233
Otrabanda (Willemstad
neighbourhood), Jews living
in 88, 103, 113–14

Ouderkerk aan de Amstel Jewish
cemetery (Netherlands) 137

P
Paiewonsky, Isidor 371–2, 378, 379,
383
de Palacios, Jacob 80
Panama, Jewish merchants in 331
Paradesi Synagogue (Cochin,
India) 144 n. 5
Paramaribo (Suriname):
Ashkenazi cemetery 132, 133,
136, 137
Sephardi community 59;
cemetery 133, 136, 137, 175, 177
Pardo, David 57
Pardo, Isaac 91–2
Pardo, Josiau 74
parnasim:
of Amsterdam: authority in the
Caribbean 73, 74, 75, 80–3, 95;
banking role 70–1; and
conflicts in Curaçao Jewish
community 91 n. 26, 96, 97,
101, 103, 104, 105
of Curaçao 89, 90–1, 95, 96, 97,
99, 100, 104, 111
of Suriname 78, 85
see also Mahamad
de la Parra family 189
Parravicino family 201
paternity, of children of black
concubines 228, 231, 232
Pax, Jan Gerard 96
Peake, Osbert 356
Pearson, Robert 275
Pearson, William 276
pedlars, Jewish, in Caribbean 351
Pelegrino, Jacob 184–5
Pelegrino, Joseph 184
Pelengrino family 139
Penso, Moses 73, 95–6, 97–8, 100,
103–4, 113, 114
Peregrino, Jacob (Jerónimo
Rodrigues Freire) 185, 186
Peregrino, Manuel 185, 186
Pereira, Edgar 348
Pereira, Lea 112
Pereira family 91, 92, 112–13
Perelis, Ronnie 12

Peri ets haim (periodical,
Amsterdam) 116
Pernambuco (Brazil), Sephardi
community in 51, 196
'The Persecuted Jew' (calypso,
Atilla the Hun) 349
personal names, Eurafrican 172–4
Philadelphia, synagogues in 162
philanthropy, Jewish 209–10
Phillips, Jacob 302
Phillips, Lyons 263–4
Picard, Bernard 137 n. 10
Pijning, Ernst 206
Pimentel, Abraham 325
Pimentel, Jahacob Henriques
(Don Manuel de Humanes)
322
Pinheiro, Isaac 206, 214
Pinheiro, Vinello 214
Pinto (cantor) 284–5 n. 9
de Pinto, Isaac 72, 76, 81, 321
de Pinto, Jacob de David 97
'De Pinto Manuscript' 320
Pinto, Simcha 181
piracy 313, 314
Captain Kidd's involvement in
315
Jewish involvement in 314
see also privateering
Pissarro, Camille 385
*A Plan of the City and Environs of
New York* (Grim) 156
plantations:
in Barbados 206; Jewish
ownership 200
in Curaçao 87; Jewish
ownership 62
in Jamaica 241, 248, 249;
interests of owners 263,
268–9, 272, 273, 274, 276
in South Carolina / Charleston
289; Jewish ownership 302,
303, 305–6
in Suriname, Jewish ownership
133, 134
Plymouth, synagogue in 159
poetry:
Jamaican Jewish 12, 73, 322–8
on Jewish gravestones 135
and psychology 322

Poland, Jewish refugees from 354–5

Political Reflections regarding the Establishment of the Jewish Nation (de Pinto) 72

politics, Jewish participation:
  in America 306
  in Jamaica 11, 262–4, 265, 266–8, 269–75, 276–8

Port Antonio (Jamaica) 247

port Jews 290–1
  in Charleston 291
  Enlightenment rationalism of 304–5
  see also merchants

Port Royal (Jamaica):
  earthquake and tsunami in 311
  Jewish community of 6, 133, 138, 153, 154

Port of Spain (Trinidad), Jewish refugees from Nazism in 348

Portland (Jamaica) 245

Porto de Ale (West Africa), Jewish community 186

Portrait of a Lady (acquarel, Belisario) 125

Portugal:
  admission of Jewish refugees from Nazism to 353
  anti-Converso investigations in 324
  anti-Jewish violence in 19
  Conversos in 4, 20–1, 22, 23
  Jews in: exiled from Spain 18–19; forced conversion of 2–4, 19; migration of 19–20, 22, 23, 324

Portuguese Jewish diaspora, *see* western Sephardi diaspora

Portuguese language, Jewish use of 7, 135, 177–9, 181, 183

Portuguese Synagogue (Amsterdam) 163
  see also Esnoga

Postal, Bernard 359 n. 53

Postma, Johannes M. 41

poverty:
  Amsterdam Sephardi community dealing with 72, 87–8 n. 12

among Barbadian Jews 201
among Barbadian whites 206
among Converso migrants 25
London Sephardi community dealing with 281, 305
among St Thomas Jews 331–2, 335–7

Poznanski, Revd Gustavus 304

del Prado, Maria / Mariana 191

Precious Stones of the Jews of Curaçao (Isaac Emmanuel) 131, 369–70 n. 24

Prince (ship), Curaçao–Amsterdam voyage 35

printing, Hebrew, Amsterdam's leadership role in 73

privateering 313–14
  Captain Kidd's involvement in 314–15
  Jewish involvement with 314
  permits for 92
  see also piracy

privileges, *see* rights and privileges of Jews

Protestants, in Jamaica 261–2

Psalms 323
  Laguna's poetic paraphrase 12, 73, 322, 323, 325–8
  Spanish translation 323 n. 9

psychology, ex-Converso 319–20, 321, 322, 325

Purim celebrations, in Suriname 188

Q

Quebec, Jewish community in 161

Quedagh Merchant (ship) 314–15

Queen or 'Maam' of the Set-Girls (lithographic print, Belisario) 121

R

rabbis:
  from Amsterdam for Caribbean communities 74–5
  in Barbados 75
  in Curaçao 74, 75, 90, 102
  of North American communities 285
  in St Thomas 330, 335, 385
  in Trinidad 352 n. 32

Rabello, David Gomes 231

racial identity:
  of Barbadian Sephardim 203, 205
  of illegitimate children 238
  of western Sephardim 205, 226, 262, 307

Ramos, Rebecca 204

Ramsay, Henry 146

Randall, A. W. G. 355

Ranston, Jackie 9

Raynal, Abbé 241, 256

Razovsky, Cecilia 344–5, 348

Recife:
  Dutch conquest and rule of 51
  Sephardi community in 25–6, 52, 60 n. 82, 163, 186

Reform Judaism:
  emergence in Charleston 293, 301, 304, 306
  of St Thomas congregation 367, 379

refugees, Jewish, from Nazism 344–6, 347–8
  to Caribbean 13, 343, 346–7, 348–59

religious authority, among Sephardim 108, 115–19

religious freedom:
  in American colonies 312
  in Amsterdam / Dutch Republic 5, 48–9, 86
  in Brazil 4, 51
  in Curaçao 59–60, 87
  in North America 306, 312–13
  in Suriname 103

Remire (French Guiana), Jewish community 165

Remnant Stones: The Cemeteries of Suriname (Ben-Ur and Frankel) 131

Remonstrantie (Grotius) 100 n. 74

research:
  of early modern autobiographies 321–2
  of Jewish communities of British West Indies 224
  of Jewish diaspora in the Caribbean 1–2, 11, 361–2

research (*cont.*):
of Jewish New World
cemeteries 132, 134, 142,
171–2
of manumission records 230
responsa, *see* halakhic rulings
retail trade, Jamaican, Jewish
participation in 264–5, 266–7
Rezio, Abraham 296
Rhode Island, status of Jews on
45 n. 1
rights and privileges of Jews 8
in Britain 145
in British colonial empire 2,
54–6, 291
in Curaçao 36–7, 59–61, 64, 86–7,
103, 109
in Dutch colonial empire 291
in Jamaica 11, 78–9, 262, 291, 306
Sephardi merchants 31, 36, 47–8,
51–2, 53–6, 58–61, 64
in Suriname 54–9, 103, 134
Ritchie, Robert 316
de Rivera, Jacob Rodrigues 45 n. 1,
75
Roanoke (North Carolina), British
colony 282
Robertson, James 10–11
Robinson, Thomas 208
Robles, Joseph Athias 336
Robles de Medina, Luna 180
Rodney, Admiral 42
Rodrigues da Costa, Ishac Haim
70
Rodriques, Solomon 267, 273–5,
278
Rohde, Ira 381 n. 52
Roitman, Jessica 8
Roldão, Sarah 176
Romain, Gemma 292
Roosevelt, Franklin Delano 344
Rosenfeld, Jacob 305
Rosengarten, Dale 11
Rowe, Joshua 127

S
St Croix (Denmark), Jewish
community 164
Saint-Dominque 300

St Dorothy (Jamaica) 266
Jewish retailers of 266–7
local government of 275–6
political representation of 11,
268–75, 276–8
St Eustatius (Netherlands), Jewish
community 73, 82–3, 291, 300,
302, 317
St John (Denmark) 164
St Maarten (Netherlands),
synagogues 157 n. 48
St Thomas (Jamaica) 276 n. 42
St Thomas (Virgin Islands):
black nationalism on 375
history 374
Jewish community 14, 164,
338–9, 361, 363, 366–7; auto-
historiography 368–73, 376,
377–9, 382–5; bicentennial
celebrations 363, 364, 367–8,
373, 376–7, 381–2; and
Hurricane Marilyn (1995)
385–6; leadership 330, 335;
merchants 329, 331; Sephardi
heritage/identity 363, 364–5,
367, 373, 378, 379–82; status of
women 12; synagogue 14,
338, 363, 364–5, 366, 367–8, 370,
372–3, 378, 379, 380, 385
racial relations on 377
Salamon, Hagar 173 n. 25
Salomon, H. P. 320
Salvador, Francis 305–6
Salvador, Joseph 305
Sam (Jamaican Crown slave) 249
Sambo, Captain (Jamaica) 246,
247
Sanct Thomae Tedende (newspaper)
368 n. 14
sand-covered synagogue floors 63,
76, 367, 378
Sanguinetti, Jacob 262–3
Sanguinetti, Jacob Jacob 264
Sara (captured Maroon),
testimony of 252, 253, 257–9
Sarah, as Sephardi first name 175
Sarfatti de Pinna, David 203
Sarna, Jonathan 207, 290, 306, 384
Schipper, Samuel 356
Schorsh, Jonathan 211, 223 n. 3, 226

Schreuder, Yda 197
schuilkerken (secret houses of
worship) 145, 163
*Secret Relationship between the
Blacks and the Jews*
(Farrakhan) 375
Seixada, Manoel Lopes 186
self-government of Jewish
communities 97 n. 55
in Curaçao 104, 110–11, 113
Semah David Synagogue
(Speightstown, Barbados)
152, 209
Senior, Jacob de David 111
Sephardi communities, *see under
individual place names*
Sephardi diaspora 2, 7, 46
see also western Sephardi
diaspora
Sephardi identities 10, 14, 46, 188,
238, 319
in Barbados 195, 203–4, 205, 222
in Jamaica 233
in St Thomas 363, 364–5, 367,
373, 378
Sephardi merchants 290–1
in Brazil 51
commercial networks of 5, 6,
7, 21, 22, 29, 63, 70, 283, 284,
286–7
in Curaçao 7, 36, 62–3, 64
rights and privileges granted to
31, 36, 47–8, 51–2, 53–6, 58–61,
64
in St Thomas 329, 331
in slave trade 39, 41–2, 54, 298,
303
success of 46–7
in transatlantic trade 2, 5, 36–7,
45–7, 63, 87, 289–90
Sephardi women 12, 190, 286
Seven Years War (1756–63) 42
Seville, anti-Jewish violence in
(1391) 17
sexual abuse, of enslaved women
227–8
Sha'ar Hashamayim congregation
(Gibraltar) 157
Sha'ar Hashamayim congregation
(London) 145, 146, 147

Sha'ar Hashamayim Synagogue/
    congregation (Kingston) 154,
    155
Shannon, Elizabeth Margaret 217
Sharpe, Sam (slave) 127
Sharpe, Samuel (lawyer) 127
Sharpe, William 208
Shearit Israel Synagogue/
    congregation (Charleston)
    305
Shearith Israel Synagogue/
    congregation (New York)
    144, 155–6, 318
Shearith Israel Synagogue/
    congregation (Quebec) 161
Sheridan, Richard B. 374
Shulḥan arukh 117
da Silva Horta, José 186
Simha, as first name for Eurafrican
    Jews 139, 173
Simonhoff, Harry 300–1 n. 63
Simonsen, David 332, 334, 337
Siporah, as first name for
    Eurafrican Jews 174 n. 28
Sketches of Character (Belisario)
    121, 123, 125, 128
skull-and-crossbones imagery 137,
    138
slave–Jew relationships 10–11,
    123–4, 225
  in Barbados 204, 210–21
  in Jamaica 10, 122, 126, 223,
    229–30, 233–8, 239, 264–5
  see also black–Jewish
    relationships; Eurafrican Jews
slave revolts in Jamaica 127, 242–3,
    243–51, 252–4, 256–9
  and Jewish 'treason' 10–11, 243,
    251–2, 253, 254–5, 257, 258
slave societies, Jamaican 227–8,
    261 n. 2, 343
slave trade:
    Curaçao's role in 37–9, 40–1, 42
    Sephardi involvement with 39,
    41–2, 54, 298, 303
slavery:
    abolition of 126
    halakhic rulings on 116–17
slaves:
    bequests of 201

female 227–8
female ownership of 232
  Jamaican 123, 249
  Jewish ownership of 226, 228;
    on Barbados 211, 212, 218, 221;
    in Curaçao 61; in Jamaica
    123–4, 230–1
  in Suriname: conversion to
    Judaism 10, 169–70, 176, 183–7,
    192; family names of 189
  see also manumission of slaves
Sligo, Marquess of, see Browne,
    Howe Peter
Sloane, Hans 121 n. 1
Smith, David 272, 274
Smith, M. G. 265 n. 16
Smith, Paul Julian 319 n. 2
social welfare activities:
    of Amsterdam Sephardi
      community 23, 25, 49, 74
    in Curaçao 94 n. 46
Society of Virgin Islands
    Historians 374
de Sola, Samuel Mendes 90, 91–2,
    95–6, 97, 98, 104, 112, 113,
    117–18
de Sola Pool, David 285
Solomon, George 264
Sorkin, David 5
South Carolina, Jewish
    communities in 291, 292
Soyer, François 2 n. 3
Spain:
    anti-Jewish violence in 17–18
    expulsion of Jews from 2, 18
    Maroons seeking alliance with
      246
Spanish America, Dutch trade
    from Curaçao with 36–7, 38,
    39–40, 42–3
Spanish language, Jewish use of
    179, 180
Spanish Town (Jamaica):
    Jewish community 133, 241, 266,
    273
  synagogues 154
Speightstown (Barbados):
    anti-Jewish violence in 209
    synagogue at 152
Spooner, John 215

Sranan Tongo (Creole language),
    use in Suriname 176, 181, 182
Stanton, Miriam 359
Stern, Malcolm 294, 359 n. 53
Stewart, John 122, 123
Stiefel, Barry 9–10
Stiles, Ezra 45 n. 1
Stone, Carl 278
Stork, David 290
Stuyvesant, Peter 60, 61 n. 84, 94,
    312
sugar production and trade:
    on Barbados 149
    Sephardi participation in 4, 21
Sunday Gleaner (journal, Jamaica)
    359
Surat (India), Jewish community of
    313
Suriname:
    Ashkenazi Jewry in 132, 136, 137,
    180, 317
    creolization in 211 n. 48
    Dutch colonial rule of 56, 58,
    188
    economic development of 57
    Eurafrican Jews in 10, 139,
    169–72, 192–3; conversion to
      Judaism 10, 169–70, 176, 183–7,
      192; Jewish identity of 187–92,
      225, 226; language use 181–3;
      names 172–6, 189, 190
    language use in 176–7
    Sephardim in 6, 53, 118, 133, 134,
    225; cemeteries/burial
      practices 9, 53, 131, 132–3,
      134–6, 137, 138–40, 141, 142,
      171–2, 177, 185, 189–90;
      conflicts 85; language use
      76, 77, 177–80; rights and
      privileges 54–9, 103, 134
    synagogues in 56–7, 133, 137–8,
    157 n. 48, 164
Suriname River, transportation of
    deceased on 141
Surowitz-Israel, Hilit 8
synagogues:
    in Amsterdam 48–9, 76, 147, 163,
    164
    in Barbados 149–52, 197, 198–9,
    209, 210, 359

synagogues (*cont.*):
  in Brazil 149, 163, 196
  in Britain 145–7, 154
  in British colonial empire 143–4,
    152–8, 165–6
  in Canada 161
synagogues (*cont.*):
  in Charleston 305
  construction of 9–10, 76, 137–8,
    143–4, 150–1, 158–9; financial
    support for 156, 284, 318
  in Curaçao 63, 88, 97, 113–14
  in Danish colonial empire 164,
    166, 338
  in Dutch colonial empire 157,
    159, 162–4, 166
  in French colonial empire 165
  in Gibraltar 157, 160, 161–2
  in India 144 n. 5, 153
  in Jamaica 153, 154, 155
  in New York 144, 155–6, 312, 318
  in Newport 160–1
  in St Maarten 157 n. 48
  in St Thomas 14, 338, 364–5, 366,
    370, 372–3, 378, 379, 380, 385;
    bicentennial celebrations of
    363, 364, 367–8, 373, 376–7,
    381–2
  in Suriname 56–7, 133, 137–8, 157
    n. 48, 164

T
Tajfel, Henri 195
taxation:
  of Caribbean Jews 78–9, 255
  of Jamaican Jews 277, 296
textile industry, Dutch 35
'Theorizing Heritage'
  (Kirshenblatt-Gimblett) 386
Thistlewood, Thomas 228
Through the Sands of Time (Judah
  Cohen) 384–5
Titchfield (Jamaica) 247, 249
tombstone inscriptions 77, 131,
  135–7
  see also epitaphs; funeral
    practices
de Toralto, Manoel de 36–7
torture, use of 248, 253 n. 39
tourism, Jewish 14
  to St Thomas 367, 370, 372, 378–9

Touro, Isaac 284
Touro Synagogue (Newport)
  160–1
Toussaint Louverture 301 n. 63
trade, international, *see* Atlantic
  trade; colonial trade; trading
  systems, Dutch
trade, slave, *see* slave trade
trading systems, Dutch 30–1, 33,
  34–5
  illicit trade of Dutch with
    Venezuela 40, 42
  Sephardi participation in 7, 29,
    31, 34, 36, 37, 42–3
Treadway, Jonathan 315–16
Tree, Ellen 125
Trinidad:
  admission of Jewish refugees
    from Nazism to 13, 345, 346,
    348–51, 352
  American administration of 352
    n. 32
  Jewish community of 258, 351,
    352, 358, 359
Trinidad Guardian (newspaper)
  348–9, 350–1, 352, 359
Tsur Israel Synagogue/
  congregation (Brazil) 163
Turner, John C. 195

U
Ulloa, Daniel 206
The Umbilical Cord (Willocks) 375
Ungar, Sydney 352 n. 32
Union of Utrecht, freedom of
  conscience in 48
United States:
  admission of Jewish refugees
    from Nazism to 346 n. 7
  Civil War 299–300, 301–2, 304,
    307
  religious freedom in 306, 312–13
  War of Independence 42, 302,
    306
  see also North America
Uscher, Rabbi 357 n. 46
Usque, Samuel 20
Usselinx, William 86
Uziel de Avilar, Samuel 192 n. 134
Uziel de Avilar family 140

V
Valentine, Simon 294–5
Valverde, Abraham 210
Van Beek, Nicolaas 95
Van Campen, Nicolaes 49
Van Limborch, Philipp 320
Van Musaphia, Mariana 181
Van la Parra, Annaatje 189–90
Van Schagen, Jan 91, 98, 101
Van Scharphuysen, Johan 59
Van Walbeck, Johan 109
Van Wijngaarden, René 338
Van Wyngarde, Abraham 190
Venezuela, Dutch trade from
  Curaçao with 36–7, 38, 39–40,
  42, 63
Venice, Sephardi community 20,
  97 n. 55
  model for Amsterdam 75
de Vera, Andres 39–40
Vink, Wieke 181, 190, 193
Virgin Islands:
  black nationalism on 373, 374–5
  history of 374–6
Virgin Islands Daily News 370 n. 25
visual art, of Jamaican Jewish
  community 9, 121–2, 123,
  124–9
de Vries, Moses Isaac 318
Vrij, Jean Jacque 184–5

W
Wagener, Zacharias 25–6
Wagg, Mordecai Gomez 298
Wallack, James 125
War of the Spanish Succession
  (1701–14) 42
Warren, Frances 227
Watson, Karl 10
wealth:
  of Barbadian Jews 201–2
  of Newport Jewish community
    45 n. 1
Webb, John 161
Weissbach, Lee Shai 365 n. 11
West Africa, Sephardi
  communities in 185–6
West India Company (Denmark)
  164

West India Company (WIC,
    Netherlands) 4, 8, 50, 92–3,
    105, 163
  adjudication of Jewish intra-
    community conflicts by 85,
    91, 92, 95, 96–101, 104–5
  in Brazil 50–1
  in Curaçao 32, 86, 93, 94, 111
  religious freedom supported by
    86
  rights and privileges granted
    Sephardi merchants/settlers
    by 31, 36–7, 54, 59–61, 86–7,
    109, 134
  slave trade by 39, 40, 41
  in Suriname 58
western Sephardi diaspora 17–18,
    26–7, 46, 52, 67–8, 107–8, 239,
    362–3
  Amsterdam's leadership role in
    8, 23, 49, 68–9, 70–1, 73–8,
    109–10, 115–18, 148

Judaism of 24
  Portuguese dialect of 177
  religious authority in 108
  research on 1–2, 11, 361–2
White, Celestino 375 n. 39
white identities, of western
    Sephardim 205, 226, 262, 307
Whiteman, Maxwell 297
WIC, see West India Company
Wiegers, Gerard 321
Wijngaard family 189
Wijnhard, Wadily 189 n. 122
Willemstad (Curaçao) 30
  Sephardi community, see
    Curaçao: Sephardi
    community
William IV of Orange-Nassau
    (prince, stadhouder of Dutch
    Republic) 101, 114
Willocks, Harold W. L. 375
Wilmot, Swithin 10, 11
Wiznitzer, Arnold 51, 197

women:
  enslaved 227–8
  epitaphs for 239–40
  manumission of slaves by 232
  Sephardi 12, 190, 286
Wood, Sarah Simpson 221
Woodhouse, Joseph 270
'A World of Difference'
    curriculum (St Thomas) 377
Wren, Christopher 146
'Writing Atlantic History' (Canny)
    107
Wyngaarde, Abraham 190

Y
de Yllan, João 36, 37, 60, 69, 87, 109

Z
Zacks, Richard 315
Zemon Davis, Natalie 169
Zucker, Eric 378 n. 47
de Zuñiga y Avellaneda, Felix 40